AF528884

KASHMIR
THE
Bermuda Triangle of India

KASHMIR
THE
Bermuda Triangle of India

Sharad Mohan

Foreword by

Walter Andersen, PhD
Former Chief of the US State Department for South Asia
Professor at Johns Hopkins University, Washinton DC

Manas Publications
(We Convert Fighters into Writers)
New Delhi - 110 002 (INDIA)

MANAS PUBLICATIONS
(We Convert Fighters into Writers)
(Publishers, Library Suppliers, Importers & Exporters)
4402/5-A, Ansari Road (Opp. HDFC Bank)
Darya Ganj, New Delhi - 110 002 (India)
Phones: Off.: 011-23260783, 23265523, Res.: 011-23842660
E-mail: manaspublications@gmail.com
manaspublications@yahoo.com
Website: www.manaspublications.in

ISBN 978-81-7049-549-9

₹ 1495

Designed by
Veronica Grafic Arts

Printed in India at
R.K. Print Service, Delhi
and published by Mrs Suman Lata for
Manas Publications
4402/5-A, Ansari Road (Opp HDFC Bank)
Darya Ganj, New Delhi - 110 002 (INDIA)

To

Kashmiri Youths

Kashmiri Pandits

Kashmiri Mothers

Kashmiri Women

Kashmiri Muslims, Sikhs, Buddhists and Hindus

Kashmiri Working and Labour Class

Security personnel posted in Kashmir and their families

Contents

Part Three

Disclaimer

This is a work of non-fiction. No names have been changed, no characters invented, no events fabricated to the best of my understanding. I would like to thank the members of the various political families portrayed in this book. I recognize that their memories of the events described in this book may be different than my own. They are each fine, decent and nationalist people. The book is not intended to hurt these families. Both my publisher and I regret any unintentional harm resulting from the publishing and marketing of this book. However, my narrative on historical events, abide by the generally known facts of the life and also common perceptions expressed and travelogues written by the folks who saw those events first hand. The photographs, maps, charts etc used in this book adhere to the Government of India's stand, the author has no intention to bypass those directives. Map of Kashmir and naming of the region is in accordance with the Government of India's declared policy and the author totally endorses that stand.

This book reflects the author's research and various scholars (stakeholders) recollections of their experiences over time. I have been corrected on some points, mostly of chronology and historical dates. I have sometimes quoted from many such works, letters, passim etc available in public domain just to use as a reference to give more punch to the narratives. Most of the data have been sourced from the authentic sources, but in case of opposite interpretation please consider it as a different view on the same event, as the intent is more on the storytelling using the data, rather than making data the gospel of truth as the statisticians may want it to be. Facts remain the same and will not change. It's the interpretation of a glass having water, half full or half empty. I've allowed some of these points to stand, because this is a book bringing unconventional narrative, the other side of the coin and such perspective has its own story to tell. But I have done my best to make it tell a truthful story.

Foreword

I am pleased to write a foreword for Sharad Mohan's book on Kashmir. We spent a delightful afternoon on a late October (2017) afternoon discussing the book. I was impressed by the thorough research he had done. It was clearly a labour of love and he had dedicated hundreds of hours to this engagement. The book is not only a fine example of analysis, but unlike so many books on topics like this, it is an enjoyable read. There may be few differences in our approaches to the treatment of specific issues but where I will wholeheartedly agree with the author is that this is not a simple political problem or just the territorial disputes between India and Pakistan inherited from the partition, but much more. The narratives of Kashmir are many and much depends on who is telling the story. There is the British imperialist perspective and that comes through in some early works on Kashmir by writers from the UK and India comes out badly in the telling. There is a Pakistani perspective and an Indian perspective and several Kashmiri perspectives. Some seven decades after the events, it is probably a good time to take another look as we now have much more material available and the emotions aroused by the partition of India (and Kashmir) have cooled, but not disappeared as the annual celebration of a Kashmir day in Pakistan demonstrate as well as the periodic terrorist attacks within Indian Kashmir.

There have been many books on Kashmir, its history, problems, politics leading from Mughal era to contemporary India; and up to Narendra Modi becoming Prime Minister in 2014. However, with the multiplicity of opinions, it is not easy to make out the truth about what is the cause and happening at the ground zero. Kashmir remains a place of great beauty but also of the tragedy. This book, *Kashmir – The Bermuda Triangle of India,* covers the vast stretch of historical, political and different perspectives relating to the current puzzle. Most books on Kashmir discusses the reason for the crisis in great detail, citing from personal experiences, travelogues and views of the various experts directly or indirectly; detailing at the micro level on what went wrong. Very few of these experts have suggested solutions for the complex Kashmir situation. Perhaps one thing is a given, India will not relinquish its control. Whether India and Pakistan can work out a creative solution that recognizes this given is the key bilateral issue between the countries.

Four wars have been fought between two nuclear States, India and Pakistan. Still, the issue is unresolved. Nehru's promised plebiscite has never been held, thanks to Pakistanis for that; and endless peace talks have failed. Two-thirds of Kashmir is with India - which includes the beautiful Valley of Kashmir, the sparsely inhabited, yet magnificent regions of Leh, Ladakh and Jammu. One-third is occupied by Pakistan and this region includes the narrow strip of land watered by the Jhelum river which leads tantalizingly onwards to the Valley called Gilgit-Baltistan. Lastly, part of the former princely State - Aksai Chin in the north-west and a slice given to China by Pakistan in the north - is occupied by China and its future depends on an agreement between India and Pakistan.

Sharad Mohan, through this book, has taken a positive step to analyse the many proposed solutions in the last chapter along with his views on what it would take to get a long-lasting solution. His analysis and style of presentation make for an enjoyable read for a broad audience that would include general readers, experts and policy-makers. Any proposal to be accepted by both sides, in my view, would have to address the sovereignty issue and would almost certainly have to avoid any fundamental shift in the present lines of control. Pakistani General Musharraf put forth such an approach based on a measure of shared governance, but no shift in sovereignty. Both sides rejected it ultimately. Other proposals have called for the autonomy of both sides of the Line of Control, but they too have been rejected. No solution, in my view, will be possible until relations between India and Pakistan improve significantly. Kashmir, in my view, is not the source of the often tense relations between India and Pakistan, but a symptom of it.

Walter Andersen

Walter Andersen is an expert on South Asia, handling Afghanistan, Pakistan and India covering topics like Intelligence, Ethnic Conflict, Strategy and Security, Terrorism and US Congress - Foreign Policy. He has proficiency in English, German and Hindi. He has a good understanding of the South Asia region and its people. He has served as the chief of US State

Department's South Asia division. He also held some critical positions including special help to the Ambassador at the US Embassy in New Delhi, member of the Policy Planning staff in Washington, DC. He is also being involved in academics and have taught at the University of Chicago, College of Wooster and is also affiliated with Tongji University in Shanghai, China. Currently, he is a senior Adjunct Professor at Johns Hopkins University and a good friend and supporter of the Indian diaspora.

Preface

Shiv chuy thali thali rozan; Mo zan Hindu La Musalman.
Truk ay chuk pan panun parzanav; Soy chay Sahibas sati zaniy zan.

(Shiva lives everywhere; do not divide Hindu from Muslim. Use your sense to recognize yourself; that is the true way to find God.)

– Lal Ded aka Lalla Arifa
Mystics poetess of Kashmir

Gar firdaus bar-rue zamin ast, hamin asto, hamin asto, hamin ast.

(If there is a heaven on earth, it's here, it's here.)

– Amir-e-Khusro Dehlavi

My poem below describes what Lal Ded's and Amir Khusro's Kashmir has become today, from Paradise to Perdition, a sad state.

O' Kashmir how sorrowful have you become, something is chocking your life out.
Smoke in the winds of conspiracies and the moon has the blood clot.
People fleeing burning homes splits the heart.
The grass is no longer green as the pallet sprays every part.
The alienation has driven away the migratory birds, as warmness of Kashmiriyat diminishes.
O' Kashmir the crown of India, every Indian heart bleeds and will not rest till the Perdition vanishes.

– Sharad Mohan (author)

This book tries to give you a glance of Kashmir rich culture, geography, people and the conflict which has eclipsed this paradise. I have divided this book into three parts and I want my readers to read a simple and understandable story, giving them a 360-degree view of Kashmir as seen from my eyes.

But before I can dare to suggest any solution or more appropriately any approach has to briefly introduce myself and my humble background, so many big names in last 70 years of contemporary India and 200 plus years from Kashmir past history pre-1947 have tried and unfortunately the conflict continues, taking many lives and causing great distress to humanity.

My credential is interesting, I am first of all not a Kashmiri, not married to any Kashmiri lady, I am not a Sunni Muslim, though have many close friends from the community, not a politician though have friends and family from this category, not an army man though again has family and friend from the army, policeman. I may not have public persona needed for someone who should take such a serious topic on Kashmir. What makes me think that I can do justice to this vast, complex and very sensitive subject. Do I even think like a Kashmiri to even comprehend the pain and anger they are going through? Have I faced a terrorist to even understand how the army works day in and day out in such a tough terrain? I do not claim any such perceived credentials for this topic.

What I guess I have, are "sensitivity, awareness, practical approach and problem solving" attributes; as have seen some part of this vast and beautiful world. I have travelled, lived and or worked as the corporate executive in more than 20 countries, talking, meeting and closely observing various cultures and civilizations and how they conduct themselves. Have some learning because of that, thanks to my corporate job.

I have spiritual connect with Kashmir, Lord Shiva is my *ishta devata* having massive footprints in this Himalayan State and my Hindu gotra is 'Kashyapa' from Kashyapa Muni who founded this city. I am from Bihar where Yusuf Shah Chak, independent Kashmir's last ruler is buried. Chak died in exile in Bihar after Mughal emperor Akbar annexed Kashmir in AD 1586. His grave is in village Biswak of Nalanda district. Research also found out that the 16th-century famous commoner poet-queen Habba Khatoon alias Zoon, was in fact buried at Biswak village in Nalanda, Bihar alongside the grave of her husband, Yusuf Shah Chak.

Now back on the topic, Maurya Dynasty from Bihar had entire Kashmir as one of its region and Patna was the capital. So the connection exists from the very long period.

The idea of the book came to me in the year 2016, when in May, I was invited by some activists in New Jersey, USA to join them for a peaceful protest in front of UN against Pakistani Prime Minister Nawaz Sharif's speech on Jammu and Kashmir State of India. I have never participated in such procession, so anxiously joined them. This was an eye-opening event where I met Kashmiri Pandits, heard their real painful stories, met Balochistan leaders, heard about their pitiful life. This is where I felt I need to understand the problem and became curious to know why this conflict has not been resolved even after 70 years. Was any sincere effort made, what is the hope for millions of Kashmiris, will they continue in this same state forever?

All these pertinent questions motivated me to do research and lot of reading on the topic and beyond, I found tons of artifacts which I have used in my book, read many blogs from both sides of the border to get the feel. I took a sabbatical from my current job, plunged into reading, researching, travelling, compiling and writing. I realized the problem is complex, but the solution is simple, you have to be honest to solve this issue, everything comes next. Be it a territorial solution or cultural solution and or people-centric solution, it is straightforward, are we honest to solve this, which will move millions of Kashmiris from both sides of the border from this daily pain, suffering and humiliation to calmness and prosperity. Do we have political and military intent to solve this? Again it has to be in due consultation and agreement with the right stakeholders.

I soon found that the solution however practical or hypothetical depended with whom I was talking to, an Army, a Policeman, a Teacher, the Separatists, the Hindu Pandits, the Sikhs, the Kashmiri Muslims, other Muslims from outside Kashmir; all had their own opinions which were always contradicting, so never the twain can meet. It was like two shores of the ocean, promising to meet only at the horizon. I decided to talk to those folks who may not have vested interest in Kashmir and also those who are spiritual leaders in the service of God, as that's the last resort one mostly turns to when the ship is sinking. This I thought will give more balanced perspective.

Mehbooba Mufti, Chief Minister of Jammu and Kashmir, resigned on 19th June 2018 after BJP withdrew support from the coalition government. BJP General Secretary Ram Madhav told, "It has become untenable for the BJP to continue in the alliance government in Jammu and Kashmir." Prime Minister Narendra Modi won in 2014 election, vowing to end the insurgency in Kashmir but militant violence has worsened in recent months.

General elections were held in Pakistan on 25 July 2018, after the completion of a five-year term by the outgoing government. As a result of the elections, the Pakistan Tehreek-e-Insaf (PTI) became the single largest party at the national level, both in terms of popular vote and seats. In the lead up to the elections, there had been allegations by some international journalists and scholars about pre-poll rigging being conducted by the judiciary, the military and the intelligence agencies to sway the election results in favour of the PTI and against the PML-N. Almost all parties, excluding Pakistan Tehreek-e-Insaf, alleged large-scale vote rigging and administrative malpractices.

There have been allegations by some international journalists and scholars, claiming that there was a plan between judiciary and military bodies to influence the outcome of the election. These allegations were also made by the outgoing PML-N following Nawaz Sharif's disqualification for corruption. It was suggested that alleged goal of these attempts was to halt the party of Nawaz Sharif from coming into power and to bring the results in favour of PTI, so that Imran Khan - who is alleged as close to the military - can be installed as the Prime Minister. There have been reports that candidates belonging to PML(N) have been coerced by ISI to switch to those parties whose future government can be better controlled by military. There have also been reports of election engineering by army and intelligence agencies in Balochistan province in favour of Balochistan Awami Party.

Reports further suggested that there was evidence of collusion between the judiciary and military, in that two military officials were appointed to the Joint Investigation Team to investigate corruption allegations against former Prime Minister Nawaz Sharif, which were further strengthened by the circumstances of the Avenfield case verdict against the Sharifs. There have been allegations that the micromanagement of political parties and the censorship of the newspapers, social media and TV channels is to further influence the election result. An official from the Human Rights Commission of Pakistan stated that the "level of army interference and political engineering is unprecedented." Another institution, the National Accountability Bureau has been described as being used by military intelligence agencies, including ISI, to bring politicians in line by threatening to bring corruption cases against them. Due to interference by military and intelligence agencies, *The Financial Times* described these elections as the 'dirtiest in years'.

The EU observer mission released their report after the election stating that there were "systematic attempts to undermine the ruling party", "lack of equality of opportunity", pressure on the media, far stronger efforts than usual to encourage switching parties and judicial conduct had all negatively influenced the vote.

Claiming victory in Pakistan's general elections, Imran Khan offered to hold talks with India to improve relations and highlighted the importance of close trade ties, but at the same time reiterated that Kashmir was a core issue and referred to human rights violation by Indian security agencies in the volatile State.

In a letter addressed to Prime Minister Narendra Modi, Pakistan Prime Minister Imran Khan sought the resumption of Indo-Pak negotiations regarding border conflict and cross-border terrorism. Imran Khan wrote to Modi, "Building on the mutual desire for peace between our two countries, I wish to propose a meeting between Foreign Minister Makhdoom Shah Mahmood Qureshi and the External Affairs Minister Sushma Swaraj, before the informal meeting of the SAARC Foreign Ministers."

The decision to agree to Pakistan's proposal for a meeting between the Foreign Ministers of the two countries in New York later this month was in response to the spirit reflected in the letters from the new Prime Minister Imran Khan and Foreign Minister of Pakistan. India accepted the offer and agreed to a meeting on the sidelines of the United Nations General Assembly (UNGA) meet. A meeting was arranged between both the Foreign Ministers in New York. India had to cancel the meeting between the Foreign Minister Sushama Swaraj and her Pakistani counterpart. India highlighted how Pakistan created the conditions for cancellation of the meeting in New York. External Affairs Minister Sushama Swaraj blamed the latest brutal killings of Indian security personnel by Pakistan-based entities and the recent release of a series of twenty postage stamps by Pakistan glorifying a terrorist and terrorism.

Dear readers it's over to you now....

New Jersey, USA (2016)
Bangalore, India (2017-18)

Sharad Mohan

Acknowledgements

I would like to express my gratitude to many people who saw me through this book; to all those who provided support, talked things over, read, wrote, offered comments, assisted in the editing, proof-reading and design. I would like to thank all the editors, Vivek Garg and Niraj Kumar (Expert on Asia) for enabling me to publish this book. Above all, I want to pay my obeisance to my late grandparents and dearest parents for their blessings all the time. I would also like to thank wife Jyoti, son Rohan and daughter Annika and the rest of my family and friends, who supported and encouraged me in spite of all the time it took me away from them. It was an exciting journey with them. I would like to thank Rupa, Manish, Siddharth, Unnikrishnan uncle, Krishnan Mahadevan, Walter Andersen, Mrinalini Andersen, Mahesh & Karuna Chaudhury, Dr Yogita Rana (Collector, Hyderabad), Rashneek Kher (founder of the Roots in Kashmir), Jeannette DuVal, Aditya Satsangi and Iftikhar Geelani (Editor, *DNA* and son-in-law of Hurriyat leader Syed Ali Shah Geelani) for helping me to be objective, focused and building high EQ, as per the need of this emotive topic. I would also thank all those people whose work posted on the public domain have been referenced. Thanks to Manas Publications, my publisher for the support and endorsement. Thanks to my late aunt and all my teachers; especially late Father George Hess and Shivkumar Sir who shaped my raw age during my childhood, without them, this book would never have found its way. Last but not the least I beg forgiveness to all those who have always been there for me and did not see their names mentioned, I sincerely thank you all from the bottom of my heart.

Sharad Mohan

Part One

Prologue

Kashmir Kaleidoscope

'3 Ms' of Kashmir History

1. Prologue

Humanity has to achieve a lot, as British scientist late Stephen Hawking predicts, we have only 100 years left before we are either going to be attacked by the hostile aliens and or hit by the asteroids which have alluded mother earth far too long and she may soon be running out of her luck. Its been seventy years and no solution to this enigma, going by Hawking's prediction Kashmiris have only hundred more years left for getting this solved before another set of invasion happens and this time it may be worst than the Afghans, Mughals or Dogras rulers. No UN or any human power will be able to give Azaadi from their invasion. So let's hurry up, time is passing fast. This book on Kashmir is divided into three parts, each containing chapters that cover important topics related to Kashmir and its people.

Part One: Starting with Prologue which gives primary construct of this book. Then I move to 'Kashmir Kaleidoscope', which introduces the demography of Kashmir and which gives us a view of the immense beauty and opportunities this great land has to offer. This is for those readers who do not know what Kashmir is made up off. This is a perfect setting for the rest of the book, as you are made aware of the subject before you read its ailment and some suggested succour. Even to understand the history of the place you need to understand the geography, culture and demography better so that the actions and reactions of its people recorded in history are understood appropriately. After knowing the demography then next important insight is about the history of this great land.

How it has shaped from Mythological times to date. What sort of rulers and people inhabited this land, bringing their values and cultures, making this land a melting pot of some ancient civilizations. "The '3 Ms' of Kashmir's History – From Mythological Times (M1) through Medieval Times (M2) to Modern Times (M3)," covers this aspect in detail. All the great historians, perception makers and narrative generators are welcome to read and provide the critical feedback. This is how I understood history reading the textbooks, religious books, travelogues, some architectural findings and views from all walks of life. Social media was one great influencer in forming some of the views similar to travelogues.

Part Two: In this section I have dealt with two important topics. Kashmir conflict which is the oldest UN conflict seems to be hanging in there forever and no sign of hope. Also what exactly is the reason for this problem? Everyone has their own story to tell. It looks like the Bermuda Triangle mystery which modern science has not been able to answer with confidence. Why do I call Kashmir issue the Bermuda Triangle of India? Can there be any solution, if yes timeline? Like the Bermuda Triangle analogy, Kashmir as I see has three vertices or coordinates of the triangle which are Kalashnikov (Terror), Kahwa (Rich Culture/Paradise) and Kaffir (Changing of Sufism and Kashmiriyat to Wahhabi/Salafi Islam, having circumscribed lacuna for the non-Sunni Muslims. Even Ahmadiyas and Shias, two Muslim communities are also targeted).

Talk Talk Talk – With Whom? This section uses anecdotes on why, how and with whom to communicate within Pakistan for the conflict resolution. Meaningless talks are the sheer waste of time and eventually bringing the motivation level down. Even when a war is ongoing, there has to be back-channelled communication link established and it should continue working on arriving at the best and mutually agreeable Agreement. Keep in touch and in communication with the rival, gives you an understanding of his SWOT, as suggested by the great Indian thinker Acharya Chanakya. Democratic India should not shy from talking with Pakistani Army directly and negotiate on resolving the conflict in a time bound manner. Working with the weak political set-up in that country has not let India anywhere and the result is Kashmir keeps burning causing despair, alienation and unfortunate deaths. Moreover, communication is the foundation of all human relationship. Communicating helps people to express their ideas and feelings and it, at the same time, helps us to understand emotion and thoughts of the others. As a result, we will develop affection or hatred toward other people and positive or negative relationships will be created.

Part Three: Most of the books and research I have read on Kashmir talks about the past and present history and some political proposals to bring the hostilities and sufferings of the people down. No, where I have seen writers trying to provide potential solution approaches. Giving a spin to the event that has already happened is no brainer. You as a writer should show your skill in helping solve this conundrum. I have dealt in this section two potential solutions approaches - Off-the-Shelf Solutions and Out-of-Box Solution. I have tried to compile all the past, present and future suggested solutions on the Kashmir Conflict from various thinkers, academicians, historians, political (left, right, centre) and military (India, Pakistan, US) leaders, residents and non-residents of Kashmir, victims, aggressors and international agencies like UN, known and some unknown bloggers on the social media all in this section. This will give my readers perspective on what hybrid solution can be yanked out of all these suggestions. If my suggested '7 Cs' mantras are followed, then the unresolved Indian Bermuda Triangle will move from 'End of the Beginning' stretch to the next phase, 'Beginning of the End'.

So what is Kashmir Issue? If you see this in the context of the entire historical journey of Kashmir which I have discussed in the subsequent Chapters, Kashmiri people faced brutal weather due to it being in the Himalayan region, the continuous attack by the foreign invaders, be it Turks, Afghans, Mongols, Mughals and later allegedly by Sikhs and Dogras. This has made them what they are today an insecure, disturbed, not very happy community.

Kashmir has been a bone of contention between India and Pakistan over the last seventy years. Pakistan was formed as a reaction against secular India and this mindset continues. But there are other interesting dimensions to this Kashmir fiasco, which may be beyond India and Pakistan formation and their relationship since 1947. It is the History of Kashmir, which is the real cause of its current miseries. People know very little about this fact. Here it goes.

Kashmir, the land of 'Neela Nag' - son of Kashyapa Rishi and his wife Kudru, supposedly serpent girl, who produced 'half-human and half-snake' children. The beautiful valley of river Vitasha (Jhelum) has no one to blame but its history for its current miseries. Many believe, since 1820, Kashmir has been under the spell of the curse of its history. Let me share with you a weird but mystic logic how both curse and cure of Kashmir problems lies in its history and interestingly this came from an unknown Kashmiri, the more I read about Kashmir's history, more I am enamoured by the sheer veracity of this logic.

Grand Chakra of Kashmir History – A Hypothesis

- Approximately 800 years of Kashmir's recorded history, it is under the domination of a particular religion. This period is called Grand Chakra of Kashmir History.

- Every Grand Chakra is further subdivided into Three Sub-Chakras of 275 years each approx.
- First Sub-Chakra relates to 'Emergence, Development and Progress' of a particular religion.
- Second Sub-Chakra pertains to 'Consolidation and Prosperity' of the religion.
- Third Sub-Chakra leads to 'Decay and Degeneration' of the predominant religion and emergence of a new religious philosophy.
- The first two Sub-Chakras make the golden period of Domination of a Religion. The term 'Religious Domination' is to be read as 'State Patronization' of the philosophy of 'Worship and Rituals' by human beings in a particular manner.

1st Grand Chakra

We do not have any recorded version of history before this. It ended around 1050 BC. But all legends tell us it was the abode of Lord Shiva and his followers were of Naga race. Recall from *Mahabharata*, Prince Takshak, who killed Parikshat – Arjun's son; he was a Naga referred as a serpent in *Mahabharata*. *Rajatarangini* begins with the year 1184 BC when Gonanda I, a 'Shivite' king was ruling Kashmir. The grandson of Gonanda I was Gonanda II who was deposed by one Harandeva a brother of 'Janamejaya' and Grandson of Arjun. Most western and Indian Historians agree that *Mahabharata* war took place around 1000-

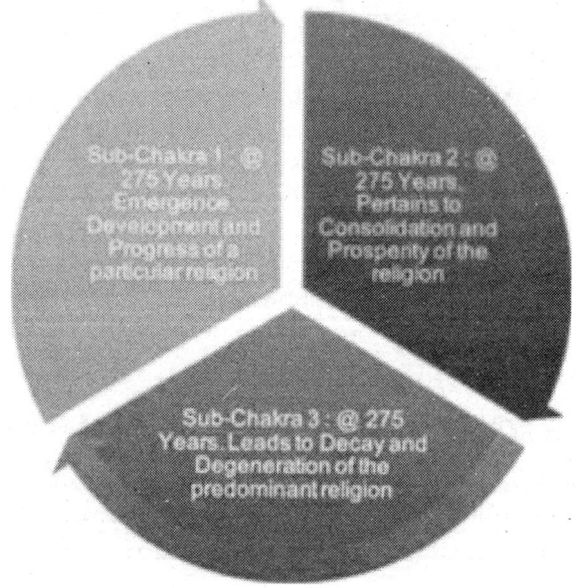

1100 BC, although some Indian scholars put the date around 3000 BC based on new findings. Let us go by the existing opinion. The 'Shaivism' period in Kashmir ended with the deposition of Gonanda II by Harandeva a Vaishnavite.

2nd Grand Chakra

Began around 1030-1050 BC. 'Vaishnavism' dominated it and it ended around 250 BC when great 'Ashoka' came to Kashmir and founded Srinagar (summer capital of Jammu and Kashmir, in honour of goddess Laxmi, Hindu goddess for wealth). Note, he was a Buddhist king and he established a city in the name of Vasihnav goddess. It explains that cults (or so-called religions of today) had no separate identity. They were intermixing and intermingling. This is one hypothesis in the absence of any western recorded history.

3rd Grand Chakra

Heralded Buddhism in Kashmir and ruled the roost in between 250 BC to AD 530. 'Kushan' kings patronized it. 'Kushans' came to Kashmir from China around 260 BC. They were followed by Shakas and Huns. This grand cycle ended with the emergence of Huns (a Chinese tribe), its first king of Kashmir was Mihirkula, a known tyrant in history.

4th Grand Chakra

Established 'Hinduism', began around AD 530, when Gopal Ditya, Mihirkula's son, come to the throne. It is he, who gave religious recognition to the term 'Hinduism' as we know it today. Here-to-fore, the term 'Hindu' was used only as a geographical identity for the land east of river Indus. It is pertinent to note the word 'Hindu' had a Persian origin and derived from 'Sindhu' a Sanskrit word. 'Sindhu' was the name given to river Indus (From Sindhu it became 'Hindu' in Persian and from Hindu, it became 'Indus', Indic or Indi in Greek). Ancient Persians pronounced 'S' as 'H', so 'Sindhu' became 'Hindu'.

No Vedic literature or religious scriptures mention the word 'Hindu,' whether it is 'Vedas,' 'Upanishads' or the great epics of *Ramayana* and *Mahabharata*. In the written form, the first time the word 'Hindu' appears on a tablet dated back to 518 BC when king Darius–I was ruling Persia. He used it to describe the geographical extent of his kingdom up to and beyond river Hindu (or Sindhu or Indus). It was a Chinese Hun, who gave 'Hinduism' its religious identity as a composite 'Culture of the Way of Living' of people. This

Grand Chakra of 'Hinduism' flourished in between AD 530-1325. It ended when Rinchen Shah, a Tibetan prince, came to power after marrying Rani Kota Devi, whose husband had run away when the Turks invaded Kashmir in AD 1324.

5th Grand Chakra

Brought in Islam, began around AD 1325 when Rinchen Shah, the King, converted to Islam (with the influence of a Sufi saint) he was snubbed by a Brahmin Dev Swami, who stopped him from converting to Hinduism. An outsider, Gopalditya – a Hun, had initiated the reign of Hinduism in Kashmir, but another outsider was prevented and he brought in Islam. This is interesting fact not known by many. Even before this, all famous Buddhist kings of Kashmir had been outsiders (in today's context) – Kushans from China such as Jalushka, Haluska and Kanishka. Do not forget Harandeva (great grandson of Arjuna of *Mahabharata* fame), was also an outsider. So an interesting correlation, outsiders are an inherent part of the Kashmir polity.

For 500 years Islam ruled Kashmir, up to AD 1820 – till Maharaja Ranjit Singh annexed it from Sikh dynasty. The third sub-chakra of the 5th Grand Chakra began around AD 1820. This sub chakra is of Decay and Degeneration. If you add other 265-275 years to the AD 1820, this Grand Chakra will close around AD 2085-2095 (this is 2018, so technically, 75 plus years more).

6th Grand Chakra

Has not yet happened. In other words, by the end of 21st century, this will take over. What will be its ingredients? It could be more liberalized 'Pluralism' or 'Co-existence' or maybe No-existence. Humanity would have entered the Cosmic Age to face the Aliens Ancestors.

Kashmir has a history of over 5,000 years. May look mythological to some liberal elites as they lack understanding and study of a very old civilization, anyway moving ahead the last couple of thousand years till about AD 12th century have been more or less authenticated by Sir Aural Stein in the *Memoir on the Geography of Kashmir*.

Kashmir had known tyrants in its history: from 'Jaldevs' in the ancient times to 'Mihirkulas' in the medieval times. All were outsiders. Today's Salahuddin, Masood Azhar, Musa and their elk are the replicas of yesteryears 'Jaldevs' and 'Mihirkulas'. History of Kashmir is using the terror groups to move on its pre-ordained path. History will find a cure at the right time. Wait until the end of the century. Sad but unfortunate situation. This is the hypothesis one school of thought has on Kashmir and stops us from moving proactively and hence keep adding to the Kashmiri's suffering.

The way Kashmiris have been suffering for over last three centuries makes one think that there is a curse on this 'Paradise on Earth'. Even in earlier times, there have been many episodes of suffering due to natural calamities or man-made causes such as internecine wars. Another interesting but unproven theory is about Jewish incursions in Kashmir which claim Kashmiris to be part of the missing tribe of the Israelites who were dispersed all over the world after the destruction of the second temple by the Romans. Jews too as mentioned in *Holy Quran* were cursed by God after their ignominious behaviour mentioned in Sura Bakara. In either case, there seems to be a curse on Kashmir which refuses to go away.

Most of the earlier travellers visiting Kashmir have been critical of the character and the behaviour of Kashmiris. The reasons for this behaviour have been given as the endless persecution of the local people by outside rulers. One cannot expect a person being persecuted continuously to exhibit any traits of decency, honesty and integrity. A person whose very existence is threatened can be expected to go to any length to save his self. The worst traits and failings become part of the character and the concerned person feels no compunction in professing these without any moral or psychological remorse. These things get ingrained in the human psyche and a person considers these to be the expected normal behaviour.

Let me share with you an interesting anecdote. Once Nehru and Ghaffar Khan (Frontier Gandhi/Bacha Khan) were invited by Sheikh Abdullah to Srinagar, this was summer of 1945. The Lion of Kashmir had laid on a Mughal-style welcome for his VIP guests. The guests were taken downriver on lavishly decorated Shikaras. Barred from gathering on the four bridges along the route, Abdullah's local Muslim opponents stood on the embankment, dressed in Phirans (traditional Kashmiri dress), long tunics which almost touched the ground. In the summer months, it was customary in Kashmir to not wear underclothes (Wow). As the boats approached, the male protesters lifted their Phirans to reveal their pencils (private parts), while the Caucasian-looking blue-eyed Kashmiri women turned and bared their backs by lifting their Phirans. Nehru, when asked about the incident at dinner, said, "Punjabis are crude, Bengalis are hysterical and the Kashmiris are simply vulgar."

After the devastation and displacement caused by the recent flood, one would have expected people to remain in shock for a long time. However, daily stone pelting and terrorist attacks on the security personnel's gives an impression that nothing has changed and the people are behaving as they used to do. There has been no chastisement as one would have expected from such a natural disaster attributed by many to be the 'Divine Retribution'. People are on the path to usher in the same lot of so-called leaders who turned Kashmir into a virtual den of corruption, dishonesty and immorality.

Incidentally, the first victims of the curse were Kashmiri Pandits who got thrown out en masse from the place where they had lived for centuries. The same Muslim neighbours who kicked them out also had to go through the worst period, like meeting the natural justice. Allegedly over a hundred thousand were killed, thousands were maimed, hundreds of women were raped and properties worth crores were destroyed. Even such terrible happenings did not make them change their attitude. The same story continues endlessly. One wonders when and how will the 'Visoka's Curse' go off from the vale of Kashmir? Will it ever go?

Now let us analyze the transformational journey of this land. I have not yet found another parallel in the history, where a 'rich' culture like Kashmiri Shi'ites got converted en masse to Islam. This happened not due to the cultural and spiritual superiority but due to the brutality of the Mongol rulers and by a sagacious Persian Sufi, Mir Sayyid Ali Hamadani buried in Tajikistan. He played a key role in that perspective, influencing Hindus psyche. Be it spirituality, devotional songs or objectifying the Dargah, this was the copy paste of Shaivism blueprint. Now after making inroads into such a large population, Islam slowly became the religion of the ruler giving Kashmiri's a sense of superiority vis-a-vis their Hindu Pandit counterparts. The main reason for conversion through history has always been coercion or social status enhancement. Egyptian followed pagan rites, adopted monotheism, returned to Isis and Osiris, embraced Christianity and finally were submitted by the Islamic tribes. Spanish Inquisition and expulsion's politics played a central role in Jewish and Muslim conversions.

Today Islam is the world's fastest-growing faith, while the world's population is projected to grow 32% in the coming decades, the number of Muslims is expected to increase by 70% – from 1.8 billion in 2015 to nearly 3 billion in 2060. In 2015, Muslims made up 24.1% of the global population. Forty-five years later, they are expected to make up more than three-in-ten of the world's people (31.1%) according to the Pew study. This has caused many countries and societies to change their equilibrium and hence to cause massive

Tsunami or in Corporate lingo enormous disruption and whenever an equilibrium is changed things starts in motion.

As Hardy-Weinberg says in his famous Equilibrium Principle, that Equilibrium can be disturbed by many forces and currently the momentum of growth of the Islamic believers is huge causing some disturbances in the equilibrium status of a society and hence all these clashes and conflicts around the globe. Europe is one example. The world's other faiths have not yet come to terms with Islam's rampaging juggernauts, fear of this disruption has pushed a counter-reaction by simply making it a villain and vilify all, rather assimilating the Muslims into the western societies, this has caused alienation and may not be the right strategy. No one likes to be continuously put under the radar of suspicion and be branded as a terrorist group after some time that stigma goes away and they become defiant and that's what happens with many Muslim youths of the Kashmir valley. Majority Islamic terror victims are Muslims themselves, but this in no way absolves some Muslims who are radicalizing the Muslim youths and making this world a dangerous place to live. As they say, almost all terrorists are Muslims but not all Muslims are terrorists.

Kashmiri youths are the slightly different case; their alienation may not be totally because of not being assimilated to the larger Indian mass, as they are in the majority in their State. They have surely faced invaders, army and wars for a very long stretch of time in their long, turbulent history. Even the Jews and the unfortunate concentration camp episode was less than a decade. So the kids borne from these parents in Kashmir will surely have genetic evolution or metabolism changes due to the environmental situation and hence the survival genes dominance takes the evolutionary path and makes them in '24 × 7' confrontational path with the prevailing systems, be it their local police, local government, federal army, or the security forces. Same stone-pelters line up for army job recruitments in large numbers and next day will have stones in their hands. This asynchronous behaviour needs to be researched further for any lasting people's solution. These poor kids need healing touch and some understanding of their mental metabolic shift. This is the topic of research and beyond the scope of this book.

Kashmiri Muslims started converts and hence were in a constant love-hate relationship with their Kashmiri Pandit neighbours - their genetic brothers. The situation was under control till the rulers were Muslims. As Sikhs and Dogras dynasties came, Muslim majority Kashmiris started complaining (sometimes for right reasons), the typical complaints were, Hindu and Sikh rulers were not kind to the

Muslim majority population, various taxes were put on the poor classes, less or no opportunity in jobs, educations, etc. When any non-partisan historian compares this with the brutal conversion and killings by the Muslim rulers in other parts of India, burning of millions of important artefacts and books from Sarnath library or breaking of so many holy and archeologically ancient Hindu temples or using their plinths for constructing mosques, it is nothing. One cannot justify any wrong doings but citing past historical events as the reason for mistrust among both the communities resulting in majority Kashmir valley residents choosing Pakistan as the natural ally, hence the shout of 'Azaadi' and 'Kashmir Banega Pakistan', causing colossal heartburn to India.

The large presence of the Indian army men, allegedly 7,00,000 in numbers gives the entire valley a war zone look. Federal government explanation is that it's the border State with a defined enemy nation as its neighbour and with continuous terror attacks both inside the region and also at the LoC. This is an unfortunate reality. Things can be worked out to address this but for that valley has to get back to its normalization. Kashmir has undoubtedly changed from Sufi Islam where there was room for others also to co-exist, today's Salafi/ Wahhabi Islam influence have closed that room, many Kashmiri intellectuals and moderate separatist leaders will not accept this but this is the fact. For separatist it's the security personnel who are creating terror among the locals and folk like Burhan Wanis of the world is the product of such atrocities. Whatever logic and rationality one can bring in their argument, one thing is sure if Kashmiris does not accept the definition of the Nation-State and think India has occupied them and keep raising Azaadi, their pain will continue. They have to find a solution by mingling with the rest of India. Far too long it was Delhi trying to reach out and appease Kashmiris. I will not say Delhi was always right as they have goofed up multiple times in past, money never reached the needy in the J&K State. But the current mood has changed and this time the alienation is from the rest of India for the Kashmiri people.

Now coming to the *'Kashmir mange Azaadi'* (freedom) slogan, well there are States in India which are more miserable than Kashmir and have always felt that the Central Government gave them step-motherly treatment, but they never wanted to break away from the Union. Tamil Nadu and Punjab had momentarily got influenced during Prabhakaran and Bhindranwale eras, but these were tiny fringes and it died after the Sri Lankan and Indian armies killed Prabhakaran and Bhindranwale respectively. Kashmiris surely needs help from siege mentality, identity crisis, suspicion by rest of India, joblessness, hopelessness, terrorism, insults, self-esteem loss, war zone related crimes, allegedly rapes, unaccounted killings of the youths, this should surely be addressed by the State and federal government, as in spite of everything Kashmiris are Indian citizen first, protected by the Indian Constitution. The unfortunate stones in the hands of the Kashmiri kids should convert into laptops, books, cricket bats and flowers. 'Kashmiriyat', 'Jamhooriyat', 'Insaniyat', each of these words must be translated into useful principles, for they represent key make of the Kashmir psyche and hence the solution. This maybe a mirage in the current situation and hence the herculean task to bring peace in this beautiful Himalayan State.

Kashmiris have no connection either spiritually or socially with rest of the Indian Muslims and they do not marry, invest or buy properties at each other's place. Problem with Kashmir conflict, the so-called unfinished agenda of Partition as Pakistan puts it, is that the majority Muslims do not want to be ruled by a democratic government as they have mind block that these folks are primarily Hindus. Even MA Jinnah, the founding father of Pakistan, had left the Indian Congress party in the 1930s, partly because he was uneasy about Gandhi's use of Hindu religious imagery. Ridiculous but unfortunately true.

Kashmiris have Article 370 implemented which stops any business house to invest there be it tourism or agriculture or education of the State, it has to be only via government agencies and hence the implementation will suffer as the case for any developing country, governments are not supposed to do business, run schools, factories etc for you.

When millions of Hindu population lived under Muslim rulers for 500 years, paid Jazia and got killed, their women population raped and their temples brutally destroyed what makes Kashmiris so unique that they cannot live in a democratic set-up where the government may constitute more of Hindu employees than say Muslims but have total freedom to preach and practice their faith. Is the government implementing *Manusmriti* rules or the Constitution of India for the governance? What is this Azaadi demand? Territorial Azaadi or freedom to preach and practice one's faith?

Yes, there has been a lousy treatment of Muslims under Dogras rule, but then Kingship had no rationality and logic and was purely personality driven governance of a King, that's why we do not have Kings anymore across the globe (some symbolic ones left). So the complaint is baseless as the Government of India does not share blood lineage with the Dogra kings. What has a democratic and independent Republic of India to do with these kings and their past deeds? If there is a question on the way Indian Constitution is written which affects someone's Azaadi, then it makes sense for carrying out Kashmir Azaadi Movement. But that is not the case.

India evidently goofed up some elections in Kashmir causing undemocratic rule in the valley, but then for that matter, all the States of the cow belt of India faced similar electoral results during '70s and '80s before the EVM came into existence. This was the natural progression of a country that had just broken the shackle of slavery from the colonial powers (France, Portugal and British) and became independent and was learning to set the institutions and governance, just to use that as an argument for alienation is again poppycock.

Kashmiri Pandits because of their focus on education in spite of being ruled mostly by the brutal Muslim rulers kept their edge on the education and grabbed whatever little opportunity they got in the jobs post-Independence. They might have discriminated against the local poor Muslim Kashmiris and hence societal enmity is possible but to orchestrate ethnic cleansing of the entire Kashmiri Pandit community and then to say Kashmiriyat is Zinda and the Kashmir conflict is only political and not radicalization maybe pushing the envelope little too far. Rest of the Muslims in India feel sorry for the Kashmiris but due to the self-imposed Kashmiriyat (false sense of superiority) and constitutional Articles like 35A and 370 negatively affects the social bondings also due to no inheritance or owning of properties no marriage happens with outside folks, the assimilation of the society with outside world is blocked and hence right mentorship, flexibility and openness suffers.

Indian policy-makers have not helped solve this due to myopic, no will-power and hiatus strategy which recalibrates after each federal election, held every five years. There is no continued and long-term well thought out strategy. First Islam, a religion of peace has to be taken out of this debate, Hindus should accept and understand that Islam is fastest growing religion, so bond with them know them better and from a close angle and then learn to respect and co-exist and do not unnecessarily vilify the entire community. This is one genuine complaint I came across talking to so many Muslim friends from the Valley.

If India has to be proud of her secular and plural character (thanks to majority Hindu population), then they should invite their Muslim friends to their house and share the kitchen and have them reciprocate as food is the fastest way to reach one's heart. The only issue here is the suspicion of 'beef' being part of Muslim kitchen, discuss and address mutually, *Quran* also preaches to respect others' faiths and sentiments. I think society has not matured enough. Long years of appeasement policy of the minorities did not give space for any healthy discussion and everything was tagged as communal and hence taboo. This appeasement policy created a false sense of unnatural parity, which ignored the fascinating fact that minority and majority can still lovingly and peacefully co-exist with no unfair treatment to each. Parity *vs* Uniqueness has to be better understood.

Even Almighty Creator did not make all of us same and he made all of us unique. Even our body parts are not identical; we have different size fingers in our palm, the parity as understood has created unnecessary problems, no one becomes *Chota-Bara* (big-small). This is no way demeaning or lessening of anyone's position. Now when you know that, you will have lessor communal nuisance, which muhalla to take Tazia processions or request to change the Durga Puja or Ganesh Visarjan processions routes passing through a minority neighbourhood. All these events happening in the rest of India communally charges the Kashmir valley.

Hindus as always due to their majority status in India have a bigger role to play and have to focus on the upliftment of their community and also minorities along with them, issues like Cow Vigilante, Love Jihad, Ghar Wapsi, should be inevitably not brushed under the carpet if it affects them, but have it first addressed with both side communities leaders, make them see it from more balanced perspective before outsiders can sprinkle communal salt. The minority should be aware and also be sensitive to majorities eating habits, faiths and culture, etc, especially in India, cow has a different status, now good or bad, one has to be sensitive and respectful. I guess a middle path can emerge with community elders involved and for that healthy environment with proper communication channel need to exist.

The government should not interfere to decide its citizen's menu as far as possible, maybe when India becomes little more advanced and mature as society issues like beef, pork, alcohol, etc which have been banned by the various State Governments will become more acceptable. I firmly believe (except cow, due to religious belief) government should not have any say to decide its citizen's kitchen menu. But having said that even in the liberal democracy like the USA, horse meat is banned and is not a delicacy. Maybe cow (not the bull or buffalo) gets into endangered species category due to its firm religious belief by majority citizens if that helps. All these issues suddenly popping up in India post-right-wing federal party government has given separatists and Indian enemies across the border ammunition to communalize the Kashmir Valley, influence and push the Sufi land kids to the Islamic caliphate fold. Their propaganda machinery surely has better storytelling capabilities and thanks to social media, twitter, WhatsApp, Facebooks and Instagram technologies, has brought massive disruption and the reach has become millions of times more, so the impact is large and fasts sometimes beyond State machinery and security groups to comprehend and control.

Kashmir's political space is usually contested between Hurriyat, Jamaat, militant and mainstream parties. This contest can get complex as the new militant campaign driven by the idea of Sharia and the Caliphate is striving to capture the imagination of the people, particularly the youth. Kashmir has a huge youth population that is hesitant to step out because of lack of awareness, empowerment and apprehension. The spirit of entrepreneurship too is hardly developed. Kashmir's potential economic wealth remains much under actualized because of the prolonged disturbed situation and also lack of requisite skills and enterprise. Fortunately, infrastructure like the internal road network is better than several other parts of the country. To optimize Kashmir's economic potential all, the three arteries connecting Kashmir to the other parts of the Country via Sinthan, Pir Ki Gali and of course Banihal need to be developed.

By connecting economics with security and education, it is possible to actualize the untapped economic potential and also provide meaningful employment for the youth. With this potentially more virulent brand of Sharia-Caliphate driven militancy striving for popular support, time is of the essence. If all the instruments, ie, politics, security, diplomacy, economic, social, information, education and justice get connected and focused, it is possible to turn the tables on Kashmir.

Muslims should also learn to co-exist as you cannot have all the secular rights when you are in minority status and want different rule when in majority status (governed by Sharia) this won't happen in India or any developed nations. There are some 50 plus Muslim countries and they practice and preach Islam with little to no religious rights for the other faiths. But in India, there is parity with the larger majority population, thanks to the Indian Constitution. This should be acknowledged and respected; sometimes majority also needs some praise by the minorities on such beautiful democratic set-up. The population of Muslims in India post-1947 has reached 170 million from 35 million. India's number of Muslims is growing at a faster rate than the country's majority Hindu population and is projected to rise from 14.9% of India's 2015 population to 19.4% (or 333 million people) in 2060. On the other side, a country formed on the two nation theory concept had minority Hindu population reduced from 24% in 1947 to 1.6% 2017. This fact has to be appreciated.

Hindus got influenced by Sufi Islam though many of my Sunni friends will keep saying that this is fake Islam and they do not want objectification of a *dargah,* please believe whatever you want as you have right under Indian Constitution but do not allow folks like Zakir Naik to venomize the youths and Muslim population by daily sermons on how his faith is the only right faith, others are fake and it will not stop here, its followed with conversion, this is direct trespassing into others territory and hence the reason for many of the today's problems and destruction of the social harmony. *Quran* never spoke of not respecting other faiths. Do not allow anyone who says this in your Friday sermons and these half-baked moulvis should be immediately taken to a correctional facility, making mandatory one-year reading and preaching of the Indian Constitution.

> *Pakistan se rishta kya? La ilaha illallah, Azaadi ka matlab kya? La ilaha illallah, Nanga bhookha Hindustan, jaan se pyaara Pakistan.*
>
> (What is our bond with Pakistan? There is no God but only Allah. What does freedom mean? There is no God but only Allah. Naked, starving India take a note, Pakistan is more precious than life itself).

Unfortunately, this reverberates in the valley after Friday prayers.

Pakistan to me is one important stakeholder and unfortunately can't be ignored. So what will you talk and with whom, this has been a question with the Indian policy-makers? Well definitely with the elected government, their army which has the country and their ISI's. Top Pakistani Generals, when they retire, get a considerable bonanza of land and money, on an average $20 million deposits happens in the UK and other Western countries, their kids get a visa to educate and live in these safe countries. This comfort zones should be intruded in the strategy formulation by India, raise the cost of the continued proxy which Pakistan is playing by carrot and stick policy.

This can be done by first showing them the bigger picture of peaceful existence and using India's clout, to help them become the leaders of the Muslim world, make them beneficiaries of the various water and power projects emanating from Indus and other Kashmiri rivers, let these ISI and Pakistani Army top bosses, some 50 in numbers enjoy the financial packages post-retirement. If they backstab or play double cross, then hurt them most where it hurts using various statecrafts. The fear of no safe heavens when perpetrating a crime, sitting happily in some far place and continue bleeding Kashmir and its beautiful people, should not be allowed.

I am for modifying Article 370, which may give more power to local Kashmiris to govern themselves, but the State has to be integrated with the rest of India. Article 35A should go, AFSPA should have a timeline, SOP to tackle the local terrorists, stone-pelters, sympathizers should be defined and educated to youths and their family via TV before implementing it. No Politicians to overrule the defined SOPs. Political prisoners should not be kept in Kashmir and send to other State's prison of India.

Recently, in a major goof-up, Pakistan's permanent representative to the UN Maleeha Lodhi flashed a picture of an injured Gaza girl with no connection to India. Lodhi, on the floor of the UN General Assembly, held up a photograph of a woman whose face was peppered with alleged pellet gun wounds. "This is the face of Indian democracy," Lodhi roared. Soon India was choosing their right to respond, lashed out by pointing at this embarrassing and shameful error terming Pakistan as 'Terroristan', a new name. All this pours cold water on any hope for this conflict resolution pushing it further away in the future.

Historiography has rarely been neutral in South Asia post-1947. If we take the Partition, for India - according to the State-approved traditional nationalist interpretation - it was the unwelcome outcome of Britain's policies of divide and rule. In Pakistan's official narrative, it represented the State's founding moment: the result of a struggle by some of India's Muslims to have their separate political identity recognized. For Bangladesh, the partition represents a false dawn, one that arguably became a necessary prelude to its emergence as a Nation-State from 1971 onwards.

The subaltern studies has brought non-elites into the freedom movement story, made a seismic impact on South Asian history writing. Likewise, the historians' interests have shifted from the larger picture to the smaller details - to see what was happening in localities where broader political occurrences could be placed in their immediate circumstances; this has been further emboldened by the emergence of the influential social media and its reach within large youth population.

History writing, when done well, never involves a static re-enactment of, or a one-way engagement with, the past. Those who write contemporary history knows that the reader is not a passive vessel to receive the text placed before him or her. The reader is also a citizen, a critical citizen, with individual political and ideological preferences. These preferences direct and dictate the reader's view of the past and of leaders and lawmakers most particularly. We live with the consequence of decisions taken by modern politicians, dictators, army heads and often presume that an alternate choice - someone modelled on oneself would have made probably better decisions.

Contemporary historians thus face a challenge from their readers. The scholar who chooses to write on the Lincoln Assassination already had strong views on the topic. For the historians as well as the citizen, the closer one gets to the present and the more judgmental one tends to become. In writing this book, I have honestly been driven by the curiosity rather certainty, by the wish to understand rather than the desire to pass judgment. I have sought to privilege primary sources over retrospective readings, thus to interpret an event of, say, 1989 concerning what was known in 1989 rather than in 2018. This book is an attempt to tell the history of Kashmir from mythological era till today, covering various aspects, beliefs, thoughts, blogs, books, travelogues, words of mouth, as there cannot be one single source that can claim the originality alone. It is an account as well as analysis and also sometimes narrative of the significant characters, controversies, themes and India's *'Chalta hai'*, *'Jugaad'* approach to most of her problems.

However, the manner of the storytelling I have taken has been driven by two fundamental ambitions; to pay proper respect to the diversity, pluralism, mutual co-existence of various religious faiths of India and to unravel the Kashmir puzzle and hence the name of the book *Kashmir – The Bermuda Triangle of India*, that has for so long confronted scholars, historians, citizens and enemies alike. Herman Kahn, a German made his name in the '60s and '70s when futurology was a fashionable pseudo-science. He predicted a world flush with the gadgetry of high technology, populations with masses of leisure time and little work to do, the elimination of famine and disease, a man approaching the resolution of all problems - man's way. He believed that the threat of nuclear war would end.

Herman Kahn is now dead, not his ideas. Kashmir surely would like to believe that Herman prophecies will come true sooner than later helping them get their problem solved humanely.

2. Kashmir Kaleidoscope

Disseminating Kashmir Silhouette

Nehru, India's first Prime Minister was undoubtedly idealistic and romantic about Kashmir. He wrote: "Like some supremely beautiful woman, whose beauty is almost impersonal and above human desire, such as Kashmir in all its feminine beauty of river and valley...."

The term Kashmir refers to the former princely 'State of Jammu and Kashmir'. Pakistanis use the term Kashmir for Kashmir Valley or even POK, the region under their control. The term Kashmir is very important for Pakistan because of the name of their nation, Pakistan, is an acrostic in which the 'K' in the acrostic Pakistan. Pakistanis most of whom are Sunni Muslim (like Saudi Arabia) are interested in the Indian part of Kashmir Valley which is very beautiful, strategically located and reservoir for all the rivers which flows into Pakistan and India from Himalaya. Cashmere is not the right term and is mainly used by some business firms in the west to protect any patent lawsuit when imitating and selling original Kashmiri products. Kashmir came into the economic limelight when the world famous Cashmere wool was exported to other regions and nations of the world.

The Indian Kashmir has three regions, Jammu, Ladakh and Kashmir Valley (where the conflict and separatist movement happens). Pakistan forcefully seized some part of Kashmir just when India and Kashmir King were discussing and finalizing the deal of instrument of annexation, that annexed part of Kashmir land constitutes 35% of the total area of Kashmir, called POK (Pakistan Occupied Kashmir) by India and POK (Azad Kashmir) by Pakistan. This POK constitutes Gilgit region, Baltistan region and POK region. This was annexed by force from King of Kashmir on 24th October 1947, two days before Hindu King Hari Singh of United Kashmir accession to India as per the guidelines laid by British to all the small and big princely States at the time of Indian subcontinent freedom.

For the readers not aware of the region, this book tries to give some glimpses of the place through this chapter. The role of religion is also a factor that needs to be understood in relation to both J&K and its residents. In 1947, religious differences played a major part in instigating the dispute over whether J&K should join India or Pakistan. Hinduism was very broad and was able to accommodate a myriad number of beliefs and practices, including a path for skeptics or even atheists known as Carvaka. Islam, on the other hand, was very tough even on their Ahmadias, they oppose them violently as they consider them as apostates. Not surprisingly, in 1947, almost all J&K Hindus wanted to join Kashmir princely State to India, so too did Buddhists from neighbouring Ladakh. They felt very comfortable with J&K joining this secular nation in which the 'State' gave freedom to practice one's faith with no biasedness. Conversely, the fact that Islam would dominate Pakistan and Pakistani politics made such people feel uncomfortable.

The name Kashmir conjures up images of the boatman in Shikaras on mirrored lakes, majestic mountains, poplar-lined roads, intricately-carved houseboats for use by tourists and beautiful handicrafts, particularly shawls. Equally this name 'Kashmir' also reminds one of the Kashmir dispute. India and Pakistan were both keen to obtain possession of the prestigious princely State of Kashmir. Some of the reasons were J&K was the largest native region in the area, second, it had strategic significance, apart from sharing international borders with China and Afghanistan, three major Himalayan rivers flowed through the princely State and into Punjab (undivided India), these were Indus, Jhelum and Chenab. The Ravi river also ran adjacent to south-eastern J&K. Thirdly India calls Kashmir the crown of India, the very idea of India which is secular where a State has no role in the religion of its citizens has been showcased in Kashmir, where Muslim majority and Hindu minority chose in 1947 to live with newly independent secular India.

Pakistan which was created on the concept of two nation theory wanted to validate its very creation theory by forcefully annexing Kashmir with its territory as it felt that the Muslim majority regions should not stay with non-Muslim State and hence should be annexed at any cost. It is this fundamental conflict in the very definition of each of these two countries and hence the conundrum continues similar to the Bermuda Triangle, making this the longest running UN conflict. Before we get into history and the events that lead to his situation, let's get acquainted with what this paradise constitutes and why it is called Switzerland of East.

Kashmir Region

Kashmir region is the north-western region of the Indian subcontinent. Historically the term Kashmir was used to refer to the valley lying between the Great Himalayas and the Pir Panjal range. Today Kashmir refers to a larger area that includes Jammu and Kashmir (comprising Jammu, Kashmir and Ladakh), the Pakistani occupied regions Northern Areas and POK and the Chinese occupied region of Aksai Chin. Kashmir was originally an important centre of Hinduism, Buddhism and later Islam. Since 1947, when Pakistan separated from India, on the idea of two nation theory, meaning Muslims need a separate country and cannot live with the Infidels (non-Muslims), the region has had a Muslim majority. In the seventeenth century the Mughal emperor Jahangir set his eyes on the valley of Kashmir and believed that if paradise could be experienced anywhere on the earth, it was in Kashmir.

Geography

Millions of years back enormous tidal waves arose from the Indian ocean and layer after layer of silt and rock deposited to make the Himalayan range of mountains. The rock formations are seen today confirm this theory. These waves brought water with them. The receding waters left infertile foothills and the shelving shores. The name 'Kashmir' means "a land desiccated from the water." According to Hindu mythology, sage Kashyapa drained a lake to produce the land now known as Kashmir. There is evidence of a former extensive lake in the physical geography. China borders the Kashmir region to the east, India to the south, Pakistan to the west and Afghanistan to the north. Aksai Chin, which is Uyghur for 'Chin's desert of white stones' and is referred to as the Soda Plain, is a vast desert of salt at heights of 16,400 feet (5,000 metres).

The Kashmir region has a total area of 2,06,552 sq miles (3,32,413 sq km), which is bigger than California but smaller than Texas. Areas of the component territories are: Jammu and Kashmir – 1,38,091 sq miles (2,22,236 sq km), Kashmir Valley is 5,992 sq miles (15,520 sq km); POK, 5,134 sq miles (13,297 sq km); Northern Areas, 43,477 sq miles (69,971 sq km); and Aksai Chin, 19,850 sq miles (31,945 sq km). Jammu and Kashmir can be divided into four geographical regions: the Siwalik Hills, the Kashmir valley and the surrounding Himalayas, the Pir Panjal range and the Indus river basin comprising of Leh and Kargil. Aksai Chin is geographically part of the Tibetan Plateau and the Chang Tang, The region is almost uninhabited and sees little precipitation due to the Himalayan and other mountains to the south soaking up the Indian monsoon.

The Kashmir Valley is famous for its beautiful mountainous landscape; Ladakh is renowned for its remote mountain beauty.

Mountain ranges include the Pir Panjal range, the Himalayas, the Zanskar range, Karakoram range, the Nun Kun range and the Shivalik range. The main Kashmir valley is 62 miles (100 km) wide. The Himalayas divide the Kashmir valley from Ladakh. This densely settled and beautiful valley has an average height of 6,000 feet (1,850 metres) above sea-level, but the surrounding Pir Panjal range has an average elevation of 16,400 feet (5,000 metres). Pakistan Occupied Kashmir or POK boasts some of the most scenic mountains and river valleys. The region includes a significant part of the Himalayas. The Northern Area has the Karakoram Range and the western Himalayas. The Pamir Mountains are to the north and the Hindukush lies to the west. Among the highest mountains are Godwin-Austen (K2), the second highest in the world at 28,251 feet (8,611 metres) and Nanga Parbat, the ninth highest in the world at 26,656 feet (8,125 metres), one of the most feared mountains in the world. Three of the world's seven longest glaciers are in the Northern Areas - the Biafo Glacier, the Baltoro Glacier and the Batura Glacier. The Deosai Plains, located above the tree line, is the second-highest plains in the world at 13,500 feet (4,115 metres). The Deosai Plains is snow-bound for half the year, cover almost 1,158 sq miles (3,000 sq km).

The climate in the region ranges from subtropical in the south-western lowlands to alpine in the high mountain areas. Precipitation is variable - it is heavier in areas west and south of the great ranges affected by monsoonal winds and is sparse to the north and east. In the south around Jammu, rainfall averages 1.6 to 2 inches (40 mm to 50 mm of rain per month between January and March. In the hot season, temperatures in Jammu city can reach up to 104°F (40°C), while in July and August, heavy though erratic rainfall occurs with monthly extremes of up to 25.5 inch (650 mm). Srinagar receives as much as 25 inch (635 millimetre) of rain, with the wettest months being March to May with around 3.3 inch (85 mm) a month. Across from the main Himalaya Range, even the south-west cloudbanks break up and the climate of Ladakh and Zanskar is extremely dry and cold. POK is cold and mountainous in the north while it has a hot and subtropical climate in the southern Mirpur regions. The climate of the Northern Areas varies from region to region.

River Jhelum is the only major Himalayan river which flows through the Kashmir valley. River Indus, Tawi, Ravi and Chenab are the major rivers flowing through the State. Jammu and Kashmir is home to several Himalayan glaciers. There are several high altitude lakes in the Northern Areas, including Sheosar Lake in Deosai Plains and Satpara Lake in Skardu.

The Jammu and Kashmir region has a loamy soil rich in magnesia, as well as clay, sandy soils and peat. The area is rich in pines, conifers and medicinal herbs. In Jammu, there are maples, horse chestnuts and silver fir. At the higher altitudes, there are birch, rhododendron, Berbers and a large number of herbal plants. In the hilly regions of Doda, Udhampur, Poonch and Rajouri, fauna includes leopards, cheetahs and deer, wild sheep, bear, brown musk shrews and muskrats. Varieties of snakes, bats, lizards and frogs are found in the region. The birds in Jammu include chakor, snow partridge, pheasants and peacocks.

The most magnificent of trees in Kashmir is the giant Chinar. Mountain ranges have dense deodar, pine, fir, walnut, willow, almond and cider, while the dense forests contain ibex, snow leopards, musk deer, wolf, markhor, red bears and black bears. There are ducks, goose, partridge, chakor, pheasant, wagtails, herons, water pigeons, warblers and doves. In the arid desert of Ladakh, some 240 species of local and migratory birds have been identified including a black-necked crane. Ladakh has Yaks, Himalayan Ibex, Tibetan antelopes, snow leopards, wild ass, red bears and gazelles.

Jammu and Kashmir is an area of high earthquake risk, classified as zone four risk, a high damage risk zone, with areas classified as very high damage risk. Srinagar, the ancient capital of Jammu and Kashmir, lies alongside Dal Lake and is famous for its canals and houseboats. Srinagar, with an altitude of 5,200 feet (1,600 metres) served as a favoured summer capital for many foreign conquerors who found the heat of the northern Indian plains in the summer oppressive. Just outside the city are the beautiful Shalimar, Nishat and Chashmashahi gardens created by Mughal emperors. POK capital is Muzaffarabad. Gilgit town and Skardu are respectively the capitals of Gilgit and Baltistan. Other important towns include Anantnag, Jammu and Leh.

The climate of the State varies from sub-tropical in Jammu plains to semi-arctic cold in Ladakh with Kashmir and Jammu mountainous tracks having temperate climatic conditions. The average annual rainfall also varies from region to region with 92.6 mm in Leh, 650.5 mm in Srinagar and 1115.9 mm in Jammu. A large part of the State forms part of the Himalayan Mountains. The State is geologically constituted of rocks varying from the oldest period of the earth's history to the youngest present-day river and lake deposits.

Economy

Kashmir's economy is centred on agriculture and tourism. Traditionally the staple crop of the valley is rice. Indian corn comes next, while wheat, barley and oats are also grown. Blessed with a temperate climate unlike much of the Indian subcontinent, it is suited to crops such as asparagus, artichoke, seakale, broad beans, scarlet runners, beetroot, cauliflower and cabbage. Fruit trees are common in the valley and the cultivated orchards yield pears, apples, peaches and cherries fine quality. The chief trees are deodar, firs and pines, chenar or plane, maple, birch and walnut.

Kashmir came into the economic limelight when the world famous Cashmere wool was exported to other regions and nations. Kashmiris are adept at knitting and making fine quality cashmere wool shawls, silk carpets, rugs, *kurtas* (a loose shirt falling either just above or somewhere below the knees of the wearer and worn by both men and women) and pottery. Kashmir is home to the finest saffron in the world. Efforts are on to export the naturally grown fruits and vegetables as organic foods mainly to the Middle-East. Srinagar is also celebrated for its silver-work, paper mache and wood-carving, while silk weaving continues to this day.

Tourism

Tourism forms an integral part of the Kashmiri economy. Often dubbed 'Paradise on Earth', Kashmir's mountainous landscape has attracted tourists for centuries. The Vaishno Devi cave shrine, important for Shakti Hindus, is nestled in the Trikuta Mountains. In 2017, nearly 8 million pilgrims visited Vaishno Devi, making it one of the most visited religious sites in the world. There are numerous pious mosques, such as the Hazratbal Mosque, situated on the banks of the Dal Lake. The sacred hair of the Prophet Mohammad, is said to have been brought there by the Mughal emperor Aurangzeb, kept in the Hazratbal shrine.

Srinagar City, which attracts millions of tourists, has numerous gardens along the banks of Dal Lake. Nishat, Cheshma-i-Shahi, Shalimar and Harven gardens, built by the Mughals, feature the maple-like graceful Chinar trees. Dal Lake was renowned for its size, which stretched for more than 50 sq miles, but has shrunk to less than 10 sq km. Amalgam, at the junction of streams flowing from Shashank Lake and the Lidder river and once was a humble shepherd's village with astounding views, is Kashmir's prime tourist resort, which is cool even during the height of summer. There is a positive impact of tourist inflow on employment generation, ie, with the increase in tourist inflow, total employment also rises. This is directly related to the political and security situation in the Valley.

Amarnath Cave is a Hindu shrine located in Jammu and Kashmir, India. The cave is situated at an altitude of 3,888 m (12,756 ft), about

141 km (88 miles) from Srinagar, the capital of Jammu and Kashmir and reached through Pahalgam town.

The Amarnath Cave was discovered by a Muslim shepherd of Batakot, Buta Malik, when he lost his flock and found that it had strayed into the sacred spot some 150 years ago. Even today his family receives some part of the alms offered by pilgrims. While the earliest reference to Amarnath can be seen in the *Nilamata Purana* (v 1324), a 6th century Sanskrit text which depicts the religious and cultural life of early Kashmiris and gives Kashmir's own creation, the pilgrimage to the holy cave has been described with full topographical details in the *Bhringish Samhita* and the *Amarnath Mahatmya*, both ancient texts said to have been composed even earlier.

Indian mythological era mentions the legend of the Naga Sushruvas, who in his fury burnt to ashes the kingdom of King Nara when he tried to abduct his daughter already married to a Brahmin youth and after the carnage took his abode in the lake now known as Sheshnag (Kashmiri Sushramnag), Kalhana writes: "The lake of dazzling whiteness [resembling] a sea of milk (Sheshnag), which he created [for himself as residence] on a far off mountain, is to the present day seen by the people on the pilgrimage to Amareshwara." (*Rajatarangini*, Book I v 267. Translation: MA Stein). This makes it very clear that pilgrims continued to visit the holy Amarnath cave in the 12th century.

Demographics

Jammu and Kashmir population in 2017 was approximately 14.12 million. This is the only Indian State with a greater Muslim population. Islam is followed by around 68.3% of the population, while 28.4% follow Hinduism, Sikhism (1.9%), Buddhism (0.9%) and Christians (0.3%). Around 96.4% of the number of inhabitants in the Kashmir valley are Muslim trailed by Hindus and Sikhs. The Shia population is 15 lakh in Jammu and Kashmir, which is 14% of the whole State population. The populace density of Jammu and Kashmir is 56 persons per square kilometre. The pre-Independence Census of 1941 recorded Muslims as constituting 72.41% of the population and Hindus 25.0%. Current Sex ratio is 889 females/1,000 males in Kashmir. POK has a population of 4.5 million.

Ethnicity

Approximately 67% of the population of Jammu is Dogra, a northern Indo-Aryan ethnic group. Most Hindus are either Dogras or people who migrated from Kotli, Mirpur and the Kashmir Valley. The Kashmiri people are of a Dardic ethnic group. Originally, the

Kashmiris were Hindus, later some became Buddhists, however, after the conquest of Kashmir by Mughal invaders, most of the Kashmiri Hindus and Buddhists converted to Islam, a religion of the ruling class. There are Sikhs also who live in the Kashmir region. The population living in the Valley of Kashmir is primarily homogeneous, despite the religious divide between Muslims and Hindus. They share a common culture, language, customs and history, which is no doubt the basis of 'Kashmiriyat', which has been passed from many centuries, even before the advent of Islamic Sufism.

Pakistan Occupied Kashmir has 99% ethnic Punjabi population (not Kashmiris), consisting of variants such as Sudhans, Rajputs, Gujjars and Mirpuris who are the closest cultural relatives of the Potohari Punjabis. While the POK people, just like the Ladakhis and Jammuites, are considered Kashmiri as citizens of the Kashmir State, they are however not ethnically Kashmiri and do not have any linguistic, cultural or genetic affinity to the Ethnic Kashmiris who are of Dardic origin.

Ladakh has a blend of many different races, predominantly the Tibetans, Mons and the Dards. People of pure Dard descent predominate in Dras and Dha-Hanu valleys. The residents of Dha-Hanu, known as Brokpa, are followers of Tibetan Buddhism and have preserved much of their original Dardic traditions and customs. The Dards around Dras, however, have converted to Islam and have been strongly influenced by their Kashmiri neighbours. The Mons are descendants of earlier Indian settlers in Ladakh. They mostly work as musicians, blacksmiths and carpenters.

The Changpa nomads who live in the Rupshu plateau are pure Tibetans and it was probably herders like them who first settled in Ladakh and Baltistan. Since the early 1960s, their numbers have increased as Chang Tang nomads from across the border flee to Chinese-ruled Tibet. There are about 3500 refugees in Leh alone. Muslim Arghons, descendants of Kashmiri or Central Asian merchants and Ladakhi women mainly live in Leh. The appearance and lifestyle of both central and eastern Ladakhis and Zanskaris reflect a strong influence from Central Tibet, which diminishes westwards, being replaced by that of Dards. The Baltis of Kargil, Nubra, Suru Valley and Baltistan, however, show strong Tibetan links in their appearance and language and were Bonpa and Buddhists until recent times.

Kashmiri Wedding

A Kashmiri Muslim wedding starts with a thap. The boy and girl meet in a public place, often at a mosque or the Mogul gardens. When the couple accepts each other, jewellery is given to the bride by the groom's family and sometimes rings and flowers are exchanged and the boy and the girl become engaged. In the next few days, the girl's family sends Wazvan, an exclusive meal consisting of 50-60 dishes, to the boy's house. This signifies the announcement of the engagement of the boy. There are two types of engagements - the *nikaah* ceremony after which the bride and the groom are considered married and the *mabadh* ceremony. The engagement period can be for a couple of months or a couple of years.

When the boy's parents decide to bring the bride home, a wedding function, which takes the form of a three-day get-together of the two families, is organized. Activities over those three days include the bride plaiting her hair, which is unplaited by the married women of the family, the bride's hands and feet being decorated with *mehndi,* a temporary skin decoration of henna, a dinner, an elaborate wedding procession with its own musical band and dancers, the bride being bathed by her mother and aunts and the bride being dressed in the traditional *salwar kameez,* a traditional dress worn by both women and men. When the wedding procession arrives at the girl's house, the women sing traditional wedding songs; the groom is showered with coins and almonds, the groom is served dinner. The amount of the *meher,* a sum of money which the husband must give his wife any time after marriage and in case there is a divorce the amount has to be given immediately, is fixed.

The next seven days see a plethora of guests bearing gifts and dried fruits, visiting the respective homes of the boy and the girl. On the third or the fourth day after the wedding, the bride and the groom visit the girl's home, where they are served an elaborate dinner. On the seventh day, the bride's aunts visit her, have a small party, then take the bride with them for a few days. At this time the formal part of the wedding is over. If the marriages don't work out, then there's Talaq and Halala.

Language

The people in the Jammu area speak Hindi, Punjabi and Dogri (which is close to Punjabi). The inhabitants of the Kashmir Valley and the Pakistani areas speak Koshur and Urdu respectively. The Kashmiris speak the Kashmiri language known as Koshur. The dominant language of POK is Northern Hindko. The Hindko dialects spoken in POK are both distantly related to Punjabi. Pashto is spoken by a sizable minority, brought by the sizable migrant Afghan community in the Mirpur area. Urdu, Kashmiri and Gojri are the official languages of AJ&K (Pakistan controlled), it's primarily Pahari language. Arabic script is used as their writing script.

The principal language of Ladakh is Ladakhi, a Tibetan dialect that is different enough from Tibetan that Ladakhis and Tibetans often speak Hindi or English when they need to communicate. Urban Ladakhis usually know Hindi/Urdu and often English. Within Ladakh, there is a range of dialects, so that the language of the Chang-pa people may differ markedly from that of the Purig-pa in Kargil, or the Zanskaris, but they are all mutually comprehensible. Ladakhi has had no written form distinct from classical Tibetan, but some Ladakhi scholars have started using the Tibetan script to write the colloquial tongue. Administrative work is carried out in Urdu and, increasingly, English.

Urdu is the *lingua franca* of the Northern Areas, understood by most inhabitants. The Shina language (with several dialects) is the language of 40% of the population, spoken mainly in Gilgit, throughout Diamer and some parts of Ghizer. The Balti language, a sub-dialect of Ladakhi and part of Tibetan language group, is spoken by the population of Baltistan. Minor languages spoken include Wakhi language spoken in upper Hunza and some villages in Ghizer, while Khowar is the major language of Ghizer. Burushaski is an isolated language spoken in Hunza, Nagar, Yasin (where Khowar is also spoken), some parts of Gilgit and some villages of Punyal. Another interesting language is Domaaki, spoken by the musician clans of the region. A sizable minority speaks Pashto.

Culture

One of the India's oldest calendars the 'Saptarishi Samvat' is from Kashmir. It dates back to 3076 BC. This is one big contribution of J&K to the world. There are different traditions regarding food, dressing, ceremonies, etc. Rice is the staple food of Kashmiris. Besides that, the majority of the people have their farms, so they grow their wheat, corn, vegetables, fruits, herbs, etc, they also raise farm animals like cows, goats, chickens. In the region of Muzaffarabad, people do their breakfast with yogurt, naan, Kulcha and pink tea. At the time of ceremonies, the food served must contain 'Lobia Daal Chawaal'. Also, pink tea and Black Tea (Kahwa) are compulsory items after food. Another important thing to be noticed is that Kashmiris use salt in the tea (black tea with milk). Kashmiris are good in handicrafts, carpet weaving, shawls and wood carvings. Sandal made of Rope (Baan) and LooI (Men Shawl) are also famous. The caste system is very active in POK. People are known, identified and judged by their castes. Key castes are Rajputs, Sudhans, Watt, Chughtais, Syeds, Daars. Kashmiri lifestyle is essentially slow paced, irrespective of the different religious beliefs. Mostly they are peace-loving people; the culture has been rich enough to reflect the religious diversity as tribes celebrate festivities that divert them from their otherwise monotonous and conflict-ridden life.

Clothing

The authentic dresses of Jammu and Kashmir are renowned for their embroidery and intricate designs that reflect the richness of the culture and landscape of the region. The form of clothing is designed primarily to counter the cold climate of the region. Such cultural influences along with influences on tradition coupled with the climatic factors are mirrored in the traditional attire. Most of the garments are made of wool, cotton and silk designed with intricate embroideries. This long gown has a lot of beautiful embroidery work on it consisting of floral motifs.

Kashmiri women are renowned for their beauty in India. It is said that they possess "an English rosiness of complexion behind the Eastern tan." Their hair colour ranges from golden red to brunette and their eye colour varies between green, blue, grey and black. Besides being boats, women and farmers, the women of Kashmir lend their men-folk a helping hand in shawl making, embroidery and other handicrafts.

A Hindu woman's Pheran could touch her feet whereas a Muslim woman's Pheran is knee-length, loose and embroidered in front and on the edges. It is tied at the waist for the sake of smartness and is made of a folded material called lunge. The long loose sleeves are decorated with brocade. The head-dress called Taranga is worn with this type of costume and is tied to a hanging bonnet. It tapers down to the heels from behind.

After the 'Reform Movement' of the thirties, the women of the State took to the sari. However, on the wedding day, women would wear the Taranga ceremonially. It is covered with the end 'palav' of the bride's wedding sari. In contrast to Hindu woman's Pheran, which imparts her Roman look, the Pheran of Muslim women is delightfully embroidered in front. Their headgear, the Kasaba, looks very different from the Taranga. It is red, tied like a turban and held tight by an abundance of silver pins and trinkets.

The traditional outfit for both males and females in Kashmir is the Pheran and Poots. They consist of two gowns, one over the other. The traditional Pheran and Poots extend to the feet, which was popular up to the late 19th century CE. However, a relatively modern variation of the Pheran and poots extends to below the knees, which is worn with a *suthan* (the loose form of *shalwar*) similar to the styles worn in Afghanistan. Salwars (or *shalwars*) are loose pajama-like trousers. The legs are wide at the top and narrow at the bottom. The *kameez* is a long shirt or tunic. The side seams (known as the *chaak*) are left open below the waist-line, which gives the wearer greater freedom of movement. In Afghanistan and Pakistan, it is the preferred garment of both sexes. It is optional to wear the suthan with a long Pheran as traditionally lower garments are not worn with Pheran.

The outfit has been vogue in Kashmir since before the 15th century.

Hindu females use a 'taranga', a headdress which becomes smaller down at the back, towards the heels. Islamic Kashmiri females use a red headwear known as the 'kasaba'. The kasaba is padded employing a turban and is pinned together by brooches. A pin-scarf revoked from the kasaba descends towards the neck.

Cuisine

Cuisine of Kashmir is famous for its delectable vegetarian as well as non-vegetarian dishes. The style of cooking is different for Hindus and Muslims of the rest of the India or Pakistan. Traditional Kashmiri food includes dum aloo (boiled potatoes with heavy amounts of spice), tzaman (solid cottage cheese), rogan josh (lamb cooked in heavy spices), zaam dod (yogurt/curd), yakhayn (lamb cooked in mild spices), hakh (spinach-like leaf), rista-gushtava (minced meat balls in tomato and curd curry) and of course rice, the staple food of Asian cultures.

The first main influence on the cuisine was the food of the Kashmiri Pandits. Kashmiri Pandit cuisine usually uses yogurt and turmeric and does not use onion and garlic. The cuisine was then influenced by the people who invaded with Timur from the area of modern Uzbekistan, as well as by Persian and Afghan cultures.

The traditional 36-course wazwan is considered the height of Kashmiri cuisine. Probably no other cuisine in the world has so many courses. The preparation is considered an art and is traditionally done by a vasta waza or head chef, with the assistance of a court of wazas or chefs. The wazwan is most often prepared for a big event, especially marriages.

Literature

Kashmiri literature has a history of at least 2,500 years, going back to its glory days of Sanskrit. Early names include Patanjali, the author of the

Mahabhashya commentary on Panini grammar, suggested by some to have been the same to write the Hindu treatise known as the Yoga Sutra and Dridhbala. In medieval times the great Hindu school of Kashmir Shaivism arose. Its great masters include Vasugupta (c 800), Utpala (c 925), Abhinavagupta and Kshemaraja. In the theory of aesthetics, one can list the Anandavardhana and Abhinavagupta. The use of the Kashmiri language began with the poet Lalleshvari or Lal Ded (fourteenth century), who wrote mystical verses. Another mystic of the time, equally revered in Kashmir and popularly known as Nunda Reshi, wrote powerful poetry like his senior Lal Ded. Later came Habba Khatoon alias Zoon (sixteenth century) with her own LOL style.

Arthur Anthony MacDonnell, the great Professor of Sanskrit at Oxford University, once remarked, "History is the one weak spot in Indian Literature." But the twelfth century Kashmiri Pandit scholar, Kalhana, putting aside the Hindu question of existence being 'dream and delusion', penned the magnum opus, *Rajatarangini* (River of Kings), which is counted among the world's most extraordinary historical works. In the tenth century, the great Abhinavagupta wrote thirty-five works, including *Tantraloka,* a treatise on Kashmir Shaivism and *Abhinavabharti,* a splendid commentary on the Natyasastra, the seed of the Indian performing arts. The eleventh-century poet Kshemendra wrote *Brihatkathamanjari*, a collection of stories representing the lost tradition of brihatkatha (big story). From the same text, Somadeva, prepared the famous *Kathasaritsagara.*

The eleventh century Pandit poet Bilhana had a secret affair with a king's daughter. When it was discovered, he was thrown into prison and ordered to be executed by beheading. Even while facing the prospect of execution, he wrote poetry. It was in the darkness of prison that he wrote his *Chaurapanchasika* (collection of fifty verses by a love thief). Many centuries earlier, Kashmiri Pandit scholars made immense contributions to Buddhism, which came to Kashmir with emperor Ashoka around 250 BC. It was in Kashmir that Buddhist scriptures were written in Sanskrit for the first time. Kumar Rajiv, a Buddhist monk, whose father was a Kashmiri Pandit, who translated the Buddhist *Lotus Sutra* into Chinese in AD 406. Guru Padmasambhava alias Rinpoche also referred as second Buddha, spent time in Kashmir. A Kashmiri Pandit woman named Lakshmi travelled to Tibet and taught Anuttarayoga Tantra. It was in the fifth century in Tibet that Pandits got a title of Bhatta or Bhats meaning the learned one. By the arrival of the 8th century, Buddhism was a waning philosophy on the horizon of Kashmir. The local faith which had hitherto been greatly influenced by Buddhist thought and philosophy, was fast returning to its Tantric, Shaivite and Agamic roots. Such was the time when Shankaracharya is believed to have set foot on the pious land of Sharda.

In the pursuit of demystifying Shankaracharya reanimating the corpse of the dead king. GC Pande makes the following observation:

> "Presumably the legend arose from a misunderstanding. Kamakala did not merely mean erotic's, but had a technical significance in Tantra Shastra for which Kashmir was famous. This sense may be seen in *Kamakala Vilasa*. Shankara could have acquired a knowledge of the strongly Advaiatic Tantra Shastras in Kashmir, which would fit in with the tradition that ascribes the *Saundaraya Lahari* and the Prapanchsara to him as also the fact of the currency of Srividya among his followers. A commentary of the Prapanchsara records that the work was compiled by Shankara in Kashmir."

Music and Dance

Kashmiris are known to enjoy their music in its various local forms and the dress of both sexes is quite colourful. The dumhal is a famous dance in Kashmir, performed by men of the Wattal region. The women perform the rouff, another folk dance. Kashmir has been noted for its fine arts for centuries, including poetry and handicrafts.

Kashmiri music is closer to Central Asian music, using traditional Central Asian instruments and musical scales. Kashmiri music uses a wide variety of musical scales, everything from musical scales which are very similar to the Byzantine scale and harmonic minor scale, to the more melodic sounding major and minor scales. In some Kashmiri music, vocals are given the central role, but in many other varieties, the instruments lead. Traditional Kashmiri vocals are harmonized.

Sufiana Kalam is popular in Kashmir, where the practice of Islam has heavy Sufi influences. This form of music is accompanied by a 70-stringed instrument called the Santoor, a trapezoid-shaped hammered dulcimer often made of walnut, along with the Kashmiri saz, a long-necked lute. Sufiana Kalam has been popular in Kashmir since arriving from Iran in the fifteenth century and has been the music of choice for Kashmiri Sufi mystics. The dance based on the Sufiana Kalam is the hafiz nagma. Music in Kashmir performed by Hindus is mainly influenced by Indian classical music, using instruments such as the sitar. Sarangadeva who wrote the famous *Sangeet Ratnakara* was a Kashmiri. Music and musical instruments where-mentioned in the earliest texts like the *Nilamata Purana* and *Rajatarangini*. The most popular folk instrument is santoor linked to the Goddess Sharada, the Goddess of learning and art in ancient Kashmir. Henzae is a music form sung by Kashmiri Pandits on religious and cultural festivals.

Popular dances in Ladakh include the khatok chenmo (only when headed by an aristocratic family member), kompa tsum-tsak (meaning three successive steps), jabro (dance steps from Western Ladakh), chaams (sacred dance by Lamas), chabs-skyan tses (dance carrying a pot), raldi tses (sword dance) and alley yaato (Zanskari dance and song sequence). A feature of a Ladakh marriage is the recitation of lengthy narratives by singers in unusual costumes.

Religion

Reason for the Partition of Indian Subcontinent and Current Kashmir Conflict: Ignoring the geographical impediments and natural ramparts, Kashmir had maintained close relations with the neighbouring Khanates of Central Asia since ancient times. The Buddhist missionaries from Kashmir, which stood a high centre of Buddhism, extended their work beyond the Hindukush in Central Asian territories, China and Tibet. They traversed the problematic routes for the propagation of the Buddhist philosophy in these lands.

Modern researchers reveal that most of these missionaries, who worked in these regions, hailed from Kashmir or were educated in Kashmir. Buddhist scholars from different parts of Central Asia, Tibet and Afghanistan were provided schooling in Kashmir. In Tibet, Buddhism made a compromise with the traditional 'Bonism' and formed 'Lamaism', which today dominate the whole area including Ladakh region of India. The Buddhist scholars from China and Iran also came to Kashmir in search of truth and salvation.

Afghanistan was once a stronghold of Zoroastrianism and Buddhism. In the AD 7th century, Huen Tsang, the Chinese pilgrim, found the traces of Buddhism there. Even today, the vast but neglected statues of Lord Buddha are located in the different parts of that country. It was with the conversion of Kaffiristan, now called Nuristan, to Islam in AD 1895 that Afghanistan became a completely Islamic country. The commercial relations were maintained not only with the principal trade centres of Central Asia like Yarkand, Khotan, Samarkand, Bukhara and Khurasan; but also with China, Bhutan, Egypt, Syria, Iran, Nepal and Iraq. Sericulture was introduced in Kashmir from Tibet.

However, with the downfall of Karkota dynasty (AD 950), these relations received a severe setback. Dulacha or Zulju, a Mongol from

Turkistan, invaded Kashmir in AD 1320, shook the Hindu power and paved the way for the establishment of Muslim rule. With the foundation of Sultanate in AD 1339, the whole strategy about Kashmir changed. It became the magnetic attraction for the Muslim missionaries, Sufis, saints and ulema from Central Asia - who propagated the message of Islam in the region. The territory was formally connected with the Islamic world. Central Asian culture, customs, habits, usages, manners, dress, diet, language and ideas penetrated into this little Valley; which brought a sociocultural change here. This ascendancy was so vigorous and dominating that it could not be washed off for centuries and is reflected even today.

The food habits in Tajikistan, Uzbekistan, Iran, Afghanistan and Kashmir are almost same. The credit of Islamizing the society of Kashmir goes to Iranian saints, Sufis, artisans and other scholars. The internal turmoil and Timurid incursion in Iran and other parts of Central Asia compelled these emigrants to abdicate their native land and move towards Kashmir. In Kashmir, Shaivism was the main belief among majority people, Hindu deity Lord Shiva was worshipped as Mrityunjay.

The Muslim missionaries had a confrontation with Shaivism. However, the Muslim emigrants exerted every effort to create a Muslim society in Kashmir. Saint Sayyid Ali Hamadani, who planted the sapling of Islam in the Valley, was from Hamadan in Iran. Baihiqi Sayyids, who came from Baihiq (Khurasan) were received with great respect and provided prestigious positions. But due to their involvement in the local politics, they were exiled, then resettled and finally slaughtered. The intellectuals and scholars from Iraq also found Kashmir as the best springboard for their activities. The scholars were encouraged and even provided 'Jagirs' in Kashmir. Mir Shams-ud-Din Iraqi, who visited Kashmir twice, was the founder of Nurbakhshiya order, a sect of Shaivism, in the Valley. The mission of Mir Shams-ud-Din was to strengthen the roots of Islam here.

In the AD mid-16th century, the relations between Kashmir and Iran suffered due to the sectarian frenzy between Sunnis and Shias in the Valley. Mirza Haider Dughlat, who ruled Kashmir from AD 1540-1551, sowed the seeds of discord between these two sects of Islam for his selfish political motives. This religious rivalry between the two sects even continue today and the so-called religious-political leaders - who are bigoted with the ultra-Islamic mentality, exploit the situation for their own personal and individual interests.

The religious fundamentalism and its related turmoil in the Valley of Kashmir is the creation of these so-called leaders and guardians of society. Kashmir, which was a great centre of Buddhism and Shaivism in the past, consummated a dignified place in the Islamic world when in AD 1699, during the reign of Aurangzeb, the Sacred Relic of Prophet Mohammad arrived here. The Sacred Relic was brought by Nur-ud-Din Ishbari, an affluent Kashmiri merchant, from Bijapur (Deccan/southern India) and lodged in Hazratbal Mosque at Srinagar.

With the advent of Islam in Kashmir, an interwoven Hindu-Muslim culture emerged. Both communities influenced each other. The newly converted Muslims never gave up their Hindu customs. The Hindu shrines and spots of pilgrimage were considered sacred by these converts. Even inter-religion marriages took place in the upper classes. The Muslim rulers married Hindu ladies and allowed them to profess their religion. Hindus learned Persian and became great scholars. However, Sanskrit learning remained confined to Hindu community only. But Islam could not dominate the traditional society of Kashmir like the way it was in their place of origin. The people of Kashmir were cognizant and perspicacious. They established a separate identity for themselves since ancient times.

Zoroastrianism was the religion of the Persians before their conversion to Islam. It is traditionally derived from its great Prophet/ Zoroaster (Zarathustra) and its sacred literature is *Zend Avesta*. The religion teaches that Ormazd, Lord of Light and Goodness, wars ceaselessly against Ahriman and the hosts of evil. Ormazd created man to aid Him and finally, the good kingdom will be attained.

Tajikistan (ex-USSR) has a special bond with the Muslim lineage of Kashmir. A lot of Kashmiris participates in 'Global Islamic Dawaati Sunnah Conference' organized by Karwani-Islami to visit the shrine of Shah Hamdan. Thousands of people from different parts of the Valley and religious scholars from across the globe participated in the day-long religious conference. Kashmiris were awakened and educated by Mir Syed Ali Hamdani. Due to his preaching, there was an improvement in the education, culture and religion in Kashmir. Subcontinental Muslims have long followed various interpretations of Islam, Sunni, Shia, Ismaili, Sufi inspired, Deobandi, Barelvi, Ahl-e-Hadith, Salafi, Wahhabi, Ahmadi, Qadiani.

Hindu Holocaust to Halcyon

During the reign of Timur in Samarkand, close relations were maintained between Kashmir and that country. The policy of Timur towards Kashmir was quite contrary to what it was towards India. In AD 1389 Timur sacked Delhi King, but at the same time, he sent two envoys along with gifts to the ruler of Kashmir, Sultan Sikandar. Both the rulers had a great mental affinity and were sworn enemies of the Hindus. Timur looted India, and took away the priceless Peacock throne from India which today worths twice the construction cost of the Taj Mahal!

Sultan Sikandar - the Iconoclast, destroyed the grand and old Hindu temples in the Valley; and used their plinths and friezes for raising mosques. The stones and bricks which once configured marvellous and splendid temples or monasteries, now hold up mosques. Hindus were offered three choices - death, exile or conversion. Some of them fled Kashmir, many were executed and most of them were converted to Islam. In fact, there was mass conversion, totally ethnic cleaning. About seven maunds of the sacred thread of the massacred Brahmans were burnt. The sacred books of Buddhism and Hinduism were either destroyed or thrown into Dal Lake. It is said that there virtually remained only eleven Hindu families in Kashmir. Sultan Sikandar flattered himself that he had extirpated Hinduism from the Valley.

'Hindukush' is formed of two parts: Hindu + Kush. 'Kush' is the later from of 'Koff' of old Persian from which we have got 'kooh' in Iranian and 'koh' in Indian pronunciation. Thus the word means Hindu koh or Indian Mountain, which divide India from Central Asia including Afghanistan. The earlier reference to the range of mountains is to be found in *Meteorologica* of Aristotle under the name Parnasos. After Alexander's invasion of India in 326 BC, the Greeks called it Paropamisus and then as Indian Caucasus. Ibn Batuta, who crossed the mountain range in AD. All the Encyclopedias and National Geographic agree that Hindukush region was the place of Hindu genocide (similar to Dachau and Auschwitz).

Jesus and Kashmir Connection

The Roza Bal or Rauza Bal or Rozabal is the name of a shrine located in the Khanyaar quarter in the downtown area of Srinagar in Kashmir, India. The word rauza means tomb, the word Bal implies place, often a landing place by a lake, hence 'place of the tomb'. Locals believe a sage buried there is Yuzasaf or Yuz Asaf (or Youza Asouph) and Mir Sayyid Naseeruddin. The shrine was relatively unknown until the founder of the Ahmadiyya Muslim Community, Mirza Ghulam Ahmad, claimed in 1899 that it is the tomb of Jesus. This belief is shared by many Ahmadis today, though the local Sunni caretakers of the shrine believe that "the theory that Jesus is buried anywhere on the face of the earth is blasphemous to Islam." However, multiples sites in the world such as the Church of the Holy Sepulchre in Jerusalem also claim to be the tomb of Jesus.

Theory of Kashmiri Descent from Lost Tribes of Israel

In a book titled *The Real Eve: Modern Man's Journey Out of Africa,* the prominent Oxford University scholar Stephen Oppenheimer has synthesized the available genetic evidence together with climatology and archaeology with conclusions which have a bearing on the debate about the early population of India. Much of Oppenheimer's theory is based on recent advances in studies of mitochondrial DNA, inherited through the mother and Y chromosomes, inherited by males from the father. Oppenheimer makes the case that whereas Africa is the cradle of all humankind; India is the cradle of all non-African peoples. The man left Africa approximately 90,000 years ago, heading east along the Indian Ocean and established settlements in India. It was only during a break in glacial activity 50,000 years ago, when deserts turned into grasslands, that people left India and headed north-west into the Russian steppes and on into Eastern Europe, as well as north-east through China and over the now submerged Bering Strait into the Americas.

Oppenheimer argues that the Eurocentric view of ancient history is also incorrect. For example, Europeans didn't invent art, because the Australian aborigines developed their own unique artistic culture in complete isolation. Indian rock art is also extremely ancient, going back to over 40,000 BC, so perhaps art as a part of culture had arisen in Africa itself. Similarly, agriculture didn't arise in the Fertile Crescent; South-East Asia had already domesticated many plants by that time.

Oppenheimer concludes with two extraordinary conclusions:

> "First, that the Europeans' genetic homeland was originally in South Asia in the Pakistan/Gulf region over 50,000 years ago; and second, that the Europeans' ancestors followed at least two widely separated routes to arrive, ultimately, in the same cold but rich garden. The earliest of these routes was the Fertile Crescent. The second early route from South Asia to Europe may have been up to the Indus into Kashmir and on to Central Asia, where perhaps more than 40,000 years ago hunters first started bringing down the game as large as mammoths."

In more recent time, the theory of Kashmiri descent from the lost tribes of Israel states that the Kashmiri people of India and Pakistan originally descended from the Ten Lost Tribes. Some consider the Kashmiri people descendants of one of the Ten Lost Tribes of Israel.

According to Rabbi Marvin Tokayer, the Kashmiri people have many Jewish cultural traits, including feasts, appearance, business practices and other customs. He also asserts that a significant number of Kashmiri names and words derived from Hebrew. Furthermore, side locks, although never worn by Muslims, are very commonly worn by the Kashmiris. The Ahmadiyya movements also support an Israelite origin for Kashmiri people. The theory was first suggested by Abu Rayhan al-Biruni, the famous 11th-century Persian Muslim scholar. According to al-Biruni, "In former times the inhabitants of Kashmir used to allow one or two foreigners to enter their country, particularly Jews." François Bernier, a 17th-century French physician and Sir Francis Younghusband, who explored this region in the 1800s, commented on the similar physiognomy between Kashmiris and Jews including 'fair skin, prominent noses', and similar head shapes.

Some researchers have found the resemblance of names and toponymy between Kashmir and Hebrew. The theory is essentially based on the purported similarities between Kashmir place names and Hebrew words and phrases. The name Kashmir locally known as kasher itself is said to be based on the Hebrew word Kashir, 'like Syria'. The Kashmir valley said to be the dwelling place of the Ten Lost Tribes, is called Bagh-i-Suleman (Garden of Solomon) in local parlance, the connection between Kashmir and ancient Israel is strengthened further by such Kashmiri place names as 'Tomb of Moses' and 'Throne of Solomon'. There is also a Kashmiri tradition that the 40 years of wandering in the desert covered the ground from Asia to Kashmir and that Kashmir is, in fact, the Promised Land.

The names of approximately 350 towns and villages in Kashmir bear some resemblance to place names in the Holy Land. These include: Bandpoor (similar to Beth Peor), Naboo Hill (similar to Mount Nebo), Pishgah (similar to Mount Pisgah) and Mamre (similar to Mamre).

3. '3 Ms' of Kashmir's History

I believe that imagination is stronger than knowledge. That myth is more potent than history. That dreams are more powerful than facts. That hope always triumphs over experience. There is no comprehensive, objective history. To understand Kashmir history better, I have divided it into three Time periods and calling it the '3M' of Kashmir's history. They are the Mythological Times, the Medieval Times and the Modern Times.

A large number of accounting historians appear to pay closer attention to social and political factors and the address overlooked episodes and segments of society. The range of theories brought to bear in accounting history scholarship since the advent of new accounting history has included Marxism/labour process theory; Foucauldian methods of archaeology, genealogy, disciplinary power and knowledge; Giddens' theories of structuration; neo-institutional theory; Latourian concepts; gender theory and more.

In history, postmodernism is a denial of the stability of the past, of the reality of the past apart from what the historian chooses to make of it and thus of any objective truth about the past. Few new accounting historians have embraced postmodernism. They have moved beyond merely examining non-traditional areas that include gender, culture, households, displaced workers and suppressed peoples to a philosophy that rejects as naive and unachievable, the efficacy of factual evidence, the attempt to reconstruct the past and the search for historical truth(s). Sociologically-oriented new breed of historians is driven by a desire to theorize and generalize, rather than to particularize and a wish to critique society.

What the traditional historian sees as an event that occurred in the past, the postmodernist sees as a 'text' that exists only in the present – a text to be parsed, flossed, construed and interpreted by the historian, much as a poem or novel is by the critic.... In postmodernist history, as in postmodernist literary criticism, the theory has become a calling in itself. The modernist historian follows a line of reasoning from his sources and evidence to a historical reality hidden behind the causes. On the other hand, in the postmodern view, the evidence does not point towards the past but to different interpretations of the history; for that is what we, in fact, use evidence.

There are innumerable inequities in society, both in the past, the present and undoubtedly the future. For example, deadly terrorist acts directed against innocent, unarmed civilians are deeply troubling to us as human beings. But as historians, we believe that we are not well-qualified or best situated to advocate particular pathways to a better, more equitable, terror-free world. Those tasks are more appropriately undertaken by politicians, public ethicists and social activists, all of whom have greater access to public forums and, as importantly, can be held accountable for their recommendations and undertakings.

The human intellect demands accuracy while the soul craves meaning. Keeping this in mind have tried to visualize Kashmir's history from the very ancient times to the current days. Events and society developed as the time passed, what past renounced historians might have knowingly or unknowingly missed, evidently caught my eyes and had tried to unearth such hidden or lost facts of Kashmir along with other stories. The corporate background in the financial sector undoubtedly helped me develop an eye for details. The advent of 'Small Data', post 'Big Data' revolution help connects people with timely, meaningful insights (derived from big data and 'local' sources), organized and packaged - often visually - to be accessible, understandable and actionable for everyday tasks. Let me start Kashmir history with the famous Sanskrit shloka from Nasadeeya Sukta which is part of Rigveda (Sanatan Dharma is popularly known as Hinduism and Rigveda is the revered book)

Srishtee se pehle sat nahin thaa, asat bhi nahin
(before creation there was no truth, or untruth)
Antariksh bhi nahin, akash bhin nahin thaa
(no universe, not even the sky)
Chhipaa thaa kyaa kahaan, kisne dhakaa thaa
(where was it hidden, who hid it?)
Uss pal to agam, atal jal bhi kahaan thaa
(at that time there was no water)

Srishtee kaa kaun hai kartaa
(who is the creator?)
Kartaa hai vaa akartaa
(is He the creator or something else?)

Oonche aakash mein rahtaa
(who stays up there in the sky)

Sada adhyaksh banaa rahtaa
(who is in charge)

Wahin sachmuch mein jaantaa … Yaa nahin bhi jaanataa
(he truly must know everything, and maybe not.)
Hai kisi ko nahin pataa, nahin pataa,
(no one knows … no one knows)
Nahin hai pataa, nahin hai pataa
(no one knows … no one knows)

Weh tha hiranyagarbh srishti se pehle vidyamaan
(he was born out of the depths … before creation)
Wahi to saare bhoot jaat ka swami mahaan
(he is the lord of all life)

jo hai astitvamaana dharti aasmaan dhaaran kar
(the one who is there over land and sky)
Aise kis devta ki upasana karein hum avi dekar
(who is this god who we pray to?)

Jis ke bal par tejomay hai ambar
(he whose strength the sky is held up with)
Prithvi hari bhari sthapit sthir
(and the earth lies green and stable)

Swarg aur sooraj bhi sthir
(the heaven and the sun stay stable)
Aise kis devta ki upasana karein hum avi dekar
(who is this god who we pray to?)

Garbh mein apne agni dhaaran kar paida kar
(In whose womb lies fire)
Vyapa tha jal idhar udhar neeche upar
(who controls here, there and everywhere)

Jagaa chuke vo ka ekameva pran banker
(who gives rise to life)
Aise kis devta ki upasana karein hum avi dekar
(who is this god who we pray to?)

O. Srishti nirmata swarg rachiyata purvaj raksha kar
(creator of creation, the heavens and who looked after our ancestors)
Satya dharma palak atul jal niyamak raksha kar
(who keeps the truth, justice and the essence of life)

Phaili hain dishayen bahu jaisi uski sab mein sab par
(whose hands seem to stretch over all there is)
Aise hi devta ki upasana kare hum avi dekar
(this is the god who we pray to)

I started with the Mythological era, researching sacred Hindu books to get historical facts from those time. The history of written text was still a distant dream. Moving on to the Medieval period when India was the cradle of commerce and richness attracting all kind of immigrants. Some plundered her, some became part of her and some brought love and knowledge from their origin place. Under the contemporary era, post-1947 history, I have covered issues like legal nature of Kashmir problem, international aspect of this problem, unilateral and bilateral attempts for its resolution, concerns of minorities, Kashmir's tryst with democracy, impact of cold war on Kashmir issue, changing nature of agitations, shift from Look East Policy (policy of eighties) to militancy uprising (in nineties) to look Middle-East (pro-Palestinian support).

M1: Mythological Times – Ancient History of Kashmir

As per Hindu mythology, Rishi Kashyapa's settled the land thousands of years ago. 'Kashmiri Shaivism' is a group of several monistic and tantric religious traditions that flourished in Kashmir from the latter centuries of the first millennium CE through the early centuries of the second millennium. These traditions have survived only in an attenuated form among the Brahmans of Kashmir, but there have recently been efforts to revive them in India and globally. These traditions must be distinguished from a dualistic Shaiva Siddhanta tradition that also flourished in medieval Kashmir. The most salient philosophy of monistic Kashmiri Shaivism is the Pratyabhijna, or 'Recognition', system propounded in the writings of Utpaladeva (c 925-975 CE) and Abhinavagupta (c 975-1025 CE). Abhinavagupta's disciple Kshemaraja (c 1000-1050) and other successors interpreted that philosophy defined the significance of earlier monistic Shaiva theology retrospectively.

In the *Rajatarangini*, a history of Kashmir written by Kalhana in the mid-12th century, it is stated that the valley of Kashmir was formerly a lake. According to Hindu mythology, the lake was drained by the great rishi or sage, Kashyapa, son of Marichi, who was the son of Brahma, by cutting the gap in the hills at Baramulla (Varahamula). When Kashmir drained, Kashyapa asked Brahmans to settle there. It is still the local tradition and in the existing physical condition of the country, we may see some ground for the story which has taken this form. The name of Kashyapa is by history and tradition connected with the draining of the lake and the chief town or collection of dwellings in the valley was called Kashyapapura, which identified with Kaspapyros of Hecataeus (apud Stephanus of Byzantium) and Kaspatyros of Herodotus. Kashmir is also believed to be the country meant by Ptolemy's Kaspeiria. Cashmere is an archaic spelling of Kashmir and in some countries, it is still spelled this way.

According to the *Mahabharata*, the Kambojas ruled Kashmir during the epic period with a Republican system of government from the capital city of Karna-Rajapuram-gatva-Kambojah-nirjitastava, shortened to Rajanpur, which identified with modern Rajauri. Later, the Panchal as is stated to have established their sway. The name Peer Panjab, which is a part of contemporary Kashmir, is a witness to this fact. Panjab merely is a distorted form of the Sanskrit term Panchala. The Muslims prefixed the word peer to it in memory of Siddha Faqir and the name after that is said to have changed into Peer Panjal. According to legend, Jammu was founded by Hindu King Raja Jambu Lochan in the 14th century BC. During one of his hunting campaigns, he reached the Tawi river where he saw a goat and a lion drinking water at the same place. The king was impressed and decided to set-up a town after his name, Jamboo. With the passage of time, the name was corrupted and became 'Jammu'.

Nilamata Purana (compiled c 500-600 CE) contains accounts of Kashmir's early history. Kalhana's *Rajatarangini* (River of Kings), all the 8,000 Sanskrit verses of which were completed by 1150 CE, chronicles the history of Kashmir's dynasties from mythical times to 12th century. It relies upon traditional sources like *Nilamata Purana,* inscriptions, coins, monuments and Kalhana's observations borne out of political experiences of his family.

Rock carvings found in many parts of Ladakh, showing that the area has been inhabited from the Neolithic times (c 8500 BCE). Ladakh's earliest inhabitants consisted of a mixed Indo-Aryan population of Mons and Dards, who find mention in the works of Herodotus, Nearchus, Megasthenes, Pliny and the geographical lists of the Puranas. Kashmir was a centre for Sanskrit scholars. According to *Mahabharata,* the Kambojas ruled over Kashmir during the epic period, about the sixth century BCE. The capital city of Kashmir (Kamboj) during historical times was Rajapura. Epic Rajapura identified with modern Rajauri. Later, the Panchalas established their sway.

Earliest Neolithic sites in the floodplains of Kashmir valley dated to c 3000 BCE. Most important of these sites are the settlements at Burzahom, which had two Neolithic and one Megalithic phase. The first period (c 2920 BCE) at Burzahom marked by mud plastered pit dwellings, coarse pottery and stone tools. In the second phase, which lasted till c 1700 BCE, houses were constructed on a ground level and the dead buried, sometimes with domesticated and wild animals. Hunting and fishing were the primary modes of subsistence though evidence of cultivation of wheat, barley and lentils found in both the phases. In the megalithic phase, large circles constructed and grey or black burnish replaced coarse red ware in pottery. During the later Vedic period, as kingdoms of the Vedic tribes expanded, the Uttarakurus settled in Kashmir.

Kanishka inaugurates Mahayana Buddhism in Kashmir. In 326 BCE, Porus asked Abisares, the king of Kashmir, to aid him against Alexander the Great in the Battle of Hydaspes. After Porus lost the battle, Abisares submitted to Alexander by sending him treasure and elephants. During the reign of Ashoka (304–232 BCE), Kashmir became a part of the Maurya Empire and Buddhism introduced in Kashmir. During this period, many stupas, some shrines dedicated to Shiva and the city of Srinagari (Srinagar) built. Kanishka (127–151 CE), an emperor of the Kushan dynasty, conquered Kashmir and established the new town of Kanishkapur. Buddhist tradition holds that Kanishka held the Fourth Buddhist council in Kashmir, in which celebrated scholars such as Ashvaghosha, Nagarjuna and Vasumitra took part. By the fourth century, Kashmir became a seat of learning for both Buddhism and Hinduism. Kashmiri Buddhist missionaries helped spread Buddhism to Tibet and China and from the fifth century CE, pilgrims from these countries started visiting Kashmir. Kumarajiva (343–413 CE) was among the renowned Kashmiri scholars who travelled to China. He influenced the Chinese emperor Yao Xing and spearheaded translation of many Sanskrit works into Chinese at the Changan monastery.

Hephthalites (White Huns) under Toramana crossed over the Hindukush mountains and conquered large parts of western India including Kashmir. His son Mihirakula (c 502–530 CE) led a military campaign to capture all of north India. He was opposed by Baladitya in Magadha and eventually defeated by Yashodharman in Malwa. After the defeat, Mihirakula returned to Kashmir where he led a coup on the king. He then conquered Gandhara where he committed many atrocities on Buddhists and destroyed their shrines. Influence of the Huns faded after Mihirakula's death. After the seventh century, significant developments took place in Kashmiri Hinduism. In the centuries that followed, Kashmir produced many poets, philosophers and artists who contributed to Sanskrit literature and Hindu religion. Among notable scholars of this period was Vasugupta (c 875–925 CE) who wrote the Shiva Sutras which laid the foundation for a monistic Shaiva system called Kashmir Shaivism. Dualistic interpretation of

Shaiva scripture was defeated by Abhinavagupta (c 975–1025 CE) who wrote many philosophical works on Kashmir Shaivism. Kashmir Shaivism was adopted by the common masses of Kashmir and strongly influenced Shaivism in southern India.

Some scholars from Vedic school believe that Gandhar Pradesh (present Afghanistan and NWFP of Pakistan) included Kashmir also. There are specific symbols and sacred things of Hinduism which were and are, found in Kashmir only. I mean to say that Kashmir valley is the only place where all of them found. Some of them are: srichakra fish (sacred as matsyavatora and worshipped here even now) lotus (connected with Brahma, Vishnu and Lakshmi) bhoorjva (bhoj-patra on which ancient scriptures were etched), devadaru tree, kesar, kustoori, snow, the snow white god Shiv (him-rund-endu-karpur-varna), mountains, water, nag and sarp (not only in human form), som (found in the mountains of Kashmir towards sharada teerth), kesar dhatura (used in Shiv worship) and kasturi all have an essential place in our ancient traditions and also in present religious rituals.

The boat of Manu, when it was floundering in the floods of the khand-pralaya had found its final resting ground at a place called manoravsarpan, which is situated in the Pakistan Occupied Kashmir. Manu was the adi purush from whom sprang the modern human race and Kashmir was the place where the first human of the present civilization originated. Seals of the Indus-valley civilization have been deciphered and it has now been proved that they contain the picture of the Shiva in makhanasan mudra. Scholars have been trying to squeeze the Vedic, *Ramayana* and *Mahabharata* periods between 1500 BC (when Indus valley civilization was destroyed) to 600 BC, to prove that the movement of Aryans had been from the west to the east, the time of Buddha (600 BC) a historically confirmed fact.

If we assume that the Indus valley civilization is a Vedic civilization and destroyed earlier than 1500 BC, then the movement of Aryans will be from the east (from India) to the west (to Iran and other parts of Europe). The creation of Vedas, their reduction into writing and the spread of their oral tradition, the influence of Aryan culture to the eastern parts of India, the time-lag between the Vedic and *Ramayana* period, the *Ramayana* and *Mahabharata* periods, the *Mahabharata* and Buddha periods and the gradual evolution (or degeneration) of the Vedic language into Sanskrit and of Sanskrit into Pali could not have taken place during only 900 years (between 1500 BC to 600 BC). Thus, when it has been proved that the Indus valley civilization is post-Vedic (not pre-Vedic as some foreign scholars have been trying to project), the movement of the Aryans seems to be from the East to the West and their original home was Kashmir. It is a different matter that around 80% of the people of the Aryan stock in Asia are now Muslims and they inhabit the areas of Kashmir, Pakistan, Afghanistan and Iran.

There is another point of importance. The Jews who migrated from the city to their present country of Israel in about 4000 BC have a mention of this movement in their scriptures but nowhere in the Vedas is a mention that the Aryan had come from anywhere outside India. The Kashmiri language is the apabhransha (degenerate form) of the Vedic language (not of Sanskrit).

1. Lord Krishna himself had come to Kashmir to put on the throne the widow (Yashomati) of the Kashmiri king defeated by him. There are hints in the *Mahabharata* that the forces of the king of Kashmir had taken part in significant Indian war though they were on the side of the Kauravas and that Takshak (Nag), who belonged to Kashmir later killed Raja Parikshit.
2. During the Buddhist period, Kashmir was a high centre of Buddhism and it was from Kashmir that this faith spread (through Khotan) to China, Mongolia, Japan and Turkey (from where it was eliminated later). The last Buddhist congress during the times of Kanishka was held in Kashmir.
3. Panini, the great grammarian of Sanskrit, was also from Kashmir. Gandharadesh (Today's Afghanistan) and Kashmir were part of the same region in olden times.
4. It is a well-known fact that even today the old Vedic rituals of marriages and yajnas are followed only by the Brahmans of Kerala, Kashmir and Karnataka.
5. After Takshila and Nalanda, the centre of Sanskrit studies shifted to the Sanskrit university Brajbihara in Kashmir, which was, along with its vast library, later destroyed by Sikander Butshikhan.
6. A majority of the major poets and scholars of Sanskrit of India were Kashmiris - Kalidas, Kshirswamin, Kalhan, Bilhan, Mammat, Anand Vardhan, Vaman, Kshemendra, Abhinavgupta, Rojanak Shitianth and others. The first historically viable book of history in Sanskrit is *Rajatarangini*.
7. The Kashmiri Shaivism and tantra schools are also distinct contributions to the ethos of India. Even Vamachar is a contribution of Kashmir to Indian rituals.

Thus Kashmir has been the home of Vedic culture and religion, Buddhist faith, Sanskrit scholarship, Shaivism, Islam, Sufism (Kashmiri Sufism is a little different from the Sufism which developed in other parts of the country) and Sikhism. Kashmir symbolized not only a 'paradise on earth', but also a celebrated space of 'multiculturalism'. Its people accordingly imbued with symbiotic traditions embodying many values and customs. Among them, few associated with the individual and group faith in different spiritual beings or objects for sacred and mundane ends: these precisely termed as the 'religious-cultural traditions'. What exactly were these traditions? Where did they emanate from? How and when did they find a space in Kashmir? What was the role of the State to this effect? To what extent did they influence the mindset of the people?

Several customs and traditions owe their origin to religion which has always been a dynamic social institution in all global communities. It represented the peoples' "belief in the living and non-living things for attaining salvation and blessings and expressing extreme devotion there unto them." The given belief formalized through a set of commonly shared rituals and ceremonies about which the French sociologist, Emile Durkheim, maintains: "religion is a unified system of beliefs and practices which unite together all those who adhere to them." Talcott Parsons (1907–79), another prominent functionalist, argues that beliefs, rituals, practices and other social norms are quite useful for the functioning of a certain system though conflict theorists like Robert K Merton hold otherwise: "these may not always contribute to the society."

Many of them may turn dysfunctional, at a particular time, due to their inbuilt weakness to resist or adapt themselves to a given social system." The conflict sociologists further maintain that racial, occupational, social and religious conflicts always dilute the unified spirit of the societies across the globe. The two groups of sociologists evenly lock horns on the nuances of the word culture. The ethnocentrists believe that some cultures are essentially dominant and superior to others which, however, the relativist group of sociologists negates by arguing that a "certain culture can be inherently good or bad concerning its system than the systems from outside."

Applying the views of functionalists vis-a-vis Kashmir society and culture, one can assume that different religious-cultural rituals and practices formed the core of human activity in Kashmir society notwithstanding dynastic changes, civil wars and ethnic conflicts. Such routines and methods evolved in the wake of the mutual intelligibility of the peoples of Kashmir and South and Central Asia to share their ideas thought, faith and culture during their onward march to civilization. True subscribing to extraneous influences should not be initiated without 'cultural shock' to the ethnocentric people of Kashmir. Gradually, however, they appreciated them for mutual benefits, social sustainability and human togetherness. Naturally, the given optimism was bound to forge marked cultural affinities between the two geographical spaces, broaden the peoples' worldview and develop among Kashmiris a sense of religious tolerance and progressive thought.

One may recall that Kashmir was an indispensable part of the centralized power structure of the Indo-Bactrian Greeks (190 BC), Sakas (Scythians) and Parthians (90 BC–AD 64), Kushanas (AD 1st–2nd century) and Hunas (AD 5th century), Karkotas of Kashmir (8th century), Mughals and the Afghans (16th–19th century). Thus, from early times, Kashmir was hooked to its Central Asian neighbourhood through regional, cultural, economic and political integration. (A) Iranian Influence (i) Pre-historic Period: The process of Kashmir's multi-vector amalgamation with outer world commenced with the importation of primitive forms of snake and fire worship from Iran. The former obtained among the anthropoid apes since Paleolithic times; they "worshipped serpents and buried them with a supply of insects in their graves as a provision for their future life."

A universal phenomenon though, the serpent (*naaga*) cult was brought by the so-called Aryans from Iran to Kashmir across the northern areas in Gilgit, Astor, Dah, Hano, Garkun, Kargil and Durchik Ladakh. Interestingly the *naaga* cult was present and practised within tribes of India and also by the ancient Sri Lankans. With its induction, the existing set of Kashmiri beliefs in natural forces and their allied divines supplemented. Subsequently, however, the early settlers of Kashmir became the faithful serpent worshippers; hence, styled as the Nagas after the name of the snakes. In Kalhana's *Rajatarangini*, the Nagas described as the civilized humans, male-female, who unlike their rival group, the Pisachas, lived around the home of the snakes, springs and lakes.

Like anthropoid apes, the Kashmir Nagas buried and revered snakes as semi divines and thought them containing supernatural powers with which they guarded human "dwellings, treasures and the graves of their progeny." With this belief in mind, the natives (Nagas) offered milk to the snakes (Nagas) to invoke their blessings for a variety of ends. Not surprising, therefore, to notice Kashmir abounding with scores of such sacred springs, Anantnag, Sheshnag,

Nilanag, Padmanag, as were named after various names of snakes. Indeed, the impact of serpent cult was so piercing that the natives carved their images in sculptures: the roughly dated 11th-12th century Kadroo stone sculpture retrieved from Pulwama in South Kashmir and the 16th century stone structured bowlies from Jammu, the other division of the Jammu and Kashmir State in India, offer the typical examples in this behalf. Even the sparsely distributed religious structures in Kashmir carry the graven images of the serpents.

The 16th-century Mughal chronicler, Abul Fazl, in his monumental work reports about seven hundred such places that possessed graven images of snakes and about which 'wonderful legends told' albeit most of them excepting those of the sixteenth century is without designs and the motifs. In any case, the serpent tradition was and continues to be a common practice among Kashmiri Pandits as well as the Muslims for the attainment of variegated desires. That the Kashmiri Muslims practised it during the medieval period is forthright vindicated by Mirza Haidar Dughlat, Abul Fazl and Haidar Malik Chadoora. Their belief amply certifies its influence on them in considering the killing of a snake next to a sin. Besides, they splashed grains at shrines and graves to express regard unto snakes and other animals, besides earning blessing there against for their ancestors.

The Kashmiri Pandit community also remembers the snakes on the eve of puja and other religious ceremonies. Likewise, the primitive cult of fire worship was central to Iran though it emanated in the 6th century BC at Balkh in the neighbourhood of Iran, Central Asia and Afghanistan. Founded by one Ahur Mazda, the Zoroastrian ideology emphasized on the worship of several Iranian gods and among them, the fire god was perceived to be powerful enough to purify the human body from all evils and allow it attain peace and salvation. Much like the serpent cult, it travelled in the train of Aryan migration to Kashmir around the 8th century BC and in due course of time, it got embedded into the innate religious-cultural texture of Kashmir through several practices about Shali maintains:

> "In the performance of Shraddha rites, the Vedic deities receive worship through the fire, Shaivite through the phallic emblem of cooked rice and Shakta through a lamp."

Accordingly, the Kashmiri Pandits subscribed to fire worship in diverse forms. They circumambulated a fire to formalize yajna, hawan and other religious-marital rituals perhaps under the Parsi or

Zoroastrian influence. Under the same weight, the Kashmiri Muslims celebrated Frove, an extent local festival of lights and bonfires after the name of a revered Kashmiri saint, Zain Rishi, at Ash Muqam in South Kashmir. On a particular day, the devotees burn a chip of pinewood, tie it to a sturdy willow stick and carry it up to a hill housing the cave of the saint and chanted slogans: 'This is the fire of Zain Rishi" meant to kill the demon and register victory of good over wicked forces. The local ceremony of Vayuk is again near to the Iranian style of Farvardin.

On a specific day of a month, the Kashmiri Muslims remember their dead, visit their graves and distribute loaves of rice, the Rohan Posh, among the needy. (B) Central Asian Influences (ii) Ancient Period: In addition to Iran, Kashmir borrowed multiple influences from the Tajik land as is vividly vindicated by the common Tajik-Kashmir heritage. The Paleolithic and Neolithic sites of Sarazam, Penjikent and Kuldara in Tajikistan and Burzahoma and Gufkral in Kashmir dating around the same period, 5000-3000 BC, reveal the coexistence of an irrevocable Tajik-Kashmir bond in terms of the collective human habitat along the river beds and forest slopes, settlement pattern and the material finds comprising charcoal, hearths, grains, chisels, bone and stone made celts, grinders, querns, needles, awls, arrow heads, spears, beads, combs, bodkins, harvesters, scrapers, choppers, cores, flakes, pits and pit chambers.

The mode and form of ancestral, animal, sun, river, tree and the worship of like natural forces, also suggest a shared history of mutual influences and cultural affinities between Tajikistan and Kashmir. However, these bilateral ties strengthened with the advent of Buddhism, an ethical-moral philosophy founded by Lord Buddha in Bodhgaya Bihar, India, in the 5th century BC. The said philosophy demanded the humans undergo self-introspection, shun malice and other evil designs and subscribe to right thinking, the right approach, right action, etc to become perfect and immaculate, the Shakyamuni. Given its popularity especially after the death of its founder, Buddhism transformed into a formal faith, which reached Kashmir during the reign of Mauryan King Ashoka in the 3rd century BC.

He popularized it through various measures which included engaging Kashmiri monks in the religious congregations at Pataliputra and constructing a large number of religious structures, the stupas and chaityas, in the Valley with a symbolic representation of Buddha's footprints, tree and chakra. On the fall of the Mauryas, the Indo-Bactrian Greeks (190 BC) under their famous kings, Demetrius and Menander (Milinda), pronounced Buddhism by building numerous viharas and stupas in Kashmir. It is either from Kashmir or their Gandhara capital in Taxila that they transported Buddha's symbols and images to China and Central Asia.

Personally, King Menandra held discussions with an eminent Buddhist monk, Nagasena and built Milindavihara after his name in Kashmir implicitly to allow free intellectual debate on faith and its existential realities and develop a sense of inclusiveness among the Kashmiris. Besides, the Indo-Greeks promoted Kashmir's trade with Central Asia and introduced Gandharan art in Kashmir which is candidly evidenced by material finds from Semthan (modern Bijbehara) in South Kashmir. The Indo-Greeks succeeded by the Sakas (Scythians), Parthians and the Kushanas [1st century BC–AD 3rd century].

All the three dynasties especially the Kushanas under their veteran kings, Kanishka, Hushka and Jushka (AD 1st-5th century) legitimized Buddhism by declaring it the State faith. They designed Buddha's images and symbols in sculptures, constructed and granted rent-free land grants to viharas, stupas and their keepers and permitted complete freedom of religion. King Kanishka personally held religious dialogue with many people including the then Buddhist scholar and saint, Nagarjuna at Sadarhadvana (modern Harvan) in proper Srinagar. Importantly, he organized the fourth (some say the third) Buddhist conference in Kashmir which was undeniably a landmark in the history of Kashmir for it assembled hordes of Buddhist monks from South, Central and South-East Asia on the one platform for exploring the hidden secrets and existential realities of Buddhism. Its findings inscribed on the copper plates. While few of them spotted from the North Kashmir, many others are known to one Kashmiri scholar Yusuf Teng.

Kashmir was strategically logged on to the higher Buddhist world. No doubt, the Buddhist kings extended every possible support to Buddhism in Kashmir. They juxtapose accorded adequate, if not equal, patronage to other ideologies to uphold the innate Kashmiri tradition of human coexistence, mutual forbearance and religious toleration. Perhaps with the same consideration, Mauryan King Ashoka revered Vedic and Shaivite deities and semi-deities, built two Shaivite temples at Bijbehara [named Ashokeshvara] and replaced the stucco building material [specific to Buddhist Viharas] by stone [particular to Shaivite Temples]. His purported son, Jaluka, a staunch follower of Hinduism though, is also reported to have shown liberality unto Buddhism by constructing a Buddhist vihara at Kitsahom (modern Baramulla) in North Kashmir.

Besides religious structures, the numismatic evidence also certifies to the Kashmir's tradition of religious-cultural pluralism under extraneous influences. That Kushanas considerably patronized Buddhism but regard unto other religions especially Shaivism is not far to seek in their coins and material remains. Kanishka's coins depict Buddha's images as well as a four-armed standing Shiva with a drum, gourd, goat and a trident in his hands, indeed a living example of Kashmir's rich heritage of 'inclusiveness'. His successors too demonstrated optimum liberality towards the non-Buddhist or Shaivite faith as is borne by different types of coins: Hushka's coins, for instance, take the impressions of Vedic or Hindu gods (the sun with a halo of rays); Vasudeva'ṣ coins carry the image of the Greek legends and the coins of the Kidara depict the impressions of a Hindu goddess. In addition to Buddhist, Brahmanical or Shaivite influences, their coins exhibit the images of Greek and Zoroastrian deities: the latter was characteristic of the Scythian and Parthians before them.

The Semthan finds and the 7th century Chinese account of Huen Tsang, authenticate the confluence of Buddhist, Hindu, Vedic, Greek and the same influences during the Buddhist rule. This presupposes that the Buddhist kings preferred 'inclusion' and 'tolerance' to 'exclusion' and 'intolerance' notwithstanding degeneration in the rank and file of the monks due to excessive absorption in wine, fish, meat, gambling and Tantric practices of sorcery, magic and sexual or physical union with the Shakti: The Hindu priests too absorbed by the Tantric forms of faith. During the religious transition, Kashmir formally experienced the introduction of Shaivism or Hinduism. It started with Jaluka, the son of Ashoka and went down to the nomadic tribes of Hephthalites or White Hunas (AD 410–569) from North China. In reality, the rule of Hunas was a breakthrough for it elevated Hinduism to the pinnacle of the State faith. Being ardent devotees of Shiva, Toraman in general and Mihirkula in particular constructed Shaivite temples in every nook and corner of the Valley and settled a considerable number of Gandharan Brahmans in Kashmir.

The local ruling dynasties, the Karkotas (600–855), Utapalas (AD 855-939) and the Loharas (1003-1101) also nurtured the Shaivite and Vaishnavite ideologies by building and carving out Brahmanical images of Indrani, Vishnu and Shiva on the religious structures and providing rent-free land grants to temples and the Brahmans for their maintenance. Only the Hindu King Harsha was an exception to this general pro-Brahmanical policy. He ruthlessly destroyed temples and siphoned off their centuries-old wealth partially under economic compulsions and partly under the influence of Abhinavagupta's Trika

Shaivism (11th century) which signified a robust social reaction against the Brahmanical rituals. Simultaneously, however, the Hindu kings demonstrated toleration unto Buddhism by building monasteries, granting rent-free land grants to them and the monks for maintenance, allowing representation of Buddha's images in sculptures at Pravarsenpura and Ushkur and celebrating Buddha's anniversary along with the anniversaries of the Brahmanical Gods.

The Semthan finds, Harwan tiles and rubble structures and the 8th century Martand and Avantiswamin stone temples certify the union of Tokharian (Buddhist) and Shaivite influences on Kashmir culture and architecture. To this effect, the Karkota rule is remembered as a golden period in Kashmir history for it saw the convergence of Buddhism, Vaishnavism and Shaivism into one religious-cultural basket. All the three religious ideologies assimilated, excreted and shared mutual influences with each other. Whereas Hinduism exported polytheistic and Tantric beliefs to Buddhism, it instead borrowed the scriptural form of art from Buddhism. Such a triangular confluence sufficed to the co-existence of diverse faiths, ideologies and skills in Kashmir under her age-long experience in multiculturalism.

Hindu Rajas of Kashmir – Mythological Times To 14th Century

In distant past the land we call Kashmir had remained submerged in water for two thousand years. In those days, it was called Kashyapa Sar. In its neighbourhood there dwelt a married hermit named Kashyapa. He made supplication to God Almighty for dry land where he could pray. Then God Almighty sent three angels commanding them to drain off the water to make dry as much of land as was required by him. The area which they dried was named by them Kashshile, which means a 'chiselled stone'. It is said that subsequently a person named Bekdarat sowed many kinds of seeds in the muddy soil and raised crops and developed the place extensively. A large number of people came from other parts of India to settle on this land. Their king, the exalted Raja, was Turkshil; Turkshil means "unmatched in fortune and dignity".

This land has been called Kashmir. The source of the Ganges also lies here, though it is not accessible to the people. Mountains protect Kashmir. At their feet occupy vast, bright and attractive lands; these are called tavar. It comprised seventy-two sectors and spread over one hundred and eight kuroh. Amidst this area is situated the city of Kashmir, from which emerged people of sixty-four classes. Prominent four were the Brahmanas, the Kshatriyas, the Vaishyas and the Dalits.

The ruler who first founded the city of Kashmir was Pravarasen. It widened under his stewardship. After his death, his tomb cracked and he rose to heaven near Maheshwar. He was succeeded to the throne by his son Ratnaditya, who reigned for sixty years. After him, his son Onta Dev reigned for four decades. Lalitaditya who descended from him ruled for eighty years. The people of Kashmir call him Zu'l-Qarnain. It is said that he brought under his sway the entire world from the borders of China to the farthest west. Many of the idol-houses in Kashmir have been built by him. He also developed a city named Parihaspora, which means a 'peerless city'. In it, he built idol houses, in which he installed huge idols. Each Idol measured sixty yards in height. It is said that in those days it was the usual height of human beings and a man's shoulders were as broad as he was tall. Whatever Zu'l-Qarnain asked of the idol, it was granted to him.

In those days there lived a man who possessed two jewels. The attribute of one of the jewel was that if cast into an ocean, it could dry up all its water, making it possible for anybody to walk across the dried-up path. The property of the other jewel was that when held in front of an ocean, the first one would be drawn to it and water would recede to its original level. Zu'l-Qarnain wanted to buy these two jewels, but the owner declined to part with them, saying that none but Shakyamuni was capable of taking them away from him. Shakyamuni means one who can transfer his soul into another body. The owner of the jewels said that he had been freed from all privations and hardships employing these two jewels.

After the sixth year, he (Zu'l-Qarnain) returned to Kashmir and entrusted the city of Kashmir to his grandson named Ratnatir. Then he proceeded to conquer foreign lands; he did not return nor did anyone bring the news of how he died. His grandson Vinayaditya continued to conquer foreign lands and captured many cities. At last, he came to a town in the East. Its king was made to fear Vinayaditya; he consulted his ministers and nobles to seek their opinion in this matter. His senior ministers submitted to him that Ratnatir was a mighty king and they could not stand against him in battle. His Chief Minister said to him that it was challenging to repel his attack. But now that the king had asked for his counsel, he would advise him to surrender to Vinayaditya. It enraged him and he ordered that his nose chopped off which followed by his expulsion from the city. After his nose would be chopped off and following his expulsion, he would join the enemy and devise some plan of destroying him.

When the enemy came to know of the minister's affairs and the news reached Vinayaditya, he made him his associate in conquering the neighbouring lands. The crafty minister, full of deceit and guile as he was, led Vinayaditya to take a route where no water was available for ten to twelve days [of their journey] and a relatively large number of his men and beasts perished. Seeing through the deceit and craftiness of the minister, Vinayaditya asked him what his objective was in doing this. The minister told him that he wanted to get rid of him so that the country of his king was spared of the scourge that he was. When Vinayaditya heard this, he gave him a robe of honour and other rewards and also extended the favour to his king.

From there Vinayaditya went to the countries of Kesh and Bahrain where he met with a disastrous defeat resulting in heavy loss of men and material. Along with a handful of his followers, the king fell into the hands of the king of Bahrain who placed them all in the custody of his mother, so that she could keep an eye on them. One day Vinayaditya threatened her with dire consequences for her son. Utterly bewildered, she asked him how his capacity for retaliation had grown during his captivity.

Meanwhile, there blew a strong gale and he, as well as the mother of the king, embarked for Mabar. In that place, there was a man-eater and the king found himself unable to kill it. Vinayaditya put his left hand into the jaw of the lion and with his right-hand rent it asunder, which surprised the king of Mabar. He summoned him to his presence and bestowed upon him robes of honour and other rewards and gave him his daughter in marriage. A large contingent of troops was dispatched under his command to conquer the country of Pars. He brought those lands under his sway and subjugated their people. Then he went back to Kashmir to continue with his rule over that land.

Once, while he was riding a horse, his whip slipped out of his hand. Thereupon he bade one of his attendants present there to reach him the lash. The attendant declined to oblige him saying that it was not his job. He was a courier called Potkan in Kashmiri. Enraged by his audacity, the king ordered that he be given a proper assignment forthwith. Then he wrote down a message, handed over the document to him and directed [him] to carry it to the ruler of Lank, which is a big and famous city of India. The name of the ruler of this city was Dados. The message was that the King of Gang dispatches one thousand and five boats to him to build a fort. Hardly had the messenger embarked when an enormous fish gulped down the boat along with all the passengers.

The messenger had a sword with which he pierced the belly of the fish which caused its death. The carcass was cast ashore near the city of Kajendan. The messenger emerged from the belly of the fish which amazed the people of Kajendan. They enquired of him about this happening. As a proof of what he had told them, they found the letters of command from [the king of Kashmir] on his person and carried these to the king of Gang. On knowing all that had happened, the king of Gang dispatched along with the Potkan a convoy of one thousand and five boats. When he reached the outskirts of the city of Kashmir, he informed the king about the coming of the demons of the ruler of Gang. The ruler of Kashmir sent pulses and many thorny fruits for them. The daily quota of ration for the demons, consisting of legumes and cereals was sent to them till the fort completed at Andarkol. Here the king reigned for seventy years. Then he handed over the reins of government to his son named Bardanatant. The kingship then passed on to Kashshil and then to Rama Chand and after his death to Onta Dev. He was miserly and so greedy for wealth that he ordered his daughters to take to prostitution in the streets to extract money from people.

There was a man, Brahman by name, who was notorious for his licentiousness. After his death, he was survived by his wife and son, who fell in love with the daughter of the king. On learning of her son's passionate love for the princess, his mother admonishingly told him that he had hardly inherited anything from his father which could help him in realizing his objective. All that his father had left behind was a dinar which had been put in his mouth at the time of his cremation. On knowing this, he visited the spot where his father's dead body had been cremated. There he was able to find the coin which he, later on, presented to the princess and succeeded in fulfilling his desire. Next day, along with other girls, she went to see the king. He was delighted to see the standard coin and bade his nobles to summon its owner.

The Brahman's son presented himself before the king. He asked him how he had procured the dinar and asked him questions about his passionate love for the princess. After knowing the whole story, he sought from his sagacious minister an answer to the question whether a person carried with him any worldly possessions after his death. The minister told him that a dead man brought with him nothing but memories of his good deeds, his even-handed justice to his subjects and of his acts of enduring benevolence. On hearing these words, the king repented over his deeds. He then ordered the building of schools, laying of the foundations of prayer-houses and construction of bridges and roads. He distributed all his worldly possessions among the destitute and the mendicants. He then restored to his subjects their due rights. Of his line, there were nine [persons], who ruled one after another over a period of three hundred and sixty years. During their reign, they amassed three hundred and sixty treasures, which were ordered to be sealed.

In those days, there lived a distraught person, who held a stone under his arm, went to the king advising him to bury his treasure, the stone along with his wealth. The king said, "O you mad person. What you have is a stone and not a treasure." He replied that a profitless treasure, a hardened heart and untimely anger were of a lesser value than that stone. The king uttered a cry, beat his head and told him that he was right. He added that one should pay attention to words and not to the person who utters them. He opened his treasures and distributed the wealth among soldiers, destitute and the poor. Soon after, the king breathed his last. During his days, there lived a hermit who, on hearing the news of the king's death, expressed sorrow for the loss of his charitable acts. He transferred his soul into the body of the dead king and brought him back to life. The king expressed his thanks to God for having been revived to life after his death. This news spread through the lands of India. Learned men assembled to submit to the king that inquiries be made if someone had expired recently. These revealed that a hermit had died and his body had been burnt immediately lest the soul returned to it. After that, the king ruled for thirty-six years before he died.

His death led to dissension among the nobles. They resolved that whosoever entered the city gate first on the next morning would be proclaimed king. The first to do so next morning was a mendicant. He was made a king and the crown and the throne was given to him. His descendants ruled for four hundred years. The last of their house was named Harshid. He invented the art of carving idols out of wood, stone, chalk and clay, whereas formerly these used to be cast in gold and silver only. Another king who lived in those days had two sons. Harshid decided to kill both of them because his nobles were favourably disposed towards them. On learning of Harsha's intention, both of them fled for their lives. He pursued them but was unable to lay his hands on them. However, he killed their parents and returned [to his place]. The boys received the news of the killing of their mother and sought assistance from the rulers of neighbouring regions. They marched against Harsha. In the fighting that ensued, he was defeated and killed. His domain, crown and throne passed on to the elder of the two brothers, who meted out justice [to his people]. Twelve persons of his line reigned successively; the last of them, Shiv Dev ruled in AH 750 (AD 1349).

Ashoka Introduces Buddhism

Ashoka (304 BCE to 232 BCE), an Indian emperor who ruled the Maurya Empire across the Indian subcontinent, introduced Buddhism to the Kashmir valley and the adjoining regions around Srinagar became a centre of Buddhism. Ashoka renounced violence, established welfare as a right for all citizens, promoted religious tolerance and promoted respect for all life, for parents, for teachers and the importance of spiritual awareness. In the first century CE, Kashmir and Ladakh were under the control of Kushans and several rulers of this dynasty strengthened the Buddhist tradition. Buddhism came to western Ladakh from Kashmir in the second century when much of eastern Ladakh and western Tibet was still practising the Bon religion.

In the late fourth century CE, the famous Kuchanese monk Kumarajiva, born to an Indian noble family, studied Dirghagama and Madhyagama in Kashmir under Bandhudatta. He later became a prolific translator who helped take Buddhism to China. His mother Jiva is thought to have retired to Kashmir. Vimalaksa, a Sarvastivadan Buddhist monk, travelled from Kashmir to Kucha and there instructed Kumarajiva in the Buddhist texts Vinaya. Vikramaditya (of Ujjain) and his successors probably ruled the region just before Srinagar fell to the control of the Huns in the sixth century and Mihirkula was the most dreaded ruler of the city and the valley.

M2: Medieval Times – Post-Hindu Mythological Era to India's Partition and Independence

The ancient legacy of religious toleration and cultural pluralism was also upheld by the early Muslim rulers in medieval Kashmir. No doubt Islam incorporates a monotheistic ideology based on the belief in "No God but their God (Allah), the Supreme Creator of the Universe" and denunciation of all sorts of polytheistic forms of stone, idol, image and shrine worship. However, it could retain its egalitarian character only in Arabia whereas, in Iran

and Central Asia, it was constrained to make a kind of compromise with pagan, nomadic and tribal traditions. Consequently, Central Asian Islam combined the essentials of real faith and the age-old un-Islamic customs and traditions. However, for the given support from both the nomadic and sedentary peoples, it developed into the 'folk Islam' with the high social appeal, which even the Wahhabi Movement of Sayyid Sharie Muhammad of Madina could not tear apart in AD 1912.

Since Islam did not arrive directly from Arabia to Kashmir, it naturally carried with it mixed Iranian and Central Asian influences, which were gradually absorbed in the native Kashmiri traditions. Initially, therefore, the neo-converts to Islam continued visiting temples, performing Hindu ritual yajna, dressing in Hindu attire and invoking stones, idols, images and deities for blessings. They did not complete the Islamic practice of circumcision and instead perpetrated acts of un-Islamic innovations. Even for expediency, their Islamic preachers did not object to these fundamental violations lest they enter into conflict with the neo-converts; hence, render their whole mission abortive. More so, they delivered religious sermons, not in Arabic but local languages and used local Hindu religious idioms of *Avtar, Deva, Nirguna, Pran, Paap, Punya, Surag, Ahankar* and *Krodh* in their speeches. Likewise, they made the Rishi cult identifiable with Hinduism by subscribing to celibacy, vegetarianism, non-violence and no injury to animals and abstaining from the use of garlic and onion, etc in food.

The most popular missionary saint, Sayyid Ali, from Hamadan in Iran, permitted group *dhikr* or collective chanting of religious literature in a chorus to undercut the loud recitation of mantras in Hindu temples. Neither *pardah* nor Islamic education was made mandatory for Muslim women. Law of succession and the adoption of a son was not objected to despite being un-Islamic and this practice is still in vogue in Kashmir. Under the circumstances, the age-long traditions featuring a mixed brand of pagan, Zoroastrian, Buddhist and Hindu practices continued to have space in the existing religious-cultural basket of Kashmir.

Over the years, however, the Kashmiri Muslims learned to differentiate between monotheism and polytheism and, as such, stopped visiting Hindu temples. They denounced the Hindu deities and Brahmanical forms as these ran across the belief in inevitable, inalienable and indivisible reality of God. In fact, the rejection of the Brahmanical ritualistic forms was not a new phenomenon but rather a continuation of the reaction articulated by an eminent scholar, Abhinavagupta and the ablest King Harsha, in the early and late 11th century. It was later upheld by Lalla, a Shaiva Yogini and Sheikh Noor-ud Din Rishi or Nund Rishi, a revered Kashmiri saint, in the 14th century. Lalla was fearless enough to recognize the 'oneness of God' and condemn (like her Indian Bhakts) stone worship in all its forms and manifestations: "He is here, there and everywhere. The idol is but a stone. The temple is but a stone. From top to bottom all is stone."

In the same century, Sayyid Ali Hamadani adopted Lalla and Nund Rishi's philosophy as the local base for advocating Islamic monotheism. The scores of his accompanying Central Asian missionaries, artisans, craftsmen, scholars and scientists, toured villages and towns and sensitized the Kashmiris to the essentials of Islam. Many of them permanently settled and formed their diaspora in Kashmir and were thus termed as the Kashanis, Badakhshans, Bukharis, Geelanis, Andrabis, Sayyids, etc. However, despite their mass awareness about what is often termed as the 'high Islam' or 'puritan Islam', the Kashmiri Muslims took recourse to the 'folk Islam' embodying, besides all else, the native customs and traditions. No doubt, their mindset changed from temple to mosque, but their association with the pre-Islamic values and customs continued there with them. It was somewhat re-energized by the Sufistic philosophy and the cult of the shrine and saint worship for being above ethnonational and religious-sectarian considerations as was the case elsewhere in Iran, Central Asia and Afghanistan.

The devotees dedicated shrines, tombs and the mausoleums to the eminent Sufis, Imams, Sayyids and ascribed great miracles to their supernatural powers to animate the dead and inspire people with a "feeling of reverential awe and mysterious influence." Consequently, whole Valley and its Central Asian borderlands were replete with such shrines which the devotees invariably thronged, tied tags and lit candles on to invoke blessings for curing ailments, bearing children, auguring bumper harvests for few ends. They comprised all social and gender groups, men, women and children especially among the peasantry who, more often than not, donated cattle, slaughtered animals, etc at the shrines.

Undeniably, their attitude was reflective of a cardinal contradiction in their belief and practice. While, they practised Kalima, Namaz, Hajj, Zakat, Roza, Circumcision, Marriage and other Islamic rituals and rites, they simultaneously visited and esteemed tombs and shrines in total disregard of the Quranic injection: "And they set-up (idols) as equal to Allah, to mislead (men) from His path. In hell, they will burn; therein, an evil place to stay. There is no other God but Allah, the Eternal and Absolute. Those who believe not are arrogant. You should worship none but Allah." The given dichotomy was probably the outcome of the continually pouring in religious-cultural influences from across the borders in Iran, Afghanistan, Central Asia, China and India. Nonetheless, such extraneous influences germinated fair deal of cultural affinity between Kashmir and its South and Central Asian neighbourhood.

One glaring example is manifest in the practice of preserving and displaying the relics of the revered Prophet Mohammad (PBUH) at several shrines in contemporary Kashmir. The said practice was implicitly the continuation of a similar tradition of around AD 1st century in ancient Eastern Turkistan or Chinese Central Asia or what currently forms Chinese largest province called the Xinjiang Uighur Autonomous Republic, where people preserved and demonstrated the relics of the Buddha, the begging bowl and the tooth, as a token of reverence unto and seeking blessings from the said high soul [Lord Buddha]. Another Kashmiri practice termed Nafl was the replica of a 13th-century method in Eastern Turkistan. Processions were taken out while holding up in hands the long wooden poles tied with scraps of cloth and this was to ward off famine or other natural calamities. After going through different streets in Srinagar, the marching crowd terminated at Eidgah for prayers and confession of past sins. No significant difference obtained in these two practices except that the Eastern Turkistanis held out a small meteorite believing that since it had fallen from the sky as a 'stone of heaven', it would, as such, redeem them from the drought severities.

Similarly, the Rishi cult of medieval Kashmir had its counterparts in Eastern Turkistan. According to the medieval accounts, the Rishis resemble the Buddhist, Hindu, Vaishnav and Muslim saints and Sufis for they (i) lead an austere life, (ii) abstain from worldly allurements, (iii) disregard polytheism, Brahmanism and ritualism, (iv) avoid taking meat, (v) plant trees, (vi) speak people's language, (vii) and tread long distances to preach monotheism, peace and non-violence. They were held with great respect by the Kashmiris, who paid obeisance at their shrines and abstained from meat or fish on the eve of their anniversaries to show their association with them. The Kashmiri Rishis were, as such, identifiable with the specific groups of ascetics in the Eastern Turkistan about whom Marco Polo avers:

> "There is a particular class of devotees, who live in communities, observe strict abstinence in regard to eating, drinking and refrain from any sexual indulgence, in order that they may not give offence to the idols whom they worship."

Similar types of affinities were marked in the architectural specimens of Kashmir and Turkistan as a whole. The pagoda type of Chinese building structure together with the mixed use of stone, wood, stuccoes, dab and wattle and earthen roofing in different ancient and medieval compositions of Kashmir, attest to the incoming influences from China, Central Asia, Afghanistan, Iran and other parts of India; hence, reflective of 'continuity within change'. In fact, few extant

Muslim shrines or mosques in Kashmir were raised on the already existing temple or monastery structures to maintain, among other things, links with the Buddhist and Hindu past. Little wonder to notice some Buddhist chaityas transformed into Hindu temples first and subsequently into Muslim mosques, graves or shrines. The Shah-i-Hamdan shrine offers one such example in proper Srinagar. The Kashmiri Pandits esteemed it for their premises housed the Kali temple during the medieval Kashmir. Thus the centuries-old legacy of multiculturalism was legitimized with the arrival of Islam and mystic ideology of Sufism to Kashmir in the 14th century. It brought with it not only a revolutionary social movement but also scores of customs and values related to individual and group behaviour vis-a-vis birth, death, marriage, faith and other social norms. These were, willy-nilly, adopted and embedded by the natives in their native cultural fabric.

In any way, the net result of exotic influences culminated in marked compatibilities in the nature, composition and performance of a variegated set of customs and traditions over a vast geographical space spanning Kashmir, Iran, Central Asia, Afghanistan and China. The common practices and rituals allied, for instance, to the naming of a new-born baby, the wedding of a couple and the performance of rituals and rites of the deceased by a Buddhist monk, Hindu Brahman or a Muslim Moulvi or Imam, prove the point. In short, the Kashmir's tradition of religious-cultural pluralism symbolized a conglomerate of customs and values which were an indispensable part of 'cultural universals' than any particular group, region, faith and people or country. They came into being in a sequence of constant human interaction by the interchange of give and take relationship. These included the rites and rituals meant, per se, to appease the living and non-living beings and objects for the variety of ends.

Consequently, these customs and traditions had a great social appeal and were least infringed by racial, occupational, social or religious conflicts, negating thereby the above-argued views of the conflict theorists on the negative role of religion on culture and society. Instead, they marginalized the scope of reactionary and revolutionary movements in both quantitative and qualitative terms. Apparently, the ideological void between Buddhism, Hinduism and Islam and even between 'puritan Islam' and 'folk Islam' did not stretch that much during the ancient and medieval periods. The reasons were more than evident. These customs and traditions promoted close-knit relations between individuals and groups, guaranteed them social security against man-made and God-made forces, inculcated in them a sense of peace, harmony and social togetherness, capacitated them to distinguish between sacred and profane values, sensitized them to social changes and challenges, made them immune to complexities of life and consoled them in the event of stress and strain.

Ladakh Dynasty

In the eighth century, Ladakh was involved in the clash between Tibetan expansion pressing from the East and Chinese influence exerted from Central Asia through the passes and control over Ladakh frequently changed hands between China and Tibet. In 842, Nyima-Gon, a Tibetan royal representative annexed Ladakh for himself after the break-up of the Tibetan empire and founded a separate Ladakh dynasty. During this period Ladakh underwent Tibetanization resulting in a predominantly Tibetan population. The regime spearheaded the second spreading of Buddhism, importing religious ideas from north-west India, mainly from Kashmir.

Islam Influence

In the thirteenth century, Islam became the main religion in Kashmir. The Muslims and Hindus of Kashmir lived in relative harmony since the Sufi-Islamic way of life that ordinary Muslims followed in Kashmir complemented the Hindu Rishi tradition of Kashmiri Pandits. This led to a syncretic culture where Hindus and Muslims revered the same local saints and prayed at the same shrines. Famous Sufi saint Bulbul Shah was able to persuade the king of the time, Rinchan Shah, who was the prince of Kashgar Ladakh, to adopt Islam and hence the foundation of Sufiana composite culture was laid when Muslims, Hindus and Buddhists were peacefully co-existing.

Few Kashmiri rulers, such as Sultan Zain-ul-Abidin, were tolerant of all religions. However, several Muslim rulers of Kashmir were intolerant. Sultan Sikandar Butshikan of Kashmir (1389-1413) is often considered the worst of these. The *Tarikh-i-Firishta* records that Sikandar persecuted the Hindus and issued orders proscribing the residence of any other than Muslims in Kashmir. He also ordered the breaking of all golden and silver images, depicting Hindus god and goddess. But faced with Islamic conquest in the thirteenth century, Ladakh chose to seek and accept guidance in religious matters from Tibet. Lhachen Bhagan was a Basgo king who united Ladakh in 1470 by overthrowing the king of Leh. He took on the surname Namgyal (meaning victorious) and founded a new dynasty, which survives into the twenty-first century. For nearly two centuries, until about

1600, Ladakh was subject to raids and invasions from neighbouring Muslim States, which led to weakening and fracturing of Ladakh and partial conversion of Ladakhis to Islam.

Mughal and Durrani Rule

Mughal ruler Jalal-ud-Din Akbar (1556 to 1605) conquered Kashmir between 1586 and 1592. Mughal is the Persian word for Mongol and was used to refer to Central Asian nomads who claimed descent from the Mongol warriors of Genghis Khan. Mughal rule lasted until 1751. As elsewhere, the Mughals adopted the local religion, which in Kashmir at the time was Islam. The Mughals defeated Ladakh, but it still retained its independence. In the late seventeenth century, Ladakh sided with Bhutan in a dispute with Tibet, which resulted in an invasion by Tibet. Kashmiri help restored Ladakhi rule on the condition of that a mosque is built in Leh and that the Ladakhi king converts to Islam. The Treaty of Temisgam in 1684 settled the dispute between Tibet and Ladakh, but its independence was severely restricted.

When the Mughal Empire started to disintegrate after the death of Aurangzeb in 1707, infiltrations to the Kashmir valley from the Pathan tribes increased and they ruled Srinagar for several decades. The Durrani Empire was a State that included modern day Afghanistan, Pakistan, parts of eastern Iran and western India. Ahmed Shah Durrani and his descendants ruled Kashmir from 1756 until 1819. During the reign of Muslim kings in Kashmir, three supplements to *Rajatarangini* were written by Jonaraja (1411-1463 CE), Srivara and Prajyabhatta and Suka, which end with Akbar's conquest of Kashmir in 1586 CE. The text was translated into Persian by Muslim scholars such as Nizam Uddin, Farishta and Abul Fazl. *Baharistan-i-Shahi* and Haidar Malik's *Tarikh-i-Kashmir* (completed in 1621 CE) are the essential texts on the history of Kashmir during the Sultanate period. Both the books were written in Persian and used *Rajatarangini* and Persian histories as their sources.

In the eighth century, Karkota Empire established themselves as rulers of Kashmir. Kashmir grew as an imperial power under the Karkotas. Chandrapida of this dynasty was recognized by a royal order of the Chinese emperor as the king of Kashmir. His successor Lalitaditya Muktapida lead a successful military campaign against the Tibetans. He then defeated Yashovarman of Kanyakubja and subsequently conquered eastern kingdoms of Magadha, Kamarupa, Gauda and Kalinga. Lalitaditya extended his influence of Malwa and Gujarat and defeated Arabs at Sindh. After his demise, Kashmir's supremacy over other kingdoms declined and the dynasty ended in c 855–856 CE. Utpala dynasty founded by Avantivarman followed the Karkotas.

His successor Shankaravarman (885–902 CE) led a successful military campaign against Gurjaras in Punjab. Political instability in the 10th century made the royal bodyguards (Tantrins) very powerful in Kashmir. Under the Tantrins, civil administration collapsed and chaos reigned in Kashmir till Chakravarman defeated them. Queen Didda, who descended from the Hindu Shahis of Kabul on her mother's side, took over as the ruler in the second half of the 10th century. After her death in 1003 CE, the throne passed to Lohara dynasty. During the 11th century, Mahmud of Ghazni made two attempts to conquer Kashmir. However, both his campaigns failed because he could not siege the fortress at Lohkot.

Muslim Rule: Kashmir Sultanate (1346-1580s), Mughals (1580s-1750s) and Afghans (1750s-1819)

The oppressive taxation, corruption, internecine fights and rise of feudal lords (Damaras) during the unpopular rule of the Lohara Dynasty (1003–1320 CE) paved the way for foreign invasions of Kashmir. Suhadeva, last king of the Lohara dynasty, fled Kashmir after Zulju (Dulacha), a Turkic-Mongol chief, led a savage raid on Kashmir. Rinchana, a Tibetan Buddhist refugee in Kashmir, established himself as the ruler after Zulju. Rinchana's conversion to Islam is a subject of Kashmiri folklore. He was persuaded to accept Islam by his minister Shah Mir, probably for political reasons. Islam had penetrated into countries outside Kashmir and in the absence of the support from Hindus, who were in the majority, Rinchana needed the help of the Kashmiri Muslims. Shah Mir's backstabbing of the Rinchana's successor secured Muslim rule and the rule of his dynasty in Kashmir.

In the 14th century, Islam gradually became the dominant religion in Kashmir. Islamic preacher Sheikh Nooruddin Noorani, who was traditionally revered by Hindus as Nund Rishi, combined elements of Kashmir Shaivism with Sufi mysticism in his discourses. The Sultans between 1354–1470 CE were tolerant of other religions except for Sultan Sikandar (1389–1413 CE). Sultan Sikandar imposed taxes on non-Muslims, forced conversions to Islam and earned the title But-Shikan for destroying idols. Sultan Zain-ul-Abidin (c 1420–1470 CE) invited artists and artisans from Central Asia and Persia to train local artists in Kashmir. Under his rule, the arts of wood carving, paper-mâché, shawl and carpet weaving prospered. For a brief period in the

1470s, States of Jammu, Poonch and Rajauri which paid tributes to Kashmir revolted against the Sultan Hajji Khan. However, they were subjugated by his son Hasan Khan who took over as ruler in 1472 CE. By the mid 16th century, Hindu influence in the courts and role of the Hindu priests had declined as Muslim missionaries immigrated into Kashmir from Central Asia and Persia and Persian replaced Sanskrit as the official language.

Around the same period, the nobility of Chaks had become powerful enough to unseat the Shah Mir dynasty. Mughal General Mirza Muhammad Haidar Dughlat, a member of ruling family in Kashgar, invaded Kashmir in c 1540 CE on behalf of emperor Humayun. Persecution of Shias, Shafi'is and Sufis and instigation by Suri kings led to a revolt which overthrew Dughlat's rule in Kashmir. Kashmir did not witness direct Mughal rule till the reign of Mughal king Akbar who visited the valley himself in 1589 CE. During successive Mughal emperors many famous gardens, mosques and palaces were constructed. Religious intolerance and discriminatory taxation reappeared when Mughal emperor Aurangzeb ascended to the throne in 1658 CE. After his death, the influence of the Mughal Empire declined. In 1700 CE, a servant of a wealthy Kashmir merchant brought Mo-i Muqqadas (the hair of the Prophet), a relic of Muhammad, to the valley. The relic was housed in the Hazratbal Shrine on the banks of Dal Lake.

Nadir Shah's invasion of India in 1738 CE further weakened Mughal control over Kashmir. In 1753, Abdul Khan Isk Aquasi, a General in Ahmed Shah Abdali's army, invaded Kashmir and established the rule of the Durrani Empire of Afghanistan. Afghan rule in Kashmir was ruthless and oppressive, particularly for the Hindus. Locals were extorted from, captured and forced into slavery during this period. The dominance of Afghans declined after Ahmed Shah Abdali's death in 1772, but they ruled Kashmir for another 47 years.

Sikh Rule

The Mughal emperor Aurangzeb had forbidden anyone from removing the decapitated head and body of the ninth Sikh Guru, Tegh Bahadur. The residents of Delhi, who had just witnessed the guru's assassination, were struck with fear. Many among them were devotees of Tegh Bahadur, the eighth spiritual descendant of Guru Nanak. The Sikh spiritual movement that had centred around Kartarpur Sahib (now in Pakistan) at the death of Guru Nanak had by then spread to far-flung regions of Punjab and beyond. His followers came from all backgrounds, bringing their material as well as human resources.

Official Mughal records, describing the reasons for the assassination of Guru Tegh Bahadur in 1675, states that he moved around with several thousand followers. With the rise in the political and material influence of the institution of guruhood, the Sikh gurus were increasingly seen as political rivals by petty kingdoms of the Mughal empire. Their power and strength were also visible to the Mughal emperor. The days of political obscurity under Guru Nanak were long gone. Several accounts are there explaining the motive behind the assassination of Guru Tegh Bahadur on Aurangzeb's orders. Sikh tradition states that the guru stood up for the rights of Kashmiri Pandits who approached him to intercede on their behalf with the emperor and ask him to revoke a recently imposed jizya (financial tax).

Convinced by his son, Gobind Rai, who later became Guru Gobind Singh, to stand up for the protection of the Kashmiri Pandits, Guru Tegh Bahadur travelled to Delhi. Here, at the Mughal court, he was mocked and asked to prove his guruhood by performing a miracle. He wrote a magic spell on a piece of paper and tied it around his neck with a thread. He told the Mughal authorities that as long as the spell remained linked to him, his head would not be separated from his body even if the blade of the executioner fell on his neck. But when the blade struck the guru's neck, it severed his head. Later, when the Mughal authorities opened the magic spell that the guru had written, it read, "He gave his head, not his secret."

In 1752, the Sikhs under Maharaja Ranjit Singh (1780-1839), who ruled from his capital in Lahore, annexed the Kashmir valley in 1819 and held it until in 1846. Although he was of the Sikh religion, his empire was effectively secular, as it did not discriminate against Sikhs, Muslims, Hindus or even Atheists. In 1780, after the death of Ranjit Deo, the Raja of Jammu, the Hindu kingdom of Jammu (to the south of the Kashmir valley was captured by the Sikhs under Ranjit Singh. Ranjit Deo's grandnephew, Gulab Singh Dogra, sought service at the court of Ranjit Singh, distinguished himself in later campaigns, especially the annexation of the Kashmir valley and, for his services, was created Raja of Jammu in 1820. With the help of General Zorawar Singh, Gulab Singh soon captured Ladakh and Baltistan, regions to the east and north-east of Jammu.

A Ladakhi rebellion in 1842 was crushed. The Ladakh Namgyal family was given the 'Jagir' (small territory granted by the ruler to an army chieftain) of Stok, which it nominally retained to the twenty-first century. In the 1850s, European influence increased in Ladakh – geologists, athletes and tourists started exploring Ladakh. In 1885, Leh became the headquarters of a mission of the Moravian Church. Sikhs always in the forefront facing the radical Islam and conversion force propagated by the Mughal rulers. Below I have tried to give the glimpse of events happened then. A sad bloody part of Sikh history.

Sri Guru Arjan Dev Ji – the first Sikh Guru to be Martyred by Mughal Emperor Shahjehan (one who built Taj Mahal) for not converting to Islam. Sri Guru Tegh Bahadur Ji – the Ninth Guru who was martyred by Emperor Aurangzeb at Chandani Chowk Delhi, for not converting to Islam. Bhai Satidass Ji went along with Guru Tegh Bahadur and was martyred at Chandani Chowk Delhi. Bhai Dyal Dass Ji also went along with Guru Tegh Bahadur to Delhi and was martyred at Chandani Chowk Delhi. Chhote Sahibzade were the young sons (not even teenagers) of Guru Gobind Singh who were captured by the Mughal Governor of City of Sarhind, Wazir Khan. He martyred seven and nine years old Sikh Sahibzades for not converting to Islam.

Mata Gujari Ji, Guru Gobind Singh's mother, left this world after hearing the martyrdom of her grandsons. Haqiqat Rai at the tender teenage was a proud Sikh which became a cause for his martyrdom by the Mughals at Lahore. Bhai Mani Singh Ji was the pious Granthi of Golden Temple who was given option either to convert or to be cut into pieces. He picked death to be cut into pieces and with Gurbani on his lips he attained martyrdom. Many Sikhs were martyred by the cruel Mughal Governor of Lahore named Zakriya Khan. Mughals captured Bhai Taru Singh Ji while he was feeding Sikhs who were hiding from the tyrant Mughal ruler. They martyred him but only by cutting his scalp and not his hair. Bhai Subeg Singh and Bhai Shahbaz Singh were father and son who were martyred on specially created wheels. The Khalsa Sikh women and children were martyred by Meer Mannu for not converting to Islam. The bloody history of Kashmir has so many innocents blood mixed in its soil.

Dogras Rule

The Dogras were an Indo-Aryan ethnic group, spoke their language and were mostly Hindus. The First Anglo-Sikh War, which broke out in 1845, led to the treaties of Amritsar and Lahore in 1846, resulted in Gulab Singh Dogra, of Jammu, becoming the Maharaja of the great Himalayan kingdom between the rivers Indus to the west and river Ravi to the east. This established a buffer State for the British between their Indian empire and the empires of Russia and China.

After the India's First War of Independence in 1857, in which Kashmir province sided with the British and the subsequent assumption of direct rule by Great Britain, the princely State of Kashmir came under the paramountcy of the British Crown. Soon after Gulab Singh's death in 1857, his son Ranbir Singh added the emirates of Hunza, Gilgit and Nagar to the kingdom. The Dogra Rule lasted until 1947 when the colonial British first partitioned India and then gave her freedom.

M3: Modern Times – India Divided into Three Parts: India (Today's India), East Pakistan (Bangladesh) and West Pakistan (Today's Pakistan)

Ranbir Singh's grandson Sir Hari Singh, a Hindu who had ascended the throne of Kashmir in 1925, was the reigning monarch in 1947 at the partition of the British Indian Empire into the newly independent Union of India and the Dominion of Pakistan. Both countries had agreed that the rulers of princely States would be given the right to opt for either Pakistan or India or remain independent. A section of the Muslim population of Kashmir demanded accession to Pakistan. Sir Hari Singh, resisted, Pakistan launched a guerrilla onslaught, the Maharaja signed the Instrument of Accession to the Indian Union and Indian soldiers entered Kashmir and drove out the Pakistani-sponsored guerrillas. The United Nations mediated a ceasefire agreement between the two nations in January 1949.

A 'Line of Control' formed the boundary between the Indian- and Pakistani-controlled sections of Kashmir. India has control of about half the area of the former princely State of Jammu and Kashmir; Pakistan controls a third of the region, the Northern Areas and POK. But before we get into more discussions, let us try to get some perspective into the personal relationship among the leaders of the United India, who were signatories to the Partition and Freedom Agreement.

Tale of Indian Political Leaders at the Time of India's Independence

It is very important to know what was the state of mind, the relationship between the principal political leaders of undivided India. Their relationship and their exposure to strategic thinking, geography, their mindset on religion, their ideology, understanding of the global politics, etc shaped India and Pakistan and impacting millions of people which included United Punjab, United Bengal and United Kashmir mainly. By mid-1949, the Constitution-making process was drawing to a close and the need to choose a President, to act as head of the new Republican State, was looming. For this post, Nehru preferred Rajagopalachari, a scholar-politician from Madras. Rajaji, as he was fondly called, was already Governor-General at the time and appointing him President would involve nothing more than a change of title.

Patel, though, had other ideas and supported Bihar Congressman Rajendra Prasad instead. To some extent, this split was driven by ideology. Rajaji and Nehru agreed with each other on the type of secularism India should follow, an idea Patel did not quite buy into. The Sardar would once call Rajaji "half a Muslim" and Nehru "the Congress only nationalist Muslim". Rajaji had also, back in the day, opposed and eventually dissociated himself from the Quit India Movement, a fact that irritated with many Congressmen. Patel's choice, Rajendra Prasad, was like him a social conservative. As President, Prasad would bitterly oppose Nehru's Hindu Code Bills. He would also help rebuild the Somnath Temple, after the Sardar's death. His most exciting clash with Nehru though was over the very date of Republic Day; Prasad wanted it moved because he thought the day to be astrologically inauspicious.

Patel Outmanoeuvres Nehru

His decision made, Patel privately communicated his support to Prasad. He did not, however, publicly reveal his hand, preferring to bide his time. Rash and impetuous, with characteristic disdain for the nitty-gritty, Nehru preferred to take a more direct and ultimately imprudent approach. With murmurs swirling around in the Congress of Prasad's candidature, Nehru wrote directly to him on 10 September 1949, expressing the opinion that "Rajaji might continue as President" and Prasad was not welcome since "it would involve a change and consequent re-arrangements."

Privately supported by Patel, Prasad wrote back, belligerent, refusing to bow out of the race. Publicly, however, Patel kept his cards close to his chest. In his communication with Nehru, Patel gave the impression that he did not have a say in this fight, telling him that is for Nehru to "deal with the situation now," giving off the impression that he would back him. Blithely unaware of what was going on behind the scenes, Nehru kept on writing to Patel complaining about vigorous canvassing has taken place on this subject and there is a vast majority who favour Rajendra Babu.

On 5th October, Nehru called a meeting of Congress MPs to decide the matter. As he proposed Rajaji's name for President, his words were loudly interrupted by the MPs present. Given Nehru's stature and his standing, this was quite astonishing. Disoriented by the intensity of the opposition, Nehru turned to Patel for support and, of course, at that crucial moment, the Sardar played his hand: he did not back Nehru. Stunned by this turn of events, Nehru stopped his speech and sat down as MP after MP attacked Rajaji's candidature. The meeting had all but wrecked Rajaji's chances of becoming President. It had also profoundly embarrassed Nehru – in public. So much so that Nehru threatened to resign, the first of many such threats.

Seeing that he had been outmanoeuvred, a desperate Nehru exchanged the stick for the carrot. He tempted Prasad first with the Chairmanship of the Planning Commission and then the Presidentship of the Congress, but Prasad did not bite. Defeated, Rajaji announced his retirement. Later on, he would be inducted into the Cabinet as a Minister without Portfolio and, after Patel's death, he would go on to become the Home Minister.

After swearing-in Prasad as President, Rajaji wrote him a congratulatory letter wishing him "strength and support." While Rajaji must obviously have been smarting at these turn of events which forced him to become a martyred pawn in a Nehru-Patel battle, he was above complaining directly about it. In his typical wry humour though, he ended the letter to Prasad with a postscript: "Please show this to Jawaharlal and Vallabhbhai. I am not writing separately to them."

Coming to Jinnah, he was aware that his politics was akin to riding a tiger, which he would eventually not be able to get off. There was as much vicious anti-Muslim behaviour going on during the time of India's independence, as the opposite. And these people were followers of the Congress. Gandhi didn't realize it. There was (for instance) that scene of Noakhali (the riots in October-November 1946, in Chittagong (Current Bangladesh) district in un-partitioned Bengal in which 5,000 Hindus were killed). Gandhi did not understand that some of the things he was saying there were inciting Hindus to kill Muslims.

In Bihar riots broke out in Chhapra and Saran districts in late October 1946, as a reprisal for the Noakhali riots, killing anywhere upwards of 5,000 Muslims; the death toll figures varied widely. At the very top level, all these leaders – Nehru, Jinnah and Gandhi – were very far from their followers, the long run to the freedom movement and their fast riping age all caught up with them. They were mostly in Delhi operating from their drawing rooms. Negotiating with each other and they were so used to the kind of rhetoric you would use in a courtroom. The things they would say, the things they would write in the press. I don't think they quite realized the impact those words would have at the ground level. In that case, I would hold all of them guilty of the United India's partition, obviously the hidden game plan was by the British.

They all didn't understand that the negotiations they were doing - the kind of brinkmanship, the hard-line positions they were taking, all part of the talks were happening against the backdrop of these increasing tensions all around the country. They were too focused on what was happening in their little room and didn't understand this was having an impact elsewhere. Nehru once admitted discussing the Partition of Punjab that he had not gone into any great detail about how it would happen.

So Nehru's wrongdoing was not just alienating his rival Jinnah but also not understanding the nitty-gritty of how Partition would unfold? They were all, perhaps, guilty of being vague about the details. None of them were administrators. None of them had ever held executive positions. They were all trained as lawyers and had become politicians.

So if you asked Nehru: "Okay you want to split the Punjab - how are you going to divide the education part of that?" he would have had no idea. (Or about.) The police force, the administration. All stuff that the British had handled until that point. They again didn't understand the reality of the impact of the things they were doing.

There is a view that had Congress knew about Jinnah's poor health, the formation of Pakistan could have been avoided and hence no Kashmir problem? This has come up all the time. His illness (Jinnah was suffering from tuberculosis since the 1930s). He evidently hid his Tuberculosis disease as it was great social taboo during those times and was more akin to poor people and Jinnah was feudal and rich in mindset and it would not have gone well with his personality, his rival, the charismatic Nehru and his Muslim followers. He had been a sick man for many years but successfully hid the truth. In 1947, had to take a whole month off and recuperate in some village outside Karachi. The year before, he had done something similar.

The majority in India believed then and also now that India's interests would have been served better if Sardar Patel, in place of Jawaharlal Nehru, had been the country's Prime Minister. Of all the leaders, Maulana Abul Kalam Azad, Nehru's friend, guide and philosopher came to the same conclusion after watching Nehru as an administrator. Azad was in Nehru's cabinet and saw him from close quarters. Azad told his Secretary, Humayun Kabir, that they should have made Nehru the country's President and Patel its Prime

Minister. Azad was secular through and through and boldly faced the charge of 'Hindu show boy' that the Muslim League made against him. He did not flinch even for a second to say publicly that the formation of Pakistan would be injurious to the health of Muslims.

Patel's most significant achievement is that he got 562 princely States integrated into the Indian Union. Patel refused to release ₹ 64 crore to Pakistan. This sum was part of assets which India had agreed to transfer while conforming to the partition details. Patel argued that how could he release the money when India and Pakistan were engaged in a war over Kashmir. Gandhiji had to go on a fast unto death to make Patel relent. The Hindu-Muslim unity was a matter of faith with Gandhiji, not part of the policy.

On Kashmir, Nehru did not allow his Home Minister to take an independent decision and the result is in front of us.

> "We want the entire territory and battle for the whole of Kashmir." – Sardar Vallabhbhai Patel, July 23, 1949

The man, who would have been the first Prime Minister of India, chose to accept Mahatma Gandhi's advice and remain happy to be the Home Minister in Jawaharlal Nehru's cabinet. As history tells us, the Congress held a Presidential election in the knowledge that its chosen leader would become India's head of government. Eleven Congress State units nominated Sardar Vallabhbhai Patel, while only the Working Committee suggested Nehru.

Sensing that Nehru would not accept second place to Patel, Gandhi supported Nehru and asked Patel to withdraw, which he immediately did. Poor decision, personal emotional connect with Gandhiji overruled his much larger duty for the nation. Let history and its future readers judge this event. I am a very small writer to comment on these great stalwarts. A man of highest personal integrity and a transparent public life, Sardar not only gave India without any ulcers but also had Lakshadweep integrated in time, which was eyed by Pakistan immediately after August 15, 1947. He had the prudence to send naval ships to the island, barely informed of the independence and thwarted a Pakistani navy attempt to seize the strategically located and almost 'out-of-sight' island.

Patel integrated 562 princely States with the swiftness and alacrity of a Bismarck. Nehru was given the task to have J&K merged. He not only turned it into a permanent pain in the neck but during his reign, we lost 1.25 lakh sq km of Indian land to China and Pakistan. Survey of India's map showing the J&K area is incomplete in the sense that India has to still take back the Aksai Chin and Gilgit region from China and Pakistan, which were annexed in 1947-48 by them.

Another anecdote to understand the leader's action and mindset that shaped India comes from Maniben's diary written on September 20, 1950. It says that Sardar told Nehru that Babri Masjid's renovation was different from the reconstruction of the Somnath Temple, for which a trust was set-up that raised nearly ₹30 lakh for the purpose. Government money was not spent on restoration of the Somnath Temple, Sardar told Nehru, following which the Prime Minister kept quiet, Maniben's diary notes on September 20, 1950. As Sardar Patel's wife, Zaverba, died very early, Maniben had taken up the multiple roles as daughter, secretary, washerwoman and nurse to the 'Iron Man' till his death on December 12, 1950.

After India's Independence and the accession of Junagadh State into the Indian Union, Sardar Vallabhbhai Patel, the then Union Home Minister, pledged that Somnath will be reconstructed and restored to its original glory. When Patel broached this subject with Mahatma Gandhi, Gandhi endorsed the plan but said that the contribution for the reconstruction of the temple should come from the public. Patel accepted this advice.

With the demise of Patel, the task of the restoration of the temple was ably led by KM Munshi, a Cabinet Minister in the then Prime Minister Jawaharlal Nehru's government. Munshi wrote,

> "I was clear in my mind that the temple of Somnath was not just an ancient monument; it lived in the heart of the whole nation and its reconstruction was a national pledge."

However, Nehru never liked the idea of restoring this ancient monument and "more than once criticised" Munshi for working for its reconstruction. Munshi was referred to in the Cabinet as someone 'connected with Somnath'.

In the early months of 1951, just a few weeks before the temple inauguration, the matter came to a head. At the end of a Cabinet meeting, Nehru called Munshi and said:

> "I don't like your trying to restore Somnath. It is Hindu revivalism."

Nehru had revealed his cards. He was haunted by the spectre of 'Hindu revivalism'. Restoring an ancient monument, a place of immense veneration, which had repeatedly been obliterated, was according to Nehru an act of Hindu revivalism.

Munshi was incensed like others. Without replying to Nehru's insinuation, he left the meeting in the middle and the very next day wrote to him a long letter, stating:

> "Yesterday you referred to 'Hindu revivalism'. I know your views on the subject; I have done justice to them; I hope you will equally do justice to mine.... It is my faith in the past which has given me the strength to work in the present and to look forward to our future. I cannot value freedom if it deprives us of the *Bhagavad Gita* or uproots our millions from the faith with which they look upon our temples and thereby destroys the texture of our lives ... this shrine once restored to a place of importance in our life will give to our people a purer conception of religion and a more vivid consciousness of our strength, so vital in these days of freedom and its trail."

Nehru evidently wasn't too convinced. When the then President of India, Rajendra Prasad, was invited to inaugurate the temple, Nehru shot him a letter, admonishing,

> "I confess that I do not like the idea of your associating yourself with a spectacular opening of the Somnath Temple. This is not merely visiting a temple, which can certainly be done by you or anyone else but rather participating in a significant function which unfortunately has a number of implications."

It seems by 'number of implications' he meant that Rajendra Prasad inaugurating a temple would be a challenge to the secular fabric of the Indian Republic. Rajendra Prasad ignored Nehru's advice and added,

> "I would do the same with a mosque or a church if I were invited."

So, on 11 May 1951, Rajendra Prasad, while presiding over the opening ceremony of the temple, gave a stirring speech. He said that the physical symbols of our civilization might be destroyed, but no arms, army or king could destroy the bond that the people had with their culture and faith. Till that bond remained, the civilization would survive. He added that it was the creative urge for civilizational renewal, nurtured in the hearts of the people through centuries that had once again led to the *praan-pratishtha* of the Somnath deity. Somnath was the symbol of economic and spiritual prosperity of ancient India, he said. The re-building of Somnath will not be complete till India attains the prosperity of the yesteryear. This speech was covered widely in the press but was 'cut out from the official organs'.

Many years later, reflecting on the Somnath incident, Munshi, penned the most devastating critique of Nehruvian secularism. He stated:

> "In its (secularism) name, anti-religious forces, sponsored by secular humanism or Communism, condemns religious piety, particularly in the majority community."

KM Munshi said:

> "In its name, again, politicians in power adopt a strange attitude which, while it condones the susceptibilities, religious and social, of the minority communities, is too ready to brand similar susceptibilities in the majority community as communalistic and reactionary. How secularism sometimes becomes allergic to Hinduism will be apparent from certain episodes relating to the reconstruction of Somnath temple. These unfortunate postures have been creating a sense of frustration in the majority community. If however, the misuse of this word 'secularism' continues ... if every time there is an inter-communal conflict, the majority is blamed regardless of the merits of the questions; if our holy places of pilgrimage like Banaras, Mathura and Rishikesh continue to be converted into industrial slums..., the springs of traditional tolerance will dry up."

Written in the sixties an erstwhile member of Nehru's Cabinet, truer words were perhaps never spoken. This is the flawed secular model congress followed and spoiled the plural character of the country. Kashmir is still paying the price.

Kashmir – A Thorn in India's Side for Decades

Since 1936, Maniben had started maintaining a diary in which she recorded her illustrious father's daily events and comments. (But with one caveat, her interpretations of great man's thinking may not necessarily be correct always.) Another entry, on September 13, 1950, quotes Ghanshyam Das Birla as saying:

> "Nehru's whole family would have embraced Islam if they had not come in contact with Gandhiji."

Particularly significant are Sardar's views on Communists, Muslims and the conversion of Hindus as chronicled by Maniben. It says Nehru tried to go soft on the Hyderabad action, apparently to appease Muslims. But the Sardar told C Rajagopalachari in no uncertain terms that nothing would stop him from pursuing a vigorous effort to remove 'an ulcer', and that Nehru should remain within his limits.

The diary says:

> "Sardar Patel bluntly told Rajaji that he would not want the future generations to blame and curse him for allowing an ulcer in the heart of India. On one side is western Pakistan and on the other side eastern Pakistan with their idea of a pan-Islamic bloc (they want to) come to Delhi and establish the Mughal empire again. Once we enter Hyderabad, it is no longer an international affair. It is the State ministry's function. How long are you and Panditji going to bypass the ministry of the States and carry on?" (September 13, 1948).

Patel's hold over the Congress party organization was undoubtedly greater. Nehru considered Sardar a rival who could dethrone him. Maniben's diary, however, reveals Patel had no such ambition, particularly after he had given his word to Gandhi. Upon the Patel-Nehru differences played many others, notably Rafi Ahmed Kidwai, the socialists and even Maulana Azad. The diary reveals their manoeuvrings to oust Sardar from the Cabinet. Significantly, Nehru consistently ignored the many allegations of corruption against Kidwai, a fact that puzzled many Congress leaders. Maniben records:

> "Sardar Patel was not happy with the Nehru-Liaquat Ali Pact as it did not stop the exodus of Hindus from East Pakistan which went on increasing and a large number of Hindus continued to migrate to India. Sardar Patel observed that he was not so much worried about the killings after all 30 lakh people had died in the Bengal famine, but he could not stand assaults on women and their forcible conversion to Islam." (April 5, 1950)

Sardar Patel further said:

> "Hindus had been finished in Sindh, Punjab, Balochistan and Frontier Provinces. It was being repeated in East Pakistan and people like Hafizur Rehman, who had stayed on in India, would be clamouring for (a) homeland in India. What would be our position then? Our posterity would call us traitors." (April 24, 1950)

Sardar Patel did not trust the Communists either. He told MO Mathai, Nehru's special assistant:

> "If we have to build up the nation, Communists would have no place there." (September 13, 1948)

He didn't know then that his photo would be used on the Congress manifesto and that the same people would join hands with the Communists whom he had despised most.

Maniben's diary further says:

> "Sardar Patel was very unhappy that Nehru had taken the Kashmir issue to the UN which tied India's hands. His idea was that India should extricate itself from the UN patiently and then solve the Kashmir problem forever. He was also unhappy when reports came that the fertile land left behind in Jammu by Muslim zamindars who had migrated to Pakistan was not being given to Hindu refugees. Instead, the Sheikh was insisting on settling only Muslim refugees on such land (May 1, 1949) (there were reports) that the majority of government employees were pro-Pakistan."

Nehru was a close friend of Sheikh Abdullah, while the Sardar didn't trust him at all. The diary reveals that even Bakshi Ghulam Mohammad, the former Prime Minister of Kashmir, felt that the Sardar could have solved the Kashmir issue if Nehru had not intervened.

> "Bakshi Ghulam Mohammad, on the other hand, was insisting that the Sardar should settle the Kashmir issue as he had done Hyderabad. But Nehru would not allow it. Iyengar reported that the Sheikh wanted to have an independent Kashmir. Upon hearing this, the Sardar said he would ask the Maharaja to return to Jammu as he did not place any trust in Sheikh Abdullah." (May 12, 1949)

Maniben also refers to a discussion by some Nehru loyalists about the possibility of the partition of Kashmir, which involved India retaining Jammu and handing over the rest of the State to Pakistan. Patel retorted:

> "We want the entire territory and battle for the whole of Kashmir." (July 23, 1949)

When India got Independence on August 15th, 1947, four prominent States; namely, Kashmir, Hyderabad, Mysore and Junagadh, present-day Gujarat; had still not signed the Instrument of Annexation with either Pakistan or India. The British divided India into two nations and three parts, they divided British India into the lines of final solution by Radcliffe, now infamously called the Radcliffe line and allowed these two nations to negotiate with the princely States as they didn't have direct jurisdiction within these princely States governed by often maverick and highly incompetent rulers who ruled their States in the autocratic fashion. At the time of Independence, India had around 560 odd princely States governed by Hindu Rajas and Muslim nawabs. Their estates could be as big as a State of Jammu and Kashmir or as small as a small village. Fortunately, India had a strong leader in Sardar Patel, the Home Minister of Independent India. His efforts and strong arm twisting often forced these princes and nawabs to sign the Instrument of Annexation. Now the Instrument of Annexation was an agreement designed by VP Menon, an IAS officer who was the Personal Secretary of Patel.

Post-August 1947 Era

Barring few States, all the princely States had signed the instrument and were annexed by India and Pakistan respectively. Now, many States who had Hindu majority, but were ruled by Muslim nawabs (Gujarat and Hyderabad) were in not favour of signing the instrument with Hindu majority India. Kashmir was the only primary State to have a Hindu ruler and a majority of Muslim population. Of the four troubled States, three States were annexed by force (Indian government had asked the military to take control of the State of Hyderabad, Mysore and Gujarat by force. It was a military coup). The Nawab of Junagadh (present-day Gujarat) ran away on a chartered plane to Pakistan, the Nizam of Hyderabad announced the signing of the instrument on All India Radio and Mysore followed through as well. The story (or rather the problem) of Kashmir start from the Hindu ruler of Kashmir.

Raja Hari Singh was not known for his articulate nature or his remarkable personality. He often used to be drunk and was never really interested in ruling the State. He knew that if India annexed Kashmir, he would lose all the riches and spoils that he had. He didn't want to annex with Pakistan as well. He wanted an Independent Kashmir and wanted to generate revenue by showcasing Kashmir as the Switzerland of the East. He refused to meet Patel or Jinnah and even banned VP Menon. His antiques were a headache for Patel as it was paramount to make Hari Singh sign the instrument, or else Pakistan can try to annex Kashmir by force. Pandit Nehru was also anxious for Kashmir as it was his home State and he couldn't let Kashmir go in Jinnah's hands.

On the other front, Jinnah got fed up with the immaturity of Hari Singh and decided to attack Kashmir by training the Afghan Pathans and tribesman, the warrior tribes, in the name of jihad, Islamic war against the non-Muslims. Some Pakistani army soldiers disguised as tribesman also attacked Kashmir along with the Pathans and captured a large chunk of Kashmir. Patel begged Mountbatten, the then Governor-General of Independent India, to send the army to Kashmir but he refused as Kashmir was not officially a part of India. Scared by the invading Muslim army, Raja Hari Singh agreed and signed the instrument and then the Indian army was sent overnight to force the Pakistani Kabalis out of Kashmir.

In the meantime, Nehru went to UN and offered to conduct the plebiscite in Kashmir under UN supervision. Patel was dead against it. He did not want any western nation or any organization to interfere in Kashmir issue as it was India's internal matter. Besides, there was a real threat that majority of Kashmiri population may go with Pakistan. Besides Kashmir had already signed the instrument; hence there was no need of plebiscite. Pakistani army refused to vacate the POK and demanded a referendum. Kashmir's then Prime Minister, Sheikh Abdullah, who was a great friend of Nehru; suggested changes in the Constitution. He asked BR Ambedkar, to introduce a temporary law under Article 370 which gave special status to the State of Jammu and Kashmir. Under this Article, except security, communication and external relations, Kashmir had zero interference from the Indian State. This Article officially recognizes Kashmir as a unique State with different rules and regulations. This Article specifies that the States must concur in the application of laws, except those that pertain to Communications, Defence, Finance and Foreign Affairs. It can have a separate legislative assembly, can force any non-Kashmiri out of the State, can ban any non-Kashmiri from buying land or establishing business in the State of Kashmir.

Article 370 effectively separates Kashmir from rest of India and therefore, is the only piece of law in the Indian Constitution, which gives strength to Pakistan's claim on Kashmir problem. The Article was supposed to be scrapped off from the Constitution after the 'issue' has been resolved. It is still present and the current Kashmir government (and the one before that) would do anything to keep the *status quo* for their political gains. Having finalized the text of Article 370 with Sheikh Abdullah, Nehru brought in Gopalaswamy Ayyangar, IAS, as a Minister without Portfolio to help him deal with Kashmir portfolio and plead the case of Article 370 in the Constituent Assembly. Gopalaswamy Ayyangar had been Prime Minister of Kashmir for six years with Maharaja Hari Singh. When Sardar Patel expressed his misgivings, this is what Nehru had to say on December 27, 1947.

> "Gopalaswamy Ayyangar has been specially asked to help in Kashmir matters. Both for this reason and because of his intimate knowledge and experience of Kashmir, he had to be given full

latitude. I do not know where the States Ministry (Sardar Patel's ministry) comes into the picture except that it should be kept informed of the steps taken. All this was done in my instance and I do not propose to abdicate my functions regarding matters for which I consider myself responsible. May I say that the manner of approach to Gopalaswamy was hardly in keeping with the courtesy due to a colleague."

Sardar Patel thereupon resigned and the matter fell in Gandhiji's lap to bring the two colleagues together. During this period, V Shankar, IAS was the Personal Secretary to Patel and had maintained a record of all events. It is clear from these documents that Nehru finalized the draft of Article 370 along with Sheikh Abdullah without even informing Patel. After that, it fell to Gopalaswamy Ayyangar to get the draft passed in the Constituent Assembly discussions. The proposal was torn to pieces by the Constituent Assembly and also Congress Party Executive.

Nehru, who was abroad at the time, swallowed his pride and rang up Patel and requested him to get the Article 370 approved. It speaks volumes of Patel's loyalty to a colleague that despite his own and others misgivings, he managed to convince the members of Constituent Assembly and Congress Party Executive. But to V Shankar he said, "Jawaharlal Royega". V Shankar, in his record, has described the meeting of the Congress Executive Committee "The meeting was one of the stormiest I have ever witnessed barring the party meeting which discussed the proposition relating to Rajaji becoming the first President of Indian Republic. The opinion in opposition to Gopalaswamy's formula was forcefully and even militantly expressed and the issue also brought in the sovereignty of the Constituent Assembly to draw up the Constitution without being tied down to the apron-strings of the Kashmir State Constituent Assembly. In such a situation even Maulana Azad was shouted down.

The Party was in an uproar. The Sardar had to plead that because of the international complications, a provisional approach alone could be made leaving the question of the last relationship to be worked out according to the exigencies of the situation and mutual feelings and confidence that would have been by then created. Once the Sardar had taken charge, all opposition to the draft was silenced. And how Nehru responded to this great act of loyalty on the part of Sardar. On 24 July 1952, after Sardar was no more, Nehru made a detailed statement on Kashmir in the Parliament on the slow integration of Kashmir into the Indian Union and mentioned that "Sardar Patel was all the time dealing with these matters." Even

Gopalaswami Ayyangar was dismayed at this blatant lie and mentioned to V Shankar,

> "It is an ill return to the Sardar for the magnanimity he had shown in accepting Panditji's point of view against his better judgment."

Partition of India: Creation of a New Country 'Pakistan'

British barrister Sir Cyril Radcliffe arrived in British India for the first time on July 8, 1947. He had precisely five weeks to draw the borders between an independent India and the newly created Pakistan. He chaired two boundary commissions, one for Punjab and one for Bengal, consisting of two Muslims and two non-Muslims.

The resulting boundary award was announced on August 17. Partition along the Radcliffe Line ended in violence that killed one million people and displaced 12 million. Radcliffe burnt his papers, refused his ₹40,000 fee and left once and for all. While drawing the border, Radcliffe was faced with unyielding demands on both sides, communal tensions, doubtful census numbers, strong economic, administrative and defence considerations and some say even interference from Viceroy Mountbatten. Was Radcliffe biased? Was he ill-informed? Here's one of the criticisms of Radcliffe and his 1947 job by the poet WH Auden in "Partition":

> Unbiased at least he was when he arrived on his mission,
> Having never set eyes on the land he was called to partition
> Between two peoples fanatically at odds,
> With their different diets and incompatible gods.
> "Time," they had briefed him in London, "is short. It's too late
> For mutual reconciliation or rational debate:
> The only solution now lies in separation.
> The Viceroy thinks, as you will see from his letter,
> That the less you are seen in his company the better,
> So we've arranged to provide you with other accommodation.
> We can give you four judges, two Moslem and two Hindu,
> To consult with, but the final decision must rest with you."
>
> Shut up in a lonely mansion, with police night and day
> Patrolling the gardens to keep the assassins away,
> He got down to work, to the task of settling the fate
> Of millions. The maps at his disposal were out of date
> And the Census Returns almost certainly incorrect,
> But there was no time to check them, no time to inspect

Contested areas. The weather was frightfully hot,
And a bout of dysentery kept him constantly on the trot,
But in seven weeks it was done, the frontiers decided,
A continent for better or worse divided.

The next day he sailed for England, where he could quickly
forget
The case, as a good lawyer must. Return he would not,
Afraid, as he told his Club, that he might get shot.

Ranbir Singh's grandson Hari Singh, who had ascended the throne of Kashmir in 1925, was the reigning monarch in 1947 at the conclusion of British rule of the subcontinent and the subsequent partition of the British Indian Empire into the newly independent Union of India and the Dominion of Pakistan. An internal revolt began in the Poonch region against oppressive taxation by the Maharaja. In August, Maharaja's forces fired upon demonstrations in favour of Kashmir joining Pakistan, burned whole villages and massacred innocent people.

The Poonch rebels declared an independent government of 'Azad Kashmir' on 24 October. Rulers of Princely States were encouraged to accede their States to either Dominion - India or Pakistan, taking into account factors such as geographical contiguity and the wishes of their people. In 1947, Kashmir's population was '77% Muslim and 20% Hindu'. To postpone making a hurried decision, the Maharaja signed a standstill agreement with Pakistan, which ensured continuity of trade, travel, communication and similar services between the two. Such a deal was pending with India. Following considerable riots in Jammu, in October 1947, Pashtuns from Pakistan's North-West Frontier Province recruited by the Poonch rebels, invaded Kashmir, along with the Poonch rebels, allegedly incensed by the atrocities against fellow Muslims in Poonch and Jammu. The tribesmen engaged in looting and killing along the way. The ostensible aim of the guerrilla campaign was to frighten Hari Singh into submission. Instead, the Maharaja appealed to Mountbatten for assistance and the Governor-General agreed on the condition that the ruler accedes to India.

Once the Maharaja signed the Instrument of Accession, Indian soldiers entered Kashmir and drove the Pakistani-sponsored irregulars from all but a small section of the State. India accepted the accession, regarding it provisional until the will of the people can be ascertained. Kashmir leader Sheikh Abdullah endorsed the accession as ad-hoc which would be ultimately decided by the people of the State. The Maharaja appointed him the head of the emergency administration. The Pakistani government immediately contested the accession, suggesting that it was fraudulent, that the Maharaja acted under duress and that he had no right to sign an agreement with India when the standstill agreement with Pakistan was still in force.

It remained unclear how much Jinnah wanted Partition. Or whether he pursued the idea more as a tactic to increase Muslim clout within a larger India? Partition - Could this had been avoided? This is the famous debate - whether Jinnah was demanding Pakistan merely as a bargaining chip, or not. The honest truth is that no one knows. The best guess is that it started out as a bargaining chip and at some point, probably very late in the process, perhaps as late as 1946, it became something more. During the war, the demand for Pakistan became more widely popular than maybe even Jinnah might have imagined it would. After the war, he was both pushing the demand and was also being carried along by it.

Up until the spring of 1946, a political compromise that would have preserved a united India was still possible.

The Congress, Nehru, in particular, would have had to grant the Muslim areas that (eventually) became Pakistan more autonomy than he was willing to allow and have had to accept a weaker Central Government than he wanted.

Abandoning that compromise was the fatal mistake. Nehru couldn't just dismiss this demand as illegitimate and say you weren't going to deal with it. You had to accommodate it somehow. And as the larger, more powerful party it was their responsibility to adjust it. You don't ask the weaker side to make the concessions. You have to be generous.

Nehru for his reasons chose not to. I think that was the last real chance to avoid Partition and preserve a United India (Akhand Bharat). The 1947 partition of South Asia has had lasting repercussions not only for the region but also for the larger international community. Border tensions between India and Pakistan have taken on a new magnitude since both countries carried out nuclear tests in May 1998. Surprisingly, historians have paid little attention to the creation of the Indo-Pakistani boundary, a vital element of the 1947 division. Let's analyse the problematic procedure and format of the body responsible for delineating that boundary through the province of Punjab, the Radcliffe Boundary Commission.

The Commission takes its name from its Chairman, Sir Cyril Radcliffe. In the end, his boundary-making effort was a failure concerning boundary-making, but a remarkable success regarding providing political cover to all sides. The British seized the opportunity to withdraw from their heavy Indian responsibilities as quickly as possible; the Indian National Congress, the avowedly secular but primarily Hindu party, headed by Jawaharlal Nehru and Sardar Patel, took control of India, as it had desired for so long. The Muslim League, which claimed to represent South Asia's Muslims and was led by Muhammad Ali Jinnah, won Pakistan, the sovereign Muslim State for which it had campaigned.

Although the British had, in 1946, considered leaving India piecemeal, transferring power to individual provinces as they withdrew, they concluded that such an approach was impractical. Without defining the entity or entities that would come into force, they found that such an approach was unrealistic. It would not be possible to hand over power without making it clear what international entity would take on that power; to define a new global existence, a new boundary between the Majority India and a Muslim India was necessary. From an individual perspective, however, a rigorously and adequately delineated boundary was not required to accomplish these political ends – any boundary line would do. Due to this fact and to a myriad of political pressures, the Radcliffe Commission failed to draw a geopolitically sound line delineated and demarcated by the accepted international procedure. The Punjab's population distribution was such that no line could neatly divide Hindus, Muslims and Sikhs. For precisely this reason division of Punjab, Bengal and to some extent Sind should never have happened, partition line divided these three great cultures forever. Radcliffe's line was a Himalayan proportion blunder and history will never forgive the man and his people who did this to India.

Radcliffe destroyed all his papers before he left India – in keeping, his biographer claims, with a lifelong habit of discarding material he no longer needed. As a result, it may be impossible ever to clarify Radcliffe's thinking completely. If Radcliffe had withdrawn his services once he reached India and was informed of the August 15 deadline – the outcome could have been dramatically different. The story of the Radcliffe Commission concerns individuals attempting to do what they saw as best and as a result, both bowing to and struggling against the pressures of larger structural forces.

Historical Context

Many historians, imperialist and nationalist alike, trace the roots of the partition to the Morley-Minto Reforms of 1909. These changes increased Indian participation in their governance, anticipating an eventual move to self-rule. By creating separate electorates for different religious groups, however, these reforms also "embed[ded] deeply in Indian life the idea that its society consisted of groups set apart from each other. The result was the flowering of a new communal rhetoric and ultimately, of the Pakistan movement." Politicians found religious rhetoric useful for rallying support, with dangerous results. The elections of 1937 and 1945-46, in which both Congress and the Muslim League rhetoric played on communal themes, provided further evidence of a lack of political cooperation at the highest levels.

With the onset of the Second World War, the Government of India found itself in an awkward position. HMG declared war on India's behalf, without even a pretense of consulting Indian leaders. Indian politicians and public opinion were outraged. The prospect of civil unrest loomed. In 1942, with the Allies in urgent need of a reliable Indian base, Churchill dispatched Sir Stafford Cripps to India at the head of a Cabinet delegation charged with exploring the possibility of self-government after the war. Cripps offered an implicit promise that if India fought in World War II, it would be granted freedom; Congress rejected this offer with Gandhi's memorable phrase that it was a "post-dated cheque on a bank that was failing." In the aftermath of Cripps's failed mission, Gandhi launched the 'Quit India' movement, which the British repressed violently. Most Indians subsided into more or less supportive attitudes.

With the end of the war, Indian leaders and people alike expected to be repaid, with independence, for their wartime backing. In Britain, the Conservatives were voted out and the Labour Party took power, under Clement Attlee. Meanwhile, the India Office was losing patience with its Viceroy, Lord Wavell. Relations between the India Office and Wavell had been steadily worsening throughout 1946. Wavell, a career military man whose stolid exterior concealed a bent for writing poetry, had been Viceroy of India since 1943. Left with the difficult job of guiding India through treacherous post-war waters, he sent increasingly blunt warnings to London that their Indian policies were misguided and inadequate to the challenges ahead. Lord Pethick-Lawrence, Britain's Secretary of State for India, resented these warnings and paid less attention to them as time went on. In particular, Wavell's outline of potential partition boundaries, the first serious discussion of the issue, received little attention. However, Wavell's 'Breakdown Plan', calling for a withdrawal of all British presence in South Asia, alarmed HMG.

Attlee sent another cabinet mission to India in hopes of negotiating a less drastic outcome. The resulting proposal, known as the 'ABC Plan', called for a loose federation to consist of three groups of provinces, each of which had the option to 'opt out' of the federation. This proposal met a curious reception. It was first accepted, then rejected, by Congress; the Muslim League initially announced that it would cooperate, but in the aftermath of the Congress decision it renounced constitutional methods and declared 'Direct Action Day' on August 16, 1946. 'Direct Action Day' became the 'Great Calcutta Killing', and the next thirteen months saw rioting and violence across north India.

By the beginning of 1947, Pethick-Lawrence and Attlee had lost all confidence in Wavell, regarding him as 'frankly defeatist'. In February 1947, they asked him to resign, appointing Lord Louis Mountbatten, a career naval officer and cousin to the king, in his place. Although Mountbatten was given a June 1948 deadline by which to disentangle Britain from India, he concluded shortly after his arrival in India that a rapprochement between the various parties was impossible. Within a few months, he decided to move the decolonization deadline up, to August 15, 1947.

Analysis of the Boundary Decision

The final boundary, known as the Radcliffe Award, allotted some 62% of the area of undivided Punjab to India, with 55% of the population. The boundary ran from the border of Kashmir State south along the Ujh river, leaving one tehsil of Gurdaspur district to Pakistan and allotting the remainder to India. Where the Ujh met the Ravi river, the boundary followed the Ravi south-west, until it reached the existing administrative line dividing Amritsar district from Lahore district. Radcliffe was careful to specify that the relevant regulatory boundaries, not the course of the Ujh or the Ravi, constituted the new international boundary. The boundary then ran through Lahore district, along tehsil and village boundaries, leaving the district's easternmost corner in India. When the Radcliffe boundary met the Ferozepore district line, it turned to follow the river Sutlej along with the administrative boundary between Ferozepore and Montgomery districts. The Radcliffe line ended where it met the border of Bahawalpur, a princely State whose ruler, like the Maharaja of Kashmir, had the choice of acceding to Pakistan or India.

The primary feature of this line was that it divided Amritsar, now in India, from Lahore, which went to Pakistan. By and large, it followed important administrative divisions, although it did meander between villages in the Kasur region south-east of Lahore. The two most controversial elements of this line involved Gurdaspur and Ferozepore. Pakistani critics interpreted Radcliffe's decision to grant most of Gurdaspur district to India as an attempt to provide India with a land link to Kashmir. As one element of the beginnings of the Kashmir conflict, this allegation remains controversial. It is worth noting that no all-weather road linked Kashmir and India in 1947; when the first Indo-Pakistani war began in late 1947, India airlifted troops and supplies into Kashmir rather than take an overland route. The other controversy was over Ferozepore's allocation to India; this decision came as a surprise in the wake of early August leaks indicating that Radcliffe would allocate a section of Ferozepore to Pakistan.

Following Mountbatten, Nehru and Jinnah's demands that he completes his work before August 15, Radcliffe submitted his award on August 12. By this time, Mountbatten had changed his mind (for reasons discussed below) and asked Radcliffe to delay the award until after August 15. Radcliffe refused, but Mountbatten had his way, choosing not to release the award until August 16, when he discussed it with the Indian and Pakistani leaders at a meeting in New Delhi. On August 17, the award was finally published.

The Problem of 'Other Factors'

One of the most difficult questions facing the Commissions was the respective significance to assign to various 'other factors'. In his awards, Radcliffe himself noted that "differences of opinion as to the significance of the term 'other factors' and as to the weight and value to be attached to these factors, made it impossible to arrive at an agreed line." The Congress argued that the unreliability of the 1941 census figures meant that 'other factors' must be given greater weight in the Punjab; the Muslim League maintained that the census figures were valid and thus 'other factors' could be all but ignored. Over the years, observers have speculated on various factors that may have motivated Radcliffe, including communal bias, pressure from Mountbatten, economic considerations, current administrative borders, defence needs and existing infrastructure.

Years later, Mountbatten offered this curious appraisal of Radcliffe's reasoning:

> "I'll tell you something ghastly. The reasons behind his award weren't very deep-seated at all. I am quite certain they were based on some rule of thumb about the proportion of the population."

Given the fact the Mountbatten's government gave Radcliffe the mandate to focus on religious demographics, it seems odd that the former Viceroy thought it 'ghastly' that Radcliffe had not come up with 'deeper' reasons for drawing his lines. Mountbatten's sentiment may indicate an awareness among British officials that the categories they had set-up were inadequate for the job at hand.

Even by Mountbatten's standards, this statement about Radcliffe's 'rule of thumb' is rather peculiar. Perhaps by the time Mountbatten gave this interview, in the early 1970s, he had developed reservations about the partition process. Until his death, Mountbatten staunchly defended his actions in 1947, making it unlikely that he would openly question himself. However, Mountbatten had a great capacity for remembering history differently than other observers, invariably along lines most flattering to himself. Given Hodson's statement that it was the Viceroy himself who brought up the notion of 'balance', one wonders whether Mountbatten subconsciously transferred responsibility for his idea onto Radcliffe's shoulders, before criticizing it. This speculation may seem rather convoluted, but Mountbatten was notably a twisty individual. A colleague famously told him, "Dickie, you're so crooked that if you swallowed a nail, you'd shit a corkscrew." Mountbatten's biographer records that this was a remark which Mountbatten remembered and repeated, though characteristically changing the recipient of the insult.

Some observers felt Radcliffe gave too much weight to economic considerations, neglecting his mandate to determine the 'contiguous majority areas' of religious groups. For example, the Chittagong Hill Tracts in Bengal were awarded to Pakistan despite the fact that the Muslim population amounted to only 3%. On August 16, Nehru complained to Mountbatten about Radcliffe's decision. Radcliffe apparently thought these economic necessities more critical than the overwhelmingly non-Muslim population.

Whenever possible, Radcliffe used existing administrative borders. The Commission's terms of reference directed it to draw its lines within the two provinces of Bengal and Punjab, so the existing provincial administrative boundaries were not an option. Within provinces, however, Radcliffe seems to have preferred existing lines, using district, tehsil, thana and even village boundaries. His textual description of the boundary relies very little on 'natural' landmarks like crest or rivers. In the Punjab award, Radcliffe repeatedly notes that although nearby rivers present apparently logical natural boundaries, the new boundary must run along the existing district or tehsil borders.

Mountbatten recalled later that he had counselled Radcliffe "not to take defence considerations under judgment in making the award." In a memo dated May 11, 1946, Field Marshal Sir Claude Auchinleck, Commander-in-Chief of the Indian Armed Forces, discussed the repercussions of Partition for Imperial and Indo-Pakistani defence. He concluded that without a united India, the British military position in South Asia would be irreparably damaged. Furthermore, although he considered the possibility of Indo-Pakistani conflict, he saw no way to define a defensible frontier. Radcliffe himself seems to have consistently operated on the assumption that India and Pakistan would have good relations after independence.

Other decision-makers - and those impacted by the divisions - took this view as well. Radcliffe repeatedly expressed hope that India and Pakistan could work together to solve some of the most challenging infrastructure problems created by his boundary award. Mountbatten himself seemed optimistic that inclusion in the Commonwealth would keep India and Pakistan on mutually friendly terms, emphasizing that Dominion Status meant membership in a community of cooperative nations.

Although the prominence of 'other factors' in Radcliffe's thinking remains unclear, his awards demonstrate the importance of infrastructure considerations. In both the Punjab and Bengal awards, Radcliffe discusses canals, headworks, roads, railways and ports before turning to population factors. In the Punjab awards, he explicitly states that "there are factors such as the disruption of railway communications and water systems that ought to result in this instance to displace the primary claim of contiguous majorities." In the Bengal award, he demonstrates a similar concern with maintaining "railway communications and river systems," as well as preserving the relationship of the Nadia and Kulti river systems with the port of Calcutta.

The irrigation systems and other infrastructure of Punjab and Bengal had been built under a single administration. They were never intended to be divided. No partition line Radcliffe could have concocted would have allowed Pakistan and India to operate their infrastructure separately, without cross-border interference. In the few weeks he had, Radcliffe seems to have tried to minimize infrastructure disruptions, but he was well aware that his proposal was flawed. In his attempt to draw the boundary near the Suleimanke headworks in Punjab, for example, he emphasized that he intended to award this equipment to Pakistan and acknowledged that the reality of the terrain might necessitate that "the boundary shall be adjusted accordingly." Several months later, the Suleimanke headworks were 'reallocated' in a clash between Indian and Pakistani soldiers. In an optimistic moment, Radcliffe expressed the hope that "a solution may be found by agreement between the two States for some joint control of what has hitherto been a valuable common service." Events soon proved this optimism unfounded.

The Boundary Announcement Delayed

Radcliffe had prepared his decision by August 12, as the various parties, including Mountbatten, had insisted. As the transfer of power approached, however, Mountbatten chose to delay the boundary announcement until after the independence ceremonies. In public statements, Mountbatten declared that he merely wished to avoid spoiling the joyous celebration of independence by announcing news that would undoubtedly distress all parties. However, in private government communications and in the minutes of the Staff Meeting at which the decision was taken, it becomes clear that Mountbatten's primary motivation was avoiding the appearance of British responsibility for the disorder that inevitably would follow the announcement.

It is difficult to see how these concerns, either for Indian or Pakistani national joy or the evasion of British national responsibility, could outweigh the potential benefit of making administrative, military and constabulary arrangements before the actual transfer of power took place. Governor Jenkins of the Punjab had begged Mountbatten repeatedly for notice of the award. On July 30, Jenkins told the Viceroy that "even a few hours would be better than none." As it was, in some border regions whose destiny was uncertain, both Indian and Pakistani flags were raised. In some cases, Pakistani officials set to work in territories that later became Indian. As August 15 drew closer, many administrators joined the last-minute flow of refugees themselves, disrupting administrative access across India by leaving their posts empty. In short, the Punjab found itself in administrative chaos, ill-prepared to deal with the impact of partition.

When Mountbatten released the award to the Indian and Pakistani leaders on August 16, both sides objected furiously to various aspects of the boundary. In the end, they agreed to issue the decision as it stood, with no public statement of their disappointment. When the award was finally announced, on 17 August, the border forces in place were inadequate to stop the communal massacres.

Violence was particularly severe along the new border areas, although there was cruel bloodshed in Delhi as well. The first Indo-Pakistani war broke out in late 1947; both Pakistan and India sent troops into Kashmir, where they remain today. Subsequent wars in 1965 and 1971 made it clear that Radcliffe's boundaries were not neat lines but raw and restless divisions.

Repercussions of Partition

The partition resulted in extreme violence and one of the largest migrations in history. Partition deaths throughout India and Pakistan numbered between one million, while some twelve million migrants moved across the new borders in Punjab and Bengal. Also, tens of thousands of girls and women were raped and abducted. Violence was the most dramatic repercussion of partition, but the boundary award contributed to other disruptions: long-term border tensions, infrastructure problems and the lasting conflict over Kashmir.

First, the high casualties and tremendous population dislocation that burdened both India and Pakistan during and after partition proved awkward responsibilities for fledgling States. In Pakistan, the position of mohajirs, or migrants from India, remains a dangerous political problem. Second, the boundaries that Radcliffe defined turned out to be restless divisions and in both the 1965 and 1971 wars India and Pakistan battled over their Punjabi border. Third, the Radcliffe Line also cut through the Punjab's well-developed infrastructure systems, disrupting road, telephone and telegraph communications, but most importantly, interfering with the region's vital irrigation system. In a rare success story, the 1960 Indus Waters Treaty mostly resolved Punjab's water-related problems. However, those original water problems were related to the final and most dangerous issue plaguing current Indo-Pakistani relations: Kashmir.

Jinnah's address to Muslims of Jammu and Kashmir in the year 1944 –

> "As I said at the moment I reached Jammu, it is not the policy of the Muslim League to interfere with the internal administration of this State or the grave and serious issues that face the Maharaja and his government, as between him and his people, but we are certainly very deeply concerned with the welfare of the Mussalmans in the State and I must say that even a casual visitor cannot but be shocked to see the condition of the people in this State, even in matters of their elementary needs and necessities. Sir BN Rao has just taken charge as the Prime Minister of the State and now the people are looking up to him and expecting that he will take effective measures for their betterment.

As regards the Mussalmans, as I said, we are vitally concerned with their welfare, but I regret that although Sheikh Abdullah and his party and the Muslim Conference discussed matters with me in Delhi and in Lahore before my arrival here and were good enough to accord me a great reception and were anxious that I should hear both sides and bring about a settlement, when I, after careful consideration, suggested that the Mussalmans should organize themselves under one flag and on one platform, not only my advice was not acceptable to Sheikh Abdullah but, as is his habit, which has become a second nature with him, he indulged in all sorts of language of a most offensive and vituperative character in attacking me. My advice to the Mussalmans is that the differences can only be resolved by argument, discussion, exchange of views and reason and not by goondaism and one thing that I must draw the attention of Kashmir government about is that goondaism must be put down at any cost and there should be constitutional liberty of speech and freedom of thought, which is the elementary right of every citizen under any civilized form of government."

Maharaja's Accession Offer to India

Legal Document: Text of letter dated October 26, 1947, from Sri Hari Singh, the Maharaja of Jammu and Kashmir to Lord Mountbatten, the Governor-General of India.

My dear Lord Mountbatten,

I have to inform your Excellency that a grave emergency has arisen in my State and request immediate assistance of your government. As your Excellency is aware, the State of Jammu and Kashmir has not acceded to the Dominion of India or Pakistan. Geographically my State is contiguous to both the Dominions. It has vital economic and cultural links with both of them. Besides my State has a common boundary with the Soviet Republic and China. In their external relations and Dominion of India and Pakistan cannot ignore this fact.

I wanted to take time to decide to which Dominion I should accede, or whether it is not in the best interests of both the Dominions and my State to stand independent, of course with friendly and cordial relations with both. I accordingly approached the Dominions of India and Pakistan to enter into Standstill Agreement with my State. The Pakistan government accepted this Agreement. The Dominion of India desired further discussions with representatives of my government. I could not arrange this given the developments indicated below. In fact, the Pakistan government are operating Post and Telegraph system inside the State.

Though we have got a Standstill Agreement with the Pakistan government permitted steady and increasing strangulation of supplies like food, salt and petrol to my State. Afridis, soldiers in plain clothes and desperadoes with modern weapons have been allowed to filter into the State at first in Poonch and then in Sialkot and finally in the mass area adjoining Hazara district on the Ramkot side. The result has been that the limited number of troops at the disposal of the State had to be dispersed and thus had to face the enemy at the several points simultaneously, that it has become difficult to stop the wanton destruction of life and property and looting. The Mohara powerhouse which supplies the electric current to the whole of Srinagar has been burnt. The number of women who have been kidnapped and raped and makes my heart bleed. The wild forces thus let loose on the State are marching on with the aim of capturing Srinagar, the summer capital of my government, as the first step to overrunning the whole State.

The mass infiltration tribesman drawn from the distant areas of the North-West Frontier coming regularly in motor trucks using Mansehra-Muzaffarabad Road and fully armed with up-to-date weapons cannot possibly be done without the knowledge of the provincial Government of the North-West Frontier Province and the Government of Pakistan. In spite of repeated requests made by my government, no attempt has been made to check these raiders or stop them from coming to my State. The Pakistan Radio even put North-West Frontier coming regularly in motor trucks using Mansehra-Muzaffarabad Road and fully armed with up-to-date weapons cannot possibly be done without the knowledge of the provincial government of the North-West Frontier Province and the Government of Pakistan. In spite of repeated requests made by my government, no attempt has been made to check these raiders or stop them from coming to my State. The Pakistan Radio even put out a story that a provisional government has been set-up in Kashmir.

With the conditions obtaining at present in my State and to the significant emergency of the situation as it exists, I have no option but to ask for help from the Indian Dominion. Naturally, they cannot send the relief asked for by me without my State acceding to the Domination of India. I have accordingly decided to do so and I attach the Instrument of Accession for; acceptance by your government. The other alternative is to leave my State and my people to fee-booters. On this basis, no civilized government can exist or be maintained. The choice I will never allow to happen as long as I am Ruler of the State and I have a life to defend my country.

I may also inform your Excellency's government that it is my intention at once to set-up an interim government and ask Sheikh Abdullah to carry the responsibilities in this emergency with my Prime Minister. If my State has to be saved immediate assistance must be available at Srinagar. Mr Menon is fully aware of the situation and he will explain to you if further explanation is needed.

In haste and with kindest regards.

Yours Sincerely,
Hari Singh
The Palace, Jammu
26th October 1947.

"I do hereby accept this Instrument of Accession. Dated this twenty seventh day of October, nineteen hundred and forty seven."

(Mountbatten of Burma, Governor-General of India)

Post-1947 – History of the Dispute

The State of Jammu and Kashmir was part of India when the vast empires set-up by the Mauryas (3rd Century BC), the Mughals (16th to 18th Century) and the British India (mid-19th to mid-20th Century). All these empires included not only present-day India and Pakistan but some other countries of the region like Afghanistan and even some part of Iran. Until 1846, Kashmir was part of the Sikh empire. In that year, the British defeated the Sikhs and sold Kashmir to Gulab Singh of Jammu for ₹7.5 million under the Treaty of Amritsar. Gulab Singh, the Maharaja, signed a separate treaty with the British which gave him the status of an independent princely ruler of Kashmir. Gulab Singh died in 1857 and was replaced by Ranbir Singh (1857-1885). Two other Maharajas, Pratap Singh (1885-1925) and Hari Singh (1925-1949) ruled in succession.

Gulab Singh and his successors ruled Kashmir; they were Hindus from Dogra community, Muslims constituted more in numbers and always kept complaining of being ruled by a Hindu king, some of them thought Dogra rule was a tyrannical and repressive way. The people of Kashmir, nearly 80% of whom were Muslims, rose against Maharaja Hari Singh's rule. He ruthlessly crushed a mass Muslim uprising in 1931. In 1932, Sheikh Abdullah formed Kashmir's first political party - the All Jammu and Kashmir Muslim Conference (renamed as National Conference in 1939). In 1934, the Maharaja gave way and allowed limited democracy in the form of a Legislative Assembly. However, unease with the Maharaja's rule continued. The Instrument of Accession was a legal document first introduced by the Government of India Act 1935 and used in 1947 to enable each of the rulers of the princely States under British paramountcy to join one of the new dominions of India or Pakistan created by the Partition of British India. 565 princely States existed in India during the period of British rule. These were not parts of British India proper, having never become possessions of the British Crown, but were tied to it in a system of subsidiary alliances.

The Government of India Act 1935 introduced the concept of the Instrument of Accession, wherein a ruler of a princely State could accede his kingdom into the 'Federation of India'. The Indian princes initially opposed the federation concept, but the accession of all the princely States was almost complete when World War II occurred. In 1947 the British finalized their plans for quitting India and the question of the future of the princely States was a conundrum for them. As they were not British, they could not be partitioned by the British between the new sovereign nations of India and Pakistan. The Indian Independence Act 1947 provided that the suzerainty of the British Crown over the princely States would simply be terminated, effective 15 August 1947. That would leave the princely States completely independent, even though many of them had been dependent on the Government of India for defence, finance and other infrastructure. With independence, it would then be a matter for each ruler of a State to decide whether to accede to India, to accede to Pakistan, or to remain independent

Accession of States to the New Dominions

The Instrument of Accession was the legal document designed to bring about accession, where it was decided upon. It was executed by the Government of India on the one hand and by the rulers of each of the princely States, individually, on the other hand. Among the more momentous of such accessions was that executed by Maharaja Hari Singh, ruler of the State of Jammu and Kashmir, on 26 October 1947. It gave control of Jammu and Kashmir to the Government of

India. The accession of Jammu and Kashmir was accepted by Lord Mountbatten of Burma, Governor-General of India, on 27 October 1947. In 1947, India and Pakistan went to war over Kashmir. During the war, it was India which first took the Kashmir dispute to the United Nations on 1 January 1948. The following year, on 1 January 1949, the UN helped enforce a ceasefire between the two countries. The ceasefire line is called the Line of Control.

It was an outcome of a mutual consent by India and Pakistan that the UN Security Council (UNSC) and UN Commission for India and Pakistan (UNCIP) passed several resolutions in years following the 1947-48 war. The UNSC Resolution of 21 April 1948 - one of the principal UN resolutions on Kashmir - stated that "both India and Pakistan desire that the question of the accession of Jammu and Kashmir to India or Pakistan should be decided through the democratic method of a free and impartial plebiscite." Subsequent UNSC Resolutions reiterated the same stand. UNCIP Resolutions of 3 August 1948 and 5 January 1949 reinforced UNSC resolutions.

Kashmir Issue – the Pakistani View

The current agitation in Indian Kashmir is rooted in the struggle of the people for the exercise of the right of self-determination. Peaceful processions chanting demands for freedom were fired upon by Indian Army and police. Thousands of men, women and children have been killed or wounded.

1. New Delhi's allegation of assistance to the Kashmiri people from the Pakistan side is unfounded. Objective reports in Foreign media testify that the Kashmiri agitation is indigenous.
2. Pakistan upholds the right of the people of Jammu and Kashmir to self-determination under the resolutions of the United Nations Security Council. These resolutions of 1948 and 1949 provide for the holding of a free and impartial plebiscite for the determination of the future of the State by the people of Jammu and Kashmir.
3. The primary points about the UN resolution are that:
   - India initiated the complaint relating to Kashmir in the Security Council;
   - The Council explicitly and by implications, rejected India's claim that Kashmir is legally Indian Territory;
   - The resolutions established self-determination as the governing principle for the settlement of the Kashmir

dispute. This is the world body's commitment to the people of Kashmir;

- The recommendations endorsed a binding agreement between India and Pakistan reached through the mediation of UNCIP that a plebiscite would be held, under agreed and specified conditions.

The Security Council has rejected the Indian contention that the people of Kashmir have exercised their right of self-determination by participating in the 'election' which India has from time to time organized in the Kashmir.

Pakistan continues to adhere to the UN resolutions. These are binding also on India.

The Shimla Agreement of 2 July 1972, to which Pakistan also continues to adhere, did not alter the status of Jammu and Kashmir as a disputed territory:

- Para 6 of the Agreement lists "a final settlement of Jammu and Kashmir" as one of the outstanding questions awaiting a settlement.
- Para 4 (ii) talks of a 'Line of Control' as distinguished from an international border. Furthermore, it explicitly protects "the recognized position of either side." The recognized position of Pakistan is the one, which is recognized by the United Nations and the world community in general.
- Article 1(iv) obviously refers to the Kashmir issue when it talks about "the basic issues and causes of conflict which have bedevilled the relations between the two countries for the last 25 years."

UN Mediation of Kashmir

The United Nations had played an essential role in maintaining peace and order in Jammu and Kashmir soon after the independence of India and Pakistan in 1947 when a dispute erupted between the two States on the question of Jammu and Kashmir. India took this matter to the UN Security Council, which passed resolution 39 (1948) and established the United Nations Commission for India and Pakistan (UNCIP) to investigate the issues and mediate between the two countries. Following the ceasefire of hostilities, it also established the United Nations Military Observer Group for India and Pakistan (UNMOGIP) to monitor the ceasefire line.

Following the outbreak of the Indo-Pakistani War of 1947, India's Governor-General Mountbatten flew to Lahore on 1 November 1947 for a conference with Muhammad Ali Jinnah, proposing that, in all the princely States where the ruler did not accede to a Dominion corresponding to the majority population (which would have included Junagadh, Hyderabad as well Kashmir), the accession should be decided by an "impartial reference to the will of the people." Jinnah rejected the offer. The Prime Ministers Jawaharlal Nehru and Liaquat Ali Khan met again in December, where Nehru informed Khan of India's intention to refer the dispute to the United Nations under Article 35 of the UN Charter, which allows the member States to bring to the Security Council attention situations "likely to endanger the maintenance of international peace."

India sought resolution of the issue at the UN Security Council on 1 January 1948. Following the set-up of the United Nations Commission for India and Pakistan (UNCIP), the UN Security Council passed Resolution 47 on 21 April 1948. The measure imposed an immediate ceasefire and called on the Government of Pakistan "to secure the withdrawal from the State of Jammu and Kashmir of tribesmen and Pakistani nationals not normally resident therein who have entered the State for fighting." It also asked Government of India to reduce its forces to minimum strength, after which the circumstances for holding a plebiscite should be put into effect "on the question of Accession of the State to India or Pakistan." However, it was not until 1 January 1949 that the ceasefire could be put into effect, signed by General Gracey on behalf of Pakistan and General Roy Bucher on behalf of India. However, both India and Pakistan failed to arrive at a Truce agreement due to differences over interpretation of the procedure for and the extent of demilitarization. One sticking point was whether the Pak army was to be disbanded during the truce stage or at the plebiscite stage.

The UNCIP made three visits to the subcontinent between 1948 and 1949, trying to find a solution agreeable to both India and Pakistan. It reported to the Security Council in August 1948 that "the presence of troops of Pakistan" inside Kashmir represented a 'material change' in the situation. A two-part process was proposed for the withdrawal of forces. In the first part, Pakistan was to withdraw its forces as well as other Pakistani nationals from the State. In the second part, "when the Commission shall have notified the Government of India" that Pakistani withdrawal has been completed, India was to withdraw the bulk of its forces. After both the withdrawals were completed, a Plebiscite would be held. The resolution was accepted by India but efficiently rejected by Pakistan.

The Indian government considered itself to be under the legal possession of Jammu and Kashmir by the accession of the State. The assistance given by Pakistan to the rebel forces and the Pakhtoon tribes was held to be a hostile act and the further involvement of the Pakistan army was taken to be an invasion of Indian Territory. From the Indian perspective, the Plebiscite was meant to confirm the Accession, which was in all respects already complete and Pakistan could not aspire to an equal footing with India in the contest.

The Pakistan government held that the State of Jammu and Kashmir had executed a Standstill Agreement with Pakistan which precluded it from entering into agreements with other countries. It also held that the Maharaja had no authority left to perform accession because his people had revolted and he had to flee the capital. It believed that the POK movement, as well as the tribal incursions, were indigenous and spontaneous and Pakistan's assistance to them was not open to criticism.

In short, India required an asymmetric treatment of the two countries in the withdrawal arrangements regarding Pakistan as an 'aggressor', whereas Pakistan insisted on parity. The UN mediators tended towards parity, which was not to India's satisfaction. In the end, no withdrawal was ever carried out, India insisting that Pakistan had to withdraw first and Pakistan contending that there was no guarantee that India would withdraw afterward. No agreement could be reached between the two countries on the process of demilitarization.

Scholars have commented that the failure of the Security Council efforts of mediation owed to the fact that the Council regarded the issue as a purely political dispute without investigating its legal underpinnings. Declassified British papers indicate that Britain and Western powers have let their cold war calculations influence their policy in the UN disregarding the merits of the case. Pakistan attacked Kashmir in October 1947. The Maharaja signed the instrument on October 27 [Instrument of Accession (Jammu and Kashmir)] and the war began immediately. After a couple of months fighting in the brutally cold mountains, Nehru finally called up the UN in January 1948. He had a fairly strong case there. The UN then took a sweet eight months and then brought a resolution in August 1948. The war was not over then. India and Pakistan didn't immediately agree to the UN resolution and kept fighting. By November the troops were already in a war for more than one year and the second winter was already there.

Why did India Decide to Approach UN?

India was running out of ammunition as it had to fight a parallel war to take control of Hyderabad State [much bigger than the size of

Austria] from the Nizam [possibly the richest person in the world of that time] who was trying to become independent. And in the north-east, Manipur and other parts still had not joined India and the leaders were busy making sure that they don't go independent. There was the resettlement from the partition and dealing with the aftermath of Mahatma's assassination. And a Constitution was being worked on another track.

British Left India in Mess and Chaos

It was a chaos Indians got and had to deal. In the history of the modern civilization, hardly anyone had the responsibility to patch so many 562 territories [with a seventh of world population] in such a short time. An endless war there could have broken the finances of this young nation and there could have been a massive civil war and an implosion.

Nehru Confused Telegraph to British Prime Minister

Excerpts of a telegram dated 26 October 1947 from Jawaharlal Nehru –

> "For Prime Minister the United Kingdom from Prime Minister India. We have received a vigorous appeal for assistance from Kashmir government. We would be disposed to give favourable consideration to such request from any friendly State. Kashmir's Northern frontiers, as you are aware, run in common with those of three countries, Afghanistan, the Union of Soviet Socialist Republics and China. Security of Kashmir, which must depend upon control of internal tranquillity and existence of stable government, is vital to the security of India especially since part of the southern boundary of Kashmir and India are common. Helping Kashmir, therefore, is an obligation of national interest to India. We are giving urgent consideration to question as to what assistance we can give to State to defend itself.
>
> I should like to make it clear that question of aiding Kashmir in this emergency is not designed in any way to influence the State to accede to India. Our view which we have repeatedly made public is that the question of accession in any disputed territory or State must be decided following wishes of people and we adhere to this view. It is quite clear, however, that no free expression of the will of people of Kashmir is possible if external aggression succeeds in imperilling the integrity of its territory. I have thought it desirable to inform you of the situation because of its threat of international complications."

That telegraph made British Prime Minister to think that Nehru is not interested in J&K and a socialist India not in the interest of the Western world. This telegram is also seen as Nehru against Independence Act (which Nehru was always). "Even a lawyer working at district court knows that if you take a complaint to the court of law, then it is your responsibility to provide proof for the mistakes committed by the accused. But the accused has the only job of denying the accusations." "Jawaharlal Nehru has committed such an incorrect decision that he will have to repent and cry badly one day" - Sardar Patel after coming to know that Nehru has taken Kashmir Conflict to UN without cabinet's approval.

UN Security Council Plebiscite Resolution

The Security Council of United Nations on the complaint of Government of India concerning the dispute over the State of Jammu and Kashmir passed United Nations Security Council Resolution 47 (1948). This resolution required among other things that Pakistan withdraw from the areas of Pakistan-administered Kashmir which it had captured in 1947 immediately and conditions be created for a free and impartial plebiscite to decide the future of the State. The Indian Army should withdraw and maintain a skeletal force to ensure proper functioning of the civil affairs of the State after satisfactory withdrawal of Pakistani tribesmen and forces. It recommended to the governments of India and Pakistan to restore peace and order in Jammu and Kashmir and provide full freedom to all subjects of the State, to vote on the question of accession.

Furthermore, it recommended to the Government of India to establish Plebiscite Administration to hold a fair and impartial referendum as soon as possible, a nominee of the Secretary-General of the United Nations to be appointed as the Plebiscite Administrator, release all political prisoners, invite the major political groups to share the administration at the ministerial level while the plebiscite is being prepared and carried out. UN Official statement: The boundaries and names shown and the designations used on the map do not imply official endorsement or acceptance by the United Nations. The Dotted line represents approximately the Line of Control of Jammu and Kashmir agreed upon by the Republic of India and the Government of Pakistan since 1972. Both the parties have not yet decided upon the final status of the region.

Status of Jammu and Kashmir

Meanwhile, elections were held in the Indian territory of Jammu and Kashmir, which brought up the popular Muslim leader Sheikh

Abdullah, who with his party National Conference, generally supported India. The elected Constituent Assembly met for the first time in Srinagar on October 31, 1951. Then the State Constituent Assembly ratified the accession of the State to the Union of India on February 6, 1954 and the President of India subsequently issued the Constitution (Application to J&K) Order under Article 370 of the Indian Constitution extending the Union Constitution to the State with some exceptions and modifications. The State's own Constitution came into force on January 26, 1957, under which the elections to the State Legislative Assembly were held for the first time by adult franchise the same year. This Constitution further reiterated the ratification of the State's accession to the Union of India.

The Government of India states that

> "the external artificial boundaries of the Republic of India, especially concerning the international borders under its jurisdiction created by a foreign body are neither correct nor authenticated."

Status of Pakistan-Controlled Kashmir

However, these tidings were not recognized by Pakistan, which asks for a plebiscite to ascertain the wishes of the people. The people there set-up, now called Azad Jammu and Kashmir in the West help by Pakistan that it controls. The much larger region of Pakistani Kashmir in the North-West, which was an exclusive dependent territory named Northern Areas in the erstwhile State, generally bore no mention in Pakistani laws and Constitution as being of any status, until in 1982 the Pakistani President General Zia-ul-Haq proclaimed that the people of the Northern Areas were Pakistanis and had nothing to do with the State of Jammu and Kashmir. The Government of Pakistan stands provisionally and unconditionally, that the 'Accession of Jammu and Kashmir' to Pakistan or even to the Republic of India remains to be decided by UN plebiscite and an official referendum for a final settlement of the dispute. It accepts UN's map of the territory. It also states that the designations and the presentation of the Kashmir's regional map based on UN practice, do not imply the expression of any opinion whatsoever on the part of the Commonwealth Secretariat or the publishers concerning the legal status of any country, territory or area, or of its authorities, or concerning the delimitation of its frontiers or boundaries. There is no intention to define the status of Jammu and Kashmir, which has not yet been agreed upon by the parties. It further says that boundaries must be based on religious, cultural, racial, historical, geographical and not political orientated.

Gilgit-Baltistan (GB) is one of the two parts of Pakistan Occupied Kashmir (POK), the other being 'Azad Jammu and Kashmir'. GB has an area of 72,000 sq km and comprises about 85% of the total area of POK. Despite its strategic location - providing land access to China, containing vast reservoirs of fresh water and the China-Pakistan Economic Corridor (CPEC) passing through it, GB does not form part of the territory of Pakistan.

The territory was handed over on a platter to the newly created State of Islamic Pakistan in November 1947 by the action of a British officer of the Gilgit scouts. Despite being in the service of the Hindu Maharaja of Kashmir, he revolted and joined Pakistan. Instead of being court-martialled, he was rewarded by the British in 1948, quite possibly because he was working on their instructions rather than those of the Maharaja. Posthumously, the Pakistan government also decorated him with the Sitara-e-Pakistan.

The impediments Pakistan faces in making GB its 5th province are many. Two UN resolutions of August 13, 1948 and January 5, 1949 established a link between GB and the Kashmir conflict. Pakistan was faced with two issues in the UN resolution; First, the August 13th resolution mentioned that "pending a final solution, territory evacuated by the Pakistan troops will be administered by the local authorities", second, GB was Shia-dominated and Pakistan was apprehensive of setting up a Shia State in its north. The Shia political conference had opposed Jinnah's two nation theory and saw few opportunities for themselves in an overwhelmingly Sunni Pakistan. Not surprisingly, Pakistan has been deliberately altering the ethnic and religious balance in the region.

To circumvent these issues, Pakistan arranged to have the Karachi Agreement of April 28, 1949, signed by Mustad Gurmani, Pakistan's Minister without Portfolio, Sardar Ibrahim Khan, the President of Azad Kashmir and Chaudhry Ghulam Abbas, head of the Muslim Conference. There was no representative from GB. With this agreement, the administration of GB was handed over to Pakistan by those who had no *locus standi* on the issue. The deal was kept secret and its existence revealed for the first time in judgment of the POK high court in 1993. Making GB, its 5th province would thus violate the Karachi agreement - perhaps the only instrument that provided doubtful legal authority to Pakistan's administration of GB - as well as the UN resolutions that would damage its position on the Kashmir conflict.

Any such move would also be violative of the 1963 Pak-China boundary agreement that calls for the sovereign authority to reopen negotiations with China after the settlement of the Kashmir dispute between Pakistan and India and of the 1972 Shimla agreement that mentions that neither side shall unilaterally alter the situation. Several courts verdicts have averred that GB is a part of J&K. The most notable is the 1993 POK high court verdict. The order was set aside in 1994 by the POK supreme court that held that GB was part of J&K State as it existed until 1948. Pakistan would also have to overcome the adverse reaction of Kashmiris on both sides of the LoC.

How the Aksai Chin became the Bone of Contention?

China began military manoeuvres in the eastern Kashmir border areas in the 1950s. By 1956–1957, China had completed a military road through the Aksai Chin area to provide better communication between Xinjiang and western Tibet. India's belated discovery of this route led to border clashes between the two countries that culminated in the Sino-Indian War of October 1962. China has occupied Aksai Chin since 1962 and, an adjoining region, the Trans-Karakoram Tract, which was ceded by Pakistan to China in 1965.

Indian and Chinese troops often get into face-off in the Aksai Chin region. How this cold and windswept desert became a seemingly intractable dispute is a tale worth telling. It's not so well-known how the ambition of Maharaja Ranbir Singh led to the cartographic annexation of Aksai Chin into the kingdom of Jammu and Kashmir. Article 4 of the Treaty of Amritsar stated:

> "The limits of the territories of Maharaja Gulab Singh shall not at any time be changed without a concurrence of the British government."

But this is precisely what the Maharaja did and saddled posterity with the Aksai Chin problem.

Aksai Chin covers an area of about 14,380 sq miles. The area is mostly a vast high-altitude desert with a low point on the Karakash river at nearly 14,000 feet above sea level. In the south-west, mountains up to 22,500 feet extending south-east from the Depsang plains form the *de facto* border (Line of Actual Control or LAC) between India and China. When Jawaharlal Nehru told Parliament that it was "a place where not even a blade of grass grows." The Congress MP, Mahavir Tyagi, riposted that the Prime Minister's head did not have a single hair, but that didn't make it useless?

In this context, WH Johnson's 'advanced boundary line' of 1865 merits attention, especially since after that, the Johnson boundary continued to be shown in one trans-frontier map after the other.

India's claims to the Aksai Chin plateau rests on Johnson's map. This boundary line first found concrete shape in the Survey of India's 1868 map and the Kashmir Atlas. It was based on the Kashmir Maharaja's outpost at Shahidulla. This made Johnson opt for the Kuen Lun watershed as the divide and not as some later surveyors were to do, on the main of the Karakoram.

It has been suggested that Johnson, a civil sub-assistant at the Survey of India, while at Leh on the eve of his historic journey to Khotan in 1865, colluded with the Kashmir Maharaja's Ladakh Wazir who provided him with money, a sizable retinue for safe conduct, apart from generous supplies of transport and food. Then there was the matter of some silver ingots the Khan of Khotan had given him to be carried as a gift to the Viceroy, but which never got that far. In 1872 Johnson quit joining the Kashmir ruler's service as Wazir of Ladakh. If the above presumptions are correct, Johnson was more receptive to the idea of showing Aksai Chin to be part of British India. The fact remains that the map prepared on his return showed the entire plateau area in the Maharaja's province of Ladakh.

Viceroy Lord Lansdowne minute on 28 September 1889:

> "The country between the Karakoram and Kuen Lun ranges is, I understand, of no value, very inaccessible and not likely to be coveted by Russia. We might; I should think, encourage the Chinese to take it if they showed any inclination to do so. (Who gave these colonial rulers, the power to offer a land that should have been part of India?) This would be better than leaving a no-man's land between our frontier and that of China. Moreover, the stronger we can make China at this point and the more we can induce her to hold her own over the whole Kashgar-Yarkand region, the more useful will she be to us as an obstacle to Russian advance along this line."

On the other hand, responding to Captain Francis Younghusband's report on his famous meeting with his old Great Game rival, the Russian explorer Colonel VL Grombchevsky, near Yarkand in 1889, Major General John Ardagh, Director of Military Intelligence at the War Office in London, recommended claiming the areas 'up to the crests of the Kuen Lun range', ie the WH Johnson line. However, in 1890, before Whitehall could make up its mind, the Chinese occupied Shahidulla. Following this occupation, it is instructive to note the opinion of the Secretary of State for India in Whitehall, Lord Curzon:

> "We are inclined to think that the wisest course would be to leave them in possession as it is evidently to our advantage that the

tract of territory between the Karakoram and Kuen Lun mountains be held by a friendly power like China."

In 1893, Hung Ta-Chen, a senior Chinese official at Kashgar, handed a map of the boundary proposed by China to George McCartney, the British Consul-General at Kashgar. This boundary placed the Lingzithang plains, which are south of the Laktsang range, in India and Aksai Chin proper, which is north of the Laktsang range, in China. McCartney agreed with the proposal and forwarded it to the British Indian government. A border, along with the Karakoram Mountains, was suggested and supported by the British for some reasons. The Karakoram formed a natural boundary, which would set the British borders up to the Indus river watershed while leaving the Tarim river watershed in Chinese control. Besides Chinese control of this track would present a further obstacle to the feared Russian advance from Central Asia.

The British presented this line, known as the McCartney-MacDonald, to the Chinese in 1899 in a note by Sir Claude MacDonald, the British Minister to the Qing Dynasty Empire of China. The Qing government did not respond to the note and the British took it as Chinese acquiescence. Although no official boundary had ever been negotiated, China believed that this had been the accepted boundary. It may be pointed out that the 1899 McCartney-MacDonald line, by and large, corresponds with the Chinese claim line.

In 1941, Military Intelligence in Delhi got reports of Soviet troops garrisoning in Xinjiang. It was then decided to push the boundary outwards to the old Ardagh-Johnson line, after which Aksai Chin once more became part of J&K, though it was just on some maps only. The India map of the original Constitution of India adopted in 1950, the longest written Constitution of any sovereign country in the world, containing 448 Articles in 25 parts, 12 schedules, 5 appendices and 98 amendments leaves the boundary between India and China at Aksai Chin as an airbrushed blank without a line running through it.

In 1962 the PLA advanced to a line, which more or less coincides with the McCartney-MacDonald line. However, the present dispute between the two sides mostly stems from overlapping perceptions about where the Line of Actual Control is? This is where we are now. And this is why 'stand-offs' happen. Aksai Chin is a high altitude cold desert with a large number of soda lakes. It is the region between Karakoram Ranges and Kun Lun Ranges

Strategic Importance of Aksai Chin

For India, it was country's only gateway to Central Asia after the partition in 1947. For China, the remote western provinces of Tibet and Xinjiang were effectively separated by possession of Aksai Chin and prevented India from the movement of armed forces from Tibet. Sometime in the decade of 1950s, Chinese decided to construct a road joining Tibet and Xinjiang illegally, in the Indian territory. The Indians consider border at Lanak La Pass (Johnson Line 1865) and Chinese consider border at Kongka La Pass (McCartney-MacDonald Line 1899 accepted by PRC until 1959).

India's Claim on Aksai Chin: Shimla Accord (1914)

A tripartite meeting of the British administration in India and representatives of Tibet and China was held in 1913 at Shimla in India. A draft treaty was agreed upon during this meeting. This agreement is known as Shimla treaty. According to the terms of this treaty, the relationships and borders between these three countries, namely India, Tibet and China, were fixed and agreed upon. However, even though the Chinese representative attending the meeting, Ivan Chen had initiated the draft treaty, he refused to put his country's official seal on the paper. Subsequently, the government in Beijing declared that this treaty was unacceptable to China. According to representatives of India and Tibet, since the treaty was mainly about the relationships and the borders between two sovereign countries, India and Tibet, they believed that the Chinese representative had merely attended the meeting as an observer and his approval or disapproval had no bearing on the proceedings of the treaty. Eventually, another meeting was held in July 1914 between representatives of India and Tibet and the draft treaty was finally approved, initialled and sealed. In the Shimla Accord of 1914, it was agreed that a region spread over 14,380 sq miles and known as Aksai Chin: located east of Ladakh, between Karakoram mountain range and Kun Lun mountain ranges, would be part of British India. The region of Ladakh in those days was part of the princely State of Jammu and Kashmir. In fact, old references show that the State administration used to have a small police outpost at Shahidulla (located on present Tibet-Xinjiang road) in this region.

Political Map of British India (1908)

According to the explorer William Moorcroft who extensively travelled in Himalayas, Tibet and Central India and was employed by East India Company put India-Tibetan Border at Lanak La. There is substantial Kashmiri government record for the area of Chang Chenmo Valley between Lanak and Kongka La Pass. In addition to the revenue records, Ladakh Settlement Report (1908), Report of several survey team, J&K Game Preservation Act (1951), Kashmiri document relating to the construction and maintenance of trade routes, rest houses and storehouses in the Chang Chenmo valley. All of them placed the entire valley up to Lanak La pass within the Ladakh. Indian sources state that there were no Chinese troops in the area till 1952, that Indian troops patrol till Lanak La Pass until 1958 and there was Indian Flag planted there until 1956.

Status of China-Occupied Kashmir – Aksai Chin

The Communist government of the People's Republic of China maintains its control over what is known as the Chinese Occupied Kashmir of Ladakh plateau. China states that Aksai Chin is a part of Chinese provincial region the Xinjiang Autonomous Region and does not recognize the addition of Aksai Chin to the Kashmir region. China did not accept the boundaries of the princely State of Kashmir and Jammu, north of the Aksai Chin and the Karakoram that was proposed by the British Empire. China settled its border disputes with Pakistan in the Trans-Karakoram Tract of 1963 with the provision that the settlement was subject to the final solution of the Kashmir dispute.

Princely State of Jammu and Kashmir

We shall begin by discussing the origins of the independence movement in Kashmir. There are two propagated pre-1947 histories of the Kashmir Valley. The first, recounted by the minority Kashmiri Pandits, talk of the butchery perpetrated under Afghan rule in the 18th and 19th centuries, in which tens of thousands of them were either brutally murdered or forcibly converted to Islam. The second is that of the majority Kashmiri Muslims and the alleged discrimination they faced under the Dogra rule from 1846 to 1947. The likely truth is both these histories are indeed true. The Kashmiri Muslims, many of whom had been converted to Islam from Hinduism by the Afghans, were discriminated against by the Dogras.

The Dogra Kingdom of Jammu and Kashmir, ruled by their Maharaja, had originated from the Jammu region of the newly created State. The Dogras were a neighbouring race of Hindus who paid the British in 1846 a lump sum to buy the rights to the Kashmir Valley as part of the Treaty of Amritsar. The British missionaries who reached Kashmir in limited numbers in the late 1800s saw a "poor, illiterate and leaderless" Kashmiri people. They were allowed to open several schools to educate the Kashmiri people and many attended their schools. The Kashmiri Pandits are the Kashmiris who practice the Hindu religion. They are the original inhabitants of the Kashmir Valley and trace their history back thousands of years. They have survived the coming of Buddhism, Islam and finally Sikhism into the valley.

However, Muslim religious leaders frowned upon the modern education system and so most Muslims remained formally uneducated. Those Kashmiris that were educated then faced the reality of high unemployment and limited access to government jobs in a poorly developed land. There was a lot of faith in the young Maharaja Hari Singh when he succeeded his uncle's throne in 1925. However, due to his reliance on his advisors, he lost touch with his subjects and became dangerously oblivious to their grievances.

Muslim Conference – Start of the Communal Polarization by the Muslim Press

In 1931, a fierce propaganda campaign against the Dogra Maharaja's rule was initiated from Lahore, in neighbouring Punjab, by the Muslim press. Leaflets and journals spoke of the deliberate suppression of the Muslims and instigated the people to rise against the Maharaja whom they claimed were influenced by his Hindu advisors. They proclaimed that Islam was in danger. There was a handful of formally educated Kashmiri Muslims, many of whom studied politics in universities in other parts of British India. Among them was Sheikh Abdullah, who would become the leader of the Kashmiri people.

It was the Dogras who mostly made up government jobs, during this time Hari Singh had spent much time in his youth trying to understand his people and had been concerned with both their welfare and development. Sheikh Abdullah was a compelling orator who delivered eloquent and fiery speeches in various mosques around Kashmir inciting a communal uprising of his fellow Muslims against their Hindu rulers. He rose to further prominence when he was jailed in June 1931 for an anti-government speech he gave. His subsequent trial became quite a spectacle and excited large crowds of thousands of Muslims to assemble near the court during the proceedings.

Adoption of Secularism

In the mid-1930s several Muslim Conference leaders stepped down citing that their colleagues were more interested in propagating their personal religious beliefs than fighting for the people's political rights. They lost the support of many Muslims and had no support from the non-Muslim minorities. In his Presidential Address to the Muslim Conference in 1938, Abdullah changed tack in response and declared:

> "Like us, the large majority of Hindus and Sikhs in the State have immensely suffered at the hands of the irresponsible government. Sooner or later these people are bound to join our ranks. We must end communalism by ceasing to think regarding Muslims and non-Muslims when discussing our political problems."

The Muslim Press concerned itself in alleviating the sufferings of Muslims in Punjab and neighbouring areas, including Kashmir. Its members mostly comprised of a small educated class and they faced difficulties in getting their message through to the broader uneducated public. This loss of support was primarily from within the organization itself.

In 1939 the Muslim Conference changed its name to the National Conference and made a concerted effort to reach out to non-Muslims. The Father of Pakistan, Muhammad Ali Jinnah, demanded a separate homeland for Muslims within British India, as explained by a 1940 speech:

> "The Hindus and Muslims belong to two different religious philosophies, social customs and literature. They neither inter-marry nor inter-dine together and, indeed, they belong to two different civilizations which are based mainly on conflicting ideas and conceptions."

Freedom Struggle

In his famous 'Quit Kashmir' speech in 1946, Abdullah rallied his people:

> "The tyranny of the Dogras has lacerated our souls. The Kashmiris are the most handsome people, yet the most wretched looking. It is time for action. Sovereignty is not the birthright of a ruler. Every man, woman and child will shout 'Quit Kashmir'. The Kashmiri nation has expressed its will."

In July 1947, just a month before partition, Mahatma Gandhi found time to visit Kashmir where he said that in an India which had become dark all around, Kashmir was the only hope with its peace amongst religions. However, Maharaja Hari Singh could not decide between India and Pakistan before the British Empire relinquished power. His indecisiveness caused immense harm to India and the Kashmiris cause. His son Dr Karan Singh is currently a respected leader in the Congress party of India.

Independent Kashmir

Following the independence of India on August 15th, Kashmir became an independent nation, with an understanding that it would soon decide its future. The Kashmir Socialist Party announced in September 1947, after careful consideration of the options facing Jammu and Kashmir that "in the best interests of the poor and backward people accession to Pakistan is desirable. The Kisan Mazdoor Conference also agreed in September 1947 that the State should cede to Pakistan.

The Kisan Mazdoor Conference was a group of farmers who discussed the issues facing Kashmir. Most were not landowners, as the rich Dogras based in the Jammu region owned much of the farmlands in Kashmir. So Pakistan not only offered them a practical option by way of their reliance on Lahore but a way for them to free themselves of their Dogra landowners who would have no place in a communal Islamic Pakistan. Sheikh Abdullah and his National Conference colleagues weren't released from prison until September 29, 1947 and immediately took to the task of deciding on Kashmir's future. They signed standstill agreements with both Pakistan and India so the Kashmiri people could have time to decide.

In a hangover from Mughal days, the Muslims of India had developed a habit of inflating their leaders with fancy titles. In this scheme, Sheikh Abdullah became Sher-i-Kashmir, the lion of Kashmir and his beautiful wife, Akbar Jehan, Madri-i-Meharban, the kind mother. Sheikh used his wife to meet his political goal when he was in prison, as Miss Akbar Jehan would meet visitors and she was very good at it plus her pieces of advice were valuable. Akbar Jehan who later gave birth to India's most outspoken Chief Minister of Kashmir, Farooq Abdullah, was the daughter of Michael Harry Nedou, an Austro-Swiss hotelier and Mirjan, a Kashmiri milkmaid.

The Nedou family had arrived in India at the turn of the last century and had invested its savings in the majestic Nedous Hotel in Lahore, Srinagar and Poona. Harry Nedou first caught sight of Mirjan when she came to deliver the milk at his holiday lodge in Gulmarg. He was immediately smitten, but she was suspicious. "I might be poor", she later told him but not for sale. Harry pleaded that he was serious, that he loved her that he wanted to marry her. In that case, she retorted wrathfully; you must convert to Islam, I cannot marry a non-believer. To her amazement he did. They had twelve children. Akbar Jehan was one of the daughters of this love-couple.

In 1928, when the seventeen-year-old Akbar Jehan had left school and was back in Lahore, a senior figure in British Military Intelligence checked in to the Nedous Hotel on the upper mall. Colonel TE

Lawrence, complete with Valentino style headgear, had just spent a gruelling few weeks in Afghanistan destabilizing the radical, modernizing and anti-British regime of King Amanullah. Disguised as 'Karam Shah', a visiting Arab cleric, he had organized a black propaganda campaign designed to stoke the religious fervour of the more reactionary tribes and thus provoke civil war. His mission accomplished, he left for Lahore. Akbar Jehan must have met him at her father's hotel. A flirtation began and got out of control. Her father insisted that they get married immediately, which they did.

Three months later, in January 1929, Amanullah was toppled and replaced by a pro-British ruler. On 12th January, Kipling's old newspaper in Lahore, the imperialists *Civil and Military Gazette,* published comparative profiles of Lawrence and 'Karam Shah' to reinforce the impression that they two were different people. Several weeks later, the Calcutta newspaper *Liberty* reported that 'Karam Shah' was indeed the 'British spy Lawrence' and gave a detailed account of his activities in Waziristan on the Afghan frontier. Lawrence was becoming a liability and the authorities told him to return to Britain. Karam Shah was never seen again. Nedous insisted on a divorce for his daughter and again Lawrence obliged. Four years later, Sheikh Abdullah and Akbar Jehan were married in Srinagar. She was an intelligent lady and soon started taking part in her hubby's political affairs. She also crucially advised her husband, alerting him, to the dangers of succumbing to Nehru.

Pakistan Conquers the Area in J&K which Now Called the POK

On October 22, 1947, an impatient Pakistan invaded Kashmir from the north with an army of soldiers and tribesmen armed with modern weapons. The tales of the invader's brutal sackings of towns and mass killings reached the people of Srinagar soon after and created mass hysteria. Kashmir, without an army, was under serious threat. The intention of Pakistan had been to instill fear into the Kashmiris so that they would surrender quickly. 1947-48 War: First attack by Pakistan to capture Kashmir, currently known POK (Pakistan Occupied Kashmir).

Afghan Tribals captured some part of Kashmir now called POK by India - Pakistan Army asked every Pathan tribe in the North-West Frontier Province of Pakistan to form Lashkars (Army) of 1,000 men. They were all told to assemble at Abbottabad (same place where US biggest terrorist Osama was hidden by the ISI and Pak army) and they were provided with arms by Pakistan and led by army regulars. Mind you this is just a few months from the time it was carved out from its parent country India, so they were in the game very early, now was that social cause or land expansion would leave for the readers to decide. The operation was named Operation Gulmarg and it commenced on October 22, 1947.

First State Policy to Support Terrorism – Plan by Tribal Raiders

The Plan - Six Lashkars to advance along road Muzaffarabad-Srinagar via Domel, Uri and Baramulla, capture Srinagar Airfield and advance to Banihal Pass. Two Lashkars to advance from the Haji Pir Pass to Gulmarg and secure the right flank of the main advancing force from Muzaffarabad. Two Lashkars to advance from Tithwal through the Nastachhun Pass and capture Sopore, Handwara and Bandipur. Ten Lashkars to operate in Poonch, Bhimbar and Rawalkot area with the intention of capturing Poonch and Rajauri before advancing to Jammu. Locals were to be used as guides and porters. 7 Pak Infantry Division and one Infantry Brigade were kept in readiness to exploit the success gained by the raiders. Muzaffarabad was captured. Many cities were captured. Even the Indian cities of Poonch, Uri, Baramulla were captured. Everywhere, the raiders resorted to looting the rich wealth of Kashmiri markets, raping and killing Kashmiris. It was after Baramulla fell and the stories of what had happened to the people of Baramulla - the plunder, the rapes, the killings spread like wildfire that the king was woken up from his slumber. He was now desperate to fight back, for in two days, Srinagar, the capital of Kashmir, would have the same fate as Baramulla.

India was still coming to terms with its Independence from British and also the division of the country. Raja Hari Singh (Hindu Dogra Ruler) sought the help from India to fight against the Muslim raiders, but India refused any help unless Kashmir signs the Treaty of Accession. Reluctant Raja Hari Singh finally signed the Treaty of Accession on 26th October 1947. Immediately, India, living up to its promise for help, sent its Army to the new Indian State of Jammu and Kashmir. On the early morning of 27th October, 1 Sikh Regiment was airlifted to Srinagar by Indian Air Force (then Royal Indian Air Force) and civilian Dakotas. They were just in time to save the Srinagar airstrip and city from being overrun by the militiamen. (On a busy day up to a hundred planes landed daily bringing in troops, ammunition and supplies and evacuating casualties and the refugees. The RIAF and civilian pilots of these Dakotas challenged the mountains, weather and fatigue to crush the evil designs of the raiders.) The main objective of the Indian Army was not to let the raiders to capture the Srinagar airfield. They had two options:

- Deploy the meagre forces around the airfield and wait for the enemy.
- Take the fight to the enemy away from the airfield and fight a series of delaying actions, thus buying time for more troops to be inducted into Srinagar.

The commander of the forces Col Ranjit Rai, chose the second option. Leaving behind a few troops to guard the airfield, he marched with a Company to Baramulla which had already fallen to the raiders. The regiment was launched into operations with no detailed plan, no recce and no intelligence of the enemy strength or dispositions.

Baramulla War

Ranjit Rai planned to stop the Lashkar at the mouth of the funnel which opens east of Baramulla into a wide valley as one advances towards Srinagar. Had the Lashkar gone on, there was nothing between them and Srinagar; however, the tribesmen sole motive obviously was not just liberation of Kashmir. A brave local young man Mohammed Maqbool Sherwani also contributed to the delay of the Lashkars advance. He went around on his motorcycle telling the tribals who had stormed Baramulla not to advance towards Srinagar as the Indian Army had reached the outskirts of Baramulla. His bluff worked, the enemy froze in its tracks for four days. By then, 1 Sikh had landed in Srinagar and marched to Baramulla. He was finally captured, shot and crucified. He remained like that for two to three days. The 1 Sikh regiment halted the Raiders for three days. Meanwhile, 1 Para and 4 Kumaon divisions were inducted through to the Srinagar airfield. With this, the balance of strength tilted in favour of the Indian Army. On 7th November, 1 Sikh along with 1 Para and 4 Kumaon fought the battle of Shalateng and broke the back of the raiders advancing towards Srinagar.

Pakistan had lost its first decisive battle with India just two months after it was first carved out from its parent country India, herself. There was no country or the culture in the human history named Pakistan before 14th of August 1947. In a last bid to capture Srinagar, a group of Pakistani tribals had managed to reach Badgam, a village just a few kilometres away from the Srinagar airfield on 3 November. A company of 4 Kumaon commanded by Major Somnath Sharma which was on a fighting patrol in Badgam village, was soon surrounded by three sides and sustained heavy casualties. Somnath Sharma's last message to Brigade HQ received a few moments before he died was:

"The enemies are only 50 yards from us. We are heavily outnumbered. We are under devastating fire. I shall not withdraw an inch but will fight to our last man and our last round."

Major Somnath Sharma was awarded the Param Vir Chakra, India's highest gallantry award. By the time the relief company of 1 Kumaon reached Badgam, the position had been overrun. However, the 200 casualties suffered by the Raiders made them lose their impetus to advance to Srinagar.

Places Captured Back by India

1 Sikh captured Baramulla avenging the death of their Commanding Officer on 8 November and advanced towards Uri. On 12 December, a fierce fight took place near Uri in which the Sikhs suffered heavy casualties, but they ensured that the raiders suffered heavier casualties. Uri was captured. With the capture of Uri, the remotest chance of any future threat developing ever again to Srinagar was removed. In February 1948 the battalion retook Handwara, Kupwara and Trahgam. The 163 Brigade group captured Tithwal, which is yet another story of tenacity and bravery of the Indian Army. India made sure that the residual Jammu and Kashmir did not suffer the same fate as the Pakistan Occupied Kashmir did. India made sure the people of Jammu and Kashmir will live to see another day.

By now, you must be wondering why, if Indian Army was so fabulous, why was it not able to capture the whole of POK? (Pakistan Occupied Kashmir, some 35% of the Kashmir total landmass.) As per a retired Brigadier of 08 JAK LI, the reason for the ceasefire in 1947 and India not going militarily to liberate the lost POK was purely a political decision. It was all due to then Prime Minister Nehru who went to the UN and asked for a ceasefire and then proposed for a plebiscite in J&K. That was for the first time in the history of the world that a country with an upper hand in the battlefield asked for the ceasefire. Had they got two more days, then entire J&K would have been under Indian army's control and the J&K issue would have been finished once for all. This is a scenario where the then Prime Minister made a mistake and generations have to pay the burden. At Nehru's request, UNSC passed resolution 47 and made a ceasefire and created the LoC. That created POK.

In World War II when Germans went very deep into USSR and offered ceasefire to them. Soviets knew the reasons as winter was closing and re-supplying German troops there would be much difficult. Hence Russians did not agree to the ceasefire and they hammered them so badly that ended with the fall of the Nazis. Same was the reason of the Chinese ceasefire in 1962.

Kashmir Initial Years with the Indian Union

Sheikh Abdullah had probably preferred an independent Kashmir himself in 1947, for he would have undoubtedly become the leader. However, due to the invasion by Pakistan he too needed India's help and thus promptly accepted the State's accession. It would be wrong to say that only the Kashmiri Muslims desired independence. The famous writer and Kashmiri Pandit Premnath Bazaz published *Freedom Struggle in Kashmir* in 1954 in which he also defended Pakistan's stand in Kashmir. He had been banished from Kashmir along with another Kashmiri Pandit Kanhayalal Kaul, by Sheikh Abdullah in 1949. Abdullah explained his reasoning for joining India in 1948 when he declared:

> "We the people of Jammu and Kashmir, have thrown our lot with Indian people not in the heat of passion or a moment of despair, but by a deliberate choice. The union of our people has been fused by the community of ideals and common sufferings in the cause of freedom."

He also later reflected that the one million non-Muslims of the State would have no place in Pakistan and as the Kashmiris had always preached secularism their ideological home was India.

In September 1951, the first ever elections were held for the Constituent Assembly in the State. The National Conference won all 75 seats unopposed. Article 370 of the Indian Constitution was passed in 1952 and was the compromise between the demands of Indian secularism and Muslim sub-nationalism. But by 1953 Abdullah had become confrontational with his cabinet and began speaking of revoking the accession and forming an independent Kashmir on several occasions. In August 1953, Sheikh Abdullah was arrested for having turned corrupt and autocratic. Abdullah's intolerance of opposition, his tight control over the press and the dominance of his party within the government made autonomy ideal for him as he would not be held accountable, as other leaders in India were. Speculation suggested his dealings with the Americans and British, worried Nehru of his future intentions. He was replaced by his friend and deputy, Bakshi Ghulam Mohammad, under whom the Constituent Assembly ratified the State's accession to India in February 1954.

Dissecting 1948 War

Almost everyone who has followed the history of Indian policy on Kashmir is intrigued by at least three questions. Why did India, which today has made a mantra of bilateralism, take the issue to the UN in 1948? Why did India not vacate Pakistan-sponsored aggression from all of Kashmir before accepting the UN Security Council's ceasefire call in 1949? And why did India not respond to Pakistan's invasion by taking the war into enemy territory, as it did later in 1965? Much of the blame for these decisions have often been put on India's first Prime Minister, Jawaharlal Nehru. Many have suggested it was a Nehruvian idealism that prompted Delhi to move the issue from the Valley, where India had a comfortable advantage, to the hostile terrain of the UN. Nehru, it has been vigorously argued, believed Delhi would get real justice from the multilateral body.

Similarly, it is often argued that Nehru did not want to permanently scar relations with Pakistan by taking the war into its territory, believing as he did that India and Pakistan needed to begin their history on a relatively harmonious note. And that it was Sheikh Abdullah who forced him to stop the army from moving the aggressors even further from what the Line of Control is now as Abdullah's influence did not extend beyond the Valley. But new shreds of evidence show it was also the British colonial mindset which was very anti-India that resulted in the Kashmir complication which has brought the world on the verge of nuclear war. Most of the early decisions were not made by the full Indian cabinet, but by the cabinet's Defence Committee chaired by Governor-General Lord Mountbatten, whose "affection for India never interfered with his pursuit of British interest." British strategic interests had a distinct pro-Pak tilt. Therefore, it was the British who, through persuasion, manipulation and often deceit stopped India from expanding the war and made it approach the UN. Mountbatten's treachery was of a lesser order compared to the skulduggery of Lord Noel-Baker, then Secretary of State for Commonwealth relations, who won a Nobel Peace Prize later. He advanced proposals in the Council that involved the unqualified acceptance of Pakistan's demands and the outright rejection of Indian views. Indeed, if he had succeeded, Kashmir would have been placed under effective UN control.

Did Cold War Era Friend Russia, Diluted India's Military Win in 1965?

The US, which was embroiled in a bloody war of its own in Vietnam, acted mostly through the United Nations. However, the defining western aim was to see their satellite Pakistan get through the war without getting battered. This view is amply summed by YB Chavan, India's then Defence Minister, he wrote about British Prime Minister Harold Wilson's ceasefire proposal at a time when India had the upper hand:

> "I insisted on military advantages being maintained. The UK proposals look like a trap."

As three divisions of the Indian Army were slicing across Pakistani defences and thundering across the Ichhogil canal to Lahore, Wilson sent a message to Prime Minister Lal Bahadur Shastri and Ayub Khan:

> "Both governments bear responsibility for the steady escalation which has subsequently occurred and today's attack in the Lahore area presents us with a completely new situation."

Wilson's message implied that India was as much to blame for the war on the subcontinent as Pakistan. "Shastri more or less brushed aside that message," says Pradhan. "Bias on the part of Britain would rule out the UK from playing any effective role in events after the ceasefire."

Conflict over Kashmir resumed again in early 1965 when Pakistani and Indian forces clashed along the border between the two nations. Hostilities intensified that August when the Pakistani Army attempted to take Kashmir by force. The attempt to seize the State was unsuccessful and the second India-Pakistan War reached a stalemate. This time, the international politics of the Cold War affected the nature of the conflict.

During the 1950s, US officials regarded Indian leadership with some caution due to India's involvement in the Non-Aligned Movement, particularly its prominent role at the Bandung Conference of 1955. The United States hoped to maintain a regional balance of power, which meant not allowing India to influence the political development of other States. However, a 1962 border conflict between India and China ended with a decisive Chinese victory, which motivated the United States and the United Kingdom to provide military supplies to the Indian Army. After the clash with China, India also turned to the Soviet Union for assistance, which placed some strains on US-Indian relations. However, the United States also provided India with considerable development assistance throughout the 1960s and 1970s.

US-Pakistani relations had been more consistently positive. The US government looked to Pakistan as an example of a moderate Muslim State and appreciated Pakistani assistance in holding the line against Communist expansion by joining the South-East Asia Treaty Organization (SEATO) in 1954 and the Baghdad Pact (later renamed the Central Treaty Organization, or CENTO) in 1955. Pakistan's interest in these pacts stemmed from its desire to develop its military and defensive capabilities, which were substantially weaker than those of India. Both the United States and the United Kingdom supplied arms to Pakistan in these years.

After Pakistani troops invaded Kashmir, India moved quickly to internationalize the regional dispute (very bad strategic move by a relatively stronger party). It asked the United Nations to reprise its role in the First India-Pakistan War and end the current conflict. The Security Council passed Resolution 211 on September 20 calling for an end to the fighting and negotiations on the settlement of the Kashmir problem and the United States and the United Kingdom supported the UN decision by cutting off arms supplies to both belligerents. This ban affected both belligerents, but Pakistan felt the effects more keenly since it had a much weaker military in comparison to India. The UN resolution and the halting of arms sales had an immediate impact. India accepted the ceasefire on September 21 and Pakistan on September 22.

The ceasefire alone did not resolve the status of Kashmir and both sides accepted the Soviet Union as a third-party mediator. Negotiations in Tashkent concluded in January 1966, with both sides giving up territorial claims, withdrawing their armies from the disputed territory. Nevertheless, although the Tashkent agreement achieved its short-term aims, conflict in South Asia would re-ignite a few years later. Following the war, most Kashmiri people had turned strongly anti-Pakistan as they were seen as the aggressors. In May 1964, Indian Defence Minister Yashwantrao Chavan visited the Pentagon, the HQ of the American defence department. Chavan, who was trying to modernize the Indian military rapidly, requested the Americans to sell India the F-104 Starfighter - the most advanced jet fighter of that era. Although the US had supplied the F-104 and the F-86 Sabres in large numbers - virtually free of cost - to Pakistan, India's request was rebuffed in an extremely crude manner.

The 1965 War remains memorable for two things. One was a monumental miscalculation by Pakistan. President Ayub Khan egged on by his scheming and feckless Foreign Minister Zulfikar Ali Bhutto, sent a top-secret order to his army chief General Mohammed Musa:

> "As a general rule, Hindu morale would not stand for more than a couple of hard blows delivered at the right time and the right

> place. Such opportunities should, therefore, be sought and exploited."

Secondly, India's leadership – as it has done consistently over the past 2500 years – frittered away on the negotiating table what the soldiers won on the battlefield. Pradhan writes: "In a way, India's leadership, out of its sense of restraint, fair play and endeavour to seek enduring peace and goodwill with the neighbour, seems to have missed opportunities to solve the problem." At the end of a bruising 22-day war, India held 1,920 sq km of Pakistani territory while Pakistan only held 550 sq km of Indian land. The Haji Pir Pass was also captured by Indian soldiers after an epic battle. And yet India surrendered everything at the Tashkent Declaration in January 1966.

Russia, which was following the events with deep interest, maintained its traditional stand that Kashmir was part of India. Pradhan writes Moscow accepted the disturbances in Kashmir had been created by infiltrators from Pakistan. Russia also backed India at the United Nations. K Vijaykrishnan writes in "The Soviet Union and the India-Pakistan War, 1965", "Support was available for India on some important technical points and objections India had raised," he says. Russia supported the Indian position that the Security Council should only deal with "questions directly connected with the settlement of the armed conflict" and not drag in the Kashmir issue. Fending off China was a trickier affair. Russia did not want an open confrontation with Beijing, but Moscow decided it would not remain a passive spectator if India had to battle on two fronts. According to Vijaykrishnan, during the thick of the conflict, India received a reassuring message from Russian Premier Alexei Kosygin indicating support in the event of a Chinese attack.

Sisir Gupta writes in *India and the International System* that India was aware Russia would never like to see India humbled or weakened.

> "A strong and friendly India occupying a pre-eminent position in South Asia was very much a Soviet foreign policy interest. Notwithstanding the fluctuations in the Soviet attitude and the zig-zag nature of the course it pursued, there was throughout a broad assumption underlying Soviet policies towards South Asia, that India was the key factor in the region and that any policy which created distrust and dissension between the two countries was to be avoided."

China got the message and backed off despite Pakistani appeals for help. Chinese strongman Mao Tse-tung was reported to have told

Ayub Khan that "if there is a nuclear war, it is Peking and not Rawalpindi that will be the target," writes GW Chaudhury in *India, Pakistan, Bangladesh and the Major Powers: Politics of a Divided Subcontinent.*

Road to Tashkent

With the US disinterested in the conflict and the UK showing its true anti-India and pro-Pakistan colours, it was left to Russia to play honest broker. It was after some initial hesitation that both India and Pakistan accepted the Russian offer. Ayub Khan later said that Pakistan went to Tashkent as it did not want to risk a veto by Moscow. There was another reason for Pakistan's eagerness for talks. According to Pradhan, "The continued presence of Indian troops on the east side of the Ichhogil canal, facing Lahore city, was hurting Pakistan's pride." The heat was clearly on Islamabad.

Before leaving for Tashkent, Shastri - who was hero-worshipped by Indian soldiers - had promised his victorious troops that he would not return the land captured from the enemy after so many sacrifices. But after six days of talks, Shastri proved once again that Indians are bad negotiators. He gave away everything. What a led down from war perspective, even by the hugely respected Prime Minister Shastri. Was Shastri feeling the pressure from the international community? Most likely not, but perhaps he felt - like his successor Indira Gandhi after the 1971 war - that showing leniency towards Pakistan would buy its goodwill.

Mystery of Prime Minister Shastri's Death in Russia

If you were Shastri, you would dread having to face the Indian soldier back home. Hundreds of them had died while capturing the strategic Haji Pir Pass, which if India had kept, would have forever nullified Pakistan's advantage in Kashmir. On the night of January 10, 1966, the diminutive Prime Minister but a giant among men died of a heart attack. It was his fourth cardiac seizure and was likely triggered by his anxiety at having to face an irate public and having to look into the eyes of his jawans - soldiers - whose hopes he had dashed. There have been all sorts of conspiracy theories, but the reality is that none of the major countries benefited from his death. Russia had scored a spectacular diplomatic coup, America fully supported the Tashkent Agreement and Pakistan was happy to get its land back. That the Indian Prime Minister died of a heart attack comes from a most unlikely source. Shortly after Mikhail Gorbachev's liberalization policies in 1991, *Soviet Land* magazine in India published an account by an ex-KGB officer. According to the former intelligence agent, the KGB was spying on both the Indian and Pakistani delegations to find out how much each country was willing to yield during the negotiations. When Shastri started getting a seizure, the KGB was listening but decided not to alert his aides because that would give away their game and lead to a diplomatic showdown with India.

Prelude to Tashkent

Having dissected what transpired at the negotiating table, we need to discuss the prelude to Tashkent. Although Pakistan was on the verge of being trounced – unlike in 1971 and 1999 when it got hammered – India generously agreed to a ceasefire after repeated pleas from the major powers. Why did India stop fighting when it had Pakistan reeling? Why did Chavan and Shastri, who swatted away the western pressure and gave a free hand to the Indian military, cave in? The problem was Army Chief Jayanto Nath Chaudhuri. The Kolkata-born General came from an affluent background and had become army chief purely on the back of family connections and pure luck. He was elevated following the resignation of another Sandhurst-educated General, Pran Nath Thapar, the army chief of the 1962 War. Chaudhuri's mentors were the Sandhurst educated British Generals – who had utterly failed before the Germans and Japanese during World War II – and predictably he also lacked warfighting qualities. "He was so good on paper that Chavan often wondered how good he would be in warfare."

Chavan mentions in his war diary that Chaudhuri would frequently lapse into depression. Each time the Indian army suffered a setback, the General would walk into the Defence Minister's room and Chavan had to give him a pep talk. Chaudhuri so completely lacked courage that Chavan often forced him to visit the front and personally take stock.

Pradhan writes,

> "On September 20 when the Prime Minister asked Chaudhuri whether India could expect to gain if the war continued for a few days more, he informed the Prime Minister that the army was coming to an end of its ammunition holdings and could not sustain fighting for much longer. Chaudhuri advised acceptance of the ceasefire proposal. It was later discovered in overall terms only 14-20% of the Indian Army's ammunition stock had been used up. At the moment of our greatest advantage, the army chief's non-comprehension of the intricacies of the long-range logistics deprived India of a decisive victory."

In contrast, Pakistan had expended 80% of its ammo. It had also lost 250 of its latest US-supplied tanks.

Chaudhuri was also criticized for his lack of daring. When the Pakistani cities of Sialkot and Lahore could have been easily taken after the dash and bravery shown by Indian troops, Chaudhuri told Shastri: "We must move with the caution and wisdom of an elephant. We will take them in God's good time." In fact, when the Pakistan Army attacked in the Khem Kharan sector in Punjab, Chaudhuri ordered the Army Commander Harbaksh Singh to withdraw to a safer position. The commander refused and what followed was the Battle of Assal Uttar – the greatest tank battle since Kursk in 1943. The Indian counter attack on the night of September 10 was so ferocious that by the morning they had knocked out 70 Pakistani tanks. But what the Battle of Assal Uttar will be memorable, the 25 enemy tanks found abandoned with their engines running and wireless sets on. It was the perfect metaphor for the plight of the Pakistan Army. Had India kept its head, today we'd have a lot more to celebrate. Indian Politicians gave it away.

Kashmir Accord

The Plebiscite movement had failed to achieve anything and after the 1971 War in which Pakistan was not only defeated by India but split in half, Abdullah and Kashmir moved closer to India. In 1972, Abdullah announced, "our dispute with Government of India is not about accession but is about the quantum of autonomy." The 1975 Kashmir Accord, signed by Prime Minister Indira Gandhi and Chief Minister Sheikh Abdullah further strengthened India's control over legislation in Kashmir (however Article 370 remained).

The 1971 War – Creation of Bangladesh

This was a watershed that led to the division of West and East Pakistan, biggest in the history of the World Wars. From India's viewpoint, it weakened Pakistan by carving out Bangladesh and asserted India's military might. It also seems to have created a psychological fear among Pakistan as well as Kashmiri Muslims. The realization came about that it would be impossible to obtain Kashmir through military means. Kashmir had very much become a part of India by this time. Popular Indian films were shot in the beautiful and picturesque Kashmir locales with its gardens, mountains and lakes providing scenic backdrops. The Indian upper class would venture to Kashmir in the summer for weeks at a time, socializing in the cooler climate of places such as Gulmarg (near

Srinagar). So while the Kashmiri people retained their own distinct culture within the mosaic of India, they were a part of India's multicultural ways by the 1970s.

US Republican Party's Controversial President Nixon and His not Very Friendly India Policy

Although Andrew Johnson and Bill Clinton are the only two Presidents to have been impeached, two others came very close to being charged with crimes. One of them, Richard M Nixon, was certain to be impeached and convicted in 1974, but the 37th President of the United States resigned before he was to face prosecution over the 1972 break-in at the Democratic Party's headquarters in what became known as the Watergate scandal. An impeachment resolution was introduced in the House of Representatives again after his veto of a bill angered lawmakers. The impeachment initiative failed. Nixon liked Communist China more than the democratic India.

Nixon to Kissinger on December 4, 1971: "Let's Blame India"

Freshly declassified documents of US foreign policy provide new insights into how Nixon and Kissinger conducted an almost personal war against India during the 1971 Bangladesh crisis. "What is history but a fable agreed upon?" Napoleon Bonaparte once remarked decisively. In the days of the court historians that would probably have been true. But in the age of electronics where every conversation, telegram or letter can be accurately recorded for posterity, history does not lie. It usually isn't very comfortable either for those that made history to have it replayed to them. Former US Secretary of State Henry Kissinger found that out last week when the US State Department released a detailed study of declassified papers of what it termed the South Asia Crisis of 1971.

That crisis saw India and Pakistan go to war resulting in the liberation of Bangladesh. The war was brutally short and swift-just 13 days and it changed forever the history and geography of the subcontinent. It saw Indira Gandhi emerge as the Iron Lady of Asia. It also saw American Seventh Fleet to the Indian Ocean to browbeat India. The undiplomatic language used by two of the world's most powerful men, Kissinger and US President Richard Nixon, in their private conversations to describe Indira had its shock value.

In one such conversation, at the Oval Office on November 5, 1971, Nixon describes his meeting with Indira a day earlier saying:

"We really slobbered over the old witch."

They then went on to discuss the crisis brewing in East Pakistan, with Kissinger telling Nixon:

> "The Indians are bast**** anyway. They are starting a war there. While she was a bit**, we got what we wanted too."

After strong protests from the Congress party, Kissinger even apologized, telling an Indian television network,

> "I regret that these words were used. I have extremely high regard for Mrs Gandhi as a statesman. The fact that we were at cross purposes at that time was inherent in the situation, but she was a great leader who did great things for her country."

While much of the history of the differences between the US and India over the 1971 crisis is known, what's important about these documents is that they provide a rare, unbiased insight into the Nixon Administration's handling of a critical moment in subcontinental history. What comes through starkly is that the campaign is conducted by the White House, primarily by Nixon and Kissinger, who was then his assistant for National Security Affairs. There is evidence of deep divisions between the White House and the State Department on the course of action to take against India. Nixon and Kissinger made it clear that they need to preserve their new-found friendship with China forged that year even at the expense of relations with India.

That in the desire to back an ally and old friend, Pakistani dictator Yahya Khan, they were even willing to risk a war with the Soviet Union, who was backing India then. Also that they had misread India's true intentions and believed that India wanted to annex the whole of Pakistan. Lt-General JFR Jacob, Chief of Staff of India's Eastern Army Command, who had played a key role in the liberation of Bangladesh, says:

> "It's amazing that they believed so when we never had a plan to annex territory in West Pakistan. What's evident throughout the papers is Nixon's tilt towards Pakistan."

That is apparent right from the day the war begins.

Kissinger told the members of the Washington Special Action Group on December 3, 1971:

> "I've been catching unshirted hell every half-hour from the President who says we're not tough enough. He doesn't believe we're carrying out his wishes. He wants to tilt toward Pakistan and he believes that every briefing or statement is going the other way."

The next day Nixon is still hopping mad and wants Kissinger to cut off all US aid to India, including what was given as relief for the thousands of refugees who fled to India even before the war. Nixon tells Kissinger:

> "By God, I can't emphasize too strongly how I feel. We told Mrs Gandhi we're going to cut off that aid.... And you're examining every other possibility of how we can squeeze India right now."

In the same conversation, they chalk out a strategy to blame India for starting the war in Pakistan.

They ignored the fact that Khan had failed to respect the huge mandate given to Sheikh Mujibur Rahman by East Pakistan in the general election of December 1970. That he then had Rahman arrested in March 1971 and launched a brutal war of suppression that saw millions of refugees fleeing to India, putting an enormous strain on the country's resources.

Nixon, brushing aside advice from his State Department, coolly tells Kissinger:

> "I think it's very important to put the burden on India on this, Henry."

Then they discuss why they should get tough, with Kissinger saying:

> "It was bad enough when, with our money, they dragged us around in the UN. When have these bastards ever supported us?"

Nixon replies: "Never." And Kissinger adds:

> "What can they do to us that they aren't doing now? I mean, if they want to be Russian stooges and have the Russians spend a billion dollars there a year, we can't prevent it."

Nixon shows no remorse when he reviews what US public opinion would be, telling Kissinger:

> "I know all the arguments that well then we're choosing sides, we're not neutral. Of course, we're not neutral. Neither are the Indians. They're always neutral against us."

That there is a division between the State Department and the White House is evident in many of the conversations. In one such, Secretary of State W Rogers tells Kissinger on December 5, two days after the war began:

> "I think we shouldn't act just in petulance."

The next day, frustrated by the US inability to make any impact on India's war plans, Nixon tells Kissinger:

> "This woman suckered us. But let me tell you she's going to pay."

Nixon saw China as offering perhaps the best prospect of putting pressure on India.

> "I think we've got to tell them that some movement on their part, we think towards the Indian border, could be very significant. Damn it and I am convinced that if the Chinese start to move the Indians will be petrified."

On December 6, 1971, Nixon tells Kissinger:

> "Threaten to move forces or move them, Henry, that's what they must do now. Now, goddammit, we're playing our role and that will restrain India."

They also discuss getting China to put pressure on India. Nixon tells Kissinger:

> "The Chinese have not warned the Indians that they're going to come in. And that's the point, they've got to warn them. All they've got to do is move something. Move a division. You know, move some trucks. Fly some planes. You know, some symbolic act."

The frustration shows with Nixon angrily asking for a concerted effort to publicize India's role in the crisis:

> "Get a white paper out. I want the Indians blamed for this and you know what I mean? We can't let these goddamn sanctimonious Indians get away with this.... Here they are raping and murdering. They talk about West Pakistan. These Indians are pretty vicious."

On December 12, 1971, the White House had information that the Chinese are finally showing some interest in making threatening moves against India. That raised the question of the likelihood of Soviet military action against China and its implications. Kissinger said:

> "If the Soviets move against them and then we don't do anything, we'll be finished."

Nixon shockingly asks:

> "So what do we do if the Soviets move against them? Start lobbing nuclear weapons in, is that what you mean?"

Kissinger responded:

> "If the Soviets move against them in these conditions and succeed, that will be the showdown. We have to and if they succeed, we will be finished. We'll be through."

Kissinger tentatively suggested:

> "Then we better call them (the Chinese) off."

But then quickly concluded:

> "I think we can't call them off frankly."

His reason:

> "If the Russians get away with facing down the Chinese and if the Indians get away with licking the Pakistanis-we may be looking down the gun barrel."

November 5, 1971

Nixon: "We slobbered over the old witch."

Kissinger: "Well, the Indians are bas***** anyway. They are starting a war there. To them, East Pakistan is no longer the issue. I found it interesting how she carried on about West Pakistan. While she was a bit**, we got what we wanted too. She will not be able to say that the US didn't give her a warm reception and in despair, she has got to go to war."

Nixon: "I'll make the meeting today a rather cool one."

November 24, 1971

Nixon: "Yahya is a thoroughly decent and reasonable man. Not always smart politically but he is a decent man."

W Rogers (Secretary of State): "If Yahya steps out of the picture, then Bhutto will...."

Nixon: "Yeah, Bhutto (ZA) hasn't changed. That son-of-a-bit** is a total demagogue. Ayub Khan in 1967 gave me a rundown on him and said this fellow is just bad news."

December 6, 1971

Nixon: "We have got to tell China that some movement on their part towards the Indian border would be very significant."

Kissinger: "We shouldn't urge them to do it ... we could say if you take certain actions we want you to know that you should not be deterred by fear of standing alone."

Nixon: "Right. That's right. Damn it. I am convinced that if the Chinese start to move the Indians will be petrified."

December 12, 1971

Nixon: "What do we do if the Soviets move against China? We start lobbing nuclear weapons in, is that what you mean?"

Kissinger: "If the Soviets move against them in these conditions and succeed, that will be the showdown. We will be finished. So then isn't it better we call the Chinese off?"

Nixon: "No. Nothing works out unless you do something about it. That's the trouble with the world."

But as it turned out the Chinese had not decided upon military action in support of Pakistan but more to go along with the US in the UN resolutions for a ceasefire and mutual troop withdrawal. A little later, Nixon gets the message that he has been waiting for-the Russians assure the US that India would not annex West Pakistan. Turning to the decision made earlier in the morning to confront the Soviet Union with military force if necessary in support of China, Kissinger said:

> "What you did this morning Mr President was a heroic act."

Nixon ruminates over how difficult it is to get the government to move and says:

> "It's the whole attitude, the whole government, the whole American establishment would say, well, don't borrow trouble. It's all going to work out. Nothing ever works out unless you do something about it. That's the trouble with the world."

Nixon may have been kind to himself in his memoirs. But history, unfortunately, can be a much harsher judge. Nixon led USA people and the value system down, the USA was formed on high morals and that's the reason why it is such a great country and power on the planet earth till date.

Sheikh Abdullah's Final Years

In 1977 the State Congress Party withdrew its support of the Abdullah government, thus ending the National Conference-Congress alliance of the time. In retaliation, two years after signing the Kashmir Accord and thus reaffirming Kashmir as an integral part of India, Abdullah began speaking about a plebiscite and even independence. In 1979, Pakistani Prime Minister ZA Bhutto pledged to "fight for a thousand years for the cause of oppressed Kashmiri Muslims." In his will, the Sheikh asked for his body to be taken to the waters of the Arabian Sea rather than be buried in Kashmir (as per normal Muslim custom) as he considered Kashmir to be an enslaved territory. His reference to the Arabian Sea, as the Indian Reasons for this sudden shift, are unclear. One view is that independence would have served his gain. Another explanation details his leaning towards Pakistan that surfaced as he realized he was reaching the end of his life and thus turned religiously conservative and anti-secular. More importantly, he may have been responding to the Kashmiri bureaucrats who were scared by the Kashmir Accord.

Islamization of Kashmir

In 1980, the Islamization of Kashmir began with full force. The Abdullah government changed the names of about 2,500 villages from their original names to new Islamic names. For example, the major city of Anantnag was to be known as Islamabad (same name as the Pakistani capital). The Sheikh began giving communal speeches in mosques as he used to in the 1930s. Further, in his autobiography, he referred to Kashmiri Pandits as *'mukhbir'* or informers (of the Indian government. There was an orchestrated public relations campaign to change the Kashmiri people. There was the distribution of a pamphlet titled the "Tragedy of Kashmir". Suddenly thousands of copies of Pakistani writer Muhammed Yusuf Saraf's book *Kashmiris Fight for Freedom* appeared in the Valley, as did *On Guerrilla War* by Che Guevara. Then an elected Member of State Parliament released a pamphlet called "The Conspiracy of Converting Kashmir Muslim Majority into a Minority". With Abdullah's death in 1982, the secessionist leadership emerged in full force. Despite having Abdullah's support in his final days, they turned against him and his National Conference. Farooq Abdullah, who succeeded his father as leader of the National Conference lost the 1984 State Election.

The Saudi Influence

The exact role of Saudi Arabia cannot be known due to lack of evidence currently, but there are clear indications showing their influence. Many Saudi religious personalities and scholars held an Islamic Conference in Srinagar in 1979 and often visited after that. Further, they set-up the Jhelum Valley (JV) Medical College in 1980, through which they were able to funnel large sums of foreign exchange money into Kashmir and also provide seats for the children of Kashmir's elite who could not gain admission at other colleges based on their results. Anecdotal evidence suggests it was the doctors in this hospital that began spreading the message of radical Islam and communalism. Further, armed militants later were captured with documents showing they had received Pakistani currency from the JV Medical College.

Nowadays even Pakistani sources confirm the extensive use of Saudi money that went towards setting up facilities, such as madrasas that trained jihadis in the region. From the early 1980s, madrasas started spreading throughout the Kashmir Vale and these institutions planted the seeds of Islamic fundamentalism in Kashmiris. It appears that the reasons for this sudden and seemingly contradictory shift were politically motivated. The secessionists wanted victory and the easiest way of doing this was by vilifying the National Conference for being 'pro-India,' even though the National Conference had changed tack in recent years.

Children were instructed to 'fight for Islam', and hatred for their Kashmiri Pandit counterparts was bred extensively. Anecdotes suggest that classes being taught the alphabet learned that "B is for Batta, M is for marun, Batta chu marun", where Batta refers to local non-Muslims, marun is to kill, hence "The local non-Muslim has to be killed." Initial Outbreaks of Violence. In early 1986 were the first clear outbreaks of violence when Muslim fundamentalists attacked the minority Kashmiri Pandits. The exact reason for the outbreak remains unclear, but at the end of it dozens of Pandits had been killed and 24 Hindu temples had been burnt by Muslim mobs.

Violent disturbances such as these were all carried out in the name of Islam. The Governor of Kashmir at the time, Jagmohan, observed that most of the disturbances that took place occurred on Friday nights as crowds dispersed from the mosques. Mosques became a platform for religious sermons intermingled with fiery political speeches. The people delivering these speeches were often trained mullahs, who had been sent to Kashmir from Pakistan for this specific purpose. A Kashmiri who attended Mosques during this period commented that such provocative language and distorted facts were used that even deep-thinking and highly learned persons who listened to these would certainly arise too. Thus, on Friday nights it became quite common for public vehicles to be stoned and police to be attacked.

Radical Islam

Before the 1980s, there were pockets of Islamic Fundamentalism present in isolated parts of Kashmir, notably in Sopore and around the Anantnag region. It's important to appreciate the difference between Kashmiri Islam and the more mainstream fanatical Islam which took over the rest of the Islamic world in recent centuries. In

Kashmiri Islam, a variant of Sufism, there is much Hindu Vedanta influence stemming from the fact that most Kashmiri Muslims were originally Hindus who had been converted between AD 1300-1800. In fact, Kashmiri Islam is based upon the teaching of their Rishis, a word borrowed from their original Hindu philosophy meaning learned scholar.

The Kashmiri Rishis, some of whom were also Hindus, formed their form of peaceful Islam that had become secular, democratic and very liberal in thought. And so it was this clash of Islams that came to the fore in the early 1980s.

This division was only later highlighted when in 1995 notorious Afghan mercenary Mast Gul burned down the sacred Sufi shrine of Sheikh Noor-ud-Din Noorani. The subsequent outcry from the general Kashmiri Muslim population resulted in large numbers of the Kashmiri insurgents pulling out of their militant groups which were based in Pakistan and in fact giving up their weapons altogether. What happened in 1995 was not foreseen by the Kashmiri Muslim youth in the late 1980s. They had believed they were victims and that to be true Muslims they needed the strict Shariat Law and thought Pakistan was there to help them. One former militant leader has said they had been manipulated by the Pakistanis as they were young at the time, but had been responsive to them as they were frustrated by New Delhi's lack of response to their plight.

The publication of *The Satanic Verses* in Britain in 1989 by Salman Rushdie, a Kashmiri Muslim, caused major protests in Kashmir. Ayatollah Khomeini of Iran banned the book, claiming it was blasphemous and critical of Islam and Prophet Mohammad. The Kashmiris, never having seen the book, felt it was their duty as Muslims to protest. In fact, the triumph of the Ayatollah in the Iran Revolution of 1979 gave much confidence to the secessionist fundamentalists. The Ayatollah talked of Islamic Revolutions in all the countries of the world to liberate the enslaved Muslim people. The Jamaat-e-Islami party spread rumours that the Ayatollah's ancestors had come to Kashmir and that he was thus related to Kashmiri Muslims. This became a great matter of pride for them, never mind that he was a Shia and most of them were Sunni Muslims.

The Jamaati directed people to buy weapons instead of colour TVs and Ghani Lone, a current member of the Hurriyat, implored all local women to sell their jewellery to help finance the purchase of weapons. In fact, the Jamaati claimed that the Pandits (presumably Indian agents as they were Hindus went the argument) were secretly collecting weapons and so the Muslims should follow suit.

Next Generation

The growing political dissidence is difficult to correlate with a lessening of political or religious rights of Kashmiris. In fact, in the 1980s, freedom of speech was flourishing in the Valley. There was a rapid expansion of educational institutions and a growth of press and television coverage. Indeed, this very fact created a more politically conscious younger generation. In fact, even today, after more than a decade of stagnation, the State of Jammu and Kashmir ranks fourth amongst all Indian States by way of per capita income. In fact, with few Kashmiri Muslims paying the amount of taxes they indeed owed, the State always faced a budget deficit and needed India to continuously pay the large difference to keep the State from bankruptcy. The Indian taxpayer effectively financed the State.

With about one-third of the former princely State under Pakistani occupation, there was a direct influence from the Pakistan side into the Indian side byways of Islamic Fundamentalism. The Islamic radicals formed the Jamaat-e-Islami party to contest elections on the platform of introducing the strict Islamic Shariat laws into Kashmir. They won a few districts and were able to influence those predominantly rural areas. In the 1970s, the Jamaats offered education to the Kashmiri Muslims and their conservative teachings included criticism on non-Muslims and anti-India messages. To finance themselves, their members had to pay 10% of their earnings to the party. In fact, Abdullah had banned these Jamaati madrasas in 1975 for 'spreading communal poison'. The result was many of these teachers were simply employed by government schools where they continued to spread their propaganda until more madrasas came up.

By as early as 1983, the Government of India received reports of Kashmiri youth returning home after receiving training somewhere on the border. By 1984, the theme 'Islam is in Danger' was the sentiment that mobilized the youth, rather than aspirations for independence. This fact is often disregarded and most sources incorrectly state that the first batch of youth to cross the border for arms and training was in 1987-88, as a direct result of the rigged elections. By 1989, the Indian government estimated that about 10,000 Kashmiri youth had gone to Pakistan to undergo training.

Not only was this emerging younger generation of Kashmiri Muslims indoctrinated with Islamic fundamentalism, but they were also faced with declining economic conditions. Exact figures of youth unemployment are not available. However, even amongst the educated, figures were quite high. In 1987 nearly 10,000 university graduates were unemployed and between 40,000 and 50,000 school graduates suffered from unemployment. This youth group did not belong to the elite who had dominated Kashmir. Furthermore, when they crossed the border to become trained jihadis, they were often supplied with substantial amounts of money and financial support.

However, the draw of militancy was much stronger than a matter of simple economics. Some former militants now speak of the sheer emotional power they felt when they held a gun in their hands, with the future of their homeland lying within their grasp. There were also some mounting social pressures that quickly became part of mainstream culture. For instance, it became a status symbol to have some mujahedin in the family. Most weapons did indeed come in from Pakistan. The Indian Border Security Forces, underpaid and posted in isolated mountain ranges in the bitter cold, later admitted to taking money as bribes from the many people who crossed the border between India and Pakistan. They did not realize that money and weapons were being transferred.

1987 State Election

Dasgupta presents an interesting explanation of the allegedly rigged 1987 State Elections which many cite as a major cause of the Kashmiri people affording further support to the insurgents. The Muslim United Front (MUF) was a coalition of parties including the Jamaat-e-Islami, who rejected the Accession and the Ummat-i-Islami, which demanded more democratic rights for the people. The electorate was already sceptical of the National Conference-Congress alliance and so when there were incidents of malpractice in the counting process, they were quite perturbed. Not only did the National Conference win 40 seats and the Congress 26 for a landslide victory for the alliance, but the MUF also won only four seats out of 76. This was despite the estimated 32% total support for the MUF and 53% for the alliance.

The tallying procedure considered whoever was first past the post Union: The Politics of Autonomy as the winner and this policy which is common in all democracies favours alliances. So while the MUF had the widespread support it only had the majority in 4 seats, the rest of its voters were spread amongst the other seats as a minority. This mathematical explanation on the inherent difference between popular vote and actual seats appeared likely in a democracy style system but did not sit well with the people as the opposition parties claimed the elections were fraudulent. Without any recourse to channel their grievances in a democratic manner, candidates such as Abdul Ghani Lone, Yasin Malik (JKLF) and Syed Salahuddin (Hizb-ul-Mujahideen) became the face of the insurgency.

Insurgency

Contrary to the popular view that the insurgents picked up their guns in response to an undemocratic political system, in no way was the movement fighting for greater democratic rights. In fact, as already shown, they had already picked up their guns before the election. Their cause was religiously and ideologically fuelled. In many ways, the ruling National Conference party had encouraged this atmosphere through a range of propaganda campaigns. Even as far back as the 1984 election, Farooq Abdullah and the National Conference deliberately tried to create revulsion against India for their political ends. These propaganda ads tried to demonstrate that India's iron fist was bleeding Kashmir. There is little evidence of Indian repression in this period and it seems likely that the National Conference was trying to use this as a way to hide the poor and corrupt performance of the State Government. Indeed, perhaps if India had done more to intervene in State affairs, it could have abated the insurgency that followed.

Role of Pakistan

Having failed to take Kashmir by force and unable to win the hearts of the Kashmiris by offering them a democracy when they had a military dictatorship, Pakistan had to woo the Kashmiris by its ideology of communalism. Before the insurgency in Kashmir began, there was an insurgency movement in neighbouring Punjab, which had also been split between India and Pakistan in 1947. That died out by the late 1980s when the Sikhs that had taken up arms against India had realized they were being used by their Pakistani sponsors and gave up arms. And so Pakistan's attention turned to Kashmir. One major reason Pakistan needed to sponsor insurgency in India was to gain intelligence on India and its army. After suffering three consecutive defeats, each time after attacking India unprovoked and by surprise, Pakistan was fearful India would be tempted to launch a pre-emptive strike against Pakistan to destroy its army to ensure Pakistan never again attempted to invade India.

The Pakistani view is that they are providing moral support to the Kashmiri People in their fight for freedom against the brutal Indian Army who commits excessive human rights abuses on the oppressed Muslims living in India, a non-Muslim country. The Indian perspective is that they are dealing with a proxy war by Pakistan who has never accepted the Kashmiri's democratic reaffirmation of their accession to India. The Kashmiris themselves are split between supporting Pakistan, India and independence. But while the Pakistanis and Indians live in relative peace, it is the Kashmiri who suffers the most while the issue remains unresolved.

The slogans: "Pakistan se kya rishta? La ilaha ilallah" (What is the relation with Pakistan? There is no God but God.) Followed by "Azaadi ka matlab kya? La ilaha ilallah" (What is the meaning of freedom? There is no God but God.) Indicate that Pakistan for Kashmiris meant Islam and freedom for Kashmiris meant Pakistan. Those who coined and floated these slogans went on to form the Jammu Kashmir Liberation Front (JKLF). The JKLF wanted to liberate Kashmir. In fact, its founder, Hashim Qureshi, later fled to Western Europe for asylum after the Pakistanis hijacked his organization and used its members to fight India as part of a religious struggle rather than for the independence he had desired. In 1990 a report showed that almost a thousand of the elite Kashmiri Muslims were on the payroll of the ISI. In 1993, with pro-independence insurgents separating from the pro-Pakistan factions, Pakistani border troops shot and killed some thirty Kashmiri youth on their way to POK for training. Slowly but surely the ties between Pakistan and the Kashmiri youth were being severed.

India's Republic Day (January 26th)

In addition to the Afghan War, local Kashmiris also watched on TV as mass movements against authoritarianism arose in East Europe and Central Asia. The most significant of these was in Romania, where on Christmas Day 1989, dictator Nicolae Ceausescu was executed. Less than a month later was to be Kashmir's turn. The Pakistan ISI got legitimacy from the Pakistani government by providing commercial and logistic transactions in Afghanistan and Kashmir. Perhaps the most significant event was the successful kidnapping of Rubaiya Sayeed, daughter of India's Home Minister, by the insurgents. In December 1989, there was a change in the federal government in India, with Rajiv Gandhi losing to VP Singh's government. Singh's deputy, the Home Minister, was Mufti Mohammad Sayeed, father of the former Chief Minister of Jammu and Kashmir, Mehbooba Mufti.

Exodus of Pandits, the Bloody Chapter of the Kashmir Conflict

One reason why Kashmiris were uncomfortable in joining Pakistan was its large non-Muslim minority, who would have no place in

Islamic Pakistan. Hence by resorting to the systematic killings of Hindus, as well as spreading fear amongst them through newspaper ads and pamphlets ordering them to leave or face death, Pakistan was able to overcome this major obstacle. With most of the Hindus gone by January 1990 and the secular-minded Muslims powerless to help them return, Pakistan was able to strengthen its claim on Kashmir. There was religious indoctrination, by misusing mosques and other available platforms, in a bid to frighten the secular Muslims.

The crimes against humanity perpetrated against the Kashmiri Pandits were tragic. While genocide occurred on a small scale, it is more likely that the objective was to drive them away rather than wipe them out. The dozens of killings and rapes were always followed by warnings for Pandits to get out, which suggest that the attacks were more as a statement rather than intent for mass genocide. But what was most surprising to Pandits was how there were large demonstrations in several Kashmiri cities by common Kashmiris with the slogan: *"Asi gachi Pakistan, batni rosin batta gatssin."* In Kashmiri, this means: "We will become a part of Pakistan, Pandit women can stay with us, but Pandit men must leave." They could understand why the extremists wanted them to leave but were shocked when the masses joined in.

The Momentum Dies

The list of innocent persons who fell prey to the bullets of terrorists is again illustrative of the Islamization drive. The victims included prominent educationists and subscribers to secular ideals. Not only Pandits, but Muslims such as Professor Mushir-ul-Haq, Vice Chancellor, Kashmir University and Maulana Mohammad Syed Masoodi, a renowned Muslim scholar were among such victims at the hands of the terrorists. Libraries of Universities were destroyed for having un-Islamic books and freedom of speech was suspended. It was clear the movement was not against India, but all things un-Islamic in their eyes.

While comparisons to Nazi Germany are fraught with danger, it does seem the population was caught in a mass hysteria that they now admit a mistake. I have heard many anecdotal stories from others who have met with Kashmiri Muslims in Kashmir who have shown much resentment in not doing anything to stop the fundamentalists. It is difficult to determine if they genuinely wanted the Islamic State of Kashmir, or if they merely followed the trend as if it were a fad.

The movement was not merely an indigenous one but influenced by Pakistan. This is corroborated by the fact that with the Pandits gone, the majority Sunni population then turned on the minority Shias. There had previously been no tension between the two groups in Kashmir. However, Pakistan has always been troubled by Sunni-Shia conflicts and thousands have been killed by each other in riots by mobs over the years. So I argue the fact that the insurgents turned on the Shias indicates they had adopted Pakistani principles rather than their own.

In 1986 Jagmohan had argued that

> "Article 370 is nothing but a breeding ground for the parasites at the heart of the paradise. It skins the poor. It deceives them with its mirage. It lines the pockets of the 'power elites'."

He explains how over the years it has become an instrument of exploitation by the ruling political elites and other vested interests in bureaucracy, business, judiciary and bar. The Article merely facilitates the growth and continuation of corrupt oligarchies. In fact, Article 370 disallows such Indian legislation such as the Wealth Tax, the Urban Ceiling Act, the Gift Tax and other beneficial laws from helping the poor Kashmiri and leaves them impoverished. There has been a complete dominance by this oligarchy, which makes up a small minority of Kashmiri Muslims. By cleverly playing India against Pakistan and using the masses as pawns in their game, they have kept a stranglehold on the running of the State.

Kashmir Muslim Bureaucracy

Top bureaucrats met in Odeon Hotel, Srinagar, in early 1949 to chart a strategy for a pro-Pakistan movement. Their immediate concern was forging separate Muslim Identity for Kashmiris. Their strategy was not to dismantle the old autocratic structure of administration but to supplant Pandit and Dogra in-service cadres by Kashmiri Muslims. Muslim educated youth were inducted into sensitive positions. Islamization of society was the basis of this thinking.

Kashmiriyat

Even some National Conference leaders had reservations about accession to India. The quest for Muslim precedence was given the name of Kashmiriyat, which came into sharp conflict with the religious minorities inside the State as well as secularist operatives of the Union Government. Article 370 of the Indian Constitution is the result of a conflict between the imperatives of Indian secularism and Muslim sub-nationalism. It continued even after 1953.

Beginning of Alienation

Family oligarchy emerged in Kashmir between 1948 and 1953. Blackmailing tactics worked. Corruption and misrule brought alienation in the trail. Those who protested were branded as pro-Pakistani. Local bureaucracy behaved arbitrarily like the area commanders of Kashmir insurgents. People identified them with Indian agents. This was the beginning of alienation of people in Kashmir.

Plebiscite

Before we talk about Plebiscite, let us understand it little better. A plebiscite or referendum is a type of voting, or of proposing laws. Some definitions of 'plebiscite' suggest that it is a type of vote to change the Constitution or government of a country. Others define it as the opposite. Australia defines 'referendum' as a vote to change the Constitution and 'plebiscite' as a vote that does not affect the Constitution. There are two types of result. Mandatory – meaning the government must do what the result says. Advisory – meaning the result of the vote is only to help the government make the final choice. It usually depends on the country's history and Constitution what sort of referendum/plebiscite is used. In Switzerland, a referendum is usually mandatory, because the people are seen as the source of the government's mandate (power) to govern.

In the United Kingdom referendum have only been advisory, because the government says that the people elected to Parliament make the decisions. The referendum on the independence of Scotland was an exception. It was legally binding, but it was not a referendum of the UK electorate. It was restricted to present residents of Scotland. An example of a proposed plebiscite was the 2011 decision by Greek Prime Minister George Papandreou to let the Greek people vote on whether the heavily indebted nation would accept a €130 billion bailout package from the European Union. The idea shocked eurozone nations, as a 'No' vote could mean Greece defaulting on its national debt and leaving the European Union and the eurozone. However, the vote was cancelled.

Another example was the voting on the European Constitution in 2005. The vote took place in some countries. France and Netherlands had a referendum on the subject. In both States, the voters said 'No' to the proposal and no Constitution was made. The separate simultaneous referendums held on 24 April 2004 in the Turkish Republic of Northern Cyprus and the Republic of Cyprus on the comprehensive settlement plan of the UN Secretary-General provides yet another example of such a vote. The Plan was approved in the

Turkish Cypriot referendum by 65%, while it was rejected in the Greek Cypriot referendum by 75%.

Many political problems can be solved by asking the people their opinion because the supporters of the argument will be forced to accept the decision of the people. However:

- It is feared that the electorate do not have sufficient political knowledge to truly understand what they are voting for.
- Philosophers Plato and Madison thought voters are too easily persuaded by their internal feelings of matter instead of focusing on the good of the nation. That is to say, they vote selfishly.

Nehru's commitment to a plebiscite, which he had clearly and forcefully stated in writing to the UN Commission for India and Pakistan in the context of UNCIP Resolution of April 13, 1948, meant expression of free will through elected representatives. But with that, a negative consciousness dawned upon the Kashmiris that a factor more powerful than India served a cue for the choice of reversal of existing relationship with India. Now the problem with Indian democracy is Nehru as a Prime Minister of free India never consulted his council of ministers or got Parliament to approve this resolution of taking Kashmir case to UN. It is the generosity of the various Indian governments of the day from different political spectrum to keep honouring the international commitment agreed by one individual.

Many in India have questioned this approach and with 70% youth population asking how can one individual take such a decision in the democratic system, time is not far when India will all together stop going to UN or even bothering to acknowledge Plebiscite. World's 3rd largest army with $ 25 billion-plus annual defence budget and with most of the state of art weapons in its armoury, will not be overly worried about views which goes against its national interests nor will be too bothered of any potential sanctions. Current Islamic fundamentalism has also convinced India that it has to fight its battle, rest of the world will continue doing lip services. It's opponent, 1/7th times small continues giving Nuclear threats. It knows it has to live in this region.

USA Influence

In May 1953, Foster Dulles met with Nehru. The Weekly Message from Delhi reported that Dulles had put forward a plan for a tri-zonal division of Kashmir with a zone each going to India and Pakistan, the valley being either 'internationalized' for a certain period till a plebiscite was held under the UN control or being ruled by a semi-independent government. Nehru sounded Mohammed Ali Bogra, the Pakistani Prime Minister. Both asserted that Kashmir would not be allowed to become another Korea. Their joint assertion was a rebuff to the imperialists. Nimitz prepared to resign. Under the agreement, an impartial plebiscite administrator was to be appointed by the J&K government. Within a month, Pakistani Prime Minister resiled and demanded that plebiscite is held under the aegis of the UN. It seems that external forces had lobbied well. Soon the US began exploring a military agreement with Pakistan.

Accord of 1975

Plebiscite Front had kept the secessionist sentiment alive in Kashmir. It exposed post-1947 generation of Kashmiri Muslims to the Pakistan ideology. The question may be asked: why could pro-Pak groups not emerge in a big way at this point? The answer is:

(a) Sheikh Abdullah had a long legacy of anti-Pakistan posture.
(b) Plebiscite Front had appropriated other platforms of pro-Pak groups.

By 1972, realization dawned in Plebiscite Front that subversion from outside would not work. Hence subversion from inside was to be tried. GM Sadiq's regime had initiated liberalization policy more an antidote to the hegemonic regime of the Sheikh and arbitrary rule of Bakshi. The ground was prepared for 1975 Accord. 1977 elections were termed by the National Conference as a referendum on the status of Kashmir. National Conference cultivated secessionists selectively and promised to open Rawalpindi road. Its moves were subtle – rock salt, green kerchief, etc. It spoke in prattles of rock salt, *shalwar* and *kameez* and green handkerchief. Dressed in flowing *kurta* and *shalwar*, the Sheikh offered namaz in his secretariat office.

Onwards of Accord

This was ushered in an era of diatribes and antics of National Conference. It claimed that the right of self-determination had never been ruled out. However, it said strategic re-adjustment was worked out. Lack of ideological cohesion in National Conference now forced its downslide. It had started dilatory and divisive tactics on the finality of accession. 1979 is a watershed in the growth of the subversive movement in Kashmir. ZA Bhutto had pledged to fight for a thousand years for the cause of 'oppressed Kashmiri Muslims'. Bhutto's execution unleashed mad frenzy against the Jamaat-e-Islami cadres in Kashmir. Zia had called them the progeny of the Brahmins.

But sooner than later, Kashmiris changed the trend and now the erstwhile *'Zia kodeh'* (the whip wielder) of their description became "Mard-i-Momin Mard-i-Haq, Ziau'l Haq Ziau'l Haq" (the faithful among the men, the truthful Zia). Other slogans reflected religious ties with Pakistan. Thus Pakistan for Kashmiris meant Islam and freedom for Kashmiris meant Pakistan. Those who coined and floated these slogans went on to form the 'secular' Jammu Kashmir Liberation Front (JKLF). Curiously, Kashmiri Muslims seldom tried to look up for democratic and progressive forces in Pakistan to draw inspiration from them.

ISI and Istekhbarat Comes together with a Plan Named 'Greater Muslim Kashmir'

In 1970, the plan of 'Greater Muslim Kashmir' was drawn jointly by ISI and the Saudi intelligence (Istekhbarat) at International Islamic Foundation Movement (Rabitau'l Islam) in Saudi Arabia. Ar-Rabita has over a hundred branches spread all over the world. It was concretized into what came to be known as Operation Topac. The Rabita has been given the Wahhabi orientation, and Dr Ayub Thakur (in London) directed the movement in Kashmir. Greater Muslim Kashmir, to which Selig Harrison refers, envisaged not the only secession of Kashmir from India but also incorporates grand design to destabilize India through ethnic and communal separatist movements carried on through terror and subversion. Saudi role in 1979 mob violence in Kashmir may not be known precisely. Grapevine has it that Saudis played a mediator role between the National Conference leadership and different fundamentalist and separatist lobbies in Kashmir. Part of the exercise was holding of international Islamic conferences in Srinagar for the first time in which important Saudi 'religious personalities and scholars' were invited.

The real purpose was to inspire Muslim solidarity and jihad against India. In 1981, the sister of the Saudi king paid two successive visits to Kashmir. The chief of the Saudi intelligence stayed with a local carpet dealer in Jawaharnagar, Srinagar in 1982. A few details of this story were covered in an issue of the journal titled *Probe*. Outsiders do not know what transpired in the meeting among Saudis, National Conference and the Jamaatis. As a result, Jamaat stopped criticizing the Sheikh. The government in New Delhi turned a blind eye to the funds funnelled through a section of National Conference leadership to various subversive and fundamentalist groups functioning against national interests.

As the honeymooning proceeded, Jamaatis became emboldened. They began attacks on Communist workers, non-Muslim business establishments and Hindu worshipping places. A group of 50 Jamaatis attacked Harkishan Singh Surjeet, the Secretary-General of CPI(M) in Srinagar in June 1982. The National Conference government took no action, Surjeet is reported to have expressed reservations about Article 370 - the cornerstone of the left perception on India. Surjeet was asked why he did not take up the Jamaat issue with the Centre. He said that would provoke Hindu reaction. This is the opportunistic antics of the left in Indian politics. Later Surjeet begged the Government of India to treat 'secularist' JKLF differently from 'communal' Hizbul Mujahideen. It is JKLF whose criminals killed Abdus Sattar Ranjoor, the CPM leader of Kashmir. While CPM spoke about autonomy and right of self-determination, it never said a word about three hundred thousand Kashmiri Pandits extirpated from their homeland and now living as internally displaced persons. National Conference patronized the Jamaat to the extent that the then Vice-Chancellor of Kashmir University, Rais Ahmad, was physically assaulted for his progressive views.

1980, saw a beeline of American diplomats and officials coming to Kashmir. Rockefeller visited in 1980 and had talks with the Sheikh. His mission supplemented the liaison established between the Sheikh and the Saudis. Then came William Saxebe, the US Ambassador in New Delhi. There was the further exchange of ideas on Greater Muslim Kashmir idea. President Reagan dispatched his close aide and his roving ambassador Charlton Heston, an actor colleague of his Hollywood days to Kashmir. Heston's visit was completely blacked out by the local press. An obscure weekly published from Calcutta took notice of the event. To alley suspecting eyes, Heston stayed at Nishat on the northern bank of the Dal Lake in the guesthouse belonging to a non-Muslim. The result of the visit of these high ups was forging unity between different elite groups of professionals in Kashmir Muslim society - university teachers, lawyers, engineers, doctors particularly those who had connections in Saudi Arabia, Iran and Libya, a powerful and well-knit section of the State Muslim bureaucracy, local political leadership, etc. One regional English daily wrote in 1990 that the ISI had nearly one thousand people among the elite of Srinagar on its payroll.

Sheikh's Antics

In his will, the Sheikh said that his dead body is consigned to the waters of the Arabian Sea because Kashmir was an enslaved territory. Why did he not choose the Indian Ocean, which is far bigger and deeper than the Arabian Sea? This was the Sheikh after signing the Accord. His speech at Ganderbal in 1979 and his last one made at Hazratbal shrine in 1982 were fully besmeared with communal tinge and even moderate Muslims were greatly incensed by these. By 1980, campaign for Islamization of Kashmir had begun with full force. The Sheikh changed the names of about 2500 villages from their original to Islamic names. It was to take divorce from the pre-Islamic history and tradition of Kashmir. Pakistani historians were imitated.

The Hindus of Kashmir who were the descendants of ancient Kashmiri race were puzzled. A vicious campaign against the Indian army and the local Hindus was also floated. The local Hindus came to be called the *mukhbir* or informers. This is how the Sheikh has characterized them in his autobiography *Aatish-e-Chinar*. In July 1980, local police contrived a clash between the local civilians of Srinagar and the army personnel. The National Conference workers set on fire some shops of the Hindus in Amira Kadal locality. The Jamaatis compared this minor incident to the Soviet intervention in Afghanistan.

Sheikh Abdullah's Death Creates a Vacuum

With the Sheikh's death, secessionist leadership emerged in full force. Common man developed the hatred for the Sheikh and National Conference leaders and their clannish corruption. Omar Mukhtar film ran for hundreds of shows. Elite and secessionists drew a parallel from the film. A book *Yih Kis Ka Khun Hai Kaun Mara* by Shabnam Qayyum attacked the Sheikh's legacy. Resettlement Bill was floated. ISI was in close liaison with National Conference. Pakistan apprehended unrest among the Kashmiris who migrated to POK. It wanted their return to Kashmir valley to get rid of them. Its other objective was changing the demographic complexion of Jammu.

Sensing Indira Gandhi's reaction against the Resettlement Bill, Dr Farooq adopted more confrontational posture. He held out threats to the numerically negligible community of Pandits in an election campaign in Habba Kadal constituency with Pandit concentration. This he did in spite of the dilution of this constituency, what we call gerrymandering. He accused them of looking to the Indian army for security forgetting he did the same thing. Indian army had guarded his father's family in Bhopal when the armed tribal marauders attacked Kashmir in October 1947 and he had secretly evacuated them. Dr Farooq is said to have hobnobbed with the insurgent elements in the Punjab including Bhindranwale and took no action against the hooligans who created a scene when the West Indies came to play a cricket match in Srinagar.

NC-JKLF Interface

Some National Conference cadres maintained links with JKLF from the times of Al-Fath under the patronage of Plebiscite Front. Azam Inquilabi, a known separatist leader, had termed Dr Farooq Abdullah as 'our senior leader'. In Muzaffarabad, Farooq had taken a vow to liberate Kashmir from Indian occupation. In 1974, some of the top leaders of Kashmir Liberation Force (KLF) visited Srinagar and in the company of Dr Farooq Abdullah addressed a rally in Lal Chowk chanting the slogan *"choon desh myoon desh Kashmir desh Kashmir desh"*. It was a subtle way of conveying the message that Muslims on both sides of the LoC considered United Kashmir as their homeland. POK people, grossly discriminated against by Pakistan, are enamoured of United 'Independent Kashmir' slogan. With a strong diaspora in the UK, they are financing the movement.

The Mirpuris have made Chinar leaf their national insignia without ever having to see what a Chinar tree looks like. They ask their women to wear Kashmiri dress, but Pakistan government has imposed a ban on attiring themselves the Kashmiri way. Maqbul Bhat, the executed founder of JKLF, stayed in a guest house near Srinagar planning insurgency. National Conference cadres would meet him often. Local Muslim elite openly spoke of secession, Jamaat-e-Islami told people in villages to purchase arms in place of luxury goods. Late Ghani Lone had told a rally in Kupwara that Muslim women should sell their jewellery and gold and use the money for purchasing guns.

Preparing for ideology

Incriminating literature appeared on the stands in Srinagar. Some government officials distributed copies of a pamphlet titled Tragedy of Kashmir. Muhammad Yusuf Saraf's two-volume work *Kashmiris Fight for Freedom* was smuggled into the valley in large numbers. It also focused on earlier terrorist movements. *On Guerrilla War* by Che Guevara suddenly appeared on the bookstalls in Srinagar. A fiction insurrection titled *Assignment in Kashmir* and authored by Aamir Ali described the involvement of two Swedish persons in smuggling of arms into Kashmir for Kashmiri guerrillas for the separatist movement. A newsman wrote that Kashmiri boys were going to Pakistan Occupied Kashmir (POK) for training in arms. He was sacked.

Aatish-e-Chinar - Sheikh's biographer calls Hindus, 'Spies of India' - the compiler of the Sheikh's autobiography, later on, to be rewarded with a berth in the upper house, used venomous idiom against the Kashmiri Hindus calling them informers or spies of India. Sahitya Akademi, the highest awarding national organization, awarded the book. Maligning the minority did not move the National Minority Commission. Congress workers blackened the face of a senior official of Sahitya Academy for awarding a Punjabi book *Janan di Rat* alleging the author had lionized the assailants of Indira Gandhi. Ministry of Human Resource moved quickly to ask for the review of the book and censured the concerned official. Not a single political worker, a single newspaper asked Sahitya Academy why it awarded the biography of the Sheikh when he had so forcefully and vehemently maligned a minuscule religious minority.

Training Camps

Sikh separatists had established a training camp for their cadres in Shajamarg, Kashmir in 1984. Farooq government kept it under wraps. Attacks on Amirakadal temple stirred no reaction in his government. At Tulamula, on the occasion of Jyeshta Ashtami festival of the Hindus, Farooq told the Assembly that Bhindranwale was the 11th guru. In 1983, GoI received reports of Kashmiri youth returning home after receiving training somewhere on the border. This belies the argument that the cause of militancy lay in the rigged elections of 1986-87. The methodology of bringing down Farooq government was a failure.

Jamaat-e-Islami (JI)

During GM Shah's tenure, two battalions of Jamaat-e-Islami were raised to augment State police force. It became the crucial element in massive internal subversion and a communal wing of the Hizbul Mujahideen. Shah had no popular base and hobnobbed with fundamentalist elements for support. Jamaatis were recruited as teachers in a large number. Shah did not fight Farooq politically but aligned himself with communal forces like Qazi Nisar of Anantnag. Political rivalry between GM Shah and local Congress leadership resulted in Congress under the presidency of Mufti Mohammad Sayeed inciting communal riots in Anantnag in 1986.

Ugly Side of the Flawed Kashmiriyat

The ideology of Greater Muslim Kashmir was given the name of Kashmiriyat. Few Kashmiri Muslim scholars wanted Urdu as the official language. The elite wanted to fraternize with the Pakistanis who had accepted Urdu as the national language. Nobody told Kashmiri Muslims that Pakistan meant Punjabi hegemony and Punjabi language was the language of hegemonists and not Urdu. Urdu would bring them closer to the Mohajirs and not Punjabis. And Mohajir is pitted against the Punjabi. Most of the Muslim children born after 1970 adopted Pakistani cricket players' names or Arabic names. This was the Kashmiriyat of the elite. On the one hand, local bureaucracy asked for huge development packages and on the other it foisted alienation.

Kashmiri Muslim youth changed their lifestyle. Trekking, playing cricket in streets and villages and towns became common. Trucks driven mostly by Sikh drivers carried suspicious contents and dumped these at identified places at night. A large number of brick kilns surfaced in the border areas. Owners were given hundreds of thousands of rupees as industrial loans. These were used as dumping grounds. President Zia of Pakistan paid a visit to Jaipur to witness cricket match. This was an indirect message to Kashmiri youth to prepare for better physical fitness. Bureaucrats and big business class formed nexus obstructing the opportunities of common Kashmiris. Training, employment, promotions, lucrative jobs, contracts, etc went to the wards of the elite. Blackmailing by the bureaucracy and the political elite continued at a high rate. Whenever local leadership came into conflict with the Central leadership, it brought in the element of religion.

Erosion of National Conference

National Conference adopted a dubious way in Kashmir but a different stance beyond the mountain range of the Pir Panchal. National Conference began losing the ground. Command went into second and third rung of leaders. They were not committed. It was crude demagogy, browbeating nationalists and Indians through Kashmiriyat. Fratricidal war paved the way for malevolent elements to become brokers. JI and Peoples League pushed their activists into National Conference through Youth National Conference. From this illegal marriage of the Peoples League, Jamaat-e-Islami and the National Conference emerged the so-called secular offspring called Kashmir Liberation Front (later on Jammu Kashmir Liberation Front). Others also joined it later on. The Peoples' United Front of Maulavi Abbas Ansari had earlier been Muslim United Front (MUF). It comprised two streams: Jamaat-e-Islami and non-Jamaatis. Their ideology was Islamization and Muslim communalism respectively. At times they locked horns. At present, the conflict between JKLF and Hizbul-Mujahideen (HUM) – if there is any conflict – is not between secularism and communalism but between the shades of Muslim communalism. Most of the Jamaatis are important JKLF members. Ghulam Qadir Wani, a hard core Jamaati, was the mastermind behind the JKLF. All earlier killings of Kashmiri Pandits were carried out by the JKLF.

Rigged Election of 1986-87

Many National Conference workers expecting a mandate from the party were refused and joined the ranks of the MUF and later on JKLF. Sons of Congress and Plebiscite Front workers were to be found in the ranks of HuM. Gradually through political diatribe like the philosophy of living with honour and dignity (*izzat wa abru ka muqam*) got exposed, thus coming closer to ghettoizing confines of the Muslim sub-nationalism, patronizing regressive bureaucracy, defending its myopic vision, withholding the Kashmiris from joining national mainstream through the creation of fantasies like 'Third Nation' etc, the National Conference contributed liberally to the process of alienation of Kashmiris from Indian national mainstream. After 1979, National Conference never confronted JI's growing secessionism. National Conference's administrative mechanism became susceptible to corruption, nepotism, favouritism and inefficiency. The nexus of bureaucracy, business class or the elite and politicians with vested interests created conditions for subversion from within. It was heading for the fascist movement. National Conference began a negative campaign under the slogan of Kashmiriyat with undertones of sectarian Muslim identity. This alienated even the Shias besides the Gujjars and the non-Muslims of Kashmir, Jammu and Ladakh.

Jamaat and Insurgency

ISI wanted the JI to become the main instrument to take up the secession. Jamaat infiltrated all organizations. It had credibility among the masses and started militancy through non-Jamaat organization JKLF. It needed a cover. Jamaat-e-Islami has created a massive structure over three decades for indoctrination of Muslim children with fundamentalist ideology. Muslim elite became a support to the Jamaatis and the ISI in Kashmir. The aim was twofold – (a) creating theocratic polity and (b) merging with Pakistan. Maudoodi believed in Islamic *ummah* (community) and not nationalities. But when UP Muslim feudal joined hands with Punjabi feudal, Mowdoodi had to be silent. He had first opposed the creation of Pakistan. Jinnah had never envisaged a theocratic Pakistani Muslim State.

JI Kashmir was independent of JI of India, a subtle way of saying that it did not accept the finality of accession. Founded in Shupian in 1947, it was banned in Kashmir for the third time during the Governorship of Jagmohan. Earlier Bakhshi had utilized their support to suppress pro-Sheikh elements. Mir Qasim lifted the ban and again used them. He got five of his partymen belonging to Sadiq group (Congress I) defeated at the hustings. The JI candidate standing against him withdrawn and in return, JI was given five Assembly seats. Thus JI established links with the administrative cadres. Mir Qasim succumbed and handed over power to the Sheikh. Incidentally, Qasim's son, a doctor in the USA, is an active worker for the secession of Kashmir. Qasim facilitated the work of Jamaat. By 1970, the young generation of the Jamaatis responded. It had its schooling in *dargahs* (religious seminaries). It talked of Nizam or socio-political system. Jamaat expanded its influence in bureaucracy, secretariat, police force, Home Guard, Bar Association, Soura Medical Instate, Muslim medicos, schools and colleges in Kashmir and Doda, Hindustan Machine Tool Factory, etc. Hindustan Machine Tool Factory and Kashmir University campus were its important centre of activity.

Islami Jamiat-e-Talaba (IJT)

In autumn 1977, the students' wing of Jamaat-e-Islami called IJT, was created. Its public pronouncements were patently secessionist. The State Government took no steps to curb it. The Afghan guerrilla documentaries were screened in the house of the Chief Minister. Ashraf Sahrai, its founder President, spoke in the first annual session in July 1978 in Srinagar and compared Kashmir struggle with liberation movement elsewhere. In 1986, the number of its basic members rose to ten thousand. It ran 300 *madrasas* (religious seminaries) where indoctrination was the rule.

Iranian Link

Iranian clerics took care not to give sectarian colour to the concept of export of Islamic revolution. Moderates like Ayatollah Taloghani and Ayatollah Shariatmadari were sidelined and extremists like Ayatollah Mohtashami were catapulted into the seats of power. Iranian clerics courted Kashmiri Muslim youth. JI liked Khomeini type of uprising in Kashmir. Khomeini's descent was traced to Kashmir. Tajamulu'l-Islam appeared as a firebrand of JT and preached for an armed insurgency in Kashmir. Police wanted him, but the bureaucracy shielded him. He escaped to Iran via Nepal. The Iranian Ambassador in New Delhi prayed in Jama Masjid of Srinagar, traditionally a stronghold of the Sunnis who did not allow Shias to enter it.

Allahwale Movement

Ahl-e-Hadith (Traditionalists) active in Kashmir for more than a century wanted to purge Islam of indigenous elements. It meant freeing popular Islam in the valley of its pre-Islamic roots. Bakhshi Ghulam Mohammad, Kashmir Chief Minister, believed in the Rishi (mystic) tradition or indigenous tradition of Kashmir. However, as the concept of Greater Muslim Kashmir developed, the resultant social-religious schism posed a big challenge. Allahwale were to counterpoise a section of Kashmiri Muslims that believed in popular Islam with rich indigenous content and tradition. Allahwale, Ahle Hadith and JI worked along common lines. Ahle Hadith worked among the elitist group, Allahwale with the common people because their idiom and lifestyle were like those of the common people.

It is the best-organized fundamentalist movement with branches in Africa, Europe and Pakistan and also in Russia and China. They undertook to do the remaining work of the Saudis after the patch up in Kashmir. To allay the fears of the Central Government they posed as religious and good Muslim. Tarjumanu'l-Huq was the newspaper they published. It attracted even doctors and top bureaucrats who would take leave and join its *tableeghi* (propagation) programme. After 1980, Allahwale spread out in entire Kashmir adopting a low profile. Silently they preached of drawing a line between *kufr* (heresy) and *iman* (faith). The communal divide was brought about carefully. Allahwale stuck to the rural base. Majority of Kashmiri militants come from the rural Kashmir. The symbols of independence give them the upward position in the social hierarchy and status ladder. Before 1988 they had organized three conferences in the valley. They had strict instructions to campaign strongly in North Kashmir, especially in Baramulla and Kupwara districts. This was the time when the 'Operation Topac' was to be launched. Many mosques sprang. The Baramulla mosque functioned as the zonal headquarters of Allahwale in northern India.

In 1988, around the time of launching Operation Topac, Allahwale held a big convention in Idgah in Srinagar. The Allahwale movement has its centre at Aligarh Muslim University.

Jamiat-e-Talaba

It concentrated on non-elitist sections. Its headquarters is in Batmaloo, Srinagar. Its leadership formed the core of JKLF. It held weekly meetings almost in every educational institution. People's League was its sister organization with leaders like Maqbul Bhat and Mohammad Altaf or Azam Inquilabi (also a Jamaati). On November 1, 1982, Mahaz-e-Azadi (Plebiscite Front), People's League and Jamiat-e-Talaba (JT) met to discuss how anti-India activities could be enlarged. Earlier on October 20, Muslim Conference called by Inquilabi had passed a resolution, which asked for implementation of the UN resolutions on Kashmir. It asked for acceptance of cultural demands of setting up an Islamic university, ban on co-education in the State, teaching of Arabic from the primary to post-graduate level, banning of cinemas, indecent ads and liquor shops.

They agreed to form United Liberation Front to fight against India. Some university teachers as members of JT asked for implementation of Sharia law in Kashmir. Interestingly, while JT demanded a ban on cinema, Omar Mukhtar film went on for hundreds of shows because it showed imaginary Muslim mujahid fighting a jihad. JT secretly distributed the guidelines of Pakistan's action plan on Kashmir. A booklet titled *Hizb-e-Islami* was published by it containing this confidential scheme. After giving the highlights of the insurgency plan, it concluded by saying,

> "Islam is our aim, the *Quran* is our constitution, jihad is our path, war till victory, God is Great."

Hizb-ul-Mujahideen (HuM)

JI formed its armed wing called HuM. It also formed women's wing called Dukhtaran-i-Millat. In the first phase, about 500 activists went over to receive training. It concentrated on the State police organization. Some well-trained commandos in the State Police organization joined HuM. Governor Jagmohan dismissed some of them. Earlier three JI MUF leaders had resigned on the understanding that Pakistan was about to attack and they would head the government in Kashmir. Initial killings of the Kashmiri Pandits were undertaken by the JKLF. But after 1990, most of the killings of Pandits took place at the hands of JUM, which now wanted to eliminate all potential opponents, not only the Hindu minority. The killing of National Conference leaders became their concern. Mir Mustafa, Maulana Masoodi, Molavi Muhammad Farooq and others fell victims to their bullets.

It is the best-armed outfit with a regular supply of arms and ammunition from Pakistan. Logistical directions come from ISI and military intelligence. Afghan mujahideen are also represented in its ranks. Top leadership has Pakistani commandos as their bodyguards. Sudanese have also joined the outfit. Kashmiris receive training in Afghan training camps, particularly in Khost. Some died during the American attack on Osama's camp. Three HUM militants captured by the Indian security forces said they were trained at Eram Park near Meshad in Iran. JI split was part of its tactics. The so-called moderate wing joined the State administrative cadres. Moderates initiated a debate that Islam is incomplete without a government. Hard core Jamaatis say their destination is not only Kashmir but also Balkanization of India.

American Perception Before and After 9/11

Before the implosion of the Soviet Union, Americans concern was about the containment of communism. America was never reconciled to Non-Aligned Movement, as that would neutralize the Muslim support. Pakistan suits the US for a specific role in the region and even globally. However, after the Soviet implosion situation had changed. America did not commit to fighting Islamic fundamentalism as part of the new world order based on what they call pluralism, democracy and human rights. Expediency decides her priorities. Anglo-American group had two priorities in Kashmir. One is keeping a regional conflict alive albeit below its flash-point level and the second to carve one more Muslim segment on the Indian subcontinent complementary to their sphere of influence. China and Central Asia are two regions not far away from Kashmir.

On disclosures made by the sections of Press about Iran's involvement in Kashmir uprising, the US looked with some concern at Islamic Fundamentalist Kashmir. It is interesting to note that personalities like Senator Cranston and Talbot took special interest to warn India about the implications of Iranian involvement in the imbroglio but not on Saudi role.

Aftermath 9/11, USA agreed that the terrorists from Pakistani soil infiltrated into Kashmir. In the course of dealing with Pakistan in the matter of containment of al-Qaeda and Taliban from spreading into Pakistan, the US talked to Gen Musharraf that cross-border infiltration should be stopped. General Musharraf, in turn, said he had made no such commitment.

Russia Blocked UN Veto #100 on Kashmir

Russia's 100th veto in the United Nations Security Council was in support of India's position on Kashmir. The veto of June 22, 1962 "smashed an Irish resolution" and dealt a body blow to the West's aim to pries the disputed territory from India's control and hand it to Pakistan. What infuriated the western bloc was that the 99th Russian veto, in December 1961, had also been in India's favour. That veto was on a resolution calling for a ceasefire when "India blitzed Portuguese-held Goa." The mood in the western bloc was, therefore, vehemently anti-India. Russia was portrayed in the Western media as a roadblock to the UN's functioning.

The Irish resolution, which urged India and Pakistan to enter direct negotiations for settlement of their dispute over Kashmir, was supported by 7 Security Council members. These included the other four permanent members – the US, France, UK and China (at that time the Republic of China, not the People's Republic of China) – plus three non-permanent members, Ireland, Chile and Venezuela. Russian delegate Platon Dmitrievich Morozov voiced a loud "nyet" (no) after the Indian delegation declared the Irish resolution unacceptable. Romania, a Russian ally, opposed while Ghana and Egypt abstained.

Adlai Stevenson, the chief American delegate, condemned Russia's latest 'paralysing action' in the UN. Morozov loudly interrupted his speech three times, saying,

> "These are Cold War manoeuvres in their worst manifestations. The right of veto is not a bad thing. It keeps certain powers in their place. It compels them to take their feet off the table when they put them there in proper American fashion."

During their 1955 visit to India, which laid the foundations for an extended partnership between the two countries, the Soviet leaders Khrushchev and Bulganin travelled to Srinagar.

In a public reception there, Khrushchev proclaimed that "Moscow was just across the border and if there is any trouble in Kashmir, Delhi should just give a shout. Moscow kept its word and exercised its veto in the UN Security Council to block Anglo-American moves on Kashmir in the 1950s." The Russian vetoes did the job of pushing the West back on the Kashmir issue. However, India got the Kashmir bogey off its back at the UN only when it stopped caring and treated the resolutions with the contempt they deserved. Here's how India's new Kashmir strategy at the UN panned out. Three years after Russia's 100th veto, Kashmir was once again the focus of world attention when Pakistan violated the ceasefire and invaded the Indian side of the territory. When India declared war and as its army rolled into Lahore in September 1965, Pakistani Foreign Minister (and later Prime Minister) Zulfikar Ali Bhutto raised the Kashmir issue at the United Nations. In response, the Indian delegation walked out of the Security Council.

The world was stunned as it did not believe the followers of Gandhi would take such a step. This was because until then (to borrow the words of a well-known analyst), the strategy was that if India was slapped on both the cheeks, India felt bad it did not have a third cheek to show. K Natwar Singh, former Indian Foreign Minister (who was posted at India's permanent mission at the UN), said India's walkout was a 'turning point' for the UN on Kashmir.

> "As a result, there was hardly any reference to Kashmir for the next few decades at the UNSC, barring one resolution after the

> 1971 War. The Soviet Union helped, by vetoing many of the resolutions Pakistan tried to push and after the Shimla Agreement of 1972, which committed to a bilateral resolution, the UNSC references to Kashmir ended entirely."

The figures back up Singh's claim. Between 1948 and 1965 the Security Council passed 23 resolutions on Kashmir. After India's 1965 walkout, the UN body passed just one resolution (Resolution 307, December 21, 1971), calling on India and Pakistan to "respect the ceasefire line" after the Bangladesh war. India seems to have taken Singh's advice to heart. Well, this was cold war era and India was a very close ally of Soviet Union.

The Cold War is an ancient history now. New equations are constantly forming and yesterday's foes are becoming today's frontline States against terror, despite the irony of it all. With America withholding military and economic aid, Pakistani Generals – who form the deep State that runs the country – are interested in building bridges with Russia. It is Pakistan's strategic location – providing easy access to the Silk Route, West Asia and Central Asia – that has made it attractive to the world's leading powers. Russia is no different. There may be Kremlin insiders who believe normalizing relations with Pakistan doesn't hurt. Whether it will push India even closer to the US is something these diplomats should ask themselves. At any rate, India's best strategy against Pakistan – or for that matter any country – at the UN is to ignore the body's resolutions. It should take a leaf out of Israel's book. Tel Aviv is one of the most isolated countries (in terms of the number of friends) plus it has faced innumerable resolutions passed against it. Its response has been to send more and more settlers into the disputed territories. This approach has worked wonders. When was the last time you read about a UN resolution against Israel?

In September 2017, it was junior diplomat Eenam Gambhir who responded to Pakistan Prime Minister Nawaz Sharif's speech on Kashmir. Dismissing Sharif's speech as 'a long tirade', she labelled Pakistan as the 'Ivy League of Terrorism'. I was outside the UN when Sharif was making his presentation with the Kashmiris and Baloch people protesting against Pakistani premier. India should stop going to UN on Kashmir, but rather go as the solution provider for any other global problems; it is a way to the big nation and an emerging power to be affected by continuous Kashmir quagmire. It also has to see that it always does not end up standing against the USA for all UN driven resolutions. It has to learn to give and take and stand with the strategic partner. Gone are the days of neutrality or non-aligned stand. As a maturing power, India should learn to shrug off irritants. Possession is nine-tenths of the law and India holds the best and largest parts of Kashmir and Ladakh plus Jammu.

Hindus Hardline Views

"Muslims are bullies and Hindus cowards," Mahatma Gandhi once said, though he was not a Hindu hardliner. He was right - at least about Hindus: there has been in the past 700 years since the first invasions started, very few Shivaji Maharajs and Rana Prataps to fight the rule of the foreign invaders, or hardly any Rani of Jhansis to stand against the humiliating colonial yoke of the British.

Because of Nehru's absurd and naive 'Hindi-Chini bhai-bhai' policy, the Indian army was routed in 1962 by the Chinese, a humiliation which rankles even today. Beijing is still able to hoodwink Indian politicians, by pretending it has good intentions, while quietly giving nuclear know-how to Pakistan, as well as the missiles to carry their atomic warheads to Indian cities, arm separatists groups in the north-east and continuing to claim Arunachal Pradesh or Sikkim. In Kashmir, the land of yogis, where Hindu *sadhus* and sages have meditated for 5000 years, Hindus have been chased out of their ancestral home by death, terror and intimidation: there were 25% of Hindus at the beginning of the century in the Kashmir Valley (only Valley not the entire J&K State) and hardly a handful today.

It is not for us to condone violence: but how long can the Hindus be the butt of killings and persecution, be sacrificial lambs that meekly go to slaughter? For in a way, Gandhi might have been correct, Muslims are bullies, they have bullied India and they continue to bully majority population of India, as Pakistan demonstrates time and again by shelling in Kashmir, which make the other powers apply pressure on India to 'negotiate' with Pakistan. Remember how Musharraf deceived New Delhi by receiving a well-meaning, but naive Vajpayee at Lahore, while its soldiers were quietly invading the heights above Kargil.

When Gandhi said they were bullies, he was very nice or very polite. Forget about the millions of Hindus killed during the five centuries of Muslim invasions, probably the worst Holocaust in world history; forget about the hundreds of thousands of Hindu temples razed to the ground, whose destruction - whatever the "secular" friends say - was carefully recorded by the Muslims themselves, because they were proud of it (see Aurangzeb's chronicles); forget about the millions of Hindus forcibly converted to

Islam and who sadly are now rallying under a banner, a language, a scripture which have nothing to do with their own ethos and culture.

Tomorrow, Pakistan might wage, with the blessing of the Muslims world (OIC group), the ultimate jihad against India ('Ghazwa-e-Hind'), which if necessary, will utilize the ultimate weapon, Islamic (Nuclear) Bomb and by wrongly interpreting the *Holy Quran* message "Choose not thy friends among the Infidels till they forsake their homes and the way of idolatry. If they return to paganism then take them whenever you find them and kill them", there will be no one but Hindus themselves to be blamed. Strength respects strength.

Does Islam Allow any Room for Secularism, Does Islam Believe in Nation-State?

Lots of Hindus and other non-Muslim communities think that Islam due to its very nature cannot be secular and does not respect a Nation-State concept and hence 'Nation State's rule of law' *vs* 'Sharia law' confuses many. There are 50 plus Muslim countries where non-Muslims cannot build temples and have to live as second-class citizens when compared to Muslims and the Sharia law is applied to them in case of blasphemy, etc. Now when Muslims are in minority status in other democratic countries, they eloquently demand the rule of law, the Constitution of land, etc to protect their minority status but do not give similar treatment to others when they are in the majority. This is not writer's view but has been mentioned by many non-Muslim friends. In case of India accepting a uniform civil court, it is made into interference in one's religious belief, but there is dead silence on the same thing when non-Muslims claim similar rights in a Muslim majority country or region. This is a controversial view but needs to be examined with unbiased mind if there is any merit to this allegation.

Secularism

Modern Secularism is a philosophy rooted in the 16th century when European Protestants struggled against the rule of the exploitative Catholic Church. These dissenters were not without religion; they simply wanted social, political and economic freedoms. Secularization is the result of the social and political processes that followed, influenced by rising capitalism and scientific discoveries. The tumults of secularization spanned a century, up until the Treaty of Westphalia (1648).

The distancing of State, from religion does not mean, the absence of religion or anti-religion. It means rearranging State laws and policies so that they are neutral and treat citizens of all faiths without prejudice. Secularity - the principles of secularism - means that religion should have no influence on public institutions and services and religious privilege must not influence government. It limits moral issues to the private, personal sphere. Secularization - the transfer of socio-political power away from religious governance - does not force people to become atheists or stop observers from going to church or temple. It does prevent using places of worship for practising politics which does not happen on every Friday prayer in Kashmir or any other Muslim nations, there is a regular feed of Israelis, West-bashing and occasionally India bashing as well in the name of Babri Masjid, Godhara riots and Kashmir so-called Azaadi demand and huge alleged human rights violations.

The encounter with secularism for Muslim societies in the 20th century has not been a happy meeting for many reasons, but not necessarily due to perceived philosophical incompatibility. Some Arab regimes created State Islamic orthodoxies as part of their brand of 'Arab secularism homogeneity' to persecute resisting Islamic dissenters and groups - pitting religion against religion under the guise of secular governance. Regardless of its origins, secularism (like modernity and technology) has many different models. In France, secularity aims to protect the republic and public space from religion. In the US, secularity means protecting religion from being exploited in public institutions. Secularity in India means pluralism, where multiple faiths are officially recognized and may practice in public.

Muslims are fundamentally, philosophically and socially non-secular because they are committed to religious activity and institutions, some may be politically secular by not voting for religious parties or policies. Grass-root Muslim leaders reject secular ideals as futile fantasies of the 'elite' but, ironically, think that socialism and Marxism are pragmatic, electable options for the masses. Condemning secularism as elitist falsely validates religious politics as inherently proletarian. Islam does speak of brotherhood and hence Muslims support for fellow Muslim brothers across the globe, but when it comes to their nation, they are diehard nationalists. Though a large number of critics may not agree to this and will want us to believe that for Muslims, nationhood does not matter. These views may be biased sometimes but give the reader a perspective of complexity involved with Kashmir conflict and the potential solution.

Bahujan Samaj View

With more than 25% of Indian population comprising of Scheduled Castes and Tribes, their views on issues of national importance makes it important to be seriously discussed. They have been in the forefront of social discriminations due to the old practice of caste hierarchy in the society and also have been the main community for conversions. Below view is the series of distinct views coming from various groups that I have used in this book to bring the complete 360 exposure of this topic covering the vast Indian mass.

Kashmir has always been considered as 'Naag bhumi'. Ferguson, mentions that a century before Christ, king Damodara, as per *Rajatarangini,* was converted into a snake because he offended some Brahmin and also mentions many Naaga kings. When Hiuen Tsang entered the valley in AD 632 during the reign of Baladitya, Buddhism was flourishing, though the King was against Buddhism. He repeats the usual story of the valley being a lake in the past but adds that fifty years after the Nirvana of the Buddha, a disciple of Ananda, converted the Naaga Raja, who quitted the tank, built 500 monasteries and invited bhikkhus to dwell in them.

Wherever Buddhism spread, it always spread by persuasion and never by force. Kashmir was no exception. Ferguson has observed:

> "No war was ever waged by Buddhists, No faith was ever so essentially propagated by persuasion as that of Buddha and though the Buddhists were too frequently persecuted even to destruction, there is no instance on record of any attempt to spread their faith by force in any quarter of the globe."

Kashmir was in Ashoka's empire. A bhikkhu, named Majjhantiko, was sent to Kashmir and Gandhara by Ashoka after Third Sangiti (Council) in 253 BC. Aravaalo, the Naga king ruling there, tried to terrify the bhikkhu, but was ultimately converted to Buddhism.

The first people to get converted were the Naga tribe of Kashmir out of 14 tribes there. That is the reason why Naaga is a suffix of many places in Kashmir, such as Anant Naaga, Sheshanaaga, Neelanaaga, Naagabal, Kokaranaaga, Sukhanaaga, etc [Gayakwad Vijay, *Kashmiratil Buddha Dharma Cha Itihas* (Marathi), published by author, Ulhasnagar, 1990, p 6]. It was Ashoka, who established the city of Srinagar, says *Rajatarangini.* His son Jalouka became king of Kashmir, who built 'Krutyakama Vihara'. Kashmir was under King Milinda, who had discussions of 'Milind Panha', 12 yojanas away from Kashmir valley. Two Kushana kings, Hushka and Jushka also ruled Kashmir, before Kanishka.

Arab invasion in AD 712 of Sind, over king Dahir, hardly left any marks in India, but Ghaznavid invasion, three centuries later has left permanent scars. Various invasions took place and Sultanate was established in Delhi in AD 1206. In spite of the opposition of orthodox

Muslim religious heads and also of royal princes, the Sufi cult flourished. The Sufi cult, which should be given the credit of making many devotees from Hindus also, was founded by the saints. The founder of the cult is supposed to be Data Ganj Bakhsha of Lahore, who died in AD 1072. Khwaja Muin-ud-din Chishti of Ajmer, who came from Gazni in AD 1161, acknowledged his greatness. The followers of this cult were called Chishtis, who spread all over and included both Muslims and Hindus.

The credit of converting Kashmir to Islam goes to one and only, fakir Bulbulshah.

Views of a controversial Dalit scholar Kancha Ilaiah, of Osmania University about the spread of Islam. He observes:

> "Islam seems to have emerged more as a reaction to the Vedic inequality as an anti-caste social synthesizer. The birth of Islam, it appears to me, has taken place to establish a total civil societal homogenization within the sphere of religion. It put the religious equality of the people who embraced it on much more solid foundations. This could have been one of the reasons why more and more SCAs (Shudras, Chandalas and Adivasis) embraced Islam in India in the second millennium."

How Kashmir became Muslim centric region? In the thirteenth century, a boy of tender age by name Ratanju came to Kashmir. Somehow, he got a place in the court of king Sahadeva and reached a high rank. He had neither any religion nor any nationality of his own. Moulana Mohammed Kazam Muradabadi writes in his history book that Ratanju had a great love for Hindu religion. He wanted to embrace it. But the Hindus were not ready to accept him in their society. He used to listen to the story of *Gita* every day from the Pandits. One day the Pandit, while explaining him the meaning of verse 47 of chapter 18, told him that it is fearful to accept another man's better religion and one must not leave one's religion though it had many disabilities. On this Ratanju asked, "Can I not join your religion?" The Pandit said "Absolutely not." Getting disappointed by this reply, Ratanju resolved to accept the religion of the person, whom so ever he will see first one in the morning. One Muslim fakir, by name Bulbulshah, got to know the decision of Ratanju. Next morning, he went to the palace of Ratanju. On seeing him, Ratanju came down and asked him, "Would you accept me in your religion?"

The door of Islam is open to all human beings. A prominent political officer wishes to become my brother in religion (dharma bandhu). What could be the more pleasing thing for me other than this, replied Bulbulshah. Ratanju became Muslim. His son Shahamir usurped the throne and brought home forcibly the queen Kona, wife of king Sahadeva's son. But the queen committed suicide by stabbing herself. It is said, those Pandits, who refused to become Muslims, were put in gunny bags and drowned in river Jhelum by Ratanju and Shahamir. The place in Srinagar where they were drowned, is famous even now by the name of 'watta mazaar'. The refusal of a low caste prominent political personality like Ratanju by the Brahmins of Kashmir led to the propagation of Islam in Kashmir with all further complications, for which all further generations of Indians may thank the Pandits of Kashmir of those times.

Communists View

"A Marxist Critique of the 'New Atheists'" (Workers Vanguard Number 1009, 28 September 2012) it is noted that: The State of Pakistan was deliberately created as an Islamic political entity in 1947 when the British partitioned the Indian subcontinent, over which they were no longer able to maintain colonial rule. The article makes the point that, contrary to some leftist groups like the [former co-thinker of the International Socialist Organization, the British] Socialist Workers Party (SWP), there is no basic conflict between British imperialism and Islamic fundamentalism. It goes on to quote John Foster Dulles on the common bond between imperialism, religions of the East and anti-Communism.

In 1950, Dulles, soon to become Secretary of State, observed: "The religions of the East are deeply rooted and have many precious values. Their spiritual beliefs cannot be reconciled with Communist atheism and materialism. That creates a common bond between us and our task is to find it and develop it" (quoted in Paul Baran, *The Political Economy of Growth*, 1957). The British imperialists have maintained that the partition of India was aimed at creating a homeland for Muslims where they would be protected from Hindus, a claim belied by the fact that far more Muslims were left behind in India than those incorporated in the new entity of Pakistan. Besides, in the provinces that became Pakistan, the Muslims were dominant; they were neither threatened by post-Independence Hindu domination nor were they interested in a separate Muslim State. In fact, the majority of Muslims were fearful of the economic and social impact of uprooting and relocation.

They resented the fact that they would be confined to the two corners of the subcontinent and have to abandon the heartland of India, where Muslim rulers held sway for over 600 years before their defeat by the British and in which lie some of the magnificent symbols of past Muslim power and glory such as the great forts of Delhi and Agra, Taj Mahal and others. Muslim merchants and businessmen opposed the partition out of concern for the loss of a long developed market. The sizable Shi'ite Muslim population, dreading living in a Sunni-dominated Pakistan, was opposed to the partition scheme.

Up until World War II the British depended on the strategically situated India as a military base to safeguard their interests - in the Middle-East, South-East Asia and their colonies across the Indian Ocean in East Africa. As India's independence dawned, the British, fearing that the Hindu nationalists who would rule post-Independence India would deny them military cooperation, settled for creating a weak, truncated entity that would serve their imperialist interests, would depend on Britain for its defence and would be ruled by their pliable lackeys of the Muslim League of Muhammad Ali Jinnah. Through their divide-and-rule policy and using religion as a tool, the British drove a wedge between Hindus and Muslims, built close ties with Jinnah, in whom they nourished separatist aspirations and recognized him as the sole spokesman of the Muslims of India.

On 5th May 1945, the same day Germany surrendered, Churchill ordered an appraisal of the long-term policy required to safeguard the interests of the British Empire in India. The report presented to him stressed the strategic importance of India "from the north-west of which British air power could threaten Soviet military installations." Churchill told Lord Archibald Wavell, then Viceroy of India, to "keep a bit of India." A more candid Lord Wavell, who prepared a blueprint of the partition borders as early as February 1946, grasped the fact that:

> "The breach to be caused in Britain's capacity to defend the Middle-East and the Indian Ocean area could be plugged if the Muslim League were to succeed in separating India's strategic north-west from the rest of the country, a realizable goal considering the close ties that Lord Linlithgow, Wavell's predecessor, had built up with the Muslim League leader Muhammad Ali Jinnah."

Dulles' idea about utilizing reactionary religious forces as a battering ram in the Cold War against the Soviet Union echoed British imperialist schemes. In his writings in the late forties and early fifties, British colonial official Olaf Caroe posed the question: "Will Islam stand up to communism?" He advocated turning Pakistan into a base for a community of Muslim States that "would show the way for reconciliation between the Western and Islamic models." A major architect of the partition, Caroe served in British India as the Viceroy's Chief Adviser, Foreign Secretary and Governor of the North-West Frontier Province, which later became incorporated into Pakistan.

By the early 1950s, Pakistan became, in the words of a Pakistani leader, "America's most allied ally in Asia." In 1954 it signed a mutual defence agreement with the US. Later that year Pakistan became a founding member of the South-East Asia Treaty Organization (SEATO), even though the country is thousands of miles away from South-East Asia. The next year Pakistan joined the Anglo-American sponsored Baghdad Pact along with Turkey, Iraq and Iran, constituting what Dulles called "the northern tier" that linked the southernmost member of NATO, Turkey, with the westernmost member of SEATO, Pakistan. Pakistan went on to host secret bases for the CIA. Following the entry of Soviet troops in 1979, Afghanistan became the front line of the imperialists' relentless drive to destroy the Soviet Union. As the CIA undertook its biggest covert operation ever, Pakistan played a strategic role. The US, Britain, Pakistan and Saudi Arabia, among others, armed, funded and trained reactionary mujahedin (holy warriors) to kill Soviet soldiers. The Soviet Red Army intervened on the side of a regime that sought to introduce minimal social reforms and faced a jihad (holy war) led by reactionary landlords, tribal chiefs and mullahs. That war, in which imperialist-backed forces threatened the southern flank of the Soviet Union, posed an acid test for revolutionaries.

Following the counter revolution in the USSR, the end of the Cold War meant that Pakistan's usefulness to the West was greatly diminished. Pakistan, unlike India, is a prison house of peoples, a legacy of three centuries of British colonial divide and rule that culminated in the partition of the Indian subcontinent. Pakistan's claim to constitute 'one nation' of all Muslims masks the domination of the Punjabi ruling class over Pashtuns, Baluchis and other oppressed nationalities. Kashmir epitomizes the seething complex of national and communal conflicts that extend from Afghanistan to Pakistan and India. For their part, Pakistan's rulers can ill afford to support independence for Kashmir, which would pose the same question for the minorities within their borders. The task of liberating all the exploited and oppressed of the Indian subcontinent demands the forging of Leninist-Trotskyist vanguard parties dedicated to the revolutionary overthrow of the bourgeoisie in India, Pakistan and Bangladesh and the establishment of a socialist federation of South Asia. (Now how much of the Communist view can be taken as factual data is for the readers to decide. But one thing we know they have played their part in mudding the Kashmiri water.)

The Indian Communists also rejected the reality of Indian history. The Muslims in the Communist Party also insisted upon the rejection of the Indian civilization as a reality. Their denial of the Indian history was inspired by different considerations. In the static economic order which the Communists in India underlined as the basis of the Indian history, they identified the Marxist categories of dialectics of history such as the classes, with castes in India and caste-war with class-war. They identified the ethnic centralism, including Muslim separatism, with independent nationalities. The self-determination for nationalities which the Communist Party of India adopted as the basis of the freedom of India, was a negation of both the unity of the working class as well as the unity of India. The Muslim intellectual class rejected the civilizational unity of India and the continuity of the Indian history out of the commitment to the separate Muslim nation in India and its separate freedom. The Communist Party in the Punjab and Bengal suffered dissolution in 1947, due to its commitment to the freedom of the nationalities in India.

The Communist Party cadres in Kashmir began to disintegrate under the pressure of the Muslimisation of the State. NN Saraf (Raina) ran away to England. The other senior leaders wobbled in frustration. The outlook of the Communist Party of India, still under the shadows of Adhikari doctrine, which in effect sought to Semitise Marxism almost on the lines Lenin had done in Russia, identified the Muslimisation of the State with the class conflict in Kashmir. It reduced the Communist cadres in Kashmiri to mercenaries performing the 'historical role' of facilitating the Islamization of the political culture of Kashmir. Communist was called as 'pongas'. It was perhaps nickname coined by the ruling elite of the State during the fifties for the Communists in the State. It has been derived from Kashmiri word 'pog' meaning inauspicious, used against Mogul soldiers who were called as 'poga-Mogul' after Akbar's invasion of the State.

Notwithstanding the nickname, the fact remains that the Communists occupied the intellectual space of the State for about two decades. It started with the birth of National Conference in 1938. National Conference was born out of the womb of the Jammu and Kashmir Muslim Conference - an organization that articulated the suffering of the Muslims. Eighty per cent of the population under allegedly brutal Maharaja rule provided an opportunity for the Communist ideologues to occupy the intellectual space of Kashmir and use the State "as a laboratory for testing socialist ideology. In 1947, when the question of State's accession with India and Pakistan arose both Jawaharlal Nehru and Quaid-e-Azam utilized the services of intellectuals and writers with left leanings to for seeing Kashmir joining their domain. Nehru deputed a whole brigade of the Communist writers to woo Sheikh Abdullah. Equally, Quaid Azam deputed Mian Iftikharuddin, Faiz Ahmad Faiz and Dr MD Taseer to Kashmir to invite Sheikh Abdullah for discussing future of Kashmir.

In 1953, when Sheikh was deposed, some progressive writers like Nadim had played a dubious role in providing grist to the propaganda mill about Sheikh conspiring with the USA for an independent Kashmir. Some historians have tried to establish connectivity between Indian freedom struggle and Kashmiri uprising against tyrant autocracy forgetting that the Congress leadership got interested in Kashmir only after Prem Nath Bazaz sent an SOS to Gandhi and Nehru after July 1931. Kashmiris, in fact, had drafted a manifesto for their struggle in 1925, in the shape of memorandum presented to Lord Reading. However, an Indian turncoat Dr Iqbal ("Saare Jahan se Achcha...", fame poet) played an inspiring role in Kashmir struggle against. Tyranny. Communists played communal cards for the first time in Kashmir by branding Sufi poets progressive writers forgetting their poetry was inspired by the love of Prophet (Peace be upon him) and not out of any dogmas.

As India had been groaning and writhing under the ruthless blood sucking British rule, the Indian National Congress had already spearheaded a struggle for liberation from the British hegemony and the Communist Party of India with its feeble political base had no option but to append itself to the Congress on the assumption that the anti-imperialist struggle had to be strengthened and fortified by the broad mobilization of patriotic forces.

The Communist Party failed to take deep roots in India for the fact that it had no feel and appreciation of the enormous heritage of India and that was how its evaluation and perception of the Indian reality never harmonized and had no compatibility with the depths and psychology of India, more than most with its leviathan of culture and civilization. The same theme-song of 'Proletarian Revolution' and 'class struggle' with hatred as its cosmic principle were plucked out of the Marxian book to shape the Indian reality for a revolution and crude attempts were harnessed to explicate the shaping processes of Indian history in the light of Marxist tenets distilling ersatz of the Indian substance anomalous to its tone and temper.

The potent and only factor that impeded and nearly stifled the steady growth of Communist ideology in Kashmir was the hide-bound Muslim mind indoctrinated and deeply steeped in 'Kufra' and 'narrowness of the spirit' shaping out into an absolute abhorrence to everything that is not Islamic. As the Communists in India had set a precedent, the Kashmiri Pandit Communists also functioned as a pressure group within National Conference, which had the same ideological goals and moorings as that of the Muslim Conference. The pre-1947 and post-1947 history of National Conference testifies to the fact of pursuing an anti-Kashmir and anti-Pandit thrust and agenda with the same overt and covert communal vigour as that of the Reading Room Party which finally incarnated into the Muslim Conference.

Much in the line of Ahmadiyas and Ahrars, the Muslim Communists from Lahore and elsewhere descended upon Kashmir to add vigour to the Communist ideology. The study circles where they flaunted their learning of the Marxist texts and the tactical line pursued by the Communist Party were largely attended by the Kashmiri Pandit converts to Marxism. As the Muslim League with its agenda of Pakistan as the destiny of Muslims had emerged on the political scene of India, communally besmeared ideological content was provided to the National Conference to fight out the Maharaja as representing the decadent feudal system, but not a word was said about the Muslim League as representing the same feudal and parochial interests.

The strategy and socio-political framings as chalked out by the Muslim Communists from the Punjab for political action was not the people of Jammu and Kashmir versus British Imperialism but the people of Kashmir versus Maharaja Hari Singh. Fazal Illahi Qurban and Abdullah Safdar pursued the same strategy in Kashmir with trappings of fixation as they felt satisfied that the ends of revolution were better served by pitting the Muslims against the Hindu Maharaja in particular and Hindus in general.

Of immense political significance was the arrival of BPL Bedi and his European wife Freda Bedi in Kashmir. They as Communists from the Punjab pioneered a new Communist Manifesto for Kashmir in the form of New Kashmir document, a pious statement of Marxist cliches, supposed to concretize the goals that were sought to be achieved through the force of a struggle against the Maharaja. The role of two prominent Kashmiri Pandit Communists Dr NN Raina and late Moti Lal Misri was highly laudable in drafting the document, but was diluted and never recognized for their Hindu credentials by the National Conference which was principally a Muslim organization preserving and battling for the Muslim interests at the expense of other ethnic and religious groups. The document of New Kashmir apparently egalitarian with an accent on minority rights was supposed to pave the way for and establish a rational democratic order and with that end in view the Communists organized and held study circles to acquaint the lumpens with the social and political content of the document and to their dismay the Sheikh swooped on them, de-legitimized them, got the study circles stopped on the plea that they were propagating communism among the Muslim youth though the fact was that the Muslims by and large detested and shunned communism for its atheistic approach and premise.

The Kashmiri Pandit Communists glued to the pursuit of guidelines issued out by party bosses deft in doling out cliches and off-ground phantasies were lacking in Hindu lore and orientation and passed for extreme liberals which trait of theirs was misunderstood, never swallowed and appreciated by orthodox Muslims mired in illiteracy and obscurantism. Liberalism as a cornerstone of Hinduism flaunted in an extremely backward society propped upon the tenets of bigotry encouraged an elusive mutual concourse weakening the resisting barriers that could have saved the Pandits from the Muslim onslaught. The rapport that developed thick and fast in the wake of Nehru's intervention dizzied the Muslims from oblivion into an identity which till then was a missing quantum.

The Pandit Communists and many Pandits in National Conference without any commitment to the community, thus rootless, surrendered the will of the community to the Muslim majority and also through their closer interface with Muslims appeared to have contributed to the growth of pernicious trends which compromised and diluted the Hindu position of Pandits. As borne out by history, Hindus have perpetually-been the butts of Muslim onslaught and this fact of history was completely overlooked as nought and much to the chagrin of general Hindu opinion, such onslaughts and any piquant situation of communal dimension were brushed off in ambivalent and lacklustre fashion and positions were taken as could be characterised capitulatory and uncouth defences were put up for the Muslim demeanour that has been absurd and irrational.

The Hindu Communists bright people by all standards got a lifetime shock, when few Muslim Communists subscribing to the 'instinctive tilt of Muslim psyche for Pakistan' theory denounced them as reactionary Brahmans and anti-Muslim and made a concerted bid to capture the Communist Party though the Pandits as a matter of fact formed a bulk of its membership. They were beaten and thrashed, moneys on them snatched and looted, humiliated and put to crass contumely. The Muslim Communists and hired goons in a joint operation looted and captured the Party run bookshop at Lal Chowk, Srinagar and they say that the whole operation was the brainchild of Mohinddin Qarra, the oriole of Kashmir, in accompaniment with Pir Abdul Ahad, who in post-1947 scenario in his disgruntlement with Sheikh Abdullah broke away from National Conference and without any contrition formed Political conference with pro-Pakistan politics as its pivotal agenda.

As expected the Communist Party suffered a dip and a split on communal lines and dismaying as it is, the Pandit Communists alert as they should have been failed to learn from the brash communalization of Communist politics and continued with their unflinching loyalty to National Conference which their party bosses had regimented them to believe that Kashmir with its so-called radical programmes would lead to a Communist revolution in India with waves flowing in from Red China. Pandit Jia Lal Kilam, a signatory to the National Demand, had the grace and independence to lodge appealing protest against Sheikh Abdullah's utterances against the religion of Hindus and raised the issue in the Working Committee of National Conference and offered his resignation when the Sheikh unexpectedly thundered that he was first a Muslim and last a Muslim. The National Conference would have sundered apart had not Pandit Nehru intervened for a patch-up to save the ship from sinking. But the Pandit Communists as per their history in Kashmir have maintained stony silence on issues of vital concern to the community though the fact was that they were taken for Kashmiri Pandits and if the rag came off, it was firmly suck back and when the State power moved against the Pandits whole hog, they were not left out for special treatment or even consideration and were vandalised and discriminated and met out a raw deal the same wise as the mass of Kashmiri Pandits were.

Pandit Jia Lal Taimiri, a veteran politician without a blemish, cultured and soft-spoken – was highly detested for the eye he had on scams and kitties of National Conference ministers. Nothing deterred him from setting a brilliant and inimitable precedent when he openly confronted and opposed Sheikh Abdullah for the appointment of Mohammad Sultan at the expense of PN Ganju on religious grounds and considerations. A Gandhian to the core, Taimiri tailed to digest the injustice and staged a *dharna* at the National Conference Headquarters demanding the withdrawal of unjust orders by the Sheikh who as a doyen of secularism and nationalism lost no time in axing and weeding out Pandits thus paving the way for ethnic cleansing.

Not emulating the example of Taimiri the Pandit Communists not only maintained intriguing silence, but also formed a part of National Conference gendarme in the execution of a policy of blatant communalism by the State with Sheikh Abdullah telling the Pandit young men though competent and qualified to go to greener pastures available for them in rest of India. The minorities were put on the hit-list of the government, were harassed and tyrannized and driven into dire straits. Had the Pandit Communists followed to the dot the Taimiri precedent, it would never have conflicted with the Marxist dicta and doctrine.

The Pandit Communists and also the Pandits drawn into the dragnet of National Conference after dissolving their parent body might not have been conversant with the precautionary history of how the Muslim intolerants with their prejudices subjected them to a pogrom which had no semblance of a human face, how a genocide was triggered off to transmute the religious complexion of Kashmir and how the Hindus had been forced to march out of their native abode five times, to say the least. The dispensation incarnated from the forces with a fanatic and sectarian visage could not on a sudden vie with catholicity of outlook and secular demeanour. How was it that the loot of 1931 and again the loot of 1932 were ignored and blotted out of focus? How was it that the dismal and gory drama of 1947 with all the ingredients of a crusade was painted rosy despite its murkiness?

The Pandit Communists following the behests of the Communist Party of India played a vigorous role in laying bare Sheikh Abdullah's hobnobbing with the western powers who were deeply aware of the strategic importance of Kashmir in the Himalayan watershed and hence a focus of their not too benign attention. In their unstinted support to the new dispensation led by Bakshi Ghulam Mohammad, the Communists created the fronts and fortified the forces to put up an ideological battle against the instrumentalities of destabilization and national insecurity. *Kashmir* as an official organ of the Communists in Kashmir published editorials and lead-articles that highlighted and put forth a reasonable analysis of the game-plan of Imperialist powers to wrest Kashmir from the Constitutional organization of India to establish its independence as a requirement of cold war politics of Dullesian vintage.

Sheikh Abdullah with a deep streak of vengeance and vindictiveness in his personality wits in no mood to forgive the Pandit Communists for their so-called betrayal in 1953. But aware of their political fertility and acumen as Pandits, he invited a brilliant thinker of the stature of late Moti Lal Misri to participate in the people's convention hastily organized as a political gimmick to smoothen his highway for a somersault ensuring his ascendancy to the seat of power and also to dole out fake and false impression that he was convinced of the absurdity of the Plebiscite Front politics of which he was the pioneer and innovator too. Despite opposition from many quarters the Sheikh was hastily and even impolitically under a quaint arrangement installed as the leader of Congress Legislature party and in the wake of quirks and heaves of history he entrenched himself as the elected Chief Minister of the State and the weapon used was to feign illness to invoke public sympathy. And dismaying as it is, he launched a diatribe against the Pandits by labelling them as 'Fifth Column', a Muslim calumny and canard motivated by his antipathy towards the Pandit Communists formulating his distasteful role in the formulaic phrase of 'unconscious votary of imperialism'.

Flaunting the credentials of a progressive, GM Sadiq maintained a close rapport with the Pandit Communists whom he used at will as a support-plank to foment and perpetuate his self-promotion and self-aggrandizement in pre-1953 and post-1953 political scenario. With no mass appeal, but still wielding political power under all dispensations, he as a matter of the first choice dictated by religious culture embarked upon an antediluvian policy-path of formalizing the wanton discrimination against the Pandits by the issuance of a satanic government decree purporting religion-based quotas in recruitment and admissions to the study programmes. Superseding the orders brazenly and clandestinely issued and implemented, the said-order practically reserving the whole pie for the Muslims proved the first convoluted exercise in generating Islamic paranoia about the Pandits who as the branded enemies of Islam had to be expelled to the Siberia of the Indian plains. The order proved a landmark in the history of discrimination and relentless elimination of the Kashmiri Hindus. Violative of the Constitutional provisions, the orders were outrageously communal making religion as a determining factor for entry into services and admissions in professional colleges. What was shocking that such orders were issued at the behest of GM Sadiq who had pretensions to secular and progressive credentials.

Harkishan Singh Surjeet once known as an Akali Communist, has been overseeing the functioning of his Party unit in Kashmir and directing its affairs before the split of the Communist Party and continued with the over-lordship even after the Party floundered into groups and sub-groups. His Jaunts between Delhi and Kashmir undertook with the objective of proliferating and strengthening the base of CPI(M) unit in Kashmir and his successes and failures in this behalf are within the knowledge of people interested in political affairs. As is common knowledge, his sphere of activities in Kashmir has been limited to a house in Khanyar, Srinagar, which is owned by Yusuf Zargar, a Muslim activist, but a comrade in Communist parlance. It was at the same house situated within the tangle of narrow lanes and bylanes of the locality that Comrade Surjeet dilating on the political scenario of Kashmir was said to have expressed his shirking doubts about the relevance and efficacy of Art. 370 and was said to have advocated its repeal. The meeting though not largely attended was suddenly wound up when hundreds of Muslims lying in wait surrounded the house and lapidated it and let loose a barrage of abuse and curse against the owner of the house and filthily denounced Surjeet, his Party and the atheistic philosophy of Marx in so loud tones as to rend the sky.

The Scene was set for manhandling the Comrades. But, before Comrade Surjeet could be bashed and thrashed in the native Muslim fashion, his party men, pale and panting, led him out of the house through the back-yard door merging into the labyrinthine of lanes and drains to the house of a Kashmiri Pandit, late JL Dhar, not a comrade, where he cooled his heels and felt safe and secure and reassured. Invested with an exceptional capacity of mind and intelligence, Surjeet should have promptly measured the trend of ominous events shaping in the secular skies of Kashmir and despairing as it is he without touching the hornet's nest maintained wooden silence and thought it highly prudent and sagacious not to broach the subject with the powers that be then at the Central capital and perhaps fearing loss of face concealed the incident fraught with nefarious designs of ominous proportions even from ills own party circles to which he was responsible if responsibility is a principle informing the Communist politics. The Muslims who had surrounded the house as the venue of Communist activists and had virtually bade for their blood were the same fanatic brigands churned out from the madrasas functioning as the seminaries of fanaticism and bigotry and upholding the agenda of converting the valley into a haven of Islam through its annexation with Pakistan.

Aware as every cawing crow is of the tact that Kashmiri Pandits as a distinctive religious minority have been expelled from their native birthplace lock, stock and barrel by the armed Muslim killers earning not covert but overt support and collaboration from large sections of Muslim majority, but comrade Surjeet set on the trail of faceless opportunist refuses to identify and cognize the stark reality and call a spade a spade. If he does, the apple-cart of hollow secularism as conceived and practised in the country will turn turtle and that is why he and his party as votaries of the same phoney secularism have not politically necessary and expedient to issue out a single statement on the cruel expulsion of the entire Hindu minority from the Muslim Kashmir. He can be unflinching in his support to the creation of Mallapuram, a citadel of Islamic Sevak Sangh, but he cannot afford to pay even lip-service to the cause of the three lakh Hindu refugees wallowing in dust and dirt lest it should taint his secular image which in fact is nothing more than a mask to conceal his anti-Hindu motivations.

How many of the Communists remember that in the mid-forties EMS Namboodiripad led processions of Muslims in Kerala along with the late AK Gopalan shouting 'Pakistan Zindabad' and 'Moplistan Zindabad'. A few will know now how he got the revered Gandhian, Kaliappan, arrested for trying to rebuild a temple just because the Muslims objected to it. It was he who distorted the Mopla rebellion in 1921 into an agriculturists' fight against landowners. EMS had the honour of equating communism with anti-Hinduism which was taken up by all other leftists and so-called progressive Indians.

RAW Views

Any suggestion for talks with Pakistan while terror continues legitimizes Pakistani terrorist activity in India. This is often seen as favouring the illegitimate Pakistani position, especially when the situation flares up. After nearly 70 years, we should treat Kashmir without special laws and its never-ending dispensations. It is time we developed our response that makes Pakistan's rulers pay a price they cannot afford. Since we have inalienable rights to Kashmir, we should stop being defensive about this and make magnanimity, a foreign policy virtue.

This phenomenon of the Valley coming out for a militant's funeral will happen and will grow unless the government acts. The past is full of incidents which have strengthened militancy through appeasement. It continued even during the Chief Ministership of Mehbooba Mufti, whose penchant for playing with fire is well-established. We had militants being released in the past for her sister Rubaiya Sayeed; the first act of appeasement. Her father, Mufti Mohammad Sayeed, was then the Union Home Minister. We then had the Delhi-Kathmandu flight hijacked to Kandahar in 1999. Three prominent militants in custody were released, including Maulana Masood Azhar of the Jaish-e-Mohammed. This was followed by an attack on our Parliament in December 2001, with Azhar being the mastermind. Appeasement only leads to the strengthening of the militants' morale, while demoralizing that of one's forces.

It was after the failure of Zulfikar Ali Bhutto's Operation Gibraltar in 1965 that the ISI escalated its involvement in Kashmir. When the holy relic of the Prophet was stolen in Srinagar in 1964 and riots broke out, all that was required to quell the riots were four Punjab Armed Police battalions. Look at the force level today? This is not the fault of the Army or the other security forces, but a confused Kashmir policy that has brought the current situation to the fore. The Army can contain a situation to a point; it is then for the Government of India (GoI) to take whatever political initiatives are required. The trouble is that before the Army brings Kashmir to the point necessary for negotiations, dabbling commences and the first casualty is the Army itself.

The Army must be allowed to bring militancy under control to a point where those professing it realize that the time has come to talk. Yes, people will die in the ensuing action, then so be it. Kashmir is Indian territory. If those owing allegiance to Pakistan's ISI continues to create instability, then they must face the music. The Burhan Wanis may be the glamour boys for many, to India they are the perpetrators of violence and separatism. Let them not live with a mistaken belief that they have the upper hand.

The Government of India must allow freedom of action to the Army. The directive must be just one: "Bring a situation in the State where the writ of India runs and not that of the ISI." Yes, in the ensuing clashes collateral damage will take place. No soldier likes such action. He is trained to face the enemy, not protecting his back from treacherous elements. We have had this experience in Nagaland, Manipur, etc. The British army considered their Northern Ireland commitment before peace with the IRA, in the same light. It was the IRA which finally decided to talk peace when they could not face growing military pressure.

It would be appropriate to end with a quote from President Obama's statement on the recent violence against the police in Baton Rouge, Louisiana: "I want to be clear: there is no justification for violence against law enforcement personnel. None. These attacks are the work of cowards who speak for no one. They right no wrongs. They advance no causes".

Pakistan Dubious Game in the Region

Is Pakistan a friend or a foe in the fight against terrorism? Question asked by the US and its NATO allies. While Pakistani officials and forces have assisted the US in hunting senior al-Qaeda figures at times, Pakistan's overall strategy is pro-jihadist and therefore puts it in the foe category. Pakistan does battle some terrorist groups within its borders, but it only does so because these groups pose a direct threat to the State. Pakistan myopically supports a host of terrorist groups in Pakistan, Afghanistan and India to further its goals in the region. Pakistan backs these groups despite the fact that they are allied with and aid the very terrorist groups that fight the Pakistani State. Also, many of the jihadist groups sponsored by Pakistan are allied with al-Qaeda. Let us discuss six major groups directly supported or tolerated by Pakistan's establishment and the Hafiz Saeed factor: the Afghan Taliban and its subgroup, the Haqqani Network; the Mullah Nazir Group, Lashkar-e-Taiba, Harkat-ul-Mujahideen and Jaish-e-Mohammed. Each of these groups is used by Pakistan as an instrument of its foreign policy. These six groups are by no means the only terrorist organizations supported by Pakistan; they are merely the most prominent.

Pakistan uses these six groups and others as a counterweight against what its policy makers perceive to be Pakistan's greatest threat: India. However, the jihadist ideology has also spread throughout Pakistan as a result of policies adopted by the country's military elite. Therefore, we should not underestimate the degree to which these groups are supported for ideological reasons. Pakistan, a country of 182 million people, does not possess the manpower to counter India, a nation of 1.25 billion. Pakistan and India have been in a virtual state of war since Partition in 1947. The two countries have fought four active wars in 1947, 1965, 1971 and 1999. Each of these wars was initiated by Pakistan and ended in defeats. Pakistani strategists have determined that to counter India, it must use unconventional means, including supporting jihadist groups.

Strategic Depth

To compensate for its inability to achieve victory on conventional battlefields against India, Pakistan implemented its version of "strategic depth" in Afghanistan. Pakistan has supported groups in Afghanistan to deny India influence in its backyard, as well as to allow the nation to serve as a fallback in case of an Indian invasion. Pakistan capitalized on the chaos in Afghanistan post-Soviet withdrawal and hunted for a group that would serve its purposes.

With the rise of Mullah Omar's Taliban faction in the early 1990s, Pakistan military and intelligence officers assigned to implement strategic depth saw the perfect partner: a powerful jihadist political movement that was gaining popularity throughout the country and was capable of sustaining military advances. Pakistan provided military and financial support to Omar's faction, which successfully established the Islamic Emirate of the Taliban in 1996 and controlled upwards of 90% of the country until the US invasion in 2001. In addition to securing a friendly government in Afghanistan, Pakistan used the country as both training and a recruiting ground for a host of jihadist groups that fight in various parts of Jammu and Kashmir.

Good *vs* Bad Taliban

To justify its policy of support to jihadist groups, Pakistani elites have attempted to distinguish between what are referred to as 'good Taliban' and 'bad Taliban'. Simply stated, the so-called 'good Taliban' are groups that advance Pakistan's foreign policy goals and do not threaten the State or wage war within its borders. 'Good Taliban' and other groups deemed acceptable by the Pakistani establishment include the Afghan Taliban, the Haqqani Network, the Mullah Nazir Group, Lashkar-e-Taiba, Harkat-ul-Mujahideen and Jaish-e-Mohammed. These groups conduct numerous heinous acts of terrorism in the region and are directly responsible for the deaths of thousands of American soldiers and civilians, and yet are supported by the Pakistani State.

'Bad Taliban' are any jihadist faction that challenges the primacy of the Pakistani State. These groups include the Movement of the Taliban in Pakistan, the Turkistan Islamic Party and the weakened Islamic Movement of Uzbekistan. The Pakistani military has pursued these groups in the Federally Administered Tribal Areas (FATA) and Khyber Pakhtunkhwa province with some success. However, when targeting these groups, the military has avoided pursuing groups such as the Haqqani Network, which provided shelter and support for the 'bad Taliban'. Pakistani officials have denied that it pursues a policy of strategic depth and differentiates between 'good and bad Taliban', or have claimed it will no longer differentiate between the two. However, these claims are false. This is demonstrated in Pakistan's continuing support for the groups as mentioned above and others, as well as an unwillingness to round up leaders and key operatives of these groups.

Afghan Taliban

Pakistan's support for the Afghan Taliban is well-documented. It helped establish the group in the 1990s and continued to support it to this day. Hamid Gul, the former head of the Inter-Services Intelligence (ISI) Directorate, Pakistan's military intelligence agency that developed and implemented the policy of strategic depth, is known as the 'father of the Taliban' for his role in directing support to the Taliban. (Gul is also known as the 'Godfather of terrorism' for his support of global jihadist groups.) The term 'father of the Taliban' isn't reserved only for Gul; Maulana Sami ul Haq, the Director of the radical Darul Uloom Haqqania Madrasa, also hold this title. His madrasa feeds thousands of recruits to the Taliban on a regular basis.

Afghanistan's insurgency continues to be fuelled by Pakistan's military and intelligence services to this day. The Taliban's Quetta Shura, or supreme decision-making council, has been based in the Pakistani city of the same name as well as elsewhere. The Taliban's four regional military commands all are named after Pakistani cities (Quetta, Peshawar, Miramshah, Gerdi Jangal).

The Taliban's top leadership has been based inside Pakistan, with the knowledge and approval of the military and ISI. The Taliban's first two emirs died while in Pakistan. Mullah Omar, the Taliban's founder and first emir died in a Pakistani hospital near Quetta in April 2013. His successor Mullah Mansour was killed by the US in a drone strike in Balochistan two months ago. They and another senior, middle and lower level leaders have operated inside Pakistan without consequence. Pakistan's border areas with Afghanistan serve as the lifeblood of the Taliban.

While all of Pakistan is jihadist friendly, the provinces of Khyber Pakhtunkhwa and Balochistan are flush with Taliban recruiting centres, training camps, safe houses and financial hubs. Taliban commanders freely admit that the ISI arms them and provides safe haven and training camps inside Pakistan.

Meanwhile, radical madrasas throughout the country indoctrinate Pakistani youth into the jihadist worldview and send them off to fight for the Taliban and other allied groups.

Haqqani Network

HQN is listed by the US as a Foreign Terrorist Organization for its support of al-Qaeda and other terrorist groups. It is an integral part of the Taliban. Its founder, Jalaluddin Haqqani, is a member of the Quetta Shura, while his son is one of the two deputy emirs to Mullah Haibatullah, the new leader of the Taliban. Thirteen senior HQN are listed by the US as specially designated global terrorists; most, including Sirajuddin, have been directly linked to al-Qaeda. Several top al-Qaeda leaders were killed in US counterterrorism operations while being sheltered by HQN. Deadly HQN attacks inside Afghanistan have been directly traced back to Pakistan. In one instance in 2011, HQN handlers, including Badruddin Haqqani, directed an assault on a hotel in Kabul from Pakistan, according to Afghanistan's National Directorate of Security. A similar attack took place in Jalalabad that same year.

In Pakistan, the HQN is based in North Waziristan and has a presence in other Pakistani tribal agencies, such as Kurram. The Haqqanis run the notorious Manba Ulom madrasa in Miramshah, North Waziristan. Despite the HQN's overt links to al-Qaeda, the group remains a darling of Pakistan's military and ISI. When the Pakistani military conducts operations in the FATA, it deliberately avoids the HQN. While Pakistani leaders insist the Haqqanis are not excluded from operations, not a single senior, mid-level, or junior leader has been killed or captured during Pakistani operations in the FATA from 2008 to date.

Mullah Nazir Group

Mullah Nazir Group is a Pakistani Taliban faction that operates in South Waziristan. The US government listed it as a specially designated global terrorist entity in 2013 and said it "has run training camps, dispatched suicide bombers, provided safe haven for al-Qaeda fighters and conducted cross-border operations in Afghanistan against the United States and its allies." Its current leader, Bahawal Khan and his deputy, sub-commander Malang, are also listed by the US as specially designated global terrorists.

Its former leader, Mullah Nazir, who was killed in a US drone strike, identified himself as a leader of al-Qaeda and said he shared the group's views on global jihad. Multiple al-Qaeda leaders have been killed while sheltering with the Mullah Nazir Group. The Pakistani military provided the Mullah Nazir Group with direct support when it clashed with rival members of the Islamic Movement of Uzbekistan. Despite the Mullah Nazir Group's direct ties to al-Qaeda, Pakistan has viewed it as an ally in the tribal areas. Like the Haqqani Network, the Mullah Nazir Group was left untouched when the Pakistani military launched operations that targeted the Movement of the Taliban in Pakistan.

Lashkar-e-Taiba

LeT is perhaps the most blatant example of Pakistan's support for jihadist groups. Listed by the US as a Foreign Terrorist Organization, it was founded by its leader, Hafiz Saeed, along with Osama bin Laden and Abdullah Azzam, the godfather of international jihad. Osama bin Laden helped LeT establish training camps in Afghanistan's provinces of Kunar and Paktia, where it continues to operate to this day. LeT shares al-Qaeda's goal of establishing an Islamic State in South Asia and beyond.

LeT operates openly inside Pakistan and has offices throughout the country. Markaz-e-Taiba, its headquarters in Muridke near Lahore, is a sprawling complex that is used to indoctrinate future jihadists before they are sent off for military training. The provincial government of Punjab has financed Markaz-e-Taiba in the past. This terrorist infrastructure was used to conduct egregious terrorist attacks in India and Afghanistan.

The most prominent attack took place in Mumbai (India) when a suicide assault team fanned out across the city and targeted multiple locations, including a theatre, a train station, hotels and a Jewish centre and killed 164 people. The attack lasted for three days. Indian intelligence traced phone calls back to handlers in Pakistan as the assault was ongoing. The handlers directed its fighters to execute non-Muslims, often brutally and laughed when their instructions were carried out. After the attack, Interpol issued arrest warrants for two serving senior Pakistani army officers and a retired major.

Despite LeT's overt ties to al-Qaeda and its campaign of terror in India and Afghanistan, the Pakistani government refuses to crack down on this group. Its complexes in Muridke and throughout the country remain open and its leaders operate unfettered. Hafiz Saeed is feted by Pakistani officials, who refuse to hold him and other LeT leaders accountable for their actions. Not a single member of LeT who has been implicated in the Mumbai attack has been prosecuted.

Harkat-ul-Mujahideen

HuM is yet another Pakistan-based jihadist group that has been listed by the US as a Foreign Terrorist Organization. Its emir, Fazlur Rehman Khalil, is also named by the US as a specially designated global terrorist.

In an update to the US designation of HuM in 2014, the US noted that it "operates in Pakistan and engages in terrorist activity in Kashmir, India, Pakistan and Afghanistan" and "also operates terrorist training camps in eastern Afghanistan." These camps are thought to be in existence to this day.

Khalil, like LeT's Saeed, is a madman inside Pakistan. In 2011, it was reported that he lived openly near the capital of Islamabad. Khalil is one of the jihadists Osama bin Laden consulted before issuing his infamous *fatwa* declaring war against the US in 1998. Khalil also signed the fatwa. Osama bin Laden's courier was reportedly tied to HuM, which may have played a role in the al-Qaeda master's support network inside Pakistan. HuM has also acted like a feeder organization for al-Qaeda's newest regional branch, al-Qaeda in the Indian Subcontinent (AQIS), which was officially established in September 2014. Asim Umar, the emir of AQIS, is a former member of HuM.

Khalil has "dispatched fighters to India, Afghanistan, Somalia, Chechnya and Bosnia, was a confidant of Osama bin Laden and hung out with 9/11 mastermind Khalid Sheikh Mohammed," the Associated Press (AP) reported in 2011. "Pakistani authorities are aware of Khalil's whereabouts," AP continued. "But they leave him alone, just as they tolerate other Kashmiri militant groups nurtured by the military and its intelligence agency to use against India."

And like LeT, Pakistan has done nothing to crack down on HuM and its activities in Afghanistan and Kashmir.

Jaish-e-Mohammed

The US government has listed Jaish-e-Mohammed (JeM) as a Foreign Terrorist organization and its leader, Masood Azhar, as a specially designated global terrorist for their ties to al-Qaeda and other jihadist groups.

Like LeT and HuM, JeM is supported by Pakistan's military and ISI because it is hostile to India and wages jihad in Afghanistan. In its 2010 designation of Azhar, the US Treasury Department said that "JeM recruitment posters in Pakistan contained a call from Azhar for volunteers to join the fight in Afghanistan against Western forces."

JeM was implicated along with the Lashkar-e-Taiba as being behind the December 13, 2001, attack on the Indian Parliament building in New Delhi. Sheikh Ahmed Saeed Omar, a close associate of Azhar, was behind the kidnapping of *Wall Street Journal* reporter Daniel Pearl. Pearl was later beheaded. Most recently, Indian officials implicated JeM in the January 2016 assault on a Pathankot Air Force Base in India. Like other attacks, Indian intelligence intercepted phone call of Pakistan-based handlers directing the assault team as they attacked the base. Despite JeM's terrorist activities, Pakistan has not taken action against the group. India has made repeated requests for extradition of Azhar, only to be ignored.

Hafiz Saeed Factor

Hafiz Muhammad Saeed is a Pakistani Islamist who is the co-founder of Lashkar-e-Taiba and the chief or emir of Jama'at-ud-Da'wah, which operates mainly from Pakistan. Saeed is a wanted terrorist by India and the United States for his alleged role in masterminding the

2008 terror attacks in Mumbai that claimed 166 lives. He has $10 million rewards on his head and is designated terrorist in UN list. Pakistan's ex-President and former military head Musharraf had recently called himself as the 'biggest supporter' of the LeT and its founder Hafiz Saeed. The former President added that he was always in favour of terrorist action in Kashmir and the LeT and the JuD were the biggest forces to take on the Indian Army in the State. Saeed announced that he would be contesting the upcoming general elections in 2018 from the newly-formed Milli Muslim League (MML). Musharraf's party is proposing to align with him and who knows in 2018 by the time this book comes out, he may be the Prime Minister of Pakistan forcing me and the publisher to revisit the book and take out the terrorist tag.

US-Pakistan Relationship Like a 'Critically Ill Patient'

"The relationship with Pakistan is kind of like a critically ill patient. You know you get up every day, you take the pulse, you deal with whatever fever has set in overnight and you just try to keep it alive for the next day. That's how I thought about Pakistan when I was there. It's a relationship you've got to have, but it is tough to maintain" said former Secretary of State Condoleezza Rice, who served as the National Security Advisor and the Secretary of State under the Bush administration.

Part Two

Kashmir Conflict - The Bermuda Triangle of India

Talk Talk Talk - With Whom?

4. Kashmir Conflict – The Bermuda Triangle of India

Kashmir Conflict – Like the Bermuda Triangle Mystery for India

The Bermuda Triangle, situated between Florida, Bermuda and Puerto Rico has long been known as a region where many Ships and Planes have vanished. One of the earliest disappearances was of Flight 19, a training mission involving five torpedo bombers. The planes left Fort Lauderdale on December 5, 1945, on routine training and never came back. To make it creepier, the search plane dispatched also vanished. More than 1,000 ships and planes have disappeared in the Triangle area over the past five centuries and such mysterious incidents on the Atlantic continue to take place even at present days.

The Bermuda Triangle, also known as the Devil's Triangle, is a region of the north-western Atlantic Ocean in which some aircraft and surface vessels have disappeared. Some people have claimed that these disappearances fall beyond the boundaries of human error or acts of nature. Some of these disappearances have been attributed to the paranormal, a suspension of the laws of physics, or activity by extraterrestrial beings by popular culture. Though a substantial documentation exists showing numerous incidents to have been inaccurately reported or embellished by later authors and numerous official agencies have gone on record as stating the number and nature of disappearances to be similar to any other area of ocean, many have remained unexplained despite considerable investigation.

By the time author Vincent Gaddis coined the phrase 'Bermuda Triangle' in a 1964 magazine article, additional mysterious accidents had occurred in the area, including three passenger planes that went down despite having just sent 'all's well' messages. Since then, scores of fellow paranormal writers have blamed the triangle's supposed lethalness on everything from Aliens, Atlantis and Sea monsters to Time warps and Reverse gravity fields, whereas more scientifically minded theorists have pointed to magnetic anomalies, waterspouts or huge eruptions of methane gas from the ocean floor.

In all probability, however, there is no single theory that solves the mystery. As one sceptic put it, trying to find a common cause for every Bermuda Triangle disappearance is no more logical than trying to find a common cause for every automobile accident in Arizona, USA. Similar to Bermuda unsolved answer, lies the Kashmir conflict with no identification of the cause, if you read the Kashmir history from the mythological era, it talks about the curse. If you read the medieval history it is full of bloodsheds by Afghans, Mughals, Dogras (few) tyrant rulers and now the Pakistani non-State actors in alliance with radicalized minds in the valley for last 70 years. Kashmir has always been like this not just since India's independence but much before that and hence no one knows the real cause why this beautiful part of the world is in continuous suffering and bloodshed.

If you see from Pakistani's perspective different answers will come, if you see from Kashmiri perspective, it will be different from Pakistanis and if you see from Indian perspective, they will be most concerned about terrorism put on them from across the border. The very idea of India they think is under attack, hence no potential, the solution as the problem statement itself is not defined or rather has multiple definitions based on which stakeholder is being asked. Is it a Political problem or an Islamic Radicals war or a Water war or a Geo-strategic location dominance war or is it just for the Scenic beauty related commerce war, no one knows that and hence a mystery, very much like Bermuda Triangle mystery. Kalashnikovs, Kahwa and Kaffirs form the most appropriate three vertices of this Kashmiri Bermuda Triangle of Uncertainties and hence the name of this book. Like Bermuda Triangle, it has sucked in golden years of India, Pakistan and Kashmiris, with so many lives, capital and energy of the nation.

For India, the region belongs to her as the last king had signed the instrument of accession to join India. Its history and culture is similar to the rest of India. For Pakistan, the region belongs to her as the three-fourths of the region was Muslim at the time of partition in 1947. The geography favours her too as Pakistani capital is just an hour drive from Kashmir border and the valley is accessible through multiple roads from Pakistan. Added to that, the main water supply for Western India and Pakistan – Indus, passes through Kashmir and controlling the State provides a strategic advantage when it comes to water (the most scarce commodity in South Asia and world).

Pakistan has encouraged the separatists for decades and China has involved herself by aiding her ally – Pakistan. Essentially, it is a two-party conflict (between India and Pakistan) where external parties are quite interested to make their imprint. For the US the road to Afghanistan crossed through the Karachi port of Pakistan and hence soft approach towards Pakistan an estranged shrewd ally. Right from the beginning, The Muslim League claimed Kashmir for Pakistan. But when the actual partition happened, the British gave 'princely States' the power to decide whether to accede to India or Pakistan. While Punjab's and Bengal's fate was decided by the Radcliffe Line, no such lines were drawn for princely States of Kashmir, Junagadh and Osmania (Hyderabad Presidency). Also, fates of NWFP and the princely State of Balochistan were left undecided as well. While the Khan of Kalat (Kalat was Balochistan's capital under the monarch) chose to accede to India, NWFP in a referendum voted to join Pakistan with 49% in favour of India.

What ensued after the British left is that India started annexing all those tiny Princely States that wanted to stay independent. India also annexed Junagadh that wanted to accede to Pakistan. India then annexed Osmania that was ruled by a Muslim Monarch (albeit the territory was a Hindu majority). India also annexed Laccadive Islands that had 99% Muslim population (still does). This was the great vision of the India's greatest Home Minister Sardar Vallabhbhai Patel.

Pakistan followed suite and annexed Balochistan and started annexation of Kashmir. Kashmir has always been part of the Punjab empire. Dogra Maharaja Hari Singh sought the help of Indian army to defend the Kashmir nation against the invading Pakistani army. The Indians refused except on one condition: Kashmir accede to India. But before acceding to India, from August 14th to 15th 1947 when Pakistan and India got independence respectively, to 26th October 1947, Kashmir remained an Independent province and was as per the partition rule laid by British had to choose between India or Pakistan. These two months of free/azaad status is the only time when it was azaad under the Hindu King Raja Hari Singh, this is when Pakistan army in the disguise of kabalis (first act of State-sponsored non-State actors proxies) plus Afghan mercenaries attacked part of Kashmir and captured 35% part of Kashmir from Raja Hari Singh, which now India calls POK (Azad Kashmir, Gilgit-Baltistan region). The Maharaja signed accession papers and off went the Indian army to defend Kashmir.

They managed to significantly claim back territories from Pakistan, but the war was abruptly intervened when Nehru, the first Prime Minister of Independent India, decided to stop the war and go to the UN. India had the accession papers and thought they would win back Kashmir. But Pakistan didn't bite – it argued that India had annexed Osmania and Junagadh and so Pakistan had every right to annex Kashmir, a Muslim majority region. Pak refused to give up what's now POK and Gilgit-Baltistan. Whilst India maintained that it can't give up Kashmir because of its religious importance to Hindus/ Sikhs and because of majority Buddhist population in the eastern Leh-Ladakh region that wouldn't be safe if the territory was to be handed to Pakistan (a 98% Hindu-majority territory, Chittagong Hill Tracts, that was awarded to East Pakistan, bore witness to the systematic cleansing of the native Hindu tribes).

Interesting bit of trivia: Pakistan doesn't officially confer any Constitutional province-hood to POK or Gilgit-Baltistan. India confers autonomous 'Statehood' to the province of Jammu and Kashmir – the only Indian State to be fully independent of the Central Government. In fact, it's one of the two Indian States to have its flag. And from what I know, the Indian government recognizes all 'Pro-Freedom' parties (parties that demand secession from both Pak and India) as a Political Party. What an Irony and it is India that faces Azaadi call in the valley. So this cannot be a political or territorial problem only.

Pakistani military used the Kashmir issue to their advantage and created ISI and started eating into Pak's budgets. They cite Kashmir as a reminder that the 'Hindu' India is a perennial threat to the sovereignty of Pakistan. India was vilified in the Media, kids got taught revisionist history (thanks, Ayub Khan) and everyone thereon started hating all things Indian – so much so that most believed they descended from Arabs and Central Asians (Persians) and that they had no Indian lineage. Similar things happened in India. Media, on both sides of the border, still spread hate. A little digression, but thought of showing the current picture.

Then 1965 happened, then 1971 happened (Bangladesh seceded from Pakistan with Indian help. And taking Kashmir from India now seemed like a perfect revenge), then 1984 happened (LoC being drawn, Siachen conflict) then 1989 happened (radicalization of Kashmir starts, mujahids, Ghazwa-e-Hind, thanks to Zia-ul-Haq), then 1999 Kargil happened (Pak's response to 84's Siachen conflict). And all these events have made the matter more complex and no light at the end of the tunnel. Add that to the nuclear arsenal and we have a perfect deadlock. India with all its military and economical might can't bring itself to wage war on Pak, while ISI continues to wage proxy war via terrorists (2008 Bombay attacks, 2001 Delhi Parliament attack and so many that list has become as exhaustive as the Bibliography section of this book.

It's unfortunate and one is left to wonder what if Sardar Patel had assumed the Prime Ministership, what if Maulana Azad's proposal had been accepted by the Cabinet Mission. What if the partition never happened? Partition of British India has caused more harm than good and all this animosity, all this hate, all this violence is a legacy of three men – Mountbatten, Nehru and Jinnah. Creation of Pakistan was never a long-term solution. (And this is the data/history/narrative India should put forward in UN for the lasting global terrorism fix, as out 19 plus US recognized terror outfits, 13 have Pakistani linkages.) It was short-sighted and void of any vision. Muslims of subcontinent paid the heavy price for this split-up and they continue to suffer from this complexity.

To know why a civil war was a distant possibility, let's rewind 80 years and relive history a little bit – the prime justification for Partition as cited by Congress (the largest party) was that a civil war was inevitable had the partition not happened. That's baseless. Mahatma Gandhi, Maulana Abul Kalam Azad, Badshah Khan could see that nothing like that would ever happen and even if it did, it would not have lasted long enough and wouldn't have broken up the country. Remember that Gandhi was still alive and so was Badshah Khan – two men who had an immense following and were saviour-like to their followers. Jinnah himself said in an interview just after the formation of Pakistan in Karachi that he never thought 'Pakistan' would be a reality in his life time. What does that say to you?

The whole 'civil war' thing came up when the protesters in Calcutta turned to violence on the Direct Action Day in 1946 (after Congress, led-by Nehru backed out of the Cabinet-plan). Muslim League in 1940 made it crystal clear that they didn't need a separate nation but a 'federated' nation of India and Pakistan – just like the Great Britain). Nehru was a socialist and wanted a 'strong' Central Government (and seeing how that has turned out for India, we now think the Cabinet-mission should have been supported to go ahead with the plan, but we are talking about two highly egoistical people here – Nehru and Jinnah), whilst Jinnah wanted a federated government with a weak centre. 'Direct Action Day' was a result of lack of respect from Congress for their Muslim counterparts and the outcome scared them. Muslim League announced themselves as a strong opposition and promised for more say for the Muslims (mainly Feudal and Nawabs).

There are many angles to what lead to the creation of Pakistan, here are some political angles to it:

1. Muslim League leaders were feudal and were against Congress proposed land reforms.
2. The western powers that be were wary of such large chunk of Asia succumbing to the Soviet Union and Communism (remember that Nehru was a Socialist).
3. Congress wanted total power (power makes a man corrupt).

With Muslims fighting and getting their own country, one has to wonder why wasn't Congress fearful of the south Indians, Dravidians (they too were culturally different and spoke a different language) asking for a separate country? It's a bit unfortunate what happened. Point to think and analyse.

Now, for reasons why there had never been a civil war in India:

1. Jinnah, though galvanized Muslims in the subcontinent under one banner, a majority of them were against him and were aware of his political ambitions.
2. The Mullahs of United Provinces (Patna - Bihar, Lucknow - Uttar Pradesh, Delhi) were against the creation of a Muslim State (although a majority did move to Pakistan after the partition and still treated as Muhajirs, the second class citizens).
3. Muslim League wasn't popular in Punjab a province that is the largest (both area-wise and population-wise in the present-day Pakistan). Muslim League couldn't even win an election there, let alone rule the State.
4. Muslim League wasn't popular to the present day Khyber Pakhtunkhwa, Pakistan and FATA. The Muslims there were fully behind Badshah Khan and his non-violent ways. (It's tragic that most terrorists and terrorist organizations have their roots in Khyber Pakhtunkhwa, Pakistan and FATA, Badshah Khan would be turning in his grave at the present state of affairs there.) In fact, 49% of Muslims voted to be a part of India during a referendum.
5. The Khan of Kalat wanted to accede to India and made no secret of his desire to do so. Kalat was the capital of Balochistan (Pakistan). People in Balochistan had no *hamdardi* (sympathy) for the Muslim League.
6. The Muslims that did support the Pakistan movement were majority Bengalis. Bengalis and Bengal could have asked for a separate State (not on the basis of religion, but on the basis of ethnicity) and that would have been a valid claim from their side. And Bengal was notoriously difficult to rule (no different

even today, ask Chief Minister Mamata Banerjee). They had have revolted, but they were a small minority compared to Muslims that wanted a peaceful co-existence.

7. The Muslims of United Provinces were also strongly supportive of Pakistan and could have caused trouble along with the Bengalis, but they had to face strong Indian army of that time under the able control of Patel to achieve their goal. And with leaders of stature of Gandhi, Badshah Khan and Azad still alive (and with the Mullahs still on the side of the Congress), a civil war would have been reduced to mere rioting.
8. Jinnah was ailing and was on the brink of death. Besides Liaquat Ali Khan, Muslim League had no real leaders. No one (look up the history books) was fit enough or charismatic enough to lead Muslims into an election, let alone a war.

Partition was never a necessity, but a convenient, rapid way to get rid of the Muslim elite that Congress could afford for short-term political gain (and vice versa for the Muslim League). It was a necessity of the West that partition happened. And because it happened the way it did, has left a permanent blemish on the United India's souls (more Indians died during the Partition than US Soldiers in WW2) and continue to die, due to the nasty power struggle that's never-ending. Kashmir is a mirror image of that with Elite Muslims wanting to separate from India and form a buffer State between India and Pakistan or at least merge with Pakistan as its new province, not gonna happen.

If anything Partition of British-India should have mobilized various separatist movements in the country which would have led to the inevitable Balkanization of the State, but it never happened. So for the readers wondering why we are discussing Pakistan more than Kashmir, they are interrelated. India cannot bypass Pakistan for solving Kashmir, Pakistan will not budge an inch for the mutually agreed resolution, the very creation of Pakistan itself has been the mother of this problem, so how can one solve Kashmir quagmire? Bermuda Triangle fear might have reduced with the advent of better technologies of monitoring, but the answer of disappearance still evades and so does Kashmir conflict resolution even after 70 years of India and Pakistan sovereign existence from British rule.

Kashmir directly challenges the very definition on which India and Pakistan were formed in 1947. Pakistan was formed purely on religious line, i e, Muslims cannot leave with majority Hindu India for practising their culture and for having a separate identity from majority Hindu population. On the contrary the idea on which India was formed was secular credentials in spite of she being a Hindu majority (80%) State.

The Indian Constitution made her plural in nature and the rule of law was primary. Hindus, Muslims, Christians, Sikhs and Buddhist can co-exist and have full freedom to practice and believe in their faiths, it even allowed conversion of religion (good or bad is a separate discussion), whereas Pakistan was totally based on the religious ground and became an Islamic republic (with the legal sanction of the blasphemy law, mostly against non-Muslims or non-Sunni Muslims). The Pakistani Penal Code prohibits blasphemy against Islam, providing penalties ranging from a fine to death, mostly deaths in practice. Hindus minorities were wiped out, their number dwindled from 20% in 1947 to 1.5% in 2017 and even Muslim Ahmadiyas and Christians are daily killed and prosecuted and made to live like a second-class citizen.

In this background, if India agrees to cede Kashmir to Pakistan it will be putting Jammu and other parts of Kashmir's Hindus, Buddhists, Shia Muslims, Sikhs and non-Feudal and poor class Muslims under harm's way, as it is the paramount duty of Government of India to take care of its citizens. Now the other option which Indian Kashmiri separatists have been floating around of becoming an independent country, a buffer State between two nuclear powers States (in fact to me its 4 nuclear powers, to some extent Russia (erstwhile Tajikistan connection to Shia Kashmiris) and China with Aksai Chin which they claim to be part of their Xinjiang Uyghur Autonomous Region, plus the $57 billion CPEC pipedream project. It will be impractical for Kashmir to get this type of solution, whatever cost incurred and also is it even worthwhile? No UN driven Plebiscite can rescue them. Just not possible.

The Kashmir problem can't be solved unless India and Pakistan agree to find an amicable solution to it. The founding fathers of India and Pakistan did not envisage antagonistic relations between the two countries. Even though Gandhi opposed the creation of Pakistan, he took fast unto death for the release of ₹ 55 crore to Pakistan towards the second instalment of arrears to be paid to it under the terms of division of assets and liabilities. In the past seven decades, India and Pakistan never seriously tried to put an end to the Kashmir crisis. Whether it's the Tashkent Declaration, Shimla Agreement, Lahore Declaration, there was no urgency and time-bound approach plan to resolve the vexed Kashmir crisis.

Historian Stanley Wolpert wrote in Jinnah's autobiography:

> "Few Individuals significantly alter the course of history. Fewer still modify the map of the world. Hardly anyone can be credited with creating a Nation-State. Muhammad Ali Jinnah did all the three."

Well said Mr Wolpert, I guess this is where Nehru, Gandhi, Rajaji, Maulana Azad and entire Indian Congress leadership failed and how miserably they failed, costing one million subcontinent precious lives! They should have had never succumbed to Jinnah's blackmail, he was weak fragile and had a very small minority support in the Akhand Bharat (United India). One man Jinnah *vs* all these Indian Congress stalwarts and how convincingly Jinnah won carving a new country that never existed in the human's history, taking away the key strategic parts that could have connected India to Central Asia and hence would have given invaluable geo positioning advantage and bringing the entire world powers at its door.

I am really surprised and disappointed, with the Indian leadership of that time, they were all western educated and highly read and well-travelled across the globe, still missed the knowledge of geography and meekly agreed to the boundary suggested by the British officer Radcliffe, totally taking out India's advantage of strategic and historical location importance. They should have declined to accept Pakistan carved out like that by not accepting Independence for some more time. What a letdown, still paying the price and will continue doing for many decades to come.

Talbot, an expert on South-East Asia, highlights the regional dimension of South Asia's past and present by noting the existence of clear regional patterns in apparently disparate local developments. This dimension underlines the region's distinct subsequent developments such as the way in which the State – in India, Pakistan and Bangladesh alike – has "often been drawn into" internal conflicts because of its own citizens' "resistance to its policies of cultural, administrative and political centralization." These conflicts have created a 'fearful' South Asian State, determined to prevent further "Balkanization." The consequences have been obvious in each of the three countries: as the State has sought to address separatist demands as law and order problems, those seeking greater autonomy have ended up raising arms. The story across the region has been a remarkably similar one.

The consequence of the 'downsized Pakistani State' (post-1971) had the effect of exaggerating its asymmetrical power relationship with India. This, in turn, has intensified three long-term policies that have had a huge impact on Pakistani politics, as well as regional political developments: the search for external allies to counterbalance India, resources being channelled into defence expenditure, ignoring other needs and the "use of Islamic proxies to destabilize India's position in Kashmir".

From the second half of the 19th century, privately-owned canals across the Indus basin started making way for canal colonies constructed and managed by the colonial State on a massive scale. In the long run, the State was able to extend its control through these canal colonies, a process that continues to the present day. But the State itself has been neither monolithic nor uncontested. After 1947, the division of a single hydrological system between competing for national interests has had profound implications, which subsequent treaty agreements between India and Pakistan have not been able to resolve fully.

There's two consistent lines of argument about the Indus waters dispute in the post-Independence period. It first contends that territoriality and sovereignty were central to water politics in the basin, with the control of water flows within national territory being essential to making a State sovereign, a necessary part of State building. The dispute was, thus, as much a political problem as an engineering one. Secondly, the dispute, more broadly and the Indus Waters Treaty, more specifically, occupied a very particular historical moment - the ideas about sovereignty that Indian and Pakistani leaders attempted to enact were a product of the two States' political development after decolonization, set within a global Cold War context. From the perspective of those on the Pakistani side, its political leaders asserted a bargaining position on the principle of territorial integrity.

Pakistani assertions of territorial integrity should be interpreted in broader notions of the legitimacy of the State. Proving to its population in the years following independence that it could go head-to-head with India in order to secure water resources may have been critical to the new Pakistani State's claims to be a legitimate successor to the British colonial power and authority. But, importantly, the rhetoric of the river's geographical integrity did not eventually preclude compromise: "South Asian territoriality was under construction" during those years; while Pakistani politicians, like their Indian counterparts, made fairly consistent claims regarding territory, sovereignty and water rights", these did vary, with sovereignty over water and space continually contested.

Indus Waters Treaty was used as a model for India-Pakistan cooperation in Bengal during the late 1960s. The short-lived attempt highlighted potential opportunities as well as pitfalls bound up in applying a relatively successful model of collaboration in a different setting. So as you see now, the resolution of Kashmir issue is directly tied to the idea of Pakistan and India, as the respective Nation-States and no one will change their definition and hence the Kashmir issue will keep hanging in Limbo. Our current concerns and priorities mean that we often read history backward, searching in the past for answers to questions that challenge us today. Kashmir is no exception.

Dissecting Britain's Role in Keeping Bermuda Triangle of India Unresolved

The beginning of the Kashmir conflict was a tumultuous experience that defined the terms of the crises in its later years. Struggles in Kashmir have been a long, drawn-out debacle of politics, terrorism and war. For the past seventy years, India and Pakistan have used both peaceful negotiation and war in an attempt to control the land known as Jammu and Kashmir, which are the same principality. Problems between the Hindu minority and the Muslim majority in Kashmir dates back to 1846.

1. A Hindu maharaja was on the throne there for one hundred years and maintained horrible conditions for the Muslim majority of Jammu and Kashmir. These issues between the Hindus and the Muslims were a larger problem for British India as a whole, which eventually led to the partition of British India into two countries: India and Pakistan.
2. Independence for British India was not an easy achievement and the difficulties of securing Muslim rights led to the creation of Pakistan. Ever since India and Pakistan earned their independence from the United Kingdom in 1947, there has been strife between the two nations. Jammu and Kashmir became a problem because each nation had important reasons for controlling the territory. Great Britain also had its interests in the Kashmir conflict. Britain had maintained a presence in the region for over 200 years and controlled the area known as British India from 1858-1947.
3. This was the reason for the Indian subcontinent to become vital for Great Britain's economic and foreign policy. Even when India and Pakistan gained their independence, Britain did not want to lose these economic and strategic military advantages. Though India and Pakistan were no longer colonies of Britain, the British continued to manipulate their

affairs. In 1947, the Cold War was just beginning and fear of the Soviet Union spreading Communist ideals around the world consumed the foreign policy of Britain. Because of this, military bases were needed in Asia to encircle and spy on the eastern regions of the Soviet Union. India and Pakistan are located south of the Soviet Union and close enough that any attack from the British Royal Air Force could reach any target in the USSR. Thus, the Cold War foreign policy of Britain depended on maintaining military bases in India and Pakistan even after they had lost political control.

4. India and Pakistan also held vital economic importance to Great Britain, through both resources and trade relations with other nations. The Middle-East's oil was an important commodity for Great Britain in 1947 as it still is today. Britain did not want to lose access to this oil because it was such a vital resource and one of the most important items in their economic policy. They believed if they allowed Pakistan to lose Kashmir, then the Muslims of the world would become furious with Britain.
5. On the other hand, India could not lose territory either because Britain wanted to maintain their primary position in the Commonwealth as a trade partner; Pakistan was also in the Commonwealth, many argue that Britain determined that it was in its interest for the Kashmir conflict between India and Pakistan to be unresolved and that, from the outset, Britain intentionally prolonged the situation there to better serve its political and economic interests. Archival material found in secondary sources and documents examining the situation from the perspective of the United Nations demonstrate this clearly. Specifically, the archive material includes letters and telegrams between the United Kingdom Cabinet and Prime Minister Clement Attlee.

Also, there are secret orders given by India's Governor-General, Lord Louis Mountbatten and the commander of India and Pakistan's armed forces, Commander Auchinleck, that describe how the British set-up their manipulations in Kashmir. Besides, to the British perspective on this conflict, sources from India's Prime Minister Jawaharlal Nehru and Pakistan's representative at the United Nations, Sir Muhammad Zafrullah Khan, also show how India and Pakistan viewed the British role at the beginning of the dissent. To understand the British role in this discord, the time covered in this paper is from October 1947, the date when this hostility began, until January 1948, the date of the first important meeting of the UN Security Council over the dissension. The focus here is how Britain's Cabinet was able to implement their manipulations on India and Pakistan. These manipulations concentrated on finding a peaceful solution in which neither India nor Pakistan regretted the loss of Kashmir.

The idea presented here is a new topic because it is not in support of either India or Pakistan acquiring Kashmir. By examining these motives, people can realize that fighting and terrorism continues today in Kashmir because of British desires at the outset. When historians discuss the Kashmir dispute, the topic of Britain's involvement is not often addressed. Because the struggle has now entered in its seventieth year and many horrible events have occurred, Britain's involvement, in the beginning, has been lost in the historical record. Also, since the Cold War, a side effect of this is that authors writing about the discord in Kashmir are only now realizing how influential Britain was in the beginning. Another common aspect in the historiography is that authors tend to favour the position of either Pakistan or India because the conflict is ongoing.

There has been a lack of information on Britain's involvement in the Kashmir hostility in historical works. This is often the case because the topic of diplomacy is not the author's focus, such as Praveen Swami's *India, Pakistan and the Secret Jihad: The Covert War in Kashmir, 1947-2004*. This is noticeable in Swami's book because he is concentrating on the covert operations that India and Pakistan unleashed against each other in Kashmir. Swami's work is an example of most books about Kashmir because, as his main argument portrays, there are recent problems to confront and solve, such as terrorism: "In essence, this book presents a new map of Jammu and Kashmir, a re-drawing of events with the jihad and its authors at the Centre."

6. Kashmir is not just two-nation theory offshoot, it is an ideological war. One Hindu king ruled for 100 years and the Muslim majority junta lead by Sheikh Abdullah had a problem, the entire India with 90% Hindus were ruled by a tyrant like Aurangzeb, etc and they now have to let plebiscite in their Kashmir for Muslim majority of the valley to choose Pakistan, UN and history has no issue with this? Nehru and others easily surrendered to Jinnah blackmail and partitioned

India, resulting in 12 million people displaced and 1 million brutally killed, both sides of the border. In the entire history of humanity, not even a small village is conceded without any blood and here in some unexplained rush, Nehru and the Indian Congress leaders, accepted to partition united India parting with huge land, throwing away the advantage of the strategic region of POK, Balochistan, etc.

Nehru was not a practising Hindu, was more of atheist elitist, understood but what about Patel, Gandhi, even Maulana how did they forget that the Indian civilization originated from Harappa and Mohenjo-Daro, parting away with this Indian cultural symbol, the great Indus Valley civilization was a Himalayan blunder. What a goof-up by the Indian political leaders, most of them came from reputed western universities and exposed to outside world. People should posthumously ask them these questions. They had no right to displace 12 million Hindus, Muslims, Punjabis, Kashmiris, Bengalis and Biharis and UPites from their million years old origin. Muslims were also badly affected as they had to move to Pakistan

7. Britain had ulterior motives before and during the incident from 1947-1948. These motives led the issue to last all these years, seventy now. The focal point of his arguments was that the Kashmir conflict could have ended within the first year, in India's favour, if Great Britain had not interfered. Dasgupta's, an eminent historian, point is that Great Britain remained in charge of both India and Pakistan armies. From there, he speaks about Great Britain's economic interest of keeping Pakistan a nation because it allowed good relations with the rest of the Muslim world. As Admiral Cunningham, a prominent leader in Britain's navy, explains: "if Pakistan's application were rejected it would shatter Britain's relations with the 'whole Muslim world' to the detriment of her strategic position in the Middle-East and North Africa." This theory of British Imperial interests was present in India too as Dasgupta reveals: "For two centuries, the Indian Empire was both the object and the instrument of British strategy in the Indian Ocean."
8. Facts such as these allow the argument of British interfering in the conflict to draw it out to keep both its interests intact to be quite convincing. While Dasgupta sees the involvement of the United Nations as a delaying tactic used by the British, Mark Mazower maintains that Britain was, in fact,

supporting the ideals of the United Nations alongside their interests in his book *No Enchanted Palace: The End of Empire and the Ideological Origins of the United Nations*. Mazower does not concentrate on the British in this piece but on the origins of the United Nations. It was not meant to be a utopian answer to the problems of the world, but a tool to maintain the interests of the world's superpowers. In this book, Mazower tries to confront the two most common ideas about the origins of the United Nations: "one is that the United Nations rose – like Aphrodite – from the Second World War, pure and uncontaminated by any significant association with that prewar failure, the League of Nations. And second, that it was, above all, an American affair, the product of public debate and private discussion in which other countries played little part."

9. Though he does digress, Britain was, in fact, a major player in the creation of the United Nations and this was because it was a part of the Big Three: Great Britain, the USSR and the USA.
10. With this information, Mazower tries to show that the UN was not created originally to solve all of the problems in the world but in fact to help the more powerful nations, such as Great Britain, to maintain their interests in the world. Then there are authors like DN Panagrahi who look at the influences of the Cold War on the Kashmir conflict. DN Panagrahi's *Jammu and Kashmir: The Cold War and the West*, is a unique and recent work because it concentrates on the influences of Great Britain and the United States on the Kashmir conflict. Besides, Panagrahi focuses on the beginning years to see how Great Britain orchestrated India's failure in obtaining Kashmir. Unfortunately, this work is completely in favour of India, so information about the issue makes India look like the victim of Great Britain and the United States' indirect interventions: "The western powers looked at the Kashmir problem as an Indian creation and wished to see that it was either amalgamated with Pakistan or made an independent State."
11. This bias towards India is understandable because DN Panagrahi is a modern India specialist and works for the University of Delhi; nevertheless, his work is still valuable toward understanding the Kashmir dispute. The Cold War and the West, Routledge, Dasgupta and Panagrahi share the common ideal that Great Britain was more deeply involved in the politics of India, Pakistan and, subsequently, Kashmir.

Their focuses are different in that Dasgupta believes Great Britain allowed the Kashmir issue to escalate out of fear of either India or Pakistan losing, but he still supported the idea of India being the victor in the issue. Panagrahi believed that Great Britain was trying to subvert India and support Pakistan. Mazower focuses on how the United Nations was created to serve the interests of more powerful nations.

The conflict in Jammu and Kashmir between its Hindu and Muslim population began with the Treaty of Amritsar in 1846. The British sold Kashmir to a Hindu Dogra King Gulab Singh; he received an amazing deal from Great Britain. As the representative of the UN Commission for India and Pakistan explains about this acquisition of Kashmir by Gulab Singh: "He sold the entire Kashmir Valley for a paltry sum of 7.5 million rupees (about $2,250,000).

12. The mistreatment of Muslims did not emanate from the Dogra dynasty itself but deeper religious and social differences. Hinduism and Islam are religions with distinct societal practices. British India has always had a small Muslim population compared to its number of Hindus. In addition, British India did not comprise the entire subcontinent; they only controlled 75% of the total population directly while 25% of it remained under the rule of local princes as per the United Nations Security Council Commission for India and Pakistan.

13. A rough estimate for British India's population was that there was about a three to one ratio of non-Muslims to Muslims. According to Sir Zafrullah Khan's speech before the Security Council on January 16 and 17, 1948:

    "The two main blocs – the Moslems and the non-Moslems – have, in most spheres of life, kept apart all through. The one outstanding cause is that the bulk of Hindu society is based on the principles of caste and untouchability."

14. Muslims did not approve of Hinduism because it was a polytheistic religion. Islam is monotheistic. Hinduism believes in a trinity of gods that represent the creation, middle and the destruction of the universe; Islam believes that there is no god but Allah and Muhammad is his prophet. This became a problem when determining the independence of British India.

15. To understand the Kashmir conflict, it is necessary to explain how British India gained its independence. India, Pakistan

(Bangladesh later gains independence from Pakistan) used to be part of the British colonial province known as British India. British officials were in charge of important economic and government positions in British India by the rule of a Viceroy. Pakistan was not an official State of British India and its creation is a result of the discord among the prominent indigenous figures of British India and their inability to come to a compromise plus the British manipulation. If they were so concerned about Muslims' situation in British India, they could have created a separate Muslim province/State within their rule.

16. Prominent Hindu figures included Jawaharlal Nehru, India's first Prime Minister; Sardar Patel and Mahatma Gandhi, the Indian philosopher of peace. For the Muslims, such prominent figures were Muhammad Ali Jinnah, the leader of the Muslim League; and Liaquat Ali Khan, Jinnah's right-hand man and Pakistan's first Prime Minister.
17. Equal representation was the issue that eventually split British India apart. Jinnah and Ali Khan wanted to have equal representation in both the government and society of British India between the Hindus and Muslims of India; Nehru and his followers, members of the India National Congress, did not allow this.
18. These political debates and issues were prominent throughout the early 20th century and it did not approach a conclusion until Lord Louis Mountbatten, Earl of Burma and the last Viceroy of India, arrived. Lord Mountbatten was the last Viceroy of India and his rule began in March 1947. He was charged with managing a smooth transition of British India towards independence. He concluded it was necessary to partition British India into two States, India and Pakistan and allowed the 600 or so scattered princely States to decide which nation they wanted to join; Kashmir was no exception. Mountbatten helped India and Pakistan to gain their independence on August 14 (Pakistan) and August 15 (India) 1947. He had only been Viceroy for five months.
19. India allowed Mountbatten to serve as Governor-General of India to help them create order amid the chaos of partition. Maharaja Hari Singh asked Mountbatten for help in order to have Kashmir not fall into chaos and to protect him from whichever nation he did not join: "He also assured him on behalf of the Government of India that if the Maharaja decided to accede to Pakistan, India would not regard it as an unfriendly act."

20. By allowing this, Mountbatten tried to create order in the chaos of partition. Partition effected both India and Pakistan greatly, leading to approximately one million deaths and the largest mass migration in human history.
21. Hindus, Muslims and Sikhs had to flee across the newly created borders to avoid being in the wrong country. Sir Cyril Radcliffe, a British barrister, created the Boundary Commission that determined where, exactly, Pakistan would be. The boundaries split in half the Punjab region and the Bengal region (modern-day Bangladesh), a fact which was not known to the public until a day after independence.
22. The UK Cabinet knew that chaos would ensue over these boundaries no matter where they drew the line and realized that the Radcliffe Boundary Commission was the fastest way to secure independence for India and Pakistan. This caused people who had lived in their homes for generations to make a mad scramble to avoid communal violence. There was ongoing violence in the months before in fear and ignorance of where the boundary line would be. Millions of Muslims had to flee into East and West Pakistan while millions of Hindus from these areas fled into India.
23. As they fled, gangs of the opposite religion attacked both Hindus and Muslims; no one was safe. Hindus were killing Muslims, Muslims were killing Hindus and riots and communal violence were occurring all over India and Pakistan. This violence was widespread and created chaos for the new governments that were trying to unite their countries and maintain order in the first years of independence. After each country became independent, they still only consisted up to half of what comprises India and Pakistan today. They had to deal with the princely States that remained.
24. Many of the princely States were in the middle of India and each of them had their maharaja and government. To try to maintain a peaceful transition of power, Britain allowed the governments and citizens of each princely State to vote on which nation they would join. Most of the princely States based these decisions on whether the population was Hindu or Muslim. Historian Alice Thorner, describes in her article, "The Issues in Kashmir," how the princely States choose to join either India or Pakistan: "The Act of Parliament of July 1947, which partitioned the eleven provinces of British India into two nations, provided that each of the 600-odd

feudatory princes (who together ruled over nearly one-half the country) might accede to one or the other or neither." Who gave British colonial ruler to decide the fate of the Indian subcontinent?

25. Each of the princely States also received advice from Lord Mountbatten about joining India or Pakistan. He advised them to take into account the economic, geographical and population statistics when deciding which country to join.
26. Kashmir was one of the most glorious and important of the princely kingdoms in the British India area. It is located in the northernmost area of British India and shares borders with Afghanistan, China, India and Pakistan. Both India and Pakistan desired to control this kingdom. Jawaharlal Nehru, India's Prime Minister, was especially fond of Kashmir being a Kashmiri by birth, in one of his writings: "My love of the mountains and my kinship with Kashmir especially drew me to them and I saw there not only the life and vigour and beauty of the present but also the memoried loveliness of ages past."
27. Hari Singh, like his Dogra ancestors, was Hindu and this led to problems in his kingdom of Kashmir where Islam was the dominant religion. The Muslims outnumbered the Hindus in Kashmir by a ratio of three to one. According to the 1941 census report in the State of Jammu and Kashmir, the total population was 4,021,616 people. Of this population, 3,101,247 or 77.11% were Muslim and 920,369 people or 22.89% were non-Muslim.
28. Therefore, when Pakistan gained independence and became a home for the Muslims of British India, Kashmir's Muslims wanted to join as well. Hari Singh brought in gangs of Hindus and Sikhs from East Punjab to control the uprising. Anyone who did not approve of his rule in August 1947. One account written by a special correspondent of *The Times* wrote that 2,37,000 Muslims were exterminated in the State of Jammu by troops headed by Hari Singh himself. This is pure allegation, have not been proved but there was deep anguish against this ruler.
29. Because of this terror wrought upon them, some of the Muslim citizens of Jammu and Kashmir revolted and formed the Azad (Free) Kashmir Movement. They tried to wrestle control from the Maharaja to join Pakistan. Economic concerns were a priority of the POK movement because they knew that Jammu and Kashmir and Pakistan were

interdependent in economic matters. This is just one reason why Pakistan needed the Jammu and Kashmir State to join them. Jammu and Kashmir, especially in the Kashmir valley, is a fertile land with good forests, fields and other useful exports. The wools and clothing are a valuable commodity for the Kashmiri to sell; timber is also an important export between Kashmir and Pakistan. Western Pakistan [modern day Pakistan] was the top consumer of Kashmiri exports. Karachi, Pakistan's main port city, was the natural and closest outlet for Kashmir to access the international market.

30. Pakistan had relied on having access to Kashmiri timber, fruit and wool to help fuel their economy, especially when they were part of British India. Trade with other parts of India existed as well, but the people from the area that became Pakistan were historical trade partners. Further, Pakistan's geography and people relied on the safety and well-being of the Jammu and Kashmir State. According to the UNCIP (United Nations Commission for India and Pakistan): "West Pakistan's three main rivers, the Indus, the Jhelum and the Chenab, flow from Kashmir into Pakistan. If Kashmir continued to be occupied by India, nineteen million acres of land irrigated by these rivers would be in danger of having their water supply cut off."
31. Violence and animosity were common between India and Pakistan, so this fear had validity. Militarily, if India gained control of Kashmir, they would be able to have two strategic fronts against Pakistan. Refugees that fled the terror of partition into Pakistan were also a problem and if three million more people had to come into their nation, Pakistan would not be able to support them all.
32. Meanwhile, India, harboured hopes that internal domestic and economic problems would cause Pakistan to want to rejoin India. India controlled more land and more technological advances, such as railways and roads; this lessened Kashmir's economic need for India. It seems that the Indian government desired to control Jammu and Kashmir to be able to control valuable economic and strategic asset of Pakistan.
33. Because of the chaotic transition to independence, India was being flooded with Hindu and Sikh refugees, but they had more land and a better economy to aid them with this. Their main goal was to stop the destruction and violence that partition created for the entire subcontinent. Sir Muhammad

Zafrullah Khan presents Pakistan's point of view on why India wanted Kashmir: "India is under no necessity or compulsion to require or to need the accession of Kashmir to itself. India has merely entered upon a gamble. If it succeeds in that gamble, it can crush and break Pakistan - and that is the object of that gamble."

34. While both countries desired Kashmir, it was essential to Pakistan, to validate her two nation theory ideology. Pakistan hoped that the POK movement would succeed and allow Kashmiris the right to vote over which nation they joined. By allowing the princely States to choose which country to join, the majority of the States entered into India or Pakistan without bloodshed. Unfortunately, Kashmir would not have so much luck in this venture of politics because Hari Singh went against the will of his Muslim citizens and opted to join India: "the Premier of Pakistan denied all accusations and warned Kashmir against joining India. On the following day, large armed bands crossed the Pakistan-Kashmir border and overpowered the State forces in the frontier town of Muzaffarabad."
35. India technically has Jammu and Kashmir as its north-west State. After Hari Singh signed the treaty to join India to save its population from Jihadi Muslim Afghan criminals and the Pakistani army in the disguise of Raiders, India invaded Jammu and Kashmir to deal with the problem. Raiders and tribesman coming from Pakistan and the North-Western provinces invaded Kashmir in an attempt to change the Maharaja's mind by force. VP Menon, Secretary for Sardar Patel, observed that Pakistan planned this from the beginning "to let loose a tribal invasion through the north-west. Srinagar today, Delhi tomorrow. A nation that forgets its history or geography does so at its peril."
36. The facts are inconsistent here because India and Pakistan believe that the conflict started on different days. India claims the struggle started when the tribesmen invaded on October 22, 1947, while Pakistan, as stated by Zafrullah Khan, "Pakistan, on the other hand, maintains that a vigorous freedom movement had already started within the State and had made considerable progress before the tribal incursion took place." They have been saying this for last 70 years now, total lie.
37. This is how the controversy and strife would become one of the first prominent international issues for the new United

Nations. Both India and Pakistan sought the help of the United Nations to settle the conflict in Kashmir and to act as a mediator in the ensuing events. Lord Mountbatten was able to convince Prime Minister Nehru to send this issue to the UN and on November 2, 1947, Nehru announced this intention in a radio broadcast to India. What a trap laid for Harrods educated Nehru, India is still facing the heat.

38. The issue was first discussed in 1948, following complaints that tribesmen and others, with Pakistan's support, were invading Jammu and Kashmir. Pakistan denied the charges and declared Jammu and Kashmir's accession to India, which had occurred in 1947, illegal. Mountbatten, one of the Guarantor and signatory of the Hari Singh accession treaty to India, kept mysterious silence, setting his long-standing envy with Nehru whose charm had enraptured his beautiful wife Edwina Cynthia Annette Mountbatten, Countess Mountbatten of Burma, an English heiress, socialite, relief worker.
39. This is how the Security Council first learned of the issue, which became an opportunity for them to show how peaceful negotiation and mediation can solve a violent issue. No major international event had yet occurred to give the recently established Security Council opportunity to demonstrate its raison d'être. The Security Council first held hearings on the issues in January 1948 when they allowed India and Pakistan to send their representatives to speak their case.
40. Throughout the coming year, the Security Council met and decided on what to do about the Kashmir struggle. The Council established a UN Commission for India and Pakistan. This Commission proposed a ceasefire, troop withdrawals and a plebiscite to decide the issue. India and Pakistan accepted, but they were not able to agree on how the plebiscite should take place. This all occurred during 1948, either through meetings in Paris, the headquarters of the Security Council at the time; New Delhi, the capital of India; or Islamabad, the capital of Pakistan. All of these events help set the stage to understand the beginning of the conflict and provides a good backdrop to Great Britain's motives.
41. From October 23 through October 26, 1947, India refused to save Kashmir from the tribesmen. Before the tribal invasion, Maharaja Hari Singh did not want to join either India or

Pakistan because he held a naive idea of an independent Kashmir, which he controlled. As Sheikh Abdullah explains in his autobiography *Flames of the Chinar:* "If he [the Maharaja] did not accede to Pakistan, he would have to agree to join India.... The Maharaja in a bid to escape a decision, avoided Mountbatten since he still nourished the hope of an independent State of Jammu and Kashmir."

42. Of course, once the tribesman invaded, he begged India for help. These three days were vital because the British government caused the situation in Kashmir to turn from a skirmish into a full-blown conflict by convincing India to respond to the invasion. Great Britain had leaders in both the militaries of India and Pakistan. Even though India and Pakistan had gained their independence from Great Britain earlier that year, Britain was able to keep their upper military personnel in each country. According to Sir Francis Tucker, Lieutenant General to all officers and men of the Indian Army in Eastern Command, the British were to remain in command of India and Pakistan's armies until a certain date: "The 1st April 1948, the date originally laid down in the Joint Defence Council order of 11th August 1947, under which the Supreme Commander's HQ was constituted."
43. This meant that the British were walking a delicate tightrope because they did not want to lose the support of both the countries even if one of them lose Kashmir at the same time, they also wanted to have each nation join their Commonwealth for economic reasons. Great Britain hoped to have India join their Commonwealth to maintain some military presence and trade. Britain was able to get Pakistan to join their Commonwealth and India seemed likely to join. To be on the safe side, Lord Mountbatten was advised by Prime Minister Attlee to make sure India became a member: "You will point out the need for continued collaboration in the security of the Indian Ocean for which provision might be made in an agreement between the two countries. At a suitable date, His Majesty's government would be ready to send military and other experts to India to assist in discussing the terms of such an agreement."
44. Because of this, India and Pakistan were poised to be significant trade partners with Great Britain while they would also be good locations for the British military; there was a problem though. Britain wanted India as a member of the Commonwealth and wanted to keep a military presence there.

The problem was that India wanted to get rid of the British officers from their military and they would not join the Commonwealth if this did not occur. India's National Congress wanted their country completely independent from Great Britain, while Pakistan desired to have British officers.

45. This reason for complete independence was viable for India because even with the chaos of partition; India had enough economic and military resources to survive on their own. This had the United Kingdom Cabinet at Whitehall worried because it would wreak havoc with Great Britain's military strategies: If the [Indian] demand for withdrawal were extended to include all British personal including those in the service of the Indian government, the fulfilment of any of our strategic requirements would be improbable. It is in our view essential that the Indian government should be persuaded to accept the assistance of the necessary number of British personnel.

46. India did allow Britain to keep their officers in command of India's army. Pakistan, on the other hand, needed the help of Great Britain because they had little economic or military resources. Because of this, both India and Pakistan were concerned about who Britain would support in the escalating discord over Kashmir. Thankfully, the British government had created a contingency plan in case of a situation as the Kashmir conflict occurred. The United Kingdom Cabinet had understood that to keep India and Pakistan happy and allow British interests to remain in effect that neither side could receive total support. On paper, it would be easy to maintain this facade of alliance with nations that hate each other, so long as neither went to war against the other.

In case a war happened between India and Pakistan, the supreme leader of all the British officers in India, Field Marshal Auchinleck, sent a secret message to all Senior British Commanders in the Indian and Pakistani armed forces on September 28, 1947: On receipt of the Code Word 'STAND DOWN' the following order will be immediately put into force: Owing to the immediate risk/outbreak of open-conflict between the armed forces of India and Pakistan, all British officers and other ranks however employed and of whatever rank shall cease forthwith to take any further part in the command or administration of the Armed Forces of India and Pakistan. You will take immediate actions to this effect and nothing is to be allowed to impede it.

Because of this, Britain did not openly help either India or Pakistan, but likewise, they could not let one defeat the other either. When other historians write about the Kashmir conflict, Great Britain's secret manipulations and motives in 1947-48 were usually just a side note in the greater picture. This is because this has been an issue for India and Pakistan for the past seventy years and has become an integral part of their society. Historians who write on the topic of Kashmir usually are either Indian or Pakistani and thus create a bias in constructing an argument to support one nation over the other.

They mention Great Britain in relation to their nations gaining independence and their motives are mentioned briefly at best. By focusing on the secret motives of the UK Cabinet in 1947-48, people can begin to understand how this problem in Kashmir grew into the stalemate it is today. To understand how Prime Minister Attlee and the UK Cabinet tried to achieve their motives, one must understand the complicated military, diplomatic and economic situations that faced Great Britain in both the Indian subcontinent and the international stage. The Partition of India was at its height at the beginning of the Kashmir strife. This meant that Great Britain had to deal with the legacy of them leaving India and Pakistan in a state of chaos and terror. Religious hatred was raging across the countryside as the extermination of Indian and Pakistani citizens occurred.

Even the members of the military wanted the extermination of citizens opposed to their religion. Sir Francis Tucker explained in his memoirs that Hindu officers in Eastern India wanted to exterminate the Muslim population: "Some pointed to the United Provinces and insisted that such large pockets of Muslims as Aligarh could not be allowed to exist right inside a Hindu population. They argued that they must be eliminated so that they should not know when war comes, the rise in rebellion in aid of the Muslim power to the north."

47. Hindu officers in Kashmir felt the same. Opinions of Hindu officers towards Muslims led Sir Francis Tucker to write this statement in his memoirs: "With the extermination and eviction of Muslims, killing far and wide over the

countryside decreased." Partition, though, was not a black and white affair, Hindus were dying too and Great Britain knew that these issues would cause problems in Kashmir. Kashmir's invasion by the north-western tribes was the catalyst for the conflict and the basis for how Great Britain's true motives were revealed.

Prime Minister Attlee was afraid of the whole situation blowing out of proportion and in this response to Nehru; Attlee explains how he hoped for peace and not hostility in Kashmir: "The immediate and grave problem... [is] to prevent Kashmir becoming the cause of a break between the dominions themselves. This cannot be a matter of concern to me and my government." British officers did not condone the use of tribesmen against Kashmir, but they allowed Pakistan to try to acquire that region because it was so close to West Pakistan. Most of the other princely States had joined the nation that was geographically close to them. Kashmir was the only instance in which this did not occur.

The barbarous actions of the tribesman without intervention reveals that Great Britain was willing to allow anything to maintain the *status quo*, even actions like those described in this lucid narration from Mir Qasim, the future Prime Minister of Kashmir in 1971: Blood-thirsty invaders swarmed the state killing and raping without discrimination between Hindus and Muslims.... The invasion and the humiliation his army suffered at the hands of the invaders unnerved him. To confound this holocaust, communal riots started in Jammu even as Pakistan imposed a total blockade on Kashmir starving it of essential commodities like salt. Violence such as this was occurring everywhere, but this was Pakistan's first attempt at using force to try to take a princely State.

Kashmir's dissent was not an original situation for India and Pakistan in acquiring a princely State; there was the problem in the State of Junagadh. The princely State of Junagadh would be the first major crisis for Great Britain in trying to keep India and Pakistan from fighting. It would also be the first test of the Stand Down orders. In Junagadh, the situation mirrored Kashmir in the sense that the Maharaja was of a different religion than his subjects; in this case, the ruler was Muslim and the subjects were Hindu.

48. What makes Junagadh's case different from Kashmir is that the princely State was inside India's territory, in what is

today the Gujarat district. Pakistan was comprised of territory that had populations with Muslims as the religious majority. Other princely States allowed a vote amongst their citizens on either to join India or Pakistan, Junagadh was not allowed one initially. India, like Pakistan with Kashmir, was worried that if Junagadh ceded to Pakistan, chaos would grow within their country. This fear was justified because the ruler of Junagadh would try to join Pakistan.

The prince of Junagadh, just like Hari Singh in Kashmir, hoped that the religious views of the elites, including himself, in his principality would determine which nation they joined. He wanted to join Pakistan, but this would encroach on the Boundary Commission, which had created India and Pakistan's current borders. Negotiations would begin between India and Pakistan over who had the right to acquire Junagadh. India already had Junagadh surrounded geographically. India's appointed Director of the Provisional Government of Junagadh, Samaldas Gandhi, explains about the citizen's choice of which nation to join: "If the Muslims vote for Pakistan, we will know who are not loyal to the Union. We cannot keep the serpents and scorpions alive moving under our pillows. We must put them to death. We will see who votes for Pakistan."

49. India grew tired of the negotiations and decided to invade; Lord Mountbatten and the UK Cabinet feared this. Lord Mountbatten remained in India as Governor-General to help the new government get on its feet and had to maintain India's interests to the best of his abilities. The Junagadh crisis would test Mountbatten's responsibilities because India wanted to provoke an armed conflict. Britain could not allow this to happen because they did not want a war between India and Pakistan. As a result, of this conflict, Lord Mountbatten asked the Cabinet what to do; he explained what he did in detail to his cousin, King George VI of England: My chief concern was to prevent the Government of India from committing itself on the Junagadh issue to an act of war against what was now Pakistan territory. My position was singularly difficult....

For the Governor-General of a Dominion to have acquiesced in action which might lead to war with another Dominion would have been completely unprecedented. But at the same time, I was aware that my physical presence as Governor-General of India was the best insurance against an actual war with Pakistan. To have compromised my position too far over the preliminary threat of war would have undermined my final position. Lord Mountbatten could not stop India from sending in its troops, which were described as a "police force," but he was able to avert a war between India and Pakistan. This was because Pakistan was not geographically connected with the Junagadh province. Because of the way Junagadh was resolved, the British hoped Kashmir might unfold the same way, but this was not meant to be. Kashmir did share borders with India and Pakistan and was right next to Afghanistan, which was a neighbour to the world superpower, the Soviet Union. A new approach to the Kashmir discord is focusing on the years 1947-48 when the Cold War was beginning and understanding how this could affect Britain to create a stalemate in the Indian Subcontinent.

By introducing the diplomatic fears that the UK Cabinet held toward the influence of the Soviet Union spreading in India and Pakistan in 1947-48, people can further understand just how delicate the Kashmir situation was in the international scheme of things. In 1947-48, Britain realized that neither India nor Pakistan could be the victor because the loser could succumb to the influences of the Soviet Union. Kashmir problem was affected by the Cold War.

Fear of the spectre, the Soviet Union, in 1947-48 heavily influenced Britain's actions involving Kashmir. Great Britain, like other major Western Powers in 1947, was afraid of the Soviet Union spread its influence to other countries in the world. This fear was viable because the USSR was one of the superpowers at the time and other nations in political turmoil were seeking ways to improve themselves; communism was one such proposition. India and Pakistan were in turmoil because of their recent independence and partition and if the war was to occur, their citizens and governments might start viewing communism as an option.

The other fear, specifically for India, was what if the Soviet Union got control of that region of the world. As the service chief of Britain's military informed the government: "If India was dominated by Russia with powerful air forces it is likely that we should have to abandon our command of the Persian Gulf and the Northern Indian Ocean routes." India was a valuable military and naval location for Great Britain. Pakistan was also important because they were next to

Afghanistan and that left Pakistan vulnerable to invasion. However, what worried the British the most concerning the Soviet Union's view towards India was Nehru's non-aligned policy towards all foreign nations. India's Prime Minister, Jawaharlal Nehru, held a political philosophy of being non-aligned and this philosophy alarmed Great Britain in regards to the Cold War. Nehru's political goal was to have India become a great independent nation and was willing to accept any help to accomplish this goal, so long as India was in control of all its institutions. He hoped for complete independence from Western foreigners, whom he considered imperialists.

This political philosophy towards the USSR and China as Nehru described to John Foster Dulles, President Eisenhower's Secretary of State in 1953, would give Great Britain reason to think India may fall to Communists: "Our minds were largely taken up by this building up of a new India and we were reluctant to get entangled in external matters. Hence our basic desire for peace, which of course arose from our whole outlook. Hence also our wish not to be tied with any other country and to retain our independence of action."

Even though Nehru stated India had no wish to become a Communist nation, their non-aligned policy greatly agitated Great Britain and the other Western powers. This fear of the Soviet Union would continue to cause problems for Kashmir when both India and Pakistan tried to settle the conflict peacefully and asked the United Nations for help. Great Britain's fear of India succumbing to the influence of communism caused the Kashmir dispute to continue for many more years. Great Britain could not afford India to lose Kashmir in fear that they might create an alliance with the Soviet Union.

This fear consumed the politicians of Great Britain so much that they ruined the best chance of a peaceful solution to the problem during the United Nations meeting in January 1948. Pakistan's representative to the United Nations, explained his suspicions that Great Britain was involved in undermining peaceful means to end the hostilities in Kashmir: Thus the failure of the Security Council to secure an early settlement of the Kashmir dispute is attributed largely to the unfortunate intervention of Attlee from London. That took place probably at the instance of Lord Mountbatten, who must have been moved by Nehru to intercede with the Prime Minister. The argument used might have been that the Security Council's persistence in laying down the conditions given in the draft resolution to secure a fair and impartial plebiscite in Kashmir might push India into the arms of the USSR; this argument has been used not only over this problem but others also.

These actions of Attlee and Lord Mountbatten were done in the name of securing peace; they just wanted to be able to have both India and Pakistan be happy with the results. Mountbatten convinced Nehru to back out because he was afraid that India form an alliance with the Soviet Union in order to secure victory in the Security Council decision: "Mountbatten warned that if the Soviet Union were to come to India's rescue by exercising a veto in the Security Council, she would appear throughout the country as the saviour of India against the machinations of the United States and the United Kingdom."

Great Britain was more partial towards Pakistan. One of these reasons was because Pakistan was a Muslim nation and the UK Cabinet wanted to maintain good trade relations with the Middle-East and the Persian Gulf. Oil was the main trade resource for the area and still is today. It remains the lifeblood of Great Britain's economic and military power. Instead of proving that Britain was more partial to Pakistan, this information will explain how complicated the economic and diplomatic matters were. This would lead Prime Minister Attlee and the UK Cabinet to desire neither India nor Pakistan to gain victory in this conflict. Pakistan was built to be a haven for the Muslims who were in British India and hence a nation with Islam as their main religion. A country's religion usually does not constitute how Great Britain views a nation but because the Middle-East and the Persian Gulf region were Islamic, this changed.

The Middle-East and the Persian Gulf, like today, had access to oil and oil was the lifeblood of Great Britain. Because of this, Great Britain wanted to keep friendly relations with the Islamic world to have access to oil. As Admiral Cunningham explained when Pakistan was appealing to Great Britain for their independence: "If Pakistan's application were rejected, it would shatter Britain's relations with the 'whole Muslim world' to the detriment of her strategic position in the Middle-East and

North Africa as well as the Indian subcontinent." This was one reason Pakistan gained its independence and would continue to be a reason why Pakistan did not fall into ruin. Problems in Palestine complicated Great Britain's position on the Kashmir conflict. In 1947, the Palestine issue in which the Jewish community was granted Israel was causing a stirring of emotions amongst the Islamic world. Great Britain had been, reluctantly, at the forefront to help Israel become a nation and was now on thin ice with the Muslim community. Because of this, Britain would be more inclined to make sure Pakistan did not lose during the Kashmir conflict.

In a letter to Attlee, Prime Minister of England, Britain's Foreign Office explains how the Middle-East should not conclude that Great Britain is opposing an Islamic nation in an international dispute: The Foreign Secretary has expressed anxiety lest we should appear to be siding with India in the dispute between India and Pakistan over Kashmir which is now before the United Nations Security Council. With the situation as critical as it is in Palestine, Bevin feels that we must be very careful to guard against the danger of aligning the whole of Islam against us, which might be the case were Pakistan to obtain a false impression of our attitude in the Security Council.

Therefore, Britain had to make sure Pakistan had support from them to maintain good relations with the Muslim world. Britain also realized that Pakistan would be a valuable military ally compared to India. Pakistan was willing to ally with the Western Powers and allow Great Britain to leave their officers in charge of their armies. This was useful for Britain's military presence in the Indian subcontinent because Pakistan was closer to the Suez Canal for their navy and closer to the Soviet Union for their Royal Air Force. It is because of these reasons that the United Kingdom Cabinet at Whitehall decided on this view of Pakistan: From the strategic point of view there were overwhelming arguments in favour of West Pakistan remaining within the Commonwealth, namely, that we should obtain important strategic facilities, the port of Karachi, air bases and the support of Muslim manpower in the future: be able to ensure the continued integrity of Afghanistan and be able to increase our prestige and impose our position throughout the Moslem world.

While the acceptance of Pakistan only into the Commonwealth would involve a commitment for its support against India, the danger would be small and it was doubtful if Pakistan would ask for more than the support of British Officers in executive and advisory positions. This decision seemed the most logical to take because it helped Great Britain maintain good relations with the Muslim community and it provided them a great military position against the Soviet Union. Therefore, Great Britain could not allow a full-blown conflict to occur in Kashmir to jeopardize its military, diplomatic and economic interests, while also not allowing British motives toward either India or Pakistan to be known to the other nation.

On October 27, India acquired Kashmir from Maharaja Hari Singh. This was because the will of the UK Cabinet was manifested through India's Governor-General. Lord Mountbatten was able to convince India that sending troop's immediately in response to the tribal invasion constituted an invasion of a neutral territory, an action that would seem barbarous to the international world. Things looked good for India because the Maharaja was afraid for his life from the invading tribesman. Therefore, Maharaja Hari Singh wrote a letter to Lord Mountbatten, which showed he decided to have Kashmir become part of India: "Naturally, they [Government of India] can't send the help asked for by me without my State acceding to the Dominion of India. I have accordingly decided to do so and I attach the Instrument of Accession for acceptance by your government."

50. Lord Mountbatten was quite partial to India and by making it seem like he was helping them, he was maintaining the facade of Britain's total support. Everything looked like India would settle this conflict before it began. Unfortunately, it was not that simple, the Bermuda Triangle of Uncertainty was in the making! Because Maharaja Hari Singh did not have a vote amongst his citizens on which nation they wanted to join, India's acquisition of Kashmir went against the Radcliffe Boundary Commission. This meant that Pakistan contested that they should have right to Kashmir. Like other cases, involving the merging of princely States into either India or Pakistan, Pakistan should have obtained Kashmir, primarily for two reasons.

First, the population of Muslims in Jammu and Kashmir was much higher than the Hindu population. A census taken in 1941 showed that about 77.11% of Jammu and Kashmir's population was Muslim. Second, Kashmir is right next to Pakistan. The partitioning of India and Pakistan was based on the geographic areas where Muslims were most prominent in British India and Kashmir is right next to Pakistan. With that argument, India was able to acquire the Junagadh principality. Great Britain understood all this and in the end, they tried desperately to find a peaceful solution but also one that suited their needs more than those of India or Pakistan.

When the Kashmir conflict was beginning, Great Britain realized that to maintain their motives of containing the Soviet Union, appeasing the Islamic in the Middle-East and keeping a military presence in the Indian subcontinent, neither India nor Pakistan could be the victor in this conflict. Britain had officers in the leading roles in both India and Pakistan's militaries. They were hoping to have both India and Pakistan become part of their Commonwealth and in this regard, India was more difficult to handle then Pakistan.

Lord Mountbatten, the last Viceroy of British India, was allowed to stay on as the Governor-General of India and was able to help keep India and Pakistan from going to war. Great Britain had already experienced the acquisition of Junagadh into India in which the Muslim ruler was going against the will of his Hindu citizens. With the Stand Down orders given to all the British officers, Britain made sure that none of their troops became involved with only India or Pakistan. Their fear of the Soviet Union's influence spreading into the India subcontinent was justified in their eyes because Nehru's non-aligned policy made Britain suspicious of India's political motives.

Also, they were afraid that if the chaos of partition caused India or Pakistan to fall into ruins that their citizens or government might consider communism to fix their problems. British military strategy relied on having their forces in the India subcontinent to maintain control of the Indian Ocean and to monitor the Soviet threat; hence, India could not lose in the Kashmir conflict. Oil was the lifeblood of Great Britain and their readiest supplier like today was the Middle-East and the Persian Gulf. Because of their support in the creation of Israel in the Palestine conflict, Britain was afraid of further angering the Muslim world and they thought if they did not support Pakistan that this would occur.

Geographically, Pakistan was in the north-west of the India subcontinent and they were fine with accepting British military officers to command their armies. Therefore, Pakistan had to be supported because the loss of economic wealth and military strategy would be a monumental blow to Great Britain. To maintain this facade of no complete support for either India or Pakistan, Britain allowed the partition to rage across the two nations. They were desperately trying to find peace to the dispute, but they wanted peace on their terms. Britain even convinced India and Pakistan to send the matter to the United Nations for peaceful negotiations while Britain worked behind the scenes to achieve political gridlock. The Kashmir discord, which is a festering wound of the political policies of India and Pakistan, has lasted for sixty-three years in part because Great Britain was not willing to accept the defeat of either India or Pakistan.

This struggle could have ended in a few months if India had been allowed to repel the tribal invaders or if India had left them alone and Pakistan took Kashmir. Either way, the Kashmir conflict remains a muddled affair in large part to the double-dealing of Britain in 1947-48.

Current Situation

The Valley of Kashmir is under siege for many years as commonly believed by the residents there. The basic individual rights like the right to life, liberty and land are at great risk. For John Locke, the 17th century English philosopher, it is the protection of these three rights that motivated people to overcome the inconveniences of the state of nature and enter into a peaceful political populace for that matter.

Thomas Hobbles once said, "my mother gave birth to twins: myself and fear." Since the 1990s Kashmiris are born under a similar threat. The Hobbesian brutal 'state of nature' finds a perfect resonance in the valley where the life of man is "solitary, poor, nasty, brutish and short." This environmental situation for prolonged time might have influenced the DNA metabolism and hence you see kids taking stones in their hand, this just cannot be mere rupees 500 impetus, has to be more.

After 2014 assembly elections in J&K which delivered a fractured mandate, Mufti Mohammad Sayeed was tempted to ally with the BJP. Apart from generous funding from the centre, he hoped that the alliance of two extremes would bridge the regional divide in the State, a brilliant move, only that it has failed so far. Because of the failure of PDP-BJP alliance, there is a sense of betrayal. There is a realization that the elections are no substitute for the settlement of Kashmir conflict, political uncertainty, continued violence and lack of development contributed to apathy.

This trend is expected to continue for the foreseeable future unless a major political initiative is taken to address the growing alienation felt even by seven years old boys and girls. Kashmiris are fed up with the status-quo. They can go to any extent to break the deadlock. No amount of exhaustion shall overwhelm them. They live a simple life and can thus sustain the movement for a long.

All those bonhomie of inviting Nawaz Sharif for the inaugural oath ceremony to landing in Lahore uninvited to attend Sharif's clan wedding went into the dustbin, post-Pak ISI supported terror attacks in Kashmir army bases. The lesson, India keeps selecting the wrong stakeholder from Pakistan, it can never be their civilian dispensation, has to be Only and always their Army COAS. Not sure what false ideology India's policy makers have in mind that stops them from doing business with Pakistani army head. The US does that; China does that, Russia does that its India that has created so many walls of morality and their understanding of democracy that the country is not able to crack problem Kashmir.

New Delhi must act now. Every killing only adds to the levels of alienation. The conflict is making inroads into new arenas of life, the universities, colleges and schools are turning into new battlefields with a battle cry and jihad to die. Pakistan is happily enjoying the show, India has fallen back on strategy and also the will to solve this mess, at least that's what it looks to me from outside the government. Fred W Riggs, an administrative thinker gave a model characterized by nepotism, corruption and formalism; a distinction between norms and realities, this is exactly the State of J&K in the present.

India-Pakistan is joined at the hip, hip being Kashmir and one has to separate for the resolution. Unfortunately, it can only be a surgical procedure which may be painful. India with world's third largest army and strong engineering and manufacturing base, with 1.3 billion people and the economy worth US $ 2.45 trillion in GDP term and $9.49 trillion in PPP term ranking, will not hand over Kashmir in the plate to anyone. Probably a small but very intense border war using land and airpower for 5-7 weeks to test the water before both countries head to the negotiating table can be one unfortunate and feasible option.

Indian bureaucrats have not been able to sell to the world more authoritatively India's plan on Kashmir. Why are they shying away from discussing Kashmir with anyone (US, China, Iran, Turkey, Russia or even Somalia), if they believe India has legitimate claim over Kashmir who will take away from them? Did world powers or UN type association solve genuine and historically correct Tibetan aspiration yet? Holy Dalai Lama is the darling of the western powers have got nothing, so the sincere advice to the Indian policy makers is to believe in their claim and work on getting Gilgit-Baltistan and POK back into unified Kashmir, maybe that's what Kashmir separatist movement wants it to do. Give them the old unified Kashmir with autonomy under Indian Constitution.

But talking to some policy makers here in Delhi I was pleasantly surprised to find utter lack consistency and no prolonged strategy for such an important and complex problem, blame it on the democracy where a change of government, changes everything and the new start happens every election. AS Dulat's book *Kashmir – The Vajpayee Years*, clearly spells out the state of affairs. Ex-Prime Minister Dr Manmohan Singh with his ten years of long uninterrupted rule was the biggest culprit whose indecisiveness kept Kashmir conflict As Is. In the Kashmir valley, the anti-India protests are mostly limited to places like Anantnag city, Pulwama, Pampore, parts of Srinagar, Butera, Handwara, Pattan. These are just a handful of small towns where the locals have been brainwashed into protesting against the Indian Army. Rest of the places people won't support any such Azaadi calls. So why should India listen to the dissenting voice from a few paid vagabonds and not listen to the silence of the majority? Wouldn't that be unfair? Well that's has been consistent policy or believe of the federal Government of India.

Modi government special representative to J&K, Dineshwar Sharma acting as an Interlocutor, has met with Hurriyat leader Abdul Ghani Bhat in Wazirbagh bungalow in Srinagar on November 27, 2017. Bhat may have been isolated in Hurriyat in talking to Sharma, but emphasized to the interlocutor the need to involve "Pakistan in talks for a breakthrough in Kashmir." There have been active back-channel talks to get Hurriyat leaders, who are playing hardball to come to the table for talks. Bhat was known as 'Professor' heads the Muslim Conference is part of the Hurriyat Conference. He is not part of the new caucus 'Joint Resistance Leadership' which has only three leaders Syed Ali Shah Geelani, Mirwaiz Umar Farooq and Yasin Malik. The trio has stayed away from the emissary of the centre. On October 23rd, Centre had appointed Sharma as special representative to J&K to initiate dialogue with stakeholders especially youth to reach out to the people of trouble-torn Kashmir Valley.

India believes that Kashmir is its integral part, which joined the union through the Instrument of Accession in 1947 making it a full-fledged State in India. So if someone has to challenge this, then the entire 600 plus princely States merger that joined India and Pakistan post-British driven partition needs to be re-visited and that should also include even Pakistan and Bangladesh as countries that were carved out from India. This is a chicken and egg situation.

Alienation and Hopelessness of Kashmiris – A Post-Independence Making or the Historical Baggage

One common thing you will hear in Kashmir from the people is how they have been badly treated by both, past and current rulers and how badly they aspire for this Azaadi (Freedom). Now this made me think and hence research on their basic traits (coming from Naga *vansha* as per mythological era history) are they habitual anti-establishment folks having issues against all their rulers irrespective of which dynasty or religion. Or, are they confused and real sufferers and poor victims. Why are they under siege mentality post-Independence in a democratic India, where they have 170 million Muslims living and practising their faith happily, coexisting with larger Hindu population. Let us understand this by going back into history again.

Kashmir wasn't always dyed in blood. The people of Kashmir had seen an intellectual renaissance under the rule of Kushans, who ruled Kashmir in the AD 1st century, after the fallout of the Ashoka dynasty. Kushans loved Kashmir, they often held their court in beautiful springs and also operationalized the Silk Route, which got Kashmir commerce and literary reforms. Lalitaditya, the great Hindu king of AD 8th century, has been praised by Kalhana, the first historian of Kashmir.

Even though, the struggles of power intensified from AD 10th century, many Hindu and Sanskrit historians have misinterpreted Kashmiri history, as the rise of Islam started emerging.

Shahab-ud-Din, first Muslim ruler of Kashmir, was married to a Hindu queen, Laxmi and he always internally consolidated all his subjects belonging from different faiths.

Akbar sees power instability in Kashmir during the reign of Yusuf Shah Chak. He invests in this opportunity and intrudes Kashmir in 1586, ousts Yusuf Shah, the last Chak ruler and convicts him in far-flung Bihar where he dies in misery and isolation. Under the guise of land reforms, nobility and grandeur, Kashmir start losing its cultural heritage. People of Kashmir were answerable to alien Mughal powers in Delhi. Mughal rule in Kashmir continued till 1707.

Afghan Vehemence

The period from AD 1752-1819 is considered the darkest period in the history of Kashmir. This was the time when Afghans ruled Kashmir and unleashed a reign of terror on the Kashmiri people, especially the Kashmiri Hindus. Under persecution, most of the Kashmiri Hindus migrated to places outside Kashmir. Those who stayed back were either forcibly converted to Islam or ruthlessly killed. It is said that only 11 Hindu families survived death. How did Afghans take over the reign of Kashmir? According to Prof Somnath Dhar, the death of Aurangzeb spelled the disintegration of the Mughal empire. The later Mughals, embroiled in internal dissensions, hardly cared for Kashmiris. Governors appointed by the Mughal emperors would nominate deputies to carry on the administration on their behalf. Hindus and Shias were persecuted in the one-year regime of one such nominee Mir Ahmed Khan.

Walter R Lawrence observed that the Mughal empire began to decay, the subahs (province) in Kashmir became independent, emperor Muhammad Shah, Abdul Gani and Mull Sharf-ud-Din had the blood of Hindus on their hands adding to the bloody history of Kashmir and its people. Kalashpura, a Hindu ward of the city, was set on fire and the Hindus-Sikhs were forbidden to wear turbans. In this reign, the subahs fought among themselves and Kashmir fell into wild disorder. By the year AD 1751, the office of subah of Kashmir appears to have become hereditary and practically independent of Delhi. Then the unfortunate valley passed into the hands of new masters and Kashmir became subject to the Pathan rule, the cruelest and worst of all. Pathan Governors were known for their savagery and inhuman treatment of Kashmiris in general and Hindus in particular.

The first Afghan chief to rule Kashmir was Abdullah Khan Isk Aquasi (1753-54). He lined up all the rich Hindu Kashmiris and ordered them to part with their wealth or face death. He extracted 1 crore rupees from the local merchants. It is said that some traders committed suicide because of his torture. About Afghan rule in general, Walter R Lawrence writes:

> "When we pass from the Mughal period to the period of the Shahani Durani, we pass to a time of brutal tyranny, unrelieved

by good works, chivalry and honour. Men with interest were appointed as Governors who wrung as much money as they could out of the wretched people of the valley. Amir Khan Jawan Sher was perhaps the best of Pathan rulers, for at least he built the Amira Kadal bridge and the palace of Shergarhi, but on the other hand, he showed petty spite in destroying the Mughal gardens on the Dal. Other Pathan rulers are now only remembered for their brutality and cruelty and it is said of them that they thought no more of cutting off heads than of plucking a flower."

Regarding the miscalculation on the part of the Kashmiris in inviting Afghans to rule Kashmir, PNK Bamzai writes:

> "Their (Afghan's) rule reduced the Valley to the lowest depths of penury, degradation and slavery. While inviting the Afghans to take over the administration of the Valley, the Kashmiri nobles had mistaken them for a branch of the civilized and humane Mughal emperors of India. They had hoped that after the break-up of the central Mughal power, Ahmad Shah Abdali and his successors would give them a stable administration. Little did they imagine that all the beauty and nobility, for which Kashmir and its people were famous, would be wiped off under their rule."

Jagmohan has this to say about the invitation extended to Afghan rulers:

> "Those who invited Ahmad Shah Abdali did not realize that they were calling a barbarous horde to their garden of nature. The unfortunate people virtually jumped from the frying pan (Mughal Rule) into the fire (Afghan Rule). And 67 years of brutal Afghan rule caused them untold miseries."

During Afghan rule, there was a custom among the Hindus to send along with the bridegroom, another boy, called 'Pot Maharaja' who would also be dressed like the groom. In case some untoward event happened to the bridegroom, the 'Pot Maharaja' would immediately take his place. It is widely believed that the custom was introduced under stress because in the Pathan times, it was not uncommon for the bridegroom to be seized as he went to wed his bride.

How cruel were Afghans and how they tortured and brutally killed people in general and Hindus in particular? According to Lawrence, the victims of these fiends (Pathan rulers) were the Hindus, the Shias and the Bombas of the Jhelum valley. First in the rank of oppressors, comes Assad Khan who boasted that the savage

Nadir Shah was his prototype. It was his practice to tie up the Hindus, two and two, in grass sacks and sink them in the Dal lake. As an amusement, a pitcher filled with ordure would be placed on a Hindu's head and Muslims would pelt the pitcher with stones till it broke, the unfortunate Hindu being blinded with filth. Mir Hazar was another fiend who used leather bags instead of grass sacks for the drowning of Hindu Brahmins. He drowned Shias and Brahmins indiscriminately.

A locality on the bank of Dal lake is still called Batta Mazar, the 'Graveyard of Hindus'. PNK Bamzai describes the terror unleashed by Afghans on Kashmiris like this:

> "Rude was the shock that the Kashmiris got when they witnessed the first acts of barbarity at the hands of their new masters. Abdullah Khan Ishk Aqasi let loose a reign of terror as soon as he entered the Valley. Accustomed to looting and murdering the subjected people, his soldiers set themselves to amassing riches by the foulest means possible."

Tired of persecution by Afghans, Hindu leader Mirza Pandit Dhar and his son Birbal Dhar secretly persuaded Maharaja Ranjit Singh to annex Kashmir. In July 1819, Maharaja Ranjit Singh sent his forces under the command of Misser Diwan Chand, Raja Gulab Singh of Jammu, Sardar Hari Singh, Jwala Singh Padania, Hukum Singh and others. A fierce battle ensued at the top of Pir Panjal and the plateau of Shopian where Afghans were defeated. Jabar Khan hastily fled to Kabul after being wounded in the battle. Thus came an end to the Afghan rule and Kashmir, after a long period of about five centuries, passed again from the Muslim rule to Sikh-Hindu rule. Sikhs gave Kashmir a better government than the Afghans and there was no brutal killing and rapes of Hindu Kashmiris.

Later, Gulab Singh, the Monarch ruler of Jammu, signed 'Treaty of Amritsar' with the British Empire and purchased Kashmir for ₹75 lakh ($120K). The clauses under the treaty were to integrate Jammu, Ladakh, Baltistan and other hill States including Kashmir under the Dogra reign, as a separate border State. The 'Treaty of Amritsar' was amended due to loyalty displayed by Ranbir Singh, in curbing the first Indian Mutiny of 1857. Now, the ruler was allowed to select an heir from his collateral family which results in the succession of Dogras, in the event of present ruler's death.

A British settlement officer, Walter Lawrence surveys Kashmir and concludes that Kashmiris live under such brute oppression which is worse than the Third Estate of the French Revolution. In 1929, Srinagar, an amalgam of graduates from Aligarh Muslim University, constitute Reading Room Party with an aim for the emancipation of Kashmiris. Ghulam Abbas, an activist from Jammu, reorganizes Anjuman-i-Islam, a Mirwaiz institution, into Young Men's Muslim Association of Jammu for the betterment of Muslims. The masses of Kashmir gain class consciousness; this was around 1931. The revolt against Maharaja Hari Singh gained momentum. It was viciously subjugated by the constabulary of Maharaja. The Muslim majority masses were not allowed to represent in the State administrative apparatus. The lands belonged to rich Hindu 'Jagirdars' who employed Muslims for tilling and, would give them paddy which would last for petty three months. For rest of the months, Kashmiris would often go to Punjab and other plains to seek industrious labour.

So as you see how blood-filled history of Kashmir and its people came as the baggage adding huge complexity to this conflict. This complexity was not the making of the India-Pakistan partition but had past legacy. Now moving on to the 1947 era which only continued following the sad historical path, adding further, to the hopelessness, alienation and radicalization of the region.

Uprising by Kashmiri Muslims against Hindu King Hari Singh in Poonch

As early as February 1947, Muslims in the Poonch region of western Jammu province, at least 50,000 of whom had acquired military experience serving in the British army during World War II, staged a 'no tax' campaign. This quickly developed into a fully-fledged anti-Maharaja uprising. The Poonchis were inspired by their dislike of feudal Hari Singh and his overbearing regime. In particular, Muslim Poonchis were disenchanted as J&K State forces sought to brutally control and disarm them. They disliked these forces efforts to suppress their strong desire for J&K to join neighbouring Pakistan.

They became dismayed as these forces redistributed some of their surrendered arms to local Hindus and Sikhs. The anti-Maharaja Muslim rebels soon congregated into a ragged militia that opposed the J&K State forces with some success. They were joined by Muslims in the neighbouring Mirpur districts, by other pro-Pakistan people in Kashmir and by J&K folks returning home from mainland India-Pakistan either following the end of temporary work undertaken during warmer months and to support the local pro-Pakistan cause. Indian government felt it was Pakistan mischief, Pakistan counterclaimed that Hindus and Sikhs from J&K were crossing into Pakistan and attacking them in the border areas. It can be true given the bloody partition that divided Punjab but no factual proof yet.

Communal Riot in Jammu Province

In September-October 1947, serious communal/inter-religious (Hindus-Muslims) violence took place in Jammu province. Protagonists sought, often violently, to ensure that J&K joined their nation of choice. In Hindu and Sikhs dominated eastern Jammu province, the large number of Muslims were killed. The very unfortunate event, the impact of bloody partition. Hindus and Sikhs who had to leave everything that now became Pakistan and was made to move to divided India, had to traverse to Jammu province, joined these killings of the Muslims as the anger of losing their home in Pakistan to the Muslims. A very unfortunate situation, communally charged, some 60,000 mostly Hindu Dogras and Sikhs arrived from Sialkot to Pathankot.

Maharaja and his forces may have been involved in some of the blood-lettings in eastern Jammu. There is some allegation on the Hindu groups as well along with the Sikhs from eastern Punjab, particularly the princely State of Patiala whose ruler had a close relation with Hari Singh the King of J&K. One unsubstantiated data is, as many as 2,37,000 Muslims were either exterminated or forced to flee. Perhaps between 20,000 and 1,00,000 Muslims were killed in Jammu Province in 1947. More research to validate this is needed, but it went into the psyche of the Muslims which later resulted in alienation. Jammu Massacre also had not only killings but rape, abductions and serious injuries. Some 4,00,000 Muslims fled to Pakistan or POK (Azad Kashmir).

While the violence against Muslims in eastern Jammu province was shameful and alarming, Muslims in western parts (Pakistan) of the province concurrently engaged in similar diabolical acts. In Mirpur districts and Poonch jagir, Muslims killed large numbers of Hindus and Sikhs. From 1,14,000 Hindus and Sikhs families belonging Mirpur, Muzaffarabad and Poonch districts were left to paltry 790. Those not killed became internally displaced.

Kabali Invasion

On 22nd October, the tribesmen from Pakistan, storm into Kashmir and integrate with Poonch Rebels as an umbrageous reaction against the killing of Muslims in Jammu and Poonch. The Kabali tribe was supported by unofficial people and leaders from Pakistan. However, the tribes also engage in plundering and despoil along the way, resulting in an exodus of over 10,000 Kashmiri Muslims as well. India accuses Pakistan of violating the 'Standstill Agreement'. Pakistan rebuts the allegations. The revolt flares up neighbouring Mirpur and

Muzaffarabad. 'Azad Kashmir' comes into existence with an independent government on 24th October 1947.

Kabali primarily Afghans were brutal killer and rapists and plundered not only Kashmir Hindus but also Kashmiri Muslims. To protect themselves and their properties from the brutal Pukhtoons, Kashmiri men and women formed a People's Militia, all this happened when India had yet not sent her army and was waiting for the Raja Hari Singh to sign the Accession Treaty and announced Kashmir's official merger with India getting British last Governor Mountbatten as the guarantor of the agreement.

The headquarters of the 25 Infantry Division in Rajouri has a sign that commemorates the massacre of Sikhs and Hindus in Rajouri in 1947 by Pakistani raiders. It has a letter written by an eyewitness who saw a Sikh kill his family one by one when cornered by Pakistani raiders. Indian army got in the nick of time to prevent the takeover of the Kashmir Valley, Poonch, Jammu and Ladakh and sent the blighters packing. Pakistan suffered the first military defeat (3 more defeats to follow later). But consider this. If the Pakistanis did not stupidly consider it to be the 'K' in its name, J&K might have remained an independent entity. The Maharaja did entertain notions of an independent existence and balked at signing the accession papers.

The first Indian troops landed at Srinagar airport even as Pakistani raiders were breaching its perimeter. (Maj Somnath Sharma of the 8th battalion of the 18th Hyderabad Regiment, later the 4th battalion of the Kumaon Regiment.) Imagine the consequences implicit for India, Pakistan and China with a supposedly independent J&K wedged in between them? Pakistan was not thinking of the consequences, but there is enough to suggest that Britain was thinking of the possibilities implicit in this and which is why British officers leading the Gilgit Scouts were the first to raise the banner of revolt against the Maharaja Hari Singh, the ruler of Kashmir before India's independence.

Sheikh Abdullah did not want the Indian Army to take more territory in present-day POK as it would have tilted the demographic balance against the Kashmiris. This needs to be further researched as this puts the eye of suspicion on India's first PM office. It is commonly believed, Sardar Patel wanted to settle refugees from Pakistan in J&K to create a new demographic reality. Like China experimented in Xinjiang and Tibet.

Pakistan claims that Maharaja had no right to initiate the 'Instrument of Accession' till 'The Standstill Agreement' was in order. Jammu and Kashmir Muslim Conference and the tribal chiefs of Gilgit advice the Maharaja against the accession of Kashmir with India. India signs an accession with The Maharaja on 26th October 1947.

Nehru's Unfortunate Speech

In August 1952, Jawaharlal Nehru gives a negative speech contradicting the settlement provided in the Delhi Agreement:

> "Ultimately – I say this with all deference to this Parliament – the decision will be made in the hearts and minds of the men and women of Kashmir; neither in this Parliament, nor in the United Nations nor by anybody else."

Kashmiri Hindus Massacre

In 1989 the Muslim terrorists operating under multiple forms of incarnations like Jammu and Kashmir Liberation Front, Muslim Janbaz Force, Ul Umur, Al Burq, Hizbul Mujahideen, Al Jehad, Ikhwan-ul-Muslim all sharing visceral hatred against Kashmiri Hindus subjected them to intimidation, panic, rape, murder and sexual assault with a view to exterminating them from the soil of Kashmir. In sheer violation of the universally accepted charter of rights and law as couched in the Universal Declaration of Human Rights and other international covenants, the terrorists debased, dehumanized and brutalized the cultured and moderate community of Kashmiri Hindus by destructing and killing them in a punitive war. In heaping death and destruction on them, the terrorists pursue the objective of the dismemberment of the State from the Indian liberal democratic order for a new political alignment based on religion.

Terror was created and violence propagated to obliterate dissent and opposition to the formulated goals of the terrorists. The elements that were deemed inimical to the terrorist campaign have been liquidated with impunity and subjected to an untold orgy of Nazi-type torture and persecution. Waves of communalism have been fanned and fuelled thereby polarizing the Kashmiri society for the furtherance of political ends. The Kashmiri Hindus as a distinct ethno-religious group have been under a conspiracy targeted, maimed and butchered in groups and put to detestable forms of violence and brutality to destruct the Indian support planks to materialist the secessionist goal thus flagrantly violating and transgressing their inherent political rights and freedoms.

With the shared ideology and agenda of thrusting a second partition on India and transforming the State of Jammu and Kashmir into an Islamic State, the Muslim terrorists have lost no time in spotting their political and religious enemies in the Hindu minorities especially the Kashmiri Hindus. Politically the Kashmiri Hindus repose full faith in and are unflinching supporters of the secular polity of India and as such do not subscribe to any trend of thought and wave of a movement aiming at snapping the historical, cultural and political ties of the State. It is pertinent to put that they have made no mean contributions to the dynamics of growth, development and consolidation of democratic and secular order and political and economic humanism allied with it and as a patriotic force have bitterly opposed the constitutional barriers which have generated the vicious and baneful forces of separatism and fundamentalism in Kashmir.

In matters of religion, the Hindus with the chequered history of torture and persecution at the hands of Muslims have rejected the antediluvian tendencies breeding religious perversion and paranoia and are wedded to the Indian discourse of allowance for tolerance and non-conformity and stand for full flow of freedom for every individual to preach and practice his religion. They have not only mocked at but held in utter contempt the Islamic police enforcing codes and *fatwas* (religious decrees).

The Muslim identity of Kashmir to the exclusion of diverse ethnoreligious minorities as an essential cog in the processes of total Islamization pursued at the State level was exposed to the shreds by the Hindu minority. That is why they have been branded as the inveterate enemies of Muslim identity which is being perceived under constant threat from India harbouring a Muslim population equivalent to that of Pakistan. With their well-known positions on politics and religion the Kashmiri Hindus as such have been opposed to any movement for Kashmir's annexation with Pakistan and are equally inimical to the retrograde Muslim programme of pushing the State into the lap of rabid fundamentalism and they, therefore, as a resisting force were mercilessly massacred and eliminated in hundreds. Some of the killed were engineers while some held positions in administrative set-up. Some victims of genocide were teachers with remarkable achievements in the domain of learning and creative thinking while some pursued legal profession.

A Hindu scientist who was brutalized to death had some research papers to his credit while another was a highbrow intellectual with enormous studies in the realms of philosophy. Some of the killed ran groceries while others held ordinary jobs hardly making two ends meet. Even a mad person was not spared. Most of the victims of the

Muslim massacre were innocent and peace-loving people who had lived in penury and had been denied opportunities under the policy of discrimination which was institutionalized by a system dominated by the Muslims.

As a weak and unarmed religious-ethnic group the Muslim terrorists put them to a mass massacre and had they not been prompted by their 'race-memory', a repertoire of the history of their persecution, to buzz off their natural habitat, the terrorists, wildly frenzied and bent upon their destruction and decimation, would have finished them off as a species.

Terror was created through threats, bomb-blasts, rumours and apocryphal allegations and the terror machine was so endemic that every man, woman and the child became vulnerable. No Hindu felt safe from the penumbra of violence and terror. Kashmir for the hapless Hindus was reduced to a killing field which was prowled about by communal and terrorist hyenas.

It was not only in violation of the canons of ethics and morality that Kashmiri Hindus as a minuscule minority were cruelly killed and tortured but also in utter disregard of decent and civilized political deportment recognized by the Charter of Human Rights Declaration and several other international agreements. The killings were monstrous and barbaric paling the killings of Jews by the Nazis into a triviality. The Hindus were abducted front homes, work-places or streets and tortured and killed in the brutal ecstasy of their tormentors. The terrorists butchered them even in their homes in the presence of their defenceless and hapless inmates. Labelling them as 'informers' and 'agents of India', they were killed in large numbers without any considerations of age, vocation and political commitments.

It is a genocide of Hindus for the political commitments that they harboured and the religion that they espoused. As members of a community with a tremendous history in time, they have been bodily and mentally harmed and injured and conditions have been created to bring about their death and destruction. The terrorists have not concealed their first resolve to destroy the Kashmiri Hindus not only as political opponents but also as religious enemies. They have generated tremendous mass support for the genocide of Hindus through the Mosque Committees, a plethora of Islamic organizations and Quranic Schools run by the Jamaat-e-Islami.

The horrendous torture deaths brought about by a resort to barbaric methods will cause a shiver down the spine of the worst Hitlerites. Burning cigarettes were applied to the naked bodies of

Kashmiri Hindus. Boiling wax was poured on highly sensitive parts of their bodies. Nails were driven into their foreheads. Their eyeballs were gouged out and tongues chopped off. Male genitals were cut off. Private parts and breasts of women were hewn open. Women were ripped into two equal parts on a wood-slicing machine. Gang rapes were resorted to. Bellies were ripped open for entrails to spill out. Hairs from the heads were plucked out. They were hanged and bullets pumped into their bodies. Kidneys were extracted from the victims and offered to their parents to chew them at the pain of death. Brains were hammered.

In absence of government computations about the killings of Kashmiri Hindus, Sikhs and Buddhists, private agencies and non-government organizations have put the number of Hindus of all shades who have been killed to 2,500 out of which Kashmiri Hindus stand out with a figure of eighteen hundred and odd. The Report submitted to the National Human Rights Commission by PKM has put the figures of killed Hindus at 319 till October 1990. BN Nissar, editor of the *Kashyapvani*, has issued out a list of 765 Kashmiri Hindus who were brutally massacred.

Siege Mentality

Talking to some apolitical Kashmiris, was made aware that the majority Muslim parents feel that due to continuous army presence in the valley and the daily security drills and grills, checking, etc has caused a sense of siege mentality. One of the main complaint and the problem that needs to be immediately addressed to bring back the youths to main stream life for their rehab, development, sense of right lawful purpose in conducting themselves and to make them again a law abiding Indian Kashmiri citizen. One of the interesting social-political-psychological phenomena which can be observed in different societies pertains to the experience of being under siege, ie, feeling as if the rest of the world has highly negative intentions towards one's society or that one's society is surrounded by a hostile world. The focus is on 'negative intentions' and 'the rest of the world'. 'Negative intentions' refer to the desire and motivation of the world to inflict harm or to hurt the society, so that they imply a threat to the society's well-being.

Especially critical is the view that the 'rest of the world' feels this way. This element is unique to siege believes; many societies probably believe that at least one other society has negative intentions towards them. But with the 'siege mentality', the situation is far more extreme and serious. Members of the society believe that their society is not only in conflict with another group, or surrounded by hostile neighbours, but they believe that the rest of the world, as a whole, is hostile toward them. This creates the tragic observation that one's society is alone in a hostile world. Usually, the described core societal belief occurs with additional societal beliefs such as loneliness, the threat to societal existence, lack of trust in other nations, expectations that no nation will extend help in time of need, or have the need to secure the existence of the society without resorting to external help.

Whenever the siege theme is central in the society's repertoire of beliefs, we can say that society members possess a 'siege mentality'. In this situation, siege beliefs not only feature prominently in the cognitive repertoire of society members and are expressed in various cultural and educational products, but also come with important emotional and behavioural implications, which have a major effect on the life of the society members and the decisions of their leaders.

The recent past and the present offer a number of examples of societies characterized by societal beliefs about siege: the Soviet society immediately following the Bolshevik Revolution, the Japanese society in the early thirties, the Jewish society in Israel, the Albanese society in the sixties, seventies and eighties, the South African White society prior to the elimination of apartheid, Iraqi society in the 1990s and North Korean and Iranian society today are all examples of societies with a siege mentality.

Causes of the Siege Mentality

The roots of the siege experience in these societies are not, of course, necessarily identical. It is possible to differentiate at least three causes for the development of siege beliefs that are not mutually exclusive.

1. The siege experience can be evoked by the society's leaders who decide to isolate the society from the world for various internal reasons (eg, Albania and North Korea). This type of siege mentality depends on the leaders' centralized authority and the needs of the society. It may end with the change of the leadership, or of internal needs, as it happened in the case of Albania. An example of self-initiated siege mentality is the present case of North Korea which, following the changes that took place in Eastern Europe, isolated itself from the rest of the world, attributing especially negative intentions to capitalist countries.

   The present leader, Kim Jong-Il, the son of Kim I-sung, explained that preventing imperialist ideology and culture from infiltrating into our country remains the key to protecting our socialism and guaranteeing the development of socialist culture. The imperialists are attempting to infiltrate bourgeois culture into the socialist world, thus to paralyse the revolutionary spirit of the people here. In line with this thesis, North Korea views other countries with extreme suspicion, minimizing relations with them (except with China) by maintaining a 'closed door' policy.

2. Alternatively, the siege mentality may stem from perceived maltreatment of the society by the world (eg, the Soviet Union after the Bolshevik Revolution, South Africa during the Apartheid). It is possible to assume that in the past, persecuted societies such as Jews, exploited societies such as the Indians in South America, or Blacks in North America, or societies which suffered extermination and genocide such as the Armenian society in Turkey, experienced isolation and maltreatment by other groups and thus formed societal beliefs about the siege. The traumatic experiences may leave their mark, even when the circumstances change.

   It also happens that the international community decides to cut relations with a particular society and usually, such decision is accompanied by punitive actions such as embargoes, boycotts, sanctions or even violent, hostile activities. This was the case of South Africa during apartheid and of Iraq after the Gulf war. In these cases, when the international community changes its isolating actions, the siege beliefs may dissipate, as it happened in the case of South Africa.

3. Finally, the siege beliefs may be maintained because of the imprint left by past collective experiences, something that greatly affects the present perception of the world. In these cases, societal channels, cultural institutions and the educational system, often support the siege mentality and therefore it is extremely difficult to change. Siege beliefs become master symbols and chosen traumas of the society. Then, even under new circumstances, society members search for evidence to validate their societal beliefs about the siege and continue to maintain them.

An example of this situation is the Israeli Jewish society, which maintains societal beliefs about the siege from 2000 years of Jewish history. As a result, as Liebman rightly pointed out:

Jewish tradition finds anti-Semitism to be the norm, the natural response of the non-Jew.... The term 'Esau hates Jacob' symbolizes the world, which Jews experience. It is deeply embedded in the Jewish folk tradition. But of special importance for understanding the Israeli siege mentality is the Holocaust. The fact that six million Jews perished, while 'the world' remained indifferent, served crucially to strengthen the siege mentality of the remaining Jews and left its marks on future generations and their experience.

In the Jewish point of view, the Holocaust does not stand alone as one grim event, but is a metaphor for Jewish history itself. Elon, for example, observed:

> "The Holocaust remains a basic trauma of Israeli society. It is impossible to exaggerate its effect on the process of nation-building. There is a latent hysteria in Israeli life that stems directly from this source.... The trauma of the Holocaust leaves an indelible mark on the national psychology, the tenor and content of public life, the conduct of foreign affairs, on politics, education, literature and the arts."

Besides, the Israeli-Arab conflict, although very different from the Holocaust, did a great deal to preserve this siege mentality. With the establishment of the Jewish State in 1948, Arab countries tried actively to destroy it. First, it was invaded by five regular armies from Egypt, Trans-Jordan, Syria, Iraq and Lebanon. Later, until the peace treaty with Egypt, all the Arab States closed their borders, declared an embargo, pressed the world to stop relations with Israel and maintained a state of war, refusing to recognize Israel and employing instead the rhetoric of the 'liberation of Palestine' and the 'liquidation of Zionist aggression'. Through its history, Israel fought several major wars with Arab States in which many thousands of Israelis were killed. Also, Palestinian terrorist attacks against Jews, which have caused many civilian causalities, also boosted siege beliefs. Finally, very often the criticism of the international community regarding Israeli policies serves as evidence of widespread anti-Semitism.

Consequences of the Siege Mentality on the Kashmiri Youth – Siege beliefs have emotional and behavioural implications that can have serious consequences for the society, as well as for the international community.

1. The threatened society with siege beliefs develops negative attitudes towards other societies, which may be accompanied by feelings of xenophobia and chauvinism.
2. The society becomes extremely sensitive to any information and cues transmitted by other societies that may indicate negative intentions. This developed sensitivity is based on

lack of trust and suspicion that society members feel toward other societies which, in their view, have negative intentions.

3. The society develops internal mechanisms to cope with the threat by increasing pressure among society members towards conformity, unity and mobilization. This pressure can take various forms, like calls for unity, calls for patching-up or concealment of disagreement within the group, as well as threatening (and carrying out) negative sanctions against those who disagree within the group.
4. Finally, a society may take a course of action without consideration of international behavioural codes. A society that feels endangered may decide that its need to survive is so paramount that all means can be used. As a result, it may decide to take a course of action considered extreme and unacceptable by the international community. In this situation, society members may disregard any unfavourable reactions from these other groups, which they consider as their adversaries anyway.

The described four consequences of siege mentality suggest that siege believes can have a serious effect on the attitudes and behaviours of the societies that hold them and Kashmiris are no exception. These beliefs dictate a particular way of life. In the cases we have looked at, they constitute the core beliefs of the societal ethos. It is possible then to characterize the societies of Albania and South Africa until several years ago and of North Korea, Israel and Iran today as having an ethos of siege because siege beliefs in these societies played or still play a very important role in the psyche of the society members and their leaders. Thus, any understanding of the behaviour of these societies must take into account their siege mentality and hence any solution to addressing Kashmiri youths have to incorporate this knowledge.

Why Kashmiris in 2018 Still Angry with India?

Suspicious that the Maharaja may not accede to it, Pakistan decided to launch a military attack on Jammu and Kashmir in October 1947 to annex the State by force. It could not use its army openly because it was still under the command of British officers. So it did so clandestinely through its so-called 'non-State actors', a myth it has kept alive to this day to wage a proxy war against India. Its 'tribesmen' invaded the Valley on October 22 and soon reached the town of Baramulla after sacking Muzaffarabad and Uri. Here, the raiders faced stiff resistance from the local population. Playing a leading role was a young man of 19, Maqbool Sherwani.

He kept the raiders back by warning them that the Indian forces had arrived on the outskirts of the town. The information conveyed was wrong, but it prevented the advance of the raiders for a few crucial days. In fact, the Indian troops had not even landed in Srinagar until then. Of course, he was soon found out, captured, tortured, nailed to a wooden cross and shot repeatedly. The tale of his bravery survives to this day. That is the story of Baramulla in October 1947.

The year 2017, the same town of martyr have words scribbled in bold letters on the wall "Indian dogs go back", and this is not an isolated example of how much things have changed in Kashmir during the last 70 years. Anantnag, Shopian and few other parts of the valley areas within Kashmir, you'll find similar sentiments painted on the wall.

The feeling of betrayal and discrimination by India runs deep in the mind of the average Kashmiri. On the issue of betrayal, the narrative runs like this:

> "The Instrument of Accession was conditional and gave India the power only over the few subjects of foreign affairs, defence, currency and communications. Over the years, India has gone back on this commitment and, despite the existence of Article 370 in the Constitution giving special status to the State, have tried in various ways to integrate it like other States." This is the perception in the valley and not the writer's endorsement of the view.

The use of pellet guns have further worsened the situation, Kashmiris feel that India did not use pellet guns during the Jat agitation in Haryana, the Cauvery agitation in Karnataka, the Patel agitation in Gujarat or any other agitations elsewhere in the country. It appears that it is specially reserved for the Kashmiris and is meant to blind their whole next generation. The use of pellet guns is the most emotive of all issues today in Kashmir.

Their present mindset prevents them from seeing things in their correct perspective. There is a readiness to believe the worst without verifying. They are blind to the excesses committed by Pakistan, including cross-border terror attacks by it. The demands most Kashmiris articulated before all-party peace mission team was to include the holding of a plebiscite as laid down in the UN resolutions, the holding of trilateral dialogue with Pakistan to unite the old Riyasat of J&K and finally grant them Azaadi.

The situation from the Indian point of view appears to use the brutal force given the present situation as radicalized militants cannot be brought on to the negotiation table as their strings are pulled by across the borders 'State' and 'non-State' actors. They ascribe the return to normalcy in the Valley to the use of force and the determination of the authorities not to flinch in the face of violence. I think you do not have to follow waterfall methodology, rather India can run two parallel tracks and there still is room for negotiation, either by force or by request. Everyone in the Valley is living under the apprehension that something terrible may happen shortly and that this time, it will be worse than anything that has happened in the past. The recently taped conversation of a Kashmir based terror groups shows they are even planning for a chemical attack to inflict larger collateral damage.

Balkanization of India, Inevitable or Delusional

If Kashmir breaks away from India, they say India will disintegrate and that's the dream Pakistani Generals, ISI and some of the Indian enemies wishes. So you see how important is Kashmir to India and the world. Now readers may ask why should the world be bothered? Well in 2018 there is no confusion on the motive of the Islamic terrorism and how radicalization have impacted the safe havens of the west. No country is immune however strong they are. Even USA felt the brunt of home grown Islamic radicalized youths, trained in Pakistan. Now let's go to Iraq, a small country when compared to India, once it broke post-Saddam, the radicalization helped give birth to ISIS and how it terrorized the world is well-covered. It has not yet been resolved and no one is safe. Imagine if India breaks and the 170 million Muslims, the second biggest after Indonesia gets radicalized and with the arguably some of the best Muslim brains to offer, the entire world will be the hell of a place and no one will be able to contain this monster, a sure Apocalypse, no 'Mayan' or 'Nostradamus' prophecies will be needed for the end of the world. It is in the world's interest to make sure India stays strong and that way even China its powerful neighbour will be safer.

Chinese cannot control small Muslim groups in Xinjiang, Gansu and Ningxia forget about ISIS type group. They should be thankful that a big country like India is absorbing all the attention, for now, will not always be like this. India may work out a deal and strategy to deflect some beyond the Himalayas. India is plural in character with federal cooperative system respecting all religions and hence it has till now able to keep its house intact. Unity in Diversity has been its national motto.

Just like Kashmir can trigger balkanization of India; similarly, Kalachakra will trigger balkanization of China. My friend and Asia expert Niraj Kumar discusses it in his new upcoming book on the "Kalacakra: The Great Wheel of Time". Kalachakra is in Motion - Eleventh Panchen Lama of China conducted Kalachakra ceremony in China for the first time in 50 years. It appears that the Kalachakra has gained the momentum. Kalachakra is the Great Wheel of Time. Kalacakra decimates the nations and the people; stars and the planets, Existence and the non-existence. It may trigger disintegration of China into 10 new Republics (Hotan, Khan, Beijing, Manchuria, Shanghai, Zhenjiang, Greater Hongkong, Chengdu, Tibet, Zhangzhung) since the internecine battle lines have been drawn among the three powerful factions at the top - Zhejiang faction led by Xi Jinping, Shanghai faction led by Jiang Zemin and Beijing faction led by Hu Jintao.

The world will have to wait and watch, unlike India where the impact will be deadly for the world it may not be the case with Chinese balkanization, the economy may be impacted but then is almost every case, China trade share with the countries of the world is in its favour. A strong China is good for Asia, but a bully China is bad for the world as it fans Islamic radicals and extremists to carry out their evil designs by supporting rouge countries to benefit its business growth. This is playing with fire and hopes an old civilization should see things beyond money and greed. For more information on this subject, we all are waiting for Niraj's next book on the Kalachakra, Foreword by none other than, His Holiness the 14th Dalai Lama.

Kalashnikov, Kahwa and Kaffir – Three Vertices of the Bermuda Triangle

The three vertices of the Kashmiri Bermuda Triangle of Uncertainty. Having said that let me explain all these metaphors. Kalashnikov represents Terrorism; this AK-47 assault rifle has been the baby in the hands of all the terror groups operating in the Kashmir Valley. Kahwa here represents the Insaniyat (Humanity) and the third vertex is 'Kaffir', used for non-Muslims and even some minority Muslim groups. This is a derogatory, communal word and should never be used in any civilized society, but here it represents radicalization of Sunni Islam (which is surely a religion of peace, as sermoned by Prophet, peace be upon him.).

Like Bermuda Triangle this Kashmiri vicious triangle of uncertainty has not been cracked yet, causing immense trouble to the humanity at large. Most of the Muslim countries for too long kept discussing that the Middle-Eastern problems as the inherent creation of the West. The 9/11 scenario destroyed whatever currency that notion once had. The dearth of freedom, radicalization, Wahhabism, Salafism, the lack of civil society, the widespread illiteracy and the dismal status of women in the Arab countries helped create a monster called Radical Islamic Terrorism. This social and communal problem has a severe consequence on the economic, political, religious and peaceful co-existence of humanity at large.

During the past three centuries, the Islamic world has lost its dominance and its leadership position and has fallen behind both the modern West and the rapidly modernizing Orient (China, ASEAN countries, Japan and India). This widening gap poses increasingly acute problems, both practical and emotional, for which the rulers, thinkers and rebels of Islam have not yet found effective answers. The Muslim world, convinced of its inherent superiority, largely ignored the spectacular epistemological and technological advances that were being made in Europe between the Renaissance and the Industrial Revolution until it was too late. Suddenly, Napoleon's armies were in Egypt, beginning a long story of decline that ended with the dismemberment of the Ottoman Empire following World War I.

It is with this defeat that the crisis of Islam opens or more specifically, it is with Osama bin Laden's commentary on that defeat. Lewis quotes him after 9/11 fulminating about the 'humiliation and disgrace' that the Muslim world has suffered for the past 80 years. As Lewis points out that reference would be almost entirely lost on a Western audience, but for many in the Middle-East, the Sykes-Picot Agreement that carved up the Ottoman Empire between the British and French after 1918 still rankles. Indeed, much of The Crisis of Islam is about the nature of historical memory. Lewis points out that for Arabs the Crusades came to be seen as "an early prototype of the expansion of European imperialism into the Islamic world." It is hardly an accident that when Osama bin Laden declared his war against the West, he framed it in part as a war against the 'Crusaders'.

Islam is "religion, a system of belief and worship" and also "the civilization that grew up and flourished under the aegis of that religion." There is a huge dependence on politics in Islam, hence its dual in nature. Islam became a State and an empire due to its political organization and it was also a religious community. The fundamentalists say that contemporary Islam is following the wrong path. They view the West as their enemy because due to them Islam is corroding away. West views the Muslims as either a threat to them or as peace-loving people who have been probably treated badly. What is

Jihad? As per *Quran* "striving in the path of God" is jihad. There's two distinct meanings of jihad, moral striving and armed struggle.

The Crusaders over Muslims and Jews caused rivalries among the Muslims and Christians, leading to The Crusades. The leaders of the Christian regime mainly attacked the Muslims for material gains and the Muslims saw this as being against their religion and towards their holy place, which leads to jihad. Muslims ruled until 1683 when Turkish siege over Vienna ended. This left the Muslims with two questions: why had the victorious Ottoman armies been defeated and how could they restore their previous dominance. They also failed to recognize and adopt the strong and powerful influence of economic expansion, competition and co-operation which marked success in Europe. When the Middle-East adopted these, it led towards the growth of their products in the West.

The European rule over Islamic lands maintained various phases of commercial expansion and armed invasions leading to conquests. The effects of imperialism were considered more harmful than the developments made regarding State's independence and social gaps. From the 20th century onwards Muslims started making agreements with various countries in the hope that they would be aided in winning their place back in the World. Pakistan China marriage is one such anecdote.

The Marriage of Saudi Power and Wahhabi Teaching created a monster child who has destroyed the peace and inter-faith harmony, and has turned Islam versus rest of the world. Rejection of modernity which has given rise to many historical movements; the most prominent being Wahhabism. Founded by Muhammad Ibn 'Abd al-Wahhabi in 1744, declared aim was the purification of Islam from all later distortions. Wahhabism was supported by the Saudi rulers of Najd who, by force of arms, spread it too much of Arabia and the Ottoman Empire. The Wahhabis were strongly opposed to any version of Islam other than their own and exposed their beliefs by wiping out people who did not meet their standards of purity.

Two developments in the early 20th century turned Wahhabis into a significant force in the Islamic world. The first was the consolidation of the Saudi kingdom by Sheikh 'Abdul 'Aziz Ibn Sa'ud. He entered into agreements with the US oil exploration companies and the corresponding inflow of money had a deep impact on the Saudi kingdom's influence on the Islamic world. Today organized Muslim public life, worship and education are to a large extent dominated by Wahhabi principles, which had it not been for the oil revenue and custodianship of the holy places, remained a small extremist sect. West should take note of this mistake.

Oil wealth also lead to adverse political effects as governments with oil revenue do not need for popular assemblies to collect taxes and therefore can afford to disregard public opinion. As a result, this discontentment has found expression in religious extremist movements. Muslim fundamentalists as those who feel that the troubles of the Muslim world are due to excessive modernization. The remedy is to return to authentic Islamic values and the most dangerous enemies are the corrupt Muslim rulers who have imposed infidel ways on Muslim peoples.

How 'Terrorism' word come to be associated with Islam in today's world. Various extremist organizations and regimes, supposedly acting in the name of Allah, are now considered to be the true representatives of Islam even though their ideologies are in direct contradiction to many of the teachings of the Prophet (Peace be upon him). Radical elements, which include groups like al-Qaeda and regimes like those in Iran and Iraq, twist the word of God to their benefit and justify their actions by referring to this extremist interpretation of the Quranic text and the Sunnah of the Prophet Mohammad. In many cases, they have even rejected those sacred verses, which do not support their radical positions by deeming them as evoked or abrogated.

Evolution of Islamic terrorism is a tactic to gain the attention of the world and has thus become a mode of psychological warfare. At the beginning of the twentieth century, Islamic terrorism was associated with a breed of rebels known as the 'Assassins' who targeted Muslim leaders whom they considered to be unworthy or unfit to rule. The Assassins have now been succeeded by the fundamentalist groups of today who identify the western world in general as their enemy. Instead of practising methods of targeted assassination, these groups target the ordinary civilians with absolutely no connection to their cause. By doing so they have managed to succeed in their purpose, ie, create psychological terror within the general masses using the rapid development of the media to their advantage.

The newly developed concept of suicide bombers has also been mentioned. Suicide has been very clearly termed in Islam as one of the greatest sins and the fact that Muslim terrorists are using it as a method of fighting their cause proves that they are fighting for their political purpose; and not in the name of Islam. Kashmir for last 25 years has been slowly and steadily radicalized from Sufi Islam to

Wahhabi/Salafi Islam bringing a large number of youths under its fold and rejecting the Nation-State concept in search of the Sharia-driven ideology.

Kalashnikov: Globalization of Terrorism/Islamic Fundamentalism/ Ghazwa-e-Hind

The AK-47 or AK as it is officially known (also known as the Kalashnikov) is a selective-fire (semi-automatic and automatic), gas-operated 7.62 × 39 mm assault rifle, developed in the Soviet Union by Mikhail Kalashnikov. It is officially known in the Soviet documentation as Avtomat Kalashnikov. Design work on the AK-47 began in the last year of World War II (1945). In 1946, the AK-47 was presented for official military trials and in 1948, the fixed-stock version was introduced into active service with selected units of the Soviet Army. An early development of the design was the AKS (S - Skladnoy or 'folding'), which was equipped with an under folding metal shoulder stock. In the spring of 1949, the AK-47 was officially accepted by the Soviet Armed Forces and used by the majority of the member States of the Warsaw Pact.

This has become symbolic of the Islamist terrorism as they love to have this weapon in their armoury. Be it Osama bin Laden, Aljuwari, Musa, Burhan, Azhar Masood, Salahuddin, etc have all videotaped themselves firing this Jihadi weapon. Kashmir home for Sufi Islam gave its way to the Islamic terrorism. In a video uploaded on YouTube on 7th June 2016, Burhan Wani, a misguided Kashmiri youth calmly informs his viewers that anyone who tries to promote Indian laws in Kashmir will face 'action'. He goes on to urge Kashmiris that instead of siding with 'Indian authorities', they should keep a close watch on the police and Army and keep informing Burhan and his associates about their movements and whereabouts. Also, with a hint of regret, he explains that they don't want to attack the local police - their people (local Kashmiri Muslims) - but as they keep helping the Indian Army and cracking down on Kashmiri youth, he is left with no choice. The Indian Army is repeatedly referred to as *'Dushman'* (enemy) in the six-minute video.

He was later killed by the Indian security forces in an encounter. His death erupted into a massive protest in the Kashmir valley. Reports suggest that over 50,000 people congregated to mourn his death and joined his funeral procession. Which brings us to the question - just why has his death brought masses in Kashmir out on the streets? Burhan, who had a bounty of ₹10 lakh on him, picked up AK-47 when he was merely 15-years-old. Burhan. His father and his friends singled out one incident as having had an outsize influence on him in his decision to take up arms against India.

Born to an affluent village headmaster, Burhan was a class X student when he went out with his brother Khalid to take a spin in the latter's new bike in Tral region, in Pulwama district where they lived. They were accompanied by a friend while continuing on their ride they were intercepted by a group of Indian Army personnel who ordered the teenagers to buy them cigarettes. Back in 2000, the friend said, this was routine.

Officers allegedly stopped young Kashmiri boys and frisked them, or asked them to buy cigarettes in return for letting them use the road during curfew hours. Khalid Wani went to buy cigarettes and returned. However, the friend said, the officers still attacked them and beat them up. Khalid fell unconscious, his new bike was damaged, while Burhan and his friend managed to run away. While fleeing, Burhan, threatened the Army officers that he is going to 'avenge' what they did to his brother. According to the same report, six months later, Wani fled his home and joined the Hizbul Mujahideen.

Burhan's mother is a post-graduate in science who now teaches *Quran* to Muslim children. His two younger brothers are still in school. Muzaffar Ahmad Wani, Burhan's father, explained why his son couldn't be held back.

> "Almost everyone here has been beaten up by the Army. You also must have had your share. But everyone didn't become a militant. It depends on how much one can take. *Yeh aap ki ghairat pe depend karta hai* (it depends on your self-respect). Someone's *ghairat* got challenged time and again, so he decided to answer back. Others decided to stay quiet. My son couldn't bear to see the atrocities and the humiliation, so he was forced to choose the path which he is on right now."

The local report suggests that several of Burhan's cousins had already joined militancy by then and it was fairly easy for him to take the leap, he already had the roadmap and mentor to take the plunge so that the alleged army atrocity could be just a catalyst. Burhan swiftly rose in the ranks of Hizbul Mujahideen and soon came to be called the 'poster-boy' of militancy in Kashmir. He is said to have recruited at least 100 people from Kashmir to Hizbul Mujahideen and was known to use social media to reach out to and urge Kashmir's youth to join the militancy group. Burhan was one of the first militants from Kashmir to reveal his face and identity on social media, belittling security forces of the country. One picture that went viral on Facebook showed Burhan, accompanied by ten recruits, sitting in forested area possibly in South Kashmir, looking smugly into the camera, Kalashnikovs strapped across their body. What the rest of the country called 'terrorism', took the concrete, believable form of a 'rebellion' for them with Burhan's face to promote it.

Young Kashmiris who support the view that Kashmir should be allowed to separate from India and resent the presence of armed forces in their home land finally found a face and a name they could identify with. What the rest of the country called 'terrorism', took the concrete, believable form of a 'rebellion' for them with Burhan's face to promote it. Burhan's throw-caution-to-the-wind stance bore his outfit rich rewards too. For the first time in a decade, the ratio between indigenous and the foreign militants had changed in favour of the former. Writing for the *Kashmir Monitor*, Seema Mustafa says,

> "He went on to discard his mask, take ownership of the path that he had chosen as a reported Hizbul Mujahideen recruit and disclosed that he was from Tral and a well-educated family."

The opening lines of the song playing in the background says:

> *Humne rasme mohabbat ko zinda kiya, zakhme dil jeet kar.*
> (We have brought love alive, by winning wounded hearts.)

Security forces couldn't trace specific attacks on armed forces back to Burhan, but he was believed to have masterminded quite a few. That apart, his overwhelming appeal among radicalized Kashmiri youth turned him into a security threat for the armed forces and other agencies. It was unfortunate that a promising youth from Indian Kashmir had to end like this, bringing huge sadness to his family and the nation.

Another interesting development happened in the valley on May 12, 2017, Hizbul threatened to behead Hurriyat leaders, hang their heads in Lal Chowk for calling Kashmir struggle political. Hizbul Mujahideen's threat is believed to be the first against the Hurriyat leadership who are acknowledged to represent the political views of a section of Kashmiris and had earlier held talks with the State and Central Governments many times. A top Hizbul Mujahideen leader has threatened to behead separatist Hurriyat leaders for calling Kashmir a political struggle instead of a religious war for the creation of an 'Islamic State' or the Caliphate.

The message was delivered through a video clip which contained a montage of slides showing Islamic quotes about Islam and Sharia. The person is believed to be of local Hizbul Mujahideen commander Zakir Musa calling Hurriyat leaders "hypocrites, infidels, kaffirs, followers of evil," the militant warned to chop off their heads "if they create hurdles in the path of making Kashmir an Islamic State." The militant also said the heads would be hanged in Lal Chowk in Srinagar, an area known as the nerve centre of anti-India protests.

In a joint statement, hardline Hurriyat leaders Syed Ali Shah Geelani, Mirwaiz Umar Farooq and Yasin Malik said the freedom struggle in Kashmir has nothing to do with ISIS or al-Qaeda. But they have been found taking funding from Pakistan to keep Kashmir on the international radar. Money to the tune of rupees 400 crore INR is used via Saudi Arabia to Afghanistan, Lahore, Karachi, Delhi-Mumbai-Kolkata to Kashmir via hawala, etc and mind you these are drugs money. So some kids or citizen in west primarily, the United States and Europe have bought this using taxpayer's money which has come to eventually fund terror operation killing security personnel and innocent civilian. Kashmiri local newspapers on Thursday gave wide coverage to the abduction and killing of army officer Lieutenant Ummer Fayaz, but stayed away from taking a stand on the murder.

None of the papers carried an editorial or an opinion piece condemning or questioning the killing of the unarmed young officer in Shopian while on holiday. Fayaz's body was found on Wednesday, a day after he was taken away at gunpoint from a wedding by suspected militants. "Army officer abducted, killed in Shopian," said the headline of leading English daily *Greater Kashmir*. The paper carried the condemnation of the killing by national and local political leaders, alongside a report on the soldier's grieving family. The paper also carried a news agency report on how Fayaz's first leave after having joined the army six months ago also became his last. Or the latest lynching of Ayub Pandith, local Muslim policeman, in the mosque premises just 3 kms from his home, that too on the sacred day of Shab-e-Quadr prayer at the holy month of Ramadan. The blood bath continues unabated. Earlier it was only non-Kashmiris security personnel or the Hindu Kashmiris, now Muslims killing Muslims and that too local Kashmiri Muslims. No one knows what Azaadi it will bring and also for whom?

Massacres in J&K by the Trigger-Happy Kalashnikov (AK-47) Gang

1989 Kidnapping of Rubaiya Sayeed (Daughter of the Indian Home Minister)

1990 Gawakadal massacre

1990 Zakoora and Tengpora massacre

1991 Kunan Poshpora incident
1993 Bijbehara massacre
1993 Sopore massacre
1993 Lal Chowk fire
1994 Kupwara massacre
1995 Kidnapping of Western Tourists in J&K
1997 Sangrampora massacre
1998 Wandhama massacre
1998 Prankote massacre
1998 Champanari massacre
2000 Chittisinghpura massacre 1
2000 Amarnath Pilgrimage massacre
2000 Chittisinghpura massacre 2
2001 Kishtwar massacre
2001 Chalwalkote massacre
2002 Qasim Nagar massacre
2002 Kaluchak massacre
2002 Raghunath temple attacks
2002 Qasim Nagar massacre
2003 Nadimarg massacre
2004 Teli Katha massacre
2006 Doodhipora killing
2006 Doda massacre
2008 Amarnath Land Transfer Controversy
2009 Shopian Rape and Murder Case
2009 Bomai Incident
2010 Kashmir Unrest
2013 Ramban Firing Incident
2014 Kashmir Valley attacks
2016 Kashmir Unrest
2016 Uri Attack
2016 Handwara Incident
2017 Umer Fayaz, young Kashmiri army officer was Kidnapped and Killed from a marriage ceremony
2017 Muhammad Ayub Pandith – Kashmir police DSP lynched in the Jamia Masjid, in the presence of Mirwaiz, he was on duty to protect the Hurriyat separatist leader. He lived just three km away from his Mosque that became his death bed.
2017 Massacre of Hindu pilgrims returning from Amarnath visit.
2018 Alas, it Continues !!!

The massacres listed was facilitated by the weapon commonly known as the Islamic Assault Riffle, 'the Kalashnikovs' and hence I have chosen this as one of the vertexes of the Kashmiri Bermuda Triangle. India does not manufacture this weapon so how does it land into the hands of the terrorists? The AK-47 has become a global brand, the Nike and Coca-Cola of small arms, with about seven million of them in Sudan alone. In Iraq there is one legally owned Kalashnikov per household; not counting those in the hands of Iraqi insurgents and al-Qaeda terrorists. Kashmir is also not far behind, thanks to the Hizbul Mujahideen group, anti-India and pro-Azaadi Kashmiri groups. There is a Santa Claus in Pakistan with name 'Hafiz Saeed' who loves sending it to his dear kids in the Kashmir valley irrespective of Christmas or no Christmas.

Before I move to the next vertex let me share a fascinating story, when an interviewer asked a Sudanese child soldier Emmanuel Jal, the rapper who was too gritty to adorn Live 8 concert at Geldof's Hyde Park, succinctly explained the attraction of the AK-47: "The gun has made me feel like a man. I knew people would do what I said because I had an AK. With an AK you can get food, respect, anything you want. Even when you are nine years old." Can the Indian government beat this attraction to bring back its young Kashmiri Kids back to becoming the innocent boys again? Can this Pakistani Santa be send to the North Pole? Probably not as he has now thrown the mask and has jumped into the political bandwagon of Pakistan which could reward him a powerful position like Quaid-e-Azam and give him access to the Nuclear button!!!

Kahwa: Insaniyat (Humanity)/Rich Culture and Warmness

Chinese Emperor Shennong (2737 BC) once instructed his people to boil some drinking water. A leaf from a nearby shrub fell into the water. Upon consumption, the aromatic flavoured drink quickly rose to fame with its herbal properties and spread rapidly across the globe. The name for the drink falls into three prominent categories: Cha (Mandarin/Canton), Tea (Min) and Kahwa (Xinjiang/Arabic) reflecting where geographically they were first linked.

Even though exact origin of Kahwa is still unclear, most Kashmiris believe that the aromatic traditional drink Kahwa dates back to times immemorial and has been a part of local consumption for ages. Certain sources also trace the origins of the drink to the Yarkand Valley in the Xinjiang area (which, with Kashmir, was part of the Kushan Empire during the AD 1st and 2nd centuries). It is likely that use of Kahwa and its spread from one region to another was facilitated and popularized in these regions during Kushan rule. Tea is made by boiling green tea leaf with saffron strands, cinnamon bark, cardamom pods and occasionally Kashmiri roses to add a great aroma.

It is served with sugar or honey and crushed nuts, usually almonds or walnuts. Some varieties are made as an herbal infusion only, without the green tea leaves. Traditionally, Kahwa is prepared in a copper kettle known as a samovar. A samovar consists of a 'fire-container' running as a central cavity, in which live coals are placed keeping the tea perpetually hot. Around the fire-container, there is a space for water to boil and the tea leaves and other ingredients are mixed with the water. Kahwa may also be made in normal pans and vessels, as the modern day urban living may not always permit the use of elaborate samovars.

Kahwa is usually served to guests or as part of a celebration dinner and saffron (Kong) is added to the Kahwa for special visitors. It is often served in tiny, shallow cups. Kahwa in Kashmir is also commonly served after Wazwan and elaborate family dinners. Sometimes milk is added to the Kahwa, but this is given to the elderly or the sick. Such a great example of Insaniyat. Kahwa in this book is used as metaphor representing the beautiful human warmness of the Kashmiri people and their rich culture.

In the good old days, Hindu and Muslim inter-faith marriages use to happen in Kashmir, with both families' consent and they lived peacefully ever after. This fairy tale continued for some time. Hindu and Muslim customs were observed in such inter faith marriages. The idea of belonging to Kashmir and the Kashmiriyat, superseded any artificial divisions by caste, class and religion and all this over the cup of Kahwa, the Hindu and Muslim could good-humouredly jostle for space. This oneness was the treasure every Kashmiri was then so proud of. This ideal pre-terrorist State left amicable room for dissension.

This is benign, congenial and cohering notion of Kashmiri oneness that the thrust of terrorist action attempts to subvert and denude. Hindus Ram Leela and Muslim Sultan Bud Shah plays were loved and talked by both the communities. The composite culture implies a blurring and melding of faiths: The Brahmin Hindus of Kashmir, unlike Brahmin Hindus anywhere else in India, happily eat meat. Kashmiri Muslims, perhaps envying their choice of gods, blurred their faith's austere monotheism by worshipping at the shrines of the valley's many local saints, its peers. It was more than evident that the mixed populace was kept together by this belief in Kashmiriyat.

But the harmony of these bygone eras has been succeeded by times that are more deceptive than any and the lurking shadows in the hearts of the younger generation are moving inexorably to a fracture. The stressed Kashmiris now begin to wonder how they could have ever believed that their beloved Kashmiriyat was best served by some association with India because India was where the churning happened. Despondency sinks in further to usher the end of whatever they have ever held dear as a people, maybe Kashmiriyat was an illusion, after all. Ultimately, the real significant loser in the whole tense situation is the frightened and downtrodden common people of Kashmir who suffer silently, not the ones sitting in the comfort of their palatial houses and with their kids happily relocated to the western countries. The decline of Hindu-Muslim harmony sees the decline of the Kashmiri culture – the wazwan loses its rich aroma, nobody has any more time to watch bhand pather and the Kahwa tastes bitter and have turned toxic.

Kaffir: Kalifate (Caliphate) transformation

Kaffir aka Infidels. First, it was Sufi Islam that helped in mass conversion of mostly Hindu Shivites from Kashmir; this created a hybrid society where Hindus, Muslims, Buddhists and Sikhs happily co-existed with a *tahzeeb* called Kashmiriyat (local name for humanity), now this paradise has become the laboratory for testing and implementing Caliphate. Very Idea of India as a nation is being challenged by these new converted radicalized minds. The rise of Islamic fundamentalism, against the backdrop of India-Pakistan tensions, threatens to cause a long internal war like situation, pointing out to the enemy hiding in the midst. The foe is now clearly labelled by Muslims in Kashmir as the 'Kaffirs' (a derogatory phrase used for the Hindus and the Indian army).

Let me start with what sacred *Quran* has to say on 'Kaffir'. 'Kaffir' is the one who does *kufr*. *Kufr* means the act of knowing the truth and then outwardly rejecting it. Mushriks are the one who does shirk. Shirk means associating partners with the one true creator.' In Islam Mushriks and Kaffirs should not be killed or even harmed just because they are kaffir or mushriks. In fact, they are not allowed to call a non-Muslim person a kaffir provided the person does not openly proclaim that he is a kaffir. This is a major misconception radicalized Muslims tries to mask. Now let's talk about the Quranic rule of how a Muslim should behave with non-Muslim, this can be categorized into two situations.

1. When Muslims are in minority or majority and the law of the land is not governed by *Quran* and authentic *Hadith* and there is the absence of Khalifa, means there is no publicly appointed

representative of the *Ummah*. In that case, no individual Muslim has the right to harm, forget about killing any non-Muslim. If someone does so, he would be dealt with the Constitution of that particular land. Even if a group of Muslim join hands and proclaim *khilafat* and start killing whoever they want is prohibited in Islam. This type of situation is there with isis and the so-called jihadist of Jammu and Kashmir. They are not only un-Islamic but even anti-Islamic.

2. When the Muslims have a majority and a publicly appointed Khalifa is there which means the rule of the land is *Quran* and authentic *Hadith*. In this case, also a common Muslim is not allowed to harm or kill anyone including non-Muslim. The Khalifa and his advisory board reserves the right to give any ruling regarding punishments and other legal matters. That too should be as per the *Quran* and authentic source. A non-Muslim has right to practice their religion and any threat to them from outside is countered by the Khalifa and the army of the land. Their place of worship and their property and their life will be under the protection of the Khalifa. No one from Muslims and outside can harm them. The only condition is that they should pay a nominal tax called *jizya* to identify them as non-Muslims and to remind the administration that they hold a minority status.

Now, when should a non-Muslim in this situation be given capital punishment. When a non-Muslim has committed murder or rape (and it has been proven) and has gone out of the way plotting against the land or country. Or they have joined the hands of the enemy to wage war against the land and these are proved. This clause relates to the Muslim as well. Presently only Saudi Arabia has been following the Quranic ruling. But here also we don't have people appointed Khalifa. So, in any part of the world, someone hears so and so Muslim or group of Muslim killing others in the name of their faith, be assured that they are not. Rather they are committing a crime against their creator and the humanity at large. So, to know Islam doesn't look at what the Radical Muslims do and unfortunately, they are everywhere and in ever growing large number. Look what the *Quran* and authentic *Hadith* says, requested by one of my close Muslim friend trying to help me get the right perspective.

The other version of 'Kaffir' concept as per self-declared champions of Islam is very gory, scary and separating brothers from brothers and turning them into blood loving monsters. Recently a video of an erstwhile pop icon and widely heard Islamic evangelist,

Junaid Jamshed went viral on the Internet, his remarks were perceived as blasphemy against the Prophet Mohammad (PBUH) and his wife Ayesha (RA). He has been charged under the Blasphemy Law (clause 295-C of the Pakistan Penal Code). Now one may say well wait a minute this is Pakistan, not India, but are these Kashmiri separatist not shouting Jammu and Kashmir to be merged with Pakistan and putting lives of millions of Hindus, Sikhs and Buddhists in the Kashmir at the mercy of this law? The spate of communally charged killings in Kashmir has spilled enough blood to ignore this very important vertex of the Kashmir Bermuda Triangle of death and sufferings.

It's Kaffirs who will do blasphemy by default, as any logic and argument they give trying to explain their faith will be taken as directed towards Islam and hence capital punishment is what he or she has to undergo. Kashmir was different for long time though has the bloody history for centuries. During the genocide of the Kashmiri Hindus, this was used to create a frenzy against the poor helpless minorities by their own fellow Muslim brothers. I will surely not like to generalize all the valley Muslims with that kind of tag, but they do have this 'Kaffir/Infidel' concept which surely differentiates between fellow countrymen and gross violation of the Constitution of the land.

Generalization of Crimes should be Avoided

What will a Christian think of Hitler killing millions of Jews in Germany? Or What will a Hindu think of the killing of Sikhs during the riots after the Indira Gandhi murder? Or What does a Buddhist monk think of Ashwin Wirathu's call for violence against Muslims in Myanmar? What will Muslims think of the destruction of World Trade Tower and Bamiyan Buddha? However hard you try to ignore this communal situation wishing for the normalcy and not the generalization, the unfortunate reality is coloured with Red. Through the centuries Kashmiri Hindus have immigrated to other parts of India because of the intolerant Muslim tyrant rulers. All Hindu homes were the prime target for destruction by burning, looting and desecration. In 1989, one fateful day the valley bursts apart, frenzied crowds and neighbours pulled Kashmiri Hindus out of their homes and then systematically raped the women in front of their husbands and children, brutally killed the Hindus who were left in the neighbourhood, as they tried to take cover. Kashmiri Hindus left 23,278 buildings and 10,112 acres land in Kashmir, which was their home for more than 1000 years. The above heart-wrenching anecdote comes from a Kashmiri Hindu, who is now living outside Kashmir in some rehabilitation camp.

Kashmir Conflict Resolution is not going to Reduce India-Pakistan Hatred for Each Other

Former Pakistani ambassador to the US Husain Haqqani told a Washington audience on February 10, 2017:

> "Even if Kashmir is resolved how would that end sectarian terrorism, because sectarian terrorism is about killing people who do not have same religious sect as you have? How would resolving Kashmir stop the Taliban, al-Qaeda, ISIS, Hizbul Mujahideen, who are radicalized at creating their old Islamic order and killing of Kaffirs."

Hizbul Mujahideen commander Zakir Musa, in his first message as an al-Qaeda operative, released an audio recording on slamming Indian Muslims for not joining Islamic jihad for 'Ghazwa-e-Hind' (the final and last battle for the conquest of India). In his rant against Indian Muslims, Musa said,

> "They are the most shameless Muslims in the world. They should be ashamed of calling themselves Muslims. Our sisters are getting abused and dishonoured and Indian Muslims keep screaming that 'Islam is peace'.... They (Indian Muslims) are the most *beghairat qaum* (shameless community) who cannot speak up against oppression and injustice. Is this what our Prophet and his *salafs* (followers) have taught us? They gave their blood during the wars and martyrdom for the honour of our sisters."

Referring to the historic Islamic 'Jung-e-Badr', he said,

> "They were 313 and ruled the world. We are crores now but only as slaves. The fact that the whole world is against one religion shows just how powerful that religion is."

The result is that Islam will win. In an indirect reference to the Hurriyat that has been insisting on the resolution of the Kashmir issue under the UN resolutions, Musa said, quoting Osama bin Laden, if they want to solve our tragedies of today in the United Nations, then they are merely hypocrites who are seeking to deceive Allah and his messenger.

The cult of the gun introduced by the Muslim fundamentalists of indigenous vintage churned out from the madrasas and Quranic schools have devastated the total fabric of Kashmir that had tolerance, the catholicity of outlook and humanism as its dominant weaves. True to their cult, the fanatic Islamists fed on the fare destruction and bigotry wrought havoc not only on them plus of learning and widely disseminated infrastructural base for human resource development but also targeted the talented and peace-loving Kashmiri State support for this hate campaign is obvious. Every day the number of those out to eliminate all Kaffirs mounts. There is nothing wrong following the faith of one's choice, but Kashmir is problematic only on account of it being a Muslim majority State, time for introspection for the Kashmiri community. If Kashmir goes, so goes the secular idea of India putting 170 million Muslims again in the pre-1947 situation, a gory memory every Indian wants to bury permanently. After all, the country was partitioned on the religious ground and the demand came from the Muslims only. Some of them did not want to live with the Kaffir Hindus and Sikhs.

Long time back the famous Kashmiri poetess Lal Ded wrote a lovely poem, still so relevant.

Holy books will disappear, only the Mystic formula will remain.
When the Mystic formula departs, nothing but Mind is left.
When the Mind disappears nothing will be left anywhere, just a Voice to be merged within the Void.

Let me end the chapter with the Persian couplet:

Har saksh hai pareshan, bechain o dil shikasta,
Koi marham inhein lagaye, ki Kashmir jal raha hai.

5. Talk Talk Talk – With Whom?

Preceding chapter touched upon the dark side of the Kashmir conflict, how monstrous and mysterious this oldest UN conflict has become, drawing similarities with the Bermuda Triangle, the modern civilization unsolved mystery. The three vertices of this Kashmir Bermuda Triangle represents what this conflict is constituted of and the challenges India and Kashmiris have to overcome the happy ending, if any. Reading all this surely makes us pessimist as one see's no light at the end of the tunnel, total melancholy. Gandhi once said, "Happiness is when; what you think, what you say and what you do are in Harmony." *Holy Quran* says:

> "Negative thoughts are those that produce bad feelings, anger, envy, jealousy, hatred, anxiety, depression and other negative emotional states. These are thoughts about the world, our wealth, our status, people we do not like or who have wronged us and so on. The cause of these thoughts is an attachment to the delusions of worldly and materialistic life that cloud the heart and prevent its purification."

Human communication is the process by which a thought is transmitted from the brain of a speaker to the brain of a listener, involves a complex interaction of acoustics, anatomy, physiology, neurobiology and psychology. The dissimilarity in the ideas and opinions result in a conflict. Conflicts and fights must be prevented to avoid its adverse consequences like War and loss of Human lives. Communication has a big role to play in conflict management. It has been observed that poor communication always results in misunderstandings and eventually conflicts. It has to be clear and precise to avoid conflicts. When we're arguing during a conflict, most of us are not listening; we are, "just talking to ourselves." One of the most important conflict resolution skills is listening. To listen well, we need to prepare. Most of us understand the importance of preparing ourselves to speak, but few of us think about preparing to listen. We take for granted that we all know how to listen. We may also assume listening is a passive activity, yet it is hard to do and we are rarely prepared to listen well.

To listen, we have to quiet our minds, most of us have a habit of taking our constant mind chatter seriously. We never stop to think about whether that makes any sense for us. 95% of what goes on in our minds is none of our business. This doesn't mean that we have to retreat to a cave or spend our lives meditating; it means that we have to consciously create a space where listening can occur, especially during conflict. 'Space' is what Pakistan and India should sincerely try to create for their meaningful and result oriented communication to re-start.

Talk Everything with Pakistanis – Bollywood, Cricket, Terrorism to Nuclear Spillage

Starting from the premise that constructive dialogue is the first step towards untangling a history of vexed relations between two nuclear neighbours, every government that has made any headway on this track has done so by first working the base at home, its politics and its message. There can be no dispute about the need for peace in the region, nor should there be any brakes on the institutional search for pathways, government or non-official, that foster sustained talks between Pakistan and India. There is no dispute about the saliency of diplomacy as quiet craft needs the space to air ideas and test limits. In fact, the state of play between India and Pakistan desperately requires a credible back channel. Because back-channel diplomacy is often used profitably by governments in taking forward complex possibilities before they are brought on board for a public push, it is important they are conducted with credibility on both sides. If not, they land the process in flames.

Both Pakistan and India have used interlocutors in the past, but both have been institutionally appointed savants, with long years of Foreign Office experience behind them and the trust of their policy establishments. From the Pakistani perspective, democracy is a gratuitous parlour game. They dismiss grassroot political parties in POK, as did Musharraf and they ignore the importance of institutional process, as well as its public message. Exactly similar mistake Sharif made disregarding the power of building consensus, let alone looping its beleaguered Foreign Office. This puts good intent at risk. Such mishandling is made even more poignant because while nay-sayers will say no, locking the mainstream political buy-in for talks, but will the army bless any such talks?

In a polarized political climate of Pakistan where civil-military relations are already strained and where a special assistant on foreign affairs has been made the scapegoat along with others for a PM House that functions only by the close cabal, consistent non-transparency only adds to tensions and questions. There is no cavil about talks with India but has to be with the right stakeholder and the Pakistan political parties are not one of them. The peril of ignoring strategic context, politics or tactics is obvious. Pakistanis think that the substance of talks with India is as important as the optics - the way they are seen to be held and by whom. In the end, there are three reasons official talks with India will never sustain. One, when they are done under public pressure to link all talks to impossible pre-conditions. Two, the Musharraf way, in which creative solutions on Kashmir are conducted so ineptly in total lockdown that they backfire on the ground when publicly floated. Three, Nawaz Sharif way, all on his own, losing the mainstream political consensus for peace with India by studiously ignoring its politics in Pakistan. Not involving Army and ISI who are the main stakeholders.

For India and Pakistan discord, Nuclear risk reduction proposals formulated more narrowly on the concrete objective of promoting strategic stability, for instance by validating the inability of given systems to deny the other side's retaliatory capability, rather than as tokens of political reconciliation or as encompassing solutions to Kashmir dispute. It also means that rather targeted proposals or steps should be considered even if they do not come as part of a comprehensive solution since individual measures might offer meaningful benefits even outside the context of a broader agreement that may be too difficult to conclude in any talk.

Nuclear arms remain highly significant in relations and strategic dynamics between India and Pakistan, not simply as symbols but also as instruments of coercive leverage in crisis and deadly weapons in the event of war. Given that tensions between India and Pakistan seem certain to persist for the foreseeable future and that the potential for these tensions to descend into outright conflict cannot be dismissed, it is vital that decision-makers, even those focused more on political than military matters - ensure that due attention is given to how their role can be managed in ways conducive to both effective deterrence and stability. Nuclear weapons do change the relations of nations. Adversary States that acquire them are thereby made more cautious in their dealings with each other.

Chances of either India or Pakistan starting a nuclear exchange are remote because of the social context of these tensions and because both countries are organically linked. But Jihadis have the different mindset and hence one cannot say it cannot happen with 100% surety. Recently held edition of the Carnegie Nuclear Policy Conference in Washington featured had obligatory alarm raised about South Asia. This year, the India-Pakistan 'nuclear flashpoint' thesis claimed that India has abandoned its No First Use (NFU) commitment and adopted a strategy, in case of an 'imminent' launch, of a pre-emptive 'comprehensive strike' against Pakistan. Such a course is being contemplated, it was argued, to spare the country the 'iterative tit-for-tat exchanges' and prevent the 'destruction' of Indian cities.

The NFU (no first use) declaration makes for fine rhetoric, distancing India from the hair-trigger situation Pakistan strives for the world to believe exists in the subcontinent. It is in Pakistan's interest to talk with the Hindu animus and predatory India because it justifies not just its nuclear arsenal but its emphasis on the first use of tactical nuclear weapons. Another view from India is that a democratically-elected government cannot morally risk the decimation of the Indian people by sticking literally to the NFU pledge.

However, certain developments in the nuclear weapons sphere do indeed make possible an Indian first strike. Such as the ongoing process of canisterising Agni missiles, including presumably the 700 km range Agni I meant for the Pakistan and Tibet-Chengdu contingencies. It, in fact, provides the country not only with a capability for launch-on-warning but also for striking pre-emptively should reliable intelligence reveal an adversary's decision to mount a surprise attack. Nuclear missiles in hermetically sealed canisters are ready-to-fire weapons and signal an instantaneous retaliatory punch to strongly deter nuclear adventurism. Thus, all nuclear weapon States keep a part of their strategic forces in the ready state; there are no guarantees that a confrontation or conflict with another nuclear power will keep to a sub-nuclear script. Having the wherewithal for pre-emptive action and launch-on-warning then is only a reasonable precaution.

Kashmir Comatose Continues – No Light at the End of the Tunnel Yet

From the very onset I never considered Kashmir issue just a political problem, as I dug into history and researched, it validated further that this conflict is not 'only' political but profoundly religious and has now transformed into a full-blown Islamic radicalism. Recently, the killing of Amarnath pilgrims, Mohammed Ayub Pandith and other local Muslim law enforcement officers of the State took place. Kashmiris killing Kashmiris is total auto sarcophagy of Kashmiriyat. Some of the people I talked and who immensely helped in collecting the data were Kashmiri people, Rushneek Kher – a Kashmiri Pandit activist, Hurriyat – Iftikhar Geelani (son-in-law of Geelani), Niraj Kumar – Asia Expert, friends from Administration, Army and Politics. What I gathered from them was little pessimist mood and no light at the end of the long tunnel. This affects so many human lives, the Kashmiris, the Security Personnels, the Peace loving citizens of India and Pakistan and the global countries at large.

Whom Should India Talk When Dealing with Pakistan?

India has invested in a freefalling stock trying to promote democratic political set-up in Pakistan by always ending up talking with the politicians of the day when it comes to resolving Kashmir or larger India Pakistan bilateral relationship. This approach has failed and will keep failing. India needs to remove its mind block and stop taking the high moral side of decision making and let go its mature democratic leader's image, has not benefited her even an inch of POK land even after four wars and each resulting in substantial wins on the battlefields. The reason is they have missed talking to the right stakeholders. Pakistan is a country where it's the Army that owns the country and not vice versa.

First time India talked to a Pakistani General was after 1965 victory and they got Haji Pir Pass, which our politician lost on the negotiating table, again in 1971 India talked to the Pakistani army and they smoothly kneeled, putting their guns down and surrendering more than 50% of Pakistan land, in return for few whiskey bottles and promise to escort them safely out of Bangladesh, in spite of all these successes in dealing with the Pakistani army, Indian politicians in the garb of becoming the champion of non-aligned grouping, democratic values, secular ideology, forget their own legendary epic *Mahabharata* and its hero Krishna who gave detailed lessons in the form of *Geeta,* on war related negotiations overcoming emotions even if the enemy was a friend or a relative, has hurt the nation a lot. Know your adversary better, is what the great Chanakya also suggested in his book *Kautilya's Arthashastra.*

The book *Inside Pakistan – Military Economy,* Ayesha Siddiqi, gives how commerce can be used as one important means for incentivizing Pakistani army establishment for coming to some resolution on Kashmir. For them, army association is a business making the profitable venture, which helps them and their families financially and their institution to continuously acquire more power and be the only power centre within Pakistan. This has to be understood when dealing with them.

The military is one of the vital organs of the State. In some countries, they become deeply involved in the politics of the State and dominates all the other institutions. In Pakistan, this does not culminate only into an annual increase in the defence budget which is very large part of the nation's GDP shape, but it also gets into commercial ventures. In Pakistan, military uses the capital for the personal benefit of the larger military fraternity, well the lion share goes to Punjabi ethnicity and also it is neither recorded nor part of the defence budget. It is a completely independent genre of capital. Is most significant component being entrepreneurial activities that do not fall under the scope of the normal accountability procedures of the State and are mainly for the gratification of military personnel and their cronies.

The top echelons of the armed forces who are the main beneficiaries of this commercial gain justify the economic dividends as welfare provided to the military for their services to the State as if they do not get the salary, interesting. This commerce is hidden from the Pakistani public and referred to the military's internal economy. On further research, it came out that this causes the officer cadre to be interested in enhancing their influence in the State's decision making and politics. For our discussion let us call this Pakistani Military Capital as PMC, as this becomes the major driver for the armed force stake in political control and hence any dispute negotiation has to keep this in mind.

Militaristic-totalitarian system of Pakistan does not allow its army to go back to barracks and over the neck involvement in money making has given an opportunity to India to understand those dynamics and cut out some deal for Kashmir resolution. There is price attached to everything, how one can negotiate with Pakistani army leadership is what India has to work on, learn to put a price and negotiate, Kashmir, Haji Pir, POK everything can be resolved. This has to be the carrot and stick approach.

Pakistan's military today runs a huge commercial empire which runs into billions of dollars. The military's business groups – the Fauji Foundation, the Army Welfare Trust, Shaheen Foundation and Bahria Foundation are some business conglomerates in the country. The businesses are very diverse in nature, ranging from small-scale ventures like bakeries (yes you read right), farms, schools, private security firms to corporate enterprises such as commercial banks, insurance companies, radio and television channels, fertilizer, cement and cereal and baby's dippers manufacturing plants, insurance businesses. Operations vary from Toll collecting on highways (now you know why they have 15K strong army deployed for illegal CPEC project protection) to gas stations, shopping malls and real estate business.

Besides these, there are multiple channels through which the army acquires opportunities to monopolize national resources and it's here the Indus water revenue sharing or electricity project revenue sharing model can be devised by India. This type of economy and their predatoriness has caused a feudal authoritarian and non-democratic, political system and this supports my argument of not talking to anyone in Pakistan except the Army.

James Mulvenon while researching the commercial activities of the Chinese armed forces and its impact on the command and control of military-run ventures and their efficiency, found corruption in the People's Liberation Army (PLA) conduct as the only major ramification of military commercialization. PLA undertook farming to contribute self-reliance and national economic development. The PLA's special war economy groups manufactured a large array of product to earn profits. The guerrilla industries donated these profits to war efforts and for financing the welfare plans of army units. Chinese realized the negative impact of running commercial enterprise by their army and introduced reforms in 1990, aimed at cutting down the non-military roles of the armed forces, by measures such as forcing the military to disinvest in the services industries sectors via Revolution in Military Affairs (RMA), though Chinese armed forces still have a role in the defence production sector. But Pakistan is no China and will never do such reforms, not soon and hence an opportunity for India.

Now India should have a mechanism for reaching out to the Pakistani people ritually and daily via electronics, prints and social media to educate them on what's going around in their country. The image of their army is so larger than life that India good gestures are not appreciated by majority yet. From Vajpayee's trip to Lahore to Modi's uninvited trip to Nawaz's farmhouse in Pakistan, gestures are not appreciated by Pakistani army who without even taking time immediately backstab in the midst of such events. Siachen, Uri list is long. The strong nexus between Pakistani feudal elites and military are collectively plundering, a concept that can be explained better through Mancur Olson's framework of Kleptocratic distribution of resources. According to Olson's concept of roving and stationary bandits, roving bandits enforce a higher cost on the settled community they pillage. By engaging in collective over-plundering, the roving bandits impose a negative externally on the society, resulting in a depletion of resources. This ultimately reduces the dividends for the bandits as well. The stationary bandits, on the other hand, are rational, since they settle down in a community and agree to protect the society against roving bandits in return for economic gains.

The entire paradigm is based on the negotiation of mutual interests. This undermines the interests of the common Pakistani citizen. For instance, land distribution tends to favour the elite at the cost of the landless peasants. The distribution of essential resources also favours the 'haves' rather than 'have-nots.' The plight of the fisherman in Sindh at the hands of paramilitary forces to the landless peasants in Okara indicates the usurpation of resources by the military.

Should the Democratic India Talk to Pakistani COAS Only?

India takes pride in its democratic values and has always taken the official line of negotiating bilateral issues only with the democratically elected government. Dealing with Pakistan, it has always struggled since its independence to talk to the right stakeholders. Pakistan is a country where Army has the country and not vice versa, in this situation my advice and approach for India will be to leave its high moral ground stand and directly negotiate with the incumbent Pakistani COAS. Give him the red carpet welcome and negotiate with firmness using the carrot and stick policy. Let's briefly discuss various anecdotes and strategies of negotiating when dealing with the radicalized minds, be it of a terrorist or of an Army, which uses such non-State actors to run their proxy wars against their stronger neighbour. Even USA, the strongest democracy of the world deals with the dictators and armies directly for peaceful negotiation of the concerned region.

President Trump once said he'd be 'honoured' to meet the North Korean despot Kim Jong Un. Egypt's President, who allowed his opponents to be shot, is doing a 'fantastic job'. President of the Philippines, who unleashed vigilante killings at home, is welcome at the White House. So is Thailand's Prime Minister, who took power in a military coup. And Turkey's President, who jailed thousands of opponents, got a congratulatory call. This is not business as usual for US Presidents. Trump's advisors portray his public praise for foreign dictators and his willingness to meet with ruthless autocrats, without preconditions in most cases, as a way to shore up shaky alliances and possibly unlock long-frozen conflicts in the Middle-East and across Asia.

Trump, they say, believes he can use his charm and negotiating skills to forge ties to despots ostracized by previous Presidents and thus bring them to his way of thinking. Critics say that outreach threatens to disrupt America's long-standing strategic partnerships, undermines the credibility of US democratic values overseas and emboldens autocrats who use bloody measures at home to suppress dissent. Prime Minister Narendra Modi too believes in personal charisma approach.

Other Presidents have bucked foreign policy orthodoxy to reach out to adversaries. In perhaps the most famous case, President Nixon set aside the GOP's anti-Communist policies to make his historic overture to China in 1972, leading to a tectonic shift in the Cold War. India surely remembers that infamous bonding. President Obama was criticized as naive and worse by Republicans and by his chief Democratic rival at the time, Hillary Clinton, after he was asked at a debate in 2007 whether he would be willing to meet separately, without condition, with the leaders of Iran, Syria, Venezuela, Cuba and North Korea. "I would," Obama said at the time. "And the reason is this, that the notion that somehow not talking to countries is the punishment to them – which has been the guiding diplomatic principle of [the Bush] administration – is ridiculous." This should be an eye-opener for India's bureaucrats and policy-makers, time to shun Nawaz Sharif and talk to General Bajwa and ISI head. During his second term, the Obama administration signed a landmark deal with Iran to curb its nuclear development in exchange for easing sanctions and restored diplomatic relations with the Communist government in Cuba, ending a freeze that began in 1961.

Trump's offer to meet such notorious leaders reflects his negotiating style, which says that "you never close off the opportunity to do a deal," said James Carafano, a fellow at the conservative Heritage Foundation who has briefed the President and his team on foreign policy. "What the President is signalling is that there is always an opportunity to talk, but that is very far from saying there are no preconditions," Carafano said. "You're always offering [the other leader] an off-ramp: 'Change your behaviour and meet my preconditions.'" Trump's National Security Council recently completed a policy review on North Korea and recommended a carrot-and-stick combination of increased pressure and greater engagement. Jim Walsh, a security policy expert at MIT, said an open channel of communication with North Korea could help prevent war. I have also suggested a policy change for India, in my proposed approach on steps to solve the conflict, one is to re-look India's policy for Iran and North Korea, India will benefit a lot strategically befriending the NK dictator and helping to mediate when the USA needs a real trust worth ally to step up. This will help stop the proliferation of Nuclear weapons which can harm India directly as portable version of such weapons will land in Kashmir via Pakistan aided by the Kashmiri terror groups JuD, JeM, HM, Taliban's, LeT, etc.

India may have pushed Pakistan to a wall making it a colony of China. India has to re-strategize and stop Pakistan from being swept away in this Chinese deluge. Does India have master strategicians and thinkers in the bureaucracy to take up this challenge and give a proactive roadmap to the government? If not, then please get folks from outside the bureaucracy, there are many around. It's challenge for the nation which is bogged down too much into daily operational level planning to strategically up its game. This will help it become a power and solve its conflicts.

Dirty Deals, Compulsion or Strategy?

The argument conventional thinkers give against negotiating with the terrorists, the dictators and the armies that use terror as a proxy for meeting its goals is simple: Democracies must never give in to violence and such extremists must never be rewarded for using it. Negotiations give legitimacy to them and their methods and undermine actors who have pursued political change through peaceful means. Talks can destabilize the negotiating government's political systems, undercuts international efforts to outlaw terrorism and set a dangerous precedent.

In practice, democratic governments often negotiate with dictators and autocratic army heads. The British government maintained a secret back channel to the Irish Republican Army even after the IRA had launched a mortar attack on 10 Downing Street that nearly eliminated the entire British cabinet in 1991. In 1988, the Spanish government sat down with the separatist group Basque Homeland and Freedom (known by its Basque acronym ETA) only six months after the group had killed 21 shoppers in a supermarket bombing. Even the Government of Israel – which is not known to be soft on terrorism – has strayed from the supposed ban: in 1993, it secretly negotiated the Oslo accords even though the Palestine Liberation Organization (PLO) continued its terrorist campaign and refused to recognize Israel's right to exist.

When it comes to negotiating with extremists, there is a clear disconnect between what governments profess and what they do. But the rigidity of the 'no negotiations' stance has prevented any systematic exploration of how best to conduct such negotiations. How can a democratic government talk to terrorists without jeopardizing the integrity of its political system? What kind of extremists are susceptible to negotiations? When should negotiations be opened?

The key objective for any government contemplating negotiations is not simply to end violence but to do so in a way that minimizes the risk of setting dangerous precedents and destabilizing its political system. Given this dual goal, some conditions must be met for talks to have even a chance of success.

Strategies and Considerations

What it takes to make talks and negotiation a viable strategy is to ensure the other party's capability of holding to negotiation agreements and to make concessions. As aforementioned, one way to ease into negotiations and retain the ability to disavow the other side, are back channel communications. Not only does this course of action encourage future talks by displaying interest in bilateral communication, but it may also establish the necessary logistics before the announcement of a fully public negotiation. Secret talks help avoid political backlash and shouting from hawkish politicians at the acting government for apparently lending legitimacy to terrorists. Secret negotiations also do not require ceasefires, allowing both sides to continue what they see as the preferable military option while simultaneously exercising the political alternative. Most importantly, it is a way for one side to gain knowledge of the other and determine if the other is willing or able to negotiate at present. The success of back-channel negotiations, in effect, makes the subject of negotiation easier to broach when moving toward the question of open negotiations. However, if all negotiations are exclusively secretive agreements made within such negotiations do not form as cohesive a set of public supporters as when the results are announced.

Regarding negotiations themselves, one boon to the process is the distinction between primary and secondary concessions. Primary concessions are the political changes the group seeks to enact, while secondary concessions concern what will happen with the terrorists themselves such as decommissioning weaponry and affording aid to individual group members. This distinction is important, although not necessary in all cases because it can allow the negotiations to divert the primary concessions to become the goal of the political alternative. Once it has been agreed that their goals are still a possibility through non-violent political action, then direct negotiations can concern secondary concessions. This avoids the apparent misgivings a democratic government may incur when seemingly surrendering to a radical change because a group was motivated enough to use violence, regardless of whether or not they renounced it. However, there is not much incentive for the terrorist group to negotiate at all if their goals are considered but declared impossible. Therefore, establishing the group's political alternative is paramount to satisfying both parties. By involving the extremist group in the political process, their radical goals or group mentality may be blunted to an extent. The political process naturally brings with it limitations on hasty action, assuming the process is at least somewhat democratic.

Speaking more specifically on the political process, the key to making the process successful is ensuring effective representatives from both parties are put forward. If there is no degree of trust that either side can keep their promises, hawkish members of the government or the terrorist group can lash out with violence and iterate on moral apprehensions to negotiation. Effective representatives are the only members on the terrorist side who can use persuasion to prevent splinter groups who feel that accords or negotiation do not apply to them. Theoretically, the biggest danger to the process on the part of the government is the maintenance of a no negotiation or no concession policy, especially considered in light of contemporary events and cultural climates. The events of 9/11 brought a new wave of polarization to conflict management, in which Nation-States which have traditionally remained absent from negotiations have now become direct combatants against terrorism.

Once negotiation is considered viable, there are other external forces still yet to consider which may affect the success of any proposed talks. Spoiler opportunities are a great danger to the peace process. When conciliatory agreements either fall short of the ideal or represent an insult to the proposed goals of the terrorists, those unwilling to negotiate within or outside the groups commit attacks. Attacks during negotiation, or the peace process, are intended to stifle moderates' efforts and provoke overreaction by government. The provocation of the peace process reinforces distrust between government and moderates thereby preventing any agreements.

Netanyahu's sudden victory in 1996 elections, following the attacks, resulted in his cancelling negotiations and pursuing more combative strategies. The targeted governments, mediators and negotiating terrorist group members all should be greatly aware of spoiler opportunities and not allow them to compromise negotiations. India has been back-stabbed by Pakistanis every time politicians have come closer to some mutual political solution. Problem with India is it has weak willpower to punish the spoiler, 26/11 was clear case of giving up in spite of international support to punish the attackers and their handlers in Pakistan.

Part Three

Potential Solutions

Off-the-Shelf (All the Known and Proposed Ones)

and

Out-of-Box (7 Cs Mantra)

6. Potential Solutions

Off-the-Shelf (All the Known and Proposed Ones) and Out-of-Box (7 Cs Mantra)

Overview

The State of Jammu and Kashmir has three sub-regions – (1) Jammu, (2) Kashmir and (3) Ladakh. In Kashmir valley Muslims are predominant. However, both in Jammu and Ladakh, non-Muslims such as Hindus and Buddhists are dominant. Some of the Muslims would like to join Pakistan, but all non-Muslims want to be with India. There is a controversy here on how many Muslims want to be a part of Pakistan. The Muslim part lies in between the Hindu part

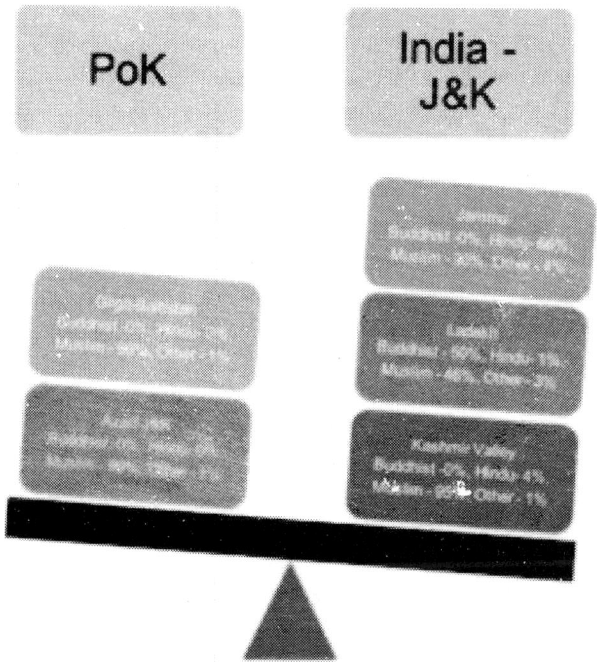

Source: Indian and Pakistani Government Censuses.

and Buddhist part. This means cutting away the Muslim part and merging with Pakistan is not easy.

The region is extremely cold (with some of the coldest temperatures in the inhabited world), snowbound, landlocked and hilly (having some of the tallest mountains in the world). Given the geography and the terrain, cutting it up is not as easy as it looks on the map. The hills are considered strategically important to both India and Pakistan. The hills of Kashmir slope into the crucial region of Punjab on both sides of the border. Controlling the hills are important for both the armies.

The region carries the Indus water that is extremely crucial for both Pakistan and northern India. Water is the most precious resource in the Basmati Rice Land (Arguably, one of the finest Rice found on the Planet) and you have to be extremely careful in how you carve the resources.

The status of Hindus in Pakistan is infinitely worse and can never be compared with the Muslims in India. Although India's minority record may also be not spotless, it has an independent Commission to take care. India has had a couple of Muslim Presidents and there are Muslim leaders in every spectrum - business, sports, entertainment, arts and sciences. That means any solution that involves Hindus from J&K moving to Pakistan is far worse than a solution involving Kashmiri Muslims continuing in India. The region adjoins extremely troubled parts such as northern Pakistan, Afghanistan, Xinjiang of China and Central Asia. This means an independent Kashmir can become a breeding ground for terrorists as a weak Kashmiri government can't prevail over lethal terrorists. It could become another Syria and a bigger headache not only for this region but the entire World.

As rightly advised, do not open the Pandora's box of Plebiscite. India is a highly heterogeneous country and removing Kashmir could embolden other separatist groups all over the nation. This is why India cannot be flexible with its own Identity of a secular, plural and the biggest functioning democracy of the world. World's secular and demographic powers should understand this and make sure India does not fail, as any adverse impact on 1.2 billion people will be catastrophic to entire human civilization. Though India is herself strong enough to take care of any such external and internal threats. Given the above facts, any proposed solution should keep this in mind that breaking of India will create such an impact that no country in the world, will remain untouched. Another point of consideration when reaching the solution is the timeline and communication to the people and stakeholders. Patience, as they say, is the virtue of the wise man, but patience, till infinity is like "justice delayed, is justice denied," and we will like the Kashmiri Pandits to return to their homes in Kashmir and start living in harmony with their Muslim neighbours with no fear or hate.

Modern India has over two thousand ethnic groups. Indian languages have evolved from Indo-European, Dravidian, Austro-Asiatic and Tibeto-Burman. India has 1652 individual mother tongues. The 2001 Census tells us that 30 languages are spoken by over a million each and 122 by over 10,000 each. India has almost 1.2 billion plus people and the Union of India consists of 29 States and 7 Union Territories, with some more being currently midwifed. Since Independence India has moved a large chunk of its population from underprivileged to the middle class and can boast around 400 million middle class which is more than the entire population of USA. But then it has still to take care of 600-700 million more population and that can only happen if it grows at the rate of 8% for next 20 years. Now if this is achieved it will make it a phenomenon power and the greatest example of what a democracy can achieve. But for all this, it needs peace and should focus on the development mantra. *Sabka Saath Sabka Vikas* (integrated development, leaving no one behind). With the current Defence Budget: $65,000,000,000, Foreign Exchange Reserves: $420,700,000,000 and Purchasing Power Parity: $7,411,000,000,000 the nation is on the right path of growth and has acquired reasonable power and stature.

It's a country of great churn, positivity, tremendous potential, the largest market for the world, heterogeneity, complexity and reasonable financial might. Its diversity makes it very challenging to run the democratic government. Now given the context of India's complexity and reasonable financial and military might how to solve Kashmir? What is the best political solution to Kashmir problem? Should Kashmir be given Independence? Is the *status quo*, the best solution? Should India conduct plebiscite? Is a referendum like Scotland the only solution to Kashmir conflict? What will be an impact of geographical separation of Kashmir on the plural and secular character of India? What happens to 170 million Indian Muslims living happily in various parts of India.

Most of the views that are floating in India related to what should be the solution for the Kashmir conflict, have been discussed in this chapter. I have read and compiled various authors and bloggers, interviewed Kashmiri people and the key stakeholders. I have also brought various solutions proposed in the past to address Kashmir conflict. The intention is to make my readers aware of all the possibilities suggested in the past, any probable solution has to have the knowledge of these options as a reference point. I have also tried to give my perspective. The UPA government never came out with any white paper on Kashmir issue. I am told that present central government which inherited this pre-partition mess is still brainstorming on what the long-term strategy should be.

For winning the game called 'Kashmir conflict resolution', there has to be a long and short-term strategy accompanied with a white paper, blueprinting of plan A, B and C using some disruptive steps to push for the desirable closure. The ego factor which has always created a wedge between India and Pakistan has to go and the parity status which Pakistan keeps expecting from India can be looked into for the larger interest of this conflict resolution.

The Kashmir solution can be grouped into two Buckets – (i) Off-the-Shelf Solutions (OSS) and (ii) Out-of-Box Solution(s) (OOB). My OOB solution has 7 Cs Mantras.

- C1: Communication (Talks with Influencers)
- C2: Catharsis (From Radicalization, Alienation to Assimilation)
- C3: Collectivism (Cooperative Federalism)
- C4: Confidence Building (In the line of Insaniyat – Kashmiriyat – Jamhooriyat)
- C5: Commerce (Cash-amir)
- C6: Class (Stratification of the Muslim Mass. Taking real Azaadi to the lowest denominator)
- C7: Conquest of the Border (Beyond the LoC)

Off-the-Shelf Solutions

India to Give Up its Claim of POK and also Control of the Kashmir Valley Region

If you directly want to jump to the solution, you will not be able to understand the real issue of Kashmir. There were several solutions proposed by both sides India and Pakistan, but the problem is the lack of trust with each other. From India's point of view, they have already lost trust with Pakistan because of several border infiltration and militant attacks not only in Jammu and Kashmir but also in Punjab and some other parts of India. 26/11, Mumbai is one big trust deficit factor. For Pakistan, Kashmir is the gateway of any conflict resolution with India and no other agenda can supersede it, be it cross-border terrorism or Indus water issue or even CPEC. It has to be 'Only' Kashmir first. For India, Terror and Talk cannot go simultaneously and hence the deadlock of the talks.

Two Approaches related to diluting the claim of POK and control of the Kashmir Valley region

Approach 1

Formalize the *status quo* and make the Line of Control into a permanent border. India would formally give up the regions that it still shows on its map and Pakistan can fully integrate its part of Kashmir. In fact, it was alleged many Pakistani political leaders have agreed to this solution in the past – although they didn't make it public given the fear of a coup by their Army and ISI (Pakistan secret service).

Approach 2

Let India and Pakistan give up their control and claim respectively, make the valley region (about 5% of the disputed area) into a quasi-independent nation with UN (if it's relevant?) or USA-China-Russia troika's control or a guarded neutrality similar to Switzerland. This could act as a sort of buffer State. India and Pakistan, two nuclear powers could provide 60:40 ratio of armed forces to this new authority. India would lose some territory but so would Pakistan, this would be more palatable to both the countries establishment. For India, the advantages are that the rest of J&K State can be merged entirely into India with no special status (Sunset Article 370 and 35A), better use of army budget currently required to protect the valley, reduction of border disputes with Pakistan and improvement of its overall brand image on the world stage. Pakistan leaders can claim a massive victory (given that they have got some territory out of India) and resume a healthy relationship with India. This might be unpalatable to many Indians, but I believe they don't have any other credible solution that could help India move on. They have other things to worry about – cannot just keep dog fighting in the snow (Siachen) and lose their precious men. Whatever difference Indian and Pakistani people may have on Kashmir, they do agree on one fact, "political parties in India and Pakistan along with ISI and Pakistani Army do not want to resolve this conflict for their interest."

Kashmir is a Muslim majority State. So, one might simplistically argue that India should vacate the place and give it away to Pakistan. But, it is not so simple as the impact on 170 million Muslims living in the rest of India will be huge and the world has not forgotten the bloody Indian subcontinent partition resulting in some 10 million human's life and 1 million in the form of worst communal killing on both sides of the border, Muslims *vs* Hindus, Buddhists and Sikhs. For meagre five million Kashmiri Muslims in the valley, India will never jeopardize lives of 170 million Muslim citizens of India. This has been a consistent policy of the Government of India, but in this proposed solution it will have to part away strategic and rich valley in some share mode with Pakistan.

Five aspects of leaving the claim of POK and control of the Kashmir Valley region.

(i) Indian controlled Jammu and Kashmir.

(ii) Nobody talks about China Occupied Kashmir (COK).

(iii) POK is where reasonable number don't want to live with Pakistan.

(iv) Khyber Pakhtunkhwa/Gilgit-Baltistan, which India claims to be its own.

(v) Balochistan, has reached out to India for helping it to get independence from Pakistan.

This will be a huge strategic give-away for India when accepting this proposal. For Pakistan, this is a huge psychological gain, but will this take the venom out of the jihadi mindset of the ISI's and Pak Army, will be a question in India's mind.

Pakistan and China will Give POK and COK Respectively to India

This looks highly implausible, but if you see India, it has so far progressed and positioned itself as a peaceful nation. China and India had three to four border skirmishes in 1962, 1967, 1987 and more recently in 2017. Apart from these they have been mostly peaceful but how long no one knows. India has the second largest Muslim population. Indian people are largely accommodative, thanks to its world's biggest diversity. Yes, there are some internal conflicts like Maoist problems, J&K problem, North-East trouble, etc but there is no civil war type situation in India as compared to so many other countries.

For COK India needs to negotiate with China. Even though COK contains soda water lakes and barren land, China has a huge strategic importance of this region with the pledge to invest US $ 50 billion for CPEC, starting from Gwadar Port in Balochistan (troubles zone) to China crossing Indian claimed Kashmir region of Gilgit/Baltistan. There is a huge economic benefit of controlling COK, CPEC road will cross Aksai Chin to China province Xinjiang reducing Chinese ships movement from Oil-rich Gulf countries via road. India needs to have a deal with China, but their current relationship on this front is affected due to Pakistan.

Chinese can be offered a peaceful run of their CPEC and OBOR if they work with India and resolve their border disputes, India can be a signatory of this, but China has to hand over the COK, first. Now if that does not happen, India needs to seriously revisit her Tibet and COK strategy, in mutual discussion with China, or UN or even getting G7 involved. If China can claim all her old historical maps and hence view its borders as per hundred years old history then India too has a rich and world acknowledged history and entire Twang and Tibet should be declared disputed and considered for negotiations and till then no road can pass from POK, India should be prepared for fighting for her sovereignty come what may or else shut their mouth and concede. There is no wait and watch in the context of CPEC. China has to take India's consent and has to pay tax for doing business in the Indian claimed region. The environmental impact of massive landscape changes in the Hindu's divine and spiritual Himalayas will have to get environmentalist and India's go-ahead for the feasibility as it will impact billion plus population of the subcontinent.

Regarding POK, Pakistan has to give either in war or agree to come on the negotiating table and agree for smooth and porous border and allow the Kashmiris to move across the entire Kashmir which includes POK and COK. India can offer Pakistan water treaty where it can get water from Indus in future on some commonly agreed terms. There will never be any curtailment of water as it will be UN approved agreement, but for that POK has to be given back to India as it was the territory forcefully seized from Raja Hari Singh of J&K just 2 days before he signed annexation treaty with India as the term for all the princely States during the time of partition.

In all the four wars that India and Pakistan fought, India never had any plan then to solve Kashmir on the battleground, things have changed and for last forty plus years of non-stop proxy war that Pakistan and its jihadi fundamentalists, ISI and army have enforced on India, it will not let go that easily this time, whenever next war happens. Again if Pakistan wins, it's over for India's claim and Pakistan can take the region but till that does not happen, POK rightfully belongs to India. A solution of Jammu and Kashmir is not a cake walk hence it should be resolved in phases so that people of India and Pakistan live in harmony and peace. Most of the Indians do not want war. People on both sides want to live in peace, harmony and with a good income.

A former Chinese diplomat had hinted that settlement of the India-China boundary dispute was possible if India agrees to make concessions in the eastern sector. "The disputed territory in the eastern sector of the China-India boundary, including Twang, is inalienable from China's Tibet regarding cultural background and administrative jurisdiction," China's former points man for India Dai Bingguo had said in an interview to Beijing-based publication *China-India Dialogue* magazine.

Dai underlined that the major reason the boundary question persists is that China's reasonable requests have not been met. "If the Indian side takes care of China's concerns in the eastern sector of their border, the Chinese side will respond accordingly and address India's concerns elsewhere."

Notably, Dai Bingguo had been China's Special Representative in more than 15 rounds of boundary talks between 2003 and his retirement in 2013. It was not until February 1951 that "the local government of Tibet (was) forced to stop its actual administration of Twang," he said, adding: "Even the British colonialists who drew the 'McMahon Line' respected China's jurisdiction over Twang." There are disputes over the eastern, middle and western sectors of China-India boundary. The biggest dispute involves the eastern section, which is vital to a fair, reasonable settlement of the boundary question.

Essential nature of the China-India boundary question is the "need to correct wrongs" made by colonialists and to restore fairness and justice. "For historical reasons, India now controls the majority of the disputed territory. The boundary question was not created by China or India, so we shouldn't be inheriting it and letting the ghosts of colonialism continue to haunt our bilateral relations," he said. Dai was China's top diplomat and held the post of State Councillor in the previous Hu Jintao administration. His interview was published by the magazine in its January edition ahead of India-China Strategic Dialogue held here last month co-chaired by Foreign Secretary S Jaishankar.

This is to be underlined that the picturesque Tawang district in Arunachal Pradesh bordering China is a very important place for India from both religious and strategic points of view. The Tawang monastery holds a special place in Tibetan Buddhism and is highly regarded by Buddhists in India as well. For China, the area of Tawang is central to Tibetan Buddhism given that the sixth Dalai Lama was born there. If Twang is that Important to China because of historical reason, then India needs to dig more into her rich history and make sure Hindus biggest sacred places like Mansarovar and many other points within the great Himalayas which is with China needs to be also negotiated for final border settlement.

Indian Foreign ministry documents on border negotiations accessed by *Mail Today* an Indian media reveal that India has signalled its readiness to let its Aksai Chin region remain in Chinese hands in exchange for recognition of Arunachal Pradesh as part of its territory. In other words, India during the UPA government was willing to give up its claims to Aksai Chin if China does the same for Arunachal. China continues to push for territorial concessions in Arunachal Pradesh, which it has been eyeing for a long time, before moving forward on the long-standing border issue between the two countries.

Publicly, India has been holding to its stated position that there can't be any territorial concessions. But behind the closed doors of the negotiating room, India has told China that it "may not be averse to *status quo* position." Simply put, it means that for China to give up its claim on the 90,000 sq km inside Arunachal, including Twang, India could agree to give up 38,000 sq km of Jammu and Kashmir. That piece of land, called Aksai Chin in the Ladakh sector, has been in dispute since Pakistan annexed it and then illegally handed 5,180 sq km over to China in 1963.

This contentious formula is not the stated position of New Delhi, but it is being considered a bargaining point. Any such proposal can only be implemented if a new government in New Delhi has an enormous political will because there is a unanimous resolution of the Indian Parliament of 1962 that India will ensure that it gets back all territory illegally occupied by China. Several documents based on the notes made by Indian officials suggest that even after 16 rounds of boundary negotiations, the talks are deadlocked efficiently. China insists it needs substantial concessions on Arunachal Pradesh and the entire disputed Eastern sector before a framework or a formula to resolve disputes in all sectors can be agreed upon.

The 16th round of boundary negotiations between National Security Advisor Shiv Shankar Menon and Chinese Special Interlocutor Yang Jiechi, a former Chinese Foreign Minister, also ended on a disappointing note, with India contesting the Chinese assertion that the boundary was never demarcated. Menon has been a tough negotiator, responding strongly to Chinese suggestions of concessions and rejecting its maximalist approach. The Indian side also says that both sides should, in the spirit of mutual respect and mutual understanding, make meaningful and mutually acceptable adjustments to their respective positions on the boundary question to arrive at a package settlement.

A consensus is building where India and China may agree to territorial concessions. It means that for China to give up its claim on the 90,000 sq km inside Arunachal Pradesh, including Twang, India could agree to give up 38,000 sq km of Jammu and Kashmir. That piece of land, called Aksai Chin in the Ladakh sector, has been in dispute since Pakistan annexed it and then illegally handed 5,180 sq km over to China in 1963. India never had *de facto* control –

the Line of Actual Control from the 1962 war was the positions held at 7 November 1959 – so India had failed to occupy it as late as then. The last written treaty (Chushul 1842) merely preserved the *status quo* and it was undemarcated till Independence (map from 1948).

China version is it was wrongly included in Indian maps of the princely State and even Chinese maps in the 1930s showed the Johnson line as the boundary. This mistake made Indian legal claims stronger there – and is the reason India was traditionally unwilling to let it go. Unfortunately, the terrain meant that neither the Princely State, the British, nor Independent India was controlling this desert. It's between two mountain ranges – Karakoram and Kunlun. Chou En-lai tried to barter Arunachal which they weren't controlling and claimed Sikkim, Bhutan and arbitrary parts of Assam and Nepal in 1959 – Nehru (rightly) refused and war broke out over a forward post. But India does have a solid claim till the McCartney-Macdonald line and China has indicated the willingness to part with some of Aksai in exchange for some parts of Arunachal. They no longer need Aksai since the road network improved in Tibet later.

The British conceded Aksai Chin to China in 1914 Shimla Accord. So, China's claim on Aksai Chin is not illegitimate though not theirs also. But the problem is China is not going to stop at Aksai Chin. Even if India gives Aksai Chin, they will demand whole of Ladakh, then Himachal and then Uttarakhand. They will not stop. On further research on China's maritime and territorial disputes with Japan and ASEAN nations. China looks to be an expansionist regime. China has also created problems for India (believed by majority Indians) in South Asia and Indian Ocean Rim.

1. It is supporting Pakistan on terrorism and anti-India agendas.
2. It has sponsored Maoist insurgency in Nepal. It is creating massive anti-India wave among Nepalese.
3. It is creating anti-India sentiment in Sri Lanka, Seychelles, Maldives and Mauritius. China has built Submarine bases in Sri Lanka. It wants to isolate India by building strong economic and strategic ties with Bangladesh, Sri Lanka, Maldives and Myanmar, by creating String of Pearls around India in the Indian Ocean.
4. It is covertly supporting insurgency in north-east India and Naxalites in Central India, India must be very candid in dealing with China.
5. Aksai Chin connects Tibet to Xinxiang province, India claims this to be part of her larger J&K region.

UN Monitored Plebiscite

After Pakistan infiltrated the region and UN helped ceasefire, it gave following solution to Jammu and Kashmir issue.

To ensure the impartiality of the plebiscite Pakistan withdraw all tribesmen and nationals who entered the region to fight jihad and that India leaves only the minimum number of troops needed to keep civil order. The Commission was also to send as many observers into the region as it deemed necessary to ensure the provisions of the resolution were enacted.

The key point here was Pakistan will withdraw all tribesmen and its army regulars but they never did it, so this solution failed. Pakistan wanted their then ally Unites State to resolve this issue and now wants China to help, India doesn't want intervention of any third party. This has been its consistent policy. India lodged a complaint under Article 35 (Chapter VI) of the UN Charter in the UN Security Council on January 1, 1948, charging Pakistan with "aiding and abetting" tribal invasion of Jammu and Kashmir which it said had acceded to the Indian Union through an instrument of accession signed by the then ruler.

In its first resolution of 17th January 1948, Security Council called upon India and Pakistan to exercise restraint. Three days later through another resolution (Resolution 39), it created the UN Commission for India and Pakistan (UNCIP) to investigate the dispute and mediate between the two countries. In another resolution (Resolution 47) of April 21, 1948, SC called for cessation of hostilities, withdrawal of all Pakistani troops and tribesmen and bulk of Indian troops (except for a minimal number required for maintaining law and order), allowing return of refugees, release of political prisoners and holding of a UN supervised Plebiscite in the princely State of Jammu and Kashmir under a plebiscite administrator to determine the aspirations of her people. It was supported by another resolution of June 3, 1948.

After deliberations with Indian and Pakistani leadership in July 1948, the UNCIP produced a proposal calling for an immediate ceasefire and a truce agreement between India and Pakistan, withdrawal from the J&K of all Pakistani tribesmen and nationals and the bulk of India's troops. India rejected it saying the Security Council failed to blame the aggressor in Kashmir. Pakistan also rejected the proposal saying that Sheikh Abdullah, Prime Minister designated on March 5, 1948, was an ally of India and by, implication, able to influence the plebiscite in India's favour. Pakistan had reservations also about she withdrawing all forces from Kashmir while India was retaining some of her troops. She argued it could potentially lead to coercion or intimidation of voters by Indian troops jeopardizing the result of the proposed plebiscite.

On December 11, 1948, the UNCIP laid out a new set of proposals that elaborated on the question of Plebiscite.... As per the proposals: The question of accession to India or Pakistan was to be decided by a free and impartial plebiscite, which was contingent upon having a ceasefire. On January 5, 1949, the Security Council came up with a new resolution on J&K focusing on the holding of a plebiscite. Its first two clauses are like this:

1. The question of the accession of the State of Jammu and Kashmir to India or Pakistan will be decided through the democratic method of a free and impartial plebiscite.
2. A plebiscite will be held when it shall be found by the Commission that the ceasefire and truce arrangements outlined in Parts I and II of the Commission's resolution of 13 August 1948 have been carried out and arrangements for the plebiscite have been completed.

Accepting plebiscite as UN's formula for resolving Kashmir issue, the Resolution proceeds to define the process of its implementation. But the Resolution makes the entire exercise of plebiscite subject to the implementation of Article 2 above. Now the SC Resolution of 13 August 1948 comprises two parts – I and II.

Part I: Ceasefire

This deals with ceasefire between the two countries.

Part II: Truce Agreement

Simultaneously with the acceptance of the proposal for the immediate cessation of hostilities as outlined in Part I, both the governments accept the following principles as a basis for the formulation of a truce agreement, the details of which shall be worked out in discussion between their representatives and the Commission.

A.1 As the presence of troops of Pakistan in the territory of the State of Jammu and Kashmir constitutes a material change in the situation since it was represented by the Government of Pakistan before the Security Council; the Government of Pakistan agrees to withdraw its troops from that State.

A.2 The Government of Pakistan will use its best Endeavour to secure the withdrawal from the State of Jammu and Kashmir of tribesmen and Pakistani nationals not normally resident therein who have entered the State for fighting.

A.3 Pending a final solution, the territory evacuated by the Pakistani troops will be administered by the local authorities under the surveillance of the Commission.

B.1 When the Commission shall have notified the Government of India that the tribesmen and Pakistani nationals referred to in Part II, A, 2, hereof have withdrawn, thereby terminating the situation which was represented by the Government of India to the Security Council as having occasioned the presence of Indian forces in the State of Jammu and Kashmir and further, that the Pakistani forces are being withdrawn from the State of Jammu and Kashmir, the Government of India agrees to begin to withdraw the bulk of its forces from that State in stages to be agreed upon with the Commission.

B.2 Pending the acceptance of the conditions for a final settlement of the situation in the State of Jammu and Kashmir, the Indian government will maintain within the lines existing at the moment of the ceasefire the minimum strength of its forces which in agreement with the Commission are considered necessary to assist local authorities in the observance of law and order. The Commission will have observers stationed where it deems necessary.

B.3 The Government of India will undertake to ensure that the government of the State of Jammu and Kashmir will take all measures within its powers to make it publicly known that peace, law and order will be safeguarded and that all human political rights will be granted.

B.4 Upon signature, the full text of the truce agreement or a communique containing the principles thereof as agreed upon between the two governments and the Commission will be made public.

Now the position is that on December 25, 1948, Pakistan formally conveyed to the Security Council its acceptance of the Resolution of 13 August 1948. India had already accepted it.

But Pakistan failed to implement its clauses and as such, the UNCIP was unable to communicate to India ratification of implementation of Resolution of 13 August 1948 by Pakistan. And with that, the question of plebiscite fell through and was never revived at the UN level. Why did Pakistan not implement the Resolution of 13 August 1948? We don't have any convincing answer. Maybe it was not confident about the outcome of the plebiscite: maybe it was apprehensive of losing the strategic Northern Areas (present Gilgit-Baltistan). The net result was that the UN Resolutions became un-implementable and plebiscite redundant. That is why former UN Secretary-General Kofi Annan had said: "that the General Assembly cannot implement the resolutions of the UNCIP."

The question is whether in the light of these realities there is justification for accusing UN of not implementing its Resolutions on Kashmir? The factual situation is that these resolutions are based on the choice between India and Pakistan; these do not allow unlimited self-determination which means a choice without limitation. If the resolutions were based on self-determination like East Timor, then under the UN Charter, Secretary-General could move the case at UN level. In that situation, he was not obliged to wait for the willingness of India and Pakistan to discuss the matter in the UN. This was precisely what two former General Secretaries Boutros Boutros-Ghali and Kofi Annan had stated.

Security Council President General AGL McNaughton's mediation in December 1949 failed to manage an agreement between the two sides. He had suggested demilitarization of Kashmir as a precursor to an impartial plebiscite. Owen Dixon replaced UNCIP in 1950, pursued demilitarization proposal but failed and proposed "regional plebiscite" now known as Dixon Plan. It suggested (a) holding a Plebiscite in the whole State of Jammu and Kashmir, region by region (b) holding a Plebiscite only in regions which were 'doubtful', the rest would constitute those regions that were expected to vote definitely for accession either to India or Pakistan. The doubtful region was meant to be the Valley of Kashmir. After the failure of Owen Dixon, Frank Graham was inducted to continue the effort of mediation as a UN representative. Graham unsuccessfully worked from 1951 to 1953 when the buck was passed on to Gunnar Jarring in 1957, but again with no success.

In the wake of the termination of the mandate of UNCIP, the UN Security Council passed Resolution 91 on 30 March 1951, which established the United Nations Military Observer Group in India and Pakistan to monitor the ceasefire line (now called Line of Control, the border that divides Indian and Pakistani controlled parts of Kashmir) in Kashmir. The UNMOGIP still maintains its presence in both Jammu and Kashmir State and Pakistan-Occupied Kashmir.

On 23 January 1957, Jammu and Kashmir led by Bakshi Ghulam Mohammad adopted a Constitution for the State and a resolution ratifying the State's accession with India. Pakistan raised the issue in the UN Security Council and a day after, the UNSC passed a resolution which reiterated the earlier UN resolutions on Kashmir that called for a final settlement of the dispute in accordance with the will of the people expressed through the democratic method of free and impartial plebiscite conducted under the auspices of the UN.

Thus the 1957 UN resolution deemed any constitutional change undertaken by India within Indian Kashmir as irrelevant to the resolution of Kashmir conflict.

However, it is to be noted that this resolution did not allude to the condition imposed by the Security Council vide earlier resolution of August 13, 1948, on determining the will of the people through a plebiscite. India argued that this was a fractured resolution and hence not acceptable. Furthermore, India claimed that the Security Council had not reacted to Pakistan declining to implement the resolution of 13 August 1948. In 1962, the Kashmir Question was again debated in the UN Security Council. However, it failed to pass a resolution because of a Soviet veto, which discouraged the UNSC from pursuing the Kashmir question after that.

The last UNSC resolution (307) that dealt with Kashmir was passed in the wake of the India–Pakistan war of 1971, where Kashmir was not at the centre of the conflict between the two countries. The resolution could be passed only after India had declared a unilateral ceasefire. UNSC's attempts to pass resolutions during the 1971 war were blocked by a Soviet veto and with the signing of the Shimla Peace Accord between India and Pakistan in 1972, which laid stress on "bilateral solutions to the Kashmir issue," the UN involvement in Kashmir was in reality dead.

The fresh delineation of the 'ceasefire line' - originally established in 1949 after the Indo-Pakistan ceasefire in Jammu and Kashmir - in Kashmir by India and Pakistan in 1972 converted the 'ceasefire line' into 'Line of Control' (LoC), which from an Indian perspective turned the temporary border in the disputed territory of Kashmir into a *de facto* 'permanent border' between India and Pakistan. Pakistan was forced to accept the change in the wake of its defeat in the 1971 war. India contended that with the formation of Line of Control, the mandate of the UNMOGIP had expired. But Pakistan supported its continuation interpreting it as a reflection of disputed nature of Kashmir.

Since 1972 India has not reported to the UNMOGIP whereas Pakistan has continued to report Indian violations of the LoC to the observer group. While the movement of the UNMOGIP is unrestricted in Pakistan Occupied Kashmir, the observer group is nowhere in sight beyond their office premises at Sonawar locality of Srinagar. With its limited mandate, the group has played virtually no role in the conflict after 1972.

In October 2001, the UNMOGIP Chief, Major-General Hermann Loidolt described Kashmir as a 'tormented country' and blamed

India and Pakistan for playing games with Kashmir. The observer also described the LoC as a ceasefire-line and a disputed border, which fell under UNMOGIP mandate. The statement evinced a sharp reaction from India, which called the UN observer's statement as 'uncalled for' and the Indian External Affairs Minister threatened to lodge a complaint in the UN against the observer.

UN effort to engage with Kashmir came during the Indo-Pak border confrontation of 2002 when India mobilized half a million troops along its border with Pakistan to pressurize it to stop aiding insurgents in Kashmir. India snubbed UN Secretary-General Kofi Annan's efforts to mediate during the crisis. Kofi Annan was not allowed to visit India and to placate Indian fears Annan stated that UN resolutions on Kashmir were not "enforceable in a mandatory sweep." It meant that no power could enforce UN Resolutions on Kashmir unless both India and Pakistan were prepared for it. Worthwhile to note is that owing to the negligence of Indian authorities, the peaceful march of a million Kashmir's to the office of the UN Observers in Sonawar, Srinagar on March 1, 1990, was the outcome of that negligence.

Why UN Failed in Resolving Kashmir? It has Failed Elsewhere as well

1. Kashmir question was profiled at the UN as a territorial dispute between India and Pakistan and not a struggle of the people of J&K for full freedom and independence. No country in the world is interested whether J&K becomes a part of India or Pakistan. If they forge relations with either of the two countries in line with their national interests.
2. India is bigger than Pakistan in size and population. World countries' regional, commercial and international relations with India are stronger than with Pakistan.
3. During Cold War era Pakistan remained camp follower of America-led NATO camp. Socialist countries and the Soviet Union (of those days) did not lend any support to Pakistan in the matter of Kashmir. Not only that, the Soviet Union at least thrice vetoed UN Resolutions that were tilted towards Pakistan.
4. Shimla Agreement recognized Kashmir a bilateral dispute. Ratification of the agreement by the UN considerably reduced its importance at the UN.

The focal point is that under the UN Resolutions Kashmiris were given the right to choose one of the two countries. This means that UN Resolutions gave a choice to Kashmiris to select one of the two countries for the permanent solution. Nations of the world have no interest in what the Kashmiris choose, be it a white, black, Hindu, Muslim, Sikh or Christian. Kashmir could not become a full-fledged international case of self-determination like Palestine, Vietnam or Algiers. Every country advised that the issue should be resolved bilaterally by India and Pakistan as stated in Shimla Agreement. That rests the case for the plebiscite expectation. The million-dollar question will be "if Kashmiris will vote for Pakistan or India."

Chatham House Survey – Year 2009

A survey which a British academic says is the first systematic attempt to establish the opinions of Kashmiris has produced 'striking results'. Robert Bradnock interviewed more than 3,700 people in Indian J&K and Pakistan Occupied Kashmir to assess their views on various issues. One of the key questions put to respondents was how they saw the future of the territory. Nearly 43% of those interviewed said they wanted independence. Without going into the merits of right or wrong and taking anyone's side, a possible answer to plebiscite question can be found in the opinion poll conducted in 2009 by Chatham House on both sides of the border.

To summarize, 43% of the participants in the poll (both sides of the border put together) favoured Independence, 21% felt that undivided Kashmir should join India, 15% felt that undivided Kashmir should join Pakistan, 14% favoured formalizing the Line of Control as the permanent border and a minuscule number chose other options, including 'don't know'. In J&K (Indian side) 43% favoured Independence, 28% that undivided Kashmir should join India, 19% favoured making the LoC permanent and 2% favoured joining Pakistan. So effectively 47% (28% + 19%) of the people polled in J&K favour staying in India, 2% favoured joining Pakistan and 43% favoured Independence. The survey found that mainly Muslim areas at the centre of the insurgency - support for independence is between 74% and 95%. But in the predominantly Hindu Jammu division to the south, support is under 1%.

Other Findings

80% of Kashmiris on both sides of the LoC say that the dispute resolution is important to them personally. Concern over human rights abuses stands at 43% on the Indian side and 19% on the Pakistani side (this will upwardly change in 2017).

Concern over unemployment is strong across the territory - 66% on the Pakistani side and 87% on the Indian side. Few are optimistic over peace talks – only 27% on the Pakistani side and 57% on the Indian side thought they would succeed.

The survey concluded that a plebiscite on the future of Kashmir – along with the lines envisaged in UN resolutions of 1948-49 – is "extremely unlikely to offer a solution today." The results of the polls show that there is no single proposition for the future of Kashmir which could be put to the population and get majority support. "The poll offers no simple fixes but offers signposts - through which the political process, engaging India, Pakistan and 'wider' Kashmiri representation - could move it towards resolution."

Methodology Followed

Unweighted sample size of the poll was 1.40 (POK): 2.38 (J&K) which was then weighted to 1.02 POK: 2.76 J&K probably keeping in mind the respective population size.

Plebiscite – Trends based on Survey and the Computation Analysis

Scenario-based results on what will happen if India goes for Plebiscite route. This covers all the three regions of J&K and two regions of Pak-occupied Kashmir. This was done a few years back and the results may vary if done today.

Jammu and Kashmir

1. **Kashmir:** Since separation and becoming an independent nation is not an option, the votes would be overwhelmingly in favour of Pakistan in all 10 districts, especially South Kashmir.
   Population: 6.1 million
   For India - 5% to 30%
   For Pakistan - 70% to 95%
2. **Jammu:** Jammu would invariably have a strong support towards India in almost all the districts, except Poonch, Doda and Kishtwar.
   Population: 5.3 million
   For India - 80% to 95%
   For Pakistan - 5% to 20%
3. **Ladakh:** Complete support of India in Leh district, while a favourable support in Kargil.
   Population: 0.2 million
   For India - 90% to 100%
   For Pakistan - 0 to 10%

Pakistan-Occupied Kashmir

1. **Gilgit-Baltistan:** Majority support for Pakistan. Dissatisfaction may lend India some voters.
   Population: 1.8 million
   For India - 1%
   For Pakistan - 99%
2. **'Azad Kashmir':** Overwhelming support for Pakistan.
   Population: 4.5 million
   For India - 5% to 10%
   For Pakistan - 90% to 95%

If a plebiscite is held today (year 2018), result may favour Pakistan and that's why they keep internationalizing Kashmir by sending terrorists to keep the pot boiling, this happens mostly when some foreign dignitaries visit India or when Indian Premier travels abroad. India had golden chance to conduct a plebiscite in 1972 after the division of Pakistan, it did not do. Indira Gandhi, Prime Minister of India missed the bus. She was advised by the people to do so. The United States government had thought that the then Indian Prime Minister Indira Gandhi might order an attack on West Pakistan to capture Pakistan-occupied-Kashmir after India's operation to create Bangladesh got over, recently declassified Central Intelligence Agency (CIA) documents says. At one of the meetings of Washington's Special Action Group, then CIA Director Richard Holmes said, "It is reported that prior to terminating the present hostilities, Mrs Gandhi intends to attempt to eliminate Pakistan's armour and air force capabilities," as per papers which are part of nearly 12 million documents CIA declassified. So two great opportunities lost, Plebiscite and Capture of POK when the enemy army had surrendered and the country was divided. Kashmir could have been solved once for all.

Mathematical Model based on Seven Scenarios

This solution is scenario-based and uses mathematical model for analysis. This analysis was done some time back by British Broadcasting Corporation under the topic Future of J&K. Government of India has not shown much interest yet but can take some scenario and modify as per the actual ground reality and government stand protecting the Constitution of India.

Scenario 1: The *Status Quo*

Kashmir has been a flashpoint between India and Pakistan for more than seven decades. Currently a boundary – Line of Control – divides the region in two, with one part administered by India and one by Pakistan. India would like to formalize this *status quo* and make it the accepted international boundary. But Pakistan and Kashmiri activists reject this plan because they both want greater control over the region.

In 1947-48 India and Pakistan fought their first war over Jammu and Kashmir. Under United Nations' supervision, they agreed to a ceasefire along a line which left one-third of the State – comprising what Pakistan calls Azad Jammu and Kashmir and the Northern Areas administered by Pakistan and two-thirds constituting of Jammu, Ladakh and the Kashmir Valley, with India.

In 1972, under the terms of the Shimla agreement, the ceasefire line was renamed, the Line of Control. Although India claims that the entire State is part of India, it has been prepared to accept the Line of Control as the international border, with some possible modifications. Both the US and the UK have also favoured turning the Line of Control into an internationally-recognized frontier. But Pakistan has consistently refused to accept the Line of Control as the border since the predominantly Muslim Kashmir Valley would remain as part of India. Formalizing the *status quo* also does not take into account the aspirations of those Kashmiris who have been fighting since 1989 for independence of the entire or part of the State and also those Pandits who have been sent to the refugee camps outside the State.

Scenario 2: Kashmir Joins Pakistan

Pakistan has consistently favoured this as the best solution to the dispute. Given the State's majority Muslim population, it believes that it would vote to become part of Pakistan. However, a single plebiscite held in a region which comprises peoples that are culturally, religiously and ethnically diverse, would create disaffected minorities. The Hindus of Jammu and the Buddhists of Ladakh have never shown any desire to join Pakistan and would protest at the outcome. In 1947 India and Pakistan agreed that the allegiance of the State of Jammu and Kashmir would be decided by a plebiscite. Had the majority voted in favour of Pakistan, the whole State would have become part of Pakistan. This no longer seems to be an option.

A plebiscite offering the choice of union with Pakistan or India also does not take into account the movement for independence which has been supported by political and militant activists since 1989. India has long since rejected the idea of a plebiscite as a means of settling the Kashmir issue. Instead, the government argues that the people have exercised their right of self-determination by participating in elections within the State. However, the demand for a plebiscite to be held, as recommended by the Governor-General of

India, Lord Mountbatten in 1947 and endorsed by the United Nations Security Council, is still considered by some as a way of letting Kashmiris exercise their right of self-determination.

Scenario 3: Kashmir Joins India

Such a solution would be unlikely to bring stability to the region as the Muslim inhabitants of Pakistan Occupied Kashmir, including the Northern Areas, have not shown desire to become part of India. In 1947, the Maharaja of Jammu and Kashmir agreed to the State becoming part of India. India and Pakistan then agreed to hold a plebiscite to confirm which country Kashmir's citizens wanted to join. The Indian government believed that the majority population, under the charismatic leadership of Sheikh Abdullah, would vote to join India, with its secular Constitution, rather than Muslim Pakistan.

If the plebiscite had been held and the majority had voted in favour of India, Pakistan would have had to relinquish control of the Northern Areas and the narrow strip of Jammu and Kashmir which it occupied militarily in 1947-48. India has long since rejected the idea of holding a single plebiscite as a means of determining the fate of the State of Jammu and Kashmir. It believes that the people made their choice by participating in elections within the State. Without including a third option of independence from both India and Pakistan, the plebiscite also fails to satisfy the demands of those Kashmiris wanting full independence.

Scenario 4: Independent Kashmir

The difficulty of adopting this as a potential solution is that it requires India and Pakistan to give up territory, which they are not willing to do. Any plebiscite or referendum likely to result in a majority vote for independence would therefore probably be opposed by both India and Pakistan. It would also be rejected by the inhabitants of the State who are content with their status as part of the countries to which they already owe allegiance. An independent Jammu and Kashmir might also set in motion the demand for independence by other States in both India and Pakistan and lead to a 'Balkanization' of the region. In the 1960s, following discussions between India and Pakistan over Jammu and Kashmir, a group of Kashmiris demanded that the entire State should become independent as it was before the Maharaja's accession to India in 1947.

The movement for independence of the entire State is mainly supported by Kashmiris who inhabit the more populous Kashmir Valley and who would like both India and Pakistan to vacate the areas they are occupying. They base their claim on the fact that the State was formerly an independent princely State, is geographically larger than at least 68 countries of the United Nations and more populous than 90. This movement is not supported by India or Pakistan, both of which would lose territory. And because of the likely regional instability, an independent Kashmir is not supported by the international community either.

Scenario 5: Smaller Independent Kashmir

An independent Kashmir could be created from the Kashmir Valley which is with India - and the narrow strip of land which Pakistan calls Azad Jammu and Kashmir. This would leave the strategically important regions of the Northern Areas and Ladakh, bordering China, under the control of Pakistan and India respectively. However, both India and Pakistan would be unlikely to enter into discussions which would have this scenario as a possible outcome. Based on the regional plebiscite if the majority of the inhabitants of the Kashmir Valley chose independence and the majority of the inhabitants of Pakistani Occupied Kashmir (excluding the Northern Areas), also chose independence, a smaller, independent Kashmir could be created by administratively joining these two areas together.

This would leave the predominantly Muslim Northern Areas as part of Pakistan and Buddhist Ladakh and majority Hindu Jammu as part of India, with the possibility that some Muslim districts of Jammu might also opt to join the independent State. Although Pakistan has demanded a change in the status of the Kashmir Valley, it depends on water from the Mangla Reservoir in Pakistan Occupied Kashmir and would be unlikely to permit loss of control of the region.

India is still committed to retaining the Kashmir Valley as part of the Indian Union and has refused to consider holding a plebiscite in any part of the State. Regardless of the aspirations of the inhabitants, to date, neither country has contemplated a situation where the result would adversely affect their interests.

Scenario 6: Independent Kashmir Valley

An independent Kashmir Valley has been considered by some as the best solution because it would address the grievances of those who have been fighting against the Indian government since the insurgency began in 1989. But critics say that, without external assistance, the region would not be economically viable. And will soon fall into ISIS type radical Islamist groups, we do not want another Afghanistan. The movement for independence in the Kashmir Valley gained momentum in the late 1980s when Muslim Kashmiris protested against their continuing allegiance to the Indian Union.

In the present day, if a regional plebiscite offered independence as an option, it is possible that the majority of Kashmiris would vote in favour of independence. With an approximate land mass of 1,800 sq miles (80 miles long, 20 to 25 miles wide) it is much larger than Monaco but only one-tenth of the size of Bhutan. Whether or not the rest of the State retained its current political affiliations, many Kashmiris, therefore, believe that the valley could be viable in its right. How? Probably wishful thinking.

Regarding livelihood, the valley could sustain itself through tourism, handicrafts and agriculture. But an independent Kashmir Valley would also need to retain good relations with its neighbours to survive economically. Not only is the region landlocked, but it is snowbound during winter. An independent Kashmir Valley would have the advantage of giving neither Pakistan nor India a victory out of their long-standing dispute. But although Pakistan might favour the creation of an independent Kashmir Valley, India would be unlikely to agree to the loss of territory involved. Autonomy of the same region under the Indian Union is also an option; Pakistan is more likely to request a 'joint protectorate' to share in safeguarding the Kashmir valley's political and religious integrity.

Scenario 7: The Chenab Formula

This plan, first suggested in the 1960s, would see Kashmir divided along the line of the river Chenab. This would give the vast majority of the land to Pakistan and, as such, a clear victory in its long-standing dispute with India. The entire valley with its Muslim majority population would be brought within Pakistan's borders, as well as the majority Muslim areas of Jammu. With the inclusion of Ladakh, which also lies north of the Chenab river, India would be left with approximately 3,000 sq miles of territory out of 84,000 sq miles.

This solution would require the voluntary agreement of India to give up territory which it wants to retain. It is impossible to see what benefit India could derive from the transfer of so much land and why the government - or the inhabitants of the region who are not contesting their status - would ever agree to such a solution. It also does not take into account the movement for independence which has been extremely vocal ever since the insurgency began in the 1980s and whose supporters have been demanding independence of all or part of the State.

Free Migration between J&K and POK Region and Maintain the *Status Quo* at LoC

Free migration between J&K, 'Azad Kashmir', Gilgit-Baltistan will lead migration of those people who believe in grass is greener on another side. Re-establishing Kashmiri Pandits: After decades, Kashmiri Pandits are still in doomsday. They need settlement with good business and infrastructure in their actual land Jammu and Kashmir.

To maintain the *status quo* is one of the best solutions provided by many historians. That means to let the LoC be the final accepted international border between India, China and Pakistan.

Removal of Article 370 and Article 35A

India is Union of States. That means any person can live and purchase a bunch of lands anywhere in any State. Removing Article 370 breaks the thin line between Jammu and Kashmir and rest of India. Removal of Article 370 will lead to more business in Jammu and Kashmir. Article 370 has been the biggest impediment to integration of J&K State into the Indian Union. That it was incorporated in the Indian Constitution by the machination of two individuals – Sheikh Abdullah and Jawaharlal Nehru is all the more regrettable. Nehru had to eat the humble pie when he had to arrest the Sheikh for his divisive and anti-national stance on 8 August 1953, but he did not let go of his concept of keeping J&K a separate entity. In 1957, some top leaders of National Conference led by Qasim split the party and formed a group called Democratic National Conference (DNC).

It had abrogation of Article 370 on its agenda. Nehru would not brook any opposition to his policy of keeping J&K a separate entity. He told the leaders that a new threat (China) is emerging and it is an inopportune time to raise this issue and force them to drop their demand. Nehru after that decided to withdraw the Kashmir conspiracy case against Sheikh Abdullah. This case had been going on since May 21, 1958. The formal orders, however, were issued by Government of India on 8 April 1964.

It is often forgotten that J&K State is not a homogeneous entity. Apart from Valley Muslims, Jammu has a predominantly Hindu population while Ladakh has a mix of Buddhist and Muslims. Then you have the Gujjar's and Bakarwal's. Why is Article 370 detrimental to the full integration of J&K State into the Indian Union. Firstly, the Central Government can make laws only with the concurrence of the State Government, practically giving it the Veto power. Article 352 and 360 for the declaration of national and financial emergency respectively cannot be applied in Kashmir. While a citizen of India has only Indian citizenship, J&K citizens have two citizenships. Anti-Defection Law is not applicable to J&K. No outsider can buy property in J&K State.

The beneficial laws such as Wealth Tax, Gift Tax and Urban Land Ceiling Act and intermarriage with other Indian nationals do not operate in J&K State. Even Article 356 under which President of India can impose his rule in any State cannot be enforced in J&K without the consent of the Governor who himself is an appointee of the President. The State of J&K can refuse to build any cantonment on any site or refuse to allot land for defence purposes.

Article 370, included in the Constitution on a temporary provision should have been gradually abrogated. This has not happened in sixty years. In fact, whenever someone mentions this, vested interests raise an outcry that legitimate rights of Kashmiris are being trampled upon. Stated agenda of National Conference is returning to pre-1953 status. Why should a State of Indian Union have a special status? It conveys a wrong signal not only to Kashmiris but also to the separatists, Pakistan and indeed the international community that J&K is still to become an integral part of India, the sooner Article 370 is done away is better. The State's Constitution was overridden by the Centre's orders. Its basic structure was altered. The Governor replaced the Sadar-i-Riyasat and State's Prime Minister was replaced by Chief Minister. Debating the Article 370 has it retained its original position or not.

Forty-seven orders have been made applicable to the State of Jammu and Kashmir from 1956 to 1994. Similarly, out of the 97 union subjects, 94 have been made applicable to the State. This shows that Article 370 has been eroded from time and became a dead provision. Thus the autonomy as visualized by Article 370 has been eroded extensively. Still for removal of Article 370, following steps needs to be taken.

Repeal Article 370. Scrap the Constitution of Kashmir and make everything that defines Kashmir as a semi-autonomous region of India irrelevant. Let people invest in Kashmir. Let people buy houses, set-up shops, move to Kashmir and open Kashmir to the rest of the country. This will dilute the issue of identities because people will start identifying with their fellow Indians more and more. This works, because it worked before. Sikkim, Hyderabad, Goa there are lots of examples. This might not solve the thorn in the leg issue of Pakistan, but at least Pakistan will know that Kashmir and Kashmiris will never tow their line anymore.

Brief Overview: Article 370 of the Constitution of India

Temporary Provisions concerning the State of Jammu and Kashmir:

1. Notwithstanding anything in this Constitution:
   (a) The provisions of Article 238 shall not apply to the State of Jammu and Kashmir.
   (b) The power of Parliament to make laws for the said State shall be limited to:
      (i) those matters in the Union List and the Concurrent List which in consultation with the government of the State, are declared by the President to correspond to matters specified in the Instrument of Accession governing the accession of State to the Dominion of India as the matters with respect to which the Dominion Legislature may make laws for that State and
      (ii) such other matters in the Said Lists as, with the concurrence of the government of the State, the President may, by order specify.

      Explanation: For this Article, the government of the State means the person for the time being recognized by the President as Maharaja of Jammu and Kashmir acting on the advice of the Council of Ministers for the time being in office under the Maharaja's Proclamation dated the fifty days of March 1948.
   (c) the provisions of Article (1) and of this Article shall apply to this State;
   (d) such of the other provisions of this Constitution shall apply in relation to that State Subject to such exceptions and modifications as the President may by order specify;

   Provided that no such order which related to the matters specified in the Instrument of Accession of the State referred to in paragraph (i) of subclause (1) shall be issued except in consultation with the government of the State.

   Provided further that no such order which relates to matters other than those referred to in the last proceeding proviso shall be issued except with the concurrence of the government of the State.
2. If the concurrence of the government of the State referred to in para (ii) of Sub Clause (b) of Clause (1) be given before the Constituent Assembly to frame the Constitution of the State is concerned, it shall be placed before such Assembly for such decision as it may take thereon.

3. Notwithstanding anything in the preceding provisions of the Article, the President may, by public notification, declare that this Article shall cease to be operative or shall be operative only with such exceptions and modifications and from such date as he may notify.

   Provided that the recommendation of the Constituent Assembly of the State referred to in Clause (2) shall be necessary before the President issues such a notification.

Why was Article 370 Incorporated?

First, why was Article 370 inserted in the Constitution? Or as the great poet and thinker, Maulana Hasrat Mohani, asked in the Constituent Assembly on October 17, 1949: "Why this discrimination please?" The answer was given by Nehru's confidant, the wise but misunderstood Thanjavur Brahmin, Gopalaswami Ayyangar (Minister without Portfolio in the first Union Cabinet, a former Diwan to Maharaja Hari Singh of Jammu and Kashmir and the principal drafter of Article 370). Ayyangar argued that for a variety of reasons Kashmir, unlike other princely States, was not yet ripe for integration (This assumption screwed the Kashmir integration and till date Indians, Kashmiris and even Pakistanis are suffering in their way). India had been at war with Pakistan over Jammu and Kashmir and while there was a ceasefire, the conditions were still "unusual and abnormal." Part of the State's territory was in the hands of "rebels and enemies."

The involvement of the United Nations brought an international dimension to this conflict, an 'entanglement' which would end only when the "Kashmir problem is satisfactorily resolved." Finally, Ayyangar argued that the "will of the people through the instrument of the [J&K] Constituent Assembly will determine the Constitution of the State as well as the sphere of Union jurisdiction over the State." In sum, there was hope that J&K would one day integrate like other States of the Union (hence the use of the term "temporary provisions" in the title of the Article), but this could happen only when there was real peace and only when the people of the State acquiesced to such an arrangement.

Second, did Sardar Vallabhbhai Patel oppose Article 370? To reduce the Nehru-Patel relationship to Manichean terms is to caricature history and this is equally true of their attitude towards Jammu and Kashmir. Nehru was undoubtedly idealistic and romantic about Kashmir. Patel had a much earthier and pragmatic view and – as his masterly integration of princely States demonstrated – little time for capricious State leaders or their separatist tendencies.

But while Ayyangar negotiated, with Nehru's backing; the substance and scope of Article 370 with Sheikh Abdullah and other members from J&K in the Constituent Assembly (including Mirza Afzal Beg and Maulana Masoodi), Patel was very much in the loop. And while Patel was deeply sceptical of a "State becoming part of India" and not "recognizing. [India's] fundamental rights and directive principles of State policy," he was aware of and a party to, the outcome of Article 370.

Indeed, the synergy that Patel and Nehru brought to governing India is evident in the negotiations over Article 370. Consider this. In October 1949, there was a tense standoff between Sheikh Abdullah and Ayyangar over parts of Article 370 (or Article 306A as it was known during the drafting stage). Nehru was in the United States, where - addressing members of the US Congress - he said: "Where freedom is menaced or justice threatened or where aggression takes place, we cannot be and shall not be neutral."

Meanwhile, Ayyangar was struggling with the Sheikh and later even threatened to resign from the Constituent Assembly. "You have left me even more distressed than I have been since I received your last letter ... I feel weighted with the responsibility of finding a solution for the difficulties that, after Panditji left for America ... have been created ... without adequate excuse," he wrote to the Sheikh on October 15. And who did Ayyangar turn to, in this crisis with the Sheikh, while Nehru was abroad? None other than the Sardar himself. Patel, of course, was not enamoured by the Sheikh, who he thought kept changing course. He wrote to Ayyangar: "Whenever Sheikh Sahib wishes to back out, he always confronts us with his duty to the people." But it was Patel finally who managed the crisis and navigated most of the amendments sought of the Sheikh through the Congress party and the Constituent Assembly to ensure that Article 370 became part of the Indian Constitution.

Third, is Article 370 still intact in its original form? One of the biggest myths is the belief that the "autonomy" as envisaged in the Constituent Assembly is intact. A series of Presidential Orders has eroded Article 370 substantially. While the 1950 Presidential Order and the Delhi Agreement of 1952 defined the scope and substance of the relationship between the Centre and the State with the support of the Sheikh, the subsequent series of Presidential Orders have made most Union laws applicable to the State.

In fact, today the autonomy enjoyed by the State is a shadow of its former self and there is virtually no institution of the Republic of India that does not include J&K within its scope and jurisdiction. The only substantial differences from many other States relate to permanent residents and their rights; the non-applicability of Emergency provisions on the grounds of "internal disturbance" without the concurrence of the State; and the name and boundaries of the State, which cannot be altered without the consent of its legislature. Remember J&K is not unique; there are special provisions for several States which are listed in Article 371 and Articles 371-A to 371-I.

Fourth, can Article 370 be revoked unilaterally? Clause 3 of Article 370 is clear. The President may, by public notification, declare that this Article shall cease to be operative but only on the recommendation of the Constituent Assembly of the State. In other words, Article 370 can be revoked only if a new Constituent Assembly of Jammu and Kashmir is convened and is willing to recommend its revocation. Of course, Parliament has the power to amend the Constitution to change this provision. But this could be subject to a judicial review which may find that this clause is a basic feature of the relationship between the State and the Centre and cannot, therefore, be amended.

Gender Bias?

Fifth, is Article 370 a source of gender bias in disqualifying women from the State of property rights? Article 370 itself is gender neutral, but the definition of Permanent Residents in the State Constitution – based on the notifications issued in April 1927 and June 1932 during the Maharaja's rule – was thought to be discriminatory. The 1927 notification included an explanatory note which said: "The wife or a widow of the State Subject ... shall acquire the status of her husband as State Subject of the same Class as her Husband, so long as she resides in the State and does not leave the State for permanent residence outside the State."

This was widely interpreted as also suggesting that a woman from the State who marries outside the State would lose her status as a State subject. However, in a landmark judgement, in October 2002, the full bench of J&K High Court, with one judge dissenting, held that the daughter of a permanent resident of the State will not lose her permanent resident status on marrying a person who is not a permanent resident and will enjoy all rights, including property rights.

Finally, has Article 370 strengthened separatist tendencies in J&K? Article 370 was and is about providing space, in matters of governance, to the people of a State who felt deeply vulnerable about their identity and insecure about the future. It was about empowering people, making people feel that they belong and about increasing the accountability of public institutions and services. Article 370 is synonymous with decentralization and devolution of power, phrases that have been on the charter of virtually every political party in India. There is no contradiction between wanting J&K to be part of the national mainstream and the State's desire for self-governance as envisioned in the Article.

Ambedkar was against 370 provision, he had added it for only a finite tenure and he had no reservations in explaining why:

> "You wish India should protect your borders, she should build roads in your area, she should supply you foodgrains and Kashmir should get equal status as India. But Government of India should have only limited powers and Indian people should have no rights in Kashmir. To give consent to this proposal, would be a treacherous thing against the interests of India and me, as the Law Minister of India, will never do it."

This is what Dr Ambedkar said to Sheikh Abdullah, the founder of National Conference and one of the most prominent leaders of Kashmir at the time of Independence. All States want less control from Delhi and which is OK and understandable, but only Indian J&K had it guaranteed under Article 370. If Islamists are gaining the upper hand, it is because Delhi will not relent on restoring what it has taken away without popular sanction.

Separatism grows when people feel disconnected from the structures of power and the process of policy formulation; in contrast, devolution ensures popular participation in the running of the polity. It can be reasonably argued that it is the erosion of Article 370 and not its creation which has aggravated separatist tendencies in the State. Only then would the slogans of Jumhuriyat, Kashmiriyat and Insaniyat make real sense. Now let's also briefly analyse Article 35A.

Article 35A

Article 35A of the Indian Constitution is an Article that empowers the Kashmir State's legislature to define 'Permanent Residents' of the State and provide special rights and privileges to those permanent residents. It is added to the Constitution through a Presidential Order, ie, The Constitution (Application to Jammu and Kashmir) Order, 1954 – issued by the President of India, "in exercise of the powers conferred by" clause (1) of Article 370 of the Constitution, with the concurrence of the government of the State of Jammu and Kashmir.

Law

Notwithstanding anything contained in this Constitution, no existing law in force in the State of Jammu and Kashmir and no law hereafter enacted by the Legislature of the State:

(a) defining the classes of persons who are, or shall be, permanent residents of the State of Jammu and Kashmir; or

(b) conferring on such permanent residents any special rights and privileges or imposing upon other persons any restrictions as respects –

  (i) employment under the State Government;

  (ii) acquisition of immovable property in the State;

  (iii) settlement in the State; or

  (iv) right to scholarships and such other forms of aid as the State Government may provide, shall be void on the ground that it is inconsistent with or takes away or abridges any rights conferred on the other citizens of India by any provision of this part.

In his statement to the Lok Sabha on the Delhi agreement, Nehru had said:

> The question of citizenship arose obviously. Full citizenship applies there. But our friends from Kashmir were very apprehensive about one or two matters. For a long time past, in the Maharaja's time, there had been laws there preventing any outsider, that is, any person from outside Kashmir, from acquiring or holding land in Kashmir. If I mention it, in the old days, the Maharaja will be very much afraid of a large number of Englishmen coming and settling down there, because the climate is delectable and acquiring property. So although most of their rights were taken away from the Maharaja under the British rule, the Maharaja stuck to this that nobody from outside should acquire land there. And that continues.
>
> So the present government of Kashmir is very anxious to preserve that right because they are afraid and I think rightly afraid, that Kashmir would be overrun by people whose sole qualification might be the possession of too much money and nothing else, who might buy up and get the delectable places. Now they want to vary the old Maharaja's laws to liberalize it, but nevertheless to have checks on the acquisition of lands, by persons from outside. However, we agree that this should be cleared up. The old State's subject's definition gave certain privileges regarding this acquisition of land, the

services and other minor things, I think, State scholarships and the rest.

So, we agreed and noted this down:

> "The State legislature shall have the power to define and regulate the rights and privileges of the permanent residents of the State, more especially regarding the acquisition of immovable property, appointments to services and like matters. Till then the existing State law should apply."

The State is empowered, both in the Instrument of Accession and the Article 370, to decree exceptions as part of an extension of the application of various provisions of Indian Constitution to the State, excluding those that pertain to Communications, Defence and Foreign Affairs. So Article 35A is seen as an exception allowed by the Article 370, clause (1)(d). Bakshi Ghulam Mohammad of the Jammu and Kashmir National Conference was the Prime Minister of Jammu and Kashmir at the time of the 1954 Presidential order. The Article 35A was added to the Constitution by the executive head without any discussion in the Parliament. The manner of its enactment has been controversial.

Permanent Resident Certificate (PRC)

The Jammu and Kashmir Constitution, which was adopted on November 17, 1956, defined a Permanent Resident (PR) of the State as a person who was a State subject on May 14, 1954, or who has been a resident of the State for 10 years and has "lawfully acquired immovable property in the State".

Jammu and Kashmir Constituent Assembly incorporated in Jammu and Kashmir Constitution discriminatory provisions under Section-51 (Qualifications for membership of the Legislature. – A person shall not be qualified to be chosen to fill a seat in the Legislature unless he is a Permanent Resident of the State), Section-127 (Transitional provisions. – Until another provision is made in this behalf under this Constitution, all the laws in force immediately before the commencement of this Constitution and applicable to any public service or any post which continues to exist after the commencement of this Constitution, like service or post under the State, shall continue in force so far as consistent with the provisions of this Constitution) and Section-140 (the elections to the Legislative Assembly shall be on the basis of adult suffrage; that is to say, every person who is a permanent resident of the State and who is not less than Eighteen years of age on such date), etc.

No person who is not a Permanent Resident of Jammu and Kashmir can own property in Jammu and Kashmir or can obtain a job within Jammu and Kashmir government.

No person who is not a Permanent Resident of Jammu and Kashmir can join any professional college run by the government of Jammu and Kashmir or get any form of government aid out of government funds.

Criticism

Article 35A was not added to the Constitution by following the procedure prescribed for amendment of the Constitution of India under Article 368. Article 370 does not anywhere confer on the President legislative or executive powers so vast that he can amend the Constitution or perform the function of Parliament. It has been brought about by the executive organ when the right of amendment of the Constitution lies with the legislative organ. Therefore, it is, allegedly, ultra vires the basic structure of the Constitution since it violates the Constitutional procedures established by law.

Besides carrying out many modifications and changes, this order added a new 'Article 35A' to the Constitution of India. Addition or deletion of an Article amounted to an amendment to the Constitution which could be done only by Parliament as per procedure laid down in Article 368. But, Article 35A was never presented before Parliament. This meant the President had bypassed Parliament in this order to add Article 35A. Where was Dr Rajendra Prasad, his silence was deafening?

The PRC classification created by Article 35A suffers from the violation of Article 14, Equality before the Law. The non-resident Indian citizens cannot have the rights and privileges, same as permanent residents of Jammu and Kashmir.

This also meant that the amending power of Parliament under Article 368 of the Constitution itself was abridged in its application to Jammu and Kashmir, another amendment, without any reference to Parliament. When the President of India does not have legislative powers, he performed the function of Parliament.

Main Objections

It facilitates the violation of the right of women to 'marry a man of her choice' by not giving the heirs any right to property if the woman marries a man not holding PRC. Therefore, her children are not given Permanent Resident Certificate and thereby considering them unfit for inheritance – not given any right to such a woman's property even if she is a permanent resident.

It facilitates the free and unrestrained violation of fundamental rights of those workers and settlers like Scheduled Caste and Scheduled Tribe people who have lived there for generations. The Valmikis who were brought to the State during 1957 were given Permanent Resident Certificates on the condition that they and their future generations could stay in the State only if they continued to be *safai karmacharis* (scavengers). And even after six decades of service in the State, their children are *safai karmacharis* and they have been denied the right to quit scavenging and choose any other profession. (What a shame.)

The industrial sector and whole private sector suffers due to the property ownership restrictions. Good doctors don't come to the State for the same reason. Children of non-State subjects do not get admission to State colleges. It ruins the status of West Pakistani refugees. Being citizens of India they are not Stateless persons, but being non-permanent residents of Jammu and Kashmir, they cannot enjoy the basic rights and privileges as being enjoyed by permanent residents of Jammu and Kashmir.

It gives a free hand to the State Government and politicians to discriminate between citizens of India, on an unfair basis and give preferential treatment to some by trampling over others, since the non-residents of the State are debarred from buying properties, getting a government job or voting in the local elections. This makes the abolition of this bad Article first step in moving in the direction of a solution.

Divide Jammu and Kashmir into Three Separate States Based on Religious and Cultural Lines

Jammu, Kashmir and Ladakh all the three regions have different cultures. While Kashmir remains disputed, people in Jammu live a peaceful life. The region consists of Dogras and Kashmiri Pandits who are proud Indians, they want to be treated like any other Indians and do not want discriminatory Articles like 370 and 35A. They want more industries and Investments in their region. Government of India can make Jammu as a separate State.

Ladakh region is mostly peaceful and doesn't have any militancy issue (though Siachen needs to be guarded against Pakistani infiltration). It also needs a lot of investment in infrastructure etc for all-round development. This can be achieved once a separate State of Ladakh can be formed merging Leh and Ladakh as a Buddhist State.

Buddhist are in the majority and are peaceful people. Like Jammu folks, they too would like to remove Article 370 and 35A for attracting investment.

Kashmir State can be formed by taking in the disturbed part of South Kashmir valley and some other area of Kashmir mostly inhabited by Muslims. This State will continue to have Article 370 and 35A along with AFSPA. Chief Minister should come from elected party and Governor from Indian Army. Security and Education will be with the Governor.

So, how will this be implemented? J&K is not like any other State of India where the Parliamentary Laws and the Constitution of India can be applied directly without getting endorsed by the State Assembly. J&K has its Constitution and all matters of the State except the defence, currency, communication and the foreign affairs are the State subjects. Government of India has no *locus standi* on the State matters. The President of India, the Supreme Court and the Parliament cannot implement any law of the Central Government or the State Government by any means. If there is no government in the State, there can be no President's Rule like in other States of India but only Governor's Rule. Governor becomes a caretaker and he has to follow the State Constitution. When a crime is registered in the State, no IPC can be applied but only RPC which is State's own Ranbir Penal Code. Now, you see why this State has so many unemployed youths. Article 370 and 35A stops any business house to come and open industries, schools and hospitals and hence both should be sunset.

Musharraf-Manmohan and Musharraf-Vajpayee Formula

After doing Kargil on India Gen Pervez Musharraf experimented with various political formulas for Kashmir conflict resolution, though it was mainly in Pakistan's favour, it's worth to take a note and maybe fine tune it for the future potential solution. The key points are as follows:

Demilitarization and Self-governance with joint supervision mechanism - Again India will not demilitarize J&K because India does not believe Pakistan. Since the inception of Kashmir, they were involved in four full-blown wars and unaccounted border skirmishes.

Free Trade without restriction - Musharraf believed in free trade between India and Pakistan. India has already given MFN to Pakistan with no reciprocation for almost a decade plus. But India already has lost trust in Pakistan. Pakistan's ISI continued bleeding India with 1,000 cuts strategy (Bhutto(s) started it) by sending jihadis and finishing in the troubled water of Indian Controlled J&K.

Self-Governance or Autonomy but not Independence - If you see Pakistan it's already messed up. Pakistan was divided in 1971 by the creation of Bangladesh. Pakistan has somewhat less influence and control on its FATA, Sindh, Khyber Pakhtunkhwa and Balochistan regions. Phase-wise withdrawal of troops from the region and a mechanism should be devised jointly - This was thought to help implement the roadmap for Kashmir conflict solution smoothly. Thus Pakistan's President Pervez Musharraf, had diluted the Pakistani position significantly and since he came from Army, it was believed at that time that there was buy-in from ISI and the Pakistani army.

Unfortunately, India did not agree, as the Agra (India) talk failed in the last minute due to some minor edits request from India at the 11th hour. Later Musharraf was thrown away and even if India had agreed on this huge step-down agreement from its current position, its implementation would have always been at risk with new army chief taking over from Musharraf. ISI also did not bless this approach.

These five major changes are:

1. Setting aside the UN's resolutions on the plebiscite.
2. Self-governance substation for self-determination.
3. Forsaking religion as a criterion.
4. Pakistan advise to Kashmiris to talk to New Delhi; and
5. Accepting the Line of Control (LoC) provided it is combined with joint management.

Musharraf-Manmohan Formula

The **first step** would be to make the LoC just a line on the Map (Making Border irrelevant). Towards this end, it was decided that cross-LoC travel and trade would be freed up.

The **second step** would be to strengthen local self-government on both sides of LoC, so that people elect their government, if necessary under international supervision.

The **third step** would be trickiest. It would entail the creation of 'joint or cooperative' institutions under the charge of Kashmiri leaders to coordinate policies on the matters of common interest. Everything except foreign policy and defence would be locally and jointly administered and these two would be handled by New Delhi and Islamabad respectively.

The **fourth step** - If all this worked and peace was restored, then the final element of peace formula would be the 'agreed withdrawal' of troops on both sides. (Source: *The Accidental Prime Minister* by Sanjaya Baru.)

Musharraf-Vajpayee Formula (Agra, India)

The plan unveiled by Musharraf envisages the treatment of Jammu and Kashmir as seven distinct regions. According to him, two of these are under the control of Pakistan (the Northern Areas and Pakistan Occupied Kashmir (POK), which is referred to as POK in Pakistan) while the remaining five are with India.

The so-called proposal of Musharraf is full of holes and contradictions. The widely held view is that the Jammu and Kashmir territory held by India has three provinces: Jammu, the Kashmir Valley and Ladakh. But Musharraf seems to base his calculation on religious, ethnic and geographical terms – Ladakh (the Islamic part between the Himalayas and the Indus), Kargil/Dras (Muslim), Poonch (Muslim, contiguous with POK), Jammu (Muslim-majority districts) and the Valley (Muslim).

Musharraf simply wanted contiguous Muslim areas to fall to Pakistan. He also had future water scarcity in mind when proposing the formula. He wanted a line drawn along the Chenab river, making Pakistan safe against any future Indian trespass into waters that belong to Pakistan under the 1960 Indus Waters Treaty. It may not be accidental that the five 'parts' or 'regions' he has presumably specified are located along the Chenab. But the famous Chenab Formula was the subject of discussion at the 'track-two' level talks between the governments of Nawaz Sharif and Atal Bihari Vajpayee in 1999.

The Chenab Formula seeks to divide Kashmir along the river Chenab, which flows down from Kashmir into Punjab, separating the Muslim-majority areas from the Hindu and Buddhist-dominated ones. The river flows through the mountainous areas of Doda, Ramban, Surukot, Salat, Reasi and Akhnoor and enters Punjab (Pakistan) at Head Marala. India has built the Salal dam on it under the Indus Water Treaty. The Kashmir Valley has a 98% Muslim population; out of the six districts of Jammu province almost three Muslim-majority districts fall on the right bank of the Chenab and will fall to Pakistan if the river is made the new boundary. According to some Pakistani experts, if the Chenab Formula is accepted, 80% of the territory of the original State, including POK and the Northern Areas, will become part of Pakistan.

The formula falls flat on just one fundamental count. The division of Jammu and Kashmir is anathema to the people of the State on either side. No Kashmiri group – within or outside the pale of parliamentary politics – has ever advocated the concept. In fact, various groups have called for the reunification of the erstwhile princely State.

Musharraf did make it a point to mention that India was not ready to accept a religion-based solution and sought to sell his formula 'in geographical terms'. However, as he said, it all amounted to the same. "The beauty of these regions is such that they are still religion-based even if we consider them geographically," he maintained. Curiously, there was no reference by Musharraf to the huge part of Kashmir conceded by Pakistan to China. In the run-up to the Agra Summit, Musharraf had said that as and when the Kashmir issue was to be settled, the territory under the control of China would also be considered a part of the deal.

Musharraf's contention that India has refused to hold a plebiscite in Kashmir as per UN resolutions and that Pakistan was not ready to accept the Line of Control (LoC) as a permanent border are not entirely correct. The Indian position has been that Pakistan did not fulfil the terms specified in the UN resolutions to create conditions for ascertaining the wishes of the people of Jammu and Kashmir and that over the years the UN resolutions had become irrelevant. Even as he talked about seven 'regions' in Jammu and Kashmir, Musharraf listed three specific steps that India and Pakistan should take. First, identify the region at stake. Second, demilitarize it. Third, change its status. The General suggested that there were many options that could then be considered and legal experts on both sides could then look at the pros and cons of ideas for joint control, UN mandates, condominiums and so on.

Musharraf said Pakistan had proposed the 'demilitarization' of Kashmir and if India asked Pakistan to do likewise in POK, it would oblige. Will India bite his bullet, never, he is seen as the guy who did Kargil on India where Pakistani army sneaked into Tiger hills when Indian forces vacated it in winter and then India had to fight a bloody war killing 2,000 or so poor Pakistani northern regiment young men to re-capture the strategic location.

The Agra Summit was a historic two-day summit meeting between India and Pakistan which lasted from 14–16 July 2001. It was organized with the aim of resolving long-standing issues between India and Pakistan.

At this meeting, a proposal was made to drastically reduce nuclear arsenals and other issues involving the Kashmir dispute and cross-border terrorism. However, the negotiations broke down and the process was collapsed, so the Agra treaty was never signed. Media and Pakistan blamed the then Home Minister LK Advani for the failure as they felt Prime Minister Atal Bihari Vajpayee was ready to sign the dotted lines with some minor changes to the draft.

Kashmir – As an Independent Country

The first references about Kashmir being an independent sovereign country are from the Greek sources. The Ptolemy's geography depicts Kashmir as a country called KASPEIRA which is supposed to enclose a large portion of land including parts of Punjab, North-West Provinces and Central India. Another curious notice is in the poem Bassarika of Dionysius of Samos. It mentions about KASPEIROI, a tribe famous for their fast feet. Even Alberuni has mentioned about Kashmiris being good pedestrians. Herodotus, who is known as the "father of history," mentions KASPATYROS as a country which is taken to refer to Kashmir.

After Greeks, Kashmir is mentioned in Chinese records. The earliest reference to Kashmir dates back to AD 541. This relates to the arrival of an Envoy in China during the early part of the reign of Tang dynasty. Kashmir is described as a country "enveloped on all sides like a precious jewel by the snowy mountains, with a valley in the south which leads up to it and serves as a gate of the Kingdom". Many other Chinese accounts of Kashmir give a similar description. Ninety years after this first mention of Kashmir in Chinese records, Hiuen Tsang visited the valley and stayed here as an honoured guest for two years.

According to him, these natural bulwarks have protected the country from its neighbours who have never succeeded in subduing it. He describes the climate as cold and snow plentiful. The soil is described as very fertile with the abundance of fruit and flowers. The people are described as light and frivolous and of a weak and pusillanimous disposition. "The people are handsome in appearance, but they are given to cunning. They love learning and are well-instructed."

The next reference to Kashmir in Chinese records relates to the Annals of Tang dynasty which mentions the arrival of the first ambassador from Kashmir sent by Candrapida and then another sent by Muktapida (Lalitaditya) of the Karakot dynasty of the *Rajatarangini*. In fact, Muktapida had entered into a treaty of military alliance with the rulers of Tang dynasty of China against Tibet which he subsequently raided with a strong Kashmiri army.

After few years of the visit of Muktapida's envoy, Kashmir was visited by another Chinese pilgrim, Ou-Kong. His account is very important regarding the routes of ancient Kashmir. He gives a very clear description of three great routes through the mountains which, since ancient times have formed the main lines of communication between the valley and the outer world. In the east, the route leads to Tou-fan or Tibet. This is the road going over Zoji La to Ladakh and thence to Tibet. In the north, the route leads to Po-liu or Baltistan which is the route to Gilgit through Upper Kishenganga valley (Gurais and Tilel) and from there to Skardu or Astor on the Indus.

The route through the western gate leads to Kien-to-lo or Gandhara. This is the famous Jhelum Valley road which was always the most frequented and easy entry to the valley. Ou-kong also mentions a fourth route which always remained closed and was opened when an imperial army honoured it with a visit. This is the route over the Pir Panjal range to the south. In fact, this route came into prominence only after the Mughals annexed Kashmir in the sixteenth century.

After Chinese, we can examine the references in the accounts of Muslim scholars. Although the first rush of Arabs into Indus Valley brought them close to Kashmir yet, they did not make any attempt to enter it. In spite of this seclusion of Kashmir, the Arabic literature has very accurate and valuable account of Kashmir. This is due to the research and critical appraisal of Alberuni who travelled with Mahmud of Ghazni up to the borders of Kashmir at the fort of Lohkot (presently Loran in Punch). This stronghold of the Kashmiri forces brought the invasion of Mahmud to a standstill and he had to ultimately retreat from here due to the onset of winter. Though this expedition failed to reach Kashmir it gave Alberuni ample opportunity to collect detailed information on Kashmir.

He refers to the pedestrian habits of Kashmiris and mentions that the nobles were carried in palanquins on the shoulders of men. He describes Kashmiris anxiety and care to protect their country. "They are particularly anxious about the natural strength of their country and therefore take always much care to keep a strong hold upon the entrances and roads leading to it. In consequence, it is very difficult to have any commerce with them. In former times they used to allow one or two foreigners to enter their country, particularly Jews, but at present, they do not allow any Hindu whom they do not know personally to enter, much less other people".

Compared to all these references in Greek, Chinese and Arabic literature, there is a lamentable lack of exact geographical mention of Kashmir in general Sanskrit literature. The most specific piece of information regarding Kashmir that Sanskrit literature outside the Valley furnishes is in the term Kasmira or Kasmiraja that designates Saffron and Kustha for which it was famous since the ancient times.

Majority in Kashmir followed the Hindu Shaivite religion till Mir Sayed Ali Hamadani (Shah-i-Hamadan) converted entire population except for 2% Brahmin rulers to Islam through his preaching. Incidentally, the Kashmiri Hindu philosophy of Trika Shaivism is a total contrast to north Indian Vedanta philosophy.

The Mughals annexed Kashmir to their empire by treachery in 1586. The four centuries of external subjugation transformed Kashmiris into virtual wretches. For last 86 years, or so they have been trying to regain their lost freedom. Due to their misfortune, they landed themselves in a mess resembling a Gordian knot during the partition of the subcontinent. They are still stuck in a mess but the new generation seems to be determined to untie the Gordian knot and reclaim Kashmir's historical position.

Steps for Independent Kashmir, as a Separate Country between India and Pakistan

Step 1: India and Pakistan should conclude that Kashmir and entire POK are disputed territory.

Step 2: Take steps to integrate both the sides of Kashmir. This means allowing free movement of people on both the sides. This will also mean having check posts at Kashmir border with Indian States to make sure only Indian citizens of Kashmir are allowed into other States.

Step 3: Before step 2, make sure a trade agreement is signed with Pakistan to increase trade between Pakistan and India many folds. This will create an economic dependence between both the countries. Pakistan to sell officially all its trade deficits to India. India should buy $30 billion trade deficit which Pakistan is currently facing. US, Russia and China along with Germany can be guarantors.

Step 4: Now this arrangement to continue for five years and once the results are positive, declare Kashmir as an Independent country, Indian Constitution will have to undergo amendments by the lawmakers. But for this saner minds needs to come to power on both sides of the border. Once all the financial and people integrations are done in a five years' timeframe, declare Kashmir as Independent country between India and Pakistan.

Step 5: Use SAARC as a backdrop and integrate the South Asian economies to such an extent that people have a hard time remembering the Kashmir problem. Wishful thinking in the current context.

Akhand Bharat – Surging Young Hindu India Vision

Kashmir se Kanyakumari - Attock se Cuttack tak and beyond. Redrawing India's older map, taking a cue from Qing Dynasty followers. The Kashmir problem at its root is a religious issue first, then a political one. It would be reasonably safe to assume Pakistan and Bangladesh were created because Muslims wanted self-determination when India was getting independence. Kashmir is an unfinished issue from the partition and flares up now and then and people including Jihadis, Kashmiris and soldiers become a casualty of the conflict. While this conflict appears to be political, it has its roots in religion. Can this problem be solved at a religious level? Instead of biuntly refusing to engage with separatists we should take off from where we were at partition but bring in religion as part of negotiations. The separatists want Azaadi because of their religion.

If Kashmir valley has to separate from India, then Pakistan has to accommodate all the Muslims from India. This might sound harsh, but do we have a choice? West Pakistan (today's Pakistan) and East Pakistan (today's Bangladesh) were created because of Muslims wanted self-determination, so let us bring this to its logical conclusion. An issue like the Kashmir where minority Hindu Pandits had to leave their place should never happen in India again. India has been magnanimous with Pakistan umpteen times to the extent of even letting the current LoC in Kashmir stay as the *de facto* border, but guess that's not helping anyone. The only solution that will have lasting and permanent peace will be the formation of Akhand Bharat (United India pre-1947), China claims Middle Kingdom prophecy based on its ancient history and civilization. India is in equal parity as far as civilization and past historical claim are concerned.

The Akhand Bharat to which Veer Savarkar and many uncompromising nationalists dedicated and sacrificed their lives include a quest for the return of India's pristine boundaries sundered at Partition. More than a desire for the reunion of lost territory (62 districts), it is a craving for the restoration of a lost civilizational harmony whose cultural-religious symbols survive in the form of 218 Tirthas (Hindus Holy Shrines) now in Islamic custody in Pakistan and Bangladesh respectively. Some of the more exalted sites include:

West Punjab (Present-day Pakistan)

- The banks of the Saraswati river, where the Saraswat Brahmins enunciated the Vedas.
- Birthplace of famous Sanskrit grammarian, Rishi Panini.
- Takshashila (Taxila), the University of Acharya Chanakya.

- Katasraj, of the *Mahabharata* yuga, where Yaksha discoursed with Dharmaraja Yudhishthira.
- Shalivahana Kot (Sialkot), the birthplace of Purna Bhakta and Hutatma, Dharamvir Bal Hakikat Rai.
- Jhelum, where Raja Puru (Porus) defeated the world conqueror, Mighty Alexander.
- Luvpur (Lahore), Kushpur (Kusur), cities established by Maryada Purushottama Rama's sons, Luv and Kush.
- Moolasthan (Multan), where Bhakta Prahlad was born and at his anguished call, the Lord Narasingha burst forth.
- Nankana Sahib, the birthplace of Sant Shiromani Guru Nanak Dev Ji, where he is reputed to have admonished Jabir Babur regarding the true sanctity of Mecca.
- Panja Sahib, where Guru Nanak Dev Ji Maharaj is reputed to have humbled Bali Kandhari.
- Gujranwala, the birthplace of Hari Singh Nalwa, the reputed General who inflicted a humiliating defeat upon the Pathans of Afghanistan.
- Murariwala, in Gujranwala, the birthplace of Swami Rama Tirtha.
- The seat of Guru Baba Pir Rattan Nath Ji Maharaj, at Purushapura (Peshawar), whose spiritual seat is now established at Jhandewalan, New Delhi.
- Tomani Sahib (Baddo-ki-Gosainyan), in Gujranwala.

Sindh (Present-day Pakistan)

- Sindh – Where King Dahir sacrificed his life while fighting the Muslim invaders.
- Shakti Peeth of Hinglaj Devi – Balochistan (present day Pakistan).
- Mahatma Jhule Lal tapasyasthal; birthplace of Deval Rishi, inspirer of the Shuddhi Andolan; and the city of the great civilization of our ancestors, Mohenjo-Daro.

Pakistan Occupied Kashmir (Present-day Pakistan)

- Sharadapeeth established by Adi Shankaracharya.

East Bengal (Present-day Bangladesh)

- Dhakeshwari Devi temple in Dhaka.
- Birthplace of great Indian revolutionaries Surya Sen (Master da), Puliyan Das, Binay, Badal, Dinesh, Hemchandra Ghosh, who were all inspired by Vivekananda.

Given the history of Indian subcontinent, it was clear to everyone that without unification of Kashmir there is no Kashmir solution and neither Pakistan nor India will ever give to another side whatever area of J&K (Kashmir) is with them. Like Bangladesh (which after separation from Pakistan demolished two-nation theory, the basis of India's partition on religious basis - hence should have been assimilated back in India but not) at some point Pakistan would have agreed to independence of at least Muslim Kashmir (on both side of LoC) if not of entire J&K in order to bring a new Muslim country (carved out of India) in existence but for the same reason India would never agree to it. Hence it left only one solution, the military solution, to Kashmir problem. Pakistan, smaller than India, tried to take Kashmir militarily in 1947, 1948, 1965, 1971 and 1999, during Kargil but India never tried to take POK militarily. Moreover, after India and Pakistan, both became a nuclear power in 1998 the only solution left was 'Akhand Bharat' (starting with unified India and Pakistan), which could become a reality under international pressure if nuclear India tried military solution against nuclear Pakistan to retrieve POK. Even Indian Judiciary High Court/Supreme Court questioned federal Government of India why it is not using military power for getting POK instead of focusing more on internal actions in Kashmir.

The idea of Sunni Caliphate started by ISIS (which did not go further because it indulged in unnecessary violence and cruelties) has now become the need of Sunni leader Saudi Arabia, also for the simple reason that the World comprises mainly of four major groups the Christians, Muslims, Chinese and Hindus. The Christians are economically and militarily powerful hence their many countries of developed West do not matter. Chinese and Hindus are solidly in one country each. It is only Muslims of developing world who are living in different countries hence are unable to become reckonable military power (crucial for deciding any international dispute/issue especially in this age of globalization) because their resources are divided into meaninglessly repetitive/similar assets and activities. Therefore, Sunni Muslims all over the world (who are bleeding and weeping profusely in many countries) find the idea of one Caliphate for them (as given by ISIS), very attractive.

The idea of Caliphate (given by ISIS) has tremendous appeal among Sunni Muslims (~85% of ~2 billion Muslim population) across the world due to one more reason. ISIS Caliphate is prepared to face militarily any power (including superpower West, the Christian USA and its Allies and Russia) to protect Islamic way of life as wrongly seen by ISS, but its so-called ultimate courage is unfortunately appreciated by the majority of the Sunni Muslims. Therefore, Saudi

Arabia will try to establish Sunni Caliphate (to start with) in geographically continuous NAME region which will not show any cowardice while protecting its vital interests. Remaining countries (out of 44 Sunni Muslim countries) may join this Caliphate or come in alliance with this Caliphate to achieve its stated objective of fighting terrorism of ISIS etc and to solve other problems being faced by Sunni Muslims. Therefore, it is only a matter of time when this Sunni Caliphate comes into existence in this region and then nuclear Pakistan is asked to join.

Once this Sunni Caliphate of Saudi Arabia crosses the geographical barrier of Iran and enters AF-PAK region then to make remaining Muslim Countries (out of these 44 countries of alliance) Bangladesh, Malaysia, Indonesia and Maldives as members, will simply be a cakewalk for this Sunni Caliphate (which will influence ~1 billion Muslims of South and South-East Asia, half the population of Muslim World). And then Pakistan is bound to press for the military solution to Kashmir problem (which, as per media and Kashmiri separatists, has already claimed the lives of ~1,00,000 Jihadis from India, Pakistan, Afghanistan, etc). Pakistan (in this Caliphate of reckonable military power equal if not bigger than India) will certainly try to achieve militarily solution to Kashmir problem without any concern for nuclear catastrophe (because at least the Jihadis of this 'Sunni Caliphate' will consider it further martyrdom in the service of Islam).

Before Sunni Caliphate claims Pakistan, the Hindu majority India should try to take POK militarily so that international community may work for 'Akhand Bharat'. As Pakistan gets weaker due to sectorial violence within and huge CPEC debt making it economically and politically bankrupt, time will come when Pakistan will find difficult to survive as a single country. This won't be too long in future. Many European and American scholars have already predicted this to happen in very near future. On similar lines to Bangladesh, we may see more pieces of Pakistan. Eventually, maybe for economic reasons, these pieces along with Kashmir can come together like the European Union. India can lead this group.

The progress India has made since the British left has been impressive. In 1947 when the British left life expectancy in India was 32 years, now it is 68 years; In 1947, India's per capita income was £20. Now it is more than £5,500; India's GDP of £7.4 trillion ranks it third after China and the US. In 1947 only 1,500 villages - a mere 0.025% - were electrified; now 97% of villages have electricity. After two centuries of British rule, only 12% of the population had seen the inside of a classroom, now 74% are literate, with Kerala close to a

100% literacy rate - this in a country with 20 languages. And all this while every change of government since 1947, has been via the ballot box, with the army not involved - something Greece, Spain, Portugal or even France can't claim. Start realizing and propagating the Akhand Bharat idea. India is ready for this big leap.

Referendums: Irish, Crimea, Scottish, Quebec and Catalonia

Eighteen per cent of Texans said that they would like to declare independence from the US as recently as 2009, hypothetically if that would have happened, will USA draw a new map? Well, it did not happen like that. Kashmiris superficial aspiration of a separate country between India and Pakistan or breaking from India and merging with Pakistan may be possible only on the battlefield. The solution of autonomy has to be found within the Indian constitutional framework and also any solution should not be for some elite Muslims and few separatist leaders. The caste line divide between Muslims, the 10% SC among Muslims plus OBC population, needs also to be brought into this gambit.

Experts point to the emergence of the European Union, which obliterated the issue of the territorial boundary in Northern Ireland. If that (rise of a Union) happens here, then the intensity of the conflict will also go away. The resolution of the diplomatic and sectarian strife in Northern Ireland through a referendum leading to the formation of a Northern Irish parliament should be studied to explore the Irish peace model feasibility in South Asia aka Kashmir crisis. The Irish model is very complicated and deeply rooted like (the problem) that India shares with Pakistan.

Sumantra Bose discusses the North Ireland type solution for Kashmir in his book *Kashmir: Roots of Conflict, Paths to Peace*. But that requires a giant leap of faith and trust between the two nations which is currently lacking. Probably influenced by the Irish history, BR Ambedkar drew on it extensively in his classic *Pakistan and the Partition of India* (1946). Had its lessons been heeded, the Partition of India might have been averted.

Irish history is instructive alike on the process for peace as well as on the shape of the product it can yield; provided that Henry Kissinger's warning is kept in mind: History teaches by analogy, not identity. No two cases are identical. After the Good Friday agreement, concluded in Belfast on April 10, 1998, between all the parties - the governments of the United Kingdom and Ireland and most of the parties in Northern Ireland - many thought that at long last peace had broken out. But on March 3 and 4, 2003, the Prime

Ministers of the two countries, Tony Blair and Bertie Ahern, met in Belfast to try to put the accord back on the rails to pave the way for Assembly elections on May 29.

The talks failed, mainly on the issue of decommissioning of arms by the Sinn Fein. When the 1998 agreement was concluded, 'a senior Indian official' based in London said on April 12 that the principles underlying it "will now have a strong bearing on all international disputes." He remarked: "Other people are getting up and doing what we at present find unthinkable." The former President of the United States, Bill Clinton, who had involved himself in both the problems, told an Indian audience on March 2, 2003: "Kashmir can be resolved along the lines the problem in Northern Ireland was sorted."

Of Northern Ireland's population of 1.6 million, just over 50% are Protestants who wish to remain part of the United Kingdom and just under 50% are Roman Catholics who wish to join the predominantly Catholic 3.5 million in the Republic of Ireland. After the Easter rising of 1916, Irish nationalists decided to set-up their State. By the Anglo-Irish Treaty of 1921, Britain recognized it and Parliament enacted the Irish Free State Constitution Act, 1922. The Northern Ulster province, however, remained part of Britain under the Government of Ireland Act, 1920.

This partition of Ireland led to a civil war. From 1920, Northern Ireland had its regional government and also elected Members of Parliament to the British House of Commons. Grave unrest began in Northern Ireland from 1969 in the wake of a civil rights movement, which campaigned for the removal of grievances of the Catholic minority. It was a procession which triggered the violence that has torn the province apart. In 1973 Britain abolished the regional Parliament in Belfast and began to rule directly from Westminster.

Two significant political developments bear notice. In 1969-70, hardliners split from the Irish Republican Army to form groups bearing the same name with the prefix 'Provisional'. It has since been dropped. The Sinn Fein is the political arm of the IRA and is led by Gerry Adams. There is the moderate Social Democratic and Labour Party (SDLP), which was formed in 1973. Its leader is the highly respected John Hume.

Majid Siraj's book *Kashmir: Desolation or Peace* reveals that the Irish precedent is present in some Kashmiri minds. It is pretentious; the logic is weird. To compare the two situations, first "as the years of violence dragged on there was a steady convergence of London and Dublin opinions and of interests," McKittrick and McVea point out, despite disagreement on objectives and policies. Both governments loathed violence, recognized that a dispute existed and sought an accord. Their Prime Ministers became friends. In Kashmir, however, Pakistan launched a war in 1965 and a covert operation in 1989 while India refuses to recognize what is obvious to the whole world - the existence of an international dispute on Kashmir and consequently, the need to negotiate. All United Nations maps mention: "The final status of Jammu and Kashmir has not yet been determined." Even 'liberals' spout shibboleths of the kind never heard on territorial disputes in any other part of the world - "Kashmir is only a symptom, not the main cause of Indo-Pak confrontation."

Even if Pakistan is given Kashmir on a platter, its hostility will not abate. India's intransigence and evasion drove Pakistan to violence repeatedly argument may not hold good. But, in all these years one basic feature has been common to both Northern Ireland and Kashmir. As Prof Richard Rose wrote:

> "Northern Ireland is an insubordinate part of the United Kingdom - governed without consensus when it is governed at all. That is the Northern Ireland problem."

That is also the heart of the Kashmir problem. Prof Hiren Mukherjee, a highly respected leader of the Communist Party of India, said on February 25, 1994:

> "Even today, perhaps the best of us do not quite realize the depth of Kashmiri alienation and are unready to ponder ways and means of overcoming it."

Rigged polls were a consistent feature in both places, though the techniques differed.

> "Gerrymandering ensured that the symbolic unionist integrity of the six counties was maintained. In British eyes at least, a nominal unionist majority in Northern Ireland would be much discounted if Derry City, Fermanagh and Tyrone fell into nationalist hands."

In 1971, Indira Gandhi was concerned about Sheikh Abdullah and Mirza Afzal Beg contesting the Lok Sabha and Assembly polls. She feared a pro-independence vote by the Assembly. They were allowed to contest the polls only after the 1975 accord was imposed on them.

Affinities should not obscure dissimilarities. A statement by Peter Brooke, Secretary of State for Northern Ireland, on November 9, 1990, greatly impressed the IRA:

> "The British government has no selfish strategic or economic interest in Northern Ireland, our role is to help, enable and

> encourage. Britain's purpose is not to occupy, oppress or exploit, but to ensure democratic debate and free democratic choice."

Its main concern was to fulfil its pledge to Northern Ireland's Protestants that they would not be forced into a union with Catholic Ireland.

In total contrast, India has legitimate strategic, political and moral interests in Kashmir. Realistically, secession must be ruled out. Equally realistically, neither India's pledges to the people of Kashmir, to the international community and Pakistan - to abide by the people's wishes - nor the abiding alienation of the people can be ignored. The challenge to statesmanship lies in reckoning with all three factors - the solemn pledge to all; deep popularization; and the stark realities, which preclude secession.

Unionist leaders were complicit in rousing sectarian passions by their pointed demonization of the nationalist and Catholic aspirations. It was precisely such 'demonization' of Sheikh Abdullah by Indian politicians and the media that led to his dismissal from office as Kashmir's Prime Minister and to his imprisonment for 11 years. It fuelled alienation. Militancy sustains itself on alienation as well as illusion. "The fantasy of militarism itself being sufficient to weary Britain of its commitment to Ulster's unionists" had its counterpart in the fantasy of some militants in 1989 that New Delhi could be made to quit Kashmir.

In both cases, militancy spawned repressive laws, torture, terrorism - the militants' and also the State's - and the State's recourse to informers and dirty tricks. Irish militants were much more sophisticated and far better armed than militants in Kashmir, Punjab or north-eastern India. Nonetheless, preventive detention (internment) was used only briefly from August 9, 1971, to December 5, 1975. There was a host of judicial inquiries into the safeguards in special laws. In 1974 the Gardiner Committee was asked to consider, in the context of civil liberties and human rights measures to deal with terrorism. In 1983 Lord Jellicoe "found that some of those powers most likely to infringe civil liberties are also the least valuable and the least used."

Amnesty International and Human Rights Watch were granted easy access to Northern Ireland. They were never allowed in Kashmir; nor were the UN Special Rapporteur on Torture and the UN Working Group on Disappearances. As in New Delhi, there were repeated claims in London that "victory was around the corner" - as if a military solution can remove popular alienation.

But in contrast to New Delhi and Islamabad, there was in London the will to settle. Endgame in Ireland traces the negotiations from 1984 to 1998 and reveals the play of the back channel. British policy was based on a national consensus. Neither Labour nor the Conservatives exploited the issue for partisan gains. When in power, each forged rapport with its Dublin counterpart. Behind the 1998 accord lay several such accords spread over 25 years. An agreed communique was issued at Sunningdale on December 9, 1973, after four days of discussions between the two Prime Ministers and the political parties of Northern Ireland. In November the ruling UUP, the moderate Irish nationals led by John Hume of the SDLP and the Alliance Party of Northern Ireland (APNI) had already agreed to form a power-sharing executive. There was to be a Council of Ireland on which both Irish governments were to be represented equally with 'executive and harmonizing' functions in specific areas and a Consultative Assembly of 30 members from the Irish Parliament.

A 'Three Strands' formula had emerged – Anglo-Irish relations, intra-Irish relations and the internal set-up in Northern Ireland. This is an apt model to emulate: Indo-Pakistan cooperation, Srinagar-Muzaffarabad relations and a mutually guaranteed democratic set-up in Kashmir as well as in Pakistan Occupied Kashmir.

On July 6, 1992, for the first time since 1920, the two governments and the major political parties met to discuss the political future of Northern Ireland. There was no objection to 'tripartite' parleys. In a Joint Declaration on December 15, 1993, Prime Ministers John Major and Albert Reynolds reiterated the principle of popular consent on Ireland's unification. They adopted 'A New Framework for Agreement' on February 22, 1995, which defined the 'Three Strands' in detail. The UK published its framework for Northern Ireland. Later, on November 28, 1995, the Prime Ministers launched a 'twin-track' process.

The Accord of 1998 rests on the fundamentals agreed earlier in the 'Three Strands'. Ireland gave up its claims to Ulster and decided to delete Articles 2 and 3 of its Constitution. Decommissioning of arms was agreed. A North-South Ministerial Council as also a British-Irish Council were set-up beside the British-Irish Inter-Governmental Conference. Power-sharing arrangements rule out majoritarian rule in Northern Ireland. Key decisions will be taken 'on a cross-community basis'.

The Irish peace process has lessons of enduring relevance on two crucial issues. One is the linkage between a ceasefire and negotiations. The other is elections as a step towards negotiations.

There are gross misconceptions on both; and not among Indians alone. No militant group has ever agreed to a ceasefire unless it is linked firmly to serious talks. No government will agree to talk except after a ceasefire. Through mediators or domestic intelligence agencies, militants are contacted and promised talks in earnest. They declare a ceasefire. The talks follow. Witness: The Sri Lanka model. Both sides must recognize, in Adams' words:

> "There was no military solution; there had to be a political solution as this was not a military problem, it was a political problem."

Adams supported the IRA's brutal recourse to violence as 'necessary and morally correct'. He was secretly a member of its Army Council. Finton O'Toole of the *Irish Times* holds that his ambiguity itself "was one of the great assets of the peace process." He persuaded the IRA to decline a ceasefire, but is unable or unwilling - or both - to make it abide by the 1998 accord. If it persists, the accord will collapse. Using its cover, the IRA operated a spy ring in Belfast. Hence the withdrawal of devolution of power to Northern Ireland last October.

Contrast this with the ineptitude of the BJP government in responding to the Hizbul Mujahideen's public declaration of the ceasefire on July 24, 2000. The Hizb expected political talks in response. Home Ministry officials presented surrender terms at the very first meeting in Srinagar on August 3. The Hizb would be given protection as renegade militants. The Hizb wanted an assurance that Pakistan would be included in the talks. This was brusquely rejected.

Prime Minister Atal Bihari Vajpayee's ceasefire on November 19, 2000, collapsed for the same reason. He had nothing at all to offer to his ally Farooq Abdullah, let alone the militants. Agra (July 2001) showed he had nothing to offer to Pakistan, either. Deputy Prime Minister LK Advani made that even more explicit on March 16. He still harps on redressing the 'legitimate grievances' and on 'devolution of power' to Jammu and Kashmir; not even autonomy. The people, on the other hand, want a decision on the future of Jammu and Kashmir through an agreement between all the parties, including Pakistan, which assures them of real peace.

Its offer of fair elections in Kashmir was not intended as a step towards a final settlement since, in its view, there was nothing to settle. It was indeed intended to legitimize and freeze the *status quo*. The polls were not to promote a peace process but to abort it. The Election Commission held a free poll in 2002. Polls were rigged in the past to conceal popular alienation. The relatively free poll exposed it.

Full texts of three Reports - by the Institute of Social Sciences, New Delhi entitled "Fair Elections: Under the Shadow of Fear" by the Rural Litigation and Entitlement Kendra, Dehradun, entitled "Jammu and Kashmir Assembly Elections: 2002. How free and fair..."; and by the Coalition of Civil Society, Srinagar and Civil Society Initiatives, New Delhi entitled "Independent Election Observers Team Report" - fully expose the falsity of official claims. Popular indifference to the polls was as palpable as the use of duress in many parts. (Vide the writer's article "A Fractured Verdict", *Frontline*, November 8, 2002.)

Thus, elections were held only to provide a mandate for talks. In the Assembly elections, voters might opt for a candidate for his qualities. In a list system, they vote for the party. This Act is of great relevance to India since we face similar situations. It also empowered the holding of a referendum. One was held after the accord to ratify it.

How is this at all different from the stand taken by the All Parties Hurriyat Conference on elections? Its Chairman Prof Abdul Ghani Bhat told in July 2000 that they were "prepared to contest elections ... for a specific purpose; namely the future dispensation of Jammu and Kashmir. If this is agreed, we are prepared for it." (Vide the writer's article "A Report on Kashmir", *Frontline*, September 1, 2000.)

Elections to the Northern Ireland Assembly were held in June 1998 but under the 1998 accord; very much as in Punjab, Assam and Mizoram after accords on each of them. The Mizo accord provided for elections after "normalcy has returned and conditions are conducive to the holding of free and fair elections."

'Real' IRA Tried to Sabotage the Process

But the 1998 Accord has established a durable framework. This was made possible only because each side was bent on compromise and tried to address the concerns of the rest. London knew that Catholics in Northern Ireland must share power; that even if the IRA were crushed, Catholic alienation would remain. The IRA knew that there was no military solution. Dublin and the Sinn Fein accepted that the Protestant majority in Northern Ireland could not be forced into a union with the South. Most important of all, London realized that while a union was out, the yearning for Irish unity had to be met and met in a manner which satisfied Dublin and Sinn Fein.

Therein lies its relevance to Kashmir. India must reckon with popular alienation in the State as well as with Pakistan's unfortunate but legitimate interests as a party to the dispute, even while ruling out a plebiscite. Pakistan has been an interlocutor since 1947. But Kashmiris have become more assertive since 1989 in their claim to be a party in their right.

A format for the dialogue will have to be devised and all the three stands put in place – power sharing in all the regions of Kashmir; India-Pakistan accord; and, in such a context, links between both parts of the State. What is necessary, above all, is leadership in India and Pakistan which is durable, creative and competent to forge the national consensus for a compromise acceptable to the people in both countries and the people of Kashmir.

The Crimea referendum was a farce that Russia enacted after it took over. The Scottish and Quebec referendums have failed to achieve independence despite promising a lot. Most such referendums are pointless and may not work for Kashmir. Jammu and Kashmir is not a monolithic entity. It is comprised of three regions – Hindu Jammu, Buddhist Ladakh and Muslim Kashmir. These regions would likely vote differently. Why should Jammu follow Kashmir valley out of India [if Kashmir valley votes for independence, again hypothetically speaking]? If the State of Jammu and Kashmir votes out of India through a referendum, then logically Jammu and Ladakh need to have separate referendums to ask if they want to be separate, join the rest of India or stay with Kashmir. Some Muslim towns of Jammu might want to stay with Kashmir, while some Hindu villages of Kashmir might want to move where Jammu and India head. One Logic will be, you can infinitely keep reducing this process until you have no more to divide.

Now the most current is between Spain and Catalonia. The regional President, Carles Puigdemont, has repeated his determination to declare independence from Spain days after 90% of participants in a unilateral referendum voted for Catalonia to become a separate State. King Felipe made a rare television address, in which he accused Catalan authorities of attempting to break "the unity of Spain" and warned that their push for independence could threaten the country's social and economic stability. One side there are people's aspirations to carve out a new Nation-State and on the other side breaking of a historic State causing colossal stability challenge and a new problem. How small one wants to divide a country with their Azaadi aspiration is a matter of emotional debate.

I can go to my rooftop and want a separate kingdom of my own that includes just my house. The government can conduct a referendum with the people of my house and they might vote with me. My vote would make my home a new kingdom separate from the existing State and I don't need the input of any other folks in this decision. Would you call that absurd? Probably, "Yes." The same is true of all the referendums above. This is not even a theoretical worry but is a current event. In 2011, South Sudan won a separate country through a referendum. Now, it is in the midst of a major pandemonium, the breakdown in South Sudan. The Nuer people there don't want to stay with the rest of South Sudan and are leading a major armed struggle. Will they get their own North-East South Sudan? At what point does such a division end?

Why will India Never Let Go of Jammu and Kashmir?

Partitions are brutal. India suffered enormously in 1947. Ten million were displaced and 1 million of them died. The Indian Constitution was built on the idea that people of diverse languages, cultures and religions can live in harmony. If Kashmir breaks away, the fundamental assumption is broken. Soon, there will be anarchy all over India. People of different religions will ask for their nations [Khalistan modelled after the earlier formation of Pakistan], then different ethnicities will ask for their own [like what is happening with ULFA and others in North-East] and different economic classes [like what Naxals are doing] too. The problem is Indian citizens have multiple identities and these claims are overlapping.

Kashmir's breakaway could break the Indian union and we might see a sea of new States warring each other. Students of Indian history know what happens to the subcontinent when it is that way. India's greatness always came when the subcontinent was unified – like under the Maurya's (Emperor Ashoka), the Gupta's (Emperor Samudra Gupta), Vijaya Nagar Empire and later the Mughals (Akbar). The Indian subcontinent was geographically meant to be a single logical unit. That would make all the rivers originate and empty within its borders and provide adequate natural borders. Splitting this arrangement does terrible things for security and water sharing. In short, there is no logical way India will give up Kashmir. India's existence depends on it and the amputation of its head [regarding geography] will happen if someone more powerful can defeat the Indian army in its home field. There exist no such powers as of now. In fact, other than Pakistan no one even pays attention to the issue anymore.

Pre-1953 Approach

National Conference President and former Jammu and Kashmir Chief Minister Farooq Abdullah pitched for pre-1953 politico-constitutional position for the State. "Our struggle is for the restoration of autonomy of the State, pre-1953 position and Article 370 in its original form as agreed in the 1952 Delhi Agreement".

A pre-1953 position is impractical and nullifies the jurisdiction of the Supreme Court of India over J&K State.

Jammu and Kashmir acceded to India, but the ruler, in the 'instrument of accession', indicated that he was giving up control over only three subjects: Defence, Foreign affairs and Communications. The State held its constituent assembly in November 1952 (Delhi Accord of 1952) to ratify the accession and New Delhi's hold over the three subjects. This is what referred to as the pre-1953 status.

At that time the Constitution of India was already framed and reasons advanced to have this changed seem completely devoid of substance. In arriving at this arrangement, the main consideration was to secure a position for the State which would be consistent with the requirements of maximum autonomy for the local organs of State Power, which are the ultimate source of authority in the State while discharging obligations as a unit of the Federation. At the talks held between the representatives of the State Government and the Indian government, the Kashmiri delegation relented on just one issue: it conceded the extension of the Indian Supreme Court's arbitrating jurisdiction to the State in case of disputes between the federal government and the State Government, or between J&K and another State of the Indian Union.

But the delegation shrewdly disallowed an extension of the Indian Supreme Court's purview to the State as the ultimate arbitrator in all civil and criminal cases before J&K courts. It was also careful to prevent the financial and fiscal integration of the State with the Indian Union. The representatives of the J&K government ruled out any modifications to their land reform programme. It was also agreed that as opposed to the other units in the Union, the residual powers of legislation would be vested in the State Assembly instead of in the Centre. But this was an ephemeral victory. It became increasingly clear, over the years, that the autonomy issue remained unresolved and anti-autonomy factions in Jammu and Ladakh did not lose their political clout.

Where this proposal for autonomy can be faulted is that it does not take into account the Accord reached between Sheikh Abdullah and Indira Gandhi in February 1975. It should have formed the bedrock of the relationship because the Sheikh has sanctified it. He took over the reins in 1975 itself. He was the one who agreed to span the distance between 1952 and 1975.

The 1975 accord authorizes parliament to make laws to prevent "activities directed towards disclaiming, questioning or disrupting the sovereignty and territorial integrity of India or bringing about cession of a part of the territory of India from the Union or causing insult to the Indian national flag, the Indian national anthem and the Constitution." Why should the Farooq government feel shy about it? Apparently, there were differences over the interpretation of the 1975 accord. In a letter to Indira Gandhi, the Sheikh had said: "As you are aware, it is my view that constitutional relationship between the Centre and the State of Jammu and Kashmir should be what it was in 1953. Nevertheless (are mine), I am happy to say that the agreed conclusions (the 1975 accord) provide a good basis for my cooperation at the political level and Centre-State relationship."

Indian Defence Viewpoints on Kashmir Conflict Resolution Approach

As per Indian Army Head General Rawat, the asymmetric proxy war in J&K, waged by Pakistan can be efficiently handled by focusing on the new Centre of Gravity (CoG), which are People of Kashmir, Ideas, Emotions and Propaganda. In military terms, CoG is the source of power that provides moral or Physical strength, freedom of action, or will to act. It is the core centre of the adversary's strength the targeting of which is essential and around which a strategy is developed.

In the First Gulf War the CoG on which the US concentrated was the Iraqi Republican Guard; once neutralized, the rest was a cakewalk. In the Second Gulf War, the US and the allied forces focused on the regime change which made Saddam Hussein the CoG. It's a little more abstract than that in asymmetric warfare, where a campaign targeting a CoG may stretch for many years.

As far as India is concerned, she correctly identified the people of J&K as the CoG and yet made a mistake, the strategy was to work towards keeping people on India's side through SOP's, development work and good governance, to meet basic aspirations of physical comfort and quality of life. However, Pakistan and the Indian Separatists Leaders were working on the minds of the people, continuously impressing on them the ideas of 'Azaadi' and Islamic affinity.

Thus, the terrorists first targeted the locals who were not in line with terrorist thinking. Second, terrorist acts against the security forces were aimed at demoralizing and weakening them. The third aspect was the most important; Propaganda targeting the people to keep them wedded to the idea of sacrifice for 'Azaadi', the need for being a part of the larger Islamic movement (as a common trend across the globe with Paris etc bombing) of resistance to non-Islamic forces to remain steadfast anti-India. Indian strategy has only revolved around countering the first two aspects, both related to terrorists. The idea of a strategy to keep the people on India's side has only been supported by the Army's Operation.

Three decisions of Rawat stand out – rather, set him apart from the routine his predecessors followed. First, the decision to give a commendation card to Major Leethul Gogoi despite all the outrage, for tying up a Kashmiri stone-pelter to his vehicle as a human shield to bring out stranded polling staff. Second, ending the periodic government-military pay commission stand-off through a new deal despite internal resistance.

And third, moving a proposal to end the deployment of combatants as *'sahayaks'* in the face of continuing internal dissent.

By publicly acknowledging Major Gogoi's actions as correct and giving him a Chief of Army Staff (COAS) Commendation Card, Rawat cut through the army's iron-cast hierarchy to send a strong message of solidarity down to the last rifleman. Gogoi, after all, is one among them, who made it to the officer cadre. The strike rate through this channel is usually low, given the tedious transformation, one has to make from the lower ranks to the officer cadre. It's not just a job change but a class transformation in a highly conservative saheb-jawaan hierarchy, which has its roots in the colonial origins of the Indian Army.

As a result, the Army Chief has also set the stage for a fresh debate on bringing amendments to the Armed Forces (Special Powers) Act (AFSPA) to nullify the Supreme Court order in the matter, which includes a leeway to register FIRs on military encounters. In many ways, Rawat has ripped open a fundamental question of whether or not the time has come to officially frame the Valley as a 'war zone' to pre-empt a repeat of the late 1980s, the last turning point when Pakistan-sponsored militancy entrenched itself in the State.

Pay and pension privileges don't usually go with strategy-making in Kashmir. But these are files that may well lie side by side on an army chief's table. Regardless of the government in power, this is an issue on which the three service chiefs have mostly presented a united front, to the extent of being criticized as an 'unionized' front. And the Army Chief, by the sheer numbers of his force, is very much the fulcrum of this solidarity.

Rawat peeled away a bit, secured and consented to a deal that addressed the concerns of majority soldiers and ended a stalemate because of which the armed forces were not getting their new salaries. While the officer cadre may not have been fully satisfied, particularly at senior levels, the message was once again sent down the rank and file. The clearest message of recognizing the army's changing profile at the entry point was Rawat's move to push a proposal to bar combatants from being made *sahayaks*. He, instead, feels a small cadre of civilians should be hired for this purpose so that trained combatants don't have to do this job.

Lastly, as part of its civic action programme, the Indian Army has been conducting Bharat Darshan Tours for the Kashmiri Kids since 1999. The main purpose of such visit is to expose the children of remote areas to the historical, cultural and technological profile of the country as also the development and progress the country has achieved. Rawat had said:

> "This is a proxy war and proxy war is a dirty war. It is played in a dirty way. The rules of engagements are there when the adversary comes face-to-face and fights with you. It is a dirty war.... That is where innovation comes in. You fight a dirty war with innovations."

Colonel Anil A Athale (Retd) warns:

> "The Pakistan army feels it can inflict a similar defeat on India in Kashmir and make it 'India's Bangladesh'.... But comparing Bangladesh of 1971 with the Kashmir valley of 2018 is like equating chalk and cheese."

On May 3, 2017, during a border skirmish, Pakistani troops and jihadi elements killed two Indian soldiers in the Nangi tekdi area of Krishna Ghati near Poonch in Jammu and Kashmir. As has happened earlier as well, the Pakistanis then carried out a ritual beheading of the soldiers and mutilated their dead bodies. As expected it has sent shock waves through the nation and calls for suitable revenge. What is the logic behind these incidents?

What does Pakistan hope to achieve through these un-soldierly acts? It is time citizens understand the mindset and strategy that lies at the root of this savagery. The Nangi Tekdi areas, where the clash took place, was captured from Pakistan in the 1971 war. The area is thickly wooded and consists of undulating hillocks, making it difficult to patrol. After the 1971 war and ceasefire, a narrow strip of land with the Poonch river behind is controlled by Pakistan. Most posts here are small strength and non-tactically located. These are vulnerable to Indian retaliation.

Could this have been a 'local' initiative? Possible, given the geography of the area. After all, how many times has one seen this kind of churlish behaviour from Pakistan? Does one remember the many time's Pakistani authorities 'accidentally' put the Indian flag upside down on vehicles for Indian dignitaries?. For the uninitiated, an upside down flag is a symbol of a defeated nation. Countless Indian army messes have captured Pakistani flags upside down on display.

Forty-six years have passed since the Pakistan army's defeat, yet it appears that the flame of revenge burns bright. It is reported that Pakistani army officers take an oath to avenge the 1971 humiliation when they are commissioned into the military. The Pakistan army feels it can inflict a similar defeat on India in Kashmir and make it 'India's Bangladesh'.

Raids on the border, support for Kashmiris fighting India, training jihadis like the LeT (Lashkar-e-Taiba) or Jaish-e-Mohammed and infiltrating terrorists into India is the methodology of this proxy war. The justification is that like India trained the Mukti Bahini irregulars in East Pakistan in 1971, so Pakistan is supporting the uprising in the Kashmir valley.

It has to be accepted that at least four to five districts in the Kashmir valley have indeed seen an uprising against India.

But comparing Bangladesh of 1971 with the Kashmir valley of 2018 is like equating chalk and cheese.

For starters, the Kashmir valley forms a minuscule part of Jammu and Kashmir, leave alone a continent-sized nation like India. Erstwhile East Pakistan was half the country and more than 50% of the population had revolted. Strategically, Bangladesh was isolated from West Pakistan and surrounded by India from three sides and blockaded by the ocean on the fourth. The Kashmir vale is neither isolated nor surrounded by Pakistan. In the early stages of the 1971 war, India destroyed the Pakistan air force in the east and had complete air supremacy. India also had superiority on the ground.

Even if one is to accept the possibility that the Chinese will take an active part (a very doubtful proposition), the Indian armed strength can more than match the deployable Chinese and Pakistan combined strength. General Rawat has made that statement already, India can take two and a half enemies together. This strategic calculus is necessary as in the case of Bangladesh's liberation, while the Mukti Bahini and popular support did play a major role, the coup de grace was delivered by the Indian armed forces. Does the 'professional' Pakistan army think it has the kind of superiority needed for this?

The Indian campaign to liberate Bangladesh evoked international support. Kashmiri separatism in the valley, with Islamic State flags on display and the possibility of the emergence of another terrorist haven, has elicited lukewarm world opinion.

In 1990, when the situation in the Kashmir valley was on the boil, Robert Gates, then the CIA Director visited India and Pakistan to defuse the crisis. Gates is reported to have told Pakistani Generals that the Americans had war-gamed India-Pakistan wars several times and in every possible scenario, it ended in defeat for Pakistan.

Finally, there is the nuclear dimension. No country in the world, including Pakistan's all-weather friend China, wants to see the use of nuclear weapons in a conflict. The basic lesson of nuclear deterrence is that it can deter an attack, but not grant any advantage in an offensive. To understand the Pakistan army's behaviour and its rationale in keeping the borders alive, we have to look elsewhere, to the internal dimension of Pakistan.

Support for jihadi organizations is dictated by the widespread public support for the Kashmir cause in Pakistan.

Besides, given its galloping population, unemployment and dire economic conditions, jihad and keeping the India-Pakistan pot boiling is the only viable option to keep the young, restive population engaged. Jihad against India is an employment opportunity for Pakistan's restive youth. Though fully aware that it cannot achieve military success against India, border incidents and killings keep the fires of India hate burning in Pakistan. This then conjures up an India threat and ensures the Pakistan army's primacy in politics and economics of that country. One possible Pakistani calculation in mutilating Indian soldiers' bodies is to be found in the logic that this will weaken support for the Modi government's Kashmir policy.

Pakistanis ought to have noted that every victim's family have felt proud of their sacrifice and wants a lesson to be taught to Pakistan. Instead of weakening the resolve, these acts have given rise to anger and the resolve to avenge. India is ready for any such false bravado surge from Pakistan and this time the plan and communication from the political leadership is very clear, "the permanent solution for Kashmir" in particular and India-Pakistan border issue in general, needs to be solved militarily. The $ 2 trillion-plus economy and world's 3rd strongest army is ready to face world 8th strongest army but with a bankrupt economy. In fact, under the able leadership of General Rawat, Army has a roadmap to take Pakistanis and Chinese armies simultaneously. The money for funding such programmes has to come from the robust economy and hence the growth rate of 8% for next two decades is paramount.

Doves *vs* Hawks Approach for this Bermuda Conundrum

Doves and Hawks are terms applied to people based upon their views about a military conflict. A dove is someone who opposes the use of military pressure to resolve a dispute; a hawk favours entry into the war. The terms came into widespread use during the Vietnam War, but their roots are much older than that conflict. The association of doves with peace is rooted in the biblical story of the Great Flood: the dove that Noah released after the rains had stopped, returned with an olive branch, the symbol of peace and a sign that the waters had receded from the ground. 'War hawk' was applied to advocates of war in the United States as early as 1798 when Thomas Jefferson used it to describe Federalists ready to declare war on France.

The juxtaposition of the two terms originates in a 1962 account of the Kennedy administration's decision making process during the Cuban missile crisis. The hawk-dove antithesis quickly became a popular way of labelling partisans in the Vietnam debate. But it also oversimplified their differences. The term 'dove' was applied both to those who supported US intervention to stop the spread of communism, but who opposed military means and to those who opposed US intervention altogether. The latter was also sometimes called other names such as 'Peaceniks'.

Hawks

Divide Indian J&K into two parts, first part a small region of the Kashmir Valley, name it 'Al-Ard Al-Mubarakah', with five million anti-India and pro-Pakistani Muslims. Remaining Ladakh, Gilgit-Baltistan, Jammu and part of Kashmir excluding Valley and also AJ&K, call it 'Himalayan Pradesh'. Stop Electricity, Water and any support Indian taxpayers give to this newly divided region, let them take it from Pakistan or China with Indian government consent, the payment, etc should be done by valley folks to these vendors. Dump entire war-related equipment and testing arsenals here and make it India's nuclear cum aggressive army command. Remove AFSPA and keep Article 370 and 35A. Governor should always come from Indian army of this newly carved State. Let them choose their Chief Minister based on the multi-party election. It should be landlocked with no outsider entry into this part for few decades. On the same line, No one is allowed to visit native American reserve areas.

For the remaining 'Himalayan Pradesh', remove Article 370 and 35A, dump billions of rupees, develop it into a most advanced State not only in India but the world. This should be shown as a real democratic State with freedom/Azaadi to do whatever within the

Indian Constitution guideline. It should have Hindu, Sikh and Sufi-Islam and Buddhist universities of international repute. Go to UN make one last presentation and announce with the big bang of India pulling the case and let the UN members feel whatever they think. India is too powerful to fall into this line of every year UN presentation and hear Pakistani's narrative every year. Have seats in this new Himalayan Pradesh for Gilgit-Baltistan and PQK giving them proper representation based on their current population count.

Allow army to go full hound anytime a terror happens either within the State of Kashmir valley or from the across of LoC. Every time we have incursion or terror attack, we should have the policy and military might of moving the border towards Pakistan near the original border by 2-5 km based on the terrain support. Separatists and Hurriyat's are Indian citizens and we cannot constitutionally deport them, even if they have venom or anger against India, will have to engage them as we have done for very long time. In a democratic set-up, you cannot take out any citizen by force. Try them in the court if the country thinks they had something provable in the Indian courts and based on the court's verdicts try them for treason or whatever. But have a clear-cut policy.

India needs to show the world how they can handle Islamists, forget about any other power – their support or criticism. Be ruthless when you unearth them or their sympathizers or funders. Just remove them once for all, no trial in civilian court. There should be a separate court formed called 'Indian-Israel-Liberal Islamist' with ETA to decide on such cases in 3-5 hearings max. Balochistan should be accepted as an independent country, have them run a government in exile like Tibetan government in exile running from Himachal Pradesh.

Resettlement for Hindus (Sikhs, Jains and Buddhists)

Resettlement for Hindus, Sikhs, Jains and Buddhists by voluntary acceptance, in response to a nationally announced scheme, which should also declare the risks involved (possible loss of life). Have 1 crore (10 million) ex-army men, other security personnel and their families identified who still can skilfully pick up arms and have them settled in South Kashmir. This should be followed by the return and settlement of the Kashmiri Pandits. Minimum one acre or more size of the land to be granted free for life per family. This will be one move that, for once, will utilize India's humongous population positively to solve this vexed legacy from the partition and beyond. China has done this in Tibet; UN will have no issue with this already implemented approach, as one of its veto power enabled permanent member has done it.

Tarek Fatah – An eminent Pakistan born Canadian writer and also a good friend of India has following things to say after his Kashmir visit. "Death to Israel", the banner screamed. Next to it was the now-familiar Muslim chant, "Death to America." Further down the road, the late Ayatollah Khomeini stared down angrily at the citizenry of India. As a large crowd of Sunday shoppers milled around an overflowing open-air bazaar, other banners showed Sayed Nasrallah of Hezbollah, with former Iranian President Mahmoud Ahmadinejad wearing his familiar sheepish grin. No, I was not in Tehran or South Lebanon. This wasn't an Alawite stronghold in Syria or scenes from Toronto's infamous annual 'Al-Quds' rally staged by Islamists belching disdain towards the West. I was in Srinagar, the summer capital of the Indian State of Jammu and Kashmir. Unfortunately, the NDA government also took the same UPA government stand when voting in UN on Jerusalem, standing with the Arabs, and going against Trump and Netanyahu. India is not going to be a strong ally of US with these non-aligned approaches.

Flaunting hatred and celebrating jihadi terrorists was once unthinkable in the city referred as a paradise on earth. Home to a people of incredible beauty, culture and cuisine, where an Islam once flourished that was bereft of the harshness of the desert and mosques took architectural inspiration from Buddhist pagodas. Pakistan-backed insurgency broke out in 1989-90 and had been largely decimated by the Indian Army and the Kashmir government, consequences of the decade-long strife remain. After all, almost the entire Hindu population of the valley was ethnically cleansed and forced to flee their ancestral homeland. The hope of one segment of the population that Kashmir would join Islamic Pakistan seems a verminous dream.

There is a recognition in the valley that being puppets in the hands of Islamabad's deep state and its State-sanctioned jihadi terror networks, offers Muslim Kashmiris no better life than what Pakistan has provided to the 100 million Bengalis who seceded from the country to form Bangladesh in 1971. It was never a nationalist cause where Kashmir's Muslims and Hindus would live as equals in a secular, liberal democracy, but now Pan-Islamism is unashamedly touted as the basis of a future State. Today's militant Islamic youth of Kashmir carry placards of Osama bin Laden in anti-India rallies and hoist ISIS flags, while Khomeini and Hezbollah inspire their Shia Muslim rivals. A senior Kashmiri Muslim police officer confided "over 50% of Kashmiris between the ages of 15 and 30 are hard-core Pan-Islamists, not Kashmiri nationalists."

Yasin Malik, Chairman of the Jammu Kashmir Liberation Front and a darling of the left parties, once said that Islam, as in the past, can still lead the whole world if Muslims unite and become one body. While New Delhi seems to believe it has put down a Pakistani-backed uprising, it will be remiss if it does not pay attention to this banner, hung across the city's Bud Shah Bridge fly-over that lies in the shadows of the State legislature; "Beware of the leaders of American Islam, whether they are in the garb of religious scholars or the shape of politicians."

India is a civilization that has a past and future. In spite of being assaulted and attacked and plundered over a thousand years, it has risen again. On the other hand, Pakistan is not a nation; it's just a state of mind. There are no such people as 'Paki' like we have Afghans in Afghanistan, Kazakhs in Kazakhstan and Balochs in Balochistan. Where are the Pak people from in history?

Top Indian strategic thinker and a renowned politician, academician and a Hindu leader Subramanian Swamy have following to say when suggesting for a solution on Kashmir and India-Pakistan in general. He suggested three parts to his proposed strategy.

- Immediate Action – More of Operating Strategy
- Medium-Term Strategy
- Long-Term Strategy

The next strategy that India can follow with Pakistan should be the removal of the Most Favoured Nation clause of trade between the two nations. Immediate closure of the Pakistan embassies in India, except one in Delhi. Their ringleader Abdul Basit has been a huge disappointment. There are some one thousand staffs in Pak embassy of Delhi and three hundred of them in Mumbai. These staffs are almost recruited by ISI with some agendas. They are playing havoc with the local Indian Muslims, as seen in case of Hurriyat's, how they are invited for photo ops during Eid and other Muslim festivals by Abdul Basit, entirely against the ethics of an ambassador in the host country.

For the Medium-term, Swami suggests Indian Army to target forty-two identified India centric terror camps operating from Pakistani soil with tactical support of their Army and ISI with the weak civilian government being fence watcher. He thinks US type drone attacks or even more surgical bombings should start for very long and sustained period. One of the residents of these 42 camps is

Jamaat-ud-Dawa (JuD) Chief Hafiz Muhammad Saeed, the most influential terrorist of Pakistan.

For long-term strategy he suggests – India should work for breaking Pakistan into four parts and should start this by recognizing Balochistan right away, giving political asylum to the Brahumdagh Bugti, son of the great Akbar Shahbaz Khan Bugti, who was brutally booted to death by the Pakistani army on the order of the General Musharraf at the ripe age of 79 and have him run his Baloch government in exile from Delhi or Jammu as India did to Tibet.

Doves

'Atoot Ang', 'Shah Rug', 'Kashmir Banega Pakistan', 'Bharat tere tukre honge hazaar, Inshallah, Inshallah' and 'Azaadi-Azaadi' dominate our image of the place, conjuring up visions of frenzied crowds and disfigured faces pockmarked and blinded. The ugly pictures of the results of crowd control measures repel sensitive Indians. The question is: what is to be done?

First, we should rule out what cannot be done. A plebiscite is not possible. Of the many resolutions the UN passed on Kashmir, only two are relevant to the plebiscite: those of August 13, 1948 and January 5, 1949. A plebiscite was to follow the complete withdrawal of tribal invaders and Pakistan forces from the invaded areas of Jammu and Kashmir, after which India would draw down its forces to a number just sufficient to maintain law and order and hold a plebiscite. Pakistan never withdrew its troops and one cannot imagine it withdrawing them now. That rules out a plebiscite permanently.

Imagining what can be done in Kashmir requires suspending prejudice and abandoning preconceived notions. The grievances of Kashmir's Muslims are not only genuine; they fester at the core of their emotional being. Any workable solution begins with recognition by Delhi that the root of the problem lies in its actions since 1953, bearing in mind that what would have worked in the '80s had lost traction in the '90s and the openings available in the new millennium may no longer work in 2018. Despite the hardline SAS Geelani and the more recent Islamist tendency among young protesters it is wrong to suppose that there are no reasonable voices left in Kashmir. It is not possible in this short piece to detail the grievances Kashmiris have against India, many real, some imagined. They have multiplied as the decades passed. The Sheikh's arrest, rigged elections, police rule under Bakshi and his successors are some.

After militancy erupted, India's record of human rights violations, the humiliations inflicted on Kashmiris and the sheer indifference to their plight only added to the alienation. India prides itself on its democratic traditions and the rule of law. Kashmiris have seen little of either. They firmly believe that Sheikh Abdullah made the wrong choice in 1947 when he chose Hindu India over Muslim Pakistan. But then who was he to make that call at that time, he was not a Maharaja? As per guidelines set by the colonial power British for the princely States, it was the King that was to choose the instrument of annexation with India or Pakistan.

Any workable solution, therefore, must address the full gamut of Kashmiri anger, even if no solution can fully assuage the intense negative sentiment about India. It is a feeling of impotence against an overbearing Indian State that propels successive generations to the increasingly violent expression of their rage. In the short run, India can hope at best to neutralize the anger. It cannot build emotional bridges, let alone win hearts.

The solution must distinguish between the Kashmir problem, which is an international issue between India and Pakistan and India's problem in Kashmir, which is a domestic matter. The Kashmir problem may never be solved, but India's problem in Kashmir is amenable to positive outcomes even now. Subtly handled it can have a favourable impact on the international issue as well. A flexible approach will allow various paths to a solution. It must be acceptable to the majority of Kashmiris as well as satisfy Jammu's Hindus and Ladakhi Buddhists and non-Kashmiri Muslims. It must provide respectable position for the expelled Pandits living in forced exile.

Amendments can always take care of constitutional impediments if they arise. In fact, the J&K Constitution will need amendment too. Separatists are prone to think of J&K as sacrosanct: it is however only the malformed and malfunctioning product of a treaty between Gulab Singh and the British, a treaty upon which Kashmiri leaders regularly heap curses.

It is possible to make the entire State autonomous as the Constitution envisages, or only parts of it, such as the Valley and if the residents want, the adjoining Muslim majority areas. Regional autonomy is possible for Ladakh and Jammu. Special relationships between Delhi and some parts of the State such as Leh can be envisaged in a deal, which gives Kashmir full autonomy over all matters outside those specified in Article 370.

Pandits who want to return should be enabled to do so, unconditionally. It is their legal right; Kashmiri Muslim clusters have come up in Jammu city without interference from its Hindus, the same principle applies to the Pandits. Government sponsored colonies are a bad idea; but what is there to prevent housing cooperatives and private realty firms?

Perhaps the point that raises the most concern is that the youth, all born in the troubled decade of the '90s or the even more troubled 21st century, are under no one's control and are operating at no one's behest other than their volition. Even the Hurriyat and its Chairman, Geelani, are being sidelined. Zakir Musa is the rising voice, threatening to overtake even Geelani, thundering that he will behead any Hurriyat leader who describes the Kashmir issue as a 'political issue', when it is, in fact, an 'Islamic' issue.

That is what makes it imperative that India talks now. There is a fundamentalist Islamic revolution unfolding in our midst, Valley's anger is at the 'humiliation' being inflicted by the Centre. Governmental conduct at State, national and regional levels had to be 'changed' so that a national consensus is evolved on 'nationally important issues'.

All the anecdotes I am trying to bring for my readers is to show the correlation between Kashmir Conflict and Islamic Superiority mindset and its direct conflict with the idea of plural and secular India. One thing is clear that separatist Muslims cannot be secular as per the definition of secularism provided in the Indian Constitution and no disrespect to them but in Islam Politics and Religion goes hand in hand and there is still a debate on whether Islam accepts the idea of the Nation-State. If Muslims are in the majority they want to be governed under Sharia laws, Fifty plus Islamic countries are examples were Minorities have negligible or no religious rights. When the Muslims are in Minority, then they need 'secular' governance protection and demand to protect their rights be it Triple Talaq, Halala, Haj grants, Ram Mandir type issues, Kashmir Azaadi and Plebiscite demands.

Now any community can have such desires, but then in the game of existence, there has to be an even play, you have to choose only one system. You can't run with the fox and hunt with the hounds. Kashmir problem as it first appeared in 1947 was plain and simple, the decision to join India or Pakistan based on what the ruler of the day chooses. This same rule was applicable to all the 562 or so princely States, now all the princely States that were in Indian region joined India and the matter was closed, only Three Musketeers, the princely States of Junagadh (Gujarat), Hyderabad (Telangana) and Kashmir (J&K), created problem for India and their smooth transition to the Indian government. The interesting correlation exists. First two had the Muslim rulers but majority Hindu population and the third one, Kashmir had a Hindu King but majority Muslim population led by a popular Muslim leader. All these three were the main proponent of anti-India tirade.

So who were the troublemakers? Muslim ruler of Junagadh, Muslim Nawab of Hyderabad and popular Muslim leader of Kashmir, Sheikh Abdullah. All these Muslim dissidents opposed the Instrument of Annexation. Pakistan still shows Junagadh (Gujarat) for their part. Question to be asked to all the liberals and human rights activists why Muslims cannot stay in secular India and govern by the Constitution of the land?

There is two-fold problem here. One is the larger political disconnect, which is deep-rooted and will not go away, irrespective of which government is in Srinagar (J&K) and Delhi, unless it is seriously addressed. The other is a sense of alienation which finds a violent expression in stone pelting that has caught the fascination of all ages, genders and areas now. Boys and girls as young as twelve are influenced. It is disconnecting and disillusionment is operating at different levels that have made space for an organized rebellious activity and India can't afford to see everything getting wiped out in front of her eyes. It has to be a multi-pronged strategy that is sensitive to various facets of the problem.

On meeting students from the valley one sense deep distress and anger. No one has ever heard them out. There's a wave of anger against local police on FIR etc probe done against them and like any Asian country they have to grease the palm to get out of these troubles. Most of them have not attained voting age and hence no political outfit interested in them as they are no vote bank. All these are making them fodder for radicalization. Thanks to the continuous pump of money from Saudi Arabia and their way of Islam, the Wahhabism. Not sure why at the government level these issues are not yet addressed.

India has to ask direct questions, why are so many youngsters being killed and injured in the firing, why aren't the people responsible for law enforcement finding innovative ways to prevent it? With all the gruesome videos that are making way into the public domain with no checks, Kashmiris resonates with every killing that took place. Burhan Wani killing was the trigger point. Every case must be thoroughly investigated; a panel needs to be formed consisting of these youths. Make them the jury giving them a sense of involvement; this will help bring them to the mainstream again. NDA government has already pardoned some five thousands of them listed for stone pelting. Good beginning but new local leaders need to be groomed.

If India views its Kashmiri youths only through the prism of law and order and doesn't come up with a cogent plan for engagement, it is not going to work, no matter how much force is used. We are dealing with a tech-savvy, sensitive, politically conscious, intelligent generation. They have no appetite for gimmickry and bluster. We have to reach out sincerely, make the administration responsive and create opportunities at all levels by improving governance. The role of those responsible for keeping order will need to be evaluated and redefined. Systems should be set in place to heal and not aggravate the problem.

The way mainstream politics is conducted currently in the State wouldn't work. We won't be able to sustain it in this way too long. We need to engage with other political parties. The opposition is not an enemy but an opponent. We need to get together and engage each other, come up with a common front. We have a lot in common and if we don't understand the seriousness of the threat against all of us, we will cease to exist sooner than later. It is not a question of power anymore. It is a question of order. We can't allow Kashmir to slip into anarchy from where there is no coming back. We have to come together to convince Delhi regarding the need for immediate de-escalation and engagement in Kashmir.

Kashmiri's opposition to the mainstream Indian system also needs to understand that our loss isn't necessarily their gain. Currently, it is a loss for all of us. We are together in this boat; we are all going to drown together. The idea of mainstream is under challenge this time. If all of us are seen as on this side of the fence and the public sentiment is on the other side, then we become the fringe. This is a reality that I am quite aware of. That is why rather than pulling one another down, should come together to reclaim the lost ground. If India has to grow as shown in the chart, it has to solve the Kashmir issue as soon as possible.

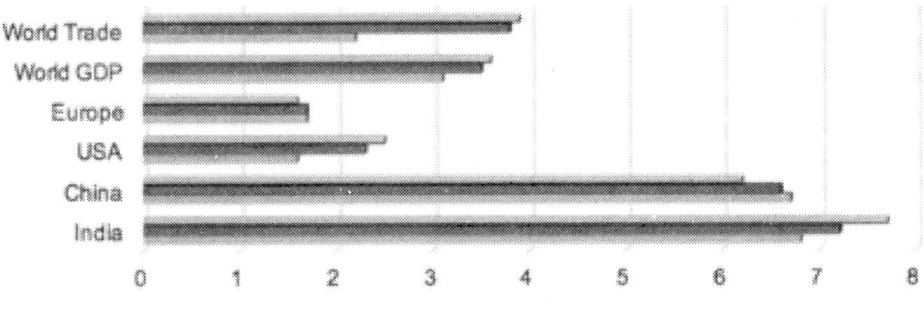

As per IMF data: YOY actual and Projected Growth Rate of the Economy

Subramanian Swamy – In Dove Avatar

There are two fixed parameters within which a solution to the Kashmir issue has to be found:

1. That neither of the parties, India or Pakistan, can be made worse off and the solution benefits both.
2. That Kashmir should not be partitioned. All the solutions proposed to date fall outside one or both of the above-stated parameters and thus are not sustainable.

Possible path to the solution are as following:

Step 1 (Year 1): The two areas of Kashmir on either side of the ceasefire line under the aegis of their respective Election Commissions should initiate the process to elect members to a Joint Kashmir Assembly, much as the independent countries of Europe do for electing MPs to the European Parliament. This forum should function on an agreed schedule of subject division and at the same time as the two existing assemblies (with the caveat that in the Pakistan-held areas, the local assembly has to be elected: the present nominated bodies cannot be accepted). Furthermore, the 5,00,000 Kashmiri Pandits must be enabled to return to the Valley and empowered to vote since ethnic cleansing is not acceptable.

Step 2: All restrictions for travel in undivided Kashmir (over a period of two years) should be removed. This would be without prejudice to known positions of the two countries on the Kashmir dispute. Hence, by Year 5, the first requirement of creating a united Kashmir would be achieved.

Step 3 (Year 7): After that, India and Pakistan should work out the common market and free trade arrangements through the SAARC.

Step 4 (Year 10): At the end of 10 years, India and Pakistan should work to have a South Asian Parliament with a charter on the division of subjects for legislation.

Step 5 (Year 11): A review to determine whether to stop here, or proceed further to even greater unity in the South Asian subcontinent. It will be at this stage that a solution to the Kashmir problem, will become visible.

Spiritual Gurus Pastoral Symphonies

Prayer is the best healers for the humanity. Before I proceed further let me share with you all a lovely prayer that was part of my childhood days.

Prayer

Make God Your Guru
Let Him tell you what to do
Listen He's calling clear and true
Take time to listen
Take courage to obey
Inner voice is calling calling you
There are voices all around me
My enemies and my friends
Do this don't do that the chorus never ends
But I shall always listen to that quiet inner voice
Which is sweet and gentle
And I have made my choice

I use to sing this often in my school's music class, I had a great school 'De Nobili School', headed by Father SA George Hess, a real spiritual guru, who influenced me with his simplicity, kindness and knowledge. He told a story to make us understand this prayer. The story is like this.

Once there was a man who went for trekking. There was some mistake that happened and he found himself hanging on to the rope when it was pitch dark. He was in a fix and didn't know whom to call, except for of course God. He called out to God for help and He immediately responded. He prayed to God to help him. God said to him "my son, just leave the rope and I shall save you." This man did not believe it and did not have the courage to do what the voice he heard said though he knew that it was God's. The next day the newspapers read "one man was found dead hanging on to a rope one inch above the ground...."

If there is total hopelessness reach out to God, the Almighty or a guru. I thought of taking my book forward from the negativism to the more spiritual treatment of a problem which many will not agree to be an only political problem. If it is also or only religious then who better than the most revered spiritual guru of our time to find solace and guidance on the potential solution for the problem, His Holiness Sri Dalai Lama, Buddhist guru and a world leader.

Dalai Lama, Tibetan spiritual leader has advocated dialogue as the only way to resolve any issue, he said:

> "Kashmiri people should live peacefully and if there is any problem, the dialogue is the only way (to resolve issues). Violence is in nobody's interest. A peaceful way is essential."

Sri Sri Ravi Shankar, founder of the Art of Living Foundation and spiritual leader once said:

> "*Kashmir ka hal Kashmiryion se hi aa sakta hai, bahar se nahi ho sakta* (the solution to the Kashmir problem can only come from the Kashmiris). Solutions cannot be found in the streets, not with stones and guns."

Cardinal Oswald Gracias of Mumbai, India – President of the Federation of Asian Bishops' Conference and Cardinal Baselios Cleemis, President of the Indian Bishop's Conference and a close adviser to Pope Francis as a member of his 'C9' council of cardinal advisers, says "We ask Jesus, the Prince of Peace, to fill India and Pakistan and the world, with his peace. We ask upon Mary, Queen of Peace, to intercede for us [so that] the Indian and Pakistani nations may walk in the way of peace."

Jain Muni Sagar Ji Maharaj – Wants Political parties and the Government of India to come out with a solution on Kashmir which does not hurt anyone's sentiment.

Maulana Wahiduddin Khan, Islamic Scholar, peace activist and Padma Bhushan awardee has below advised –

> "I have done extensive research on the Kashmir issue and my firm opinion is that it was a relatively simple matter, which became complex because of the immature leadership of Kashmir. If the real context of an issue is changed, it becomes complex. The case of Kashmir was a secular matter but it was made religious and this made it complex. They made it an issue of establishing Nizam-e-Mustafa (Establishment of Islamic Shariah). For example, Muslims in India participate in all aspects of life and avail all benefits but if Indian Muslims were to start a campaign to establish Nizam-e-Mustafa in India, they would lose everything. Muslims cannot think of progressing separately from the rest of the country, that, if they isolate themselves from the rest of India, they certainly cannot develop. Kashmir issue was a secular issue and it had to be solved within the secular parameters. The Indian government had taken the right stand in this matter by offering to grant a special status to Kashmir under the Article 370 of the Indian Constitution. The then Prime Minister PV Narasimha Rao had defined it as a case of autonomy and had given Kashmir the right to be an autonomous State while still being a part of the country. This was a great opportunity for Kashmir. This is the same as in the United States of America where fifty States exist and all of them enjoy autonomy. This has

> been the secret of America's progress and would have become the secret of success of Kashmir had they opted to go with the offer of Indian government. Unfortunately, the leadership of Kashmir could not take the right decision and this best offer was rejected. This is the only way out from this current situation."

Unfortunately not all Islamic leaders and countries endorse secularism.

The Grand Mufti of Jerusalem, **Hussam ad-Din Jarallah** in 1951, became a staunch defender of Pakistani claims to Kashmir after visiting Pakistan that year. He said let each one spend some time in prayer for peace in Kashmir, to work for peace, to become bridge builders and to commit ourselves personally to the defence and promotion of the fundamental good which is peace.

Aga Khan, spiritual leader of the 15-million strong Ismaili community worldwide, said Kashmir is perceived as an example of injustice, along with Palestine, by the Arab world. However, the Aga Khan did not elaborate on this statement.

Modi Government Policy on Kashmir

During the height of the Kargil crisis in 1999 when Narendra Modi was the Chief Minister of Gujarat State, an Indian Air Force fighter pilot mistakenly put a Pakistani military base in its sights and was ready to bomb it, but was pulled back by his superiors. According to the Indian Air Force officials who were then holding senior positions in the Air Force's Western Air Command, a flight commander was tasked to bomb Point 4388 in Kargil but he instead ended up aiming at a Pakistani military base in Gulteri through a cockpit laser designation system (CLDS).

Under the protocol, a Jaguar pilot first 'lased over' the area using the CLDS while a second Jaguar was to drop the bomb on the target coming in the pre-designated path identified by the first one. 'Lasing' refers to locking in on the coordinates of a target. Such a protocol of using two fighter jets was used then as only trainer Jaguars had the CLDS system. The Pakistani media had reported on June 25, 1999, that both Nawaz Sharif and Pervez Musharraf were present at the base when it became the focus of the Indian Air Force jet's target, even though the government – then headed by Atal Bihari Vajpayee – had not allowed the IAF to cross over the Line of Control. If the political leaders had not intervened in military decisions since Nehru's time lot of India's territorial and border problems would have been resolved. Unfortunately, this interference inside military action continued even till Vajpayee's NDA.

Now consider this, Musharraf in an interview mentioned that Pakistan was ready with the nuclear war in 2001. Imagine if they had gone ahead with it and here the Indian Air Force missile had zeroed on this General to blow the very finger which could have become the reason for million death in the subcontinent, alas only to be denied by the political masters. My point is simple, do not create a situation for war, war is destruction. But once the politician makes that decision, stick to it and let the army do as per their SOP's and capabilities.

Under Modi's leadership, things are positively changing and such political hara-kiri has changed into iron hand decision making. This has resulted in the Surgical Strike, heavy retaliatory fires on being provoked and even crossing the LoC and taking the fight directly inside Pakistan not just against non-State actors but also their army. All these decisions are now being made at the local and central level of the army with full autonomy, which missed badly during UPA's rule. The Diplomatic initiatives launched by Prime Minister Narendra Modi achieved its main objective. For the first time, the world accepted the Narendra Modi doctrine that terrorism anywhere is a threat to the human race and that Pakistan has become the epicentre of terrorism for the world over. The US went ahead and declared Hizbul Mujahidin chief Syed Salahuddin a global terrorist.

China stands out as the sore thumb, indirectly supporting the notorious terror perpetrators ensconced in the western neighbourhood and openly courting Pakistan with heavy defence and commercial investments. China last year vetoed an Indian resolution to ban Jaish-e-Mohammed Chief Masood Azhar. The timing of the Chinese action now would look as if that country was offering sops to Pakistan at a time when the world at large is beginning to look at it as a rogue State. Like Pakistan offering covering fire for terrorists to sneak into India, the dragon is spitting fire against India in a bid to divert world attention from Pakistan's discomfiture.

In the last three years, Modi has consolidated his position as a world leader. The strategic alliance he is building with Israel, Russia and the US has piqued its western neighbour. Even Russia, which at one time was moving closer to China, is today a huge trade and defence partner with India and commercial interests have made it positively disposed towards this country. Pakistan and China are further rattled by the joint military exercises India is engaged in with US, Japan, Israel and South Korea. When China opened a corridor to West Asia through Pak-occupied Kashmir, India responded by developing the Chabahar Port in Iran and a road link connecting Iran, Afghanistan and into the heartland of the Arab world.

Under Narendra Modi, India's foreign policy has undergone a sea change. It has for the first-time become India centric. It is now more national interest driven than fanciful ideology driven. Three years have gone by since Narendra Modi took over as the Prime Minister of India. What do we expect in the fourth year? Kashmir issue to get on track for the permanent solution. Kashmir resolution is of paramount importance and if not acted upon will continue to threaten the security fabric of India. Top officials in the government confirm that at least 40% of the policy in the fourth year will be dedicated to this issue. The issue is burning and can only get worse if not acted upon immediately.

The first action was seen when the Army announced Surgical Strike that had hit a post in Pakistan which aided infiltrations. There should be back-channelled talks with those who want to talk about the ambit of the Indian Constitution. However, it would be the government which will set the terms for talks and not the separatists, the ED notices to the Hurriyat leadership is showing the intent of the government, enough is enough and way too long free hand was given to the separatists. Another sign that showed that the government wants a solution to the Kashmir problem through a muscle policy was when the Army rewarded Major Gogoi after he used a human shield against stone-pelters.

The policy is to be muscular, but the government wants a solution at the earliest. Stone-pelters are handled with brute force, terrorists are being blown away along with their place of hiding. It's not only muscular approach but the government has sent an interlocutor to talk with all the stakeholders. It has given amnesty to some 5,000 first time stone-pelters to motivate youths to take more positive and nation-building paths.

Backchannel diplomacy is on hold. The only gap I see is not engaging the Pakistani army bosses, in parallel to the politicians. Now since Nawaz Sharif is gone due to corruption charges and his political future looking bleak, this makes army's role more important. Another thing, Modi government should do is to tell China officially to back off from Kashmir and stop pushing Pakistani army from behind or else there will be repercussions soon, this debate has to be won in UN. Time when Prime Minister Narendra Modi should take the bull by horns.

For the readers, Modi government's solution approach on Kashmir resonates what I have written in my Out-of-Box Solution under the 7 Cs mantra. Home Minister Rajnath Singh gave 5 Cs steps for the NDA government during his recent trip to Kashmir.

Modi Government's Five Cs

1. Compassion
2. Communication
3. Coexistence
4. Confidence Building
5. Consistency

Government does not want to leave out any stakeholders with whom dialogue should be held. Army has been given full freedom at the local and central level to plan operations as suited to them.

Huge Financial Package of ₹1 lakh crore PMDP (Prime Minister Development Package) was announced, but again there is a lack of local level leadership, Panchayats need to be made strong with more representations coming from common and non-feudal class Kashmiris.

Let me quote from two high ranked politicians from BJP. "We will find permanent solution of Kashmir." – Indian Home Minister. "Modi will solve Kashmir by 2019 permanently," says Subramanian Swamy and last but not the least the former Chief Minister of J&K Mehbooba Mufti said:

> *"Humein dal dal se koi agar bahar nikal sakta hai toh, woh PM Modi hain. Woh jo faisla karenge mulk support karega."*

Pakistan's Approach

Kashmir humari sha ragh hai, the unfinished agenda of the Partition, hence needs to be yanked out from India and merged with Pakistan

Some South Asian experts argue that India should stop the military occupation and "praetorian attacks on Kashmir's Muslim majority." They say that the people of Kashmir themselves should be permitted to choose their leaders in free and fair elections and "New Delhi should solemnly commit to supporting Kashmir's provincial autonomy and human rights of the people." Is India ready to be an enlightened democracy and address the genuine grievances of people who want to maintain a separate identity? The success of a democracy depends not only on holding regular elections but also upon giving political space to people who want to write their destiny.

If the military might cannot hold South Sudan with the North, if enlightened despotism could not stop the Jasmine Revolution in Tunisia and if thirty years of strong-armed tactics cannot curb the democratic aspirations of the people of Egypt – can the controlled and manufactured mandate in this valley kill the idea of a free and separate Kashmir? India has been threatening war against Pakistan, but there is no war in which India can ever beat Pakistan. No Pakistani is afraid of war. Pakistan will win any war against India. World War I, World War II, The American Civil War; we have never lost any war against India. In fact, the worst Pakistani performance in a war was by the actors in Bilal Lashari's movie 'Waar'.

Even there we beat India. Anyone who saw the Bollywood movie 'Border' and thought no one could make a worse propaganda movie underestimated the power of Pakistanis.

There is a reason why we have the best spy agency in the world. Every single boy in Pakistan is trained in spy missions. Trying to pick up a girl from her house in Karachi posh colonies without her mother noticing is nothing short of a James Bond mission. You have to disguise yourself as a driver, strategically park the car at an angle where her mother cannot spot it from the roof and if anybody approaches, at a moment's notice be ready to scream out, "Khuda ki kasam behan hay meri".

For years the ISI has tried to warn us of the nefarious designs of India's spy agency by screaming out to us 'RAW is WAR,' but we never listened. We were blinded by 'Aman Ki Asha' and steamrolled by the Samjhauta Express. Too long have we danced to the beat of India on all our mehndis and dholkis; too long have we asked our barbers to give us the Amitabh Bachchan and Shahrukh Khan haircuts; too long have we tried hiding our bellies in Salman Khan endorsed white vests. It is time we say enough is enough and engage in an all-out war against India. Every Pakistani is equal to 60 Indians. We will beat India on the cricket ground also, Inshallah one day for sure. We will beat India at the border. We will go to Mars and beat their satellite there. So what if we do not even get water in the most posh area of Karachi? Beliefs are stronger than science and I believe we will win. I am sure Agha Waqar can build us a satellite that runs on water.

Nawaz Sharif will beat Narendra Modi in an eating contest. Shahid Afridi will beat Sachin Tendulkar in the longest playing cricketer contest. Humayun Saeed will beat Shahrukh Khan in a 'will still play a 20-year-old in movies' contest.

Atif Aslam will beat Himesh Reshammiya in an auto-tuning contest. Bilal Khan will beat Katrina Kaif in a faker British accent contest. Imran Khan will beat Arvind Kejriwal in a 'trust me and we can still win' delusion. Mubasher Lucman will beat Arnab Goswami in a shouting match. Every Muslim lady will beat Bappi Lahiri in wearing more gold in public. Hamza Ali Abbasi will beat

Subramanian Swamy in jingoism. Every wall being used as a public toilet in Pakistan will defeat the Swachh Bharat movement.

Pakistan Army rubbishes India's claim of 'Surgical Strikes' along LoC. We are the more hip choice for people worldwide. Pakistan is the new and improved India. We can build six Taj Mahals - even if that means spending no money on building schools and hospitals. If it means being better than India, then I am sure all people dying from lack of adequate healthcare will understand. India better not challenge us to another war. There is no way they can defeat us. We will have applications pending for visas for other countries. Every Pakistani will be willing to fly a plane over India, all the way to Europe and Australia for a safe asylum. India cannot isolate us from the West. We are the West. Every geographer in the world will tell you that Pakistan is closer to the West than India. (Well the above satire says it all, the mindset and kind of people India has to deal with in her western border.)

Kashmir today stands at a historical moment. The youth of today have grown restless and are dissatisfied with the options currently available for them. They represent the third generation of Kashmiri freedom fighters. Hizbul Mujahideen (HM) has never been so popular. Kashmiris have finally started viewing it as both homegrown and as part of the Kashmiri society. HM has succeeded at using social media and internet to appeal to the youth. Additionally, the group has been steadily getting funds from Kashmiris globally through hawala and covert means.

India knows that on the ground its occupation has been rejected by the Kashmiris. Its massive military presence in Kashmir may have helped her control the territory but has invalidated its claim to it. If the territory were an integral part of India, then you would not need to keep 700K military and security forces there. But if you do, surely that means it is not yours; you are keeping it by force. And that is what India is bent on continuing doing for as long as it can.

India knows that the success of the Kashmir cause depends on two facts - the strength of the insurgency and Pakistan's support to the Kashmir cause. Kashmiris would not come thus far without Pakistan's help. So it is not just Kashmiris that stand in India's way, Pakistan does too. So the Indian strategy is twofold: on the one hand, unleash extreme repressive measures to bludgeon the Kashmiris into suppression and on the other launch a campaign of isolating and defaming Pakistan and put it on the defensive and off balance. The broader theme is to marginalize Pakistan to make it irrelevant in the dispute and then as a consequence weaken the Kashmiris and impose India's will on them.

Indian plan has been helped by its rising economic profile and geopolitical value, as a balancer to resurgent China and by the post-9/11 anti-Muslim bias and erosion of Pakistan's image. India has used its influence in Washington to harm US relations with Pakistan and by extension the causes it espouses. A legacy the present Administration is going to follow. So don't expect any help from Washington in solving the Kashmir dispute. Even China and the Islamic world pay but only lip service.

There is a sad irony here. Kashmiris' struggle has never been so energized in its entire history and the rejection of Indian occupation never so loud and clear. But in contrast to it the international community's silence has never been so deafening and the big powers apathy never so morally appalling. And Pakistan has never been so much at a disadvantage in helping the Kashmiris. The rise of their struggle is thus out of sync with the external support. That means the entire burden of realizing the aspirations of Kashmiris fall on the shoulders of Kashmiris and Pakistan alone. And that means Kashmiris because Pakistan's ability to fight for them has diminished not just because of India's clout and its negative campaign but also because of Pakistan's own mistakes, Kargil being the most egregious.

The question is how Pakistan can help? Or can it help? The answer requires some reality check. Here is the core reality. The only way Pakistan can help the Kashmiris is through a dialogue with India as the military option is unthinkable. But India does not want a dialogue. Even if India agreed to dialogue, Pakistan would be entering into it with a weak hand as Pakistan has little leverage. Or whatever leverage it has or has had is a double-edged sword and is not employable. We have seen what the Jihadis have done to Pakistan. And denial of trade and transit rights to India, the other option, does not hurt India as much as Pakistan thinks. In fact, it hurts Pakistan more. The equation, therefore, at least for now - not good for Pakistan, not good for Kashmir.

So where do we go from here? So the advice to the Kashmiris, please consider all these limitations and raise the level of your resistance. Energize and organize the Kashmiri diaspora abroad especially in the US. Learn from other resistance movements, Pakistan can help wherever it can. For Pakistan, the important point to consider is that Kashmir is embedded in Pakistan's history, identity and moral purpose. It should, therefore, continue to support the Kashmir cause diplomatically, morally, militarily (covert) and politically. But that is all it can and should do. Nothing more nothing less. It is not enough but is necessary. Beyond that, it is up to the Kashmiris.

Kashmir should remain on the agenda of India-Pakistan issues. No economic or strategic benefit Pakistan may get from India as a payoff for backing away from Kashmir would be worth the betrayal of the Kashmir cause. But Pakistan must not gamble its future over Kashmir. Then there will be nobody to help the Kashmiris. What is required is a great balancing act. And for that, you need not only great diplomacy but also focus on Pakistan's central priority – to strengthen itself first. Good diplomacy and national strength go hand in hand, always.

Just after Partition, the Pakistani State claimed the complete Kashmir as its legitimate territory which should be certified by a plebiscite by the Kashmiri people based on the fact that majority of its inhabitants are Muslims. "Kashmir humari sha ragh hay" is the major slogan sung by Pakistanis and the claim that the letter "K" in Pakistan is for Kashmir.

On the contrary, in 1963, the Pakistani side under Field Marshal General Ayub Khan announced giving Kashmir's 13,000 sq miles land to China on Kashmir's border with the Chinese region of Xinjiang. It means we were ready to give some part of our vital land as a gift to China. Then in 1972, Prime Minister Zulfikar Ali Bhutto accepted the Line of Control (LoC) as an almost official border and in 2006, President General (Retd) Pervez Musharraf gave a proposal which included two major points. Firstly, borders between Pakistan and India remain the same and secondly, Kashmir is given autonomy but not independence.

These chronological events show that Pakistan's stance on Kashmir has been going back slowly and steadily. This means that the "sha ragh" is no longer considered as such practically but only remains so in speeches and slogans. The people of Kashmir on the Indian side have not accepted Indian domination even after more than 70 years. Interestingly, India has millions of Muslims living peacefully in other parts of India, but a continuous wave of revolts and protests against the Indian regime can be seen in Kashmir. Either it is because of the continuous and deliberate interference of Pakistan in Kashmir or the brutal and inhumane behaviour of the Indian regime which includes Pellet guns, disappearances, extra judicial murders, etc, or maybe it is because of the nature of the people of Kashmir to not bow down against injustice and stand for their freedom.

Whatever may be the case, the Kashmir issue should have been properly handled rather than going again and again on the negotiating table when things get hot on the roads of Kashmir and betraying the hopes of the people by slowly stepping back from the initial claims. As far as the UN resolutions are concerned, which is the prime route Pakistan intends to take to resolve the conflict, it seems that since the UN has failed miserably for the last 70 years, expecting it to intervene and resolve the issue ahead is nothing but self-deception. It can be safely stated without any exaggeration that UN has been a useless platform when it comes to issues related to the Muslim world which include nations like Kashmir, Palestine, Iraq, Chechnya, Syria, Libya, etc.

Similarly, Organization of Islamic Cooperation (OIC) has always discussed this issue but never taken any practical steps for its resolution. It could have become a strong force in dealing with resolving conflicts of the Muslim world by using its massive influence. But it chose to remain an incapable platform. Now then, with negotiations, we are losing Kashmir, the UN and OIC are not doing anything about it. Pakistan has also tried small military operations like Gibraltar and Kargil and has failed in them miserably because of lack of political will.

It seems that in order to seriously liberate Kashmir, a sound political and military strategy is required with a sincere and determined will. Secondly, any demotivating claims like "India and Pakistan are both nuclear States and therefore we cannot do much about a military solution with India" are outcomes of a politically weak mindset. Have we not seen two nuclear superpowers in the cold war where America came out triumphed? Secondly, have we not seen how India took out Bangladesh from Pakistan? Why is it not possible then with a serious visionary leadership to turn the tide of history?

The question would remain, what if we do get the whole Kashmir, can the current Pakistani regime yield to the demands of the Kashmiri people? The Pakistani regime is already responsible for massive atrocities on its people in places like Balochistan, FATA region, Karachi, Gilgit-Baltistan, etc. Will the people of Kashmir accept such an attitude from Pakistan? Or would they then demand independence and would be dealt with the same fate as that of the people of Bangladesh?

And finally, let us assume, we give up the "sha rag" and India gives up the "Atoot Ang" and both nations decide to let Kashmir become an independent State. Would that be good for the Kashmiris or would they become a colony of either India or Pakistan or even China because of inability to take a firm stance in front of these giant neighbours? Consequently, it means that an independent Kashmir would also not prosper much, would remain in turmoil and therefore will not be in a position to make its destiny. So the bottom-line no solution shortly.

USA Connection – Historical, Political, Commercial and Democratic

India and United States relationship had some vibrant and devoted personalities making the bond deep-rooted, one of them is Samuel Stokes. He left his home in Philadelphia and set sail for India aged 22; his parents had hoped he would return home, this did not happen. Instead, Stokes made India his home. A young man from a wealthy American Quaker family, he had come to India to work for the leprosy-afflicted in 1904 and went on to become an active participant in India's struggle for freedom.

The brutality of the Jallianwala Bagh massacre in April 1919 drew him into the freedom movement. Stokes worked closely with Mahatma Gandhi and took part in the Non-Cooperation Movement. He was imprisoned for six months for sedition in the Lahore jail and refused bail, the only American to be jailed in India's struggle for Independence. The British intelligence maintained a special file on him. He fought against *begar* or forced labour that the British exacted out of Indians, which was finally abolished. He wore Khadi, married an Indian lady, learned the Sanskrit language, became a Hindu, set-up a school and introduced American apples to Himachal Pradesh. The hill State's most famous produce owes its origins to the apple cuttings Stokes had brought from America to persuade farmers to start apple cultivation. His family still maintains roots with Kotgarh in Himachal Pradesh where Stokes started it all. Stokes did not live to see India gain freedom. He died in 1946 and was cremated in the hills he loved so dearly.

His contribution to India's freedom was very substantial. He was very active in the first Non-Cooperation Movement and worked closely with Mahatma Gandhi, Lala Lajpat Rai, Motilal Nehru, CR Das and other national leaders. He wrote articles, gave speeches and organized meetings. His unequivocal support of Gandhi through these years was valuable to the cause. He did miss Philadelphia where his family and friends were based. In his early letters, he often wrote of how homesick he was and wanted to meet everyone. But this changed with the passing of time and with his involvement in his work. But he remained connected with his American roots through his correspondence with his mother. During his imprisonment, he did not want to stay in a European cell. He said he was an Indian and wanted to be treated as such. He requested for a change of his cell, but the British administration did not agree. Hope separatist forces in the valley gets inspired from this beautiful story.

Abraham Lincoln, one of the greatest American President of all time once said: "The central idea of secession is anarchy." On the similar lines Robert Lansing, former Secretary of State under President Wilson said "Self-determination of peoples - a phrase ... simply loaded with dynamite."

In past various US Presidents have tried to use their clout with Pakistan and also reason with India for coming to some solution on Kashmir. In 2009 US President Barack Obama secretly offered Pakistan that he would nudge India towards negotiations on Kashmir in place of it ending support to terrorist groups like Lashkar-e-Taiba and Taliban, but much to his disappointment Islamabad rejected the offer. Pakistan's former Ambassador to the US Husain Haqqani writes in his book *Magnificent Delusions*:

> "Since the 1950s Pakistan had wanted an American role in South Asia. Now it was being offered one. In the end, Pakistan would have to negotiate the Kashmir issue directly with India. But at least now the American President was saying that he would nudge the Indians toward those negotiations."

Again this may not be true, as then White House spokesperson denied any such rumours, but truth maybe somewhere in the middle.

This is based on Haqqani's interpretation of the secret letter written by President Obama to the then President Asif Ali Zardari, which was personally hand delivered by his then National Security Advisor Gen James Jones (Retd), dated November 11, 2009, through the letter Obama offered Pakistan to become America's 'long-term strategic partner'. The letter even hinted at addressing Pakistan's oft-stated desire for a settlement of the Kashmir dispute, he writes. Obama wrote that the United States would tell countries of the region that "the old ways of doing business are no longer acceptable."

He acknowledged that some countries - a reference to India - had used "unresolved disputes to leave open bilateral wounds for years or decades. They must find ways to come together," Haqqani writes. Obama administration view was 'the Road to Kabul runs through Kashmir'. India's problem with the Obama thesis was in the simplistic trade-off it sets up between Kashmir and Afghanistan. It was always the Republican government that upgraded its strategic partnership with India which many in India surprisingly are unaware and is traditionally Democrat supporters. I am Republican and would like to put my views across without being biased using facts and data and letting my readers decide.

George W Bush visited New Delhi and Mumbai for meetings with India's political, strategic and business establishment. In the

Indian capital, he addressed an audience of federal government officials, parliamentarians, business executives and foreign policy wonks that comprised the most receptive gathering the former American President had encountered in a long, long time. The standing ovation the 43rd President had received on his way out (a repeat of the effusive applause on his way in): "Can't think of too many countries where he'd get such a reception ... India and Israel maybe ..." "And Poland ..." his interlocutor added. "And Poland ..." the ambassador repeated, still a little dazed.

The emblem of India's fascination with Bush is, of course, the game-changing Civil Nuclear Cooperation Agreement that he pushed through between 2005 and 2008. He put his weight behind persuading Capitol Hill, the Nuclear Suppliers' Group and the International Atomic Energy Agency to, "end India's nuclear apartheid," learn to live with its nuclear weapons and permit it civilian nuclear commerce.

Bush seemed to see India exactly as Indians imagine it to be: "A vibrant, modern nation built on an ancient civilization"; "a force for stability and peace in one of the most strategically important regions in the world." On the war against terrorism–which has consumed the Bush legacy – he was categorical that it was an "ideological struggle," made no distinction between al-Qaeda and the Taliban, hoped the "free world" would not "lose its nerve" and warned "I don't think you can negotiate with extremists".

When reaching out to India as President, Bush had his eyes on history. His inspiration came, however, from geography. Pointing out that he had invited India into G-20 – the successor to G-8 as the talking shop of the world's biggest economies–he said his motivation was a belief that the locus of power was moving from "Europe and the Atlantic to Asia and the Pacific." Appropriately, Bush's only visits outside North America since he left the Oval Office have been to South Korea and India. Indians, if they had the vote, would amend the American Constitution and give him a third term, he was the President who has warned Pakistan not to play double cross on terrorism or else would be bombed to stone age.

Looking towards Washington for the resolution of the Kashmir is not out of wishful thinking, it is not out of what Christopher Brooks called as "the fantasy cycle" but rooted in the history of the Dispute. From the birth of the Dispute, in October 1947, Kashmir has topped Washington's South Asian policy. For first two decades after the UN through its resolutions guaranteed right to self-determination to people of the State three US Presidents Harry S Truman, Dwight D Eisenhower and John F Kennedy got 'personally involved' in the resolution of the Dispute. True, the later Presidents did not show same enthusiasm as by their predecessors.

Nonetheless, they continued to nudge and encourage the two countries to settle the dispute for ensuring peace in the South Asian region. Moreover, they played a pro-active role in defusing the crisis sparked over Kashmir between the two countries. In the post-1989 scenario in Kashmir, Washington once against forcefully reiterated stand it had taken in the fifties on the Dispute. It made various attempts to mediate for resolving the problem, to quote *Herald Tribune,* "switched from an overt to a quiet, behind-the-scenes role as peace broker." President Bill Clinton passionately sought to see two key South Asian nuclear players resolve the core issue and live in peace.

An Indian commentator had written on Bill's 'fixation on Kashmir was apparent in his speeches'. Comparing Kashmir to the Caucasus in his September 1993 at UN General Assembly he saw it as a 'serious threat' to the world peace. He called it a most dangerous place in the world. He made India and Pakistan Prime Ministers sit at the table in Lahore in 1999. President George W Bush also did not lose sight of the dangers for the peace in the non-resolution of the Dispute. On February 22, 2006, he strongly advocated the primacy of the people of the State in the resolution of Kashmir and tacitly supported the right to self-determination. In his words "the United States supports a solution of Kashmir dispute acceptable not only to India and Pakistan but also to citizens of Kashmir." The statement highlighting pre-eminence of people of the State was made at a time when India and Pakistan were in the thick of dialogue and it was widely believed that the two countries had reached an agreement – and it was just to be signed.

Now after eight years of Obama administration, we have a Republican President in the White House. Trump is different, he is not a typical Republican and hence a lot of uncertainties with him and his style of functioning, there was some clarity after Modi and Trump met in Washington in June-July of 2017. Modi comes from the business background and his art of making a deal with Trump will be on a test as they meet more often, so far it has worked in India's favour. The majority of people of J&K are highly sceptical about the US role in the resolution of Kashmir. This scepticism was all-time high when reports about President-elect Donald Trump's interest in mediating a resolution of Kashmir was published in the newspapers.

Trump's Indo-US Engagement

Trump called India a 'true friend' following a meeting with Prime Minister Narendra Modi and said relations between the two countries have "never been stronger ... never been better." But Trump seemed to indicate that friendship would not be without conditions. "India makes billions of dollars in trade from the United States and we want them to help us more with Afghanistan," he said. Trump had similar expectations for other powers. He has asked NATO allies and global partners to support his new strategy with additional troop and funding increase. India's Ministry of External Affairs said New Delhi welcomed Trump's "determination to enhance efforts to overcome the challenges facing Afghanistan and confronting issues of safe havens and other forms of cross-border support enjoyed by terrorists."

"We are committed to supporting the government and the people of Afghanistan in their efforts to bring peace, security, stability and prosperity in their country," the statement said. "We have been steadfast in extending reconstruction and development assistance to Afghanistan in keeping with our traditional friendship with its people." "We will fight to win in Afghanistan," President Donald Trump said in a speech at Fort Myer in Arlington, Virginia. "We have been paying Pakistan billions and billions of dollars, at the same time, they are housing the very terrorists we are fighting ... that must change immediately," Trump added. He called on India, to help more with Afghanistan, especially in the area of economic assistance and development.

US officials believe that much of the Haqqani leadership is based in Pakistan and some analysts think eliminating their safe havens is critical to stabilizing Afghanistan. Trump repeatedly mentioned the 9/11 attack as the reason for US action in Afghanistan during his speech. However, what the President will do to ensure Pakistan does change its behaviour is unclear, said Kugelman. Tactics could include cutting aid and curtailing military assistance to Islamabad, he added. "A review of whether Pakistan should be considered a State sponsor of terrorism - a draconian measure - should not be ruled out if conditions don't improve," thinks Pakistan analyst Bruce Riedel from Brookings Institution. Pakistan request for Kashmir conflict as the precursor to Afghanistan help was shot down by the Trump administration. This pretty much sums up his Kashmir approach in future.

Trump's Pakistan Probable Policy?

Ex-US Senator Larry Pressler feels that Donald Trump may turn out to be the best US President for India.

> "US must declare Pakistan a terrorist State, cut off all aid and must not treat India and Pakistan as equals."

Larry suggests that both India and the US should conduct pre-emptive strikes inside Pakistan to destroy its nuclear sites (where weapons have either already been stored or are being made). But for this to happen, Trump would have to get around the Pentagon, which always encouraged Pakistan, he said. Such encouragement emboldened Pakistan to attack India as 'the mother of terrorism' and 'predator' at the UN General Assembly. Trump's description of the Pentagon as 'a swamp' was a good sign, he noted, hoping the US President would drain it soon (as he'd promised).

Trump's warning to Pakistan on its sheltering and export of terror, linking of US aid to 'action on terror' and his request to India to "help us more with Afghanistan" signalled a recasting of relations. Larry said,

> "US must declare Pakistan a terrorist State, cut off all aid and must not treat India and Pakistan as equals. India is a democracy, Pakistan isn't. Pakistan and especially the ISI have lied to us for decades."

All praise for Prime Minister Narendra Modi, the Vietnam veteran said it was good the Modi government was tough with Pakistan. He called the denial of US visa to Modi when the latter was Gujarat Chief Minister 'a stain' on the US. Pakistan couldn't have developed nuclear weapons if the US had stopped aid. Pressler was criticised when, in the 1990s, he had expressed concerns about an 'Islamic bomb'. He said he stood vindicated today and that the growth of ISIS and similar groups led him to fear that fundamentalist organisations - and not individual States - may create a 'Caliphate'.

If Larry words have to be taken at face value, there is definite, decisive shift of the Trump government towards India. Now it is up to India's policy-makers to strike a good 'deal' with President Trump. India has to learn also to give when it's trying to address Afghanistan, the tradeoff to get tangible benefits on Pakistan. Trump art of deal-making will be the mantra, Indian diplomats and ministers need to become good at, unfortunately, India policy of appeasing both 'Israel and Iran', 'Arab world and Trump', is the same old mindset of non-aligned and will never elevate it to the main strategic partner status of US. There is no harm to pursue a nationalistic policy which takes care of India's interest, no need to be apologetic in that regard.

Trump Government Policy in the Indo-Pacific Region

On December 18, 2017, the Trump administration issued its National Security Strategy (NSS). Organized under four main principles;

1. Protect the homeland,
2. Promote American prosperity,
3. Preserve peace through strength, and
4. Advance American influence

Continuing to uphold the importance of an all-of-government approach to pursue US strategic goals, the NSS reflects the unique, "disruptive" nature of the Trump administration. It questions conventional wisdom, based on which past administrations, both Republicans and Democrats, have shaped their national strategies since the end of the Cold War and criticizes it as "strategic complacency."

For US allies and partners in the Indo-Pacific region, the NSS suggests the strategic importance this region has for the United States. For instance, the NSS signals that this administration considers the Indo-Pacific region the most strategically important geographical area by referring to the region at the top of the section devoted to discussing the regional implications of its "America First National Security Strategy." The Indo-Pacific appears ahead of the Middle-East, which has dominated past US administrations' strategic attention. The affirmation of the US leadership role in the Quad group of the United States, Australia, Japan and India (while expecting Japan and India to take greater initiatives in the region) is also a stark contrast to the reference to Europe.

What is even more significant is the portrayal of China throughout the NSS. China has not only been referred to as a US competitor that challenges America's leadership in the world and the international order, but it also has been singled out for its aggressive investment and other economic activities in the areas outside the Indo-Pacific region, including Latin America and Africa. Moreover, the NSS talks extensively about how China has been prosperous in leveraging the most advanced technologies (which the NSS points out have often been acquired through cyber and other economic theft) not only to strengthen its military capabilities but also to tighten restrictions against its people.

Overall, however, the "America First National Security Strategy" laid out in the NSS is a welcome articulation of this administration's commitment to ensuring that the United States can still play a leading role on the international stage, even though some of the approaches it takes may be unconventional. For the countries in the Indo-Pacific region, which have been struggling to respond to increasing pressure from China both on security and economic issues, this is a positive step for reaffirming US commitment to peace and security in the region.

Out-of-Box Solution(s) – 7 Cs Mantras

Writer's Perspective on Potential Kashmir Solution

> It has to be Multi-Pronged, Multi-Phased, Multi-Parties, involving the Indian Military Participation, Mothers of the Valley, Separatists, Pakistani Army, Common People representation, Political parties from the State, NGOs, Students, Labour Unions, Teachers and the non-Kashmiri Indian Muslims.

Keeping the issue hanging for ages only complicate the matter and leads to frustration - Stanley Wolpert's latest book *India and Pakistan* suggests: "acceptance of the current Line of Control ... as the northernmost international border of India and Pakistan" as the "most realistic" solution to the Kashmir conflict. Wolpert, an old hand in South Asia and an Emeritus Professor at the University of California, says that Pakistan's "failure to sustain a freely elected civil polity and its inability to control the al-Qaeda and the Taliban militants who inhabit its entire Afghan frontier and to end the nurturing of the Pakistani soil of suicide bombers, its demand for a democratic resolution of Kashmir conflict will have little credibility and win scant support."

Vivekananda once said,

> "We are responsible for what we are and whatever we wish ourselves to be, we have the power to make ourselves. If what we are now has been the result of our own past actions, it certainly follows that whatever we wish to be in future can be produced by our present actions; so we have to know how to act."

My OOB solution has 7 Cs mantras.

1. C1: Communication (Talks with Influencers)
2. C2: Catharsis (From Radicalization, Alienation to Assimilation)
3. C3: Collectivism (Cooperative Federalism)
4. C4: Confidence Building (In the line of Insaniyat-Kashmiriyat-Jamhooriyat)
5. C5: Commerce (Cash-amir)
6. C6: Class (Stratification of the Muslim Mass. Taking real Azadi to the lowest denominator)
7. C7: Conquest of the Border (Beyond the LoC)

C1: Communication

Identify the Key (Effective) Stakeholders, Identify the clear Agenda for the talk, have authority to give and take when talking. Sincerely execute the signed agreement in time bound manner. Keep honest approach for the closure of the case.

Talk, Talk and Talk that's the mantra

Darby and Mac Ginty, author of *Contemporary Peacemaking: Conflict, Peace Processes and Post-War Reconstruction,* have identified five criteria defining a genuine peace process:

1. The adversaries negotiate in good faith and do not stall with pre-conditions and non-negotiable demands.
2. The key players are linked in the process, which necessitates mutual recognition by the adversaries.
3. The central issues in the conflict are harangued - both the core and the ancestral issues.
4. The players do not use force to achieve their goals or use a ceasefire merely for rearming and repositioning their forces.
5. The players are committed to a sustained process, not just exploratory talks.

These are the ideal circumstances; the Oslo, Dayton and Northern Ireland peace processes were short on several criteria yet went ahead. In the Oslo process through Camp David, the good faith of both adversaries was questionable because of their use of or reluctance to stop coercive moves that each knew obstructed the negotiations. In Northern Ireland, some of the most divisive issues such as decommissioning and police reform were outsourced from the negotiations to post-accord commissions. Before and at Dayton, the Bosnia Serbs had to be bombed by NATO into participation in peace talks and coerced by Milosevic for compromising on borders and or signing the DPA, which they did their utmost to undermine during implementation. In the Kosovo peace negotiations, the central issue of Stateless was not decoded. Because of these shortcomings peace accords was beset by uncertainties.

India made two mistakes from the very start of Kashmir issue, its flawed non-aligned grouping and taking high moral ground on the democracy even affecting her national interest, has been a big let down. First India chose to talk to the elected civilian Government of Pakistan, a country which does not have her army but the army has the country. Given this power arrangement from the very start not sure why India has wasted so many years talking with the weak civilian government. It has only to talk with the Pakistani army, COAS, rest will be accordingly informed.

India has not used common Kashmiris as the third party from the very beginning but gives all the courtsey of hosting, housing and now hunting them. This policy has confused millions in India as well. You cannot have your legs in two boats. Kashmiris are not only Hurriyats but local NGOs, Pandits, Sikhs, Buddhists, women sections, low caste Muslims and common people on the streets. As far Indian separatists are concerned, get them also on the negotiation table by breaking the communication ice, or by force, they are needed for the last time for the final sincere try. Various Indian governments have been confused and have complicated the matter almost beyond the control and this continues even in 2018. Its now when government has appointed Dineshwar Sharma as an interlocutor to talk to stakeholders in Kashmir. It also has not seem to have yielded any fruitful result so far.

My proposed basic recommendations for this section:

1. Give notice to UN informing India's decision to pull out from UN supported Kashmir resolution. The reason, seventy years without any output. Shimla agreement of 1972 made it a bilateral issue. It was the Congress government that took it to UN.
2. Change the stand from Terror first talk and Kashmir later stand. India sometimes comes out looking bit stubborn and Pakistanis as the poor small and innocent rival. Why do the Indian MEA, relevant government officials and legal experts not confident to put forth India's case strongly anytime and anywhere in front of the International group of the nations?
3. More social interactions and communications using social media should happen among the Kashmiri youths, the Hindu Pandits, the Sikhs and the Buddhists of the State. Media should be restrained when villainizing the Kashmiris. However angry rest of India maybe, seeing stone pelting on their national army, they should be restrained. I am also suggesting mosques/maulavis to be licensed, similarly media handling Kashmir news have to be regulated and in the name of reporting cannot be opinion makers.
4. Have a separate Kashmir affair committee of prominent persons from every field for two years only to work on the conflict resolution and with all the powers to make the decision. Prime Minister of India should not be pulled into initial meetings. Grievance cell to hear and resolve problems daily with the help of concerned department.
5. Keep eliminating the stakeholders if their stance or efforts are delaying the process. If Hurriyat cannot change the anti-India stance sitting in India, then take them out once for all. But for the start of serious and meaningful discussions for any

resolution, India will need them as the country has wasted a lot of time without cultivating a second and third line of Kashmiri leaders and there's huge vacuum in the valley today. Accept these shortcomings, India is way to mature, magnanimous and mammoth country and can handle this.

When preparing for negotiations, concerned person should deliberately choose a tactical approach to conducting the interaction that takes into account the complex negotiating context. There are many options, but they can be grouped into four general approaches described in the negotiation art.

1. **Focus on Power:** Also called Contending, Competition, Distributive Bargaining, or Claiming value
2. **Focus on Interests:** Also called Problem-Solving, Collaboration, Integrative Bargaining, or Creating value.
3. **Accommodate:** Also referred to as Yielding; relevant to a party who values the relationship with his counterpart more than the negotiation's outcome
4. **Avoid:** Relevant when the Cost of negotiating is higher than the Potential gain from the negotiation, or when a party can achieve the same gain without negotiating.

The single biggest problem in communication is the illusion that it has taken place. – George Bernard Shaw

C2: Catharsis

Even if India solved Kashmir based on 100% Pakistanis expectation, which is to give the entire Kashmir to them and redraw a new map of India once again still the region will not be peaceful forever. The Fundamentalist Islamist enthusiasts, the Bangladesh creation factor, some madrasas based radicalized mindsets and the product of the distorted history, will not stop here and will want more and more. Pakistani Army and ISI are radicalized and any such move by India will be seen by them as the first winning step of the 'Ghazwa-e-Hind' prophecy coming true, which is to rule Delhi causing more mayhem in this region.

So what should India do?

There will never be a solution to the Kashmir problem in the current form, as the core definition and expectation differ among the stakeholders. Indians, Pakistanis and Chinese are not Canadians or British who would conduct a referendum to decide on a State's demand to secede. It should wrench anyone's heart to watch people fall to bullets, again and again, both Kashmir's misguided kids and also the security personnel. But, sadly, Kashmiris don't lament the soldiers who die at the Muslim terrorist hands. The killing and disfiguring of the local Muslim policemen during the holy months of Ramadan in 2017-18, by the terrorists is appalling, unholy and against Islamic values, as preached by *Quran*.

But on the other side, a large section of Kashmiris mainly from South Kashmir mourns the killing of stone-pelters or the death of terrorists killed in an encounter with the Indian security forces. Underlying the contrasting response is an explanation which no one wishes to admit, but perhaps everyone is aware. It could be stated thus: There will never be a solution to the Kashmir conflict. Nor will it have peace at least not in the "foreseeable future" - a euphemism for "our lifetime." This is because the idea of Nation-State runs deep in the Asians and has become pathological in context of Pakistan. They cannot contemplate the shrinking of their territory, as none of the other Asian countries can either, unless, apparently, they lose it in war. By contrast, they don't mind acquiring girth, as they did to gobble up Balochistan. China, a powerful country of Asia and world, has problems with 22 different countries on the border issue. Here is a list of the countries that have territorial and border disputes with China.

1. Japan: Parts of the East China Sea, particularly the Senkaku Islands and the Ryukyu Islands. The Kingdom of Ryukyu was once a vassal State of China. The Kingdom of Ryukyu terminated tributary relations with China in 1874.
2. Vietnam: China claims large parts of Vietnam on the historical precedent (Ming Dynasty, 1368-1644). Also, Macclesfield Bank, Paracel Islands, parts of the South China Sea and the Spratly Islands.
3. India: China illegally occupies 38,000 sq km (Aksai Chin) of land in Jammu and Kashmir. It also holds 5,180 km of Indian territory in Pakistan Occupied Kashmir under the Sino-Pak agreement of 1963. At the heart of Sino-Indian boundary dispute is the issue of Arunachal Pradesh (90,000 sq km), which China describes as 'Southern Tibet'. Beijing is demanding that at least the Tawang Tract of Arunachal Pradesh, if not the whole of the State, be transferred to China. Now even CPEC as it will cross from Gilgit-Baltistan, Indian claimed part of Kashmir.
4. Nepal: China claims parts of Nepal dating back to the Sino-Nepalese War in 1788-1792. China claims they are part of Tibet, therefore part of China.

5. North Korea: Baekdu Mountain and Jiandao. China has also on occasion claimed all of North Korea on historical grounds (Yuan Dynasty, 1271-1368).
6. The Philippines: Parts of the South China Sea, particularly Scarborough Shoal and the Spratly Islands.
7. Russia: 1,60,000 sq km still unilaterally claimed by China, despite China signing several agreements.
8. Singapore: Parts of the South China Sea.
9. Bhutan: Bhutanese enclaves in Tibet, namely Chamba Valley, Doklam Plateau, Cherkip Gompa, Dho, Dungmar, Gesur, Gezon, Itse Gompa, Khochar, Nyanri, Ringung, Sanmar, Tarchen and Zuthulphuk. Also Kula Kangri and mountainous areas to the west of this peak, plus the western Haa district of Bhutan.
10. Taiwan: China claims all of Taiwan, but particular disputes are: Macclesfield Bank, Paracel Islands, Scarborough Shoal, parts of the South China Sea and the Spratly Islands. The Paracel Islands, also called Xisha Islands in Vietnamese, is a group of islands in the South China Sea whose sovereignty is disputed among China, Taiwan and Vietnam disputes with Burma.
11. Kazakhstan: There are continual unilateral claims by China on Kazakhstan territory, despite new agreements, in China's favour signed every few years.
12. Laos: China claims large areas of Laos on historical precedent (China's Yuan Dynasty, 1271-1368).
13. Brunei: Over Spratly Islands. The Spratly Islands is a disputed group of more than 750 reefs, islets, atolls, cays and islands in the South China Sea. About 45 islands are occupied by small numbers of military forces from the People's Republic of China, Taiwan, Vietnam, the Philippines and Malaysia. Brunei has also claimed an exclusive economic zone in the south-eastern part of the Spratlys encompassing just one area of small islands on Louisa Reef. This has led to escalating tensions.
14. Tajikistan: Chinese claims based on historical precedent (Qing Dynasty, 1644-1912).
15. Cambodia: China has, on occasion, claimed parts of Cambodia on historical precedent (China's Ming Dynasty, 1368-1644).
16. Indonesia: Parts of the South China Sea.
17. Kyrgyzstan: China claims the majority of Kyrgyzstan on the grounds that it was unfairly forced to cede the territory

(which it had formerly conquered) to Russia in the 19th century.

18. Malaysia: Over Parts of the South China Sea, particularly the Spratly Islands.
19. Mongolia: China claims all of Mongolia on historical precedent (Yuan Dynasty, 1271-1368). In fact, Mongolia, under Genghis Khan, occupied China.
20. South Korea: Parts of the East China Sea. China has also on occasion claimed all of South Korea on historical grounds (Yuan Dynasty, 1271-1368).
21. Afghanistan: Afghan province of Badakhshan (despite a bilateral treaty of 1963, China still encroaches on Afghan territory).
22. Pakistan: Surprised, yes even their friend Pakistan but this was before their friendship had started. In 1959 Pakistan became concerned that Chinese maps showed areas of Pakistan in China. In 1961 Ayub Khan sent a formal Note to China, there was no reply. It is thought that the Chinese may not have been motivated to negotiate with Pakistan because of Pakistan's relations with India, with which China was soon to enter a war. After Pakistan voted to grant China a seat in the United Nations, the Chinese withdrew the disputed maps in January 1962, agreeing to enter border talks in March. The willingness of the Chinese to enter the agreement was welcomed by the people of Pakistan. Negotiations between the nations officially began on October 13, 1962 and resulted in an agreement being signed on 2 March 1963. It was signed by Foreign Ministers Chen Yi for the Chinese and Zulfikar Ali Bhutto for the Pakistani. The agreement resulted in China withdrawing from about 750 sq m of territory, and Pakistan withdrawing its claim to about 2,050 sq m of territory (which it had not in fact occupied or administered). China's extended territory became known as Trans-Karakoram Tract. The area is part of Kargilik County.

China has reputation for using force after carefully weighing the costs, benefits and the chances of success. The list of its militarized conflicts is long; with the USA in 1950 (Korea); with Taiwan in 1955, 1958 and 1995-96; with India 1962; with Soviets in 1969; with Vietnam in 1974, 1979 and 1988 (over the Paracels, border and Spratlys, respectively); and with Philippines in 2012 (Scarborough Reef). Instead of harping on China's strengths, India strategicians should start identifying its weakness. No country has resolved land border disputes with China on its terms. They all had to agree to the Chinese terms including Russia.

No Indian leader will agree to slice the land from India. To even think or talk of it, he or she should be prepared to write his or her political epitaph. Even Muslims outside Kashmir, suspected of harbouring sympathy for Kashmiris, will not, they know bisecting India again will invite butchery worse than what was witnessed during the Partition. (Some 1 million were killed, 10 million Indians displaced.)

Nationalism refers to the devotion for one's own nation's interests over those of all other nations. It signifies a particular love for the nation. It was an important factor in the development of Europe. In the 19th century, a wave of romantic nationalism swept the European continent, transforming its countries. Some newly formed countries, such as Germany, Italy and Romania were formed by uniting various regional States with a common 'national identity'. Others, such as Greece, Switzerland, Poland and Bulgaria, were formed by uprisings against the Ottoman Empire and Russia. More concisely, nationalism better defined these countries.

The French Revolution paved the way for the modern Nation-State and also played a key role in the birth of nationalism across Europe where radical intellectuals were influenced by Napoleon and the Napoleonic Code, an instrument for the political transformation of Europe. Revolutionary armies carried the slogan of 'liberty, equality and brotherhood' and ideas of liberalism and national self-determinism.

National awakening also grew out of an intellectual reaction to the Enlightenment that emphasized national identity and developed a romantic view of cultural self-expression through nationhood. The key exponent of the modern idea of the Nation-State was the German GW Friedrich Hegel. He argued that a sense of nationality was the cement that held modern societies together in the age when dynastic and religious allegiance was in decline. In 1815, at the end of the Napoleonic wars, the major powers of Europe tried to restore the old dynastic system as far as possible, ignoring the principle of nationality in favour of 'legitimism', the assertion of traditional claims to royal authority.

With most of Europe's peoples still loyal to their local province or city, nationalism was confined to small groups of intellectuals and political radicals. Furthermore, political repression, symbolized by the Carlsbad Decrees published in Austria in 1819, pushed nationalist agitation underground. Hegel's assumption may not be correct in today's era when the wrong interpretation of Sharia and Islamic Caliphate has become central root for all the terrorism happening around the world, the need for Nation-State has become more important and no division or new formation can be allowed on religion basis and that's where Kashmir conflict lost its political face to Islamic supremacy struggle.

For Kashmiris, Azaadi or independence call has been conceived within the framework of a Nation-State. Their only marker of freedom is to have their independent State or be granted the right to decide whether they wish to join Pakistan or remain with India. But their idea of freedom and Nation-State comes into conflict with that of the rest of Indians and mainly 170 million strong and well-integrated Indian Muslims mostly living happily in other parts of India.

The third actor in the tragedy is Pakistan, which most of the Indians think of as a villain. Many Kashmiris think of Islamabad as a friend and spiritual guide. Pakistan is interested in proving right the two-nation theory - that Hindus and Muslims constitute two separate nations - which constitutes the historical foundation of its existence. An increasingly large number of Kashmiris repose their faith in this foundational idea as well.

But because the two-nation theory was proven wrong through the birth of Bangladesh, Pakistan wishes to midwife an independent Kashmir to undercut the idea of composite nationalism, which seems ragged and in tatters - in Kashmir anyway. Until such time any success is achieved, it would wish to tie-down India in Kashmir. Tit-for-tat is the cardinal principle of international relations.

All these three actors at the table, therefore, have conceptions of the Nation-State at variance with each other. They cannot even hold an iftaar party together, let alone discuss their ideas of Kashmir conflict resolution. Azaadi (Freedom) means different things to different segments of Kashmiris. This is why some say, grant a degree of autonomy to them. Reduce the presence of armed forces and make the border with Pakistan porous. Who in India do you think will move in that direction and why should they? Not the Modi government. The credo of the Bharatiya Janata Party is the abolition of Article 370, which has been diluted over the years. Its predecessors UPA government never thought of granting autonomy to Kashmir because they were, among other reasons, apprehensive of the backlash majority Indian national could trigger.

An aspect of the paranoia that the idea of Nation-State breeds is to think of the centre as synonymous with India. Pluș, sharing a long border, some 3,323 km, so there will obviously be a significant large deployment of border patrol and internal security personnel's, not sure what is the fuss all about regarding the numbers. Not only terrorism and continuous intrusion of the terrorists into India from across the border, but the entire western region which includes Afghanistan is the world's biggest drugs supply zone and India has to be on guard to save its very large young citizens, 68% of its 1.25 billion population is under 35 years. Punjab a rich Indian border State bordering Pakistan is facing a massive problem, as there has been a large supply of drugs reaching into the hands of its young population.

Forget a reduction of troops; the Indian federal government won't even withdraw the Armed Forces (Special Powers) Act (AFSPA) from Kashmir. The thinking is it would be tantamount to loosening control – it could embolden the separatist people to start their flawed Azaadi movement. In Kashmir, it could shoot the graph of cross-border infiltration northwards. Some India critics think that the Jammu and Kashmir police are competent to provide security to the State. To have Kashmiris firing at Kashmiris will at least not project India as an occupier, which is what many Kashmiris think it is.

But the Nation-State's paranoia conjures up another dreadful scenario – what if Kashmiris in uniform decide to rebel? India doesn't have to go far and can draw a lesson from her history – remember the Indian Navy mutiny of 1946 or list further the Indian first war of Independence of 1857. So cancel out this proposal as well. But this scenario will not happen as the Kashmiri Police are very nationalistic and are geared to take the revenge of their fellowmen killed by the terrorists recently. The hate for these Hurriyat separatists and locally grown terrorist among these policemen family is sitting on a volcano that will erupt anytime to devastating effect. This will get into civil war situation where separatists and homegrown terrorist family will be identified, named and shamed and even resulting in a bloodbath. RAW, NIA and State police intelligence should be keeping an eye on this situation and can use this strategic advantage appropriately and in the larger interest of the country and its citizens.

Consider how Manmohan Singh and Pervez Musharraf were close to working out a Kashmir solution – soft borders, joint management of resources, without having to exchange territory that would have riled the hawks in both countries. First Manmohan Singh hesitated, then Musharraf panicked, after all, he was still a Muhajir (those Muslims who migrated to Pakistan from India during partition) and not a Punjabi Pakistani and hence an opportunity was lost.

But their hesitation wasn't on account of any of their traits. It was linked to the idea of the Nation-State. The two leaders dithered because they feared the people's reactions, irrespective of their two contrasting personalities. This is precisely why such opportunities will continue to be missed and why Track II diplomacy also will not yield concrete results other than study papers.

For example, it is an established fact that both India and Pakistan were close to resolving the Siachen problem. But India said it would withdraw from the icy heights after its position had been authenticated on the map by Pakistan. But Pakistan refused, believing its people will see the move as capitulation. It led India to suspect that Pakistan intended to betray it in the future, as it had in the past.

Or recall Atal Bihari Vajpayee's initiative in Kashmir as Prime Minister. He wanted to resolve the Kashmir imbroglio within the parameters of Insaniyat (Humanity), Kashmiriyat (Identity) and Jamhooriyat (Democracy). A wave of jubilation receded soon after that. Another opportunity lost. Muhammad Ali Jinnah was secular, so said Bharatiya Janata Party leader LK Advani, whose career nosedived after that. Advani's pronouncement wasn't even an opportunity.

Azaadi in Kashmir is a flame which is lowered or enhanced from time to time, as we do with a gas stove, depending on our needs. The number of pro-Azaadi Kashmiris varies from time to time. What doesn't is the number of Kashmiris who sadly detest India? You can't conceive of people who can participate in elections – for *sadak, paani, bijli* and *makaan* (roads, water, electricity and housing) and still want independence. It leads us to conclude, at every outburst in Kashmir, that yet another opportunity has been frittered away.

People say Hurriyat leaders are cowards who do not wish to prove their popularity through the electronic voting machine. They fear the intelligence agencies will ensure they lose any poll they participate in. Their other fears, never expressed, is that scramble for power could further divide the disunited lot and incur them the wrath of people and Pakistan, which could organize their assassinations should they dare to step out of line. Not sure why same fear was not orchestrated by RAW and NIA when they are physically located in Kashmir, shows these two organization in poor light when compared with their ISI counterpart.

Finally, can't Kashmiris lead a non-violent movement as Gandhi did for pre-partition India, emulate the anti-colonial struggle against the British rule? They also know strikes and *bandhs* won't make a difference to the rest of India. This is because rest of Indians are not dependent on Kashmiris, as the British were on Indians to maximize their gains. There isn't a railroad or highway in Kashmir that protesters can takeover to bring parts of India to a halt, as the Gujjars reservation movements did in Rajasthan a few years ago. Kashmiris don't supply a commodity which Indians can't forego. They can, obviously, shutter down the Valley for days. It is like closing the doors of your house to which no one has any need to come. Again thanks to Article 370 for this segregation.

Sure, widespread bandhs de-legitimize the ruling power, in this case, Delhi. But Delhi doesn't have any illusion about its legitimacy on ruling the Kashmir. Outside of Kashmir, most people think the Indian State's actions in Kashmir are legitimate. The actions are brutal because Kashmiris want independence and redrawing of a new map, no sovereign nation that too of India's size and stature will accept and hence unacceptable. Nevertheless, Kashmiris continue to take violence against the Indian security system and unfortunately sometimes court deaths, they too have drawn a lesson from the history of the national movement - that a struggle for freedom is prolonged, spread over many decades, is cyclical, the highs alternating with the lows. So they will continue to throw stones and get fired upon and die. Total doomsday scenario and hence rational mind should come together and solve the prolonged standoff.

Nuclear Flash Point

At the height of India-Pakistan tensions in 2001, there were reports that Pakistan was likely to use nuclear weapons early in a war. This was recently validated by ex-Pakistani President General Musharraf, he mulled using nukes against India after 2001 attack.

Tactical Nuclear Weapons (TNWs) are nuclear weapons with low yields of sub-kt to 10 kt - suited for military targets. The sub-kt weapons with yields from 0.05 to 0.5 kt are also referred to as mini-nukes. Because TNW is meant to inflict damage on a battlefield, these in military parlance, are also called Theatre Nuclear Weapons.

Belonging to the non-strategic category of nukes, the TNW are miniaturized weapons which can be delivered by short-range ballistic missiles, cruise missiles, air-to-surface and air-to-air missiles artillery shells and as atomic demolition munitions. Built into war scenarios, it has been argued by defence analysts that if an Indian conventional assault manages to go deep inside Pakistan, the latter is likely to use TNW to halt the Indian blitzkrieg.

Another doomsday scenario shows Pakistan using TNW early in the war to pre-crisis to the crisis. Following a war between India and Pakistan, in which 100 Hiroshima-size (15 kilotons) nuclear weapons are detonated in the large cities of these nations, 5 million tons of smoke is lofted high into the stratosphere and is quickly spread around the world. A smoke layer forms around both Hemispheres which will remain in place for many years to block sunlight from reaching the surface of the Earth. One year after the smoke injection there would be temperature drops of several degree centigrade within the grain-growing interiors of Eurasia and North America. There would be a corresponding shortening of growing seasons by up to 30 days and a 10% reduction in average global precipitation.

War with 100 low-yield nuclear weapons

Summary of Consequences of Regional Nuclear War between India and Pakistan (from studies done at Rutgers - NJ, the University of Colorado-Boulder and UCLA), war is fought with 100 Hiroshima-size weapons (currently available in India-Pakistan arsenals), which have half of 1% (0.05%) of the total explosive power of all currently operational and deployed US-Russian nuclear weapons. 20 million people die from the direct effect of the weapons, which is equal to nearly half the number of people killed during World War II.

Weapons detonated in the largest cities of India and Pakistan create massive firestorms which produce millions of tons of smoke. 1 to 5 million tons of smoke quickly rise 50 km above cloud level into the stratosphere. The smoke spreads around the world, forming a stratospheric smoke layer that blocks sunlight from reaching the surface of Earth within 10 days following the explosions, temperatures in the Northern Hemisphere would become colder than those experienced during the pre-industrial Little Ice Age these nuclear war-induced effects on temperature would be twice as large as those who followed the largest volcanic eruption in the last 500 years, in 1816, which caused "The Year Without Summer"

This cold weather would also cause a 10% decline in average global rainfall and a large reduction in the Asian summer monsoon. China will be affected. 25-40% of the protective ozone layer would be destroyed at the mid-latitudes and 50-70% would be destroyed at high northern latitudes. Massive increases of harmful UV light would result, with significant adverse effects on human, animal and plant life. These changes in global climate would cause significantly shortened growing seasons in the Northern Hemisphere for years.

World grain stocks, which already are at historically low levels, would be completely depleted. Grain exporting nations would likely cease exports to meet their own food needs. Some medical experts predict that ensuring food shortages would cause hundreds of millions of already hungry people, who now depend upon food imports, to starve to death during the years following the nuclear conflict. Effects are largest over land, but there is substantial cooling over tropical oceans, too. The warming over Antarctica is a small area, is part of normal winter interannual variability and is not significant. All these scenarios surely create fear of apocalypse and make the resolution of disputes more important.

Soon have a Counter to the Religious Radicalization

Worried about the long-term dangers radical Islam can wield amongst the world's second largest population of Muslims, India is set to draft the first ever counter-radicalization policy. In a shift from its 'hard' approach, sympathizers and volunteers of the extremist Jihadist group are 'counselled' with a humane touch, marking a new approach towards tackling terrorism. And this is surely one important point I would like to stress. The young stone-pelters and fastly growing radicalization of very young mind need to be immediately arrested. Mosques should be brought under government watch, anyone who addresses public has to have a license for doing it and needs to have credentials as a citizen.

Almost a year after the first cases of Indian nationals joining the ISIS and al-Qaeda emerged; the realization has come to hit the intelligence and security agencies that India is no more a bystander in the Global Islamic Jihad fought in the distant lands of Iraq and Syria. With 17 Indians enlisted on the ranks and files of the extremist militant organizations, India has to quickly embark on an ambitious intervention to prevent the 170 million-strong Muslim community in the country from falling sway to the savagery of the Islamic State and propel them from going down the path of terrorism and global Jihad. The counter-radicalization strategy is unfortunately still in its making and government needs to hurry up. This will put the thrust on the soft approaches like counselling, guidance and de-radicalization programmes for the suspected misguided Kashmiri youths, supporters, sympathizers, instead of detaining them behind prison walls for following a radical ideology justified in the name of religion.

Why Now?

The urgency to evolve a counter-radicalization doctrine is reflective of the school burning and kids picking guns at the tender and innocent age of 12 in Kashmir valley created by ISIS and other Islamic militant groups, who have taken the virtual world by storm to spread propaganda, promote their activities, raise funds and recruit volunteers in their brutal war. The appeal of ISIS and its black-masked, long-bearded fighters waving the group's signature flag, holding guns and beheading apostates to purify Islam, is driven by curiosity amongst the youth population who are getting acquainted with the romantic and glamorous version of Jihad on the social media and online forums.

The social media research finds out that Islamic Jihadist groups post at least 120 tweets every minute and has more than 1,25,000 accounts - where fighters and supporters are uploading information, photographs, videos and tailored views all as a part of propaganda, in real time, are a defining feature of new age terrorist is estimated that 35,000 volunteers from 100 countries including India answered the call to Jihad and arrived in Syria via the open borders of Turkey, Iraq, Jordan and Lebanon, in the last two years. Aptly, Syria which was once called the cradle of civilization is now the playground of Jihadists.

A majority of the Indian ISIS/al-Qaeda recruits are believed to have been radicalized by online charismatic handlers. Currently around 250 active online supporters are under monitoring by the intelligence agencies. These preachers or supporters use religious ideology and quote *Quran* verses on various platforms including Twitter, Facebook, Snapchat, Kik, Instagram to incite people in joining Jihad as a spiritual journey and even provide information to facilitate one's travel to Iraq and Syria. The availability of ISIS-related propaganda in the open-domain has increased the risk for radicalization through the internet and social media. In the case of Indian recruits, many have no combat or terrorism experience - they are students of engineering, a journalist and regular immigrant employees in the Gulf - and were motivated to join the Jihadist groups by such religious handlers.

What can IT Power India do?

Big Data, Small Data, AI, Analytics, Local Language-Driven Research, Subject-Driven Research, Creating the Data Set, Cybercrime, Online Money Transfer etc, India can do all of these efficiently. Millions of her strong IT resource pool does the job daily for millions of business houses around the globe. Need right team, priority and strategy.

There have been in past several attempts to study jihadist internet strategies and there is considerable research into technological products that will make it easier for security agencies to analyse data from social networking sites. The tools that are currently available consist of computer programmes that track, collect and process the data gathered through social networking sites or from the Web. These programmes enable researchers and investigators to find and structure data, but they do not provide further qualitative analysis, which is left to the human operator.

The data structuring and the resulting analysis itself also depend on human assumptions, which are too often based on factors deriving from incomplete research. This kind of research faces another well-known problem, which is the difficulty of identifying a limited and representative statistical sample of the environment that is to be studied. Certain aspects of the internet – indiscriminate, anonymous, borderless and extremely fast – when combined with the rapid growth of jihadist content, make it extremely difficult to isolate a representative sample of jihadist information operations and then submit that sample to qualitative and, especially, quantitative analysis.

To succeed in their campaign, terrorists need publicity. Sociologist Mark Juergensmeyer maintains that terrorism is strongly connected with the publicity it generates and that without an audience, terrorism would cease to exist. Social networking sites and the internet, in general, serve as these groups' communications battle horse for disseminating information about their activities and recruiting support to their cause. The reasons behind their effectiveness (or lack thereof) are briefly covered in the next paragraph.

Any approach to analysing the potential success or failure of jihadist information operations on social networking sites should take into account two major influential factors: first, the recommendations made by prominent jihadist ideologues concerning the public image of the jihad and second, the exploitation of social networking sites' capabilities by jihadists. The jihadist ideologues' viewpoints on information management, although mostly of a rhetorical nature, especially when related to the traditional and high-level leadership, can be framed to be operationalized for further analysis. Ideological divisions over the issue of organization type (centralized *vs* decentralized) for the jihad do not influence how we classify ideological perspectives on the management of the information, or meiotic, jihad.

Opinions of this nature have to be accepted and assumed to be complementary to each other, independent of the source. Previous research into and analysis of the writings and public messages of prominent jihadist ideologues yielded the following four elements, which the movement's leaders consider necessary for the conduct of a successful jihadist information operation:

1. **Quantity and outreach** – This twofold element appears in the recommendations of every prominent jihadist ideologue. Regarding our analysis, this element presupposes that activists

should fill the internet with the jihadist material through as many outlets as possible to reach the optimal audience.

2. **Networking** - Prominent jihadists recommend that spreading the call to jihad should be seen as a common effort. On this matter, al-Suri and Mohammed bin Ahmed al-Salim are the most outspoken and both offer detailed recommendations. Framed for this study, this element assumes that to achieve success, jihadists should actively participate in the common effort to spread radical content over the internet, provide feedback, expand their reach and share materials through different outlets.
3. **Specific tailoring** - Leading jihadists suggest that successful activism on the Web requires communications to be tailored to the class and customs of their specific audience. This element presupposes that jihadist information operations will tend to match their narratives to local conditions, by exploiting local languages and symbolism and offering 'solutions' to local grievances through jihad.
4. **Audiovisual media production standards** - Prominent jihadists recognize the power of well-produced messages. This element presupposes that higher audiovisual production and editing values plus originality improve the likelihood that a media campaign will be successful. These four elements, described in this way, serve as a theoretical explanation of the factors for the potential success of jihadist information operations, but to be useful for analytical purposes, they need to be operationalized. Operationalization is done through a process that takes into account the current developments and opportunities offered by the internet and, for this study, in particular, social networking sites. Generally speaking, social networking sites provide users with publicly available data on the performance of other users' postings, or other users' activity on the site.

A user may choose to remain anonymous or restrict the release of his data to third parties, but for our purposes, such users have no analytical value because our object of study is focused on extroversive uses of social networking sites. Table shows the user data that can be easily obtained by visiting two major social networking sites, YouTube and Facebook, categorized according to the four elements described earlier. Such a scheme can help us measure the performance of various jihadist information operations on social media. This just an example what can be achieved using Indian IT power.

Sample Unit of Measurement for the Parameters Identifying Jihadist Information Operations

Parameter	*YouTube*	*Facebook*
Quantity and Outreach	# of views # of likes # of dislikes # of subscriptions driven by post # of shares time watched # of comments # of videos posted by user	# of status updates, photos and videos published # of likes # of shares # of comments
Networking	Usernames of other users who interact/respond to postings of the original user Web addresses and hyper-links to other websites, or other social media sites Organization/group/individual mentioned in postings	Usernames of other users who interact/respond to postings of the original user Web addresses and hyper-links to other websites, or other social media sites Organization/group/individual mentioned in postings
Social Network Elements	Language or dialect used Date of posting (to match with important local events) Topic Name of user Location of user Other data (Description section)	Language or dialect used Date of posting (to match with important local events) Topic Name of user Location of user Other data (About section)
Specific Tailoring Audiovisual Exploitation	Quality of editing Audiovisual quality Branding Length of video	Quality of editing Audiovisual quality Branding

By using various methods of analysis that compare the data for the quantity and outreach element with the measures of other elements, it is possible to obtain qualitative insights into the overall performance of each jihadist information operation compared to others. This approach can also reveal trends and patterns of performance based on the two major influential factors mentioned earlier: the suggestions of prominent jihadist leaders and a realistic quantitative dataset extracted from the social networking sites where common jihadists and their sympathizers carry out their part in the jihad.

Jihadists will continue to use the internet as their primary tool for conducting information operations. Their transition from the use of Web 1.0 to the use of Web 2.0 applications may be slow, but it is inevitable because jihadists need to reach the wider public at any cost, whether they successfully influence it or not. Social networking sites have presented less tech-savvy jihadists with problems such as learning how to exploit such sites, along with the restrictions and dangers posed by counterterrorism bodies that mine the internet for information on terrorist activities.

By raising their popularity scores on the Web, jihadists may attract the attention of counter-terrorism personnel who can then do data analysis for reaching out to them for lawful treatment needed to be meted out to such humanity enemies. The lack of a centralized information management structure contributes to a further degradation of jihadist information operations on the Web. India has huge task cut out to achieve. Linguistics play a role here, for coming out with right algorithm building a model using a keyword search to isolate a data set that may help identify and analyse jihadist internet networks and the characteristics of their information operations.

Religious Radicalization

Apart from online radicalization in the cyber world, certain Moulvis should be under the scanner for inciting people to join Jihad a religious obligation, starting with Mirwaiz, the suit boot wale 'impeccable' English speaking, Pakistani lover and the so-called Islamic leader. Although such cases are few, mosques, institutions and charity foundations following Wahhabi/Salafist ideology are suspected to be fertile ground for indoctrination.

The Ahl-e-Hadees is primarily promoted in India by the Jamiat Ahl-e-Hadith foundation, which receives its main funding from Saudi Arabia. The Foundation claims to be the group of Sunni Muslims who adhere to the Salafists interpretation and rejects un-Islamic practices, traditions and rituals. Following Kashmir, where it first registered the foundation in 1958, the Ahl e-Hadith has spread to Maharashtra and Kerala now. All these examples should not be interpreted as this is against Islam, not at all, India largely lives peacefully with their Muslim citizens and it should always be like this.

Threat

Radicalized individuals are at a higher risk to act upon their indoctrination. Those who are unable to participate in the violent Jihad may be prompted to execute lone-wolf attacks, as frequently seen in Europe lately.

Schools are expected to be able to demonstrate their compliance with this duty, appropriate to the level of risk of radicalization in their institution. Some of the areas where schools can focus on leadership, partnership and capabilities. People in leadership positions in schools should make sure their staff understand radicalization, have the capabilities to deal with it, are aware of how important this duty is and can implement it effectively.

Schools need to show evidence of productive co-operation among parents and staff, police and other appropriate agencies. Staff should understand what radicalization means and why people may be drawn into terrorism through it. They also need to understand what kind of extremism the government is interested in and what measures are available to prevent people being drawn into terrorism.

Government of India first needs to clearly and firmly define extremism, get it discussed and debated in both the houses before making it legally binding. Some headway I can provide here, Extremism should be vocal or active opposition to fundamental Indian Pluralism and Secularism values, including democracy, the rule of law, individual liberty and mutual respect and tolerance of different faiths and beliefs. We should also include in our definition of extremism calls for the death of members of the countries armed forces fighting on the border.

The difficulty of spotting the signs of radicalization has been understandable concern about the potential of this new duty to restrict free speech and to potentially punish curiosity. Schools are places where ideas should be freely discussed and debated, not least to give pupils the necessary skills to identify and challenge harmful ideas themselves. JNU (Delhi) case may fall into this scenario. Government probably had no clue to own or disown these students. However, as the government guidance itself states, these rules are an extension of Institutions' responsibilities to safeguard their pupils from many potential harms. These also include sexual, physical and emotional abuse. Schools/Colleges/Universities might consider the potential harm from extremist ideologies and how they might be vocalized by pupils in the wider context of safeguarding against abuse. In this context, radicalization can be understood as a process of socialization by which a pupil increasingly comes to hold a potentially harmful world-view.

More longer-term and more successful approach to tackle radicalization can be found in strengthening community cohesion by focusing on the links between all communities – not just in strengthening the civil society structures of Muslim communities. Another recommendation has been for schools to be prepared to react to major events such as the Syrian conflict or why Pellet guns should be or not to be used in the Valley. It has been argued that these activities will enable students to become active citizens and to participate more fully in democracy - through hearing different opinions and learning how to critique and challenge ideas.

A similar approach has been tried in universities, by increasing the religious literacy of staff and students to facilitate better quality conversations about beliefs and values of other faiths, badly needed in Muslim majority Kashmir. This approach taps into a broader conversation about whether Religious Education (RE) in schools could be better used to educate pupils about different religions or if indeed RE needs to be re-thought to help it achieve this. A further question of literacy has been raised around how young people use the internet, highlighting the need to help young people critically appraise online sources of information. These recommendations all have their basis in academic research - although not necessarily research targeted at preventing radicalization.

Once again HRD ministry needs to come-up with some whitepaper or strategy on preventing radicalization, check extremism and de-radicalized the existing unfortunate minds. Indian Army under the able leadership of General Rawat has already started Bharat Darshan for the Kashmiri youths, to help them see how other parts of India operates, how Indian IT firms which employees millions of India's youth work and happily live with folks from different religious background or how a temples or mosques or a church co-exit harmoniously together. Kashmiri youths need lots of such interactions and also youths from rest of India needs to visit Kashmir too, the flow has to be both ways.

> Who wishes to fight must first count the cost. The greatest victory is that which requires no battle.
>
> - Sun Tzu, *The Art of War*

C3: Collectivism

Federalism in USA for the border States like Arizona, California, Texas can be used as a reference point for meeting Kashmiris aspirations this can also cover pre-1953 situation but for all such arrangement and relaxation of AFSPA type laws, one thing has to be remembered by the separatists and pro-Azaadi protesters, all has to be within the Constitution of India and a strong federal government will be paramount, rest people can handle each and everything of their State, but again who are the people? Not the few radicalized or feudals, but the majority silent oppressed and financially disadvantaged ones. Power should come in their hands for real Azaadi and a democratic way of life.

In the modern era since the French Revolution, the planners – Rousseau, Marx and the rest – have increasingly sought to remake society in their own image. In the face of this challenge, whether or not our present-minded, anti-traditional intellectuals care to admit it, America has increasingly provided the modern world's best example not only of historical continuity but also of the benefits which stem from moulding political institutions with one eye on the past. Again and again the world has learnt to its sorrow that constitutions are easily written and also amended, but meaningless unless they are the product of a nation's historical experience.

The solution to Kashmir autonomy or pre-1953 period can be found in American Federalism, the Indian policy makers and Kashmir State stakeholders needs to take leaf out of this for coming with more Indian version of cooperative federalism for all the border States of India. Have the same cooperative federalism for all of these border States, no special favour to any one of them. This will meet lot of the people's aspiration for the autonomy.

Let me briefly give you a glimpse of the most powerful democracy of the world, The USA model.

Federalism in the United States is the constitutional relationship between US State governments and the Federal government of the United States. Since the founding of the country and particularly with the end of the American Civil War, power shifted away from the States and towards the national government. The progression of federalism includes dual, State-centred and new federalism.

Federalism was a political solution for the problems with the Articles of Confederation which gave little practical authority to the federal government. For example, the Articles allowed the Continental Congress the power to sign treaties and declare war, but it could not raise taxes to pay for an army and all major decisions required a unanimous vote.

The movement was greatly strengthened by the reaction to Shays' Rebellion of 1786-1787, which was an armed uprising of yeoman farmers in western Massachusetts. The rebellion was fuelled by a poor economy that was created, in part, by the inability of the federal government to deal effectively with the debt from the American Revolutionary War. Moreover, the federal government had proven incapable of raising an army to quell the rebellion, so that Massachusetts had been forced to raise its own.

Although Cooperative Federalism has roots in the civil war, the Great Depression marked an abrupt end to Dual Federalism and a dramatic shift to a strong national government. President Franklin D

Roosevelt's New Deal policies reached into the lives of US citizens like no other federal measure had. As the Supreme Court had rejected nearly all of Roosevelt's economic proposals, the President proposed the Judicial Procedures Reform Bill of 1937 to add more members. The expansion of the Court along with a Democrat-controlled Congress would tilt Court rulings in favour of Roosevelt's policies. Lowi notes three Supreme Court cases that validated the shift in power:

- National Labor Relations Board *vs* Jones & Laughlin Steel Corporation,.
- Helvering *vs* Davis and
- Steward Machine Company *vs* Davis.

The national government was forced to cooperate with all levels of government to implement the New Deal policies; local government earned an equal standing with the other layers, as the federal government relied on political machines at a city level to bypass State legislatures. The formerly distinct division of responsibilities between State and national government had been described as a "layer cake," but, with the lines of duty blurred, cooperative federalism was likened to a "marble cake" or a "picket fence." In cooperative federalism, federal funds are distributed through grants in aid or categorical grants which gave the federal government more control over the use of the money.

Another movement calling itself "New Federalism" appeared in the late 20th century and early 21st century. New Federalism, which is characterized by a gradual return of power to the States, was initiated by President Ronald Reagan (1981-89) with his "devolution revolution" in the early 1980s and lasted until 2001. Previously, the federal government had granted money to the States categorically, limiting the States to use this funding for specific programmes. Reagan's administration, however, introduced a practice of giving block grants, freeing State Governments to spend the money at their own discretion.

New Federalism is sometimes called 'States' rights', although its proponents usually eschew the latter term because of its associations with Jim Crow and segregation. Unlike the States' rights movement of the mid-20th century which centred on the civil rights movement, the modern federalist movement is concerned far more with expansive interpretations of the Commerce Clause, as in the areas of medical marijuana (Gonzales *vs* Raich), partial-birth abortion (Gonzales *vs* Carhart), gun possession (United States *vs* Lopez), federal police powers (United States *vs* Morrison, which struck down portions of the Violence Against Women Act), or agriculture (Wickard *vs* Filburn).

In the United States, federalism originally referred to belief in a stronger Central Government. When the US Constitution was being drafted, the Federalist Party supported a stronger Central Government, while 'Anti-Federalists' wanted a weaker Central Government. This is very different from the modern usage of 'federalism' in Europe and the United States. The distinction stems from the fact that 'federalism' is situated in the middle of the political spectrum between a confederacy and a unitary State. The US Constitution was written as a reaction to the Articles of Confederation, under which the United States was a loose confederation with a weak Central Government.

In contrast, Europe has a greater history of unitary States than North America, thus European 'federalism' argues for a weaker Central Government, relative to a unitary State. The modern American usage of the word is much closer to the European sense. As the power of the federal government has increased, some people have perceived a much more unitary State than they believe the Founding Fathers intended. Most people politically advocating 'federalism' in the United States argue in favour of limiting the powers of the federal government, especially the judiciary.

Asymmetric Federalism

A distinguishing aspect of Indian federalism is that unlike many other forms of federalism, it is asymmetric. Article 370 makes special provisions for the State of Jammu and Kashmir as per its Instrument of Accession. Article 371 makes special provisions for the States of Andhra Pradesh, Arunachal Pradesh, Assam, Goa, Mizoram, Manipur, Nagaland and Sikkim as per their accession or Statehood deals. Also one more aspect of Indian federalism is the system of President's Rule in which the Central Government (through its appointed Governor) takes control of State's administration for certain months when no party can form a government in the State or there is violent disturbance in the State.

Coalition Politics

Although the Constitution does not say so, India is now a multilingual federation. India has a multi-party system, with political allegiances frequently based on linguistic, regional and caste identities, necessitating coalition politics, especially at the Union level. In Britain, an Imperial Federation was once seen as (inter alia) a method of solving the Home Rule problem in Ireland; federalism has long been proposed as a solution to the "Irish Problem," and more lately, to the "West Lothian question."

Autonomy

Kashmir Autonomy can be met with Government of India coming out with a new Centre-State model only for the border States. Let the State Government manage and raise money for their internal security and Central Government should not put its nose in such matters, the elected government has to keep its people safe. Natural calamity rule should also change and the State needs to build those institutions and manages via internal revenue. This reminds me of State of Arizona, US *vs* then federal government run by President Obama. I think that issue will give India lot of insight into formulating its border State autonomy model.

My proposed framework will help meet the aspiration of the people of Kashmir valley related to 'Azaadi' and their never-ending complain against India. Hope this new Border-State model will resolve their grievances and ends anti-India tirade on and off in their long course of disturbed history.

1. New Indian Border States-Federal Model should be worked.
2. Abolish all the existing laws, including Article 370 and 35A and form a new border State model which will incorporate most of the relevant laws from these Articles but after the people of the State have voted for such propositions.
3. Feudal and Family rule should not be allowed and if India needs to be a democracy, the lower section of the society needs to be running the government and hence class stratification and probably a new voting model only for the border States should be formed.
4. Defence, Foreign affairs, Federal GST, Home ministry and Education should fall into Central Government ambit rest all should be State Government subject. Schools, temples, mosques and NGO activities will be Central Government's responsibilities and State will be instructed how to act on it.
5. States should be financially competent to run or else that can be criteria for dissolving it and Governor Rule to be applied. No minimum number criteria to form the government, just go by the largest party concept for the government formation.
6. Elected government of the border States will get full autonomy as suggested in American or other cooperative federalism models, local police will be under State, but the IPS appointment has to come only from the army.

Federalism isn't about States' rights. It's about dividing power to better protect individual liberty.

– Elizabeth Price Foley

C4: Confidence Building

No Pellet gun anymore please, use what western countries uses for effective crowd control systems. Chili-based PAVA shells type system should be immediately considered as a replacement for pellet guns, India has maimed enough of its misguided youths. No security personnel I talked, enjoyed performing this task on their own.

Though a final decision is yet to be taken, government sources said a seven-member panel involving officers from home ministry, BSF, CRPF, J&K Police, IIT-Delhi and Ordnance Factory Board is considering their use for control crowd. The panel is expected to submit its report soon. These shells have been developed by the Indian Institute of Toxicology Research (IITR), a laboratory in Lucknow under the Council of Scientific and Industrial Research (CSIR).

In 2010, UPA government said pellet gun is a non-lethal weapon which can cause the least damage, but now NDA government feels there should be some substitute for this cruel crowd control mechanism. The Indian Army had suggested to the committee that it should opt for less lethal ammunition while controlling crowds in J&K. Northern Army Commander Lt Gen DS Hooda had also said security forces should use less lethal weapons such as sound cannons, pepper shotguns and chili grenades. "Alternative non-lethal weapons are available to disperse crowds during demonstrations. The panel sought our inputs and we have suggested that sonic weapons, pepper ammo and chili grenades could be less harmful. The government is looking at these options," he had said.

Officials said PAVA shells were on trial for over a year at the IITR and its development has come at a time when J&K is on the boil. The name PAVA stands for Pelargonic Acid Vanilly Amide, also called Nonivamide and is an organic compound found characteristically in natural chilli pepper. On the Scoville scale (the degree to measure the power of chilli), PAVA is categorized as "above peak," meaning it will severely irritate and paralyse humans, but temporarily. It is also used as a food additive to add pungency, flavouring and spicy effect to food.

The expert committee seems in favour of PAVA shells, they have recommended that the Tear Smoke Unit (TSU) of BSF in Gwalior should be tasked with the bulk production of the shells. The committee found that it was less lethal than pellet guns and equally effective. Once fired, the shells burst and temporarily stun, immobilize and paralyse the target in a more effective way than a tear gas shell or pepper sprays. The panel noted that PAVA is "bio-safe, better than chili grenade or tear smoke shell and can also be used in combination with stun and tear shells" by security forces while tackling unruly protesters.

Crowd Control: Riot Police Techniques from Ferguson to France – The scenes of violent confrontation in Ferguson, Missouri, over three straight nights show angry African-American residents protesting in response to a police shooting currently under investigation. To counter the crowds, local police have attempted to use the same techniques that security forces use around the world, including tear gas, bean bag rounds and wooden bullets.

Riot control police – wearing helmets, visors, body armour and gas masks – are called in for disturbances ranging from rowdy soccer matches and merchandise looting to anti-war protests. Civil disorder, whatever the source, can be quelled with a variety of methods, increasingly taken from the military arsenal:

Tear Gas – Deployed at demonstrations from Tahrir Square to Port-au-Prince to prevent looting, disperse crowds and promote security, one of the most commonly used riot control agents around the world is tear gas. Known as a "lachrymatory" substance for the irritation that generates teary eyes and difficulty breathing, the chemical is usually discharged from a canister that is fired from a grenade launcher towards a crowd.

CS and CN are most frequently used gases. Dispenser methods include backpacks and even drone attachments for larger aerial volumes. Pepper spray is another lachrymatory agent, whose effects can last up to two hours, considerably longer than normal tear gas. The active ingredient, capsaicin, is sprayed directly onto people – as at a 2011 tuition-hike protest at the University of California, Davis.

In Ferguson, MO, police have attempted to disperse protesters using smoke bombs – fireworks that generate smoke after ignition. A similar projectile can be used by police to break up crowds: stun grenades. Also known as a flashbang, these non-lethal explosive devices create a blinding light and loud noise to disorient people.

Baton Rounds – This category includes four separate but related types of crowd control: rubber bullets, plastic bullets, wooden bullets and bean-bag rounds. Rubber bullets, which are sometimes just rubber-coated steel bullets, can be fired from normal firearms or dedicated riot-control weapons. They are used as a non-lethal alternative to standard metal bullets but often cause significant pain and result in hematomas and contusions. As with similar weapons, they are more dangerous when fired from close range. When aimed at people's heads, they can cause fatal damage.

Plastic bullets were developed by British forces to use in Northern Ireland to be safer than rubber bullets and carried less risk of ricocheting uncontrollably. Used to quell the recent Missouri violence, wooden pellets also cause bruises and welts. Shot from a distance, the ammunition is intended to administer 'pain compliance'. Police in Oakland agreed in 2004 to stop using this technique after a lawsuit.

Bean bag rounds, also referred to as "flexible baton rounds," are fired as shells from a regular 12-gauge shotgun – often with a bright coloured tag to differentiate the weapon. The lead shot disperses through the air within a small fabric sack, spreading the impact over 1 sq inch on the target. The blow often causes a muscle spasm, temporarily disabling the subject. This method has on average caused one death per year in the US. So as not to cause internal bleeding or disrupted heartbeat, officers are instructed to aim at extremities. During Occupy protests in Oakland, veteran activist Scott Olsen's skull was fractured by a bean bag round.

Liquid Fire – When standard police vehicles are not sufficient for forcefully deploying riot officers, a department often sends horse-mounted units, busloads of additional policemen and armoured vehicles, such as Mine-Resistant Ambush Protected (MRAP) jeeps. Water cannons can spray a high-velocity stream and be first used on fireboats, before being truck-mounted in the 1930s. They were widely used during the Civil Rights Movement. While advocacy groups and vendors disagree on what form of riot control is most safe or effective, water cannons are not widely used in the US today. However, they are used in police crackdowns in other countries, from student marches in Chile to demonstrations against the gang rape in India. Stink bombs or liquids causing a foul odour are sometimes used and testing has been done on sticky foam that can immobilize rioters. Moreover, Israeli soldiers in the West Bank often use 'skunk water' to disperse protesters.

Physical Barriers – Known as kettling or corralling, police use 'containment' tactics to cordon off a crowd and either direct people towards one exit or prevent them from leaving the area entirely. The method is seen as controversial because it often traps bystanders in the same location and has been criticized as a violation of civil liberties. Trapping protesters in a confined space stop other individuals from joining and can divide a long march up into several enclosed sections to minimize mobility for the crowd. Sealing access roads and exits often tire out protesters and give police an opportunity to videotape or photograph people who might later be arrested. To disperse a crowd, security forces can move quickly in a coordinated line towards the gathering. "Baton charges" are only used as a last resort. Clubs and riot shields raised can inflict pain, forcing people away from the scene due to the actual impact or just the fear of being struck.

To prevent confrontations beforehand, long metal "bike racks" are used at public events in controlling the movement of large numbers of people attending parades, rallies and festivals. Organizers of such events deploy these objects at the venue to manage crowds. At mass gatherings, these provide a psychological and tangible way of pushing individuals away from accessing certain zones. Temporary fencing can enhance public safety or provide theft deterrence. Composed of steel or lighter-weight plastic, such barriers are often joined to prevent them from being knocked down and the standard height is 43 inches. Wooden sawhorses with the writing "Police Line - Do Not Cross" were formerly used for the same purpose.

Wave Weapons

Stun guns and Tasers use electro-shock pulses to incapacitate people. In the first half of the last decade, more than 100 people died from such police action across the US, which has led some police departments to consider less lethal weaponry. Riot police in New York City deployed Long Range Acoustic Devices (LRAD) during the Republican National Convention of 2004 and Occupy Wall Street protests of 2011 - as loudspeakers, but not as sound cannons. Weighing up to 300 lbs, the low-frequency sonic weapons emit pain-inducing tones.

Active Denial System (ADS), known informally as a heat ray, was deployed to Afghanistan and has been acquired by the Los Angeles Sheriff's Department for potential prison riot use. With a directed-energy blast, the weapon increases skin temperature with a burning sensation, using similar radiation technology to a microwave.

Ideally there should never be a situation when kids need to be fired upon with any such systems, employment generation, work on anti-alienation, DNA change related therapy followed by creating better role models for these youths then Musa and Wani to help channelize their immense energy level for more productive and legal help for the family, society and the country in large.

Take the case of Afshan Ashiq's an angry Kashmiri girl pelting stones at the J&K police, got her into national media spotlight, more so after it was discovered that she was an avid footballer. That picture, Afshan now says, not just turned around her sporting career but also helped introduce many young Kashmiri girls to what was hitherto a male-dominated sport. Afshan is now captain and goalkeeper of the J&K women's football team that is getting exposure at the national level and competing in the Indian Women's League. The 23-year-old also plays for a Mumbai club and has even inspired a Bollywood biopic on her life.

So what turned things around? This was achieved by human touch provided by the Union Home Minister Rajnath Singh. Afshan said it was a one-off reaction triggered by her "anger" at the abusive language used by a J&K cop as well as the alleged 'slapping' of a team member she was escorting to the football ground at the time.

> "I don't regret anything. I would not have picked up a stone had it not been for the misbehaviour of the police.... But now I have a reputation and image to maintain. I want to focus on football and make my State and nation proud."

Grievance Cell – Direct access to Prime Minister and President, Kashmir Governor and Chief Minister and Army Chief Twitter account.

Good Governance - Let Hurriyat run the administration for two years on the experimental basis, give them five districts with the total autonomy. Remove feudal, wealthy and dynastic leaders via real elections and empower mothers and village level genuine nationalistic citizens. Unemployment and Modern education network needs to be weaved and done with the best innocent hands with time-based monitoring of the results directly posted to Prime Minister and Chief Minister's twitter wall.

Ministry of Happiness - Siege Mentality and DNA Metabolism Change in the Kashmiri youths post-1989 generation. What can be done? New research shows DNA can be altered by trauma passed on to the offspring. While we have long known that hereditary genes are responsible for physical attributes and illnesses or allergies, scientists have discovered that the trauma experienced by one generation can alter genes and those mutations can be passed along to offspring. Researchers at Mount Sinai Hospital and the James J Peters Veterans Affairs Medical Center, both in New York, studied the genetics of thirty-two Jewish men and women who had experienced the horrors of persecution during the Nazi regime, either because they had been in a concentration camp, witnessed or experienced torture or were forced into hiding. The children of these individuals, known to have a higher likelihood of stress disorders, were also studied. The researchers then compared their findings to Jewish families who had not been in Europe during that time and the differences in DNA were noticeable.

So what I am trying to say is that Kashmiris born after 1989, the security personnel posted in Kashmir since 1948 and the Hindu Pandits of the valley needs to be addressed differently, maybe have a 'Ministry of Happiness'. This cannot be just a law and order problem, the ministry of happiness should get experts from Israel and US, this is so crucial in my suggestion for the path to conflict resolution. India has to bring back its alienated youths, silently suffering security personnel and Hindu Pandits who have been ethnically cleaned up from their land. This cannot be treated at the shallow level, has to back up with the deep research and motherly hand when treating these affected citizens.

Beef Ban Bickering

Majority of people in India thinks that India is secular because it is primarily a Hindu majority country. It follows Hindu values, Hindu customs, Hindu philosophy. Hindus treat all religions as an acceptable but different path to reach to the same God and this helps them ideologically to peacefully coexist with other faiths. This is very important fact to know when the population ratio of them *vs* rest of the minorities is 80 : 20 and that too from a large population size of billion plus. This is a great asset of India. Pandit Nehru, India's first Prime Minister echoed this view in his article "Glimpses of World History", the line of distinction between Indian nationalism and Hindu nationalism is very thin because India is the only country where Hindus are the majority population. This is the character of the nation now let's analyse the recent beef ban controversy.

Where's the Beef? The smuggling business between India and Bangladesh is worth as much as their "official" trade and is around US $ 8 billion. That could be the reason for India's little harsh action on Beef trade and eating ban and there may be potential grievances that many Hindus had from a long time before the right-wing Hindu party came into power. Regulation can be a better way to address the problem then putting a blanket ban, but again this was in the Constitution since a long time. The current government just forcefully implemented it and also thanks to media for over hyping it, showing visuals of the folks being lynched by the crowd carrying beef. Problem is somewhere in the middle.

The most talked about issue in the country right now is beef politics. Is it right on the part of the State to interfere in the eating habits of people? The State has no business in interfering in the eating habits of people. Yes, India has to save her bovine now, or else in a decade, she will be importing milk. If you promote the beef-eating habit, the environment will be finished, because India's population is in billions and not in millions like many beef eating countries. Even in the Paris climate summit promoters came with a concept of a meatless Monday. Why? Because meat has a more negative impact on the environment. Beef requires forty-eight times more water as compared to vegetarian food.

Even China is asking its people halve their meat consumption. Even if it is interference in the eating habit of the people, it is climate beneficial to do so. It is not wrong. When bovine wealth is lost and agriculture and the environment are affected, the government can put reasonable restrictions. In India, cows are not just like any other animal; it has sacred for the majority population. Under the Constitution, the government has an obligation to protect the cow and its progeny. Article 48 of the Constitution casts this obligation. The Supreme Court decided in 2005 that even aged and economically useless cows also need to be protected because cow dung and cow urine are sources of organic enrichment of the soil. The Supreme Court, in effect, said there is no useless cow. The Supreme Court held that Article 48 which stands for public good overrides individual rights of choice of food.

Today many countries are restricting beef to protect the environment. Also, 18 out of 29 States have banned cow slaughter and most of them did it when the Congress was the ruling party. Were they also interfering in the food habits of the people, they being a secular party? How is it that the cow has become communal now? In the 1970s, the cow and calf were the election symbol of the Congress. Today, the Congress is slaughtering a calf in the middle of the road and preparing food as the mark of protest steaming live on the national media. What a perverse decline.

In a State like Kerala, Hindus eat beef, unlike north India. So also Hindus in Bengal, Andhra, Tamil Nadu and the North-Eastern States. So this cannot be called a communal issue and hence not targeted at Muslims only. Rather it is targeted to protect the bovine wealth of India, agriculture and environment and may be targeted towards the farming community. But the problem is the cow vigilantes and poor use of social media or electronic media by the government to communicate to the citizens on the plan and reason for doing so. This needs to be corrected.

Kashmir Women Association (KWA), Kashmir Mother Association (KMA) and Kashmir Missing Child Mother Association (KMCMA)

Government of India should immediately form or merge any existing associations under three distinct categories of the Kashmir Women Association (KWA), Kashmir Mother Association (KMA) and Kashmir

Missing Child Mother Association (KMCMA). The responsibilities should be to handle all the social and political issues affecting the women. From Triple Talaq, to enforcement of Arab style burkha wear, to halala, to the missing childs issues, to issues related to police and security personnel continuous searches and any other issue that needs to be humanly addressed needs to be in the domain of this association. They should have power and funds to execute their programmes in the timely fashion. India needs to use this approach to bring 50% of her Kashmiri population on the track and this section can help bring other 35% kids and youths on the right track.

Not all can change, but that is OK as even Allah too did not intend for all the fingers of the hand to be same. A strong country with right fundamentals can live with this reality that the rotten apples will be there however beautiful the orchard of valley Kashmir be (*Chand pe bhi daag hain!*). But the future generation and the entire Women community cannot be left and their hearts need be won. There are grievances and strong differences in every family, but at the end of the day they still are the family and this truth can not be changed. India border State of Nagaland beautifully experimented with this concept helping the society to evolve and they become a problem solver.

Naga women from different tribes joined hands to fight social evils and went on to emerge as peace agents, that has been on the edge for decades similar to Kashmir as this is also a border State with army deployed for too long time to control insurgency, cross-border terrorism and misguided youths challenges. Naga Mothers Association members with their tiny frames, traditional attire, addictive chuckles and cooking expertise changed the hostile environment for the country. This group of Naga mothers looks what mothers are expected to do, care with no expectation. They travelled six-hour into the jungles to meet the armed groups, working with the HIV positive in the early 1990s and helping those in the long legal battles, it's clear the idea of a mother's role is one that few women or men would be equal to and no force can replace them.

The Naga Mothers Association (NMA) was formed in 1984 in response to the drug and alcohol addiction ravaging Nagaland at the time.

> "Every Naga tribe had a women's wing; women were strong in the church's activities. But with NMA they came together in an organized manner. NMA's constitution mandates that every adult Naga woman is automatically made a member with an annual membership fee of ₹1. Leaders were selected from among members nominated by each of eight Naga tribes.

> In the beginning, the biggest issue affecting homes was drug addiction," says Abei-U Meru, also a founder and now NMA President. "The mothers came together because it was hurting every home." Along with spreading information, NMA started a rehabilitation centre. In the 1990s, it played a pioneering role in tackling HIV and AIDS. In September 1991, recalls founder member former President Neidonuo Angami, they visited the HIV-affected in Manipur Jail. "Food was thrown at them; such was the stigma. We were the first to go in and shake the patients' hands."

Through the 1980s and 1990s, NMA addressed the violence that tore Nagaland apart: alleged atrocities by the security personnel against Naga groups and civilians and then years of fratricidal killings between various Naga factions. "Daily gun battles would see two or three boys shot dead outside our homes. We would bring the shrouds for them," Meru recalls.

NMA made 'Shed No More Blood' its motto – one the women have gone to great lengths to uphold. Every time tensions simmered, they took off in a car on barely-there roads into the jungles of Nagaland and neighbouring States to urge leaders of factions to talk; NMA's only demand that peace is maintained. Ever since the 1997 truce between Naga groups and the Centre, NMA's been active in negotiations to settle the vexed issue of a homeland for all Nagas. But the ceasefire hasn't meant an end to the violence.

The older women are sure a new leadership will emerge. "The elders planted the seed very well," says Neidonuo. "Many younger ones ask: Why mothers? Let's change the name to women. I say no. The NMA is for all women, unmarried or married, mothers or not. But the word 'mother' has dignity in Naga society. Everyone respects a mother. The name stays," says Vamuzo.

When India has so much inherent talent, skills and examples, why not use similar techniques in Kashmir. These women's associations should be monitored, given guidelines and left independent to make decisions and operate. Government can surely win hearts like this. Let these mothers in time bound fashion become representatives in the upper house or even lower house, this way a right representation of Kashmiri awam will get a chance to shape their destiny. Enough power for way too long have been given post-Independence to the feudal and dynastic rulers. Enough of hiding under the name of the democracy and the constitutional limitation due to Article 370 and 35A.

(i) Government should immediately stop the use of the pellet guns and move to teargas or chili guns.

(ii) Engage youths via multiple forums, giving them leadership platform to become proud citizens, use the carrot and stick policy. Incentivize them to be on the lawful track and punish the dark sheeps, if any.

(iii) Mosques and Temples need to have laws of operating and using a public broadcasting system. Anyone addressing public with their discourse even if that's for religious purpose needs to have a license (which should be yearly reviewed and renewed). No temples, gurudwaras, churches and the mosques however sacred, old or powerful they maybe, be allowed to use the public broadcasting system to voice political messages, under the disguise of religious freedom, such activities should draw immediate arrest, closure of that structure and conversion of the entire real estate into State Governments asset. This applies mainly for the border States as India's taxpayers cannot pump billions into defence to take care of cross-border terrorism, there has to be some regulation. Kashmir with approx 1% of India's population consumes more than 10% of the national GDP.

(iv) Funding from Muslim countries needs to be stopped, any funding by Muslim countries to a secular India has to be used by all Indians and in the field of poverty elimination. Religious conversions aided by these foreign aids should be declared anti-social and illegal as this creates disturbances in the society.

(v) Cow vigilantes and any such activities that affects the social harmony has to be ruthlessly handled; media needs to be regulated; currently, they do not even bother to put a disclaimer when showing lynching or any such violence on the national TV. If the TV reaches Indian homes and there is no UA certification on news programmes and violence is viewable by the two years old kid, then it has to be regulated.

(vi) 'Women associations' and 'Missing child's Mothers' association needs to be immediately formed or merged if there are any existing ones with a power given almost at par with local MLA's for the betterment of the society. They need to have the legal power to work with the law, health, finance, police etc.

(vii) Missing childs and unnamed graveyards need to be immediately addressed, even if it was used in the past by different government or security establishments, let the mothers of the missing child know the truth. A new start has to be made going forward. There should be nothing to hide from anyone as far as Kashmir conflict is concerned. '*Hamam me sabhi nange hain*', accept this and move on without repeating the past mistakes. This will work as a tranquillizer restraining the daily uprising, indoctrination, radicalization and alienation of the young minds. Winning the heart is the underlying mantra for the confidence building.

(viii) SOP has to be laid on how to conduct when army and militants are engaged in such situation. Kashmiris should be educated to follow the rule set by the government agencies for such situations, once that has been done anyone breaking it should have consequences to face. If the civilian tries to come in between the army and militant during the encounter, then not only that individual but the entire family and maybe entire street from where this disruption happened should be demarcated and no electricity, power and criminal FIR for everyone should be initiated and tried in the fast track courts. Also if the security personnel is found in any kind of breach other than agreed SOP should be immediately court-martialled. The punishment should be based on the rule of law should be for both the parties.

(ix) The disturbed regions of Kashmir Valley like Anantnag, Pulwama, Pampore, Poonch, Srinagar, Butpora, Handwara, Pattan should have special youth development programmes. Change the habit of youths, expose them more to a western way of life, modernity and comfort. Let them be 50% stakeholder in the mall or road ventures. Raise their aspiration level to what youths around the world wants. Indian Movies, foods, clothings, music, etc should be smartly used to de-radicalize. Give them the promise of good life independent of the radicalized world. Pull them out from the radicalized mosque's environment and have them integrate with more non-Muslims via social media duly incentivized by the government.

(x) Get Islamic scholars from around the world to teach the correct and liberal side of the Islam. Have the video files created and have some innovative ways to make it part of the youths' lives.

(xi) Start an international level soccer, baseball and cricket club, something like IPL, with each Kashmiri district pushed to fierce rivalry to win the cup. Have a huge prize worth million dollars to make the life-changing impact on the winning team, financially.

Optimism is the faith that leads to achievement. Nothing can be done without hope and confidence. – Helen Keller

C5: Commerce

Cashmere is another synonym used in the west for Kashmir. Commerce results in Cash, making people amir (rich). The phrase is an important part of overall Kashmir Conflict solution. Pakistan and India have invested 70 years and still going strong on this issue, totally negating any other means of getting closer and bringing prosperity in the region. Pakistan has invested unflinchingly on Kashmir issue, even after losing East Pakistan (Bangladesh), which was 50% of the Pakistan landmass and 60% of their population. This makes us think that it just cannot be for the love of Kashmiris and their so-called sufferings as perceived by the Pakistanis. This cannot be just to revalidate the two nation theory after separation of East Pakistan or the revenge for Bangladesh creation; there must be something bigger and stronger issue. Can this be 'Water War' or unethically protecting trade and commerce gateway access for Central Asia due to its strategic location or expansionist mindset to become a substantial size by getting Kashmir and Afghanistan and become a big geo-political power for the entire Muslim Ummah?

Water, because the Himalayan rivers emanating from the place affecting the entire west Punjab region from where the elite feudal political class or army bosses come from and hence their financial interest in making sure Indus water source never dries up. Also the connectivity of Central Asia, which has helped Pakistan bag the $ 57 billion worth of CPEC project. So in one-way, their continuous fight even at the brink of balkanization fear or in the past losing four wars with India have not even for a second lowered their motivation for keeping the Kashmir pot boiling.

Just like Golan Heights fight between Israel and Palestine is for the water similarly fight for having control on Kashmir which has rich water sources could be one of the key reason and hence the solution has to keep this in mind. The "War over Water," also the Battle over Water, refers to a series of confrontations between Israel and its Arab neighbours from November 1964 to May 1967 over control of water sources in the Jordan river drainage basin. Relations between Israel and its neighbours had never fully normalized following the 1948 Arab-Israeli War. In the period leading up to June 1967, tensions became dangerously heightened. Israel reiterated it's 1950s statement that the closure of the straits of Tiran to its shipping would be a casus belli and in the month of May, Nasser announced the straits would be closed to Israeli vessels.

Egypt then mobilized its forces along its border with Israel and on 5th June Israel launched what it claimed was a series of pre-emptive airstrikes against Egyptian air-fields. Claims and counterclaims relating to this series of events are one of some controversies relating to the conflict. The issue of water sharing from the Jordan-Yarmuk system turned out to be a major problem between Israel, Syria and Jordan. Small-scale water-related skirmishes had occurred following the 1949 agreements. In July 1953, Israel began construction of an intake for its National Water Carrier at the Daughters of Jacob Jordan Bridge in the demilitarized zone north of the Sea of Galilee. Syrian artillery units opened fire on the construction site. The United Nations Security Council majority (excepting the USSR) voted for the resumption of work by Israel. The Israelis then moved the intake to an economically inferior site at the Sea of Galilee.

At 1955, the Jordan Valley Unified Water Plan (Johnston Plan) was accepted by the technical committees of both Israel and the Arab League, but the Arab League Council decided not to ratify the plan on 11 October 1955. According to most observers, including Johnston himself, the Arab non-adoption of the plan was not a total rejection. While they failed to approve it politically, yet they seemed determined to adhere to the technical details of the agreement. Moreover, it continued to be taken seriously by Arab leaders. Though the Unified Plan failed to be ratified, both Jordan and Israel undertook to operate within their allocation limits.

Israel completed its National Water Carrier project, which siphoned water from the Sea of Galilee in 1964. The initial diversion capacity of the National Water Carrier, without supplementary booster pumps, was 320 million m^3, well within the limits of the Johnston Plan. Nevertheless, the Arab States were not prepared to coexist with a project which seemed likely to make a major contribution to Israel economic growth. In January 1964 an Arab League summit meeting convened in Cairo and decided that the establishment of Israel is the basic threat that the Arab nation in its entirety has agreed to forestall. And Since the existence of Israel is a danger that threatens the Arab nation, the diversion of the Jordan waters by it multiplies the dangers to Arab existence. Accordingly, the Arab States have to prepare the plans necessary for dealing with the political, economic and social aspects, so that if necessary results are not achieved, collective Arab military preparations, when they are not completed, will constitute the ultimate practical means for the final liquidation of Israel.

The Arab States decided to deprive Israel of 35% of the National Water Carrier capacity, by a diversion of the Jordan river headwaters (both the Hasbani and the Banias) to the Yarmouk river. The scheme was only marginally feasible, as it was technically difficult and expensive. A major escalation took place in 1964 when Israel declared it would regard the Diversion Project as an infringement on its sovereign rights.

In 1965, there were three notable border clashes, starting with Syrian shootings of Israeli farmers and army patrols, followed by Israeli tanks and artillery destroying the Arab heavy earth moving machines that were used for the diversion plan. The Arab countries eventually abandoned their project. Control of water resources and Israeli military attacks against the diversion effort were considered among the factors which led to the Six-Day War in June 1967. The war is referenced in the famous US anti-war 1965 song "Eve of Destruction" by Barry McGuire with the line "And even the Jordan river has bodies floating."

Internationally, the Indus Water Treaty is seen as one of the most successful cases of conflict resolution especially because it has stayed in place despite the two countries having been engaged in four wars. Signed in 1960, the IWT is an agreement that was signed by former Prime Minister Jawaharlal Nehru and the then President of Pakistan, Ayub Khan, marking out control over the six rivers running across the Indus basin following the partition of the subcontinent.

The six rivers of the Indus basin originate in Tibet and flow across the Himalayan ranges to end in the Arabian sea south of Karachi. Preceding partition, it was one common network for both India and Pakistan. However, while partition managed to draw terrestrial borders, the question of how to divide the Indus waters was something that needed to be worked out. Since the rivers flowed from India to Pakistan, the latter was unsurprisingly threatened by the prospect of being fed by the former.

Initially, the issue of water sharing was sorted out by the Inter-Dominion accord of May 4, 1948, that laid out that India would release enough waters to Pakistan in return for annual payments from the latter. The problems of this arrangement were soon realized and it was considered necessary to find an alternative solution.

Eventually, in 1960, the two countries reached a decisive step with the intervention of the World Bank wherein precise details were laid out regarding the way in which the waters would be distributed.

The components of the treaty were fairly simple. The three western rivers (Jhelum, Chenab and Indus) were allocated to Pakistan while India was given control over the three eastern rivers (Ravi, Beas and Sutlej). While India could use the western rivers for consumption purpose, restrictions were placed on the building of storage systems. The treaty states that aside from certain specific cases, no storage and irrigation systems can be built by India on the western rivers.

From the Indian point of view, the basic dissatisfaction with the treaty arises from the fact that it prevents the country from building any storage systems on the western rivers. Even though the treaty lays out that under certain exceptional circumstances storage systems can be built, the complaint raised by India is that Pakistan deliberately stops any such effort due to the political rivalry it shares with India. The matter is further aggravated by the fact that the western rivers lie in the disputed region of Jammu and Kashmir, which has been a subject of the tussle between the two countries since independence. Since the treaty's conception in 1960, the two countries have been embroiled in conflicts over many projects including the Salal hydroelectric project on the Chenab, the Tulbul project, the Kishanganga and Ratle hydroelectric plants.

While the tense political relations between the two countries have to a large extent resulted in conflicts over the treaty, to a large extent it is the framing of the treaty itself that has led to grievances. Water policy expert, Ramaswamy R Iyer writes the following in his work *Indus Treaty: A Different View*: One can immediately see how differences arise. One party can claim to be in full conformity with the criteria laid down in the treaty and the other party can say that this is not the case.

In the first place, as pointed out by Iyer, the treaty is highly technical leading to far-ranging divergences between the two countries regarding interpretations. For instance, while the treaty says that storage systems can be built, but to a limited extent, the technical details make it increasingly difficult to conclude under what circumstances projects can be carried out.

Added to this inherent limitation within the treaty is the political situation between the two countries. As per the writings of Iyer, while India, on the one hand, tries to make maximum use of the breathing space provided by the treaty to build projects on the western rivers, Pakistan on account of its suspicions towards India keeps an extra keen eye on every technical aspect of the project and tries its absolute best to get it suspended.

The current conflict is over the Kishanganga dam project and the Ratle hydroelectric project. The Kishanganga hydroelectric plant is an

$864 million worth of project that was initiated in 2007 and was projected to be completed by 2016. Pakistan took the project to the Court of Arbitration in 2010 raising six issues that they say violate the treaty. In 2013, the Court of Arbitration ruled India to go ahead with the project under the condition that a minimum water flow to Pakistan of 9 cubic metres per second is maintained. On several other issues, however, no agreement between the two countries could be reached. The 850 MW Hydroelectric power station named Ratle was initiated in June 2013 on the Chenab river. While laying the foundation stone of the project, former Prime Minister Manmohan Singh had said that it would help in the development of Jammu and Kashmir.

However, Pakistan had once again objected to a meeting of the Indus Commission held in September 2013, to the project on the grounds of violation to the IWT. Following the Uri attack in September 2016, India decided not to hold a meeting of the Permanent Indus Commission so long as Pakistan does not stop funding terrorist activities. The decision led to further delay in concluding the future of the two projects. With India now agreeing to hold the Permanent Indus Commission meeting, an agreement over the two projects is much awaited.

Water is going to be next pricey thing to the world in future as it becomes a scarce commodity and any war for water cannot be ruled out. This makes Kashmir very important region and hence the fight will continue. National Conference, the party that was in power in Jammu and Kashmir and was part of the Congress Party-led coalition that ruled at the Centre. The State's Chief Minister was Omar Abdullah, while his father Farooq Abdullah was a minister in the Central Cabinet, in charge of New and Renewable Energy. But that did not stop the State Government from asking some uncomfortable questions: who owns the water that runs through the State, the State or the Centre? If a hydroelectric project is built on a river running through the State, who has the first right on the electricity, the State or the regional grid, in this case, the northern India grid?

The questions have been raised in the past. Thrice, the Jammu and Kashmir government has passed resolutions protesting the Indus Water Treaty (IWT) because it prohibits India from holding back any water from the four western rivers in the Indus basin before they flow into Pakistan. Since 1960, when the treaty was signed, it has been the contention of the State Government that it cannot irrigate its farms because it cannot hold back the water, thanks to the IWT and that the Central Government had no right to negotiate on rivers that flow through the State. Among the western rivers mentioned in the

IWT, the Jhelum and the Chenab flow through Jammu and Kashmir before reaching Pakistan.

Globally, the IWT is often cited as a model of cooperation between otherwise antagonistic neighbours. But in Kashmir, it has always been seen as a huge problem. Shakeel Qalandar, President of the Federation of Chamber of Industries in Kashmir (FCIK), says that due to the IWT, only 40% of the cultivatable land in the State can be irrigated and less than 10% of the hydroelectric potential harnessed. The treaty has also come under increasing attack from Pakistan, which has taken India to international arbitrator's every time India has planned a hydroelectric project on any of the western rivers. In 2005 Pakistan had sought the World Bank's intervention to stop construction of the 450-megawatt Baglihar dam and the hydroelectricity power project over the river Chenab, but Bank-appointed experts cleared the project while asking India to restrict the overall height of the dam.

Earlier India had to stop construction of Tulbul Navigation Project on the Jhelum on account of objections raised by Pakistan. Last year Pakistan raised objections on the construction of the 330-megawatt Kishanganga power project by India over a Jhelum tributary and took the matter to the International Court of Justice. Kashmiris say that despite the legal wrangling India and Pakistan are still well-placed regarding the exploitation of water resources and residents of this Himalayan region should also benefit from it.

There are six rivers – Indus, Jhelum, Chenab, Sutlej, Beas and Ravi – which form the part of Indus river basin, some of which are situated in Kashmir. India is heavily dependent on these rivers for energy and water. Pakistan fears that since the source rivers of the Indus basin are in India, it could potentially create droughts and famines in Pakistan, especially at times of war.

The land was partitioned in 1947 and the waters were partitioned in 1960. According to the Indus Waters Treaty in 1960, a water-sharing treaty between India and Pakistan, Ravi, Beas and Sutlej, which constitute the eastern rivers, are allocated for exclusive use by India before they enter Pakistan. Similarly, Pakistan has exclusive use of the western rivers Jhelum, Chenab and Indus but with some stipulations for development of projects on these rivers in India. The treaty resulted in the partitioning of the rivers rather than sharing of their waters and it is a success as it has managed to survive four wars.

The Irrigation Canals built on these rivers are responsible for the agricultural produce of Kashmir, Punjab and Haryana. This has had a tremendous effect on the agricultural life in those regions. The estimated hydel potential in J&K State is about 20,000 MW, out of which projects of about 16,200 MW capacity have already been identified. These projects are techno-economically viable, besides being eco-friendly and socially beneficial.

Energy and Water-Starved India cannot Survive without Kashmir

According to the Indian Niti Ayog (Ex-Planning Commission), Kashmir has around 100 types of expenditure, 21 comes from J&K State tax receipts, 12 from Kashmir's share given to centre as central taxes (income tax excise duty, etc) and 67 as grants in aid from Central Government (central taxes collected from other States, redistributed to Kashmir). So as you see commerce plays a huge part in the solution.

CPEC/OBOR projects and its connectivity to Central Asia has brought Kashmir region in prominence. My second logic for this 'C' is connectivity to the Central Asia can be one reason for Pakistan not diluting its claim from this region, till the existing LoC is not officially accepted as the boundary, Pakistan will keep pushing for more so that when India is at the negotiating table they have some leeway in negotiating the deal in their favour. From Indian perspective CPEC is illegal and should be stopped for the part which traverses vie POK, India has the right to intervene when the project reaches India's claimed Kashmir.

China is getting overconfident by arm-twisting two major India centric propositions and making the world fall into its line, not allowing UN to ban Azhar Masood, a Pakistani terrorist and also not allowing India to become NSG member may be further emboldened to forcefully enter into Kashmir dispute between India and Pakistan as it has $57 billion at stake with the CPEC project. What strategy India has against this commerce war?

The USA, had always supported India since its independence except for a brief 1971 era when Nixon errored. Trump government is very business friendly and India has to show how it can help contribute America First policy of the Trump government when it has an ambitious policy of Make in India. Will Africa take sides? Europe may be disillusioned with Trump for now and may look towards stronger China and morality does not work in politics. The Middle-East supports Pakistan on Kashmir resolution. They may blow hot and cold with India, but when it comes to Kashmir, they see it purely from Islamic angle. Russia will never disown India, but keep mum or even advise India to mend its way on OBOR stand. Japan and Australia have no personal enmity with Pakistan neither South Korea, Vietnam, Tibet, Singapore or Malaysia.

Turkish leaders have spent several years pursuing a goal they call 'zero problem with neighbours'. Turkey is on good terms with Greece, Bulgaria and Iraq. Its leaders realize that Turkey's prospects depend on regional stability and are actively seeking to resolve disputes in the neighbourhood. Because of its size, its economic power, its history and its well-developed though still incomplete democracy, Turkey is uniquely placed to be both a model and a broker. For most of Turkey's modern history, the Muslim world has seen it as an Apostate. Atatürk's reforms pulled it so far from Islam that it seemed to have no religious legitimacy. Besides, it was perceived as Washington's lackey, stigmatized by its embrace of American policies that many Muslims found abhorrent. Neither of those objections applies to Turkey today. It is governed by pious Muslims and has its foreign policy. Its leaders are now warmly welcomed in many Muslim places where, in the past, they would not even have cared to visit.

Pakistan, on the other hand, was a great promise when it was created and had a somewhat liberal Muslim society with focus on education and nation building for two decades just after its creation. In late '80s with the coming of a military ruler General Zia, this country turned into a radicalized Muslim country, which later deteriorated to becoming an epicentre of the international terrorism radicalizing its people, army and most of the institutions. Every recent terror attacks have some Pakistani footprints. The only good thing for that country happened in the form of it becoming a Nuclear power, raising its stature from a roadside trouble maker to a nuke possessed the radicalized rogue country, aspiring to become the leader of the Muslim world. Egypt, Turkey, Iran and Pakistan have emerged to lead the Muslim world. Their societies, however, are weak, fragmented and decomposing. Indonesia a friend of India and is the more promising candidate, but it has no historical lineage of leadership and is far from the centre of Muslim crises. Pakistan and Turkey are currently in the race to become the torch bearer for the Muslim communities - one by possessing the Islamic Nuke and other due to Historical factor.

Kashmir conflict resolution is holding India, Pakistan, Afghanistan, China, Iran, Russia and the entire Central Asia on financial projects. All these unhelpful realities suggest India needs to rethink its self-isolating opposition to BRI in general and CPEC in particular. Indeed, India has an opportunity to convert CPEC to its advantage, provided Modi's advisors think innovatively and boldly. Briefly put, India should make the following three proposals to China and Pakistan they cannot refuse:

- Alongside CPEC, there should be a China-India Economic Corridor (CIEC) in line with the historical Mauryan Trade route, which, after passing through POK, enters the Indian side of Jammu and Kashmir and then into the rest of India. Central Asian countries (Kazakhstan, Uzbekistan and Kyrgyzstan), which are keen to join CPEC, will be keener still to join CIEC. India, in turn, will have land access to these countries and also to Western China. CIEC/Mauryan Trade Route will also partially address India's concern over its sovereignty and territorial integrity about POK. The proposed Mauryan Trade Route will merge with it, BCIM (Bangladesh-China-India-Myanmar) Corridor as well.
- India should offer to join CPEC at multiple points along the Punjab and Sindh border and also seek land access to Afghanistan and Iran. Remember: The Iran-Pakistan-India gas pipeline and TAPI (Turkmenistan-Afghanistan-Pakistan-India) gas project will be immensely beneficial to the Indian economy. But when it comes to POK, China has to enter a tri-party agreement with India and pay tax for using POK for CPEC.
- Just as Chinese keep quoting from their ancient historical books on the Silk Route path and giving it a modern touch by renaming it to One Belt One Road. India too has similar rich and very powerful history and can use Chola empire maritime trade route to connect Africa via Malacca Strait to Eastern Asian country and Europe. I am proposing India gives an alternate option to the entire Africa, Middle-East, South China Sea islands and countries to Europe via this route. It's always recommended not to have monopolistic options, India can be a great help to the world with its Chola Maritime Trade Route.

These three proposals have the potential to achieve comprehensive infrastructural and economic connectivity in large part of Asia, South Asia in particular.

India-Pakistan Trade Ties

India-Pakistan trade ties have three components, namely: "black" or illegal trade transacted through the land borders; the informal trade which is carried out through "third" countries and re-exported from there to Pakistan; finally, formal trade through imports/exports of merchandise through all recognized seaports, airports, land customs stations and inland container depots. The illegal trade channels are smugglers who operate along the 675 km unfenced stretch of the Rajasthan sector along the contiguous Indo-Pakistan border; besides carriers, khepias who misuse personal baggage through the 'green channel' facilities at international airports. Informal trade is conducted through agents who are stationed in free ports like Singapore or Dubai and estimated to be the US $2 billion. Thus, the combined volumes of illegal and circular trade are much larger than formal levels of trade which in reality, therefore, amounts to "pseudo" trade between the two countries.

The attraction of mutual trading between the two sides is linked to low freight costs which translate into lower prices, given the contiguous borders between these two countries. In such a situation, a government keeping in view the people's interests is obliged to ensure that commodities and merchandise are imported only from such countries. The other conducive conditions are cultural affinity, common language, similar economic and social systems which provide an ideal foundation for broader India-Pakistan trade ties.

The potential for greater trade between the two is considerable. Current trade volume is less than $3 billion, but some experts estimate that a normalized trade regime could eventually send the Sensex soaring to $40 billion. Such projections take into account, in part, the large volume of informal Pakistan-India trade, which not long ago equalled that of formal trade, more Indian cotton, petroleum products, telephones, cars, organic chemicals and tea will flow into Pakistan, while more Pakistani dates, jewellery, medical supplies and petroleum oils will surge into India. Many of these exports are now transacted informally (such as by smuggling or through third countries).

For instance, Pakistan imports iron ore from Brazil and Australia, besides tea from Kenya at higher prices, though these items could be available at lower rates from India. Similarly considering Indian pharmaceutical products are 30% cheaper than Pakistani products, it would certainly make a difference to the common citizen in that country. In turn, this would help Indian pharmaceutical products to sell larger volumes in geographically proximate markets, besides impacting positively on industrial growth.

Indian coffee which is now smuggled into Pakistan, due to the absence of formal trade in the commodity, has a scope of being a lucrative export item. Pakistan is estimated to be the second largest tea consumer in the world with a market size of around 130-150 million kg per annum and for several years it did not import tea from India. Eventually, India and Pakistan signed a contract for the sale of tea in August 1997 owing to compulsions, as the tea gardens in Kenya, Sri Lanka and Indonesia were hit by drought. Tea is not imported from India. Two major multinational tea traders in Pakistan have their tea gardens in Kenya and it is natural for them to make Pakistan a captive market. India can surely think of offering Kashmir and Assam tea and coffee farmland to Pakistani business houses with 51-49 investment model.

Pakistan's economy which is characterized by inadequate industrialization has created a demand-supply gap and drives both 'black' and informal trade for truck tyres exports from India. The size of the market in the country is one million truck tires annually and production facilities exist for only two lakh tires, of which half is taken by the government sector. This leaves only one lakh truck tires for sale in the open market. Therefore, Indian truck tires are a popular product in Pakistan. However, though the item has been placed on the 'open' import list, the high duty structure of 46.6% would make Indian tires costlier in Pakistan than tires imported through the Turkmenistan route.

India and Pakistan both being agrarian economies could cooperate in agriculture which is a core component of the GDP and the largest employment generation sector in either country. To quote, "It, therefore, makes sense for the two countries to cooperate in areas of common interests as it would be to their mutual advantage. Just as coal and steel were the 'lead sectors' in European integration, there is every possibility of agriculture emerging as the major sector in which cooperation and joint action can benefit both countries especially in the context of the liberalization of these sectors."

The food and agri-business industry have a significant impact on the regional economy. This industry has one of the highest economic multiplier effects among the various industries, even ahead of the telecom or power sector. According to an estimate, liberalized India-Pakistan trade in the agro-sector would generate around 3.0 plus lakh jobs in India and 2.0 lakh jobs in Pakistan. A research paper prepared by the Karachi Chamber of Commerce and Industry entitled, "Freer Trade with India: raison d'être and Impact" argues strongly in favour of Indo-Pakistan trade relations. The paper sees the possibility of transfer of appropriate technology to Pakistan from India; besides, that liberalized bilateral trade would give the two countries a bargaining chip in negotiating with the developed countries.

The new CARs namely Kazakhstan, Uzbekistan, Tajikistan and Turkmenistan have signed several bilateral trade and economic cooperation agreements with India. However, the continuing conflict in Kashmir is preventing the implementation of these non-political ties from taking shape with India. If peace is restored to the region,

"Pakistan will be pressed by the CARs into granting trade transit facilities to India. In view of Pakistan's own keenness to set-up close relations with the CARs in various fields, including trade, it will hardly be able to resist this pressure."

At the time of partition, both India and Pakistan inherited economies which were complementary in nature. However, their politically-driven economic policies resulted in divergence as the two neighbours promoted competition among themselves. Pakistan's economy was, therefore, resource-rich and agro-based without an adequately developed industrial infrastructure and lacked technology. Its limited manufacturing capacity included a few textile mills, cement factories and an oil refinery.

The Indian government has made a formal démarche to the Pakistan government about the MFN status and it awaits a response. MFN status stipulates that the contracting parties have to accord each other's exports and imports the same tariff and trade restrictions which are given to other nations. Today there are three views in Pakistan about liberalizing trade with India. Significantly, a section of economists and businessmen advocate trade with India as they feel that it would be a mutually beneficial proposition. However, another group of businessmen does not favour trade ties which are considered synonymous with an Indian economic invasion. Finally, the security services are opposed to economic relations with India for purely political reasons. They feel that bilateral trade ties should be formed only after the Kashmir problem is solved between the two nations.

So here are my suggestions:

1. Indus water benefits to be appropriately shared among Pakistan and India, Stat of Jammu and Kashmir to get the lion's share of the revenue.
2. CPEC revenue from POK to come to India which will eventually go to J&K (China should be assured of no harm to its CPEC investment, but it has to get into legal agreement with India as this is an Indian region of Jammu and Kashmir.
3. India should launch Mauryan trade route, encouraging Pakistan to become key investor, partner and stakeholder.
4. India to buy the entire $40 billion trade deficit of Pakistan on 1% interest. This is an important strategic recommendation.
5. India to come out with the model to help benefit the Pakistani decision-makers in the Electrical Power Projects in Kashmir River Projects.
6. MFN – should be based on some quantifiable mathematical formulae in terms the gain or loss to each.

7. India to give more room to Pakistan to run some financially beneficial projects in Afghanistan.
8. Pakistan has large feudal class and army top brass with business interests, get them a partner in commerce and give them large stakes, anti-India policy will see U-Turn.
9. India should launch Chola maritime trade route passing via Arabian sea, Indian Ocean, South China Sea via Malacca Strait.

What war could ravish, commerce could bestow and he returned a friend, who came to a foe. – Alexander Pope

C6: Class – Stratification and Social Engineering

Kashmir issue affects so many important parameters of human and society growth, be it happiness, security, environment, terrorism, commerce, health, education, religious harmony, development of the entire region. Remove anti-social issues like gender-biased marriage act, inheritance of properties etc from Article 370. Government of India should come out with a plan to reach out to two affected sections of the Kashmiri society; the mothers (especially from South Kashmir) and the low caste Muslims also known as commoners; who have not benefited so far from independent India's growth. Most of the ruling class folks are Abdullahs, Muftis, Geelanis, Mirwaiz, Hurriyat's. They all come from rich class and have feudal type lifestyles.

They will not let Article 370 and 35A to be modified but will take the stand of maintaining the *status quo.* And diluting the Articles by modifying it to benefit common poor Muslims who are almost daily forced to shut down their businesses and send their kids for stone pelting is detrimental to their political ambition of being the prominent player in this Kashmir movement. This social fault line needs social engineering type treatment, which during Mandal era Laloo and Mulayam so smartly used for their benefit, even though arguably it did not help larger OBCs and SCs population, the gain went to the so-called leaders and their kins.

Something similar can be worked out in Kashmir, maybe promote more such leaders who represent their communities for the real development and have mass reach. Does Ajit Doval has such strategy to segregate the society so that each of their aspirations can be packaged appropriately? All these foreign imported concepts of Wahhabism and Salafism will be effectively checkmated with this suggested strategy. Indians are heavily caste driven society irrespective of their religion. In India irrespective of your religion, caste is still the biggest glue to make or break any religious fundamentalist movement. Use this unfortunate caste influenced societal stratification to your benefit and eventually helping the people. It's like using deadliest COBRA's venom to make medicine. I am presenting data in the subsequent para to prove my argument for those liberals and separatists who think this may be a bigger evil and hence should not be used. Well, everything is fair in the statecraft and politics.

Social Fault Line – Now coming to the main objections raised against Article 370 and 35A.

It facilitates the violation of the right of women to 'marry a man of their choice' by not giving the heirs any right to property if the woman marries a man not holding PRC. Therefore, her children are not given Permanent Resident Certificate and thereby considering them unfit for inheritance – not given any right to such a woman's property even if she is a permanent resident. It facilitates the free and unrestrained violation of fundamental rights of those workers and settlers like Scheduled Caste and Scheduled Tribe people who have lived there for generations. The Valmiki's who were brought to the State during 1957 were given Permanent Resident Certificates on the condition that they and their future generations could stay in the State only if they continued to be *safai-karmacharis* (scavengers). And even after six decades of service in the State, their children are safai-karmacharis and they have been denied the right to quit scavenging and choose any other profession.

This is such a shameful part of the law, India cannot allow this and hence the modification or abolition of the Article needed to provide a human touch to the large section of Valmiki Muslims in the valley. They need to come-up in the society and become the part of the development and upward hierarchy movement. All the talk about human rights only caters to rich Muslims and not to the Muslim Valmiki's (the lowest in hierarchy folks), the scavengers. BSP's, Left and liberals are mysteriously silent of their state of affairs.

Caste divide between Kashmiri Muslims – In the Indian subcontinent, caste-based discrimination is not unique to Hindus only, it's found in Christians, Sikhs and Muslims. Even among Kashmiri Muslims, distinctions based on descent are pretty common and sometimes not very subtly. Sayeeds often consider themselves superior. A few years ago, a Barber happened to be at the wedding feast of a well-to-do family of the Sayeed descent. When the meal was served, in traditional Wazwan style with four persons sharing a meal of many courses from the same large platter, three young men from Sayeed families found they would have to share their platter with the barber.

One by one, each of them got up, making one excuse or another and sat elsewhere. The barber was an assertive sort and, as the meal began to be served, got up and announced that he would not eat unless those three boys shared his meal. There was a commotion as the three showed no signs of moving back. A community leader got up and offered to share the barber's meal, but the young man would not settle for anything less than those three young men sharing his meal. Finally, they had to return. In fact, washer-men, milkmen and bakers in Kashmir even have backward caste status under the rules of government recruitment. Most tourists to Kashmir never realize it but the families that run houseboats, whom tourists often presume to be Kashmiris, are commonly reviled by most other Kashmiris as Hanjis, the name of the boatmen's caste. The word Hanji sounds as if its roots are in the word Majhi, which is commonly used in the Gangetic plains for boatmen. One strain of Kashmiri lore even maintains that the Hanjis came to the valley from Kerala, with philosopher-preacher, Shankaracharya. Since they were well-versed with fishing and boats, they took to the lakes and rivers of Kashmir like, well, fishermen to water.

The degree to which Kashmiris often carry their consciousness of their own and others, caste backgrounds is sometimes amazing. Not just housewives around kitchen hearths but bright, well-educated young men will slip easily into descriptions of their own or other people's caste antecedents. Even the veteran trade union leader and former member of the All Parties Hurriyat Conference General Council, Ishtiaq Qadiri, once told without the slightest trace of embarrassment that he would not accept an invitation to dine with a milkman's family. The result of such social ostracism is that some families with a Hanji background who have taken to other occupations often adopt the surname Dar, which denotes descent from a sub-caste of distinction among Brahmin Kashmiris. Far more common among various other castes of Kashmiris is the adoption of the surname Sayeed. Indeed, if the number of Kashmiris who claim the Sayeed name are to be accepted at face value. Of course, it would also mean that all these families, at some point in history, migrated from further west.

There is an irony in that too. For, among a people so conscious of the supposed superiority of a Brahmin background, the deference given to certain sorts of foreign origin is remarkable. For instance, Khans, who have Pathan antecedents, are also highly regarded and many Kashmiris are almost as happy to have a match arranged with a Khan family as with a Sayeed. These Pathan families are not only descended from those who settled here during the highly oppressive period of Afghan rule in the first half of the eighteenth century. Some of them were also settled here as officers during the British or Dogra period.

Some Kashmiris also take such surnames as Naqshbandi or Makhdoomi after the names of Sufi saints whom they hold in reverence, although Naqshband Sahib is foreign. The name Sheikh is particularly interesting. When used before the person's name, as in the case of the Abdullah family, it denotes descent from Brahmins and often landlords. When used as a suffixed surname, it denotes the cleaner caste and so is looked down upon. Certain Kashmiri caste names are similar to Parsi names, in that they denote the occupations of those with the name. Kokru, for instance, is rooted in the word kokur, which means chicken in Kashmiri and the bearer of the name is likely to have descended from a family that ran a hatchery.

Caste first came to be identified as a principle of social stratification among Hindus. It has remained a dominant feature of social stratification in the Indian subcontinent. Sociologists have always tried to explain and analyse the social stratification in India in terms of caste. Moreover, while analysing systems of social stratification in other religions and societies, they tend quite unconsciously to follow a culture-specific definition of the institution and base their discussion on the Hindu phenomenon.

The Kashmiri society, being a part of the broader Indian society, has also been influenced by this caste system. In the pre-Islamic period, the valley was wholly peopled with Hindus, in which the Brahmins were at the top of the social hierarchy because they were considered the most knowledgeable person. They enjoyed the superiority and exploited the low castes (Shudra) for their vested interests. But it was only after the 14th century when Muslim saints reached here and started their mission by converting the people (Hindus) into the Islamic religion. They taught the basic philosophy of Islam, which is based on the equality of all. It is because of this egalitarian philosophy, most of the Pandits convert into Muslims and had a sigh of relief of the oppression which they had faced in the typical Hindu caste system. The Islamic religion, when we see from the strictly theoretical sense, is without the caste barriers. In fact, it negates the very notion of caste stratification. It emphasizes on the egalitarian system; the *Holy Quran* says:

> "O mankind. We (God) created you from a single pair of male and female and made you into peoples and tribes, that ye may know each other (not despise each other). Verily, the most honoured in the sight of God is (he who is) the righteous among you." (Surah Al-hujuraat, Verse 13)

This verse makes it quite clear that though Islam accepts differentiation based on gender and tribe. It does not recognize social stratification. It opposes to draw the line of demarcation by race, colour, creed and caste. But, at the same time, it is true only up to the theoretical understanding of Islam. But in reality, the Muslim community remains diversified, fragmented and as caste-ridden as any other community of India.

Practically, the situation in the Muslim society is somewhat different. Muslims too are stratified by caste. There had always been an element of superiority present with those castes which are considered to be at the top and a kind of inferiority present with those castes which are considered to be at the bottom. The Muslim society like the traditional Hindu society got divided into different status groups on the lineage and descent.

In Kashmir districts, those who own the land was called, Zamindars (landlords) and those who don't be called as Nangars (Landless/Serfs). This system of class stratification was known as Shaksi or Shaksiyaatic Raj (feudalism), in which the Zamindars (landlords) were at the top and the Nangars (landless peasants) were at the lowest rung. After conversion, people differentiate one another on the basis of descent and lineage. Syeds, Pirs and Ulemas sat at the top, because of their foreign ancestry and religious knowledge, whereas the Wattals, Wagays and Dums at the so-called lowest rung because of their ignorance and occupation.

Again, Islamic sanctions do not divide the community into different endogamous groups. But under the impact of traditional culture, the Muslims also developed a caste-like hierarchy and the concept of superior or inferior prevailed on the basis of birth, descent and religions knowledge. This was given due importance and Muslims also performed marriages within the same castes. At present marriages occur within caste. This is the only institution where caste system still plays a vital role.

As a complex social phenomenon, social stratification which refers to the division of the society into various hierarchical strata is as old as human civilization, while many have talked about a classless society of either the past or the future, but these ideas found very little support in historical experience. Though the phenomenon is common to all societies, its nature and forms vary from society to society and from culture to culture. Hope Doval and his team is making the strategy to reach out to all the right representatives of the Kashmiri population for the right solution to this never-ending problem.

Reservation for the OBCs, SCs and lower economic strata people of the J&K State – Chief Minister should come from special, class representing majority economic strata as the part of new stronger Article 370. Dr Aftab Alam, a political scientist who has worked on the subject, says. "Untouchability is the community's worst-kept secret." Studies have claimed that "concepts of purity and impurity; clean and unclean castes" do exist among Muslim groups. A book by Ali Anwar says while Dalits are called *asprishya* (untouchable) in Hindu society, they are called *arzal* (inferior) among the Muslims. A 2009 study by Dr Alam found there was not a single 'Dalit Muslim' in any of the prominent Muslim organizations, which were dominated essentially by four "upper-caste" Muslim groups. Now a major study – possibly the first its kind – by a group of researchers reveals that the scourge of untouchability is alive and well among Kashmiri Muslims.

A substantial proportion of the "Dalit Muslims" report that they do not receive an invitation from non-Dalits for wedding feasts, possibly because of a history of social segregation. A section of "Dalit Muslims" testify that they are seated separately in non-Dalit Muslim feasts. Almost a similar proportion of respondents confirm that they eat after the upper-caste people have finished. Many say they are served food on different plates. At least a third of them state that they are not allowed to bury their dead in an "upper-caste" burial ground. They do so either in some other place or one corner of the main ground.

Most of the Muslims offer prayers in the same mosque, but in some places "Dalit Muslims" felt discriminated against in the main mosque. Article 35A also has that caste biased incorporated, it has denied permanent resident status to husbands and children of women marrying outside the State and made sanitation workers of the Dalit Valmiki caste stay tied to their occupation. The Study Centre lists the things one loses out when denied this status: government jobs, admission to government professional colleges, voting and property rights. As for women, while they retain their status if they marry outside the State, their husbands and children can't hold property, cast their vote, get admission to professional colleges or get government jobs in the State because of Article 35A. This is a great gender bias, as the same disabilities do not apply to men marrying out of the State.

Land Reforms and Property tracking should be some measures to correct and modify Article 370 and 35A. Sheikh Abdullah also had a similar dream.

Policy for the social media – Global Jihad and Ghazwa-e-Hind will surely attract India's younger generation as social media and propaganda machinery is in a way too advanced and impactful. What narrative India has to counter this? Currently it does not even allow its army to create more brigadiers like Mr Gogoi, a youth icon. It does not even regulate its over liberal media and intellectuals when this dirty war is on. On the top of it, right-wing fringe elements come out daily with all the buried issues that will further disrupt the society disturbing the government focus on tacking all these global issues with strong supportive citizens.

I personally believe in total freedom, but each utterance has to be tied with the follow-up action. Let Kashmiri youths form a group funded by the Central Government to monitor the discussions on the web. JNU type discussion though hurtful should be entertained, even if that's calling discussion of balkanization of India or communal talks, give these kids a platform to discuss and conclude. Let the free flow of ideas be finally regulated by the groups of selected prominent Indians from all walks of lives. Let rest of India see how much innovative talent these kids have, when they say "Bharat ki barwaadi tak, Insha'Allah", or Beef Party or hacking a calf in the middle of the road, let them use this platform. India needs to know their kids, how they are shaping and what measures can be used to correct them.

C7: Conquest of the Border

C7 is the fundamental of all the above 6 Cs. Like our planetary system has Sun as the central element and the planets around it. Similarly, all the 6 Cs mantras need to have a primary mantra that energizes, activates and makes them effective. Without this core mantra; all the other Cs does not have much value. In fact, various governments in the past have tried multiple forms of these Cs, but the results have been abortive. To stop this miscarriage; Pakistan's psyche of brazen and full of bravado needs to be addressed. This is where C7 will play an important role.

As mentioned before, I do not see Kashmir conflict as purely a political or the territorial problem as talked by many renounced historians and political commentators, trying to put the onus on the history to India, Pakistan and erstwhile people of Dogra Riyasat, it is plain and simple Water war, Geographic Location control, Islamic Radicalization and Flawed Aspirations of the local people all thrown in a boiling pot called Kashmir Conflict. Now as far as aspirations of the people are concerned, who will validate this? UN, Western powers, Arabs run OIC group or liberals and Communist's media, driven by their perception.

The so-called 'Azaadi' aspiration as always quoted by Pakistan and Indian Separatists is the outcome of years of coaching is the result of indoctrination in madrasas', brilliant funding strategy of separatists and using non-State actors to keep this pot boiling by Pakistan. So I have my strong view on this so-called 'Azaadi' aspiration. Kashmiris have no issue believing and practising their faith; they do not have to compromise and still being part of the Indian union. Other issues like development, poverty, unemployment, etc are purely a governance issue and weak Article 370 that has affected the State, but then it's the Kashmiris who have chosen this set-up and hence India needs to help them get out of this mess.

As far as two nation theory is concerned, it was good till 1971, but after East Pakistan chose to break and form a new country Bangladesh this idea died, the separatist Kashmiris have to make peace with this reality or else this conflict will never end in their remaining life time. If you see today's Kashmir, the amount of freedom that people have with practising, sermonizing and making mosques as some kind of anti-India and anti-kaffir platform has gone beyond the tenants of Islam and also against the democratic and civilized society norms. The vigour with which it is done, it sometimes culminates in kaffir's bashing resulting in the ethnic cleansing of the minority Hindus from the Kashmir Valley as done in '90s to the killing of a young local Muslim DSP in 2018 in front of the famous so-called religious and political head in the now infamous mosque, Jamia Masjid, Srinagar.

Military Option – Pakistan is a special case, its strategy of asymmetric war against India has landed it in a sweet spot with zero fear of retaliation. It uses its pariah status to cross the moral threshold and uses nukes as the umbrella to neutralize India's superior military might. And in all this, they are making American taxpayers money (Yours Truly included) be siphoned to them via blackmailing our politicians into releasing funds. By sponsoring terror against India and using covert means to sponsor unrest in Kashmir, Pakistan forces global powers to focus on South Asia and uses that leverage to squeeze out more funds. Terrorism becomes a self-fulfilling prophecy. India has to hit the psyche of the Pakistan nation and that has to be continuous and deep causing the huge cost to that nation. LoC needs to be pushed towards Pakistan at least covering all the key strategic ridges. India should be ready to lose 300K soldiers and hence should in parallel raise units to replace them. The cost of these 300K soldiers should translate into minimum $15-$25 billion for Pakistan. The full power is given to the local and central command to carry on the operations best suited. India should mutilate any non-State actors caught in such operation beyond LoC. Pakistan psyche is false Islamic values and ideology they have created, India and Modi's government has to break this neck and for this even it requires aerial bombing of such faith-based structure and monuments it should be carried on.

This is not as simple as it may look to the civilized world. Take the case of the alleged Indian spy Kulbhushan Jadhav who was kidnapped by the Jihadists from Iran, brought to Pakistan and then captured and sentenced to death, based on the verdict of the Kangaroo military court. His wife Chetna Jadhav was made to wipe her bindi, remove the bangles, take out the Mangalsutra (very pious symbol for Hindu married ladies), asked to change her Indian women attire saree to a Salwar Kameez, her shoes taken; his mother was asked not to speak in the mother-tongue Marathi when talking with her son; all this when earlier agreed venue from Pak MEA office shifted to a bullet prove container and mother and wife kept behind the glass wall for thirty minutes, that too when this meeting was planned and agreed upon by the two MEAs. All this comes from a false and brazen bravado this Islamic nation's Army and ISI have woven around them. The time has come when India needs to act or else stop complaining. Stop being a cry baby and be counted as a nation that aspires to be a power. Power comes from strength. Strength has to be demonstrated always.

Under the circumstances, branding Pakistan a 'Terrorist State' makes little sense because it actively works towards such a branding. By inverting the rules of the game, the more Pakistan appears unstable, the better for it. Hence declaring Pakistan, a State sponsor of terror, far from being a deterrent, will incentivize them more to export terror. Which is why Modi will make a big mistake strategically and politically if he relies on diplomatic offensive alone to counter Pakistan's aggression against India. It has never worked in the past and it won't work in the future. The only casualty will be Modi's legacy. You have to plan every quarter one major military offensive measure costing US $ 50-100 million worth investment.

Allegedly around 22,000 widows, 1,00,000 orphans and 6,78,086 bread earners of the Kashmiri family have been reportedly affected as a result of violence in Jammu and Kashmir over the last several decades. Huge investment for any nation and much more for a democratic State. So Military option is a must to help push the solution. This will be the catalyst that was, maybe, missing. Iran was a strategic depth for Pakistan; their fighter planes were in Iranian hangers during 1971 war.... Modi has broken that depth. If Pakistan joins Saudi Arabia led the group for the boycott of Qatar, then Iran will be forced to act against Pakistan and liberation of Balochistan will be smoother and faster. India has to talk in a plain and simple language with the friend Iran, time to test the Dosti.

Raheel Sharif is leading the army of Saudi Arabia alliance; he needs to be given special treatment by India in any strategy they plan, he is the key guy whose neck has to be broken for bringing down the unwarranted false temper among Pakistani army and future recruits. This should be an important part of the strategy. During his visit to the LoC, Pakistan army chief General Qamar Javed Bajwa had talked about supporting Kashmir's freedom struggle. Through this provocation, Bajwa had all but challenged India's military power to the glee of foreign and domestic terrorists in Kashmir.

Indian politicians and the army are seething with anger as it coincided with the beheading of Indian border patrol team and rightly so, at the inhuman act and have vowed to avenge the dishonour. Experts have given out various retaliatory options short of a war on the LoC that the Indian army could undertake. These include raids by Special Forces, beheading as a tit-for-tat, use of artillery's long-range firepower to blow off Pakistani posts and surgical strikes, which have recently been incorporated in the joint doctrine of the Indian armed forces.

The Pakistan army would surely have mulled over the possible retaliatory actions before challenging the Indian might. They would have thought through the possibility of war escalation. While India should respond hard, wisdom dictates that it should go beyond tactical gains. The purpose - very much doable - should be to deter the Pakistan army by forcing them to assess that they lose more by such reprehensible acts and by continuing the export of terror.

What to Do - India should use heavy artillery guns at the LoC. This way the soft image of a large nation will be shed creating doubts in the enemy's mind and their non-stop brazen attacks will undergo rethinking, though this will not stop future attacks India has to be prepared. Another important messaging will be for China which has brazenly started working into POK region which is a disputed territory between India and Pakistan, which has to bilaterally resolve. Even after knowing this if any nation starts a road building work, means it is directly challenging the other country's sovereignty, with thousands of Chinese workers milling all along the LoC constructing the China-Pakistan Economic Corridor (CPEC), their unfortunate casualties as the artillery's collateral damage will send the message to Chinese peace loving people that how their neighbour India is confronting deadly terror which will soon reach at their doors as well and they need to better safeguard themselves from future such attacks, this may help change opinion in China and the Communist government may have to rethink its CPEC route plan.

India has two artillery platforms, the Pinaka and Smerch multi-barrel rocket launchers, with 40 km and 70 km ranges should be deployed heavily. The CPEC, which passes through Pakistan Occupied Kashmir and Gilgit-Baltistan, will fall within the ranges of these weapon systems. India should immediately declare CPEC is crossing POK as trespassing and have it known to UN, world and China on the option of military action in case India feels its sovereignty has been violated to disrupt this road construction. China has to get tri-party agreement to even put a single stone on the POK part of the CPEC.

Thirdly any retaliatory beheading of Pakistani border patrol also will not help. It goes against the moral fibre of the Indian Army and also global image; and instead of deterring the Pakistan army, it will embolden them to do more of the same. The September 2016 surgical strike was just the beginning it need not be surgical this time, it has to be motor roll inside the LoC. More use of Air Force needed, in fact, they always have to strike first, a new regiment as suggested should be dedicated to such initiatives. India needs to expand her air power many times than the current strength with better radar, satellite and cyber equipped force.

Critics of War strategy thinks that the full-scale war is not an option for India either, for five reasons. One, Pakistan will have China's support regarding war supplies to fight a long-duration war. Two, China could help Pakistan with its robust space, cyber and electronic warfare capabilities without showing its hand. Three, Chinese in Pakistan could be collateral damage in war. Four, the Indian army will need sufficient time to re-orient itself from counter-insurgency to fighting a conventional war. And five, Pakistan's tactical nuclear weapons cannot be overlooked. I do not buy this. To solve Kashmir, you have to have long-term (minimum 3-5 years') war plan in parallel to other peace initiative.

Viable Options – What should the Indian army do? Three things: It should not repair the fence on the LoC which gets damaged each year by heavy snow in winter months. On the one hand, the Pakistan army finds new ways to breach it for pushing terrorists into Jammu and Kashmir; on the other hand, symbolizing the psychological and military limit of war-fighting, it has, unconsciously, instilled a defensive mindset in the Indian army. The Pakistan army, which happily allows the Indian army to repair the damaged fence, will be worried if India were not to do so, as that will be a clear message of India ready to change the LoC. This would distract it from its three major priorities: heavy involvement in counter-terrorism tasks for internal stability; protecting the CPEC to ensure timelines are met; and its diplomatic role in support of China's 'One Belt, One Road' mega-project for global power.

Moreover, the Indian army should adopt an offensive posture on the LoC and this means ready for a long war, instead of fighting a continuous war since 1989 inside Indian territory all India needs to do to remove the fence and the war will be pushed within Pakistan. What it would also mean, is that instead of the present anti-infiltration role which involves the army looking out for infiltrators along the valleys and gorges, it should be looking at Pakistani posts and how to destroy them through heavy firepower and regular continuous raids. While the Pakistan army will surely react with equal force, it will be compelled to assess the trade-off between its other priorities and increased aggression on the LoC.

This is not all. If the infiltration supported by the Pakistan army does not abate, the Indian army could even contemplate improving its tactical positions on the LoC, especially in the south of the Pir Panjal range where it has the numbers as sufficient troops have been moved forward from the hinterland to the LoC. Were thess to happen, the Pakistan army would certainly react; there is a possibility that it could finally use its artillery and break the 2003 ceasefire, which India wants. The Pakistan army's commitment on its eastern front with India would increase dramatically, something that both Rawalpindi and China would not prefer.

To support the offensive posture and action, New Delhi should help the three defence services make up critical deficiencies, especially ammunition, on war-footing from abroad. Prime Minister Narendra Modi's visit to Israel, which had wholeheartedly supported India with war material during the 1999 Kargil conflict, could help in this. Needless to add, the three defence services would need to work out their war-plans for the Jammu and Kashmir theatre, where plenty of campaign-level (as distinct from tactical) objectives are available. If the above were to be done, Rawalpindi would be compelled to sit up and reassess its options. Its ally, China, which desires regional peace for its One Belt, One Road plan, would also nudge Pakistan to check its proxy war. And all this would not be lost on the people of Kashmir.

In 1965 war, Indian Army had captured the strategic Haji Pir Pass. During the Tashkent talks between India and Pakistan, held through the good offices of Soviet Union, India agreed to return Haji Pir Pass, Pt 13620 which dominated Kargil town and many other tactically important areas. To add mystery to the whole process, Prime Minister

Lal Bahadur Shastri died on 10th January 1966 after signing the Tashkent Declaration with President Ayub Khan of Pakistan in a foreign land. He was denounced by all and sundry for caving in to the Russian pressure and made to return Haji Pir Pass to Pakistan, resulted in two grave disadvantages to India: One – had the pass been held by us, the distance from Jammu to Srinagar through Poonch and Uri would have been reduced by over 200 kms. Two – later on Pak commenced its infiltration into J&K in 1965, through the Uri-Poonch Bulge which continues even today. This historical blunder of Shastri Ji or backstabbing by the trusted friend is under the clout with no answer till date. But whatever maybe the reason, this is 2018 and India need to undo her 1965 and 1971 mistakes related to Haji Pir Pass and removal of the fences from the LoC will be a good start.

1. Modi government should immediately allocate US $100 million each for having strategic groups formed constituting top experts from India working to take democratic aspirations of Balochistan, Sindh, Gilgit-Baltistan, POK and Karachi to the global stage and promote people's democratic aspiration. Investing in the non-State actors within Pakistan should be immediately pursued at war footing. CIA does it all the time, some leafs from its book needs to be taken.
2. Have Brahmos supersonic cruise missiles or similar missiles systems some 50 plus in numbers targeted to the major dams, roads few selected manufacturing hubs of China and Pakistan in the ready state and the total worth of those targets should be not less than US $2 trillion! The Doklam standoff and China foreign ministry declaring China's intent to enter Kashmir on Pakistan's request makes India jittery. For a proud ancient and sovereign country, this standoff and direct threat gives her total moral standing on choosing the minimum deterrence shield. I am told during cold war this helped keep the full blown escalation down substantially between the two superpowers then, will do now as well. Yes, there will be implications, have to be ready to face it. China should be informed of this act, which will be purely India's strategy of self-defence and not war, this should be followed with the abolition of no first use strategy of nukes. They are welcome to reciprocate based on their strategy and might, India will not complain. Kashmir resolution will have a price which India has to pay already she spends 10% of her GDP on J&K, increase the Defence investment from 1.2% of GDP to 6% like any powerful country.

Be ready to open front(s) with China every time Pakistan attacks Kashmir via proxies. China cities are not near India-China border, they have Tibet covering 30% of their total land bordering India as the buffer region for heavily populated east, this sense of security due to large distance maybe giving China false sense of confidence vis-a-vis India and her missiles capabilities and hence it has been lately escalating pressure at the border often and coaching and motivating Pakistanis to follow the suit. Now even former Chief Minister of J&K, Mehbooba Mufti made a statement on China wrongly influencing Kashmiri Jihadis. For India, the entire population lives around the border, so China thinks even if India goes nuclear the damage will be mostly to Tibet side, who are India's friend and hence India will never attack. India has to build a counter strategy to easily reach China's east coast via other avenues. Again I am not suggesting a war, but the deterrence has to be built, bullies will no more be taken lightly. It takes 1:3 ratios for an attacking nation when fighting on the plain and 1:7 army for the mountain terrain, this will work in favour of India as it's a peaceful nation and even coexists with small Bhutan and Nepal peacefully, unlike China.

Now why China when the topic is Kashmir conflict? I have an interesting perspective which came to me from childhood story which I heard from my granny. There was a cruel magician whose life was hidden in a bird put in the golden cage far away in some castle. His victims kept trying to kill him to save innocents from his evil design but in vain and he always kept coming back. One day a boy name Bharat Kumar found the secret and killed the bird which eventually killed the evil magician and the entire village was safe again from his evil magic spell.

The moral of the story as per my nanny was to kill the reason for the cause and the cause will be taken care. Pakistan has not only covert but overt support from China to checkmate India and to challenge her sovereignty.

What story India as a law-abiding responsible, democratic, emerging global power have to convince the global fraternity? Well the list is long, South China Sea posturing, Bhutan-China border dispute, Vietnam, Philippines, South Korea, Malaysia, Japan, making of OBOR/CPEC project blatantly in the Indian claimed part of disputed POK, Diverting of Upper tributary of river Brahmaputra affecting India and Bangladesh, the list is long. Hence India is very concerned and worried for peace to prevail in the region and has put some 50+ nuclear equipped very long distance continental missiles delivery system, both on land and in water. The world should come together to support such noble gesture for overall peace and safety of approximately 3 billion plus humanity of the region.

Few Facts to Support this Military Strategy

Land Attack: China has an army of 2.3 million soldiers and India of 1.3 million. In case of wars, the advantage always goes to defensive side in a ratio of 1:3 (one soldier for defence is equal to 3 in the offence) and this ratio becomes 1:5 to 1:7 (if on higher altitude) in hilly and mountainous terrains. So advantage India. Also, the supply line from beyond Tibet in the north Himalayas can be easily cut, with Tibet being acquired land and constitutes 30% of the China landmass.

Sea Attack: To launch a massive sea attack on India which has Seven major sea ports and many minor sea ports is nearly impossible as it will require more than Five carrier battle groups if we say the least. Considering China has only One operational carrier battle group it's impossible to even with huge submarine force to block every Indian port.

Malacca Trade Choke Point

A second thing which people should note is that nearly 80–90% of Chinese trade happens through Indian ocean. To attack China Indians don't have to attack their naval ports which maybe little far, they just have to block supplies to China which will cripple its economy and Indian navy is considered the king of the Indian ocean. So its advantage India.

Air Power: In a battle of air forces numbers matter little as an experience of pilots and technology they possess matters in the 21st century. India already have fought 2 major air force wars with Pakistan (1965,1971) and their pilots every year practices with best pilots around the globe which Chinese lack, as long as Sukhoi SU-30MKI, Rafale, Advanced F16 (to be manufactured soon in India) are in the Indian armoury, even an F-22 type state of art bird can't penetrate Indian skies and leave alone the Chinese planes (remember we are only talking of defence not offence). Israelis best radar and short distance precision driven missiles will add further to the Indian feel-good situation. So again advantage India.

Cyber/Space Warfare: If one sees the ranking of Chinese hackers compared to Indian hackers they rank pretty high but when these raking are made they only consider the people who operate from the Chinese or Indian soil. Not the huge diaspora sitting in the different parts of the world managing the entire global financial systems with perfection. That is the huge IT strength which India can leverage in a war time call of duty and Indians are pretty emotion bunch in such situations as all of them in spite of relocating has umbilical cord still intact with mother, India.

If you consider the most advanced nations and see the hackers which work for them, you will find considerable number of Indian hackers ranked among the top in the world. So if one side launches a hack attack on other it will not be limited to Indian hackers serving from Indian soil, it will be an all-out war which will be highly dangerous.

In 1962 when India lost to China that time troop ratio was in favour of China 8:1 still brave Indian soldiers did not surrender because Indians believe better to die than face shame. In 1967 there was a standoff between India and China where India defeated Chinese troops. (300 Chinese soldiers were killed and India lost 75 brave hearts.) So when Chinese media and ministry asked India to remember 1962, they should remember 1967 and 1987. In Indian Ocean, the spy satellite P-8 Poseidon and naval ships have tracked down 13 Chinese ships (these figures are real government numbers and are not shown due to secrecy) which gives some glimpse to the capability, right now it's just tracking but will not be same in the war-time and hence this proposed strategy.

India should let China know that they have been helping terrorists operating in India – the Naxalites, insurgents in the North-East. If India does even 2% of what the Chinese are doing, they will not know how to handle the Tibetans and the people in Xinjiang. India is the house of world's 2nd most Muslims and can easily start dominating the atrocities Muslims are facing in Xinjiang. China is the only nation in the world which officially protects Pakistan and North Korea. China's military strength is based on its economic strength. Economic strength depends on industrial strength. If China's economy is affected, its military will get impacted and what better then choking Malacca strait.

This will send tremor in the Western world to take India differently and also such posturing will help India shed her soft nation image. China should be told that they are not an enemy nation, India has to fight her battle against radicals and all these steps she thinks are the best military strategy to fight her dirty war with her enemy. India can guarantee China to help her built CPEC if it pays the revenue and also gets into an agreement with India as far as POK route of CPEC is concerned. India can make sure Chinese business interests and human resource working there will be protected. It has to enter into a tripartite agreement with India and Pakistan for CPEC project as it falls in the Pakistan Occupied Kashmir. If they have a vision for Rising Asia which they claim then India will like to be one of the key drivers, but will not compromise its sovereignty.

3. **Iran and Israel:** Time to choose 'one' of them to be effective, can't choose both as it neutralizes the overall advantages. Iran has been on and off related to their Kashmir stand. India in her effort to always do balancing act is making the beautiful dance look ugly. With now some movement on the Chabahar Port Iran can help strategize free Balochistan campaign. If Iran wants India to be a trusted friend, India needs clarification and non-public apology on the latest Kashmir statement made by their leader, even if that's a clerical error, India has zero tolerance for friends supporting anti-India stand on Kashmir as India cannot compromise with the very idea of India and Kashmir is the key to that idea.

   Israel has to be India's all-weather friend and should be kept from such mindless foreign policy of balancing between Muslim world and Israel. Being home for the second largest nationalist Muslim citizens, India should not be apologetic but outward looking, with India first policy. Arab relationship should be based on mutual interests and past historical connection which is strong. If this is not enough then re-define the relationship. India and Israel's relationship is non-negotiable, it's permanent and independent from any nation.

4. **North Korea Relationship:** India has gone against NK for pleasing West and what has it got, no UN seat for world's second most populous country, no clear-cut support on Kashmir and no effective support against bully China which single-handedly stopped the ban on the UN designated terrorist, Azhar Masood and entry into NSG. There has to be a Give and Take on putting NK in the terror list, or else India should do business with NK as Chinese are doing and getting undue advantage in creating a fear of nuclear attack and selling the idea of invincibility when it comes to

containing the NK dictator. This comfort zone has to be broken by India. Why create another enemy, which is going nuclear and is based in the same Asia region. This is going to be a very important policy decision and India has to barter this with her UN seat aspirations or else bury it till it can take China, which will probably be twenty years of long wait. If China can openly support a UN-designated terrorist Masood and still be treated as a world power, India can learn to use the same strategy vis-a-vis NK. India this way can be important strategic and trusted partner to help President Trump in bringing NK dictator on to the negotiation table.

5. India is the glue that holds the China-Pakistan relationship together. China's policy has been driven by power political criteria and economics has counted for very little so for the peaceniks arguments of $50 billion trade surplus as a deterrent that will stop China from any India centric misadventure, is a false assumption. China-Pakistan relations are today even more important to China than they ever had before. As China seeks to shape the Asia-Pacific, Pakistan's utility to her increases. "Now Pakistan is a central part of China's transition from a regional power to a global one." Pakistan is at the heart of the network of One-Belt-One Road, China's strategic Marshall Plan. Karachi and Gwadar are critical for China's take-off as a naval power; and, the ISI is vital to Chinese intelligence on jihadis and China's initiatives in the Islamic world.

   For Pakistan, China is the key to her future. Luckily for Pakistan, first USA needed it badly for Afghan war and now China for OBOR. What are options for India, as Pakistanis ISI and Army may be laughing at India's unfortunate situation every time? Karachi has a special bonding with India as it is home to Muhajirs the largest settlement of Indian origin Pakistanis. Altaf Hussain and his MQM need to be revived, India needs to free Dawood from the ISI imprisonment and see if he can be used as an asset for larger interests. India needs to groom a large group of non-State actors within Pakistan; this will help take out the motor mouth Army heads, ISI high-rank officers and non-State religious terrorist leaders, India has to be relentless. India LoC motor firing capability has to go 10 times notch up, for that it should ask Israel to support on a priority basis.

6. India needs to raise minimum 1,00,000 Tibetans, Gurkhas and other fighters to build a mountain strike corps for the cold start doctrine. Get your best minds from IT, Medicine,

Civil services, Other streams into the army by offering huge unmatched perks, lifestyle, adventure and a free hand on planning multiple projects to soften and disrupt India's enemies. Youth will take this challenge and if they have excelled in another stream on the global stage, they will surely take army institution to the Himalayan height. The enemy will not understand the cost by one or two surgical strikes or border bunker busting mission; the game has to be played not on the LoC but deep within the heavily populated city of West Punjab. Yes, Punjab where Pakistani ISI, Army and big non-State leaders come from or have their family and friends. This region has to pay the price of 70 years of Indian blood. Not a forlorn hope.

7. Hire International cartel to reach out to all those Pakistani hawkish and India centric army bosses moving to western society for save heaven, their family to face this ugly and dangerous situation. They say everything is fair in love and war. The earliest known origin of the sentiment "all is fair in love in war" was found in poet John Lyly's novel *Euphues: The Anatomy of Wit,* published in 1579. Still relevant and true even today.
8. Any terror attack in Kashmir or other parts of India, if found to be emanating from Pakistan, then make sure India uses heavy airpower every time to move the *status quo* of the LoC line, from the current location towards Pakistan 10-15 km each time as the terrain situation maybe and 100 kms towards Pakistan if there is any chemical attack. Even if this results in full-blown war, each time India moves the LoC towards Pakistan (International Border) it should share the new line with UN and the world. The average distance between two armies manning LoC is 50-100 kms so there is a high possibility of huge loss of lives. Indian army has nothing new to lose as it is anyway getting beheaded in defensive strategy. Consider downgrading diplomatic relations by withdrawing the High Commissioner. Declare LoC demarcation no more acceptable to India, start removing the fences, do not repair the fence broken by flood or infiltrators, in fact, remove them.
9. India cannot have world's 3rd largest army of 1.3 million strong force becoming just the pensioners; it has to weekly carry out multiple border intrusion projects supported by Air Force which has always been reluctant in all the earlier wars and have always lost the element of surprise. Though it has covered for its lapses and have achieved many victories only

to be lost by the politicians at the negotiating tables, this time India has to keep pushing Air Force for real proactive attacks. From Nehru to Shastri to Indira Gandhi and to even Vajpayee, India always lost its war gains by the weak post-war negotiation skills, it has not gained even an 'inch' of the occupied POK, so what Indian army calls four wins is no win in the real term, even the formation of Bangladesh did not help India gain any land or material advantage. The check neck area connecting North-East States continues even after liberation of Bangladesh. What a waste of the 1971 gain.

India needs to learn post-war negotiations from the US by employing some ex-American army leaders in their NDA training and also continuous training for existing political bosses handling the relevant offices. Maybe have a specialized post-war negotiating team trained and educated in western army colleges. Once the war is over the fighting Generals moves out of the scene and the negotiating team steps in. Politicians other than Prime Minister, Defence Minister and Opposition head should be part of the negotiating team, but any decision has to be on consensus and majority view. In a democratic set-up elected Politicians will have final say on declaring war, but once they have made the call, it should not be their domain to negotiate and spoil the nation's gain. Have done enough damages in the past.

10. Full-fledged war should be planned with Pakistan as the neck of the Pakistan is very thin and can be easily cut, it is only 350 to 600 km in width and the Indian army can within few hours motor its tank to the friendly Afghanistan. It can say hello to her good Afghani friends, can have the best cooked Kabuli Pulaw, Kabobs, Qurmoh offering and may also rekindle the memory of great Rabindranath Tagore's story "Kabuliwala", known to most Indians.
11. Iran which acted as a strategic depth for Pakistan in earlier wars with India by allowing Pakistan to use their hangers to hide the entire Pakistani Fighter planes is now having a good relationship with India, independent of Israel-India relationship. Iran relationship needs to be further groomed via aggressive diplomacy.

Raheel Sharif has to be targeted where and whichever role he takes post-retirement to break the pseudo bravado he had built around himself and the Pakistani army, helping jihadis to flare-up the Kashmir valley both with symbolic leadership and providing direct support to the so-called non-State jihadis.

India should adopt a complex strategy to wear down Pakistan's resistance. This strategy should encompass military and political pressure; subversion; counter-terrorism; diplomatic isolation; media and public defamation and cultural domination (Indian movies and foods are next to the Chinese in global acceptance and spread). Tarnishing the reputation and credibility of the Pakistan Army should be an important element of the strategy. It is really surprising how Pakistani people see their army, an Army which lost 4 wars, surrendered more than half the country to create Bangladesh, are bewitched by their COAS guys as some demi-god, this should be busted with continuous social media war using India's mighty IT manpower and the relationships with the global countries.

12. If India is serious to handle Kashmir, it should tell the nation that the recent statement made by General Rawat on the army readiness to face Two and a half war simultaneously, is a valid and feasible statement, if yes then what's the timeline government is looking for the preparedness. Build your strength in the 12-36 months max, there are tech and funds to expedite things. China first builds her might before calling the shots in the region. India has to have multiple military initiatives to protect her sovereignty and her commerce interest in the vast Indian ocean, as suggested earlier it has to take one major military initiative per quarter as she builds her might and sharpens her clutches for larger and longer initiatives. But do not stop after one surgical strike, it has to be continuous and relentless, you win some you will lose some, but the whole mindset of the army and also enemy will undergo favourable change. Kashmir will automatically benefit and get resolved.

13. Indus extra water which is the rightful India's share has to be taken out immediately rather allowing it to follow into Pakistan Punjab province. Stop the water flow from Indus to Pakistani Punjab in the summer of 2018. India needs to hurt west Punjab where all the master mind of anti-India happily lives and flourishes. Unless they are willing to solve Kashmir once for all. Pakistani Punjab should not be allowed to sleep peacefully when on the Indian side the poor Kashmiri mothers are made to run from pillar to post searching their missing sons. India needs to fund its defence by raising allocation percentage of the GDP. This can be used as an investment for self-defence and also commerce by selling and servicing war equipment creating jobs for millions.

14. America, the only super power has to be taken into confidence. India has to come out with a plan to show how it can help the US come out from Afghanistan and also how American interests will be protected in this conflict zone. India needs to quickly work on the strategy of balkanization of Pakistan, as terror has to be controlled and not all regions of Pakistan wants to continue Jihad with India. But unfortunately they are locked currently in Pak federal structure, regions like Sindh and Balochistan want to have a friendly relationship with India. With world's second largest Muslim population, hence India should be morally obligated to remove the dark cloud of radicalization, terrorism, alienation and image of the large South Asian Muslims around the world. Start the talk with the Pakistani people via satellite, social media or any other forum that has a reach there and it has to be relentless and Brobdingnagian.
15. **CPEC/OBOR:** ISI planted a story of how Indian Intelligence (RAW) was working with their asset within Pakistan to arm Afghan Jihadis with small tactical nuclear weapons and employed 35,000 RAW agents along the border of Afghanistan to disrupt CPEC passing via POK, which India claims disputed and their part. Now even if this is not true, this angle should be looked like an option (taking the nuclear thing out of the scope) for non-stop violence in Kashmir. The growing economy of Pakistan will fund more money anti-India, pro-Kashmir jihadi activities and which will be directly hurting India, so why should India not stop the CPEC dream trespassing into disputed part of Kashmir? India should tell Pakistan the repercussion it will have to face if CPEC passes POK in the current form and also the new proposed train line from Gwadar to Tibet, this should be seen as an act of war if it crosses POK. India can get Israel take over the Indus water administration as a vendor running and maintaining water storage, utilization and electricity development for Indian Kashmiri farmers. Government of India should get Israel's engineers and technicians to run and build aviation in and around Srinagar, Kashmir. India needs to have a friend near the nuclear flashpoint for any future help if needed.
16. India has to officially let go her no first use policy of pre-emptive nuclear attacks if there is any indication of her enemy even thinking of doing it, she has to act for the safeguard her billion plus people. Go aggressive with the strategy. India should understand it is way too big and strong nation to be

pushed for way too long by a small maverick Pakistan and its supporters. Also, old conventional and *status quo* type policymakers should make space for younger and brightest Indians to take over. The Goody-Goody, Soft and Mature nation tag needs to be immersed in the Indian Ocean. It has to take stand for saving humanity from the radicalized terror menace even at the cost of hurting herself.

China is a mature nation and will probably understand that dragons are not real but an imaginary beast, but India's national animal lion is real, ferocious and called king of the jungle. It's jungle out there, with ISIS, Taliban, al-Qaeda, Kashmiri Jihadis conglomerate and other terror groups. A wise crook is one who knows when to quit. China should take its great thinker Sun Tzu little seriously who once said **'Opportunities multiply as they are seized, they will also be the reason for your downfall.'** Greed and cunningness had led to the fall of even the mighty Anglo Empire where they say sun never used to set, such was its spread across the globe.

Conclusion

You may be wondering about this last 'C' which I introduced as a wrapper for the other 6 Cs to be more of maximalist China bashing; it is not, just trying to suggest approaches to neutralize the catalyst behind Pakistan's continuous brazen acts against India. Pakistan which so blatantly housed America's biggest foe Osama bin Laden in Abbottabad, under the direct supervision of the army HQ and still came out without being bombed by the world's only power, do you think will listen to any rational, logic, confidence building measures proposals, etc no way, it thinks it has the nuclear weapon and will continue bleeding whoever it wants, be it Afghanistan, India and now even Iran. Out of 20 UN-listed terror outfits, thirteen have Pakistani linkages. Any global country that thinks India should show its generosity and give J&K and POK to Pakistan to help resolve the issue once for all are living in fool's paradise. Peaceniks keep living in a cocoon, not going to happen.

Pakistani Generals think that what mighty USSR could not do in Afghanistan, what super mighty America could not do they have done using their non-State actors, the Taliban's, the Haqqanis, etc, do you think they will appreciate any good diplomatic gesture by their foe, India ... so conceding even an inch of Kashmir will be setting the timer for the balkanization of the country called INDIA and ferocious attacks by Islamic radicalized fanatics across the globe. No country probably with the exception of the USA, can save herself from these terrorists' onslaught. India is the only hope in this region against this apocalypse, acting as stop gate preventing the deluge of terror scars to move across, even China will benefit as they will soon have a massive issue in Xinjiang province, which is only a few hours from their national capital, Beijing.

Kashmir conflict resolution has five main players, Kashmiris (both in India and Pakistan), USA, China, Pakistan and India, if you take care of them, resolution will happen. First, handle the internal situation. There are some Kashmiris in the seven districts of South Kashmir valley who have alienated; they need to win back through various measures. Try to win those who have alienated due to no hand holding or lack of proper communication from the federal government. Second try to yank out two important constituents from this 'pro-Azaadi' population, the women section and the lower caste Muslims category and have the separate social and financial measures for them. This social fault line in the subcontinent demography has to be utilized. The way Triple Talaq helped right-wing BJP win India's biggest State election in 2017 due to unexpected support from the Muslim women in spite of the Fatwas.

Similar techniques can be employed to get 50% of the Kashmiri women population join the mainstream and I have discussed them in detail earlier in this chapter. Government should work on this very hard with good intent to uplift these people who suffer daily in the shutdown calls by the separatists. These silent but large population's day to day survival depends on tourism and daily labour which a bandh-call affects badly. They have been scared to go against these few feudal leaders in the valley who keep calling shutdown of businesses. These two sections of people who live in constant fear of losing their kids and husbands can be a good starting point for the government to deflate the artificial wall of 'pro-Azaadi' inertia.

China is one important source which has given covert support to Pakistan against India since its very formation, it was very open in 1965 war, but China was not a strong country than to play this overt role supporting Pakistan fight for Kashmir and did support Pakistan but it was more moral support then military one. Now in 2018 when the assertive China is fast becoming global power it has shed its covert face to overt face and taking anti-India stand on everything that hurts Indian interest even to the extent of supporting a UN banned terrorist Azhar Masood and in the most brazen manner suggesting Third party army can enter Kashmir (read China) on the request of Pakistan, this coming from the recent standoff between India and Chinese army in Bhutan.

In my proposed solutions, I have dealt with China in detail, giving a reason why I think they are one of the key factors in resolving Kashmir. Pakistan gets daily booster shots from his all-weather friend China to keep bleeding India and now the latest salvo which Chinese official media fired in the context of Bhutan-India-China standoff is that they can use the same logic in entering Kashmir, the covert mask is totally out in their intoxication of the tremendous financial power status, China has come open and is willing to get into the military war with India be it on Kashmir, Arunachal Pradesh, Sikkim and is also building illegal dams to block upper tributaries of Brahmaputra river. Birds of feather flock together. The enemy of my enemy is my friend. Kashmir cannot be resolved diplomatically anymore and has to have a strong military angle and hence huge cost, India has to decide if it has the economy, strategy and will-power to get into any surgical treatment of this cancerous growth.

Pakistanis are primarily Indians who got converted en masse some 200 to 600 years back and had the genetic lineage that will not allow dismantling each other. Pakistanis have distorted their entire history and teach their kids something which is total baloney. They do not allow them to read and research about their origin and have tried hard to wrongly align with the Arabic culture. Pakistan will not allow any resolution on Kashmir. Critics, peaceniks and eminent liberal historians will say well what about Musharraf's proposed solution to Manmohan Singh and later to Vajpayee in Agra. Well they may be some impulsive seizure from the equilibrium and *status quo*, but the country which lost four wars with India, lost 50% of its land is not going to stop even if you make Kashmir LoC porous, or even give them Kashmir on a plate, they want Shaheen Flag on the New Delhi's Red Fort and India to Balkanize, this is the simple agenda the Army and ISI of Pakistan believes, no string attached. To make a poisonous snake harmless, one has to surgically take out the venom gland forever and till that happens, Kashmir conflict will continue, 70 years is just a trailer.

The whiskey loving Pakistani army Generals needs different treatment as the containment strategy has failed, Kashmir can never be solved unless India builds a strong, ruthless army and follows the framework in principle covered in the seven 'C' mantras as suggested by yours truly. The pipedream of false radicalized Islamic bravado of 'Ghazwa-e-Hind' forcing Indians to the Hindukush mountain (place of Hindu genocide similar to Dachau and Auschwitz) for Shechita is not to happen, such hallucination has to be crushed for the world's peace and only India can lead the world as she has already dirtied her hands due to being pulled into this dirty radicalized war, but she would need the tactical supports and blessings from Russia, Uncle Sam, Israel and some friendly Arab nations. Again this is a military wrapper framework and hence will sound and read war like, fighting a radicalized war is no super Mario games.

Great Britain's war-time Prime Minister, Sir Winston Churchill, in 1942 after the 2nd battle of El Alamein said,

> "Now this is not the end. It is not even the beginning of the end. But it is, perhaps, the end of the beginning."

This section of the book ventilates the end of the beginning for the Kashmir conflict. A conflict which has peaked since 1989 and has seen so many of the young ones dying, residents and the security personnel, both sons of the same soil. Let me conclude this book by sharing David Phelps lovely lyrics 'End of the Beginning'.

He was born of a virgin one holy night
In the little town of Bethlehem.
Angels gathered round him underneath the stars
Singing praises to the great I Am.
He walked on the water, healed the lame and made the blind to see again.
And for the first time here on earth we learned that God could be a friend.
And though he never ever did a single thing wrong
The angry crowd chose him. And then he walked down the road
And died on the cross and that was the end of the beginning.

The Kashmir conflict is in the End of the Beginning stage, next phase will be Beginning to the End.

'Shalom'

Bibliography

Books

Abdullah, Sheikh, *Atish-E-Chinar*.

Aggarwal, PC, *Caste, Religion and Power: An Indian Case Study*, SRCIR New Delhi, 1971.

Ahmed, AG, Moses David Audu; Wagdy Loza and Artur Maximenco, "The Prevalence of Extreme Middle-Eastern Ideologies among Some Nigerians", *International Journal of Social Science Studies*.

Al-Awlaki, Anwar, "44 Ways to Support Jihad", Victorious Media: 2009.

Al-Suri, AM, "The Global Islamic Resistance Call", 2004.

Ansari, H, Cinnirella, M, Rogers, MB, Loewenthal, KM and Lewis, CA, "Perceptions of martyrdom and terrorism amongst British Muslims, 2006".

Arafa, MG, "Initiative of stopping violence and the fruits of five years of the Egyptian Islamic group", El-Islam El-Youm, 2015.

Bar-Tal, D and Antebi, D, "Siege Mentality in Israel", *International Journal of Intercultural Relations*, 16, 251-275, 1992.

Bawer, B (2006), *While Europe slept: How radical Islam is destroying the West from within*. New York: Doubleday.

Biberaj, E, "Albania Between East and West", Conflict Studies Number 190, London: Institute for the Study of Conflict, 1986.

Blaydes, L, Rubin, L (2008), "Ideological Reorientation and Counterterrorism: Confronting Militant Islam in Egypt," Terrorism and Political Violence, 20, 4, 461-479.

Braithwaite, Alex, Dennis M Foster and David A Sobek. 2010. "Ballots, Bargains, and Bombs: Terrorist Targeting of Spoiler Opportunities", *International Interactions*, 36: 294-305. (Crocker, A Chester, 2011. "Thoughts on the Conflict Management Field after 30 Years."

Chasing a Mirage: The Tragic Illusion of an Islamic State, Tarek Fatah, Published in 2008.

Country Without a Post Office, The, Agha Shahid Ali, Published 2013.

Correspondence of Sardar Patel, Durga Das.

Coser, LA (1956), "The Functions of Social Conflict". NY: Free Press.

CTX: "Social Media in Jihad and Counterterrorism" (Special Issue) 2, Number 4 (2012),

Curfewed Night, Basharat Peer, Published 2009.

Defiant Border: The Afghan-Pakistan Borderlands in the Era of Decolonization, 1936-65, The, Elisabeth Leake, Published in 2016.

Democracy: Stories from the Long Road to Freedom, Condoleezza Rice, 2017.

DNA Indian, "Hindu Janajagruti is organising Akhil Bharatiya Hindu Adhiveshan in Goa every year. In its convention, schedule has been fixed for formation of Hindu Rashtra. It states in 2025 Hindu Rashtra will form. Law for having only two children should be framed", "DNA INDIA" Published 13th January 2015.

Dunleavy, P Special to IPT News (January 9, 2015), "Another Ex-Con, Another Terrorist Attack, The Danger in Closing Gitmo".

Ecoterrorism. New York: Facts on File, Inc. Maslow, AH (1943), "A Theory of Human Motivation. Psychological".

Elon, A (1971), *The Israelis*. London: Weidenfeld and Nicolson.

El-Saeed, NM (2010), "Prince Naief a shield in front of extremism and terrorism", Al Jazirah News Paper 09/06/2010 G Issue13768.

Everton, Sean F 2012. "Disrupting Dark Networks". New York: Cambridge University Press.

Flood, Gavin D, *Body and Cosmology in Kashmir Saivism (Distinguished Dissertations)*.

Gilmartin, David, *Blood and Water: The Indus River Basin in Modern History*.

Gunaratna, R (2011) "Terrorist rehabilitation: a global imperative, Journal of Policing, Intelligence and Counter Terrorism", 6:1, 65-82.

Gunaratna, R, Bin Ali, M (2009), "De-Radicalization Initiatives in Egypt: A Preliminary Insight. Studies in Conflict and Terrorism", 32: 277-291, 2009.

Gurfinkiel, M (2015), "France's moment of truth". Middle-East Forum.

Hairgrove, F and McLeod, D (2008), "Circles Drawing Toward High Risk Activism: The Use of Usroh and Halaqa in Islamist Radical Movements." Studies in Conflict and Terrorism (May): 399-411.

Haqqani, Husain (former Pakistan's ambassador to the United States) and Lisa Curtis (The Heritage Foundation), "A New US Approach to Pakistan: Enforcing Aid Conditions without Cutting Ties".

Herald, Dawn, "Talking to India is just as important as how not to talk", by Sherry Rehman, Former Pakistan Minister and Chairperson of The Jinnah Institute.

Hindu Political Parties. General Books. 30 May 2010. ISBN 9781157374923.

History of Kashmir Shaivism, BN Pandit.

Hoglund, Kristine and Isak Svensson. 2009. "Mediating between tigers and lions: Norwegian peace displomacy in Sri Lanka's civil war." 17(2): 175-191. (Marsden, Lee. 2006. "Promoting Democracy in Northern Ireland: George Bush and the Peace Process."

Horgan, J and Braddock, K (2010), "Rehabilitating the Terrorists: Challenges in Assessing the Effectiveness of De-radicalization Programs. Terrorism and Political Violence", 22, 24.

In Search of Pakistan: A Muslim Homeland and Global Politics, Ayesh Jalal, Published 2015.

In The Line of Fire – A Memoir, Pervez Musharraf, Published 2006.

India After Gandhi – The History of the world's largest democracy, Ramachandra Guha, Published 2016.

India Betrayed – The Role of Nehru, Brigadier BN Sharma.

India, Her Civic Life and Administration. Jai Prakash Nath & Co. Retrieved 23 July 2014.

India, Pakistan and Kashmir, Stephen Philip Cohen, Published online: 4 June 2010.

India's Wars – A Military History 1947-1971, Published 2016.

Integral Humanism – An Analysis of Some Basic Elements, Deendayal Upadhyaya, Published 2016.

International Negotiation 16: 1-10. (Esser, K James and Christine M Bridges. 2011. "Negotiating with Terrorists: The Case of the Basques and Spain." Peace and Conflict: Journal of Peace Psychology 17(1): 60-76.)

Jinnah – India Pakistan Independence, Jaswant Singh, Published 2009.

Jinnah vs Gandhi, Roderick Matthews, Published 2016.

Kareema, AM (2015): "The Group of Muslim Brothers: A critical view". El-Gizera, Cairo, El-Aiat.

Kashmir – A Curse and Cure of Its History, Rajee Kushwaha.

Kashmir – The Vajpayee Years, AS Dulat with Aditya Sinha, Published 2016.

Kashmir 1947 – Rival Versions of History, Prem Shankar Jha.

Kashmir Shaivism: The Central Philosophy of Tantrism, Kamalaka Mishra.

Kashmir Shaivism: The Secret Supreme, John Hughes.

Kashmir The Case For freedom, Tariq Ali, Hilal Bhatt, Angana P Chatterji, Habbah Khatun, Pankaj Mishra and Arundhati Roy, Published 2011.

Lee, IS, Park, JU and Rhee, BJ (1993), "North Korea: After Collapse of Socialist Camp". Seoul: Naewoe Press.

Leuprecht, C, Hataley, T, Moskalenko, S and McCauley, C (2009), "Winning the Battle but Losing the War? Narrative and Counter-Narratives Strategy. Perspectives on Terrorism".

Liebman, C (1978), "Myth, Tradition and Values in Israeli society". Midstream, 24, 44-53.

Lost Decades, Nani Palkhiwala.

Loza, W (2007), "The psychology of extremism and terrorism: A Middle-Eastern perspective. Aggression and Violent Behavior", 12, 141-155.

Loza, W (2010a), "The prevalence of Middle-Eastern extreme ideologies among some Canadians." JIV, 26, 1388-1400.

Loza, W (2012 May), "Issues regarding the assessment and intervention with Middle-Eastern radicalization, extremism and its operational manifestation: terrorism". Crime Scene, Volume 19, Number 1: Canadian Psychological Association, Canada.

Loza, W Abd-El-Fatah, Prinsloo, J, Hesselink, A, Seidler, K (2010), "The Prevalence of Extreme Middle-Eastern Ideologies Around the World". Journal of Interpersonal Violence, 2011 February; 26(3): 522-38.

Makers of Modern Asia, Ramachandra Guha, Published 2014.

MB Rogers, CA Lewis, KM Loewenthal, M Cinnirella, R Amlot and H Ansari (Eds), "Proceedings of the British Psychological Society Seminar Series Aspects of Terrorism and Martyrdom", eCOMMUNITY (pp 1-5), *International Journal of Mental Health and Addiction.*

Midnight's Furies: The Deadly Legacy of India's Partition, Nisid Hajari, Published 2016.

My Frozen Turbulence in Kashmir, Jagmohan.

My Reminiscences of Sardar Patel, V Shankar.

National Post (October 27, 2014), Michael Zehaf-Bibeau. "Threatened To Act In The Name Of Allah", in Response to the Canadian Foreign Policy.

Naveed Qazi, "Chronology of Conflict: Kashmir," 21st January 2011. Countercurrents.org

Non-Stop India, Mark Tully, Published 2011.

Our Moon Has Blood Clots – A Memoir Of A Lost Home In Kashmir, Rahul Pandita, Published 2014.

Oxford University scholar Stephen Oppenheimer.

Pandit, KN, *Baharistan-i-shahi,* A Chronicle of Mediaeval Kashmir.

Partition Plan, Alan Campbell Johnson.

Pipes, D (2015), "How terrorism harms radical Islam".

Poems of Lal Ded, translated by Ranjit Hoskote.

Poetry of renowned Kashmiri Poet, Habba Khatoon, Transformed into Standardised Devanagari-Kashmiri by MK Raina, 2014.

Political Quarterly, The, 77(1): 61-70 (Miller, Carl. 2011. "Is it Possible or Preferable to Negotiate with Terrorists?" Defence Studies 11(1): 145-185. Neumann, R Peter, 2007. "Negotiating with Terrorists" Foreign Affairs 86(1): 128-138. (Pruitt, G Dean, 2006. "Negotiation with Terrorists." International Negotiation 11: 371-394.

Qazi, Ashraf Jehangir (former ambassador to the US, India and China and head of UN missions in Iraq and Sudan), "A Kashmir Statement", 2016.

Rabasa, A, Benard, C, Schwartz, LH, Sickle, P (2007), "Building Moderate Muslim Networks". Arlington, VA: Rand Center for Middle-East Public Policy.

Ramaseshan, Radhika, "Advani Fires Atal Weapon", *The Telegraph,* 16-6-2005.

Rashwan, D (2009), "The renunciation of violence by Egyptian jihadi organizations". In Bojorgo and Horgan (Eds), "Leaving Terrorism

Behind: Individual and collective disengagement". Routledge, London and New York.

Resolving the Kashmir Conflict: Pakistan, India, Kashmiris and Religious Militants, 2008, Rodrigo Tavares.

Rivers Divided: Indus Basin Waters in the Making of India and Pakistan, Daniel Haines, Published 2017.

Sageman, M (2004), *Understanding terror networks*. Philadelphia: University of Pennsylvania Press.

Secrets of the Kashmir Valley, Fahana Qazi, Published 2016.

Shaiva Devotional Songs of Kashmir (The Su Ny Series in the Shaiva Traditions of Kashmir), Constantina Rhodes Bailly.

Stein, HF (1978), Judaism and the Group-Fantasy of Martydom: "The Psychodynamic Paradox of Survival Through Persecution". Journal of Psychohistory, 6, 151-210.

Stern, J (2009), "How to Deradicalize Islamist Extremists, Mind Over Martyr", Foreign affairs, 89 Number 1, 98-108.

Spread of Nuclear Weapons: More May Better The, Kenneth Waltz, Adelphi Papers, Number 171, London: International Institute for Strategic Studies, Published 1981.

Talbot, Ian, *A History of Modern South Asia: Politics, States and Diasporas*, 2012.

Taliban, Ahmed Rashid, Published 2010.

Toros, Harmonie (2008), "'We Don't Negotiate with Terrorists': Legitmacy and Complexity in Terrorist Conflicts." Security Dialogue 39(4): 407-426.

Understanding Kashmir and Kahmiris, Chritopher Snedden, Published 2015.

Understanding Kashmir and Kashmiris, Christopher Snedden: Hurst & Company, London, 2015.

Valdmanis, R (Reuter, Ottawa Wed October 29, 2014 1:11 pm EDT), "Canada's plan to defang would-be jihadists at home".

Vashi, Ashish, "Anti-Sardar Patel Book Sold from RSS HQ in Gujarat", *The Times of India*, 27-8-2009.

What's wrong with Pakistan?, Babar Ayaz, Published 2014.

Wicker, C (2007), "International lessons learned and recommendations for combating domestic Islamic terrorism". Carlisle, PA: US Army War College, Carlisle Barracks.

Yaseen, E (2007, September 28), "Dawla dinia or islam dimokrati?" [Religious country or Democratic Islam?]. Cairo, Egypt: Al-Ahram Newspaper.

Yoga Spandakarika: "The Sacred Texts at the Origins of Tantra", Daniel Odier, Swami Lakshmanjoo.

Zena, A (June 21, 2002), "Hot debate inside Islamic communities after the initiative of the leaders of the group for apologizing to the Egyptians". El-Sharq El-Awsat News. Retrived (2015-01-10).

Articles

"Doctrine of Recognition: A Translation of Pratyabhijnagrdayam" (Suny Series in Tantric Studies), Ksemaraja.

"Doctrine of Vibration: An Analysis of the Doctrines and Practices of Kashmir Shaivism", The (Suny Series in the Shaiva Traditions of Kashmir), Mark SG Dyczkowski.

"Dynamic Stillness Part One: The Practice of Trika Yoga", Swami Chetanananda.

"Finding The Hidden Self: A Study of the Siva Sutras", Roger Worthington.

"From Early Vedanta to Kashmir Shaivism: Gaudapada, Bhartrhari and Abhinavagupta" (Suny Series in Religious Studies), Natalia Isayeva.

"Fundamentalism in the Modern World (Volume 1)", page 97, ISBN 978-1-84885-330-0, IB Tauris, Ulrika Mårtensson and Jennifer Bailey, Published 2011.

"Ideological heresy?" *The Hindu*, 2005-06-19, Jyotirmaya Sharma.

"Kashmir Shaivaism" (Suny Series in Cultural Perspectives), Jagadish Chandra Chatterji.

"Kashmir Shaivism: The Secret Supreme", Swami Lakshman Jee.

"Kashmir Shaivism", J Rudrappa.

"Kashmir Shaivism", Lakshmi Nidhi Sharma.

"Kashmir Valley", A Poem, The, Part 1 and Part 2, 2015, Mohtarma Mumtaz.

"Kundalini: The Energy of the Depths: A Comprehensive Study Based on the Scriptures of Non-Dualistic Kaskmir Shaivism" (Suny Series in the Shaiva Traditions of Kashmir), Lilian Silburn.

"Later, KM Munshi, with Gandhi's blessing, also resigned from the Congress to plead for Akhand Hindustan as a counter blast to Pakistan. Gandhi, who previously thought that swaraj was impossible without Hindu-Muslim unity, subsequently came to the conclusion that as Britain wanted to retain her empire by pursuing a policy of divide and rule, Hindu-Muslim unity could not be achieved as long as the British were there, Mahatma Gandhi". Allied Publishers, p 315, ISBN 9788170232056, Ghose, Sankar Published 1st January 1991.

"Many months ago, when the Pakistan issue was still in the melting pot, the Khan brothers determined to fight for Akhand Hindustan and challenged the League to fight the issue out before the electorate of the Province, Pakistan: The First Twelve Years". Oxford University Press, Mazhar Ali Khan, Published 1996.

"Nothing Exists That Is Not Shiva: Commentaries on the Shiva Sutra", Vijnana Bhairava, Guru Gita and Other Sacred Texts, Swami Muktananda.

"Nuclear winter revisited with a modern climate model and current nuclear arsenals", Journal of Geophysical Research, Vol 112, D13107, Alan Robock, Luke Oman and Georgiy L Stenchikov, Published 2007.

"On 5 August 1944, he issued a common letter to the leaders of various parties making a proposal to hold Akhand Hindustan Leaders' Conference. Such a conference was held on 7 and 8 October in Delhi". Encyclopaedia Eminent Thinkers. Concept Publishing Company, p 88, ISBN 9788180694929, Dr Radha Kumud Mukherji, Sharma, Jai Narain, Published 1st January 2008.

"Only by Akhand Bharat", *The Indian Express*, 2007-02-01, Manini Chatterjee.

"Political Space: Frontiers of change and governance in a globalizing world", page 155, SUNY Press, ISBN 978-0-7914-5460-2, Yale H Ferguson and RJ Barry Jones, Pubished 2002.

"Real Eve: Modern Man's Journey out of Africa", The (New York: Carroll and Graf Publishers, 2003).

"Rediscovering God With Transcendental Argument: A Contemporary Interpretation of Monistic Kashmiri Saiva Philosophy" (Suny Series), David Peter Lawrence.

"Right Wing Mobilization in India, Feminist Review", Issue 49, page 17, Routledge, ISBN 978-0-415-12375-4, Sucheta Majumder, Published 1995.

"Samvidullasah: Manifestation of Divine Consciousness", Swami Lakshman Joo, Saint Scholar of Kashmir Shaivism, Baumer; Bettina and Sarla Kumar.

"Siva Sutras: The Yoga of Supreme Identity", Jaideva Singh.

"Splendor of Recognition: An Exploration of the Pratyabhijna-hrdayam", a Text on the Ancient Science of the Soul, Swami Shantananda.

"The Aphorisms of Siva: The Siva Sutra With Bhaskara's Commentary, the Varttika" (Suny Series in Tantric Studies), Bhaskara.

"The Jew Is Not My Enemy: Unveiling the Myths that Fuel Muslim Anti-Semitism", Tarek Fatah, Published in 2010.

"The Philosophy of Sadhana: With Special Reference to the Trika Philosophy of Kashmir" (Suny Series in Tantric Studies), Debabrata B Sen Sharma.

"The Role of Nuclear Weapons in the US-Russian Relationship", Elbridge Colby, Task Force White Paper Published February 26, 2016.

"The Stanzas on Vibration: The Spandakarika With Four Commentaries: The Spandasamdoha by Ksemaraja, the Spandavrtti by Kallatabhatta, the Spandavivr" (Series on the Shaiva Traditions of Kashmir), Vasugupta.

"The Teachings of the Odd-Eyed One: A Study and Translation of the Virupaksapancasika, With the Commentary of Vidyacakravartin" (SUNY Series in Hindu Studies), David Peter Lawrence.

"The ultimate reunification of the subcontinent is a professed goal, as it is for the Mahasabha, but here, too, there is a difference in emphasis which deserves note: for the Sangh, the goal is 'Akhand Bharat', while for the Mahasabha it is 'Akhand Hindustan'." The Swatantra Party and Indian Conservatism. Cambridge University Press, p 55, ISBN 9780521049801.

Erdman, HL, Published 17th December 2007.

"The Yoga of Vibration and Divine Pulsation: A Translation of the Spanda Karikas With Ksemaraja's Commentary, the Spanda Nirnaya" (Suny Series in Tant), Jaideva Singh.

"Those who dub Shri LK Advani, the Home Minister of India and others as foreigners, must realise that the freedom struggle was a mass movement of all the people of entire Akhand Hindusthan (United Bharat)", *Rashtriya Swayamsevak Sangh*. APH Publishing, p 262, ISBN 9788176484657, Chitkara, MG Published 1st January 2004.

"Triadic Heart of Siva: Kaula Tantricism of Abhinavagupta in the Non-Dual Shaivism of Kashmir", The (Suny Series, Shaiva Traditions of Kashmir), Paul Eduardo Muller-Ortega.

"Vijnana Bhairava: The Practice of Centring Awareness", Lakshman Joo Swami.

"Why Kashmir Is So Angry With Us", Yashwant Sinha is a senior BJP leader and former Union Minister of External Affairs.

"Workers Hammer", Number 221 (Winter 2012-2013), newspaper of the Spartacist League/Britain, section of the International Communist Leagu, Comrade, Published on 23rd November 2012.

1947 Partition Drawing of Indo-Pakistan Boundary, Lucy Chester's publications include "The Mapping of Empire: French and British Cartographies of India in the Late Eighteenth Century" in Portuguese Studies (October 2000) and "Mapping Imperial Expansion: Colonial Cartography in North America and South Asia" in The Portolan (Fall 1999).

Other Sources

BBC
CNN
Constitution of India
Dawn
Deccan Herald
Indian Express
Kashmir Times
Multiple Blogs
Quora
Times of India
Wikipedia

Index

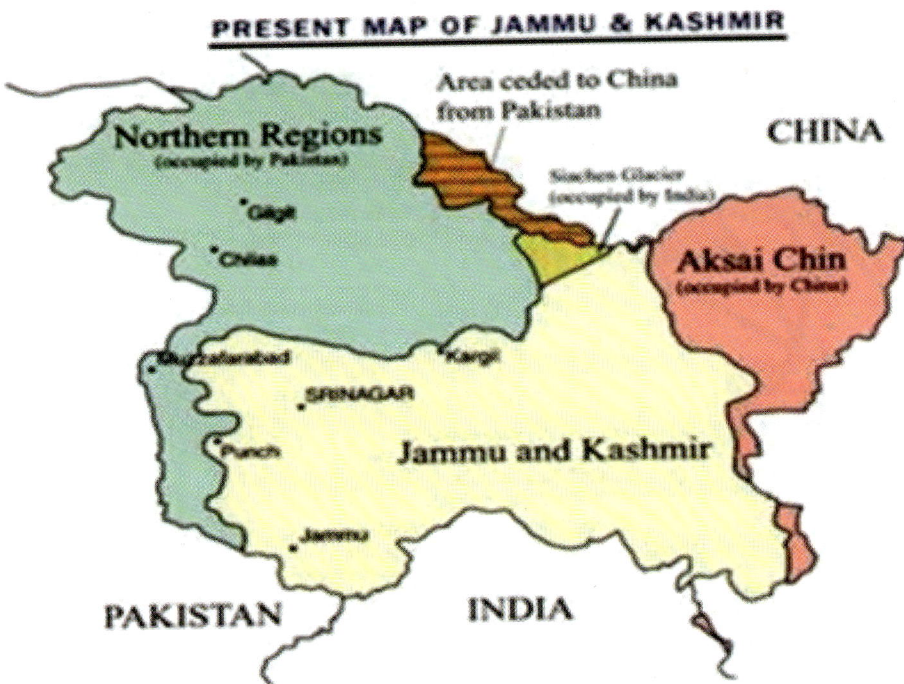

J&K map showing regions occupied by Pakistan and China (Map not to scale)

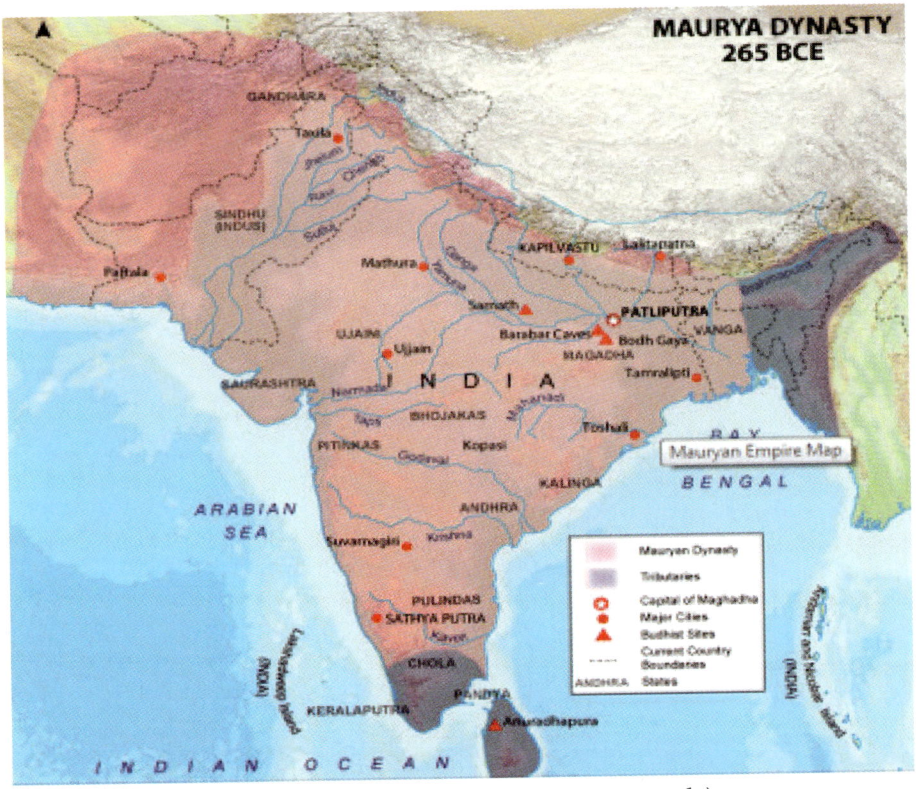

Maurya Dynasty 265 BCE (Map not to scale)

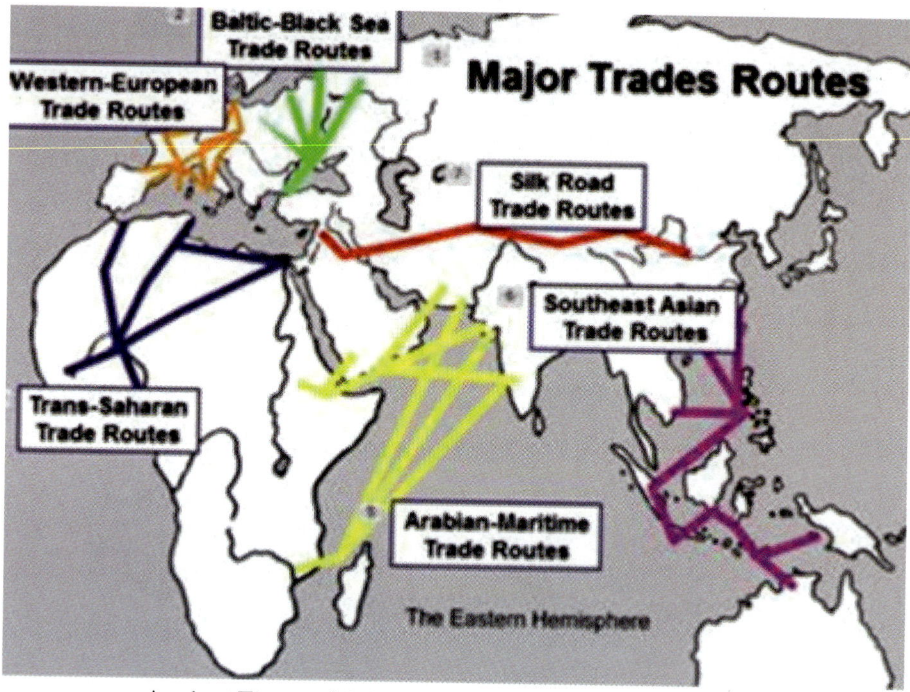

Ancient Times – Major Trade Routes (Map not to scale)

India's Map – Before Partition (Map not to scale)

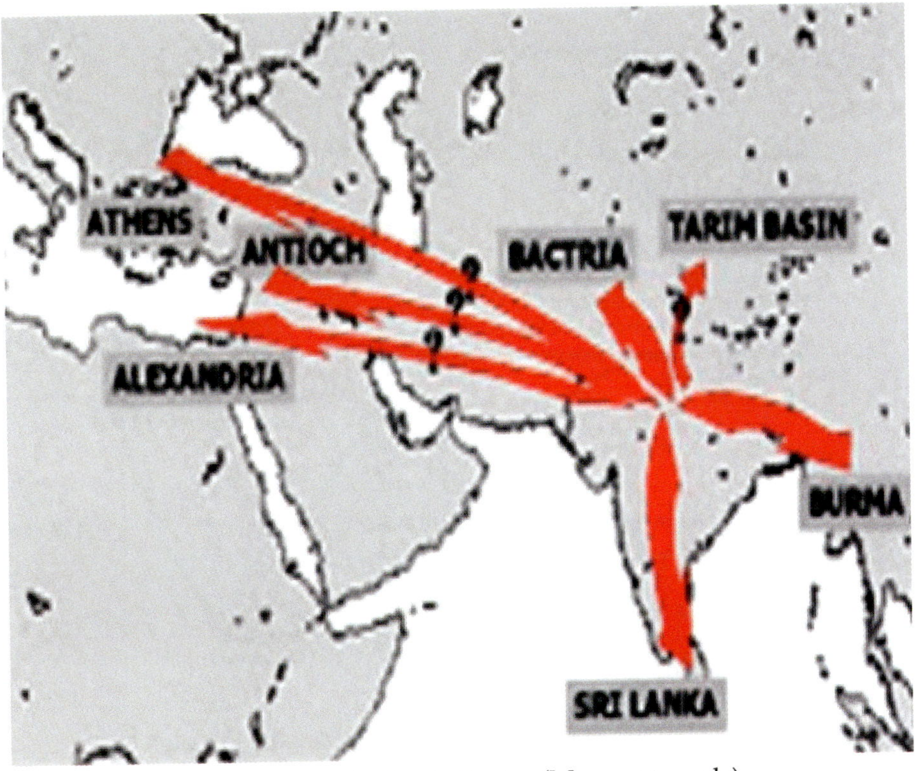

Mauryan Empire Trade Routes (Map not to scale)

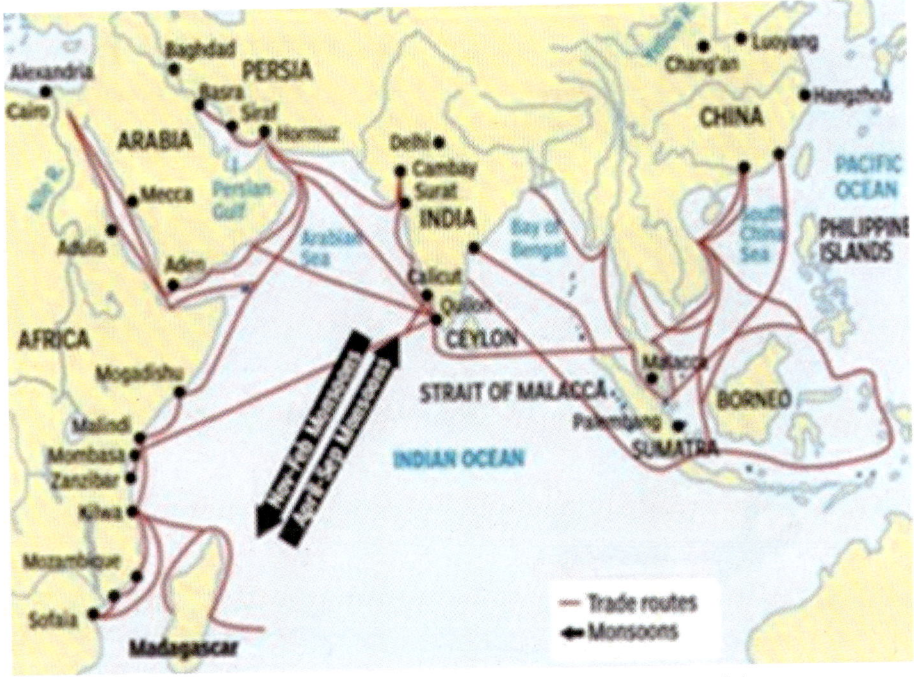

Navigation and Masuam Project (Map not to scale)

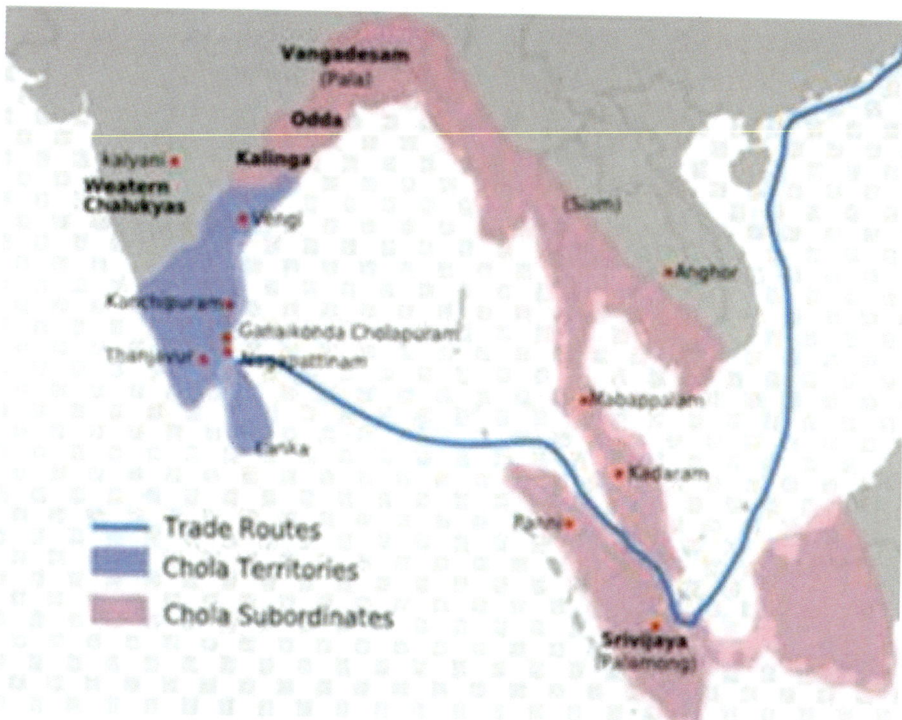

Chola Empire Maritime Trade Route (Map not to scale)

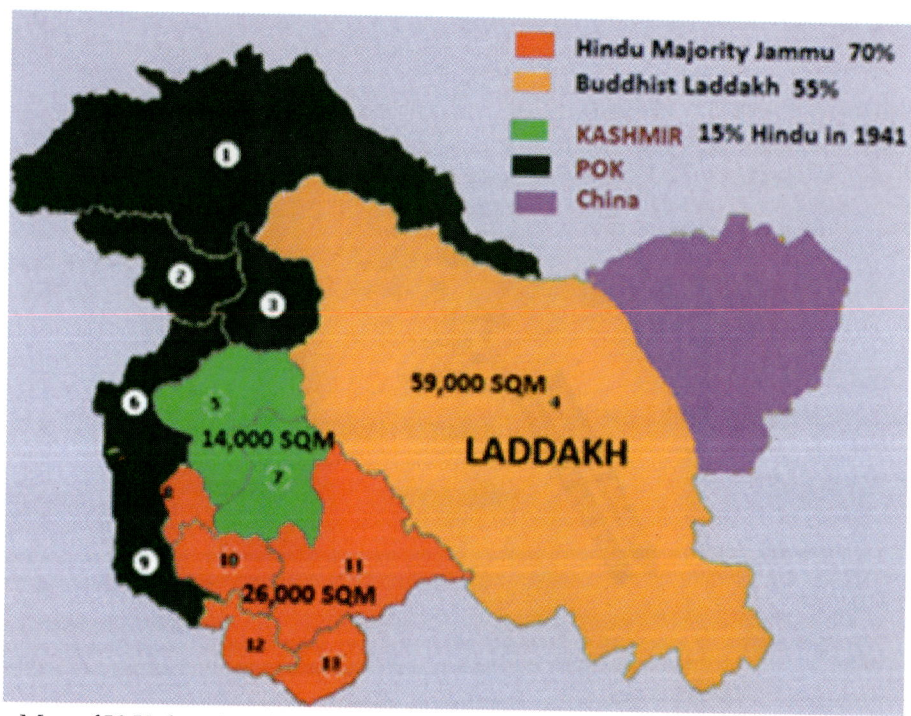

Map of J&K showing the religious spread across the region (Map not to scale)

Map of J&K showing various dresses worn in different regions
(Map not to scale)

MUGHAL EMPIRE
1530-1707

BAY OF BENGAL

ARABIAN SEA

INDIAN OCEAN

Ancient Map of India showing Mughal Empire spread (Map not to scale)

Pre-1947 Map showing the half drawn Radcliffe Line (Map not to scale)

Map of India, comparing the population of her various States mapped to some prominent countries of the world. This mapping is purely symbolic representation (Map not to scale)

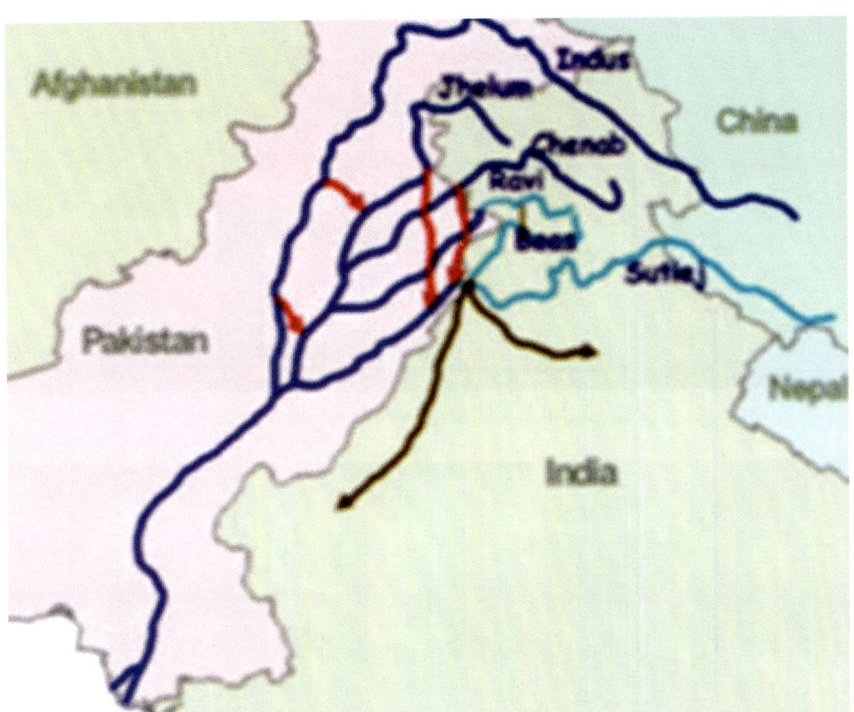

Map of Indian sub-continent showing catchment area of five rivers covering the fertile land of United Punjab (India and Pakistan) (Map not to scale)

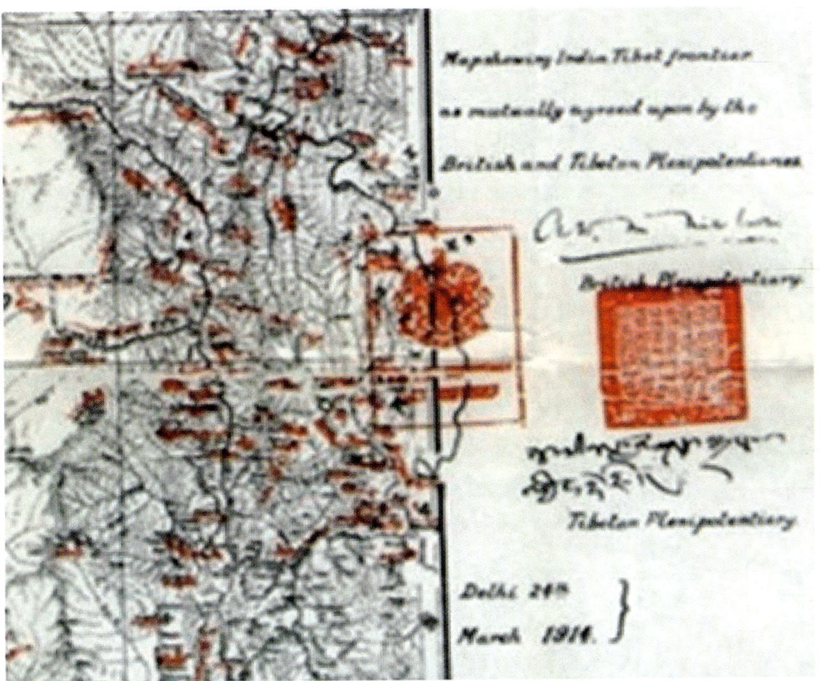

1914 – Map showing India Tibet border. Mutually agreed signed treaty copy with 'British-India' government and Tibet's head (Map not to scale)

Leh, Ladakh – Buddhist place of worship

Ladakh – Scenic View

Vaishno Devi Cave (Jammu) – Sacred Hindu Holy Shrine

Shikara, houseboat on the famous Dal Lake – Srinagar

Amarnath Cave (in J&K, Anantnag/Pahalgam) – Sacred Hindu Shrine

Neelam Valley – POK

Martand Sun Temple – Longest Hindu temple complex in India (Anantnag, J&K) built in the 8th Century CE

Holy Hazratbal Shrine – Srinagar

Habba Khatoon – An artist view of a great Kashmiri Poetess and Queen

Caucasian look – Women from Kashmir, J&K

Lal Ded, Mystic Poetess, J&K

Wazwaan – Traditional Kashmir Delicacy, served mostly during marriages

Sufi Singers

The Hindustan Times

KASHMIR ACCEDES TO INDIA

PLEBISCITE SOON ON RULER'S DECISION

SHEIKH ABDULLA TO FORM INTERIM GOVT.

The Hindustan Times – carrying historical headlines of Kashmir acceding to India on 26 October 1947

1st Indo-Pak War (1947-48) – Kabali tribesman of Afghan origin along with Pak army attacked and captured 35% of J&K territory from Raja Hari Singh before he signed the Instrument of Accession with India. POK was hence formed. J&K lost Gilgit, Baltistan and so-called Azad Kashmir (Mirpur) areas

2nd Indo-Pak War (1965) – Capture of Hazi Pir by the Indian Army (later returned to Pakistan)

2nd Indo- Pak War (1965) – One of the largest tank battle since the Battle of Kursk in WWII. Pakistan had 760 tanks vs. India's 720, more than parity and showed how Indian politicians let the country down in 1962 and 1965 as far as army buildup was concerned. The poor investment policy, made India and Pakistan army enjoy parity, considering the size of both the nations

3rd Indo-Pak War (1971) – Resulted in Defeat, and Division of Pakistan into two parts: Lt Gen AAK Niazi, Commander of Pakistan Eastern Command, signing the Instrument of Surrender in Dhaka on 16th December 1971 in the presence of Lt Gen Jagjit Singh Aurora of India

4th Indo-Pak War (1999) – Kargil heights intrusion by Pak army, after intial losses Indian army using Bofors guns and helicopters was able to free it from the Pak army, killing more than 5,000 of their Northern Command army personnel

Surgical Strike (2016) – Indian army enters across Pakistan LoC and annihilates 38 terrorists and 2 Army personnel guarding them

Rare historical picture of Patel, Nehru, Jinnah, Ambedkar, Mountbatten, Radcliffe, etc

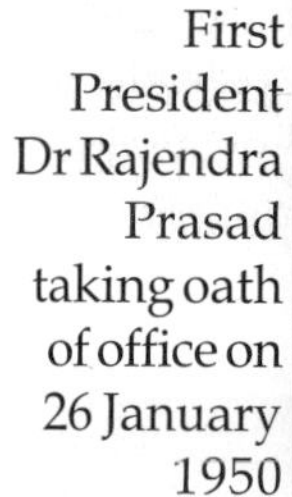

First President Dr Rajendra Prasad taking oath of office on 26 January 1950

Nehru (left) and Jinnah – two leaders who divided millions of people of the Indian Sub-Continent

Father of the Indian nation Mahatma Gandhi with Jinnah

1965: Pakistani President Gen Ayub Khan, Indian Prime Minister Lal Bahadur Shastri and Soviet Union Premier Alexei Kosygin

1965: Prime Minister of India Lal Bahadur Shastri signs the Treaty at Tashkent (Uzbekistan) to stop the war between India and Pakistan. India lets go its strategic Haji Pir Pass, won on the battlefield. This would have reduced the distance between Jammu and Srinagar by 200 kms, through Poonch and Uri. It could have been useful deterrent for checking all the infiltrations of terrorists across the western border

The Times of India

SHEIKH ABDULLAH ARRESTED

CHARGES OF CORRUPTION AND MALADMINISTRATION

Bakshi Ghulam Mohammed Sworn In As Prime Minister

POLICE OPEN FIRE ON VIOLENT DEMONSTRATORS

SOBER SATISFACTION IN DELHI

"Timely Action By The Sadar-i-Riyasat"

Sheikh Abdullah arrest news on the Indian daily newspaper

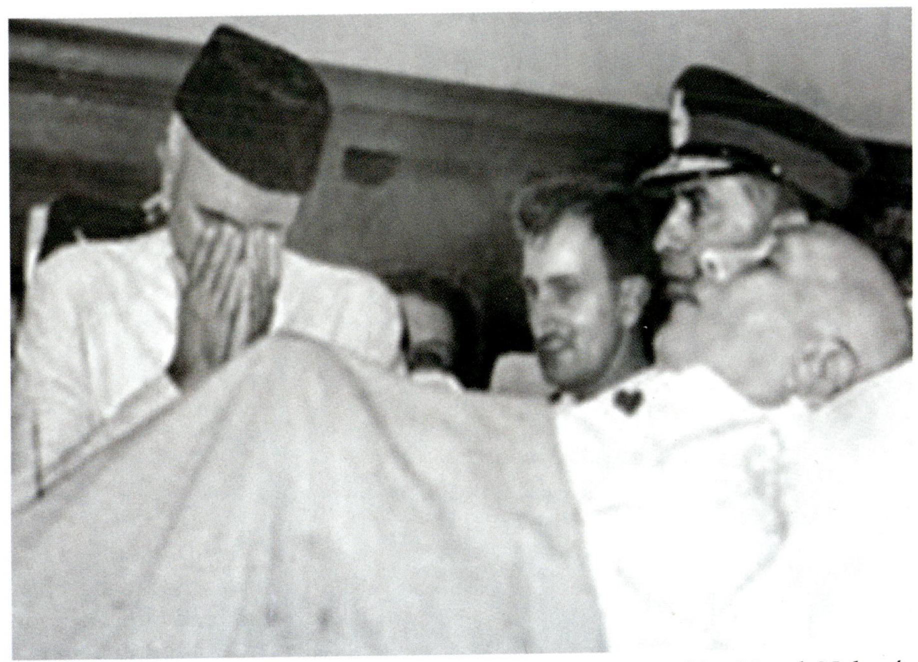

Sheikh Abdullah could not hold his tears on seeing his friend Nehru's dead body

Tallest war time Indian Prime Minister Mrs Indira Gandhi with President Nixon of USA

Pakistan PM Zulfikar Ali Bhutto and his daughter Benazir Bhutto with Mrs Indira Gandhi (in middle)

Gen Zia-ul-Haq with Imran Khan. Zia was the architect of Islamization and radicalization of Pakistan as a country along with the Army and ISI as the institutions during the '80s

PM Vajpayee and Pak PM Nawaz Sharif during Lahore declaration. The bus took Vajpayee to Pakistan via Wagah border

Failed Agra Summit – Pak President Musharraf with PM Vajpayee, LK Advani and Jaswant Singh

Pakistan President Musharraf with PM Manmohan Singh

Prime Minister Narendra Modi and Pak Prime Minister Nawaz Sharif started on a positive note in 2014 but could not take the momentum forward, thanks to ISI supported terrorrist attacks in India

Stone pelters in Kashmir Valley

Brigadier Gogoi of the Indian army used a stone pelter as a human shield to stop his friends and sympathizers from pelting stones on the Indian army personnel. Innovative action though became politically incorrect in the separatist eyes

2016, NYC, US – Yours truly, Sharad Mohan with Baloch leader Ahmad Mustkin and Kashmiri Pundits, participating in a peaceful procession in front of United Nations during Pakistani PM Nawaz Sharif's speech

Pakistani postal stamp showing Kashmir (Pakistani version)

Indian Postal Stamp showing Kashmiri bride

Last King of Kashmir – Maharaja Hari Singh (L), son Karan Singh (R) standing with their spouses Maharani Tara Devi (R) and Yasho Rajya Lakshmi (L) sitting